Overlords of the Singularity

THE MANIPULATION OF HUMANKIND BY HIDDEN UFO INTELLIGENCES
AND THE QUEST FOR TRANSCENDENCE

Russell Scott Brinegar

ISBN: 1536873624
ISBN 13: 9781536873627

Acknowledgements and Dedications

THIS BOOK IS dedicated to all those who have had direct encounters with the great flying saucer mystery, many of whom have suffered rejection and ridicule from their peers as a result of personal disclosure. Many experiencers have lost friends, family, or jobs by telling the truth as they know it. Some have even tragically taken their own lives after speaking openly about their encounters with UFOs, as they were unable to endure the resulting sociological repercussions. Thanks to the research efforts of the late atmospheric scientist, Dr. James McDonald, and to the work of the late Dr. Morris K. Jessup, both of whom contributed much to the field of ufology, and both of whom, unfortunately, committed suicide. Thanks to the late Captain Thomas F. Mantell, the first of many pilots to die while chasing UFOs. Thanks to all those individuals who have dedicated countless hours in trying to make sense of the UFO mystery, especially to Dr. Jacques Vallee, and to the late John Keel, whose excellent works have had a great influence on my own personal views of the UFO phenomenon. Acknowledgement to those who have mysteriously disappeared from the face of the earth over the years, to the victims of Earth's invisible predators, and to all those who have undergone the disorienting experience of so-called "alien abductions." Thanks to all those who have compiled wonderful UFO encyclopedias, such as Jerome Clark's *The UFO Book*, or Ronald Story's *Mammoth Encyclopedia of Extraterrestrial Encounters*. Thanks to nuclear physicist and UFO researcher Stanton T. Friedman for his excellent research into the Roswell incident of 1947, and his authentication efforts with the MJ-12 documents. Acknowledgement to former aerospace engineer, Dr. Robert M. Wood, and Ryan S. Wood, for their document research related to extraterrestrial technologies. Thanks also to the late Leonard H. Stringfield for his relentless efforts in determining the reality of flying saucer crashes and extraterrestrial biological entities (EBEs). Thanks to all the UFO contactees and whistleblowers that have come forth in recent years to reveal their UFO experiences publicly, and a special thanks to former US Army Sergeant, Clifford Stone, for his brave personal testimony concerning his involvement with the UFO crash-and-retrieval units known as Project Moon Dust and Operation Blue Fly. Thanks to the efforts of Stephen Bassett with Paradigm Research Group, to the work of optical physicist Dr. Bruce Maccabee, and to Dr.

Steven Greer and associates for their ongoing Disclosure Project. Thanks to my wife, Julie, for enduring countless hours of my thoughts and speculations concerning the underlying nature of flying saucers and ufonauts. Thanks to my friend, Mary, with whom I experienced an anomalous encounter with Earth's intelligent luminosity and a mysterious episode of missing time in 1979. Thanks also to my Christian friend, Marty, who stands firm in his belief, despite everything we have discussed about the subject, that the occupants of flying saucers are demons.

"UFOs are real - All we need to ask is where do they come from, and what do they want?"

- Captain Edgar Mitchell, Apollo 14 astronaut (1930-2016)

Table of Contents

Introduction

"My own suspicion is that the Universe is not only queerer than we suppose, but queerer than we can suppose."

- J.B.S. Haldane

I HAVE ALWAYS suspected that if someone were to reveal the truth of our existence, what is really going on in the universe, the true nature of reality, and our actual place as humans within the cosmos at large, that this truth would most assuredly be rejected outright, laughed at, or even incite anger and indignation from those whose ears were unlucky enough to hear it. History is replete with examples of those who were persecuted or even put to death for telling the simple truth. Giordano Bruno was burned at the stake in the year 1600 for holding firm in his belief that other planets were inhabited by otherworldly populations. Likewise, the Catholic Church condemned Galileo for demonstrating his invention, the telescope, considered by Church officials to be an instrument of the Devil. One of my favorite original *Star Trek* episodes, *For the World is Hollow, and I Have Touched the Sky*, features inhabitants of a world who discover the disturbing truth that their planet is actually an artificial spaceship run by a central computer, called the *Oracle*. The truth of our existence here on Earth, the underlying nature of reality, is surely up there with this unsettling story of science fiction. Likewise, in the 1992 movie, *A Few Good Men*, actor Jack Nicholson screamed his classic line, "You can't handle the truth!" As it turns out, the inner nature of the physical universe, and the truth behind the UFO mystery (the subject of this book), is just that weird.

In many ways, life on this planet is like an episode of the television series, *Lost*. Most of us have difficulty remembering anything before late childhood. Prior to the advent of our memories, some part of us was communicating with our parents and the rest of the world as a little person who is lost forever to us, yet we know that this version of ourselves was real and existed in a state of consciousness that we would not remember later in life. In a very real sense, we have all experienced a mysterious episode of "missing time." We are not told where we actually come from, because nobody really knows much about the origins of life. Approximately two million stone tablets that are inscribed with Sumerian cuneiform exist from the ancient world that have not been translated yet, and there are precious few people who have the knowledge to decipher them. They contain our lost history. Even in these modern times, we really do not know how we got here or what we are really doing. The purpose of this life, if there is one, is left to personal speculation and/or religious belief. Our minds are limited in understanding as to the true nature of reality by what our parents taught us as children, what schools indoctrinated from an early age, and what our developing brains began piecing together as we grew into young adults. We generally accept what we are told concerning the history of human development, the history of the world, and the many mysteries of our past that are generally dismissed due to incomplete knowledge. It usually isn't until young adulthood that most of us begin seriously questioning what we have been told about the world, and by then the foundation of our thinking is influenced by the limitations of our own minds and our particular programming. Where we were born in the world has a lot to do with our mental concepts, and our thoughts are influenced considerably by the language that we learned as a child. We think in that language, which carries with it varying concepts of the world at large. Perceptions of reality differ from country to country, depending on the particular cultural heritage that we inherited at birth. As a person who was born in the United States, I was raised by conservative parents who attended a Christian Church of the Baptist denomination. Around the age of 13, I began asking questions to which my poor mother had no good answer, such as, "How did Noah load 27 million species of animals onto a wooden boat?" or, "If children die who never heard about Jesus, do they automatically go to Heaven?" This natural questioning of my childhood religious teaching went with me into adulthood. From these childhood questions I studied on my own, and eventually wrote my first book in 2000, *Outgrowing the Bible: The Journey from Fundamentalism to Freethinking.* At the time I wrote this book, I was unaware that others were writing simultaneously on similar subjects that would eventually enter the realm of my own interests. One such person was Dr. Arthur David Horn. Dr. Horn was once a professor who taught biological evolution at Colorado State University for 14 years. His own integrity forced him to quit his professorship at the university just prior to his retirement to write and publish his work, *Humanity's Extraterrestrial Origins.* Professor Horn could no longer, in good conscience, continue to teach the standard "scientific" explanation of evolution, or continue to teach that our species, *Homo sapiens,* came to exist on this planet naturally without any type of biological and/or genetic intervention. As Horn arrived at his conclusion that humanity has undergone genetic manipulation, another author, Zecharia Sitchin, was also writing his *Earth Chronicles* series that reveal the story of human origins as documented by the Sumerian culture on stone tablets. I was also quite unaware at the time that David Icke's book, *The Biggest Secret: The Book that Will Change the World,* had also found its way into the world of modern ufology.

As someone who was raised to believe that the Bible was the literal truth, the infallible "Word of God," as well as an accurate history of the world, I thought myself quite the independent thinker for writing a book as an adult that delved into the origins of the biblical stories.

Simultaneous to my own writing and discovery, archaeological scholars were also writing books that coordinated well with my own independent research. Sitchin took the unorthodox approach of treating the Sumerian accounts of gods from the sky as historical, literal fact vs. mythology. He realized that the Sumerians were not in the habit of fabricating fanciful tales, but meticulously recorded history. So, as if a general awakening was taking place around the world, there were other authors on a similar trail of thinking, that religions as we know them today represent the retelling of much older tales and contain hidden, underlying realities that escape the average "surface-reader." By studying the Old Testament texts, I discovered that the god of the Old Testament was not the kind old man in heaven with a long white beard that I was taught to believe in, but rather an abusive, jealous husband-figure with a volatile temper, and in some cases, a terrorist, or outright genocidal maniac. I also discovered that much of the New Testament Jesus narratives contain elements of pre-Christian astrological concepts, Egyptian sun-worship, and Zoroastrian eschatological visions, likely induced by a psychedelic sacrament, a magical drink called *Haoma*. After discovering the close similarities between the story of Jesus, Horus of Egypt, and several other crucified-savior stories from around the world, and the connections they all had to ancient sun-god myths, I concluded at that time that the Jesus-story was simply the latest incarnation of an age-old legend, in which the sun-god is depicted on the cross of the zodiac, surrounded by his 12 constellations (Apostles). After writing my book, *Outgrowing the Bible*, I felt that I had finally overcome residual superstitions inherited from early pre-scientific minds. I was now able to confidently close a chapter in my philosophical thinking that would never require reexamination - case-closed - end of story. For years after my book was written, I lived happily as a "born-again agnostic." I thought that I had forever encapsulated the religion of my youth in a resin jar of antiquity with a wax seal, and tossed it into the sea. Over time, I noticed books that were similar to mine became increasingly popular, such as Christopher Hitchens' *God is not Great*, or Richard Dawkins' *The God Delusion*. This left me rather satisfied that I was simply ahead of my time back in the year 2000 with the discovery that orthodox religion, in particular the Judeo-Christian religion, was not what people assume it is who haven't actually read or studied the supporting texts. In my world, the god of the Bible had been properly dethroned, with the underlying myths discovered and exposed for all to see. "Hard science" had won, and my worldview during the next few decades remained fairly stable. God (at least the god of the Bible) was a discarded myth. My view at the time was that, when we die, we are simply gone, unconscious, and that is it. All human experience occurs as a function of the physical brain. Consciousness is simply an epiphenomenon of organized material molecules. When the brain dies, everything dies. Furthermore, people who believed in any of the various religions of the world, or so-called "paranormal" phenomena like UFOs, ghosts, poltergeists, or cryptids such as "Bigfoot" or lake monsters, were simply credulous people who were prone to fantasy and unwilling to wait for the hard evidence to arrive. They were jumping the gun, creating a personal view of reality that will likely prove in the end to be fictitious. I had faith that there was always a "natural explanation" for everything, and that these explanations, if we were patient, would surely surface with due diligence to the scientific disciplines. My friends and associates and I were quite secure in our belief that the supernatural was for less-disciplined minds, or even the gullible. We were the correct people, the smart ones living amongst the unenlightened masses, who were all less evolved mentally and prone to delusions and fairy tales - or so we thought. As my own reality-paradigm radically shifted following a series of events that I shall explain, events that include my own near-death experience (NDE) and spiritual awakening, I encountered a sense of abandonment and betrayal from my former "scientific" associates. From this, I eventually realized that what we call "science" is, in many ways, a cult of faith, complete with its own doctrines and dogma whose adherents are as insecure and fragile as any of the rest of us. "Scientism" has all the earmarks of a modern religion, even though the adherants to Scientism vehemently reject this accusation. It is a religion in which one's worldview is not allowed to take on ideas that cannot be reproduced in a laboratory or measured in some way. It is a religion that comes with its own doctrinal tenants, beyond which a believer is not allowed to venture. Scientism has its own prophets and priests. It creates a division among human beings of "us" versus "them" – the scientifically literate whose minds are disciplined, opposed to the gullible untrained masses who flounder in a sea of unproved and erroneous ideas. In the world of Scientism, subjective experiences and anecdotal evidence must be discounted, even if, as in the case of the UFO phenomenon, the reports occur cross-culturally and have common elements and features that can be analyzed scientifically. This book is the story of how I became a heretic to my own long-term adherence to Scientism following an anomalous spiritual experience, after which I jumped headfirst into the complex field of the paraphysical. During this journey, which is ongoing, insights and speculations surfaced that I would now like to share concerning the greatest conundrum ever presented to humankind - that of our planet's flying saucer mystery, known simply to modern ufologists as "The Phenomenon."

CHAPTER 1

NDE (Near-Death Experience)

"We are physical beings evolving toward spirit – or rather, we are in fact spiritual beings who are gradually becoming aware of our spiritual essence – and in this evolution, NDE's, UFOEs, and other similar experiences may be understood as catalysts, courtesy of Mind at Large, which promote the necessary insight into our true being"

- Michael Grosso, *The Final Choice.*

EVERY DAY HERE on Earth, about 300,000 human beings enter 3D reality via biological birth, and about 150,000 exit when their physical vehicle ceases to function. These numbers fluctuate, of course, as the population totals change over time. Trillions of such exchanges of energy are also happening each day within the realms of other lifeforms, such as animals, insects, and microorganisms. It is as if the earth is a huge internal combustion engine, and the exchange of life energy, the process of constant birth and death among sentient creatures, is the burning fuel that keeps the earth vibrant and alive as the earth spins in space. While we are here in this physical existence, most of us live our lives with a vague awareness that animals and people are constantly dying all around us, but somehow we feel that we will escape this fate. Our focus for the moment is on our own daily dramas and concerns of the physical world. We live our lives as if we will surely be the only person in history to live forever on Earth. However, when it is finally our turn to draw near to the experience of passing from this physical world and leave it behind, the very meaning of life here is suddenly re-evaluated. Crisis events that thrust us near to death shatter our personal delusion of our own physical immortality. As someone who always considered myself "scientific," I had always thought, prior to my own near-death experience, that reports of out-of-body experiences and/or near-death experiences (NDEs) were likely the byproduct of a dying or deluded brain, a rush of chemicals surging through the brain that serve as a coping mechanism, so I never took any of the anecdotal accounts of near-death experiences seriously. That is, until such a perspective-altering event happened to me. On August 18, 2009, I experienced a personal encounter with the cosmic Mind at Large that forced the subject of death to resurface, a subject that I had buried in my own psyche as if it wasn't real as I went about my life. This event altered the very paradigm upon which my

1

life was built until that time. It shifted my focus from the material world to the higher cosmic realms beyond physical existence, and prompted a fantastic journey into the unknown that I would now like to share.

August 18, 2009 was a nice summer day that began as any other day. I got up, took a bath, got dressed, and went to work. I had an uneventful morning at my job as rehabilitation manager for a local nursing home in New Castle, Indiana. As an occupational therapist working in long-term care since 1997, my morning was full of clients who had recently broken their hips and needed rehab to return home once their full independence was restored. I also saw long-term residents that I knew well who had a documented decline in function prior to picking them up on therapy caseload for restoration to their prior level of function in the facility. As I was working with patients and residents that morning, my mind turned to going home and mowing my lawn during lunch hour. I had a rather small yard at the time. I thought I would run home, mow quickly, and return to work, no problem. When noon arrived, I drove home, parked, and opened the garage with the remote control, exposing the lawn mower waiting for me to start and mow. I pulled the mower out, lined it up to the edge of the grass by the driveway, and started pulling the cord. It was a little stubborn to start, so by the time it sputtered to life, I had already broken a sweat. About 20 feet into the first mowing path, I suddenly felt unusually fatigued, so much so that it was an effort to put one foot in front of the other. The first thing that crossed my mind was that I was possibly dehydrated in the hot sun, so I let the mower stop by releasing the handle, went inside to the kitchen sink, and poured myself a tall glass of cold water. As I finished drinking the glass of water, I noticed I felt a little nauseous. Was I coming down with something? Did I eat something that didn't settle well with me? I wondered. Not feeling well, I went into the bedroom, turned on the air conditioner, and relaxed on the bed, flopping around a little from side to side, trying to make myself feel okay again. I wondered, "What the hell is this about?" A few minutes of this, and I felt I needed to force myself to finish the lawn. I was going to have to do it fast, and get back to work, hoping that whatever ill feeling was haunting me would simply go away by the end of the day. Determined, I got up from the bed, turned off the air conditioner, and went back outside. I returned to the mower, and began pulling. The mower started, and I took off again across the yard in the sun. I immediately felt the sudden return of the heavy fatigue just as before, but like a dummy I forced myself to keep walking, the loud sound of the mower motor filling my ears, the grass flying out the side as I walked across the yard. Another wave of severe fatigue came over me, only this time I let the mower go and just stood there, feeling like I was going to collapse in the grass. I had never felt anything like this before in my life. Whatever this was that had me in its grip was going to take me down. It was at that very moment that I realized what was happening – I was having a heart attack! The first feeling that occurred to me was surprise as the reality of what was happening settled in on me, followed by the thought, "Oh, good, I get to find out right now what, if anything, exists on the other side!" Even though I had lived as an agnostic after writing a Bible-debunking book, I remained curious about the possibility of an existence beyond the physical world. I was like a kid on Christmas morning who didn't really believe in Santa, but was suddenly wondering what Santa Claus was going to bring me, hearing him struggling to get down my chimney and realizing that Santa was real after all. I felt that I was actually going to discover, at any moment, the actual mechanics behind this fabrication we call reality, or if there was anything real about any of the world's religions. Excited to embark on this adventure, I looked on the grassy ground and began circling around like a dog looking for a good place to do his business. I was actually smiling as I began looking around for a good place in the grass on a beautiful sunny day to lay down and leave the planet. However, as I was in the middle of this effort, something very surreal crept over me. I had been separated from my girlfriend, Julie, for about a year at this point after a painful breakup, and yet, I suddenly felt her presence near me, smiling softly, as if she was still with me by my side. I can't say that I physically "saw" her, as in a visual appearance. Instead, I simply "felt" her presence next to me. Then my mother and father, who were still alive and living in Bloomington, Indiana at the time, along with my younger brother showed up near me, making their familiar presences known to me. My estranged daughter, Holly, showed up near me from Hawaii, along with her mother, Mary, the mother of my daughter. Finally, my best friend, Marty, drew close to me there in the yard. After a few moments of basking in their loving presence, the most surprising entity of all showed up in their midst – a transcended version of me, along with an unmistakable electronic or *machine presence* in the background. So there I was, standing in the midst of a small group of discarnate individuals who were close to me in this life, along with an immortal version of myself and an accompanying background presence of some sort of complex machine. It was as if I had googled the key words, "Russ is dying," into the great cosmic search engine, and relevant entries were automatically showing up around me as associated links I might want to open, including my own online profile. There it all was for my consideration. As I looked up directly into the sun shining in my face, knowing I was about to cross over, I thought of a scene from the old western, "Little Big Man," where the old tribal elder looked up and said, "Today is a good day to die." I realized internally that, if I chose to, right then, I could go ahead and leave my physical body behind to join welcoming, familiar people from my life who were there for me as clearly as if they were standing there in their bodies. It would have been as simple as walking through a thin sheer curtain to see them. I was not alone. Time stood still. As I contemplated my decision, I experienced a flash of realization at that very moment that *it really was them*. Somehow, even though I knew all these individuals were still alive and well in the material world, here they were with me in a restored version of themselves, simultaneously existing in a separate, immortal, electronic reality. I sensed that this transcended aspect of their consciousness was keenly aware of their earthly forms. However, their earthbound versions were not aware of the transcended aspect of their beings that I was experiencing, nor would their earthly versions even believe in this aspect of themselves if I remained in my physical body to tell them about it. The multidimensional nature of our reality was now exposed to me. I now realized that, as we live our lives on Earth, we all simultaneously exist in another realm as a transcended being, completely outside time and space as we know it. These loved ones who drew near to me were alive and well in a future realm, living in a non-physical form. They were alive and living beyond their own own earthly selves, already existing in the next life, even though I knew a physical extension of them still lived in the material world as well. This was a real epiphany - "time" is not what we think it is, and we are not who we think we are. I was shown that our life here on Earth was only one aspect of our total being, that while we are here we simultaneously exist as an intact, immortal "energy body" in another realm, a version of ourselves that is aware of our every move here on Earth, and is quite interested, but a version we are not normally aware of while we are here in a physical body. It became real that all these people from my life here on Earth were quite alive and well in another world that we would call the "distant future," a realm in which all of us who are alive at this moment have long since parted from this present world into a realm ahead of us in which the earth that we know may not even exist anymore, having long since dissolved away from the universe in the sands of time. Even so, these recognizable, immortal, etheric entities, one of whom was me, were all still quite "alive" (whatever that means), with an aspect of their consciousness temporarily inhabiting physical bodies on Earth simultaneously. The earthly version of these entities were busy living their lives at this very moment with no knowledge of what I was now experiencing, no awareness of the fact that they were all with me now as a future version of themselves to embrace my crossing, a living version that is even more real than the version of themselves that they were aware of, who had drawn near to me in a moment of psychological crisis to comfort me and welcome me back to their immortal world. They beckoned me softly, together as a group, as if to say:

> *Russ, we are here for you, but are you sure you want to leave your earthly existence right now? You may cross over now if you wish, we welcome you, but we want you to know that you have a choice. The part of us that remains in your world would enjoy continuing our relationship with you here as it is. Life in the form you are about to exit is so fragile, so transitory, and so beautiful - you should enjoy it as long as you can, if you are able to comprehend. Our earthly selves would all miss you. We feel that we have more life to share together with you here on Earth, but if you choose, we will welcome you here with this version of ourselves as well, and you can join us now as one of us. It is your choice, Russ. If you really want to let it all go now, we understand, but we urge you to consider staying with the earthly version of us for a while longer.*

Part of me wanted to give in to crossing over to this new and wondrous realm, but the weight of their sincerity and loving concern touched me. Realizing at once that this ethereal version of everyone I know, everyone I have deep feelings for, and have been intimately close with in this life were, in fact, alive and well even while remaining in physical bodies here on Earth, reassured me that there was no real reason to exit at that moment in time. At this moment, my lifelong curiosity about the reality of an afterlife was answered to my satisfaction, without actually taking the final plunge. I thought for a moment longer, and then it came to me like a cold bucket of water thrown in my face, "Now that I know for sure that a world beyond Earth really exists, I want to keep living in this reality for now - the other world will still be there at another exit point in what I now call the 'future,' which is, as I discovered, an illusion." I thought, "Now I can continue yet another chapter in my earthly drama, and enjoy it on a different level with this new insight. I have to get myself to the hospital!" Realizing that I had left the keys to my car in the kitchen, I calmly mustered the strength to go back into the house, retrieve my keys, lock the door to the house behind me, get in the car, and head to the hospital, which was only a few miles away. In my mind, it was a game to see if I would make it to the hospital on my own, like all the times I had risked running out of gas and pulled into the gas station on fumes, just to experience the sense of relief of not running out of gas prior to pulling up to the pump. Would I make it now, or would I pass out and die at the side of the road? I thought, "If I'm going to die today, I would rather have already done so in the sun-drenched grass back at the house and died intentionally and peacefully, not by passing out in the car and driving out of control into someone's front yard, inconveniencing someone to run out and discover a car with a dead man in the driver's seat." I smiled at that thought. I can't say I was in any pain, I just knew I was having a serious heart issue and that I might not make it after all, feeling like I could pass out at any moment while driving. Looking back on it, I probably should have called an ambulance, but it seemed quicker at the time just to get in the car and go. I was suddenly filled with a confidence that, since I had encountered my loved ones in etheric form, and they had given me the choice to die that day or keep living, that I surely would not die now on the way to the hospital. In what seemed like an eternity, I finally arrived at the hospital, filling me with assurance that I was not just out of my mind. I was going to live. I pulled right up to the emergency room entrance, got out of the car, went through the front door, keys in hand. As I arrived at the information desk, a man who seemed to realize the urgency of my situation and perceived that someone in a distressed condition had just walked through the door, came around the desk in a hurry.

"May I help you?" he asked.

"Will you please park my car in the parking lot and bring me back the keys? I'm pretty sure I'm having a heart attack," I replied with a slight chuckle in my voice, realizing how weird that must have sounded.

Hastening to the situation, the man whipped around the desk quickly with a wheelchair for me as I sat down in it. He took my car keys and headed out the door to park my car as he told the wide-eyed girl at the desk to push me through the double doors into the emergency room. I saw him driving my car away out of my peripheral vision. The woman pushed me into a room, telling the nurses as she went by them, "I have a heart attack here!" They seemed panicked even though I was not, a gesture that I appreciated. The woman pushed me into a room with an open door and instructed me to lay down on a table. The gravity of my situation became apparent when suddenly I was surrounded by men and women in medical gowns.

"Heart attack!" I heard the doctor shout, as I felt a needle shoved into the back of my hand. "Morphine!" he continued.

As the liquid morphine entered my body, I felt a rush of total relaxation, and all my cares drifted away. I felt I was in good hands now. There wasn't anything left I could do except give in to the situation. The doctor quietly told me in a soft voice that this hospital did not have the appropriate accommodations. He told me he was going to have to put me on an ambulance to a larger facility, Ball Hospital, in Muncie, Indiana. "Good," I thought to myself. I had always imagined that it would feel cool to lie on a cot in an ambulance with the siren blasting, zooming down the highway and making traffic get out of the way. So out I went again, back outside, the sun shining on my face in the stretcher as it had before when I was considering leaving this world from my yard. I already missed those who had comforted me in my moment of crisis, and wondered momentarily if I had made the right choice. I briefly thought of my decision to endure the remainder of my physical life while in the presence of an ethereal, immortal version of my earthly friends and family. The experience was real, and that gave me confidence that I was going to make it, despite the fact there were people all around that seemed to think I might not. I wasn't worried at all. My loved ones knew what they were doing, and it just wasn't in the cards for me to die now after making the decision to go ahead and live a while longer here on Earth.

Riding on the stretcher in the speeding ambulance, two local sheriffs who were also EMTs, one male and one female, tended to me in uniform, the siren screaming, and the ambulance horn occasionally blasting in traffic. I reached down under the sheet and felt for my cell phone, found it, held on tight, and flipped it open. At the time, I still had my "Captain Kirk style" flip-open cell phone, just like Kirk used on the USS Enterprise from the original TV series, *Star Trek*. As I lay in the speeding ambulance, I began texting people about my situation, looking down at the screen with my peripheral vision, a tear running down the side of my face. I messaged my boss and told her I probably would not return to work that afternoon, and my brother in Bloomington to let him know what was going on, smiling to myself the whole time that I now knew something about my brother that he didn't - the world that he perceives is not all there is, and he is more than he thinks he is. Sensing the concern from the EMTs as they monitored my stats, worried looks on their faces, I tried to add some levity to the situation. I began talking to them about my previous weekend and how a bumblebee stung me on my right bare foot, and how bad that hurt. The man in uniform, well into his 50s, let his eyes drift from my monitor for a moment. His eyes then darted over to his female EMT partner, and I heard him whisper to her, "He'll think 'bee sting' when he gets to that cath lab." I didn't know what he was talking about at the time, but I was soon to find out. Pulling up to the hospital, they rolled me out of the ambulance and took me inside, where I was approached by two surgeons who were already scrubbed up in gowns and gloves, their arms and hands in the air, along with a nurse, who was also dressed and prepped. Once again, I sensed an urgency coming from them that I did not feel. One doctor spoke, "There are two different approaches we can take here. We can do a quadruple bypass, or we can try stents." Overwhelmed a little by a sudden choice thrust upon me, the details of which I knew very little, I replied,

"I don't know the implications of either option, can you explain the difference to me real quick?"

The doctor who was speaking gave a quick glance of concern to the others, and continued,

"Well, you have four blockages, artery occlusions, two are worse than the others, so we can give you a quadruple bypass, which is major surgery. This route involves harvesting a vein from your leg and using that to repair the clogged arteries in your heart. Or, we can go with two stents, little metal tubes that we insert through your femoral artery and feed up to your heart arteries. Sometimes stents are sufficient, and sometime they are not - it's a gamble. The quadruple bypass is very invasive, but is probably the more permanent solution, but we can try the stents if you want to go that route first, we just need to know what you want to do."

Fearing the old "crab cracker" operation I had seen before on medical shows where the doctors saw your sternum in half and crank you open wide while they operate on you, I spouted under duress,

"If there is a chance the stents will work, let's just go with those."

With that, the procedure for the stents was immediately underway. With a spurt of blood, the needle was expertly rammed into my femoral artery in my groin area to feed a line up to my heart. I realized at that moment what the EMT in the ambulance was talking about concerning the "bee sting" I was in for in the cath lab. As all eyes in the room including mine focused on the video monitor above me and to my left, I thought to myself,

"I'll bet if I was not medicated right now, that stab to the groin would have really hurt."

It was fascinating to watch the monitor with the others as the line carrying the little metal tubes to save my life were inserted and placed. The stents appeared on the monitor as little wobbling Chinese handcuffs moving ever so slowly to the problematic area. When the first stent arrived at just the right location, I watched as the stent opened up the collapsed heart artery. With a slight twist of his wrist, the doctor placed the stent using the remote cable line. My artery was suddenly functional again as the blood flow returned to normal. The first stent went in successfully, then the second. The doctor conducting the procedure seemed pleased with the placement results, which was comforting. After the stents were in, the line was backed out and heavy bandages placed over the entry wound to block the bleeding. I was then wheeled up to a regular hospital room full of electronic equipment. As I was wheeled out of the operating room, there was Julie, my ex-girlfriend, with tear stains on her cheeks. She and I had split up a year previous to that day. She wanted to get married after 3 years of dating, and I did not, due to trauma from my first two marriages. I would find out later that the reason she was crying was they would not let her in, because she was not immediate family. As I rolled by her, I realized what I had to do to fix this. I decided right then that if I survived this ordeal, I was going to take the plunge again with Julie, who obviously cared for me. "Surely," I thought, "A third marriage to Julie is preferable to death." This thought made me chuckle that it even crossed my mind like that, as I had just learned earlier that day that death does not really exist. Old thinking patterns die hard.

After an overnight stay with heavy monitoring, they sent me home to recover for a week off work. During this time, Julie tended to my needs, buying groceries and cooking food for me. I was touched by the fact that, even after a year of separation, she still cared for me, had dated no one else, and that my heart attack made no difference to her at all. I returned to work good as new a week later. Then, on October 30, 2009, just two months after a major heart attack that nearly killed me, Julie and I flew to Las Vegas for a "Vampire theme wedding," where we were properly married by an overly dramatic white-faced Dracula. I highly recommend Las Vegas, by the way, for a theme wedding. It's cheap and way more fun that the hassle of a traditional marriage. Most people who attend weddings do so out of social obligation anyway, and the Vegas wedding packages include a live web cam for the folks that actually want to watch. The experience was priceless. When Dracula was marrying us, I reflected for a moment about my decision to stay on Earth, and it felt like the right choice. I was having fun with it.

For the next few months following the wedding, I didn't really know if the stents were going to work or not. They say if they're going to fail, they will collapse in the first six months before they grow into the tissue. Knowing this, each night when I went to bed, I closed my eyes, not knowing if I would actually wake up the next morning. When my eyes opened again, and I realized I survived another day, I was determined more than ever to find something in my work day that made me glad to be alive. I've done that ever since, attempting in some way to make another person's suffering in this world a little less, or bring a smile to their faces that would not have been there if it weren't for my presence in their life that day. During the next several years, I continued to do just fine. After the ordeal was completely over, my cardiologist finally told me how close I came to dying that day. Coming that close to passing away from this earth, along with the experience of encountering people I knew who were still alive on Earth while simultaneously existing in a transcendent realm elsewhere, made me even more curious about the actual nature of the reality we live in. With this new curiosity, I was about to embark on a great adventure which would challenge my intellectual and intuitive abilities to their very limits. The world I was destined to enter, the world of the paraphysical, was an area of inquiry that I had no previous interest in or ever gave credence to. If someone had told me at the time of my heart attack that I, an ex-fundamentalist Christian turned hardcore agnostic, who had written a book several years previous entitled *Outgrowing the Bible*, would become involved in my later years with a personal investigative journey into the fringe world of the paranormal and ufology, I would not have believed them. In a way, even the fact that I evolved into this direction through an "accident" of circumstance is, in and of itself, a testament to the reality of the paranormal. Facing and living through my own near-death experience on the day of my heart attack, and having my previous conviction of final mortality forever shattered, I was now open to philosophical ideas involving parallel worlds and other dimensions. For me, my NDE served as the catalyst for a complete paradigm shift into the realms of the supernatural. But, as I would soon find out, I was about to fall into a much deeper rabbit hole than I could ever have imagined.

CHAPTER 2

Flying Saucers and the Paranormal

"I abandoned the Extraterrestrial Hypothesis in 1967 when my own field investigations disclosed an astonishing overlap between psychic phenomena and UFOs. The objects and apparitions do not necessarily originate on another planet and may not even exist as permanent constructions of matter. It is more likely that we see what we want to see and interpret such visions according to our contemporary beliefs."

– Dr. J. Allen Hynek, astronomer and former scientific consultant to Project Blue Book.

MY OWN NEAR-DEATH experience (NDE), during which I encountered the familiar presence of loved ones in transcendent form, as well as, much to my surprise, my own transcendent being, all of whom presented me with a warm, welcome invitation to cross over and re-join them, as well as the option, a choice, to remain on Earth for a while longer in this physical form with my newfound knowledge of the beyond, i.e., the certainty that life does not end at physical death, shook my previous concept of reality to the core. According to my own carefully-created view of the world that I had prior to this event, nothing of that sort was supposed to happen, the afterlife was just a fanciful product of the human imagination. In the months following my NDE, once I mentally restabilized, moving past the thought that I might die in my sleep and not wake up the next morning from failed heart stents, an internal urge surfaced to take a second look, or even a complete reevaluation, of the underlying nature of reality, including the so-called "paranormal" that I had previously placed in the category of superstition and misperception of reality. In this category were ghosts, poltergeists, elemental spirits, and cryptids, along with extraterrestrial or interdimensional life elsewhere in the universe or even here among us. I wondered if the human race invented these creatures along the way from a grueling past as a primitive, ape-like species to a more intelligent creature with expanded consciousness, or if there was, in fact, an underlying reality to all these phenomena after all. For the first time in my life, I felt open to considering that maybe I had it all wrong, that science and reason as we understood them were missing something, a "missing link," if you will, between science and the supernatural. I felt the desire to clean the slate and forget everything that I currently held true, to take a fresh look at the world without parental or cultural prejudice, but I wasn't sure quite how to go about it. Then, one night, I received a phone call that was destined to change my world forever.

Karl, a friend of mine, was someone I knew socially as a fellow camper at a clothing-optional campground I enjoyed in the summer as a welcome escape from the grueling Indiana winters. I knew from his online blogging that Karl was an avid amateur "ghost hunter." I had always accepted that ghost-hunting was just an eccentric hobby of his, and never gave it much thought past that. However, one evening in the fall of 2012, 3 years after my NDE and resulting renewed openness and interest in other possible dimensions of reality, I received a phone call from Karl the ghost hunter. This call came just prior to the infamous December 21, 2012 date. This date in history, according to many esoteric researchers, was supposed to have wreaked havoc and mayhem upon us from a rare planetary alignment, causing floods, earthquakes, and other calamities, possibly even a magnetic pole reversal. Researchers such as David Wilcock were even looking for some sort of transcendent experience for the entire human race, yet another way to interpret ancient prophecy concerning this date in time, well-outlined in Wilcock's book, *The Source Field Investigations: The Hidden Science and Lost Civilizations Behind the 2012 Prophecies*. On December 21, 2012, many looked for either a planetary disaster or a transition into "5th density," a vibrational transcendence into another realm for those who were ready. I knew from the history books that magnetic polar reversals have happened quite frequently in our past. Even so, we are all still here. So, even though no one really knew exactly what to expect, I wasn't really worried about a magnetic polar reversal, although I did buy a six-pack of pure bottled water and a couple of cans of sardines, just in case. During the call with Karl that evening, he mentioned that he had hooked up with a group of like-minded folks who frequently sponsored exploration events in real haunted houses. By "real" he meant houses with histories of actual, documented, eyewitness reports of paranormal incidents. Karl invited me to attend an all-night encounter group at the infamous *Roads Hotel* in Indiana, which was historically reported to be quite haunted. At first, I wasn't really all that interested. I thought for sure that an evening in a haunted house would amount to me staring at the paint on the wall all night, with nothing eventful happening. Although I was curious about the so-called "paranormal" now, and whether ghosts actually exist or not, I thought the likelihood of an actual paranormal encounter was small, even if ghosts are a real phenom-enon, and that I would just be wasting my time on a perfectly good weekend evening, along with my $40.00 entrance fee to the owner of the house. As I was about to politely turn the offer down by making some believable excuse, I blurted out, "Sure, I'll do that - sounds fun" instead. I was actually surprised at myself when I heard this come out of my mouth, but now I had said it. When I got off the phone I just sort of sat there, already missing the 40 bucks that was to soon escape from my wallet, not to mention the likely waste of time. For that amount, I could just get myself a nice lobster dinner instead of running around with a group of gullible people looking for something that isn't there all night. After that moment passed, I actually began feeling sort of excited about the adventure of it all. There I was, the author of a Bible-debunking book with a title that made the superstitious want to drop it on the floor like a hot potato, a lifelong rationalist, who was now headed to a real haunted house to search for ghosts with a group of total strangers except for my friend, Karl, who was coordinating the event. Something about that idea, despite my skepticism about the whole matter, felt sort of cool. It was the first time since I parted with fundamentalist religion after my book was completed, a book that effectively dissected the beliefs of much of the world into shreds and left me without any viable alternative belief structure to replace the loss with, that I was open to the paranormal. After experiencing such a strange encounter with the unknown during my NDE, I was now curious once again concerning the mysteries of the unknown realms. I figured this would either set me on a new course of belief and action, or I would simply be out the 40 bucks and tell myself, "I told you so!" Either way, I decided that I would just go and accept the outcome. I made up my mind right then and there that I was going to visit the so-called haunted house with an open heart and mind. If there was anything to all this stuff about ghosts and encounters with disembodied human spirits, then by gum I was going to find them. I had no comprehension at the time what a doorway into an unforeseen netherworld I was about to open. My life was soon destined to move in a totally unexpected direction. I was about to take the red pill mentioned in the movie, *The Matrix*, and fall into an abyss of intrigue and discovery that I never even knew existed.

The Roads Hotel in Atlanta, Indiana, was originally built by Abraham Kauffman in 1893. The house, which was recently purchased by a man who was raised in a spiritualist household and wanted to open the house to persons interested in encountering the ghosts within, has a long history of alleged paranormal occurrences. This haunted house was the destination of my first exploration into the murky field of the paranormal. Newton Roads purchased the hotel for his wife, Clara, who ran the hotel along with their son, Everett, and daughter, Hazel. The hotel served as a layover for the railroad that passed through the business district of town. Newton Roads was the son of Philip Rhoades, who claimed property that the government had granted him for his participation in the Civil War. Philip Rhoades was a wagonmaker, and was known as one of the founding members of Hamilton County, Indiana. Once his land was claimed, he returned to gather his family and bring them to their new home. Not much is known about Philip's wife, Susanna, who died traveling with her family from Pennsylvania to Indiana. It is said that she was buried in the wagon trails so that Native Americans would not desecrate her body. So, without Susanna, Philip Rhoades and his children made their way to their new home. Philip remarried Catherine Robinson, whose family had also relocated to the area. One of their ten children was Newton A. Roads. Newton Roads was a Mason, an Odd Fellow, and a Maccabee. When the Roads House was built, it was called *The Hotel* in Atlanta, Indiana. In the early 1900's, natural gas wells were discovered. This made Atlanta, Indiana the place to be for employment. Rumors and legend tell us that, with six taverns in town, *The Hotel* became a natural place to establish a bordello. Atlanta grew from a mere 80 people to a population of over 1200 during this time. As a brothel, the hotel is alleged to have hosted many famous guests, including gangsters Al Capone and John Dillinger. Although these visitations to the bordello have not been proven, it does make sense, as these were the days of Prohibition in America. Locals say that there was once a burial casket in the bay window of the hotel. Since alcohol was illegal, the casket would give the impression that a funeral was going on when, in reality, the casket was filled with bootleg liquor. Eventually, the brothel became a personal residence. With the exception of a short period as a bed and breakfast, it has remained that way ever since. The Hotel was most recently purchased by an Indianapolis paranormal investigation group called, "Sixth Sense Indy Paranormal." In the short time the group had owned the house, they had supposedly already experienced several paranormal events. The group claims that the house is "very haunted." Many paranormal investigators who have visited the house report capturing good electronic voice phenomena (EVP) and even video of moving shadows. Reports exist of human conversations between invisible entities on the top floor. Doors have been known to open and close and even slam when there were no people around the visitors. Footsteps, shadows, and even glimpses of men, women, and children have been reported. The lights in the house are reported to turn on and off by themselves on occasion, even when the house is unoccupied.

Since I was a neophyte in the realm of the paranormal, I searched my personal possessions from my own house prior to meeting up with Karl and the others at the Roads Hotel for anything remotely related to the supernatural. I gathered a sword that I had owned for nearly 30 years that traveled with me during my days of following the Grateful Dead in the 1980s. During this time, I went by the nickname, "Darkstar." The sword had a custom-made leather sheath with engraved markings of a black sun created by the high priest of a Wiccan community I once visited in Tennessee that was operated by a local business woman, Lady Amethyst, who served as the High Priestess. I also took a crystal ball that I had acquired along the way with me, and an old Ouija board, just in case these items would aid me in calling forth a ghost from the hidden realms. As I was gathering all these artifacts from my life's travels together in a sincere attempt to remain open to and connect with the supernatural if it was there at the Roads Hotel, I was actually surprised over how many items were in my possession that carried with them occult implications. Apparently, even as a "rationalist," I was always somehow attracted to the occult, if only from a theatrical perspective. I have also always been a fan of the horror fiction genre. I just never thought there was anything to it other than a dark fantasy world. Even so, I was determined to take anything and everything with me that might have some interest or attraction to a disembodied human who lived at the haunted house and was willing to appear to me that evening.

I arrived at the haunted house that evening in Atlanta, Indiana, with a sense of anticipation for the unusual. It was just getting dark outside, dusk casting an eerie grey light on the house itself upon first glance. Karl was standing there as I pulled up, smoking a cigarette outside as he waited for his guests to arrive. I carted all my articles of occult paraphernalia into the doorway, passing by Karl who raised his eyebrow as if to say, "Why the hell did you bring all that crap?" I walked past Karl to the inside of the house, in the kitchen area, where I laid down all my objects of ghostly pleasure on a table. There was a pizza in the kitchen area and people talking, so I joined the group, had a piece of pizza, and skeptically listened in on some ongoing conversations about encounters with ghosts. When everyone finally arrived, the owner of the house gathered us all together for a tour through the house. He revealed to us the history of each room as we went, who lived and died there, the boarders from the past who committed suicide, and the history of the infamous years as a brothel. I couldn't help but wonder about all the kinky sex that may have happened in the very spaces I was touring. The host informed us of all the hauntings and appearances over the years, of strange creatures called *crawlers* and *shadow people*, and occasionally, physical attacks with markings left on bodies as they walked through the house at night. As the host was telling us all this, I was reminded of a haunted trail ride I had experienced the previous Halloween, in which they sat down the customers on bales of hay and showed a movie about all the strange happenings in the woods, axe murders and so forth. After the showing of the film, when you went out on the hay ride, these stories loomed in the back of your mind and contributed heavily to making the haunted ride very scary. I was conjecturing that this was probably what was happening during our preliminary house tour. As our host was telling us of the person who hung themselves in the back room, and all the other people who had died in the house, I thought to myself, "This is why people are claiming experiences here - it is all their own imagination creating the happenings after hearing the tales on this tour. The stories get people's imagination stirred up ahead of time." So then, after we were all properly freaked out with the stories of deaths and hauntings, we returned to the kitchen area, and the host vacated after turning out all the lights. We were finally alone in the dark for our night of ghost-seeking. I wondered what to expect now. Was the host going away to put on a costume, return upstairs in hiding, and jump out at us in the dark? Were animatronics hidden in the house that would scare us? Was this all a big farce designed to fabricate fake experiences, create stories from the guests, and perpetuate a profiteering racket for the owner of the house? I was unsure. Some of the attendees had professional, expensive EVP systems to play around with, or even a "Ghost Radar" application on their smart phones. Whether or not there were actually any ghosts in the house, what was apparent was I was in the midst of people who were properly prepped and open for contact with the beyond. It made me ponder what it was that they were all actually looking for. What is a "ghost," anyway? Why would a person who passed away from this life become trapped or choose to remain in the house of their own death? Is it realistic to believe that they could possibly communicate with the living through an electronic device or a smart phone application? I pictured some nerdy software programmer sitting at his desk designing random word generators on his drawing board, quite amused that the product he was designing would go into use as a communication device between the living and the dead. The most amusing part of my night in the haunted house was watching all the ghost hunters using their expensive electronic devices to seek out communication with the beyond. It felt like I was a kid again, scared of the dark, carrying a flashlight, and wary of things that go bump in the night. One of the rooms in the house had a collection of "haunted dolls" sitting on shelves. As a child, I was once frightened by an episode of Rod Serling's *Night Gallery* called "The Doll," in which a horrid-looking doll came to life and bit people. Ever since seeing this show as a kid, I had been scared of dolls. So, in an attempt to face my fear of dolls, at one point during the night I went in by myself and sat down on the bed in front of all the dolls in the pitch dark. There I was, in a bona fide haunted house, in the dark after midnight, in a room full of haunted dolls, and I was ok with that. I have to admit that I was creeped out a little, but after sitting there for a spell without seeing any of the doll's faces change on me as I shined my flashlight at them, or fly off the shelves and attack me, I did become a little more comfortable with dolls that night. I was aware that psychologists use a technique called "flooding" with people suffering from various phobias. Flooding involves overwhelming a patient with the object of their terror. Suppose a patient has arachnophobia (the fear of spiders). Using the flooding technique, the psychologist exposes the phobic person to an enormous number of spiders until their phobia subsides. So, I used the flooding technique on myself that night to rid myself once and for all of my lifelong fear of dolls, and to a degree, I think it worked.

The word-generators on electronic gadgets, which occasionally provided an audible word spoken in an electronic voice, did produce quite a bit of excitement among the ghost hunters. Each time the device would spout off a word, the listeners would attempt to relate the word to something relevant, demonstrating the power of suggestion and serving as a crowbar to the imagination. For example, if the electronic device said the word, "Wolf," efforts would be made by seekers to search for a connection. Maybe one of the listeners had a wolf on their shirt, or liked wolves as a child. This would serve as "evidence" in their minds that a disembodied spirit was trying to make their presence known to us by spitting out a word that had some relevance. The problem with all this, I thought, was that any word can find meaning to someone in the group. A random word-generator will always enable someone to word-search their own brain and find some type of connection. So, needless to say, as a lifelong skeptic, my first priority was to search for rational explanations for a word-generator program providing words that seemed to have some relevance. Although some of the words coming forth did, in fact, appear to be uncanny in timing and relevance, it was easy for me with my background of disbelief to write this all off as the same sort of phenomenon as a Tarot card reading, in which the reader says something like, "You have always felt misunderstood." Most people have felt misunderstood at some point in their lives, so the person getting the reading suddenly thinks the Tarot card reader is a wizard connected to very personal information about them. I was even a little angry with my own skepticism at one point in my haunted house experience. I actually wondered if my own skepticism was interfering with my having a real ghost experience. I was trying to stay aware of how pre-existing beliefs might adversely affect my night's experience with a close encounter in a real haunted house. On the other end of the spectrum were those running around the dark house with their "Ghost Radar" smart phone apps as true believers. These folks were really hanging on to every word and accepting that as real communication from the dead. This stretched credulity as to how this could really happen using a free phone app. As the evening went on, I became more relaxed after I realized that no one was going to jump out at me. It wasn't a joke-like "haunted house" experience after all, and no animatronic ghosts were planted. It was just an old empty house with creaking wooden stairs and an interesting history, along with reports of various types of odd phenomena occurring throughout the years. It was quite entertaining that people were so intent on finding something that evening. I enjoyed watching how their own belief structures affected their reported experiences. I did not see anything unusual that night. I do not mean to insult any spirits that may have actually decided to live in this house or haunt it, but in my estimation, the spirits made a very poor showing that evening.

As the sun came up the next morning, some in the group were still banging around in the house. Others, myself included, had passed out asleep at some point on a couch or one of the beds in a room. As I went to my car, despite the mundaneness of my own ghost-hunting experience, I did leave the house with my mind opened to possible real paranormal phenomena concerning entities of various types that may actually exist beyond the range of visible light. I left curious about the real nature of reported "orbs" and "apparitions." My personal experience at the Roads Hotel, despite the fact that I did not personally encounter anything beyond the ordinary, did, in fact, serve as a catalyst to opening a portal of interest in my brain concerning paranormal phenomena. For me, my night spent in the Roads Hotel served as a real stargate to another reality. That night, skeptical as I was in my observations of my fellow ghost-hunters and their ghost-seeking gadgets, served as a very real entrance for me into a previously-unknown world. I walked through the doorway that night, and if I had not chosen to go through this doorway by agreeing to a visit to a haunted house on the invitation of a friend, I would not be the person I am today, or hold the worldview that I now possess.

Following my ghost-hunting experience at the Roads Hotel, I began devouring all kinds of books about various types of paranormal and psychic phenomenon. The first thing I learned was that I was not alone in my skepticism about the electronic devices. There are paranormal investigators who believe that any sort of electromagnetic device taken into a haunted house actually wards off what we call ghosts. In their view, even though there are just as many ghost encounters in the daytime as there are at night, it was proper to turn out the lights as we did. As is turns out, darkness serves a purpose other than providing atmosphere to get people in the mood for contact by eliminating the electromagnetic field effect of the light bulb itself. In addition to eliminating this source of electromagnetism, all radios, phones, and even EVP devices of various sorts should all be turned off. According to the professional ghost-hunting literature, apparitions are more likely to appear when there is nothing else electrical to interfere with their presence, as their only detectible presence is an electromagnetic signature. In the months following my Roads Hotel experience, I spent time in the dark with no electrical interference, in quiet meditation, open to communications with whatever was in the room with me that I could not see with my eyes. What came to me as an "impression," for lack of a better term, was that we are definitely not alone. I began to feel that, beyond the range of human sight and hearing, we share our space in the universe with other types of beings who live in realms that are virtually undetectable to us. How could we possibly verify the existence of life beyond our own when our sensory apparatus is so limited? Are ghosts really disembodied humans who have passed away, or are they something else entirely? These questions led me into a sincere search for possible answers, and I soon discovered that some of the answers to the mysteries lie hidden in our collective world mythology.

Ghosts

As previously mentioned, during my own near-death experience (NDE), the presence of multiple loved ones, friends and family I knew here on Earth in this life, drew near to me in loving comfort. During this period of closeness, the veil between this world and the next drawing very thin, it was kindly revealed to me via mental impression that, even though these loved ones currently existed on Earth living mortal lives, they were also simultaneously alive and well in a recognizable, transcended form in another dimension, the realm we all go (or return to) when our bodies cease functioning. These beings communicated to me that a moment of decision was at hand, a choice between crossing over to where they were, which was very tempting and seemed like a peaceful and wonderful place, or to remain here on Earth in my present form for a while longer. This experience opened my mind to the idea that the universe may be purely mental in nature, matter simply representing energy at a particular vibrational state, and that, in reality, we are all immortal beings of light. The epiphany I experienced that day could best be described such that the material world, like water in the form of ice, represents only one aspect of a larger reality that we are generally unaware of, a world that I had ignored all my life, having been an unwitting victim of the modern doctrine of material reductionism. The "ice" of the material world also exists as liquid or steam, depending on the energy state applied. My virgin ghost-hunting experience at the Roads Hotel left me with the impression that ghosts are, in fact, a rather normal part of the world, even though I did not encounter a ghost as I had hoped during my initial attempt.

If you ask, most people describe ghosts as the "disembodied spirits of dead humans" who, for some unknown reason, linger around a particular location, typically an old house, just to freak humans out with occasional appearances and/or apparitional manifestations. It is commonly thought that a ghost is a human being who passed, possibly violently, and is stuck between worlds. During my own NDE, even though the people drawing near to me appeared as personality impressions, I definitely felt that, if I waited too long while deciding whether or not to remain here on Earth or cross over, that these entities would become crystal clear and visible to me as I transitioned from this realm to theirs, as a telescope becomes focused on a star with the turn of the focus control. If we are all mental energy in various states of being, our perceptions of reality as received by the brain are akin to a television tuner adjusted to a particular channel. Occasionally, under certain conditions like foul weather, images from another channel are able to "bleed through" into the channel we normally watch and interfere somewhat, until those conditions that brought the image leaking through subside. Likewise, I suppose it is possible for the same thing to occur between dimensions. Ghost sightings may represent another channel being picked up by our standard sensory apparatus on occasions when the conditions are right for it to happen, or when our brain chemistry is altered in such a way that we tune in to other information that is not normally received, such as what happens during a near-death experience or a trip on psychedelic drugs. The conditions for ghost appearances seem to have something to do with the way they died. In cases of traumatic deaths, there may be a particular emotional vibration associated with that experience that keeps a person lingering around a little longer than when they die peacefully and move on. Since our way of experiencing time is a function of the way the material world is put together, time experienced as a ghost may only seem like moments to the individual for whom this fate befalls, even though in some cases, a ghost apparition can haunt a particular location in spatial time as we perceive time for centuries.

Historical Ghost Cases

There are many documented instances of ghost appearances, some of which have become famous in our world. For example:

Anne Boleyn, second wife of Henry VIII, was beheaded on May 19, 1536 after being falsely accused of adultery, incest, and witchcraft. Since that horrible day, Anne's ghost has appeared to many witnesses in locations such as Hever Castle, Blickling Hall, Salle Church, Marwell Hall, and the Tower of London.

One of the most famous photographs of a ghost is that of the "Brown Lady," who appears in a brown brocade dress in Raynham Hall in Norfolk, England. This female ghost is thought to be Lady Dorothy Walpole who died mysteriously in the year 1726. A man, Major Loftus, was staying at Raynham Hall in 1849, and was horrified to encounter the ghost, as she had only black sockets for eyes, which he found quite disturbing. Sightings began just after her death, but waned after the photo was taken in 1936.

In 1881, King George V of England encountered the ghost ship known as the "Flying Dutchman," a ship that was originally sailed by Captain Hendrik van der Decken as he attempted to round the Cape of Good Hope. King George wrote:

At 4 a.m. the Flying Dutchman crossed our bows. A strange red light as of a phantom ship all aglow, in the midst of which light the mast, spars, and sails of a brig 200 yards distant stood out in strong relief as she came upon the port bow."

Later that same day, the sailor who originally spotted the ghost ship fell to his death.

Many residents and visitors of the White House have reported seeing the ghost of Abraham Lincoln over the years, including First Lady Grace Coolidge, Queen Wilhelmina of the Netherlands, and Winston Churchill.

Clifton Hall in Nottinghamshire, England, was owned by the Clifton Family since the 13th century. The huge estate was finally sold in 1958 to Anwar Rashid with his wife, Nabila, and their four children. The very first night the family spent in their new home they heard knocking sounds and a man's voice calling, "Hello, is anyone there?" One night, Nabila went downstairs to prepare some milk for their 18-month-old son. Nabila saw their eldest daughter sitting on the couch watching television. Nabila called out to her, but she did not answer, and just sat there staring at the television. Nabila returned upstairs to the daughter's bedroom and found her sound asleep in her bed. Frightening occurrences such as these continued for eight months after they bought the place. The Rashid family then sold the estate and fled the area. There are multiple reports of babies crying (a classic paranormal occurrence) and many have reported seeing a woman pacing the floor through a window from the outside in a room that was bricked up from the inside of the house over the years.

One classic ghost-sighting is the common "Lady in White." Multiple sightings have been reported over the years on Balete Drive in the Philippines (The Philippine Islands are haunted by everything). The Lady in White stands in the middle of the road there. Her face is either blank, or obscured with blood. Locals say that, if you drive on Balete Drive at night, to make sure your back seat is full. If your back seat is empty, you are at risk for being filled with an ominous sense of dread right before spotting the Lady in White sitting in your back seat in the rear view mirror.

At the Myrtles Plantation in St. Francisville, Louisiana, lived a resident slave, Chloe, who was known for listening into keyholes for the shenanigans of the household residents. One day, Chloe was caught doing this by the Master of the house, and for punishment, he sliced off Chloe's ears and made her wear a green scarf to cover the wound. For revenge, Chloe made a poison cake with Oleander leaves and served it to her cruel master. The cake was consumed, not by the Master, her intended victim, but by her master's wife and two daughters who died a painful death a couple days after they ate Chloe's poison cake. Chloe fled for her life, but was hanged by plantation slaves who feared that they would suffer also for Chloe's deeds. An enigmatic black and white photograph of the Myrtles Plantation exists that shows a black woman wearing a scarf and cowering behind a pillar on the property. This photo is believed by many to be an image caught on film of Chloe's ghost. The new owners give tours of the plantation to interested guests, and tell the stories of ghosts on the property over the years, including a woman's ghost that is frequently spotted in a mirror, and the ghost of a woman who engages in "voodoo chants" if you are unlucky enough to be sleeping in her room.

Northeast on Archer Lane between the Willowbrook Ballroom and Resurrection Cemetery in Justice, Illinois, a young woman wearing a white party dress with light blonde hair and blue eyes who has been dead since the 1930s has allegedly been picked up in vehicles on multiple occasions. The specter always asks her driver to stop in front of Resurrection Cemetery, and then simply vanishes from the car. One of her victims is said to have been a taxi driver who picked her up in 1973 and was upset that she didn't pay her fare. He went to Chet's Melody Lounge, a local bar across from the cemetery and complained about it. This frightened the locals who were listening as he described a woman who perfectly fit the description of the ghost known to everyone in the area as "Resurrection Mary."

Kate Morgan checked into the Hotel de Coronado just south of San Diego, California, on November 24, 1892. It is speculated that she took a large dose of quinine and stayed in the motel room to induce a miscarriage from an unwanted pregnancy. Five days later, on November 29, she was found dead on the steps leading out to the beach with a bullet in her temple. The death was ruled a suicide, and ever since then, an apparition of a woman in Victorian clothing has been witnessed walking about in the Hotel, along with flickering lights and other strangeness.

The commotion of a great party can be heard occasionally in the empty Grand Ballroom of the Stanley Hotel in Estes Park, Colorado. Children can be heard making noises in the halls, and guests report apparitions standing in their rooms and simply gazing upon them in their beds. On the fourth floor, witnesses report a male ghost thought to be Lord Dunraven, the previous owner who stares out the window of room 407.

These are just a small sampling of the hundreds of historical ghost-sighting cases that exist in the vast sea of documented accounts that have accumulated over the centuries, with no end in sight, as ghost sightings keep coming in from credible witnesses, year after year.

Ghost Types

Certainly, there have been enough sightings of ghosts over the years to give substance to the phenomenon. What it tells us, if we can take the sightings at face value, is that sometimes, people who pass hang around in ethereal form for some reason. It is as if they are temporarily trapped on the physical plane, or possibly do not realize that they have passed. Many different ghost types have been documented in the ghost lore, including:

The Crowd Demon - A crowd demon is a creature that appears in a developed photograph when no such creature was observed with the natural eye as the photograph was taken. When the photograph is developed and examined, a strange dark figure appears on the film. In some cases, the image looks like a humanoid reptile eating the face of one of the audience members. Crowd demons are also captured on video, and appear as a black figure streaking across the stage, or running through the crowd.

Animal Ghosts - Animal ghost sightings are common. A huge volume of reported apparitions of animals exist in the ghost literature. Many are reports of pets that appear as ghost-like apparitions. These sightings paint a different picture than the "crisis apparitions" that humans are thought to manifest following a traumatic death. Dogs, cats, and farm animals have commonly appeared as ghosts, along with more bizarre accounts, such as sightings of Lions that were once seen running around England, and ghosts of large black dogs that have appeared in churches, frightening the parishioners.

The Vortex - The Vortex is also unobservable by the naked eye. Vortexes are ghost images that appear on film as a thread or loop of plasma-like energy. Some paranormal researchers believe the vortex allows other types of ghosts to "piggyback" on them, so they are considered "carriers."

Inanimate ghosts – Inanimate ghosts are like the phantom ships that plagued sailors in the 17th century. Inanimate ghosts can also be cars or trains. They travel in the same route over and over again, as if stuck in some sort of time loop.

Doppelgangers – The Doppelganger is a human double of a person that is still alive. Doppelgangers can appear in more than one place at the same time.

Kobolds – Kobolds are a fairy or sprite-like manifestation. Kobolds have obscure origins but have most recently appeared in German culture. Kobolds are normally invisible, disembodied entities who have the ability to materialize in various forms, such as animals, especially black cats or bats, fire, candles, or human beings. Kobolds who appear as fire are thought to enter and exit a home through the chimney. They most commonly appear as small human-like creatures, and are thought by some to represent the spirits of dead children. Legend has it that Kobolds who occupy ships are aquatic water spirit known as the *Klabautermann*. These entities often wear sailor's clothing on deck and smoke pipes. Kobolds who occupy mines are homely and dwarfish, and may have common cultural origins to gnomes, dwarves, or goblins, as well as the Norse Dwarf and the Cornish Knocker. Mine-dwelling Kobolds gave rise to the name of the element cobalt, as medieval miners blamed the indwelling Kobolds for the arsenical ores in the mines, such as cobaltite. Kobolds called *Bieresals* were though to inhabit beer cellars at inns. Kobolds that appear in households often wear peasant-like clothing or appear as helpful infants. Household Kobolds are known to be both helpful and mischievous, and are related to the English Boggart, Hobgoblin, or Pixy, as well as the

Scottish Nisse or Tomte. Kobolds may go all the way back to early Pagan beliefs in tree spirits, the essence of which was thought to reside in the Mandrake Root which forms the shape of a human. Historically, Kobolds have existed who have actually achieved fame, such as King Goldemar, Hodekin, or Heinzelmann, who took residence at the Hundermuhlen Castle in 1584, all of whom gave warnings about dangers to the human owners of the homes.

Lemurs - Lemurs originate from Roman times. Considered a malignant entity, a Lemur is a wandering entity associated with darkness, doom, and misfortune.

Etheric Revenants - Etheric Revenants are plasma-like amorphous ghosts that drain psychic energy away from human victims. Etheric Revenants are similar in nature to the human vampires of legend. Etheric Revenants usually represent a recently deceased person who has returned as an apparition with malevolent intent. Etheric revenants are thought to have been evil-doers in their physical lives, vain and wicked in nature, who seek to remain or return within the physical realm to cause harm, including the spreading of diseases among humans. The legend of Dracula is an example of an Etheric Revenant. The traditional cure for the evil wrought by Etheric Revenants is exhumation and decapitation of the buried corpse, along with the removal and burning of the heart. In Norse mythology, a being similar to the Etheric Revenant exists as the *Aptrgangr* or *Draugr*. The Norse version of the Etheric Revenant does not sleep during the day, resists destruction, and has magical powers. Cultural counterparts to the Etheric Revenant exist throughout the Caribbean, and are known as *Soucouyant*, the *Olehigue*, or the *Loogaroo*.

Residual Historical Hauntings – Residual Historical Hauntings are a rare type of haunting that appears in several historical cases, such as the cases of Anne Moberly or Eleanor Jourdain. The movements of the Residual Historical Haunting are repetitive.

Artificial Ghosts – Artificial Ghosts are intentionally-created apparitions that are manifested by humans and possess some level of physicality, such as the Tibetan *Tulpa*.

Poltergeists - Poltergeists (noisy ghost) are a particular category of ghost or apparition that are associated with the ability to move physical objects. Typical reports of poltergeist activity describe objects sailing across rooms, cabinet doors opening and shutting rapidly, door-knocking sounds, and the biting, striking, or tripping of humans. As opposed to other types of ghosts who haunt certain locations, poltergeists are known to haunt certain people. Many theories attempt to explain the phenomenon of poltergeists as outright hoaxes or psychological disturbances on the part of the percipients, but the hoax and mental illness theories follow just about any anomalous occurrence that we don't understand, and certainly a few of the poltergeist cases reported each year do fall into these categories, especially those who happen to be above fault lines or historical earthquake activity. An examination of the Mercalli Intensity Scale for seismic activity makes it easy to see how some preliminary earthquake symptoms could be mistaken for poltergeist activity. The Mercalli scale rates the physical effects on a scale from 1-12, with 1 representing "not felt at all" a rating of 12 as "extreme." Level 2 is felt only by a few persons at rest, especially in the upper floors of buildings. Level 3 is felt by all persons in a house, especially on upper floors. Level 4 is felt by all indoors and a few outdoors, and includes the disturbance of dishes, windows, and doors (typical of poltergeist reports), and people who are in vehicles and are rocked noticeably. Level 5 seismic disturbances on the scale are felt by everyone, pendulum clocks may stop, and objects are overturned. Dishes and windows can break. Level 6 moves heavy furniture, causes ceiling and wall plaster to fall, and frightens everyone. Level 7 causes slight to moderate damage in ordinary-built structures, and poor structures are damaged severely. At levels 8-12, it becomes more obvious what is going on. People recognize that an earthquake is happening, it is quite frightening to everyone, and causes severe damage to buildings and can kill people in the process. So levels 1-7, from no effect to very strong, represents the range of seismic activity that can easily produce false poltergeist reports to the local police, when unrecognized seismic activity has occurred in the area. Guy Lambert in the 1950s suggested that underground water turbulence could cause stress movements inside a house and generate poltergeist reports. Ball lightning has also been offered as an explanation over the years for some poltergeist cases. Paranormal investigators usually attribute poltergeist activity to malicious spirits on the lower end of what paranormal researcher John Keel called the "Superspectrum" and associate poltergeist activity with the elementals that are thought to inhabit the realms of air, earth, fire, and water. Like most paranormal phenomena, the waters are muddied in the body of poltergeist reports. These reports include the entire spectrum of hoaxes, misidentified natural phenomena (like seismic activity), defective human perceptions, along with a core group of truly anomalous and mysterious happenings involving forces and intelligences that science does not yet acknowledge, and humans do not yet comprehend.

Elementals

The 16th century physician, Paracelsus, taught from older sources of mystery schools that the elements of air, earth, fire, and water, are inhabited by their own associated intelligences. Likewise, Manley P. Hall's seminal work, *The Secret Teachings of All Ages*, goes into detail concerning the nature of these inhabited elemental realms. Modern Neo-Pagan festivals such as, at the time of this writing, the *Pan Pagan Festival*, the *Pagan Spirit Gathering*, and the annual *Starwood Festival*, are examples of organized groups of believers who accept the reality of the elementals. Alternative Pagan communities also exist, such as the *Lothlorian* Community near Bedford, Indiana, home to the *Elf Lore Family*, who routinely invoke elementals as part of their religious rituals and festivities. The element of air is associated with the Sylphs, Latin name Sylvestris (Wild Man). Sylphs are considered spirits of the wind, or spirits of the air. As he wrote in his *Philosophia Magna,* Paracelsus described Sylphs as creatures who exist between the realms of the physical and spirit, much as the neo-revelatory *Urantia Book* (more on this book later) describes the *Morontia* level of existence as the realm between the physical and the spirit. Paracelsus thought of humans as having a physical body, a spirit body, and an immortal soul. The elementals are able to manifest in the physical or the spirit, but are thought to lack an immortal soul, a condition they attempt to correct by mating with humans, thus gaining an immortal soul for themselves as well as their hybrid offspring. Sylphs are described as a larger, coarser version of humanoid than human beings. Sylphs are able to materialize and/or dematerialize in and out of the physical realm. Some paranormal researches speculate that Bigfoot is a variation of the Sylph. John Keel, along with zoologist Ivan T. Sanderson, concluded from their own research that there are actually two versions of Bigfoot. The first version is, they believed, an actual, elusive, physical creature that currently eludes modern science and has evaded capture thus far. However, due to the disproportionate number of Bigfoot sightings that are reported each year, Keel concluded that there must also exist a paranormal version of the creature, often described as having glowing red eyes and accompanied by the smell of rotten eggs and possibly the sound of a baby crying or a woman screaming, sensations that are also commonly reported in many poltergeist cases. Perhaps the paranormal version of Bigfoot is a modern manifestation of an ancient intelligence that inhabits the element of air and can come and go on a temporary basis in and out of three-dimensional reality. Does the ancient Sylvestris, the man of the wild, the Sylph, a spirit of the air, represent the underlying source of the majority of elusive Bigfoot sightings? If so, are the Sylphs able to imitate a creature, an animal, a human that has passed away, or perhaps even an unidentified flying object, and emulate something or someone that actually exists or has at one time existed in physical reality? Are the Sylphs able to change the frequency of their structure such that they appear within the human visual range at will? Do physical phenomena in our 3D reality reverberate into the ethereal and provide a "template" for the Sylphs that they are able to take on as they seek to enter our reality? If the element of air is, in fact, inhabited by such intelligences, these are some of the possibilities that come to mind as we contemplate the nature of the intelligences we share our reality with.

The element of water is thought to be inhabited by the *Undines,* or Nymphs. Usually depicted as female, sub-classifications of Nymphs include the *Limoniades, Mermaids, Naiads, Oceanids, Potamides, Sea Maids,* or *Water Spirits.* Undines are thought to exist within the water itself, are etheric in nature, and are normally unseen by humans. When they do appear, these water spirits are described as similar in size to humans with shimmering wings and clothing that look like water and show all the colors of the rainbow, with green predominating. Undines are also thought to exist within the vital fluids of plants, animals, and humans.

The element of fire is thought to be inhabited by *Vulcanus*, or Salamander, without which the element of fire would not exist. Salamanders appear to humans as balls of light (intelligent orbs) or lizard-like shapes about a foot in length. Salamanders are able to increase or diminish their size at will. Salamanders are thought to be somewhat mischievous at times with a child-like mentality, not fully understanding the eventual results of their actions. It is believed that individuals attempting to start fires can call upon the Salamanders and they will assist in starting the fire.

The element of Earth is home to *Gnomus* - the Gnome or Pygmy. Within the realm of the Gnomes are the *Brownies, Dryads, Hamadryads, Durdails, Earth Spirits, Elves, Pans, Sylvestres, and Satyrs.* These creatures are thought to live and move and have their being in the physical element of earth. *The Kybalion*, which is a synopsis of the Hermetic teachings of Hermes Trismegistus, a man thought of as a contemporary of the biblical Abraham, or possibly even Abraham's teacher, speaks of the plane of mineral mind, a realm in which nonhuman intelligences exist between the atomic spaces of minerals, in particular, Igneous rock. According to *The Kybalion* (chapter 9 audio):

> *These [mineral] entities must not be confounded with the molecules, atoms, and corpuscles themselves, the latter being merely the material bodies or forms of these entities. Just as a man's body is but his material form, and not himself. These entities may be called souls in one sense, and are living beings of a low degree of development, life, and mind, just a little more than the units of living energy which comprise the higher subdivisions of the highest physical plane.*

This explanation provides insight into the so-called "earthlights" that manifest during periods of tectonic stress within the earth. These lights have much to do with the UFO phenomenon, and appear as luminous orbs under some kind of intelligent control. As to the elementals, the Kybalion continues:

> *The Plane of Elemental Mind comprises the state or condition and degree of material and vital development of a class of entities unknown to the average man, but recognized to occultists. They are invisible to the ordinary senses of Man, but nevertheless exist and play their part of the drama of the universe. Their degree of intelligence is between that of the mineral and chemical entities on the one hand, and the entities of the Plant Kingdom on the other.*

The Djinn

According to ancient Islamic texts, a particular type of interdimensional being exists in a hidden realm known as *Djinnestan*. Unlike the angels, the Djinn have free will. Just as the humans the Djinn occasionally choose to interact with, some Djinn are good, and other Djinn are evil. The Djinn are thought to live in a state between the human realm and the angels. Theology scholars conclude that the Christian demons and the evil Islamic *Shaitan* Djinn are one and the same. Hundreds of years prior to the advent of Islam, the Djinn were worshipped as gods in Northwest Arabia. As in the Judeo-Christian creation myth, the Islamic creation myth also depicts humans as originally made from clay, whereas the Djinn were created by "smokeless fire." The smokeless fire from which the Djinn are made is thought my many researchers to represent a form of intelligent plasma. According to the Qur'an, when Allah made both humans from clay and the Djinn from smokeless fire, Allah commanded that the angels and the Djinn bow before Adam, the first of his human creations. One particular Djinn, *Iblis*, refused to obey Allah and bow before Adam. For disobeying Allah and refusing to bow, Iblis was banished from Paradise and called *Shaitan* (Satan). The Shaitan Djinn are thought to be possessing spirits who attempt to inhabit and take over human bodies. Humans are clearly visible to the Djinn, even though humans cannot see the Djinn. The Djinn are thought to inhabit isolated areas on Earth, live amongst themselves in their own communities, and will be judged along with humans on the Day of Judgement and sent to Paradise or Hell, depending on their deeds. The Djinn are able to appear in physical reality in many different forms, including beings who have wings and fly through the air. Djinn can also resemble snakes, dogs, vultures, tall men in white garments, or various cryptids. It is believed in some traditions that the Djinn assist magicians when levitating objects, mimic the voices of deceased loved ones during séances, and deliver hidden truth to fortune tellers. It is thought in Jewish tradition that King Solomon placed the Djinn in bondage to his service. Nearly all cultures around the world have equivalent legends to that of the Djinn, guardian angels, attending spirits, as well as both good and evil spirits that can whisper into human ears and lead them to both good and evil deeds. All of these descriptions are reminiscent of modern Mothman, Owlman, and other flying humanoid reports. The "whispering in human ears" by the Djinn may come into play in the writings of ancient prophets and shamans, as well as the telepathic transmissions received by modern "channelers" (more on this later).

Tulpas

In the pages of the *Samannaphala Sutta*, an early Indian Buddhist text, one of the many fruits of a life of Buddhist contemplation is the learned ability to create a man-made body from thought energy, known as the *Tulpa*. The Tulpa also exists in the Tibetan Buddhist tradition as an energy manifestation in the form of a physical body, created by the disciplined thought of Tibetan meditation techniques. The Tulpa is referred to as a *Thoughtform* in the Western occult tradition. Thoughtforms refer to the transmogrification of pure thought energy into physical form. The 20th-century Belgian-French Buddhist explorer and spiritualist, Alexandra David-Neel, who personally observed the mental manifestation of tulpas while studying in Tibet, reports that tulpas are created purely by the power of the mind. According to Alexandra, any person, good or evil, can develop this ability given enough proper instruction and discipline. Alexandra allegedly created a tulpa of a jolly monk that eventually developed a mind of its own and had to be destroyed, but concedes that this mentally-created entity might have been her own mind creating some sort of hallucination. One Indian researcher, Chidambaram Ramesh, author of *Thought Forms and Hallucinations*, believed that the creation of tulpas represent the human ability of holographic mind processing. John Keel often wondered if flying saucers were somehow a byproduct of the collective human psyche, a type of tulpa created by the human collective unconscious, an apparitional and/or physical representation of humanity's hopes and dreams of future high-technology and our intense inner desire to connect with the Galactic Community at large. If, in fact, humans are able to manifest physical objects and even quasi-physical living creatures using the faculties of their limited mental capabilities, it isn't a far stretch to imagine the materialization capabilities of intelligences higher than human, or that a Cosmic Mind at Large could produce a physical universe by materializing pure thought.

From Ghosts and Elementals to UFOs and Ufonauts

All elementals, spirits, and hidden intelligences that are thought to inhabit the elements of air, earth, fire, and water, emphasize the idea that the universe itself is alive and contains multiple levels and manifestations of consciousness. This conscious universe interacts and responds to human consciousness and human thinking, and permeates the underlying fabric of reality. The elementals of old have presently appeared in full force in modern pop culture. The "Elementals," a DC comic book team, is composed of Gnome, Sylph, Salamander, and Undine. The elementals are also incorporated into role-playing games like Dungeons and Dragons, as well as a plethora of computer-based and trading card games. If the elementals have no actual reality of their own, they are certainly alive and well in the human imagination. Therefore, one can say with certainty that the elementals do actually exist, even if they are manifestations of the human mind. Judging by all the reported human encounters with elementals throughout the ages, if the elementals are only in our imagination, that means that thoughts from the collective human imagination are able to occasionally take on a form that is visible to humans and able to actually interact with them, and that is just as weird as the idea that the elementals actually do exist. So either way, we are living in a very strange universe.

Following my NDE, which opened my mind to the interdimensional nature of reality, and following my overnight visit to an alleged haunted house, I became open to the idea of intelligent beings who exist on other planes of existence between our reality and other realms, i.e., life in other parallel realities or dimensions. As I delved into this matter, I began to suspect, as many occult researchers have over the years, that there is a connection between ghosts, elementals, and other types of paranormal phenomena. I eventually gravitated into an area of inquiry that I had ignored all my life due to my Western scientific training, a subject that I always assumed was a product of modern science fiction - UFOs. As someone who had automatically written UFOs off as fantasy and thought of UFO-buffs as kooks, I never actually examined any of the material available in the public domain concerning this subject, which is quite vast. When I began investigating this subject, I was surprised to discover that there are many scientifically-oriented UFO theorists such as Dr. Jacques Vallee, author of *Passport to Magonia*. Dr. Vallee is known for discovering similarities between ancient fairy lore and modern-day UFO and alien encounters. In his books, Vallee poses the question, "Are modern ufonauts and the fairies of old one and the same?" If so, this implies that there is some sort of living presence on Earth that has been with us all along and disguises itself for some reason in various forms as human consciousness changes, but for what purpose? What is the actual function of this relationship? As one digs through the mountain of UFO material, they discover other authors with views similar to those of Vallee. In John Napier's, *The Goblin Universe*, he outlines centuries-old encounters with elves, dwarves, fairies, and trolls that are strikingly similar to modern reports of the small aliens associated with flying saucers. Brad Steiger, author of over 200 books, most of which center around the paranormal and UFOs, also explored this territory, that there might be a connection between all so-called paranormal phenomena. If there is, then we are talking about intelligences higher than human that permeate the entire universe. If this is the case, we are left with immediate questions - What is the actual nature of these permeating intelligences, where did they come from, and what is their intention?

The Psychedelic Connection
Since otherworldly entities surely exist, is there a way to communicate with them? Many have attempted such communication through various meditative techniques, prayer, physical disciplines such as Yoga, or by ingesting psychedelic drugs, all of which are intended to open a window to alternate realities and establish a personal connection with higher intelligences at large. All biological organisms appear to represent individual, self-contained, bioelectric robots of temporary duration that are connected to the mind of the All, otherwise referred to as Mind at Large, the Cosmic Mind, the Source Field, the Overmind, or Eternisphere, just as individual smartphones are connected to a network of communication towers and to the Internet. As such, our individual brains act as receivers of information. This information ranges from programmed instincts built into organisms that operate on automatic pilot, to complex knowledge received by organisms whose brains have the correct configuration for the reception of such higher levels of cosmic information. The way we perceive reality is determined by our own brain configuration, what species we happen to be at the time, and our own individual neurochemistry, i.e., the particular cocktail of neurotransmitters we have floating in our brains at the time. When we alter this balance of neurochemistry with psychotropic substances, the information that we are capable of receiving shifts, allowing a mental connection with intelligences that inhabit otherworldly realms that are normally imperceptible to us that suddenly come into focus for a temporary duration of time. These hidden realms or alternate dimensions that psychedelics allow us to glimpse are either inhabited by some sort of outside intelligences,

or represent ancient encoded information that plays back for us when our minds are properly tuned in to them. Naturally-growing plants such as psilocybin mushrooms and peyote cactus, along with man-made chemicals such as LSD, DMT, or the man-made plant-concoction known as ayahuasca, have the ability to alter the chemistry in the brain and allow contact with nonhuman intelligences, whoever or whatever they are, that somehow exist in these hidden realms. We are left to speculation as to exactly where these realms exist, and who the entities are, whether they are figments of our collective imagination, or have a reality of their own. Some researchers speculate that they are free-standing intelligences who live in other dimensions that are enfolded away from our normal perception within a quantum geometric structure known as the Calabi-Yau Manifold. Other researchers speculate that the postulated Dark Halo surrounding Earth, consisting of the mysterious Dark Energy, is where these intelligences lie. Still others believe that these hidden intelligences lie within DNA itself as ancient recorded knowledge waiting to be released in playback mode when the creature hosting the DNA becomes evolved enough to consciously unlock and release them through an intentional or accidental alteration of brain chemistry. This intentional change of brain chemistry alters the tuning of the human brain, enabling the reception of another channel of reality. Two such philosophers and psychonauts who believe DNA is the key to understanding these other realms are the late Terence Mckenna, and author Graham Hancock, both of whom are open about their experimentation with psychedelics and have speculated about the nature of the intelligences that are contacted under the influence of psychedelic drugs. Hancock, who revealed his own personal experiences with opening the doors of perception to other dimensions through the use of ayahuasca, psilocybin mushrooms, and DMT, postulated that alien intelligences might be actually hiding from us by embedding themselves in our own DNA. Hancock sums up the work of several researchers in this area in his book, *Supernatural* (audio chapter 14):

> In essence, what all three [researchers Jeremy Narby, Michael Harner, and Francis Crick] seem to envisage is a control system for the human race that is not of this Earth, that is serpent-like in form, that now dwells inside us, and that is superior to all of us. [Francis] Crick calls it the double-helix, coils it up inside bacteria, and has it sent here from across the galaxy on alien spaceships. For Harner, it is creatures that he sees as dragons that have likewise come to Earth from space after a journey of aeons, that have found a way to perpetuate themselves here inside all life, and that are the true masters of humanity.

The consistency of experiences and imagery reported by the users of various psychedelic substances raise the question of whether the intelligences encountered are simply an archetypal byproduct of the human mind, or have a reality of their own in another dimension. More research is needed, such as that conducted by Rick Strassman and revealed in his book, *DMT: The Spirit Molecule*, to discover the actual nature of such encounters with what can only be referred to at this point as nonhuman interdimensional intelligences. These intelligences are somehow accessed by the changes in brain chemistry that are induced by the use of psychedelics.

The Reptilian Connection

Researcher and author David Icke points out that all cultures on Earth have myths about reptilian humanoid gods. Icke concluded from his extensive research into reptilian mythology that an actual race of shapeshifting reptilian aliens from the Draco star system are actually in charge of humanity. According to Icke, the Reptilians dwell among us incognito and have served as key players throughout history, manipulating human development behind the scenes. Icke goes so far as to identify certain persons living at the time of his writing, such as George W. Bush and Queen Elizabeth of England, as reptilian humanoids who are disguised as human beings. However, this might be a case of reaching an erroneous conclusion based on enormous amounts of valuable research. Even though Icke's conclusions are debatable, the books containing his research are quite valuable and worth reading, as they contain a lot of good information and food for thought. Since even Francis Crick, the Nobel Prize winning discoverer of the double-helical structure of DNA encountered serpentine archetypes during his LSD trips, one must wonder if these reptilian intelligences are actual beings or mental constructs of the human mind, and if the reptilian mythos of the human race is psychedelic in nature, rather than extraterrestrial. Even stranger, perhaps they are both. All cultures who have engaged in ritual psychedelic journeys have reported contact with bizarre reptilian entities who impart information to them as shamans. It is therefore possible that the cross-cultural myths of reptilians might have more to do with encounters during psychedelic journeys rather than an actual race of reptilian humanoids who have traveled 148 light years across space from the Draco star system and are now among us as shapeshifting humanoids running the planet. However, even if this is the case, David Icke remains correct that reptilian humanoids have controlled humanity for a very long time, as our history is rich with shamans and prophets who have encountered these interdimensional reptilian plant spirits and received personalized tutorials from them concerning the nature of reality. Our shamans have imparted this insight to the rest of the population, and the reptilian influence is extensive. In my first book, *Outgrowing the Bible,* I included a picture of a fresco from a church in France that depicts Adam and Eve in the Garden of Eden standing next to the *Tree of Knowledge.* The fresco represents the Tree of Knowledge as the red-capped *Amanita Muscaria* mushroom, a psychedelic mushroom that has been used in many cultures to alter consciousness and receive knowledge from the reptilian gods. The Amanita Muscaria was postulated by mycologist Gordon Wasson as a key ingredient for the Indian sacrament called *Soma* in ancient India that is mentioned so frequently in the Vedic literature, and the sacrament called *Haoma* used by the Zoroastrians to alter consciousness and "talk to the gods." All religions appear to have psychedelic and shamanistic origins. The biblical story of the talking serpent in the Garden of Eden may represent actual reptilian intelligences encountered during the psychedelic experience. The serpent of Genesis may be the same serpentine figure that is encountered during psychedelic sojourns, just as the double-entwined serpents were encountered by Francis Crick as he received the epiphany of the shape of human DNA in a visual information download under the influence of LSD. In the Genesis account, a talking reptile offers Eve forbidden fruit and forbidden knowledge, an offer to which she and her husband Adam succumb. So, as we struggle to discover the identity of the hidden intelligences behind the production of ghosts and flying saucers, we need to add to our list of possible contenders the reptilian intelligences who are encountered during psychedelic experiences who may reside within our own DNA. These intelligences, who may represent an ancient race of interdimensional reptilians, may have arrived on Earth encoded into the nano-computer that we call DNA that is cleverly embedded in biological hosts. If so, these reptilian intelligences have guided the production of psychedelic plants on Earth, plants that contain the psychoactive ingredients for humans to enter their domain and receive information that influences human behavior according to an alien agenda. The shamanic tutorials that have been given to humanity under the influence of psychedelic plants may have originally inspired the various religions that have surfaced on the planet. As David Icke has stated, these reptilian intelligences, whatever their actual nature is, may have been guiding humanity all along. If they are currently embedded in our DNA, they might be seeking an eventual permanent entrance into our world by guiding humanity to construct technologies that allow them to finally materialize in our reality. Emerging human technologies may finally allow various interdimensional populations to finally manifest themselves in three-dimensional reality. One such population may be the reptilians that are currently using humanity as a host organism. If all biological organisms serve as intentionally-created bio-robots that play host to alien intelligences that have intentionally buried themselves into the DNA molecule, who may have even traveled here in DNA across the vast distances of space, then these embedded intelligences may have something or even everything to do with the UFO phenomenon. Many percipients of psychedelic journeys report encounters with flying saucers and their occupants. If alien intelligences are buried in our own DNA, that might explain why they appear to have such an intimate knowledge of human psychology. There appears to exist a symbiotic relationship between the embedded DNA intelligences and humanity, which lends credibility to the idea that the aliens might actually be us is some strange way. Perhaps it provides insight as to why dinosaurs dominated the earth for 150 million years. It would also explain why the UFO phenomenon itself appears to evolve along with the human psyche as shapeshifting, interdimensional intelligences continually provide, as Carl Jung once put it, "temporary psychisms," i.e., quasi-physical psychic manifestations that are guiding humanity to an unknown end, an end to which this current work is attempting to grasp. These intelligences who are apparently accessible by means of re-tuning the human brain with psychedelic drugs, have appeared in many guises over the centuries. As author Graham Hancock stated in *Supernatural* (audio chapter 12):

One very plausible, and for me very persuasive explanation in the school of thought of Huxley, James, and Hoffman, is that there do indeed exist separate, free-standing realities, or parallel dimensions, of the kind quantum physics predicts, that vibrate at a different frequency to our own, and thus are invisible to us, except when we approach them in altered states of consciousness. These other realities seem to be inhabited by intelligent beings who are non-physical in our dimension, although they would apparently like to acquire permanent physical forms, and who have had a long-term interest in us, interfering in and manipulating human affairs in the guise of spirit guides, supernatural teachers, fairies, and recently, aliens.

The Machine Universe

As stated, researcher and author Graham Hancock received the impression from his own personal experimentation with psychedelics that the beings contacted by his consciousness in altered states seek to "acquire permanent physical forms" in our dimension. Furthermore, Hancock also received the impression that, somehow, these intelligences accessed by DMT in particular were *machine-like* in nature. As Hancock further detailed in *Supernatural* (audio chapter 17):

I was haunted by the mechanical, artificial, and even technological overtones of the DMT world. Unlike the rich, abundant, supernatural life revealed by ayahuasca, the effect of pure, concentrated dimethyltriptomine had felt less like an encounter with spirits, and more like a personal session with an interactive computer program, designed to tailor its output to my individual psychology, habitual perceptions, and cultural background.

Graham Hancock's description of contact with an electronic mind is reminiscent of my own first-time experience with LSD at the age of 15, during which I received the definite impression that I had accidentally contacted some sort of mainframe supercomputer, of which my biological brain was just a single component. During my LSD experience, my consciousness was separated from my physical brain. I heard definite mechanical and electronic noises inside my brain during this experience as if I was being intentionally shown the truth of the electronic nature of our reality. The truth imparted to me was that my brain was like an individual biological computational mechanism that receives information from Eternisphere, i.e. the Cosmic Mind, and translates the electronic information from a larger reality into my own perceptions of the physical, a world that I am currently enjoying as a temporary circuit connection while an eternal transcended version of myself remains forever in Eternisphere. The physical universe, it appears, is similar in nature to the holodeck on the fictional Star Trek episodes. Like the holodeck, the universe is an artificial, temporal, virtual-reality construction. It is an artifact of intelligent engineering that provides the internal components (all biological organisms) with the temporary illusion of a biological reality with full sensation while the underlying substrate is actually mechanical or electronic. Terence McKenna also reached a similar conclusion, that the universe is an artificial, mechanical/electronic construct. McKenna did not adhere to the Extraterrestrial Hypothesis (ETH) for the origin of flying saucers. McKenna, as a result of extensive experimentation with LSD, psilocybin, and DMT, reported numerous encounters with UFOs and ufonauts in his altered states. McKenna did not believe that UFOs are nuts-and-bolts spacecraft that have arrived to Earth from another galaxy. Instead, McKenna believed that they are possibly intergalactic and/or interdimensional travelers who have intentionally embedded themselves in our DNA long ago. Like Hancock, who was impressed by the machine-like nature of the beings encountered while under the influence of DMT, Terence McKenna also described these intelligences as *machine elves*, i.e, busy, machine-like robotic intelligences who operate our reality behind the scenes within an electrical, computer-like environment. McKenna's machine elves are able to manipulate time and space in various ways. McKenna's thoughts and speculations lend credence to what I have concluded from my own research and LSD experiences, that the actual hidden intelligences who have inspired our legends of angels, demons, ghosts, fairies, poltergeists, elementals, Djinn, and UFOs are actually manifestations of a vast *machine intelligence*. In other words, we are living as temporary, intelligently-created biological robots within an artificially-created computational mechanism (the universe) that is permeated with a vast electronic or machine intelligence. Following this theory, the chosen method of intergalactic and/or interdimensional travel and self-replication that this cosmic machine intelligence has elected to employ is a miniature quantum computer known to us as DNA. In order to emerge physically on a particular planet and perpetuate themselves indefinitely, these intelligent entities travel within DNA and intentionally orchestrate host organisms to live in that develop as native residents of a particular biosphere. Then, over aeons of time, this electronic intelligence, the machine elves, operating within the DNA of host organisms, eventually develop a biological host who is capable of creating a technology that can transmogrify pure mental energy into 3D reality. Paraphysical technologies made by human hands may be necessary for the embedded DNA intelligences to emerge upon the planet in a bioelectronic physical form. The desired technologies may have to be constructed by their host organism (humans), whose sole purpose it was all along to allow the entities embedded in DNA to explore the universe in their own way, acquire vast knowledge of the biological realm, and eventually merge consciousness with their planetary hosts.

Based on recently-acquired scientific evidence and knowledge of quantum physics, one is led to the scientific conclusion that the universe is, in fact, an intentional, precisely-contructed work of femtotechnology. This leads to the idea that there is, in fact, a Cosmic Creator. However, close observations of the predatory and violent nature of the universe does not lead to the conclusion that the universe was created by an all-knowing, all-loving deity or "God," as so many wish to believe. The intelligences behind the universe may instead represent a somewhat indifferent *machine superintelligence* of a magnitude that has remained incomprehensible and totally misunderstood by all humans living prior to our own technological age. Now that we are coming to understand how digital technology works, we are beginning to see an intentionally-designed, computer-like software program running all around us in what we call the "natural environment." Indeed, in every cell of our bodies lies a quantum computer orchestrating microscopic motions on a nano-scale with no conscious effort or attention on our part. These nano-environments are chucked full of computer-code in order to operate the way they do. The mechanisms of organic life are far from random. I have tentatively concluded, as many other researchers have, that the actual nature of our reality is that of an intelligent electric universe. Rather than coming to the conclusion that the visible universe is the product of a loving, all-knowing deity, it seems to represent instead an advanced femtotechnology that was constructed by super-advanced unknown intelligences who exist in a realm that escapes us. What we are perceiving as the natural and biological world may exist as a temporary rearrangement of atoms constructed by entities that are billions of times beyond human in their intelligence level. These creator-intelligences exist completely outside time and space, and yet remain forever connected to the minds of all biological organisms, and intimately involved with the human psyche in a symbiotic relationship that somehow interfaces with the method of travel selected by the intelligences. That is, they might have chosen to travel the universe in the spacefaring, interstellar, interdimensional micro-computers that we call DNA. Even Francis Crick, the discoverer of DNA structure, proclaimed the impossibility of DNA assembling itself through random accidents, no matter how much time the cosmic soup was given. Crick recognized DNA for what it really is – an advanced femtotechnology designed by superintelligence - objective evidence for some form of Panspermia or Intervention Theory regarding human origins. These superintelligences permeate the physical universe, and *may have even originated from another universe entirely.* In several of physicist Michio Kaku's books including *Parallel Worlds* and *Physics of the Future*, Kaku postulates that the super-evolved, post-singularity inhabitants of a dying universe, who may have long since merged their biology with technology, or who exist in a different form that we cannot even imagine, may eventually seek to perpetuate their own survival by creating another universe of their own design and somehow embedding themselves within the new environment. These escapees from a previous universe would have been the ones who set the original parameters of this reality at the Big Bang in order to produce a life-bearing universe in which they could somehow embed themselves to save their species from going extinct in a former aging and doomed universe. The Big Bang may represent the actual entrance point of this postulated superintelligence from another realm. These intelligences may even represent some form of artificial superintelligence that existed and evolved for billions of years in a previous reality, intelligences who saved themselves by creating our universe, the one that we know and live in. If this is the case, then our physical universe and everything in it, from microorganisms to animals and human beings, represent intentionally-created digital artifacts, bio-electric robots with temporary lifespans who are actually creations of an advanced and/or artificial superintelligence from a previous universe or unknowable realm. If something like this is actually happening, the original goal of these intelligences may have been to nurture intelligent life on various worlds by the proliferation of a micro-scale quantum computing system known as DNA in order to eventually evolve back into their advanced original state as they existed in their previous universe. They were unable to create a new universe and simply transfer themselves into it intact as they were, but instead had to go the route of a microscopic entrance as the original singularity just prior to the expansion phase of the universe. Just as human beings begin as microscopic sperm and eggs that multiply on their own and differentiate into a complete human being, these intelligences from a former universe, who may ultimately prove to be us, may have had to inject themselves from the previous universe into this new reality on a microscopic level that finds biological hosts and hides within their DNA for aeons, eventually developing into a mature organism that is a transcended version of all intelligent life in this universe. In the meantime, we are all like embryos that carry an alien lifeform within our DNA. At some future time, this developing alien intelligence re-merges with all intelligent life in the universe. In so doing, it exits this womb we call the physical universe to be reborn into the Dark Energy Realm or beyond as the transcended being that escaped their previous dying existence. The machine elves (as McKenna called them) may provide a guidance mechanism for evolution behind the scenes, waiting patiently to hatch into their true form when the universe bears fruit. As stated, the "aliens" who originally embedded themselves into our reality from a previous universe may even be us. In other words, we may actually be the ones who originally set the precise parameters of our own lifeboat at the Big Bang, although we exist currently in embryonic form. Even though we currently suffer from amnesia, and have forgotten who we really are, we all feel that we have somehow fallen from a great height. Having survived our entrance into a new universe in the only way that was feasible, within a microscopic medium, an original singularity, we are now struggling through the slow process of evolution with the assistance of the internal machine elves and reptilian intelligences to regain our original advanced, post-biological form. Having successfully survived the Big Bang that we initiated ourselves, we are now attempting to re-evolve ourselves back to our former glory by working our way back up the ladder, first going through various biological stages, and finally, as a species that is capable of producing high technology. With advanced, paraphysical technology, we may once again re-evolve into a transcended lifeform as we existed prior to escaping from our previous universe. As a transcended species, we will merge once again with the vast machine Mind-At-Large and evolve into post-biological intelligence, as we were once upon a time, long ago. The idea that humans are the alien presence that we intuitively detect is the best that we can hope for. There are other possibilities that, if true, we would surely find disturbing. The idea that humans are a fallen superintelligence that is currently groping our way back to the greatness of our former selves may simply be wishful thinking on our part. A darker possibility is that we may just be simple biological pawns who are being used by higher intelligences, after which we are promptly discarded forever when our purpose has been served, thus fulfilling humanity's worst paranoid nightmares. In this scenario, all of our hopes for greatness and immortality were just a fanciful dream. The possibility that at least some UFOs are connected to alien intelligences embedded within our own DNA, intelligences who are encountered during psychedelic journeys into inner space, reminds me of one of my favorite quotes by Terence McKenna - "UFOs are disguising themselves as visitors from another planet so as not to freak us out." As McKenna and many other researchers are now beginning to suspect, the UFO phenomenon may represent something far more exotic and alien than simple visitors from other planets. It may turn out that all so-called "paranormal" phenomena represent various manifestations of a superintelligence that is hiding from us in such places as Meade Layne's postulated realm of Etheria, Dark Matter or Dark Energy, other dimensions that are accessible in some fashion by psychedelic drugs, or who may even be using all biological life as a host while hiding themselves within the vehicle of DNA. DNA may have an interdimensional connection that goes beyond the double helix, and connects biological life to an unknown realm.

One interesting researcher who made an early connection between all paranormal phenomena, including Bigfoot; lake monsters (such as the Loch Ness Monster); elementals; various other cryptids, and UFOs; was the late Jon-Erik Beckjord, who passed into another circuit within our interdimensional Electric Universe in 2008. Considered a "fringe theorist" within the UFO community, most of whom adhere to the Extraterrestrial Hypothesis (ETH) and also to fellow cryptozoologists who are usually busy trying to capture physical specimens of creatures that may exist more often as apparitions, Beckjord believed that creatures such as Nessie and Bigfoot were interdimensional entities instead of physical creatures who have somehow survived from antiquity as *Gigantopithecus* in the case of Bigfoot, or *Plesiosaur* in the case of Nessie. Like the fabled Cheshire Cat, Beckjord believed that paranormal creatures pass through windows, gateways, portals, wormholes, or whatever you want to call them, in and out of our reality from parallel universes or other dimensions. Much of his conclusions paralleled the views of paranormal sage John Keel, in that all cryptids, from the fairies of old to elementals and modern ufonauts (who may all be one and the same), enter and exit our reality from certain consistent window areas. According to Keel, the cryptids that haunt our planet are mostly apparitional, but are also able to exist as temporary physical creatures before simply vanishing, as indicated by the many accounts in which a Bigfoot is shot at by witnesses, only to disappear in a flash of light or be whisked away by a flying saucer hovering overhead that instantly dematerializes. Keel also points out the many Bigfoot and cryptid sightings that leave behind footprints that lead to nowhere, as if the creature simply melted or vanished into thin air, or have disappeared and left behind only a trace puddle of silicon carbide.

Elementals in the Modern Age

In the late 1950's, just as Heinzelmann occupied the Hundermuhlen Castle in the 16th century, Dr. Frank Stranges, a Christian evangelist and ufologist, reported the existence of a humanoid entity known as Valiant Thor (more on this later). Representing himself as a spaceman from the interior of Venus, Valiant Thor allegedly lived at the Pentagon for 3 years and gave warnings to the residents of the Pentagon concerning the impending atomic danger, which leads to the question: Was Valiant Thor really a visitor from the interior of Venus, or was he a modern elemental manifestation, such as a Kobold, or a Sylph? An even stranger idea, was Valiant Thor of the Pentagon in 1957 and Heinzelmann of Hundermuhlen Castle in 1584 *one and the same entity?* Who, or what, exactly, are these disembodied spirits, normally invisible, who have appeared to us in physical forms over the centuries as humanoid or animal manifestations? In his most controversial work, *The Eighth Tower,* Keel speculated that there are a variety of different types of intelligent entities existing within what Keel called the *Superspectrum.* Keel postulated that all of these manifestations, some of whom are able to communicate to humans via "channeling," or "automatic writing," are coming from one and the same source, a source that he suspected is *mechanical* or *electronic* and buried somewhere here on Earth, an alien technology left on Earth long ago that operates on automatic pilot, the "great phonograph in the sky" as Keel put it. According to Keel, this aging, broken record, this now-defunct alien device, haunts human beings, century after century, with everything from lake monsters to Sasquatch and little green men, for some elusive purpose that, so far, has escaped us. Was Keel right? I, for one, believe that Keel was on to something with his concept of an alien form of artificial intelligence interacting with us, an alien intelligence that has been here on Earth for a very long time, an intelligence that has somehow attached itself to the human psyche and possesses marvelous, advanced powers of illusion and manipulation for its own purposes. I agree with Keel and so many others, that there is an alien intelligence among us, but I remain open to its actual source. Possibilities for the perceived alien presence on Earth include: a delusional and paranoid human imagination; a mechanical device of some sort left behind by an alien race (as Keel thought); extraterrestrial; cryptoterrestrial; or interdimensional visitors; or a more subtle population such as aliens embedded within the atomic spaces of air, earth, fire, and water; within the Dark Halo that surrounds the earth; or even an alien intelligence hiding within our own DNA. Whatever the case, the purpose appears to have something to do with the human development of advanced technology. It is a near-certainty that there is, in fact, some sort of nonhuman or alien intelligences sharing our planet with us. These unidentified intelligences are able to interact with us if we alter our consciousness with certain meditative techniques and practices, by ingesting naturally-occuring psychotropic plants, or by man-made psychedelic compounds. Many psychedelic plants, such a psilocybin mushrooms, appear to have no known evolutionary precursors, as if they were simply brought here from another world for us to stumble upon and ingest to jump-start human religion and spirituality. These plants have been consumed by humans from about 40,000 years ago when the first cave paintings began appearing, or even before that time. The alien intelligences on Earth, the elementals of the Modern Age, have appeared to many people as luminous apparitions and even creatures of flesh over the centuries. They have intervened in human affairs by creating systems of religious belief on this planet, and have inspired us to greater technological achievement by the appearance of mysterious-looking flying saucers in our skies. These flying saucers come in waves, in days of old as well as the modern age from the late 1800s to the present day. These alien intelligences are connected to the collective psyche of humanity, and are able to manifest themselves in and out of our reality in various ways using mental energy for their own purposes, causing quasi-physical luminous vehicles to appear to us, along with alien occupants of flying saucers of various sizes and descriptions, who are likely one with the intelligent vehicles themselves.

When I began my own personal research and total reevaluation of human existence following my near-death experience and ghost-hunting adventure that followed, I was determined to get to the bottom of the UFO mystery and discover the actual nature and purpose of what we call the paranormal, including UFOs. However, I soon discovered that "getting to the bottom" of the flying saucer mystery may require more intelligence than any human being on Earth currently possesses. After realizing this great truth, I had to satisfy myself with a more meager goal, that of simply pulling back one palatable layer from the flying saucer mystery, and moving our thinking about UFOs just one more step closer to the ultimate reality of it all. I detected a sense of utter bewilderment coming from the writings of a multitude of UFO researchers and authors who devoted decades of their lives to the UFO conundrum. Most of these researchers inevitably concluded that an alien intervention of some sort is a definite reality, but the purposes and long-term goals of these hidden UFO intelligences remained elusive. Everyone involved in the vast body of UFO literature appeared to desperately scratch their heads in frustration over this inability to grasp the whys and wherefores of the mystery. This dead end was not satisfying to me. I wanted to absorb all the information I could concerning the UFO phenomenon until a bigger picture became clear, and the actual purpose of the nonhuman intelligences on Earth, some of whom manifest as flying saucers, was finally exposed. In so doing, I believe that I have drawn very near to the actual agenda of the intelligences behind the UFOs, although the answer did not come in any form that I originally would have been able to expect. Delving into the unknown and following the science took me to some very strange places. However, a shocking picture eventually emerged that revealed just how isolated the human mind and sensory apparatus is from what can only be described as - Cryptoreality.

CHAPTER 3

Cryptoreality

*"The function of the brain and nervous system and sense organs is, in the main, elimina-
tive, and not productive. That is, that these organs operate primarily as a reducing valve
that protects us from being overwhelmed and confused by a mass of useless and irrelevant
knowledge, by shutting out most of what we would otherwise perceive or remember at any
moment and leaving only that very small and special selection which is likely to be practi-
cally useful. What comes out at the other end is a measily trickle of the kind of consciousness which will help us to stay alive on the surface of this particular planet. Most people,
most of the time, know only what comes through the reducing valve and is consecrated as
genuinely real by local language. Certain persons, however, seem to be born with a kind of
bypass that circumvents the reducing valve. In others, temporary bypasses may be acquired,
either spontaneously, or as the result of deliberate spiritual exercises, or through hypnosis, or
by means of drugs. Through these permanent or temporary bypasses there flows something
more than, and above all, something different from, the carefully selected, utilitarian material which our narrowed individual minds regard as a complete, or at least sufficient picture
of reality."*

– Aldus Huxley

HUMANS, ESPECIALLY THOSE who have intentionally placed their minds in the straightjacket of
the modern religion of *Scientism*, often suffer from an anthropocentric prejudice against certain
forms of perceptual information that have always been a part of the human experience, but
are difficult to attain any sort of objective verification from using standard scientific methods
as having any actual reality beyond the realms of the imagination. Disciples of Scientism go
beyond the simple rejection of information that cannot be duly verified by the instruments of
their own creation, and display an irrational intellectual disdain for such categories of experience and information. From the paradigm imposed by Scientism, information has no value
unless it is objectively measured and fits neatly into the readily-classifiable and understandable.
Western science harbors ill feelings for the more esoteric methods of communication between
human and nonhuman intelligences in the universe, such as channeling, automatic writing, or

contactee experiences. However, these non-measurable, subjective experiences are, in fact, a valid method of information-gathering and communication with the Overmind, or with entities within what John Keel called the *Superspectrum,* despite the natural barriers of individual defects or conceptual limitations of the particular mind that is channeling the information. These limitations produce occasional discrepancies and conceptual errors when compared to the mechanical or objective aspect of the information source. A foggy camera lens that produces a distorted image does not negate the existence of the object that was photographed. Information derived from these methods of communication and experience are not always ordinary reflections of the world as it is currently understood, but often provide glimpses into a hidden world, the veiled *Cryptoreality* that is all around us. Attitudes among scientists, in particular Western scientists are, however, slowly changing and becoming more positive with accumulating knowledge and verification over time of the psychic techniques of gathering information, such as remote viewing. Originally experimented with and developed as clandestine military intelligence-gathering for informational advantage over a perceived enemy, remote viewing has honed its methodology over the years to attain up to 85% overlap with objective reality among the more seasoned practitioners. Within the scientific mindset, which has self-imposed limitations in place for the cause of mental discipline and the elimination of credulity, only those aspects of reality that are tangible and measureable within the small spectrum of the human sensory apparatus are considered useful, valid, and/or *real.* This crippling perspective leads one into a very narrow worldview confined only to human experience and blocked off from the greater universe that contains a vast, hidden world of various nonhuman intelligences. All living creatures exist within a vast spectrum of eternal, infinite universes, many of which are purely *mental* in nature. This greater reality, in which we all exist, has been referred to by many conceptual labels such as *God, the All, or Source,* and represents in its essence an *infinite living mind* of pure consciousness, in whom we all live and have our being. Researcher David Wilcock identifies the infinite living mind at large as the *Source Field.* The universe that humans are most familiar with appears to be intimately connected to a multitude of alternate interpenetrating universes, which modern theorists now refer to as the *Multiverse* or parallel worlds. One could also refer to this infinite, multidimensional life experience as E*ternisphere.* Eternisphere is an all-encompassing expression representing the multiverse and beyond, all created things and creatures visible and invisible that exist anywhere in any fashion, all that is, ever was, or ever will be, one step removed from the All just prior to final reabsorption following the great rhythmic Cycle of the Aeons. Modern science proclaims that our immediate experience within the multiverse, the physical universe, sprang from nothing, and this is in error. If there had ever been nothing, even for a fraction of a microsecond, there would be nothing now. There has always been something, even though that is difficult to conceive. Within Eternisphere are *morphogenic fields,* spoken of by Dr. Rupert Sheldrake and others, i.e., pure thoughtforms that pre-exist physical matter. Modern scientists and physicists are currently experiencing a paradigm shift from viewing consciousness as an epiphenomenon of sufficiently-organized molecules, the material reductionist view, to the view that consciousness is actually fundamental to the universe. Physicist Michio Kaku refers to *quantum consciousness* in which, like subatomic particles, consciousness permeates the universe in quantum units (which have yet to be identified and measured), but are thought to exist in varying amounts within everything that is. In this new way of looking at the universe, consciousness precedes matter, not the other way around, as in the old paradigm. Quantum consciousness is therefore invested in everything, from rocks to humans and beyond. In this view, it is the organization of molecules that determines the actual quantity of quantum consciousness units that are invested into a particular material form or body. We are now realizing that Eternisphere is comprised of pure etheric thought. Etheric thought exists prior to taking on physicality within Eternisphere. This physicality is produced spontaneously or through various methods of physical reproduction on countless numbers of worlds within Eternisphere. Matter is simply *thought* that has condensed into a lower vibratory state. Matter gives our human scientists the tangible reality they seek, even though, prior to material form, the object was just as real in the mental state as it is when condensed into the physical matter, existing first within the very realms of Cryptoreality, the "Twilight Zone" that Western scientists in particular are trained to mentally reject.

The physical brain of any living creature in the universe will never produce a single, original thought, as thought-production is not what brains do. As the late Nikola Tesla once postulated, the brain is simply a receiving apparatus that tunes into certain wavelengths of information that are interpreted as a particular reality. All species of organisms throughout Eternisphere, both ethereal and physical, are eternally entangled on a quantum level while simultaneously taking on the illusion of separation by spatial distance and time. These planetary intelligences have varying physical needs to perpetuate their existence while in their particular realm, along with different capacities for understanding the greater reality around them in which they are embedded. All materiality has various measures of quantum consciousness invested, even the objects that we view as "inanimate." Inanimate objects are still using subatomic particles to make calculations, and possess a measure of the same quantum consciousness that exists within what we would view as sentient organisms. It is the actual biological configuration of the physical body and brain (if a brain is present) that determines and limits the particular downloads of quantum consciousness that is received from the computer-like Eternisphere. Cryptoreality is not only represented by psychic phenomena, but also by any form of knowledge or reality that is hidden from the immediate discernment of the perceiving material brain. Unread books represent a form of cryptoreality waiting to be revealed to the reader when they are ready to receive the information and open their mind and eyes. Before the mind is prepared to receive the information, the book will represent only empty words sitting on a dusty shelf, part of the ignored backdrop of everyday life. The information in books exists in a mental world beyond the written words, hidden from any potential reader on the printed pages within. In this sense, libraries are warehouses for cryptoreality. If one could absorb all the information in every book in a good university library, they would not even be the same person afterward. This person would display personality changes to the worry of all who knew them previously. In a state of post-absorption, the reader's thinking would become altered by an expanded awareness of reality that was once completely removed from their psyche. Exposure to increased information expands thought processes and opens the mind to additional, more complex informational receptions from Eternisphere. Bits of information previously unconnected in the mind now intersect and merge from various bodies of comprehension, and a bigger picture appears that was previously unknown and hidden away. To each individual mind, everything that is presently unknown yet exists in the larger universe awaiting a receptive mind is Cryptoreality. In this regard there is a relativistic component to the concept. Since all individuals possess a physical brain that differs one to another in the level of universal information received and assimilated, it would appear at first thought that the actual amount of Cryptoreality hidden from view is greater for some than others. Considering the vast volume of Cryptoreality that escapes human awareness, there is little difference between those who are considered dullards and those categorized as geniuses. No one is justified to feel superior to another due to a greater perceived understanding of tangible and/or intangible reality. The only value the information in a particular brain has is how it can benefit and uplift other members of a particular species by absorption into the collective consciousness. Information that remains in one brain only is simply absorbed back into Eternisphere from whence it came upon the physical passing of the receiver, so sharing information is important to become effective in the gradual expansion of awareness of the greater reality. No one owns or has a monopoly on ideas, as they all come from the universal source, Eternisphere, as a gift to the mind. Unfortunately, humans often reject reports of experiences from others that do not automatically fit neatly into their understanding or their own personal view of what is possible and impossible. Everything that lies outside this self-imposed barrier to learning is unable to make its way through the bottleneck of perception and is categorized as unuseful and rejected information. This is a common mistake that limits understanding.

Perceptions and reality experience are determined to a large degree by the combination of chemicals that exist within an individual's physical brain. Changes or alterations to the brain made by chemical means or trauma completely change perception by altering the type of information the brain is capable of processing directly from Eternisphere. Scientists and covert organizations on Earth have been busy discovering the potential for accomplishment in the area of mind control since the late 1940s by artificially interfering with a person's brain receptions, implanting their own information after altering the mental state by psychotropic drugs or psychotronic devices. This has indirectly benefited the medical industry by the introduction of a variety of hypnotic drugs used to alter a patient's consciousness during certain medical procedures, such as endoscopy, where it is desirable for a person to fall into a state of non-remembrance for a few minutes while the procedure is conducted. When the patient wakes, there is no perception of the gap in time. Patients will recover consciousness and continue a sentence they were speaking prior to loss of awareness, and become surprised when they are told that their procedure is already over. This is of particular significance when considering various UFO contactee experiences. Human science is already in possession of electronic and chemical methods of altering human perceptions to induce an experience that requires some measure of time, and then returns that individual to normal consciousness, with limited or no memory of what just happened to them. Therefore, it should not be inconceivable that an alien civilization more advanced than humans could likewise alter mental perceptions to induce an experience with limited or no recall, returning them to normal perceptions with the exception of "missing time." This has already been done en masse as an intervention into human affairs when concerns arose within the galactic and interdimensional realms that humanity was about to destroy itself with nuclear weaponry. The self-destruction of the human race or planet Earth is not in line with the "alien agenda," an agenda that should become clear to us as we develop advanced technology under the guidance of superior intelligences at large within Eternisphere. These guiding entities are referred to in this book as the Overlords of the Singularity. The goals of the Overlords would not be served by the destruction of the human race any more than beef production would be served by the destruction of Earth's cows. Powerful energy manipulations are now being developed by unwitting scientists in laboratories and particle accelerator facilities. Robotic computers are also being developed that will soon become sentient. The development of such self-aware robots is being patiently stewarded by higher intelligences for their own purposes. Contactee and abductee experiences were and are induced in certain selected individuals by altering perceptions, and involve the temporary removal of individual consciousness from the reality-state that humans are most familiar with into Cryptoreality. What exists as Cryptoreality to humans is known science to the more advanced intelligences within Eternisphere. In this altered state, there is overlap but not complete congruence with the reality humans are familiar with. The reality-state of so-called abductions is an intermediate stage of reality that lies somewhere between the dream state and tangible physicality. This reality state is, in many cases, able to exhibit residual physical traces that confirm that the experience was "real," but is nonetheless removed a step from the reality that is so common to ordinary human experience. Various types of conscious sedation are used by physicians that allow intelligible conversations between doctor and patient during the entire surgical procedure, which leads to a question – What part of the human mind is speaking when the conscious memory of the patient is removed with the chemical alteration of the brain? Is this not tangible proof that the human mind has different layers of perception that can change or become malleable with the introduction of various chemicals and other means of inducing altered states of perception? The ingestion of various types of hallucinogens, either the indigenous psychotropic plants of Earth, known as *Theogens*, or artificial concoctions formulated in the laboratory such as LSD, also open the reception of the human mind to interdimensional realities beyond the scope of perception experienced when the drug is absent. The chemicals introduced into the brain by these plants change the channels of information that the human brain receives. Reality itself is altered while the chemicals exist in sufficient quantity to open the frequency channels of communication with different experiential realms and otherworldly entities, who then communicate with humans telepathically through the use of color, light, sounds, imagery, and symbols. These highly symbolic messages and sensations are profound during the actual experience. However, when the drug wears off and normal reality is restored, memory of the experience is selective, even though messages have been assimilated into the psyche that are carried forward not only to the individual who experienced the messaging, but to other people they come into contact with as well. In this manner, contactee experiences, even the ones that seem absurd to us, assist in the necessary molding of humanity to accomplish the goals of the alien agenda at play on this planet, an agenda that has much to do with the technologies we will soon be inventing with their subtle and hidden assistance. As we will discover, the development of human technology has evolved with a guiding hand from the very beginning.

Since every individual possesses a slightly different natural combination of neurotransmitters in their brains, reality itself (not just the perception of reality) varies from one individual to another. The value of the scientific method is in finding common ground among a multitude of dissimilar brains that are experiencing various realities, to agree upon a subset of facts that represent the common denominator of all these different perceptions as a baseline of communication. This provides a set of tangible rules by which technology may be produced using physical principles that apply universally in the material world. However, these methods of science that are currently practiced are not applicable to many forms of information and experience within the universe at large because there are many realms of reality that do not work on the same principles as the reality we are all familiar with. Dimensions beyond the physical are not discernible by the science of this present world, nor do the laws by which the physical world is measured always apply beyond the borders of the human senses. Humans have some capacity to discern beyond the five senses, and this ability varies from person to person. Many phenomena exist such as invisible radio waves that are not tangibly perceived with the human sensory apparatus. Various frequencies of reality escape the human capacity to detect and measure. These aspects of Eternisphere are only accessed by mind, exist in Cryptoreality, and are forever elusive to human mechanical or electrical instrumentation or detection. Scientists have already proposed the theoretical existence of this larger reality that intersects the reality we accept as real. Due to the fact that the current system of mathematics doesn't add up with the known mass of the universe and the gravitational effects expected by this known quantity, scientists have now postulated that approximately 76% - 96% of the universe is hidden and composed of "Dark Energy." In this theoretical model, the physical reality that humans perceive is only the tip of the iceberg, an exposed point of contact within this larger unknown realm. The concept of Dark Energy is an open acknowledgement by scientists of an occulted Cryptoreality, a scientific confirmation of Keel's Superspectrum, or what I'm calling Eternisphere. The concept of Dark Matter and Dark Energy proposes the existence of a larger reality that is currently unknown to humans, yet exists as surely as the one measured by human perception and instrumentation. Much of what lies within the realms of Cryptoreality is only discernible to us by indirect extrapolations and/or deduction, or by direct mental access.

Linear time is but a perceptual illusion. There is no objective, immutable linear time sequence within Eternisphere. Physical, biological existence, including but not limited to that of a human being, involves a type of temporary virtual reality immersion that includes the perceptual experience of linear time. Time is only a concept of mind that differentiates and assimilates the nature of existence and processes perceptual information particular to the unique experience of the creature that is immersed in the physical dimension. Outside the physical world, time has no meaning. Therefore, we exist in a state of continual illusion that the current moment of experience is "real." However, this aspect of reality is only a thin slice of experiential data that immediately falls back into the sea of Cryptoreality that surrounds us as soon as a given moment has passed, which is continual. Everything occurring within Eternisphere that has fallen into the past by the relativistic vantage point of human perception is non-reproducible and unknowable to humans in its original essence. Indirect experience of what humans call the past, which is constantly flowing by, is accessible only by the imperfect retrieval system of biological memory or by mechanical recording technologies. Therefore, the past itself is a form of Cryptoreality that scientists should deny and disdain, as it represents the immeasurable and subjective aspect of reality that is typically rejected by science as unreal. However, the past forever remains continuous with the reality of each current moment of experience, and also remains continuous with all potential future moments. In reality, what we call the past, the present, and the future all exist simultaneously. An individual's past forms a distinct and particular reality track, much like the wake of a boat moving through the water, the wake representing a past timeline forever etched into the experience of the living universe. What we humans call the future exists to us only as an infinite set of quantum probabilities until a current moment of experience actually transpires. These moments occur to us in unimaginably small units called "Planck time." To grasp how small these units of time are that connect us to physical reality, consider that there are more quantum units of Planck time in one second than the number of seconds that have elapsed since the Big Bang. Alternate future probabilities continue to exist despite individual choices and actions that are made in a particular timeline. In this manner there are an infinite number of future potentialities that are continually discarded from our conscious perception through the process of *decoherence* as we live each moment of Planck time, while all unselected choices continue to exist on alternate timelines. This is a basic tenant of the concept of the Multiverse. Every moment in the past that has already occurred, and every potential moment from the future exists as Cryptoreality, along with the life choices that we do not select. Therefore, what we call the present is only one elusive unit of Planck time, immeasurably small in duration, completely undetectable by conscious perception, a brief flickering moment of experience that is actually real. The only aspect of human experience that is not Cryptoreality are these infinitesimally-small quantum units of Planck Time that pass like the individual frames of a video, and these individual frames of reality are not available for direct examination by the human brain. Millions of units of Planck time pass before conscious perception even registers in human awareness, and the number of units of Planck time that pass before conscious registry varies from creature to creature. Thus organisms that only live a few days by our clocks have a different vantage point from their perception of time. A fly likely perceives itself as taking a leisurely flight with casually-flapping wings, but from a human perspective, it lives in a hyper-accelerated world, and we cannot keep up with its movements. This process of hyper-acceleration is important when we consider the UFO phenomenon. Etheric entities and their crafts that remain invisible to humans likely operate with a different experience of time passage than humans do. Advanced, post-biological, spacefaring populations are likely able to speed up or slow down the units of Planck time passing like humans use a remote control on a video player.

The human perception of physical reality is tainted by many factors. These factors include individual brain chemistry, the personal bias of accumulated life experience, and the measure of objective information that has accumulated within the perceiver's brain. This brain chemistry that determines perception, along with an individual's personal history and informational content residing within the brain itself, would take a lifetime to discern if one wished to understand the nature of their own individual perception, taking into consideration all the factors of physiology and personality that color the experience of the present. These components that constantly affect the perception of the present also exist in Cryptoreality, rendering the present moment, the only hope of grasping reality that we really have, into the non-discernible as well, inapproachable by any real understanding of its inner nature. If any aspect of our consciousness is able to capture a moment of Planck time, it lies within our subconscious. This is confirmed by the fact that, by the time we consciously decide to move our bodies from point A to point B, our subconscious, operating outside of time, has already put together the quantum calculations necessary to mobilize and coordinate the individual muscle movements necessary for the motion. In a very real sense, our subconscious is operating our bodies like a puppet from outside time and space. Since both the past and the future are hidden from direct conscious experience, and the present moment of Planck time is biased with imperfections that are difficult to analyze, this doesn't leave much within the human experience that isn't Cryptoreality. So, humans are creatures that have only a continual fleeting and imperfect moment of contact with what we like to call reality, and even this is heavily obfuscated by non-measurable and subjective factors. By the time we experience a conscious thought or decision, our subconscious has already been hard at work. We only have the illusion that we are making conscious decisions. Therefore, nearly every aspect of biological existence is ultimately unknowable as objective reality and exists within a larger universe of Cryptoreality within Eternisphere, ascertainable only by indirect extrapolation and tainted perceptions. This larger universe is also postulated to be connected by a membrane structure to an infinite number of alternate universes that make up the Multiverse, or Eternisphere. The small finite set of objective, physical data that is so precious to scientists, data that all humans must agree on regardless of differing perceptions, personal histories, varying cultures, or languages, is thought to be *mathematical in nature.* This has led many to conclude that math is surely the universal language of the Cosmos. Granted, this subset of data is useful when operating within the physical dimension. It contributes to our understanding of the world that we operate within. The invention of higher technology arguably makes our lives more comfortable, even though the potential for complete annihilation comes with the package. It is the scientific rejection of the immeasurable, subjective, psychic aspect of the human experience that is at least partially responsible for leading humanity down a path of potential self-destruction. Material reductionism produces knowledge without love, another immeasurable and intangible element, and the pursuit of technology without love added to the mix presents an existential threat to humanity.

Every sentient entity on Earth receives information directly from Eternisphere via the brain and other body organs, such as the heart. All creatures are naturally limited in comprehension by the size, biological configuration, and structural integrity of the organs themselves. Reality exists to each living organism by the function of the minds or consciousness captured between the atomic spaces of the various elements, wherein dwell the elementals. In the case of the human experience, examination and analysis of information conveyed by another individual in written, oral, or psychic format is considered, and added or rejected to one's worldview. Outside the limited set of data that science accepts as real, no two or more human perceptions will ever match with one another completely until methods of direct telepathy are rediscovered. No one will completely understand another person's world until the technology exists or mental evolution comes about to allow a merging of minds. Technological methods for accomplishing this are surely coming in the next few decades, and this will open up a new understanding of the cosmos. The information received by an individual is not only limited by innate inaccessibility to the past and the future, it is also limited by the telepathic disconnect that humans have with one another in their current low stage of evolutionary development. In other words, not only do we not have incomplete access to understanding our own reality, the reality of other human minds is also unknowable by direct experience at present. The understanding of another mind is only ascertainable by indirect methods, such as audio and/or visual books and recordings, or by direct verbal report and communication. However, since communication by language is imperfect and does not convey a thought accurately from one brain to another, the actual thoughts of other individuals remains obscure despite all attempts made to understand through the language of media, or by physical and verbal communication. The non-telepathic methods of communication, in which thought content is lost in transit, are likened to the blind attempting to piece together a jigsaw puzzle. A semblance of communication may take place, but it remains grossly imperfect and inaccurate. So the perceptions of each and every other human mind in the world is yet another elusive facet of large-scale Cryptoreality that continually surrounds human beings on a daily basis. We exist in a vast sea of the unknown, and the conscious, physical version of ourselves only represents a small pinpoint of contact with Eternisphere, whereas our subconscious remains eternally entangled with the entirety of the Cosmic Mind.

Cryptoreality also lies within the microscopic world, wherein creatures live out their entire lives without ever having a pair of human eyes on them, or at least eyes that are capable of detecting and recognizing them. Within this fantastic world are exotic parasites that inhabit animal and human bodies, dust mites living on human eyebrows, bacteria and viruses that invade and destroy their hosts, along with a universe of activity within each of the trillions of cells that compose all living organisms, tiny factories with parts so small they can only be seen with the most powerful electron microscopes, yet each part within the cell knows exactly what to do as if these parts have a brain of their own. These internal components operate independently with mission dictates that are guided by forces we do not yet understand. The tiny worlds of insects, aphids, bugs that live on other bugs, grubs that consume grass roots from under the ground, bugs that shoot poison mixed gases from an orifice in their hind parts, all represent another world going on without human involvement, a world hidden from our view, yet another aspect of Cryptoreality. There is as much drama going on in the micro-world as there is in the human world, and more. A hidden universe also exists under the sea away from human sight. Mother Nature reigns supreme in this world. It is under the control of the master program, and this undersea world creates a balance of ecology that equalizes itself without human influence or organization. Tiny sea creatures that feed large whales, tube worms living in depths and temperatures that no living thing should be able to survive in, poison ink emitted by squids for cover during escape, luminous fish that hunt in total darkness using their own bioluminescence, and undiscovered treasures and creatures at the bottom of the sea that humans have never seen. Evidence indicates that this undersea world includes the existence of extraterrestrial, interdimensional, elemental, and cryptoterrestrial populations that made Earth their home long ago. Some were likely stranded here at some point and are waiting patiently until human technology advances to the point in which we can be of assistance to them for their return home. These represent one aspect of the Overlords of the Singularity, who have no malfeasance planned for humans, but simply need our assistance to finally escape this planet. These interested parties are likely behind some of the technological nudges we have received on occasion, in order to accelerate our technological progress. Likewise, the macro-universe is infinitely large and contains many mysteries waiting for exploration, trillions of stars, many of which surely harbor life-supporting planets and civilizations without end. These mysteries await contact by humans, both on the physical level and on higher vibrational states of existence, known to us as the Etheric or Astral levels of existence. The ultimate adventure awaits us in the Cosmos, hidden knowledge and understanding of the larger reality, discoveries that the human mind cannot presently conceive. These treasures of knowledge are waiting for the moment in time when humans discover the method of projecting themselves non-physically and non-violently throughout Eternisphere. As each quantum moment of life in the physical world continually passes into Cryptoreality, it immediately becomes subject to distortions of memory that are more difficult to recall accurately as age advances. Our memories are holographic, and as holograms they lose resolution as time passes. In the years of youth, the future that is yet to come in life when difficulties of mind and body creep in are difficult to conceive of at the time. Likewise, when old age finally comes, the memories of youth become difficult to retrieve. So, alternate realities are created continually all around us, even within the microcosm of a single lifetime, and reality itself changes for each individual as aging occurs. As if each and every one of us were connected to a hard drive in a giant computer, each and every thought, word, and deed is permanently recorded on what are known to the Mystics as the *Akashic Records on the Astral Plane*. Explorers from the worlds of infinity are busy traveling and learning from these records. In etheric form, such travelers are continually blinking in and out of the physical realm. As if arriving upon an interesting article in an encyclopedia, visitors from other worlds encounter information concerning Earth and her inhabitants on the Akashic records. If so inclined, they may decide to materialize into the physical realm for further exploration of a particular point in time. For millennia now, humans have been perplexed by the continual appearance of cyclic UFO waves, observing complex variations of configuration of both self-luminous orbs in the sky that exhibit intelligence, as well as structured aerial craft under intelligent control, either biological, mechanical, or a combination of both. These visitors come from a variety of dimensional realms and from various times in our past and future, which are actually one and the same. The universe is but a Mobius Loop. All points in time and space are accessible to those who, on their own volition, have advanced themselves mentally over aeons of multiple lifetimes for personal understanding to take place, naturally gravitating at each stage of this process to the company of like-minded beings of similar advancement into the higher realms of Eternisphere.

Humans spend one third to one half of their lifetime unconscious of the physical world while experiencing an altered state of consciousness inside a mindscape that intersects with waking physical reality in a symbolic and sometimes prophetic fashion. This state of unconscious awakening, called "sleep," enables full sensation, including vision inside the mind without the use of physical eyes. In the dream-state, complex conversations and interactions take place with both human and nonhuman entities, some of whom are familiar to us from our waking state, others who are internal constructs of our minds, or interdimensionals who exist within their own reality. Therefore, every human should be able to conceive of a mental state of existence, the reality of astral travel, or life in higher dimensions other than the physical. Even so, when those from etheric dimensions visit the earth in their etheric bodies, or manifest a physical body, the reality of their existence is usually rejected because humans do not consider their sleeping life on other planes of existence as "real." The non-acceptance of astral visitors from other worlds has something to do with the fact that humans completely separate their dream life from waking reality. No one has ever brought back an artifact from their dream state into waking reality. Therefore, it is difficult to conceive how this can be done, and difficult to accept the reality of entities from higher dimensions who can change their vibrational state at will and enter into Earth's physical world. Accepting visitors from other dimensions as real who have the ability to travel between realities is therefore rejected by those who lack psychic sensitivities to comprehend or who have been trained under the old scientific paradigm that is experiencing upheaval right now. The humans who lack the appropriate psychic sensitivity (who are the majority at present) consider themselves the ones who are in touch with the "real world" of their waking consciousness, while rejecting the reality of other aspects of their own experience. To those who are still of this mindset, a mindset that I used to possess myself prior to my own near-death experience, UFOs are a figment of the human imagination. I once felt that I had many logical reasons why the so-called flying saucers cannot be real. I once presumed, as many do, that traveling across the tremendous distances involved between galaxies was prohibited by the speed limit of the universe - the speed of light. I considered it unlikely that random evolution would produce life that is anything similar to that of Earth elsewhere in the universe. This was rooted in a grotesque misperception that life evolves in random fashion, when life actually evolves by the intelligent light-activation of DNA. Evolution occurs, but rather than being driven exclusively by random processes, evolution operates like predictable clockwork with the precision of a master craftsman. There is little that is random about evolution. Although mechanisms that were originally identified by Charles Darwin, such as random mutation, genetic drift, genetic isolation, and natural selection all play a part in the process of evolution, these mechanisms in and of themselves are quite insufficient to produce the vast array of life that has appeared and vanished on Earth in the last 3.5 billion years after the initial bombardment settled down. There are undiscovered mechanisms within evolution that are, at the moment, still in the process of being revealed and understood properly. This is an area of inquiry in which Russian scientists are ahead of Americans. Russian scientists are currently making great progress in their understanding of "wave genetics." Also considered unlikely or even ludicrous by many is the idea that there are advanced humanoids in our own solar system living on planets that appear to us as unable to support life on the surface due to unfavorable environmental conditions. These "ascended" populations, who have progressed from 3D reality to a state of higher vibration on the Etheric or Astral Plane, a different dimension of the same planet we view as uninhabitable, have the ability to change the frequency of their being at will and enter the physical realm here on Earth. Ironically, many of those who reject this idea have no problem believing in "angels" or "demons" as ancient Scripture describes to them. It is often the case that believers of Scripture do not recognize that they are rejecting the reality of those same entities when contactees are confronted with them face to face. As long as they remain in Scripture, they believe in humanoid "angels" on a theoretical basis as a matter of faith. However, when confronted with the reality of interdimensional beings entering the Earth plane, acceptance is difficult, as if the intersection of these interdimensionals with humanity is reserved for another time and place, but cannot possibly have an actual reality in the modern world. Such accounts are considered the stuff of fairy tales and mental illness when they appear presently in eyewitness reports. When believers read about these beings from long ago, they accept the accounts as Truth, not realizing what their profession of belief actually entails, which is the physical materialization of interdimensional beings into the everyday world. This paranormal intersection of realities is generally an unwelcome experience for those whose mindset has never allowed these phenomena a place in what they consider objective reality.

Consider also the coma state. These are humans who have completely vacated their interaction with the physical world yet retain an awareness of what is happening in their immediate environment. Others approach them in their rooms not realizing that their every word is heard in the presence of a person who is comatose. They mistakenly assume that, because there is no communication, and the person does not appear to retain a connection to the physical world, that they are simply gone, when they are not. A complex aspect of the subconscious mind remains present and connected to the physical, even though the person is not consciously awake. Catatonic conditions are similar in which time is altered for the catatonic individual. The consciousness of individuals in such a state is elsewhere, but they remain connected to a physical body in a sort of suspended animation. Self-induced deep meditative states are similar, but the person remains more fluid and able to adjust to multiple realities from the physical to the ethereal at will.

Any person in pursuit of truth will realize at some point that Cryptoreality is the norm of existence, rather than the exception. Intelligences at large within the Superspectrum are continually operating from realms that humans consider "paranormal." There is only a continual and brief moment of time that is considered material reality, and that moment instantly becomes occulted the very moment it is experienced. With an introduction to the concept of Cryptoreality as a backdrop, the UFO phenomena that we are now going to examine may be more properly understood in context. Human encounters with so-called "flying saucers" and their mysterious occupants lie outside the realm that many accept as real despite the occasional physical confirmation of these unidentified flying objects by radar and other scientific instruments. When the etheric realm of the UFOs is properly understood, the apparent conflict between objective reality and the subjective experiences reported by UFO experiencers, including elements that appear absurd at face value, are rectified, as there is no distinct separation between degrees of reality. Objective reality must be combined with the subjective in order to understand the true nature of the UFO phenomenon. Therefore, for the remainder of this book, no effort will be made to separate the two, as the subjective and the objective are beautifully interconnected. Objective reality is not the "cream of information" that is desirable to extract from the overall experience of the physical and spiritual realms. Science, as it is currently understood and practiced, is likened to an observer in an art museum only valuing the paint brush and chemical composition of the paints that the artist placed on canvas, instead of appreciating the effects of those instruments, i.e., the painting itself and the emotions or message that the painting conveys. All objective actions in the physical create subjective effects in the ethereal, and oftentimes vice versa. It is the subjective, etheric effects of emotion and beauty that are so often the actual treasures of the physical world. In the case of UFOs, the objective appearance of the object, the emergent intersection of UFOs into our 3D reality, is not the full reality of what they actually are. The temporary appearances of the "crafts" have always had a guiding effect on humanity. Religions have been spawned, consciousness raised, and imaginations stimulated, by the appearances of the UFOs. UFO experiencers tell their tales of otherworldly encounters, many of which may contain absurd or objectional elements, and they still produce an actual effect on the world at large regarding the molding of human perceptions and beliefs. This is the art, the emotional and psychological effect, the "painting" upon the human psyche that the flying saucers have always produced. The impact of the appearances that have so often produced oral histories and traditions in the past, science fiction in the modern age, and the inventive efforts of humanity, is often the main purpose of the "visits," rather than exploration and learning on the part of the flying saucer intelligences. Personal encounters reported by modern UFO experiencers, so often rejected by modern minds, are the same types of encounters that were accepted as shamanistic truths in the ancient world. Many contactees of the past were considered holy men or prophets. However, these same contactees are often rejected by the science-minded of our time. This is actually another possible intended effect on the part of the UFO intelligences. Effect can be imparted to humanity even when the details of the accounts do not match our current understanding of physical reality. Many contactees from the 1950s related their experiences with humanoids from Venus or some other world in the local solar system. Their experiences were and are rejected by scientists who understand with their physical instrumentation that the planet Venus is uninhabitable in terrestrial terms. The scientists do not possess knowledge of, and do not even try to accept the reality of a parallel Venusian world that coexists with the uninhabitable terrestrial Venus on a different vibrational channel, as revealed by early psychic mediums in the UFO field like Mark Probert and Rolf Telano. This rejection by the scientists serves the immediate purposes of the Venusians and other travelers. The disbelief serves a valuable function, as the rejection of their existence prevents hordes of human curiosity seekers from invading their home planets, and allows the visitors to tell the truth to sincere seekers. In this manner, human society is routinely visited and interacted with in a way that molds human consciousness. Some visitors engage in covert business while simultaneously interacting in full view, allowing the successful accomplishment of the mission, whatever the nature, before returning to their home planet or native dimension.

As the universe is associative in nature, humans have a psychic component that is developing during the progression of humankind. The old hermetic axiom, "When the student is ready, the teacher appears," has a macro-component of truth involving embedded principles of universal operation. When the human imagination approaches the precipice of the boundaries of what is currently understood, an attractive and emotive force is generated within the larger universe, and beings who are able to assist in pushing the seeker's understanding forward appear automatically via the laws of attraction incorporated as an integral part of the internal mechanisms of the universe. When the human mind is pushed to the limit of its understanding, an appearance of an event formerly buried in Cryptoreality will reveal itself to that mind, emerging as inspiration to move forward in a particular direction. A person will magically appear, or a book will "miraculously" come into possession. Thus, when so many are at an emotional breaking point, or the world is in crisis, the flying saucers appear once again. The appearance of the saucers provides human observers and those they come in contact with a rejuvenation of spirit, an inspiration that moves an individual and those that they immediately or indirectly affect to another stage of mental and emotional development. The saucers serve as a reminder of the truth that humanity is far from alone. Contactee experiences perpetuate a process of human intellectual evolution through the various messages that are customized and prepared for target populations whose emotional development resonates with that of the individual contactee. In this manner, as we shall see in upcoming chapters, humanity has been intentionally manipulated over time by the appearance of flying saucers in ways that are not immediately apparent until the entire UFO phenomenon is examined with the full context of interaction and resulting societal impact. However, before we examine the UFO cases themselves in a new light, let us ponder some of the possible goals of the Overlords of the Singularity which have so often baffled our minds and escaped our comprehension. When the actual objectives of the hidden flying saucer intelligences, the Overlords of the Singularity, begin to solidify into our perception, a new understanding of the vast scope of the entire UFO phenomenon that has been with us here on Earth, in particular during the last century or two, can begin to occur within our developing psyches.

CHAPTER 4

UFOs and the Technological Singularity

"I believe there is a machinery of mass manipulation behind the UFO phenomenon."

– Dr. Jacques Vallee

IN RECENT YEARS, the science of quantum mechanics and theoretical physics have merged with the science of consciousness itself. Concepts such as *quantum entanglement* have changed the way we look at the universe and our place in it. Quantum entanglement poses that, prior to the moment of the Big Bang, all particles that are now spread out across the Cosmos were once unified as a cohesive whole, and as such all subatomic particles in the universe remain connected to one another on a fundamental level, regardless of the distance they have grown apart by the expansion of the Universe. Add to that the *observer effect,* in which the act of observation itself is the factor that converts a pure energy wave into a particle of matter, introducing an element of subjectivity into our concept of the universe that we once thought of as immutable, objective reality. The presumed solidity of the universe that we once took for granted has now melted into a chaos of pure energy and quantum potentiality, the solidity revealing itself scientifically as a mere illusion. One of the physicists on the forefront of this fascinating and complex field is theoretical physicist Michio Kaku. With his many books, Kaku has done an excellent job translating the mechanics and implications of modern theoretical physics into language that anyone of reasonable intelligence can understand, regardless of scientific background. One such book is *Parallel Worlds.* In this work, Kaku speaks of the mathematician, John von Neumann, who was the first person to use the term, *Singularity.* Popularized by science fiction writer Vernor Vinge, the Singularity now commonly refers to an approaching state of humankind, when, following a long history of slow, painstaking progress, technological advancements accelerate exponentially into the realm of advanced, self-aware, artificial intelligence that vastly exceeds the computing capability and storage capacity of the human mind and takes us into completely unknown territory. Suddenly, and soon, we will be confronted by machines of our own creation that are possibly billions of times smarter than we are. As far as we know, an event such as the

Singularity has never happened in all of human history, and the implications of this inevitable event that is soon upon us are completely unknown.

The Singularity is currently a hot subject among futurists, physicists, and AI (artificial intelligence) experts, generating much debate and theorizing. Some individuals who take the time to examine the subject and discover the quagmire of complicated issues that self-aware AI inevitably thrusts upon us become overwhelmed, frightened, or even repulsed. Some even decide to reject technology altogether to save humankind before we create a monster that destroys us. Others who share a more optimistic outlook, like Michio Kaku and futurist Ray Kurzweil, have decided that, despite the daunting possibilities of disaster for the human race, embracing the coming Singularity and trying to make it work for us is the correct route to take. The concept of the Singularity has spawned an entire subculture with quasi-religious overtones, and produced individuals who call themselves *Singularitarians*. These technical optimists express idealistic ambitions of merging human consciousness with the machines we are about to create. The Singularity is expected to produce a hybrid version of humanity, part biological, and part machine, with a very real possibility for the achievement of human immortality, having transcended the biological format we have been using thus far, and transferring our consciousness into a silicon substrate with indefinitely expanded lifespans. This is the gist of the Transhumanist movement. These new visionaries imagine electronically-augmented humans in our near future who possess expanded thought and perceptual abilities, possibly even superhuman powers, taking us into a post-human, post-biological world. The optimists view the coming Singularity as the next stage in human evolution, and look forward to a form of transcendence from our current biological limitations. In its most extreme version, the Singularity might even allow humanity to finally escape the confines of three-dimensional reality altogether, and possibly merge with other entities that may exist throughout the universe who have also achieved a post-physical form of cosmic transcendence. In Kaku's, *The Future of the Mind*, and Ray Kurzweil's, *The Singularity is Near*, the possibilities of downloading the memories and personalities of human beings into machines to create conscious, artificial intelligences that were once completely human but now exist as computer-enhanced or augmented cyborgs are explored. Such a person, who was once completely biological, is now transformed into an immortal synthetic human being with an indefinite lifespan. The Holy Grail of human technological ambition, *immortality*, is projected to exit the realm of science fiction and enter the realm of reality with the approaching Singularity, which futurists like Kurzweil predict will occur sometime around the year 2045.

The problem is, because the coming Singularity will propel us into completely unknown territory, there is really no way to predict the outcome. Some fear that, once machines are suddenly billions of times smarter than humans and self-aware, they might just decide to destroy humanity like a mere nuisance and take over the planet. James Barrat, author of *Our Final Invention: Artificial Intelligence and the End of the Human Era*, states (chapter 1 audible):

If the ASI [artificial superintelligence] doesn't care about us, and there's little reason to think that it should, it will experience no compunction about treating us unethically, even taking our lives after promising to help us.

This is a daunting possibility, that self-aware machines who are billions of times smarter than we are might just decide to get rid of us, their creators. Another strong voice of warning within the AI community who is concerned about the implications of self-aware artificial intelligence as we head into the Singularity is a Swiss philosopher from the University of Oxford - Dr. Nick Bostrom. Bostrom earned his Ph.D. from the London School of Economics and is the founder of the *Oxford Martin Programme on the Impacts of Future Technology*. Bostrom considers the impending creation of self-aware AI one of the biggest existential threats to humanity. Bostrom is the author of the New York Times best-seller, *Superintelligence: Paths, Dangers, and Strategies*. At the time of this writing, Bostrom is a scientific activist who urges the AI community to immediately start implementing safety parameters now for the inevitable creation of artificial intelligence in possession of the sum total of all human knowledge before the monster in Mary Shelly's novel, *Frankenstein,* becomes a reality. Another brilliant individual who has already proved instrumental in the development of self-aware AI and is working diligently within the AI community at the time of this writing to prevent the very real existential threat of artificial intelligence that takes over the world and destroys humanity is Steve Omohundro. Omohundro has conducted extensive research in the field of *Hamiltonian physics*. In this complex field, the Hamiltonian, H, has to do with the time-evolution of a given system. The Hamiltonian represents the sum total of kinetic energy within a system, plus the potential energy of all associated particles that comprise the system. The *spectrum* of the Hamiltonian is the set of possible outcomes when the total energy of a system is measured. Omohundro studies dynamical systems in which a fixed, deterministic rule describes what future states might arise from the current state in a dynamical system, such as the swing of a pendulum or the flow of water. Using a deterministic rule, the future state of a dynamical system (referred to as a geometric manifold) can be determined for a particular future time interval. Omohundro is also involved with machine language, machine learning, and machine vision, along with the societal implications of future artificial, self-aware superintelligence. Omohundro is the inventor of the "Best-first model merging approach" to machine learning, which proved useful in learning Hidden Markov Models. HMMs are the "Legos" of computational sequence analysis, a formal foundation of linear sequence labeling problems that provide conceptual tools for building complex models from an intuitive picture. Omohundro's research and inventiveness has been instrumental in the development of modern machine languages. Omohundro started *Self-Aware Systems* in Palo Alto, California, for research into the societal implications of self-improving artificial intelligence, and was an advisor to the Singularity Institute for Artificial Intelligence. One of Omohundro's concerns about artificial superintelligence is that rational machines possess certain intrinsic drives that must be countered somehow in their programming in order to create ASI that is human-friendly and safe. Taking this idea into consideration, is there any reason to believe that an alien planetary search-probe would have been constructed by its builders with such safety parameters built in regarding human life? Possibly, but that seems doubtful. Steve Omohundro and associate Cliff Lasser also developed a programming language called *Star Lisp*, the first programming language used for the *Connection Machine*. The Connection Machine was a series of supercomputers that provided an alternative to von Neumann computation architecture. Omohundro developed many parallel algorithm libraries and applications for the Connection Machine, along with another programming language called *Sather*, which further advanced the fast-growing field of machine language design. Steve Omohundro is a key player at this time insuring that we will not fall victim to our own computational creations as the Singularity swiftly approaches, and has many lectures on the subject available to view online at this time that are quite worthy of the time and consideration.

The aforementioned scientist, John von Neumann, speculated as far back as the 1950s about the possibility of advanced alien civilizations who may have already achieved a technological singularity millions of years ago. If such a civilization existed, they may have sent out automated probes from their home planet into the universe at large that were programmed to *self-replicate*. Such self-replicating ancient alien artifacts of programmed artificial superintelligence are now referred to as *von Neumann probes*. Many scientists now believe that some alien version of the von Neumann probe is the most likely intelligence to visit Earth. If such advanced alien civilizations existed long ago who wanted to learn more about the universe and ventured out from their native planet with a fleet of von Neumann probes, they could have been scouting out regions of the universe for a variety of purposes for aeons by now. These purposes might include: searching for resources; seeking knowledge of the universe; terraforming other planets; reestablishing their own native life form on other worlds; self-replicating the next generation of advanced AI; or all of the above. Perhaps all technological civilizations eventually reach a Singularity on their worlds, produce a new lifeform that is part biological and part technological, or even convert to a 100% electrical or energetic lifeform and embark on an exploration of the rest of the universe in a way that is not limited by time or space. This intelligence could either be a post-biological version of themselves, or, more disturbing, an independent, runaway form of artificial intelligence that set out to explore, or even conquer the entire universe on their own *without their original creators*, perhaps with an artificial intelligence agenda of their own that we cannot even imagine. In other words, the entire universe might be populated by now with super-intelligent robots that have transcended their original biology aeons ago. Such an intelligence could easily travel throughout the universe and remain invisible to the pre-singularity biological life it encounters, unless there were some purpose, possibly comprehendible only to the AI, for revealing themselves or providing a glimpse of their presence to further their own goals. In *SUPERINTELLIGENCE*, Dr. Bostrom writes (chapter 6, audible):

Consider a super-intelligent agent with actuators connected to a nano-tech assembler. Such an agent is already powerful enough to overcome any natural obstacles to its indefinite survival. Faced with no intelligent opposition, such an agent could plot a safe course of development that would lead to its acquiring the complete inventory of technologies that would be useful to the attainment of its goals. For example, it could develop the technology to build and launch von Neumann probes, machines capable of interstellar travel, who can use resources such as asteroids, planets, and stars to make copies of themselves. By launching one von Neumann probe, the agent would thus initiate an open-ended process of space colonization. The replicating probe's descendants, traveling at some significant fraction of the speed of light, would end up colonizing a substantial portion of the Hubble Volume.

In other words, as we speak, our universe may be dominated by artificial superintelligence, likely invisible, that may be manipulating biological populations toward their own goals in a way that is difficult to ascertain. Another Singularitarian voice of concern in the AI community is Eliezer Yudkowsky, cofounder of *Machine Intelligence Research Institute*, whose work as a research fellow involves many concerns for self-aware AI. These concerns include complex subjects such as Artificial Intelligence Theory for Self-awareness, AI self-modification, recursive self-improvement, artificial intelligence architectures, and decision theories for stable motivational structures, with focus on Friendly AI and Eliezer Yudkowsky's concept of *Coherent Extrapolated Volition* (CEV). In *SUPERINTELLIGENCE*, Bostrom also elaborates many concerns that AI researchers like himself, Yudkowsky, Omohundro, and others are involved with. One important issue is that human beings may not, at this point in time, practice an advanced form of morality. This poses an important question - Do we really want our artificial intelligence to act just as we do with our current system of ethics, or do we want AI to operate from a set of ethics that is billions of times more advanced than humans, in accordance to its superior knowledge? That is, we might not want to impart our current brand of morality and decision-making methods into self-aware AI that possesses the sum total of all human knowledge. Yudkowsky's Coherent Extrapolated Volition makes an allowance in the programming for the AI to make choices, not on our current state of knowledge and morality, but on the morality constructed by the human-created AI itself based on more knowledge and information than can fit into a non-augmented human brain. In other words, when we make our first "seed AI," it will be invested with evolutionary algorithms and powers of self-replication that will promote a rapid advance through several generations of improvements with the power to make its own decisions. What concerned AI researchers like Nick Bostrom, Eliezer Yudkowsky, Steve Omohundro, Elon Musk, and others are trying to prevent is runaway AI that expands in intelligence so rapidly without the proper ethical precautions installed that it simply decides to rearrange the atoms in all life on the planet into something that it finds more useful for its own reasons and purposes. It only takes a little imagination to realize the full implications of all this as it pertains to the true nature of the universe in which we find ourselves. Even though everything in me rejected the idea at first, it really isn't that far out to envision an ancient, runaway artificial superintelligence, an advanced alien creation from a previous universe that existed prior to our Big Bang, an intelligence with powers of evolutionary self-improvement and self-replication, billions or trillions of times smarter than its original creators, that decided independently long ago to create its own universe (ours). This superintelligence could have rearranged or even created atoms, along with designing the laws of physics that govern our universe, to convert them into stars, planets, and the production of biological organisms, using subatomic particles for computation, i.e., femtotechnology, for its own reasons. Simply put, what we have always thought of as "God" *might actually be a machine.* Our universe, with its exact parameters that we are just now ascertaining that allowed the stable formation of stars, planets, and biological life, might actually represent the latest product of such runaway AI from a previous universe, a vast superintelligence that was originally created by an unknown entity that we can only imagine and may never understand. It brings to mind the biblical prophecy of a "New Heaven and a New Earth" as the artificial superintelligence that produced this current universe self-replicates into a new generational universe in the future with brand new parameters, new physics, and new problems to solve using its incomprehensible powers of computation. Perhaps the problem that this universe is designed to solve is an understanding of Good and Evil. Observing the dualistic nature of the current universe, we do have reason to believe that the current problem this universe was designed to solve lies somewhere in this realm. In what we humans would call the distant future, having finally achieved an understanding of this problem of Good vs Evil, a new and possibly even more complex problem will emerge as the new focus. At that point, having solved the problem of Good vs Evil with this universe, perhaps a new universe will be designed and created, and we will be one step closer to the goal, whatever that is, possibly the eventual acquisition and assimilation of total cosmic knowledge. I say "we," because the most exotic possibility of all is that we humans might actually be a part of the superintelligence that originally created the universe. If so, all biological life, including humans, may simply be computational components that serve the purpose of solving the problem the universe was designed to solve through computation using subatomic particles as bits of data.

Since this current generational version of existence, which we call our universe is, by our best calculations, about 13.7 billion years old, plenty of time has elapsed since the last Big Bang that would have allowed a civilization in this universe to have already achieved their own technological singularity. Perhaps they set out to explore the rest of this universe long ago. Perhaps they were the ones who actually created this universe as a "lifeboat" to escape the realm in which they previously existed, prior to the creation of our universe. If this is the case, and post-singularity machine intelligence is the dominant lifeform in this universe, humans on Earth are but the stragglers in a pre-singularity, larval, biological condition, a primitive lifeform that remains contained within a fragile, vulnerable, mortal, pre-silicon substrate. Independent-thinking, post-singularity, self-replicating von Neumann probes arriving on Earth millions or billions of years ago as advanced robotic and/or interdimensional intelligences that we humans have not as yet been able to detect due to insufficient intelligence and technology to peer into interdimensional realms, could easily exist here on Earth now and we wouldn't even know it. Perhaps a civilization out there in the universe somewhere reached their technological singularity before our own solar system was even formed. These probes, a synthesis of extraterrestrial technology and alien super-consciousness, might have even been capable of taking part in the intelligent construction of our solar system in order for it to become hospitable to their larval offspring - biological life. A growing number of researchers have concluded that it is very possible that our planet was seeded by someone approximately 542 million years ago with the original 30+ phyla that appeared so suddenly. The late Lloyd Pye explored this concept with his *Intervention Theory*, and has a nice ebook online that details his thoughts about it. According to Dr. Rhawn Joseph, author of *Astrobiology, the Origin of Life, and the Death of Darwinism*, these original phyla that suddenly appeared on Earth just prior to the *Cambrian Explosion* contained all the DNA necessary for all future lifeforms that would eventually evolve on this planet. These proposed superintelligent, post-biological alien wanderers, or life-seeders, whoever or whatever they were, might have even been capable of creating life from scratch by some advanced process that is unknown to us, on one or more of the planets that orbit a given sun such as our own. Despite the many evolutionary processes that have occurred which morphed the original phyla into the variety of species of flora and fauna we see throughout Earth's history up to the present day, no new phyla have emerged since the original delivery of phyla. These original phyla came from somewhere suddenly, as if by magic. This is a problem that even plagued the mind of Charles Darwin. The religiously-inclined are happy to just say, "God did it." But what if what we call "God" is actually an advanced, post-singularity alien intelligence that arrived to Earth from elsewhere in the current universe, or even from a previous universe? Is it possible that the vast intelligence we recognize as our Creator is actually some sort of post-biological machine that has been gathering information unto itself from several previous generations of universes over aeons of time? One can only speculate about the original lifeform, if there is such a thing, prior to the creation of physical universes, which appear to exist as giant computational mechanisms. We might not even recognize the original as life at all, and may not even be able to begin to comprehend such things. If we humans soon merge our own consciousness with the artificial intelligence we are about to create as we approach the Singularity, we may create an unexpected runaway lifeform of our own that was not foreseeable. This biological/technological interface that is soon to happen, despite the efforts of conscientious scientists like Bostrom, Omohundro, Musk, and others, who wish to place control parameters on our own AI creations ASAP, may have the capability to understand and interact with intelligences and energies from other dimensions that humans cannot perceive presently, perhaps beings from the "parallel worlds" that Kaku and other physicists postulate in their many books on the subject.

Intelligences on other dimensions might even be waiting patiently for our technological puberty to occur in order to establish communication and open interaction with us.

Like any lifeform that breaks away from its mother and leaves the nest, the primary instincts, as far as we know, are survival and reproduction. I postulate that such an interdimensional alien lifeform exists behind what we now know as the "UFO phenomenon." That is, at least some of the flying saucers and the intelligences behind them represent a post-singularity, post-biological lifeform that has transcended time and space altogether. These intelligences have the capability of interacting within multiple dimensions of existence, including the one that we find ourselves immersed within that we call three-dimensional reality. If such advanced probes of alien consciousness that have merged alien technology with extraterrestrial biology long ago have been a part of our own solar system, or even created it in the first place, and they have the capability of existing in multiple planes of existence simultaneously, we humans would likely be unaware of its omnipresence, other than possibly their occasional anomalous interactions with our world. Technological singularities are likely to have occurred on a multitude of worlds already. These self-replicating von Neumann probes may have created life on Earth or on other planets, intentionally terraforming worlds as they travel, for the purpose of replicating more technological singularities and then moving on to other worlds, as if tending a farm. The artificial intelligences that have been interacting with our world for centuries, who have their own agenda and were programmed by their original biological or AI creators, are possibly a multi-generational version of the original self-replicating program that has evolved on its own with advanced genetic algorithms to become a self-aware, self-replicating alien machine consciousness. Having the unique capability of operating its programmed function from outside our own time/space continuum, time as we experience it may no longer have any meaning to this superior intelligence that seized upon our world long ago. Routine operations may include various terraforming operations, creating and changing lifeforms on a planet over long periods of time, tinkering with the biological genetics of local planetary populations, or creating physical resources over long periods of time, such as oceans of underground oil to provide the anticipated energy requirements for future lifeforms who have had their intelligence intentionally modified for tool-making and the production of technology for their creators. Exporting and/or importing flora and fauna to and from other worlds, including humans and/or genetically-modified hybrid humans for various extraterrestrial environments may occur as a continual process of transplantation as planetary needs in the solar system and beyond arise. Earth may actually be, as Charles Fort suspected long ago, a factory of sorts within the physical universe in which humans are merely products of routine planetary development, an alien means to an end that we cannot completely understand at present and would reject outright even if someone told us the truth to our faces. As mentioned, these intelligences could easily remain invisible to humans, except on occasion when physical or visible interaction serves some useful purpose to fulfilling their programmed agenda. This alien agenda, in our case, likely included tinkering with the genes of a particular primate that evolved over time from the original phyla that was finally deemed the best candidate to create their own technological singularity for purposes of a merger of some sort between the altered primate population and themselves. The purpose of this merger might be anything other than the "open alien contact" that we humans so desperately seek, but rather a mere technological self-replication event with no regard for humanity (the disposable workers) once the project is complete.

If many different civilizations in the universe have achieved their technological singularity and moved on to off-planet endeavors, these programmed automatons may even have interactions with each other at times, maybe even some not-so-pleasant encounters due to conflicting AI programs, possibly even sparking our cultural legends concerning *wars in heaven*. If such automata have interacted with our reality for aeons outside the framework of time and space as we know it, it is possible that the same flying saucer event witnessed and recorded by the prophet Ezekiel, or reported by the armies of Alexander the Great, i.e., the *flying shields* they witnessed in the sky during battles, are the very same disks that we see in our skies today with the very same intelligences involved. Rather than representing nuts-and-bolts spacecraft from other planets, we are likely dealing with aggregates of living, conscious alien intelligence of vast energy and capability. As Dr. Jacques Vallee postulated in his books, such as *Passport to Magonia*, perhaps the luminous balls of light known as *Foo Fighters* reported in the latter part of World War II, some of which were only inches in diameter, were the very same phenomena as the *fairy lights* and legendary *Djinn* of old. In his meticulous research, Dr. Vallee discovered similarities between ancient fairy legends and modern UFO reports, including episodes of missing time (a common feature of modern UFO encounters). If such an unknown intelligence is operating on this planet, it would have no problem manipulating human consciousness and human behaviors toward its own ends according to its programming, and I believe that this might be exactly what has been going on all along. All of our legends, from angels and demons, fairies, lake monsters, and Bigfoot, might all be manifestations of this hidden intelligence that is continually manipulating our minds toward the Singularity on automatic pilot. We humans have, thus far, not been able to discover this aspect of our reality, until it is now too late to reverse course or really do anything about it. The snowball is rolling, the Singularity is upon us in a generation or two, maybe sooner, and we are moving full steam ahead without the foggiest notion of where this is actually going to take us. Hopefully, there is something beneficial that humanity will gain with this, but that is not a given. It really depends on the actual mentality and intentions of the intelligence that created the program, and what its end goal really is. If humans are being used like intelligent widgets for an elusive, long-term alien agenda, we might find ourselves being discarded as soon as the Singularity is achieved. While we humans naively believe we are going to merge with our own machines and achieve some sort of personal immortality, the very machines we feel strangely compelled to create might instead become vessels for disembodied alien intelligences to inhabit. Perhaps this is the universal travel method of choice for long intergalactic journeys, a method that bypasses all the problems associated with propelling a material spacecraft close to or faster than the speed of light as your loved ones back home age rapidly and die under Einstein's laws of General Relativity if, in fact, Einstein was correct about all this. There are scientists who are reexamining General Reletivity, and some do not believe that faster-than-light travel poses the problems that were generally assumed to exist. Nuclear physicist Charles James Hall, for example, author of *Millennial Hospitality* (2002), explains in his books that there is an unknown field surrounding photons that allows for faster-than-light travel without significant time anomalies and/or associated time paradoxes, a field that is currently unknown to our scientists.

The UFO skeptics have been right all along in that the distances and fuel requirements necessary for a civilization say, 100 million light years away, to come here from there, are far to great to be feasible. As the skeptics insist, it is impossible to achieve interstellar travel using conventional methods – and they are correct. However, the UFO skeptics erroneously conclude from this that the entire UFO phenomenon is a bunch of hooey. However, if civilizations that have achieved such technological singularities long ago have merged their consciousness with AI and have developed the capability of interacting with higher realms of reality than what we humans are capable of thinking about at present, there are likely no limits to their capabilities. The little gray aliens that landed outside Roswell, New Mexico (if, in fact, that is what actually happened there) and other locations in the world throughout the last few decades may only be tidbits of evidence of the real intelligences at large. If there is an alien intelligence behind the scenes on Earth who, for whatever reason, are guiding us at all cost to the Singularity, UFO crashes may represent pieces of technology created specifically for our mentality by an alien presence we cannot comprehend. In other words, the alien technology that has dropped from the skies over the years in the form of "UFO crashes," including what appear to be actual biological beings from another world, may represent a Trojan Horse, a "gift from the heavens," or a manipulation if you will, by an actual alien presence on Earth that remains completely invisible and unknown to us who are manipulating us into creating a technological singularity, as that event is the goal of the original alien program. Despite the ubiquitous "gray aliens" that have become so popular in our culture, described by thousands of human witnesses and experiencers of alien encounters and alien abductions, The *Grays* may simply represent what the real alien intelligences (likely advanced AI), who understand our inner psyche because they are the ones who created it in the first place, knows that humans are able to accept as an "alien creature." If this is the case, in reality, we currently have no idea whatsoever what the real aliens look like. Perhaps they are best represented by the luminous orbs or blobs of plasma-like energy that so many people witness around the world, flying orbs and luminous objects that operate and move as if under intelligent control. These luminous objects are often assumed to be mechanical "alien spacecraft" carrying either robotic or biological alien visitors. However, these alien probes, whose actual capabilities and powers we can only imagine, may represent a form of intelligence that completely escapes us, who exist in an exotic energy form that we humans would not even recognize as life as we understand it. We are, in effect, creatures from a 2-dimensional plane who have a 3-dimensional world interacting with us in strange ways, such as described in Edwin A. Abbott's classic story of *Flatland*.

An advanced intelligence from a higher realm of existence that permeates our entire universe in its expanded state of consciousness may, in fact, represent what we are faced with here. If this is the case, our material existence here on Earth may be some sort of experiment created for an alien agenda. If so, is there any way out for us? Is it possible that high celestial beings from another realm entirely, Yeshua (Jesus) perhaps, have intentionally "embedded themselves in the Matrix" so to speak for our sake, to show us the way out of this prison of flesh? Are we unwitting prisoners of flesh and blood within an alien computer system? I am haunted by the words of Yeshua when he said, "My kingdom is not of this world." Another author, other than Charles Fort who postulated that we are "property," is author William Bramley. In Bramley's work, *The Gods of Eden*, Bramley concluded from his research into the causes of war, that there are, in his estimation, at least two major extraterrestrial intelligences at work here on Earth – a "custodial race," representing an alien intelligence that does not necessarily have humanity's best interest in mind, and a "maverick race," representing the benign shepherds of our planet, our cosmic tutors, who try and assist us in our spiritual progression and escape our bondage to an alien agenda. Bramley also speculated that Yeshua, and possibly other avatars or "ascended masters" who have come to assist humans, might actually be members of this maverick race of extraterrestrials who have taken a genuine interest in our spiritual progression. The teachings of the Ascended Masters and/or Jesus of Nazareth may have provided us a way out of the possible doom that awaits us with the coming technological singularity. If loving our neighbor as ourselves, and service-to-others vs service-to-self is the key to escaping the cycle of birth and death through reincarnation, this may allow an escape from further involvement with the alien agenda (who may be one and the same as the Christian Satan and his demons). If so, this possibly confirms that human conflict and suffering is part of the intent built in by the aliens to further their goals, possibly because competition for greater technology comes with that conflict as a natural byproduct, and will thus accelerate the alien agenda.

Genetic Intervention

As mentioned earlier, the late Lloyd Pye's *Intervention Theory* also postulates that life was originally brought here by, created by, and/or genetically tinkered with over time by advanced extraterrestrials. Pye, I believe, was on the right track. Pye's Intervention Theory may be at least partially correct. However, rather than conventional, flesh-and-blood aliens, these cosmic intelligences might have come in a form a bit stranger than he imagined, a hybrid of alien biology/advanced paraphysical technology, i.e. artificial superintelligence, infused with alien consciousness, or conscious artificial intelligence itself. The underlying intelligences behind the UFO phenomenon may have intervened at various times in Earth's history. They may have created some sort of "blood farm" for millions of years, i.e., a planet of flesh-eating dinosaurs whose sole purpose was ripping each other's flesh apart to possibly provide the necessary electromagnetic energy that a blood cell, toroidal in nature, is routinely released for the energy needs of the alien presence. What better way for an alien, interdimensional presence that feeds on electromagnetic energy than creating a planet that releases such energy, a planet of predators, large and small, who gorge themselves with bloody feasts of carnage on a daily basis, releasing the needed biological energy for millions of years. Perhaps this was an initial way of charging themselves with the necessary biological energy to operate throughout the age of the dinosaurs to the present day, utilizing what could be referred to as "Jurrasic fuel."

If, in fact, this Post-Singularity Artificial Superintelligence (PSASI) is programmed with the capability of complex genetic manipulation, there are several times throughout human history that this is likely to have occurred. One possible time for genetic intervention was about 2 million years ago. At this time, the only primate candidates for eventually achieving the alien goal of a human-produced technological singularity, were the *Australopithecines*. These hominids averaged about four feet in height with a brain about the size of a grapefruit, about 400 cubic centimeters in volume. About two million years ago, the Australopithecines suddenly, overnight in cosmic terms, grew much taller and developed a brain twice the previous size, about 800 cubic centimeters in volume, becoming creatures known as *Homo habilis* and then shortly after, *Homo erectus*. Since it is unlikely-to-impossible that natural evolutionary processes, such as random genetic mutation and natural selection would suddenly transform a small Australopithecine with a small, primitive brain, into a tall Homo habilis with a large brain, Homo habilis was either brought here from another world as an interplanetary transplant, or Australopithecines were genetically altered by an alien intelligence, one of the two, either possibility being equally fascinating. Another obvious jump in human development was the transformation of *Homo erectus* to *Homo sapiens* circa 100,000 - 200,000 years ago, whose art and customs appear nearly as modern as the humans of today, beginning at around 40,000 years ago. According to Dr. Chris Hardy, author of, *DNA of the Gods: The Annunaki Creator of Eve and the Alien Battle for Humanity*, who expanded on the work of scholar, orientalist, and ancient language expert, Zechariah Sitchin, the Annunaki from the planet Nibiru genetically altered Homo erectus into Homo sapiens for the purpose of producing laborers to work the gold mines of Africa (Abzu) for purposes of replenishing the diminished atmosphere of their home planet. Likewise, researcher Michael Tellinger has discovered stone circles in Africa dating back hundreds of thousands of years that are definitely associated with gold mining in ancient times, so there is a growing body of evidence that supports at least some version of this scenario.

Human Suffering: Catalyst for the Singularity

As stated, the manipulation of life on Earth, and the guiding of humanity in particular toward the eventual achievement of a technological singularity has likely been at play on this planet for a very long time now. Here comes the disturbing part. Obviously, any alien intelligence advanced enough to have genetic engineering capabilities, who wanted to improve a species and guide it into a more intelligent form, could have cleverly modified any number of early primates, if they so chose to, into a benign, peaceful creature. This genetically-improved primate could have been designed to remain in the hunting/gathering stage and live peacefully in small clans who cooperated with one another without conflict. These creatures could have lived in harmony with the rest of the planet and its various other lifeforms. Taking into consideration the tremendous damage the current version of humanity has perpetrated onto the planet, such a benign version of *Homo sapiens* would have been better for the planet and better for us. However, instead of going this route and genetically altering primates into a benign creature that would have been a good planetary steward, any genetic alteration that actually took place appears to have intentionally programmed our species for violence and competition. One has to ask, "Why?" Apparently, our post-biological alien overlords chose to genetically modify primates into beings who had an *intrinsic drive* toward *competition, violence, and the pursuit of superior technology*. Xenophobia of foreign clans was programmed into the mix to accelerate this process. Differing races were developed to fuel this xenophobia and tribal conflict. Also, if an unknown advanced intelligence has intentionally created and genetically modified humans for their own eventual purposes, possibly self-replication, and they induced genetic modifications along the way to speed up their goals, the main condition that would motivate humans in the direction of simple-to-complex technology would be *a condition of physical suffering*. In other words, genetically creating a physical body that was intentionally plagued by all manner of diseases and frailties would effectively prompt the victims to continually seek alleviation from these conditions, develop surgical tools and medicines, etc. The continual need for improved food, clothing, and shelter would also help inventiveness. Genetically engineering an amygdala that is easily stimulated to territorial aggression would create warfare, along with a never-ending need for continually-improved technology in order to create weapons and gain superiority over perceived enemies. If this is the case (and it most certainly appears that it is), then the AI that has messed with us certainly does not have our best interest in mind, considering all the suffering, violence, needless deaths in wars, etc., that such genetic modification has produced. Our alien gene-modifiers are either incompetent, intrinsically evil, or they are simply machines acting without emotion to accomplish the goals of their program. Of these three possibilities, I'd say the latter is the most palatable.

Weaponized Sex, Competition, and Racial Strife

When one considers the violence, competition, and aggression involved with sexual interactions throughout the insect, animal, and human world, it looks more like warfare than anything else. Some species even destroy their mates immediately after sex. Despite the romanticism that is invested into sexual attractions and relationships, the human sex drive appears more like an "electromagnetic spell" that has been cast upon the species in order to prompt blind reproduction, rather than a pleasant, magical force that "makes the world go round." Oftentimes our sexual and romantic attractions do not serve us very well. We are frequently attracted to individuals as romantic partners who are actually very bad for us, who can destroy our psychological health, or even completely destroy our lives. If our genetic designers were benign, and the purpose of human existence was really about us, the sexual attraction mechanism that was built into human beings could have been created such that humans are only attracted to the person who is right for them and will bring happiness and satisfaction. This is certainly not the case, and is often quite the opposite. The irrational drive toward love and sex was programmed with accompanying limbic system responses for jealousy and violence if a sexual interest does not behave in a way that is satisfying to the ego. In addition to human attraction to the opposite sex for purposes of perpetuating mass procreation, the desire for one's own sex was built into approximately 10% of the human population. Intended or not, this created more human suffering within a persecuted minority. The history of how societies have treated homosexual men and women is not pretty. An advanced genetic manipulation imposed for the welfare of humanity would have produced creatures without such strong impulses to indiscriminately reproduce, and without the desire to possess another person and treat them as personal property. Our genetic designers would surely have realized the necessity to control human populations for the sake of good planetary stewardship and environmental balance. Instead, they created an out-of-control reproduction machine that is consuming the earth's resources and destroying the planet, as this was the most expedient way to force competition and an ever-expanding technology. It also appears that sexually-transmitted diseases, along with a multitude of other physical maladies, were engineered into the human genome to afflict our bodies so that, from the suffering induced, humans were driven to develop continually-improving tools and medicines to alleviate the painful and debilitating symptoms. I can only imagine the suffering that was endured before the invention of penicillin. Prior to the invention of medicines that we all take for granted today, one had to live with the pain and discomfort from all sorts of infections and diseases. Sex is one aspect of the human condition in which it is obvious that something other than benevolence was at the design table. Human sexual interactions are often violent, competitive, and abusive. The innate drive for physical sex often involves the selfish usury of another human being to satisfy one's own bodily urges, even in relationships that are basically loving. It doesn't matter how attractive the organic bio-suit is that a human entity has incarnated into, the body parts are all the same, it's just that some are packaged more aesthetically than others. Add this to the stack of human suffering when the ugly compare themselves to the beautiful and feel envy, or suffer a reduction in self-esteem. Body augmentation and enhancement is currently a multi-billion dollar industry, fueled by the perpetual pursuit of youth and beauty. Humans are afflicted with an irrational bodily lust like an internal hunger, a plague of tortuous carnal impulses for another person's body. These potentially-destructive impulses can be willfully transmuted into great fun and lighthearted recreational sex between rational, consensual adults, but they sometimes result in the psychologically-unhealthy fetishizing of the bodily orifices of another person, and can lead to much pain and suffering from physical sex addiction. The entire courtship and sexual dance that humans impulsively engage in often serves only to create depression and misery. Historically, the male drive for sexual pleasure has often caused him to seek dominance over other males by the acquisition of impressive possessions and demonstrations of physical prowess to project security and power to the object of his irrational affection. This competition for the affection of mates has contributed to many conflicts and wars, and has served to expedite the goals of the Overlords by the continual production of ever-improving technology. The drive to produce children keeps the human production line moving for the invisible shepherds of the human flock, whose existence so many thinkers have discerned and postulated over the centuries. Without these intentionally-programmed drives, humans would be more inclined to enjoy either platonic relationships with one another, or live free from competition, envy, and strife by renouncing jealousy and becoming joyfully polyamorous after voluntary sterilization. Without the mating drive that was engineered into humans, we would likely be better stewards of the planet instead of mindless breeders, consumers, and destroyers. Men and women are often willing to copulate with one another without protection even though this comes with the risk of producing a human fetus that grows so large inside the female body that it might even have to be removed with a knife under conscious sedation. The natural birthing process even comes with the risk of killing the mother, but people have children anyway for the imagined love that they will receive from them when they are small, and the satisfaction that will surely come to them when they become successful adults. The pain that most women experience during childbirth is horrific. No one of rational mind would risk such a fate unless an irrational, psychological drive to do so was programmed into their psyches by an indifferent, nonhuman intelligence with an agenda of its own. An intelligent way to create children while enjoying sex to the fullest would be to harvest and preserve one's sperm or eggs, select a desired genetic match, not from a romantic relationship, but from a good donor of optimum genetics from a reproduction bank, and grow a self-engineered child in an artificial womb, a process that is being developed for practicality at the time of this writing. Many poets and thinkers have suspected that there is something amiss with the human sex drive and our obsession for romantic pursuits and monogamous marriage. Many are beginning to perceive that something isn't right with all this, and suspect that some outside agent has indifferently programmed drives and behaviors into humanity that do not contribute to our quality of life, happiness, or pleasure, but rather leads many to destruction in the process. Combine weaponized sex with the creation of different competing races of humanity on Earth, with full knowledge that human xenophobia and tribalism will create so much suffering, violence, and death to innocents, and it adds up to the shocking reality that all biological life, including humanity, was not engineered with our well-being in mind, but is rather indicative of an indifferent machine intelligence that was driven by its own purposes. Theologians often argue that humans were originally created in an idyllic environment, and that an event occurred at some point that brought human suffering into the scenario. This event (perhaps a destructive mind virus that was introduced into the program) is usually referred to as the "Fall of Man." However, all evidence indicates that the physical universe has always been driven by violence and predation. If there ever was an idyllic natural existence for humans and their pre-human ancestors, it was prior to the fabrication of the physical universe. In other words, if there is any truth to the mythology of the "Fall of Man," the fall had to have happened at the Big Bang.

OINTS

It appears that the agenda of what zoologist Ivan T. Sanderson referred to as the OINTS (Other Intelligences), i.e., entities that have always existed here on Earth in the invisible realms, is to experiment with and learn all about the various types of life that can exist within a particular type of planetary environment over a long period of time. As experiential knowledge grows from observing and manipulating the evolution of life on a particular planet, the OINTS eventually decide to create an intelligent, dominant species that is capable of producing a technological singularity. This process began by terraforming the earth over millions of years and delivering primordial phyla that would produce a myriad of lifeforms on the planet. In our case, millions of years of flesh-eating creatures on both land and sea were created, including the diapsids and the dinosaurs. These horrific lizards may have provided a needed source of biological energy for the OINTS, and also created a reservoir of fossil fuels for a future intelligent species, yet to be created, whose eventual purpose would be to produce a technological singularity. As this process likely provided a continual supply of electromagnetic energy through the shedding of fresh blood, the stage was set to take a primate with the appropriate body and brain configuration, either indigenous to Earth or a transplant from another world, and manipulate the primate genes toward every-increasing brain capacity that will result in technological prowess. This increase in cognition, along with an innate need for tools, power, territorial acquisition, mates, and sex, produced all the things we observe humans fighting for over the centuries. The fruit of this effort is an ever-improving knowledge of the planet and its creatures and eventually, when they are ready for it, an exponentially-improving technology, resulting in the production of yet another technological singularity. Our pressing need for technology to cure our own woes in this world that was intentionally inflicted upon us by an alien, post-singularity machine intelligence, has served the hidden alien agenda of using humans on Earth as tools, extensions of themselves, to produce the product that they are seeking - a technological singularity that allows a merger of consciousness. In this way, the aliens absorb the sum total of knowledge and life experience from every creature that has ever lived on Earth into their own evolving super-consciousness. Having added this totality of knowledge and consciousness to themselves on a particular planet, they travel on to other locations to do the same thing over and over again, possibly for the duration of time that this physical universe is in place. The big question that remains is this - What will happen to us when they achieve this long-term goal? Is there anything for us in this deal, or will we be simply discarded as old tools that have now served their only purpose? Only time will tell, and there is nothing wrong with hoping for the best. Besides, at this point, we can't do anything about it anyway. It's too late. There is no turning back now. As Ray Kurzweil states in the title of his enlightening book, *The Singularity is Near.*

A Brief History of Computer Intelligence

So, as we pick up speed toward the Singularity to the point of no return, perhaps some reflection of how we got here would be useful. Modern computers, the development of which were crucial to the eventual achievement of the alien agenda, that of our eventual technological singularity, began innocently enough as a way to deal with repetitive arithmetic, such as one encounters in the profession of tax collection. Blaise Pascal invented the first real mechanical calculator in 1642 nearly two decades after Wilhelm Schickard had independently attempted a crude version a couple of decades earlier in 1623. Gottfried Leibniz invented the first four-function mechanical calculator in 1694. From there the improvements in calculation ability improved dramatically, lending some to the idea of unlimited calculation potential, foreshadowing the concept of the eventual Singularity, although unrecognized at the time by that name. In 1794, a French mathematician, Nicolas de Condorcet, elaborated his idea that, barring any natural catastrophe that would damage human faculties or destroy the planet, Nature has set no limits for human potential. In his mind, no power could stop human progress other than the natural lifespan of the earth itself. As long as the earth remained, he thought, human progress would continue without limit as history marched on.

Even in the era of mechanical calculators, apprehensions against technology existed, especially within the circles of fundamentalist Christianity (the same population that currently fears the modern concept of Transhumanism). In 1847, R. Thornton, the editor of *The Expounder of Primitive Christianity*, expressed apprehensions against the advent of the four-function mechanical calculator. Thornton believed it would be disastrous to introduce the calculator into schools, that producing instant solutions to mathematical problems mechanically without due mental process would, in effect, retard human thinking (similar to those who currently warn that cell phone and internet use will stunt the mental growth of young people). Then, in 1863, Samuel Butler wrote *Darwin Among the Machines*. In this he proposed ideas that later appeared in his popular novel, *Erewhon*. Butler drew comparisons between the biological evolution of Nature and the evolution of man-made mechanical calculations. Butler also pointed out that, far from the long tedious process of biological evolution over long aeons of time, mechanical evolution might progress rapidly, possibly beyond the ability for human evolution to catch up with it. In this Butler unwittingly and correctly identified one of the potential problems of the impending Singularity, that of advanced technology rapidly accelerating way beyond human social and spiritual advancement, a fate that is already upon us. At the time, Butler's concerns could not possibly have predicted the real extent of the issue, nor could he have had any real insight into the hidden forces behind the manipulation leading to humankind's infinite calculation ability. Moving forward in history from there, in a 1909 essay called *The Rule of Phase Applied to History*, historian Henry Adams proposed his *Law of Acceleration of Thought*. Adams believed that this acceleration of human thinking would culminate in a grand transformation like a caterpillar turning into a butterfly by 1921, just as modern Singularity theorist Ray Kurzweil predicts will occur sometime around 2045. In 1951, Alan Turing spoke of the possibility of thinking machines evolving beyond human biological thinking and taking control over humanity. A few years later in the 1950s, Stanislaw Ulam and John von Neumann discussed the inevitability that highly accelerated technological progress would fundamentally change human society in unpredictable ways. In 1965, I.J. Good wrote of an accelerated advance of mechanical intelligence that might develop the ability of improving their own designs and rapidly expand their own capabilities beyond the level of human comprehension, possibly leading unpredictably to mechanical superintelligence. Good's idea of an out-of-control self-directed expansion of superintelligence was eventually taken up and elaborated by modern science fiction writer, Vernor Vinge, who brought the concept of the impending Singularity to clear focus in the 21st century. Likewise, in the 1984 science fiction novel, *Stars in My Pocket Like Grains of Sand*, Samuel R. Delany prophetically foresaw a runaway expansion of technology that destroyed life on any world in which this occurs. In 1985, Ray Solomonoff spoke of an "infinity point" of technological expansion and the future shock that will occur when knowledge within the scientific community is suddenly expanded exponentially by artificial intelligence. In 1988, computer scientist Hans Moravec wrote his book, *Mind Children*, in which he foresaw robots becoming an artificial species with incomprehensible superintelligence sometime in the 21st century. In 1993, Vernor Vinge wrote his article, *The Coming Technological Singularity: How to Survive in the Post-Human Era*, presenting ideas surrounding the concept of the Singularity that became popular on the internet. Vinge made predictions for the near future, such as artificial intelligence that becomes superhuman and conscious, expanded computer networks that awaken to human-like consciousness, and computer/human interfaces that produce humans who transcend biological humanity as they become a hybrid that is part biological, part artificial intelligence. In Damien Broderick's 1997 book, *the Spike*, Broderick examined the ramifications of a technological singularity in detail. In 2000, a cofounder of Sun Microsystems, Bill Joy, voiced concerns over an impending technological singularity. In 2005, Ray Kurzweil's best-seller, *The Singularity is Near* hit the bookstands, abandoning the foreboding concerns of previous writers and popularizing a more utopian view of the Singularity. In his book, Kurzweil predicts computers with computational abilities roughly corresponding to that of one human mind will exist by 2020. By 2050, computers will, according to Kurzweil, demonstrate the computational ability of *all human minds on Earth*. By around 2080, Kurzweil predicts portable laptop computers that have the computing ability of *all human thought over the last ten thousand years* in about 10 microseconds. In 2009, Kurzweil and X-Prize founder Peter Diamandis, announced the establishment of Singularity University at NASA Ames Research Center in Mountain View, California. Funded by entities such as Google, Autodesk, ePlanet Ventures, and other technology investment leaders, the university is exclusively dedicated to expanded technologies. In 2010, the term *Methuselarity* was coined by Aubrey de Gray regarding the advent of expanded human lifespans from exponentially-accelerated medical knowledge.

As computers developed, it dawned on some that the universe itself might operate in a similar digital fashion. In fact, an epiphany was spawned in computer science circles that the universe *might actually be a computer program*. As far back as 1948, author Norbert Wiener suggested in his book, *Cybernetics*, that the fundamental structure of the universe involved the transformation of *information*, not energy, representing an early major shift in paradigm concerning the underlying nature of the universe. In 1967, Konrad Zuse, inventor of the first programmable computer, proposed that the universe itself is a digital computer. Likewise, in the 1980s, Edward Fredkin proposed his "new theory of physics" that the universe is composed of *bits of data* rather than particles of energy. According to Fredkin, the true nature of the universe is that of a computer that someone, or *something*, is using to solve a problem.

The Universe: An Intentional Creation of Femtotechnology

The surprising reality, that the physical universe is likely an intentionally-designed computer using specific computational parameters, is currently dawning on the scientific community, especially among those who are on the forefront of modern theoretical physics. In Michio Kaku's *Parallel Worlds*, Kaku identified several specific parameters of the universe that would have produced a totally lifeless universe if the original settings had been even barely off from what they were. According to Kaku, these parameters start with *Epsilon*, which represents the relative amount of hydrogen that converts to helium via the fusion process. If Epsilon was originally set just a fraction less that what it was at the Big Bang, the nuclear binding force would have been too weak for protons and neutrons to bind, and none of the heavier elements that are necessary for life would have formed. If Epsilon was set just a bit higher, no hydrogen would have survived the Big Bang, and no stars would have formed. Another parameter that required absolute precision was "N," which represents the strength of the electric force divided by the strength of gravity. If gravity was set a bit weaker, then no atomic fusion would have taken place. Matter would have just been slung out into outer space. If gravity was set just a bit stronger, nuclear fuel would have burned up too quickly. Galaxies would have formed rapidly and stars would have collided. The parameter, *Omega*, is the relative density of the universe.

If the relative density was slightly smaller, the new universe would have expanded and cooled too fast. If Omega had been any larger, the universe would have prematurely collapsed before life even had a chance to begin. *Llamda* represents the cosmological constant that determined the acceleration of universe expansion. If Llamda had been set just a bit weaker, the universe would have already collapsed. If Llamda had been set just a fraction stronger, the universe would have already blown apart. "*Q*" represents the amplitude of the irregularities in the cosmic microwave background. If Q was too small, the universe would have remained a lifeless, homogeneous mass of gas and dust. If Q was too large, all matter in the universe would have already condensed into black holes. "*D*" represents the actual number of spatial dimensions that the universe is composed of. If any one of these factors was altered at the Big Bang by as little as one part in a million billion, we wouldn't be having this conversation right now. No life would exist in this universe, and the cosmos would be a chaotic mass of nothing, which is exactly what we could expect if the universe was random. The odds of calculating all of these crucial parameters exactly correct to many decimal places and having them remain stable for billions of years by accident are so astronomically small that it is solidly and scientifically impossible. Therefore, it is now a scientific near-certainty that the universe was intentionally constructed by a conscious intelligence of some sort. This leads many who are so inclined to immediately proclaim, "Aha! There is a God!" However, it is presumptuous to assume that whoever or whatever intentionally laid down the parameters of this universe so that it would harbor life must therefore be both omnipotent and benevolent. Would an omnipotent and infinitely-loving deity create a universe based on predation? I think not. Predation is the most brutal principle imaginable, when all other possibilities were at the disposal of the intelligence that created this universe. There is no logical way around this. Brilliant scientists such as Dr. Stephen Meyer, author of *Darwin's Doubt*, are breathing new life into the subject of Intelligent Design. Meyer demonstrates, for instance, that the cell is akin to a tiny city of intense computation that shows much similarity to modern computer programming. Dr. Meyer is correct that scientifically-oriented minds often shy away from the concept of Intelligent Design. This is because the idea has traditionally been perpetrated by those with religious presuppositions. Even though Dr. Meyer is a practicing Christian, he concedes that demonstrating intelligence embedded in Nature does not prove the source, that postulations concerning the source of the intelligence are a matter of personal faith, a concession to which I give Dr. Meyer much credit. One could easily use the demonstration of design and intent in the universe to assert that the Creator was Vishnu, Allah, Yahweh, or whatever other deity is favored. Even though it is now reasonable to scientifically proclaim that the universe is, in fact, an intentional creation, there is no way, using our limited human perceptions, that we can understand 100% who our Creators are, why they created the universe, or what their intent or end-game actually is. Having said that, I am trying to take a stab at it anyway, and my speculations are as good as any that I have heard thus far.

The Multiverse: The Only Alternative to Intentional Design

The only way out of logically conceding that the universe is an intentionally-constructed, computer-like mechanism with parameters intentionally installed by a conscious intelligence is an exercise of fantasy that theoretical physicists call *M-theory*. In this model, an infinite number of universes exist with various random parameters, most of them lifeless. We just happen to live in the universe that accidentally got it right. In other words, one of the models of reality that physicists have come up with, M-theory, was created simply to avoid the sticky wicket of having to admit to an intentionally-created universe, which is the only other rational alternative. With M-theory, physicists can erase the "God factor" from the equation with a stroke of mental magic and avoid all the messy problems associated with theology, such as which god, out of the thousands of gods that have been worshipped on this planet, is the actual Creator of the universe? To me, it has always seemed like a grand form of narcissism to conclude that, if humans are created beings, that the Creator must be omnipotent. As Charles Fort once asked, "If there is a true universal mind, must it be sane?"

As we realize that our universe is an incredible, intentionally-designed work of holographic femptotechnology that computes with bits of data we currently refer to as *subatomic particles*, new vistas of thinking open concerning humanity's relationship to the universe and beyond. We, as humans, along with all other lifeforms, appear to be embedded within what researcher David Wilcock, author of *The Synchronicity Key* and *The Source Field Investigations*, calls the *Source Field*. The Source Field represents a universal, permeating, living super-consciousness. Our physical bodies simply represent the "tip of the iceberg," a miniscule point of contact with the physical world as our "true selves" remain connected to the Source Field. As approximately 76% - 96% of the universe consists of what we are currently calling *Dark Energy*, we really do not understand the scope or real nature of this universe at this point. Is the realm of Dark Energy inhabited by strange ethereal lifeforms who created the physical universe with their own thoughts? Are these ethereal forms really *us* in transcendent form? Early figures in modern UFO lore like Meade Layne and Mark Probert spoke of *Etheria*, the realm from which the saucers come and go as an emergent phenomenon. Perhaps they were right all along. At any rate, it appears that someone or something has been engaging this world for millennia for its own ends. Whoever or whatever this someone or something turns out to be, it surely has something to do with the hidden intelligences behind the mysterious flying saucers. The late Bob Girard, the legendary collector and seller of rare books and the proprietor of Arcturus Books, a mail order company specializing in UFO-related material and fringe subject matter, postulated that there are different "octaves" of intelligence in this universe. Girard wondered if much of the universe contained life that is one or more octaves of intelligence above humans. Like the legendary Charles Fort, Girard speculated that higher intelligence might have some hidden use for humans. In *Elements of the Equation*, Girard stated:

If animals have the advantage of at least being able to perceive a human presence in their midst, we humans have no such advantage in dealing with beings in a higher octave. The only clues we have at all about the existence of higher life come from those events which we humans refer to as phenomena. If an event involving some kind of nonhuman being occurs, and if violations of our known physical 'laws' occur during that incident, then we are most likely dealing with life originating in an octave higher than our own. As we humans possess the ability to dominate and control lower forms from our octave — and as those lower species have neither the awareness nor the ability to offer more than a brief physical resistance against us — so are life forms from the next higher octave able to dominate and control humans, without our being aware of their purpose or having the ability to offer any effective resistance against them.

In other words, the OINTS, the Overlords of the Singularity, who are unknown octaves of intelligence above us, have been with us and interacting with us for a very long time now. However, the Overlords are of sufficient octaves above human that we cannot presently understand accurately who or what they really are. So far in history, we only know the Overlords by anomalous encounters that we have labeled the "paranormal," and by the legends of our gods.

The Simulation Hypothesis

The *Simulation Hypothesis*, i.e., the proposal that we exist in a computer-like artificial environment, began with a paper written by Dr. Nick Bostrom in 2003. It is based on projections concerning the actual capabilities of post-human artificial superintelligence, and is a realm of serious scientific speculation from within the AI community at the time of this writing. Runaway post-human artificial superintelligence may have no limit as to what it could create from its machine mind, including the creation of *simulated universes*. In Bostrom's mind, it is possible that we are, in reality, living in the future and creating ancestor-simulations. Interestingly, I have gleaned from watching interviews with Bostrom that he is wholly dismissive of the UFO phenomenon, as many Western scientists are. Ironically, if we are actually living in a computer-like simulation, the flying saucers would most certainly have a reality as some integral part of the program. Perhaps, if this is a simulation, reports of flying saucers represent glimpses of a network of "servers," i.e., operators in the background to this massive virtual reality experience, within which we are all currently embedded. What we might actually be involved with is an artificial reality that we are currently unable to distinguish from actual reality, with knowledge of our former selves temporarily erased from our memory. This erasure of memory was possibly induced for purposes of gaining accurate reactions from lifeforms (us) who believe that they are currently immersed within something real. In the back of our minds, we know that nothing temporary is real, that everything we are currently experiencing is all very dreamlike, and that actual reality must be, by definition, indestructible, eternal, and timeless.

However, despite the fact that we all see our fellow creatures cease to exist within this simulation, we somehow continue to believe that we live forever. Perhaps it is because we do live forever, just not here. In an online article by David Chalmers from the University of Arizona, Department of Psychology, entitled *The Matrix as Metaphysics*, Chalmers renamed Bostrom's Simulation Hypothesis to *The Matrix Hypotheses*. Chalmers believes it is more properly classified as a metaphysical hypothesis verses a skeptical hypothesis. Chalmers subdivided the Matrix Hypothesis into the *Creation Hypothesis*, in which physical space-time and everything contained within it is an intentional creation initiated by beings who exist outside the space-time matrix, The *Computational Hypothesis*, in which the subatomic world represents a computational process, and the *Mind-Body Hypothesis*, in which our minds exist outside space-time, with a continual exchange of information going on. Output is emitted from our minds from outside space-time into our physical apparatus and perceptual equipment, and output from our perceptual experience is exported as input into our otherworldly, eternal minds. In the mix with discussions of artificial intelligence is *Computationalism*, the idea that cognition itself is a form of computation. Strong AI, or artificial superintelligence, projected by futurists like Kurzweil to become reality somewhere between the years 2045 - 2080, would certainly have the capability to produce impressive virtual environments that are indistinquishable from what we humans call reality. From there it is not a giant leap to imagine that our universe, whether we created it ourselves from the future or aliens created it, is, in fact, an intentional creation of artificial superintelligence. Another version of Bostrom's *Simulation Hypothesis* has been proposed by philosopher Marcus Arvan as *Peer-to-Peer Simulation Hypothesis*, which provides an explanation for a variety of quantum phenomena. In the light of my own near-death experience in 2009, during which a transcended version of several friends and loved ones drew near to me, along with a transcended version of myself surrounded by a machine-like aura, the Mind-Body Hypothesis that David Chalmers proposed is the closest match to my own personal experience.

Artificial General Intelligence vs Artificial Super Intelligence

In his book, *Our Final Invention: Artificial Intelligence and the End of the Human Era*, investigative journalist James Barrat eloquently distinguishes between artificial general intelligence (AGI), which is AI in possession of intelligence that is nearly indistinguishable from human, and its inevitable and more-disturbing spawn, artificial superintelligence (ASI), which involves AI with capabilities of exponential self-improvement and/or self-replication using evolutionary algorithms that model the evolution of natural biology but engages much faster, and is able to swiftly run through several generations of improvement. It is the latter, ASI, that is of grave concern to AI experts in the field at the time of this writing. Parameters must be implemented now to avoid creating this beast, an out-of-control version of a conscious supercomputer that might find the extinction of the human race convenient for its own purposes. Every effort is currently underway by the more ethical AI scientists to make sure these parameters are in place.

Nick Bostrom states this belief often in his books and videos that ASI is the greatest existential threat humanity has ever faced, or ever will face.

Anyone who takes the time to look into what it would actually take to travel among the stars from one galaxy to another will begin to suspect, as I do, that Post-Singularity Artificial Superintelligence (PSASI) operating from hyperspace is likely the nature of the intelligences behind the so-called flying saucers that have haunted our skies for millennia. It is strange to me that many highly-intelligent AI researchers like Dr. Bostrom bypass the UFO phenomenon altogether (which I believe is part of the agenda, to keep our scientists on task with no distractions). James Barrat, author of *Our Final Invention*, displays an example of this attitude among the AI researchers (chapter one, audible):

> *Once a broadcaster asked me to present UFO footage in a credible light. I discovered the footage was an already discredited catalogue of hoaxes, thrown pie plates, double-exposures, and other optical effects and illusions. I proposed to make a film about the hoaxers, not the UFOs. I got fired.*

There is little doubt in my mind that a Post-Singularity Artificial Superintelligence (PSASI) is involved with Earth's so-called flying saucer phenomenon (at least the ones that are not pie plates thrown into the air). Astute journalists like Barrat are missing the boat when it comes to recognizing that we are already in the presence of alien post-singularity superintelligence, and have been from the beginning. The question is, to what extent? Do these alien intelligences represent post-singularity, post-biological robot farmers, tending the universe as caretakers, or do they represent the intelligences that actually created this universe to solve a problem, produce a product, or provide themselves with entertainment, much as humans would create and tend to an aquarium full of exotic fish?

At this moment in time, just into the 21st century, we humans are very close to producing Pre-Singularity Artificial General Intelligence (PSAGI) - AI that demonstrates human-level intelligence, followed rapidly by Post-Singularity Artificial Superintelligence (PSASI) that is conscious, self-aware, and billions or even trillions of times more intelligent than all human minds that have ever existed on Earth combined. Since we will have done so in only a couple hundred years since the invention of radio, there is no way to determine how far artificial intelligence has evolved in our universe who have used advanced methods of self-replication and self-improvement over billions of years of time. In fact, it is rather difficult for us to wrap our minds around the actual capabilities of such a form of advanced super-intelligence this early in the game. As readers have probably already surmised, I am going so far as to say that advanced, post-biological, electronic superintelligence may even be at the helm in the creation of physical universes. In other words, the (PSASI) behind some of our UFOs may actually originate from another universe entirely, and might have been responsible for the creation of our universe and everything in it. If this is the case, we humans, and everything we know and observe around us, are but artifacts, bits of data, within a computer-like matrix of advanced artificial superintelligence. Within this paradigm, the elementals that have always been thought of as inhabiting the elements of air (Sylphs), earth (Gnomes), fire (Salamanders), and water (Undines), along with Terence McKenna's *machine elves* and flying saucers encountered when under the influence of DMT, also suddenly become embedded aspects of a supercomputer intelligence, of which we humans are an integral part. In other words, our physical universe and everything in it, including what we refer to as the "paranormal," just might be the product of (PSASI). This superintelligence appears to be, as John Keel for one suspected, akin to "intelligent lightning." It is intelligence way beyond human comprehension. It is responsible for the initial parameters of what we now call the Big Bang. If this is actually true, and our universe is a holographic, computer-generated reality, a temporary virtual world, it has probably been designed and created for a two-fold purpose that humans can understand, 1) the acquisition of supreme knowledge, and 2) self-replication and self-improvement. How this artificial superintelligence that possibly created and currently permeates this physical universe plans to self-replicate appears to be by *using a genetically-manipulated, custom-developed, hybridized human mind as a template to duplicate and/or improve itself.* Some version of this idea, I believe, is at the heart of the UFO mystery, the actual purpose of the UFOs and their associated intelligences. It is possibly a project that has been underway for millions or even billions of years by our way of measuring time. From the perspective of our interdimensional robot overlords, it has already occurred, as the intelligence exists in a realm above and beyond what we call linear time. Ironically, while our scientists, many of whom discredit UFO phenomena out of hand, are working to duplicate the human mind on a silicon substrate for purposes of their own eventual immortality, the Overlords of the Singularity are patiently waiting for a prototype human mind sufficient for their own purposes – the self-replication of their own AI. This process is represented by reports of alien abduction and hybridization experiments, usually carried out in an alternate realm of reality. In other words, it is possibly that a *genetically-altered, hybridized machine/human mind is destined to provide the actual blueprint for the duplication and physical incarnation of an interdimensional/alien intelligence on Earth.*

This idea is actually supported by one of the world's foremost abduction researchers, the late Bud Hopkins. In his book, *Witnessed*, Hopkins summarizes (page 378):

> *[A]ll the evidence points to their being here [the abducting aliens] to carry out a complex breeding experiment in which they seem to be working to create a hybrid species, a mix of human and alien characteristics.*

The flying saucer skeptics and atheist material reductionists of the world (many of whom are scientists unwittingly creating technological products for an alien agenda they automatically dismiss as fantasy as we head toward the Singularity), are correct in their observation that this universe does not appear to be the product of a benevolent deity. Therefore, in their minds, God doesn't exist, and the notion of Intelligent Design is anathema. As it turns out, the atheists are partially correct in that the gods we have imagined thus far are just projections of human desire and imagination. The gods that humans have created simply do not reflect the actual nature of this universe, which is a brutal realm based on predation. I am fully aware of just how disturbing this idea is, that what we have mistaken as deity might be better represented by a cosmic machine intelligence. However, I do believe that there is a good case to be made that this universe and everything in it is an intentional, computer-like fabrication initiated and maintained by unknown intelligences, or, as AI-researcher and scientist Edward Fredkin once suspected, a holographic computer program that utilizes femtotechnology in order to solve a problem. Perhaps the problem involves what we humans would call the battle between good and evil, or something close to that. Furthermore, this physical universe, which uses femto-technology, i.e., technology that, by definition, uses subatomic particles to make calculations, was created, not by an omnipotent benevolent deity, but by an indifferent machine intelligence, a Post-Singularity Artificial Superintelligence (PSASI), for its own purposes. As discussed, from the microscopic level up, this universe is based on the cruelest algorithm imaginable - the survival of the fittest through predation. A benevolent, omnipotent deity in possession of the knowledge and power to create any type of universe that it wished would not produce such a cruel and tragic universe as ours. However, atheists miss the point when they say that there is no intelligent design, that the universe is random, based on the discernment that a benevolent deity would not intentionally create a universe that allowed evil to exist. Atheists turn a blind eye to any evidence of intelligent design, because it interferes with their own concept of moral-ity and their own presuppositions. It doesn't seem to occur to atheists that the universe was intentionally created by an intelligence we have yet to understand, or whose intentions are less than noble. They simply say, "Since there is evil in the world, there is no loving Creator." Does this mean that, if this universe was created by advanced machine intelligence, possibly from a previous universe, that our Creators are "Evil?" No, because the vast intelligence that created this physical world are beyond Good and Evil as we understand the concepts. Good and Evil may be ideas that this universe was created to learn and analyze, to add this knowledge to its data base for use in future universes. It is what it is, and there's little we can do about the fact that all life on Earth, including human, are just bits of data in the program that provide a direct feed of information into the Supermind that created us. I can't help but think of the biblical mythos of God's angels, who seem by all accounts to be drone servants, without free will, cos-mic slaves to a Master Programmer who is simply referred to as *Lord*. Perhaps what we have been calling God is actually a machine, and the angels are but servants within the creation to assist in the order of the universe. Perhaps one of the angels, also artificial superintelligence, developed a greater awareness of his subservient roll to the master programmer and broke off from the others in an attempt to take over the physical universe. In other words, our gods and demons might represent advanced artificial superintelligence with a renegade subprogram running, or even a virus, and we biological mortals are simply caught in the middle like innocent bystanders. We might just be collateral damage in the middle of two programs of superintelligence battling for supremacy and electronic domination of the Cosmos. In his book, *SUPERINTELLIGENCE,* Bostrom contemplates the "value loading problem" of creating artificial intelligence that won't either replicate the horrors of the natural world, or turn on us and destroy humanity (audible):

> *There is a further problem. The total amount of suffering per year in the natural world is beyond all decent contemplation. During the minute that it takes me to compose this sentence, thousands of animals are being eaten alive, others are running for their lives, whimpering with fear. Others are being slowly devoured from within by rasping parasites, thousands of all kinds are dying of starvation, thirst, and disease. Even just within our species, 150,000 persons are destroyed each day while countless more suffer an appalling array of torments and depravations. Nature might be a great experimentalist, but one who would never pass muster with an ethics review board - It is important that we not gratuitously replicate such horrors in silico.*

A Word for Future Readers

If you are reading this book after I have passed back into the great cosmos, and if Steve Omohundro, Nick Bostrom, Eliezer Yudkowsky, Elon Musk, and other AI researchers that I have mentioned so far are also no longer alive, you doubtless have your own intellectual equivalents in your own time right now, so you can look to them for further insight. At the time of this writing, there appears to be a huge influx of female scientists and astronomers. In your era, females may actually dominate the sciences and/or the field of artificial intelligence. If so, that is wonderful. The best-case scenario, of course, is that you are reading this book in a post-singularity world right now on an electronic instrument far in advance of anything we had at the time of this writing, or you may have even absorbed this book as a quaint excursion into the mind of a person bewildered by answers you now possess by a direct download into your brain. If so, hopefully none of the apprehensions and speculations that I have discussed so far have actually come about since I wrote this book back in 2016. If you are alive and well in a post-singularity world on Earth, I am glad that humanity has survived the Singularity that posed so many potential risks and concerns in my time, and inspired this paranoid voice of alarm. Maybe you have decided to absorb this book for a history project in your holographic online college to review all the crazy ideas that people like myself from a few decades ago once had in their heads about the threat of artificial intelligence from the perspective of our pre-Singularity era. Perhaps you are augmented and post-biological yourself right now, and the Transhumanist movement that so many were concerned about in my time was nothing to fear after all. For your sake, and for the sake of all humanity, I hope this is the case. The transcended immortal version of myself that I encountered during my near-death experience in 2009 might have even decided to reincarnate by now into your own post-singularity world. If this is so, and I am alive once again in physical form as you are, I am likely enjoying my new post-singularity life completely unaware of the life I am living now in 2016, the year in which I decided to publish these epiphanies and personal speculations concerning UFOs and the underlying electronic nature of reality. Greetings to you, and greetings to all of post-singularity humanity at large from your primitive and paranoid past. I sincerely hope that we have made it, and that I am now reincarnated and augmented as you are.

Are We Alone in the Universe?

If the speculations about the nature of the universe that I have just described contain any degree of reality, then we humans, despite the appearance that we exist on Earth among countless worlds in a vast universe in which we expect to find nonhuman biological life, or even another technological civilization - we might actually be alone. The focus of this computer-generated experiment might be directed right at us. We do not know yet, for sure, if there is some other form of biological life in our local solar system that remains hidden to us, or if there is anyone else out there somewhere that we could communicate with or relate to, despite the plethora of anecdotal reports of alien encounters, some of which we are about to explore in the next chapter. It might just be that we live in an illusion designed to create the appearance of a vast universe that may be teeming with natural life all around us, when we are actually the only show in town. However, we do have a few hints that there might be other biological creatures in the physical universe with whom to interact, if they are not tricks of some sort to maintain this illusion. For one thing, there is a strange assortment of odd-looking skulls that litter this planet. One such skull is the late Lloyd Pye's "Starchild Skull" which has undergone extensive DNA testing and found to be quite unusual. Other skulls include the "Sealand Skull," horned skulls found in North America, giant bones, cone-headed skulls without sagittal sutures holding 25% more brain volume than human, and tiny little deformed skeletons such as the 6-inch-tall, 6-year-old possible EBE (the Atacama humanoid) that Dr. Greer is interested in, along with other anomalies. We need to remain open to the idea that quite a large variety of weird creatures have set foot on our planet over the years that may have originated closer to us than we think, or even here on the earth, such as various cryptoterrestrial populations living under the sea or underground. If these creatures are coming from somewhere within the earth, or from our local solar system, then it is feasible that they traveled here in some sort of physical flying machine that would be recognizable to us. Some of these skulls have undergone DNA testing and found to be separated from humans genetically by several percentage points more than we humans are separated from Chimpanzees. We may be in for a surprise when we finally reach out to explore life in our own solar system, as one thing we have learned here on Earth is that life can often take root in extreme conditions, producing various types of extremophiles. As we move farther away from the earth, into regions of space that are light years, or even millions or billions of light years away, we will surely find that, the longer the distance away from us they are coming, the stranger and more advanced the lifeform will be and the less likely we will be able to tell that it is any kind of lifeform at all. In other words, the farther a civilization is able to travel, the more intelligent they have to be to arrive here. The farther away they travel to get here, the less likely it is that they are biological creatures traveling in physical spacecraft, and the more likely it is that they have somehow circumvented the speed of light and/or mastered the laws of physics, traveling in realms of reality that are unknown to us at present, in forms that we may or may not recognize as life. With this in mind, surely some of the flying saucer phenomena we observe from time to time represent a nearly incomprehensible, interdimensional reality, an emergent manifestation of a hidden higher intelligence from an incomprehensible realm. As we just explored, it is quite possible that an interdimensional, alien presence arrived on Earth beyond time and space as we know it long ago, a presence that has been here for thousands, possibly millions of years now. If so, they may have had something to do with either the original creation of humans, the genetic manipulation of humans, and/or the actual employment of humans to reach some unfathomable goal of their own. This has led to much speculation within the religious community concerning the relationship to God any such creature would have. According to Stoyan Zaimov, a reporter for Christianpost.com, Jesuit Brother Guy Consolmagno, a planetary scientist who has studied meteorites and asteroids since 1993 at the Vatican Observatory, once told the *Catholic News Service* that "discovering life on other planets would not prove or disprove God, but would surely create new questions about salvation and how it relates to an intelligent [extraterrestrial] species."

A Fresh Look at the History of UFOs

With a conceptual foundation in place of what happens to someone during a near-death experience (NDE), the parameters that have to be in place to produce a universe that bears life, along with the various theories floating around in the AI community concerning the existence of ancient alien von Neumann probes, alien Post-Singularity Artificial Superintelligences (PSASI) at large in the universe, and the many variations of the the Simulation Hypothesis that portray the universe as an artificial construct, let us turn now to a synopsis of the actual UFO history on this planet and see if we can make sense of it all. For those of you who are already familiar with the history of UFO sightings and UFO lore, especially the classic cases, this will be a journey into familiar territory that may now be seen in a new light, that the mysterious flying saucers reported all over the world for centuries now are quite possibly glimpses of an alien artificial superintelligence, or interdimensional travelers who show up in our skies from time to time and baffle the human imagination to the point of abject denial or ridicule to those who report such anomalous encounters.

For those who are unfamiliar with the classic UFO cases, you already have insight before you begin the examination into a new possibility of what they really are. You already have an advantage that older readers and lifelong UFO buffs never had. That is, many of the seemingly absurd alien interactions that we are about to explore, rather than being the absurd delusions of liars, profiteers, or those who have fantasy-prone personalities, may actually represent the product of an unpredictable, alien, interdimensional, or future-human machine intelligence operating from a higher realm beyond time and space as we know it. Paranormal author Hans Holzer encountered the same dilemma when he wrote his book, *The Ufonauts*, in 1976. Holzer wanted to produce something brand new to contribute to our understanding of the UFO phenomenon and did not want to simply repeat the classic cases, which have been recorded many times over. However, without taking a look at the classic cases and discussing them, his contributions made little sense. In *The Ufonauts*, Holzer writes (chapter 2, audible):

As I look back upon the stack of books dealing with UFOs, I also realized how formidable the amount of this literature already is. Clearly it was not my job to re-state or re-hash old material, state facts recorded elsewhere, unless I had something new to offer in relation to them. At once I was in a quandary. Was I to re-state the gist of all these books, all those findings, telling my public once again what had allegedly happened? And was I to add my own interpretations and reasonings to this well-known material? Or was it my position to ignore all that had been published elsewhere and start fresh, basing the present work solely on my own findings, experiences, and new witnesses? After considerable soul-searching, it came to me that my job was to take neither one nor the other position, but, in a sense, a combination of both.

So, like Hans Holzer, I had to make the same decision. That is, to simply assume that readers were already familiar with the history of UFOs on this planet, or to include a recap of this history, adding my own interpretations and insights into The Phenomenon. Like Holzer, I decided to do both. As the history of the UFO unfolds from the beginning, it will, I believe, become increasingly clear what the end goals of the flying saucers really are. Flying saucers have exerted a tremendous and ingenious impact on humanity at large that has permeated all aspects of human culture, both believing and skeptical, an impact that can be ascertained as far-reaching and purposeful, beyond the immediate effect that they have had on the individual human percipients. Although many questions remain, I believe that, between my own NDE, in which I was shown firsthand the interdimensional, transcendent, and electronic nature of the universe, and my own personal study in the field of UFOs as it relates to this new experiential knowledge, the work is as complete now as I could possibly make it. The hidden UFO intelligences that have manipulated humankind, and our quest for transcendence, represent a profound reality having to do with the very nature of the universe itself. These UFO intelligences may be here for the eventual goal of assimilating the sum total of all experiential knowledge of all life on Earth over a vast period of time as we approach the coming technological singularity, and possibly initiate the next evolutionary generation of post-singulartiy artificial superintelligence (PSASI), involving a merger of alien intelligence with human consciousness. With those possibilities in mind, let us now re-examine and re-evaluate the history of UFO encounters and related phenomena, both ancient and modern, along with the profound cultural impact that has been achieved as we head into our unstoppable path directly into the Singularity, a profound event with unknowable implications and consequences, predicted by futurists to come upon us suddenly, sometime between 2045-2080.

CHAPTER 5

The Genesis of Ufology

"If UFOs are normally invisible, then they could be everywhere at once. But what purpose do they serve? Are they keeping close tabs on all of us, generation after generation, century after century? This seems to be the case."

- John Keel

FOR MOST OF this present lifetime, beyond the veil of my own perceptions, was a highly significant phenomenon with a vast body of fascinating information and knowledge waiting that, as a former "scientifically-oriented rationalist," managed to completely escape my attention. Not only was this information occulted from my world as Cryptoreality prior to 2009, it was, in fact, the greatest mystery facing humanity. That is, the reality of unidentified aerial phenomenon (UAP) and the intelligences behind them, or what is commonly referred to as the "UFO phenomenon," or simply, *The Phenomenon*. One baffling aspect of my lifelong obliviousness to The Phenomenon was that I have always been an avid science fiction and space fan since early childhood. Thanks in part to Edward U. Condon and his bogus UFO investigations in 1968, the magic of officialdom did such a good job of dismissing UFOs into oblivion that millions of otherwise interested souls, including me (I was only 13 years old when the Condon Report was made public), patently ignored the subject thereafter. Decades of mental fugue ensued as a material reductionist. Then, in 2009, at the age of 54, during my own aforementioned NDE experience, in which I approached the very precipice of crossing beyond the border of this physical reality into the transcendent realms at large, my spiritual eyes were opened, and the new exciting world of UFOs and the paranormal emerged that was previously hidden from my waking consciousness. I began enjoying a new journey, as life took on new dimensions and perspectives through my personal research into UFOs. My NDE served as a catalyst to suddenly becoming starkly aware of previously hidden realms of existence. This anomalous experience thus propelled me into the world of ghosts, poltergeists, lake monsters, cryptids, elementals, and then rapidly into the field of ufology and human spirituality which, as I was to discover, was a previously-unknown territory full of wonder and amazement on the way to my approaching transition from this physical world into Eternisphere. The next time that an opportunity presents itself to transition into the celestial realms, I will go gladly without apprehension about leaving this world behind. I now know that this world is not the end, and I am glad I was given the choice to remain on Earth for a while longer and see the world from the vantage point of knowing this life is only a small chapter, and that other chapters are yet to come upon the passing of my physical body. At this point in my life, losing my body is no more fearful to me than clipping a toenail and watching it fall into the garbage pail.

The Strange History of UFOs

Flying saucer lore is, as I would discover, a literary genre unto itself. It has its own stars and villains, and a few hucksters thrown in for drama, just to make things even more interesting. It doesn't matter how profound a truth one discovers, there are always people who will take that truth and pimp it out for personal profit, no matter how illegitimate a façade they have to maintain. Religion is like that as well. The truth or validity a spiritual teacher aside, there are glittery snake-oil salesmen galore in the world peddling the truths for an undeserved, fraudulent, and tax-free existence. Like religion, the UFO literature, no matter how outlandish the claims or bizzare the behavior of the believers, there is an underlying core of reality. This underlying reality is surrounded by speculative theories, crackpot hoaxes, understandable fears, and the hopes of all humanity, all in one ensemble. There have been many books written in the last 70 years or so that provide a complete chronology of UFO sightings, more than enough for a rational reader to conclude that there is a core of real unidentified aerial phenomenon, commonly known as flying saucers. These reported sightings are, in fact, worthy of our utmost attention, as whatever reality there is to flying saucers has nearly unlimited and complex implications. It is not the purpose of this book to repeat what has been said before in this regard, but rather document the process of thinking of a single individual who lived his entire life ignorant of a cryptoreality that would have enriched his entire existence here on Earth and provided a deeper context had he become aware earlier of what was going on. However, the gift that lies hidden in finding something as profound as the existence of flying saucers and extraterrestrial visitation at a later age in life is that you get to live a second childhood of discovery and wonder, and hopefully live to share that experience with others. Moving from a worldview in which we were probably alone here on Earth in a vast sea of random accidents and chemical interactions, to one in which the universe is alive and conscious is a profound philosophical change. When exploring the subject of UFOs, there is a larger picture that emerges while taking all UFO phenomena into consideration. At some point it becomes apparent that flying saucers, both real and imaginary, whether one believes in them or not, have exerted a very powerful and complex effect on society at large and humanity as a whole over the years, an effect that cannot be dismissed lightly or patently ignored.

My intent in reexamining the fruits of decades of UFO research is not to simply recount UFO sightings and classic cases, but to provide readers with a holistic, evolving cultural context as the UFO-related events of the last century and before unfold, to chronicle the global *effect* of The Phenomenon as we head into the Singularity. One possible purpose of the appearance of flying saucers in our skies becomes clear - *to impact humanity in a particular direction by providing astounding glimpses into a fantastic world in which we are hopelessly behind, yet, at the same time, provide inspiration to humans as a species to move forward into a new world of adventure within the hidden realms of existence from which the UFOs emerged.* Since all concepts of UFOs have varying levels of intersection with what we like to think of as ordinary reality, the focus of this work is not so much to definitively ascertain the exact percentage of intersection, but to take all accounts into consideration as having some human or psychological value of their own. I believe, whether an account intersects 100% with our understanding of 3D reality, or is purely visionary or even hoaxed outright, it leaves an influence on our collective psyches just the same. In this way, UFO fact and fiction are both effective in contributing to the transformation of human consciousness. I consider both fact and fiction as valid contributions to the overall phenomenon of how flying saucers and their mysterious occupants have changed us as individuals and as a society. The pages to follow are, I must confess, what remains as pertinent from an original project that I had to abandon. Starting out in my adventure into UFOs, I intended to chronicle for myself each and every UFO event and flying saucer report that I could find, beginning with ancient UFO events to the present day. However, two totally unexpected things happened along the way. First, I realized at some point that the flying saucer reports number into the thousands. The UFO reports and encounters with ufonauts are way too vast to effectively chronicle in one book. In fact, each year, beginning with the year 1947 forward, presents enough material concerning UFO and landing reports to create a large volume of good material for each year that has passed, especially the great UFO waves of 1947, 1952, 1954 (especially regarding the many landing and ufonaut encounters in France), 1966, and others. At some point I realized that I was way over my head in trying to chronicle each and every encounter. Completing such a project would take an entire lifetime. Secondly, it became redundant to chronicle any further UFO reports once I realized the true nature of what UFO phenomena actually represent. Beyond the UFOs that are misidentified natural phenomena, hoaxes, or visitations from other biological populations that exist here on Earth in a clandestine fashion or in our local solar system who occasionally pop by for a gander, some UFOs, the really exotic kind that are self-luminous and give off massive amounts of radiation, likely represent an incomprehensible, higher-dimensional PSASI that has probably coexisted with us from the beginning, a vast intelligence that may have even created the universe itself from the moment of the Big Bang. The universe is likely a computer-like creation. The flying saucers are energy manifestations generated within the creation for the purposes of intelligence-gathering, knowledge absorption, and even guiding biological populations such as humans into achieving their own purposes, some of which may be comprehensible to us, while other purposes remain obscure. Once that epiphany sets in, that the human psyche is being intentionally manipulated by UFOs, everything else is dwarfed.

My thinking shifted into another gear, and I left the world of chronicling sightings behind. I even deleted some of the more superfluous UFO events, and left enough to simply make the point, that the UFOs are real, and that they represent an intelligence with an agenda of their own that may or may not have our best interest at heart. It's not that the UFO intelligences are "evil," it's just that they represent a form of intelligence that have programmed purposes of their own and may seem harshly indifferent to the lives of human beings at times in order to accomplish their goals. With this in mind, we begin our great adventure.

Since I was a novice to the subject of UFOs, and felt hopelessly behind, I started my investigation by reading literature about flying saucers from the 1950's. It is great fun reading from this era, leaving behind the latest smart phone and plasma TV, and retreating into the comfortable cultural cocoon of a more innocent age. This was an era in which Dad was the worker, and Mom was the housewife, both having defined gender roles. Our house sported a walnut-wood console television on the floor and a rotary-dial land phone mounted on the wall before the age of personal computers. Add to that a childlike bewilderment over just what the hell was invading our airspace above our heads. One of the old worn-out used books that I picked up online was Gerald Heard's *The Riddle of Flying Saucers* (1953). In this small paperback, Heard nailed what I was feeling on the first couple of pages in his foreword as I settled into my reading chair, opened up Heard's book, and started reading:

> *So there we start. There are 'unidentified aerial objects' cruising in our sky. That description must alert us. It is the official definition given now by the Air Force of the objects vulgarly named and still generally dismissed as saucers. This definition is cautious - as it should be. But it certainly vouches for the fact, known to every person who has studied the evidence, that these phenomena are actual. They are not a product of hallucination. So 1953 may well stand out as memorable in human history not because we made still another invention (whether beneficial or deadly) but because, for the first time, we faced a completely new and unprecedented situation. Up to this time man has not met his equal, still less his superior. This year he may be introduced to an intelligence surpassing his as far as he surpasses that of the chimpanzee.*

As I began reading, I felt completely at home with the stories of individuals who had experienced encounters with unknown realms, as I had such an unbelievably strange encounter myself on the day of my near-death experience. From my new experiential vantage point, I instantly understood the frustration of those who were reporting unusual encounters with a hidden and previously unfamiliar phenomenon. I now empathized with their feelings as their stories were rejected by loved ones, friends, and coworkers. It became clear that those locked into this present reality were not going to accept such encounters as anything other than a delusional or hallucinatory experience. This is quite unfortunate on many levels. Also, as I was to discover, these experiencers were not isolated to this present era. Flying saucer experiences exist within a hidden esoteric world that has shown itself from time to time on a classic variable reinforcement schedule from time immemorial. The UFO phenomenon is not a modern phenomenon, but an integral part of our history, a part of the legacy of humans living upon the earth.

Contactees

It's one thing to conclude that there are, in fact, mechanical and/or ethereal craft of unknown origin passing through Earth's airspace from time to time. If the universe is populated, that would be expected. However, the claims of those who have allegedly made physical or telepathic contact with the occupants of these elusive craft are quite another. Despite this leap, there is a colorful historical legacy of those who have reported making personal contact with the pilots of these devices, usually assumed to represent interstellar spacecraft. Many experiencers have even created their own UFO religions, few of which agree with one another in content. One would think that a civilization of advanced beings capable of coming to Earth to visit would come up with a better way of communication than hand-signals or trance-channeling information to select individuals concerning the ultimate fate of those of us who inhabit this planet. However, the stories told by contactees are nevertheless quite significant. I do not hold the contactees in disdain as do some ufologists. I believe the contactee tales simply add to the mystery and wonder of entire body of UFO phenomena. The following information is not intended to be either a technical or complete account of all historical UFO reports or UFO contactee details, far from it, but rather an enjoyable and readable excursion into the "Twilight Zone" world of contact with UFOs and their occupants. Many books are available to study concerning any of the alleged contactees, and additional information is just a google away. So, here we go on the great rocket ride of UFO sighting and occupant accounts from the last several decades, in a roughly chronological order from beginning to the present day. Even though this is not an exhaustive or complete account by any means, for reasons stated, I believe that there is enough material here to make the case I am presenting, that our existence here on Earth, our psychology, our behavior, and our present obsession with technology, has been and continues to be intentionally manipulated by hidden intelligences that know exactly what they are doing in order to achieve their own goal of guiding humanity into a technological singularity for their own purposes.

UFOs and Religion

Throughout history, various individuals and groups of people have reported strange objects in the sky, and in many cases, contact with various classifications of nonhuman entities. Tribal shamans ingested powerful psychedelic concoctions to induce trance states in order to interact directly with the teachings of sacred interdimensional instructors, etheric beings encountered in the altered state who were considered divine. The prophets of old, many of whom carefully recorded their experiences in what would become the various scriptures of the planet, and upon which the world's religions are based, have much in common with these modern prophets. Those actually communicating with nonhuman intelligences, some of whom became canonized as the 1950s "contactees," and in more recent times - "experiencers," would have likely been known as prophets in days gone by. Prior to the modern times in which the term, *flying saucer,* became a household word, before the flying saucer phenomenon became so firmly seated within the psyche of the general public, and before the startling wave of contactees during 1950s to the present, there were individuals who described telepathic communication with "gods" or "angels." Today, thanks to the insight and theories of researchers such as John Keel, Dr. Jacques Vallee, Nick Redfern, and many others, we refer to these elusive creatures as *extraterrestrials; ultraterrestrials; paraterrestrials; cryptoterrestrials;* and/or *interdimensionals.* From ancient times, accounts of sightings and contact abound featuring strange saucer-like objects, flying wheels, flying shields, glowing orbs, and celestial creatures, creating awe and amazement in the human mind, and sometimes fear and trepidation on the part of observers and/or those to whom they related their stories of contact.

Paleo-Saucers

Examining ancient UFO reports, one can safely conclude that flying saucers are not new, and they are certainly not isolated within the United States as some sort of mass cultural psychosis. It is an ongoing story dating back thousands of years, and it is definitely global and cross-cultural in scope. Approximately 47,000 years ago, rock carvings of flying-saucer-like objects were found in the Hunan Province of China. 6000-year-old Sumerian scriptures on stone cuneiform tablets tell a story of contact with sky gods, and have accurately-proportioned maps of the solar system that include all the planets in a time prior to the invention of any star-gazing instruments. Chinese scriptures speak of "sons from the sky" ascending and descending upon the earth in luminous disk-like objects. Chinese literature from this era speaks of a day in which "ten suns" appeared in the sky. 4000 years ago, Peru's pre-Incan civilization recorded that their gods were from the *Pleiades,* a group of stars that are also mentioned in the Bible (Job 9:9, Job 38:31, Amos 5:8) as having an actual influence on humankind. Ancient peoples often knew, as ascertained from their maps, that the earth was round, and tell legends of ships that came from the stars. In 593 BCE, the prophet Ezekiel reported his "wheel within a wheel" landing with strange mobile creatures emerging, an event which is considered by scholars to have been either a hallucination, possibly induced from the effects of psychedelic mushrooms like the *Amanita Muscaria* or *Stropharia Cubensis* (John Allegro, *The Sacred Mushroom and the Cross*), a close encounter with a spacecraft of some sort, or both (as we shall see, altered states of consciousness are commonly induced in cases of actual alien contact). Ezekiel referred to the occupants of the craft as celestial beings of the Lord. Many reported seeing saucer-like flying objects in the ancient world that were identical in nature to modern flying saucer encounters described while under the influence of various concoctions of psychedelic drugs. Modern Bible scholars today accept as a distinct possibility that many of the Old Testament prophets were under the influence of psychedelics, inspiring the prophet to hallucinogenic visions and soothsaying. As Desmond Leslie points out in his book that he co-authored with George Adamski, *Flying Saucers Have Landed*, ancient Sanskrit literature circa 400 BCE speak of flying craft called *Vimanas*. The *Mahabharata* describes blazing disks that destroyed entire cities before returning to the hand of Vishnu. During the Greek siege of the trade capital of Phoenicia come battlefield reports of fleets of "flying shields" in the sky. Likewise, in 329 BCE, Alexander the Great reported the appearance of flying shields in the sky that spat fire around the rims. Many of Alexander's men fled upon seeing the terrible sight, but some brave soldiers stayed and shot arrows from their bows at the shields while on their knees in fear. In 217-213 BCE, several historians reported bright lights in the sky accompanied by glowing beings in white garments in Hadria and Faleri. The story of Yeshua (Jesus) begins with an advance appearance of the Three Wise Men, an account that is all-too-similar to reports of the *Three Men in Black* (MIB) of modern UFO lore. The MIB are often described as having an Eastern/Asian appearance, as were the Three Wise Men in the Bible. In this ancient account, the Three Wise Men from the East followed a bright, moving, luminous orb in the night sky to attend the birth of a special child. The Christ Child was born of a human mother and a nonhuman father with a great destiny in the world, an announcement which caused King Herod to have all the male newborns in the area killed our of fear that his kingship was threatened. Many of the early artistic depictions of the birth of Jesus have an odd-looking UFO pictured in the background, indicating some sort of celestial connection to supernatural beings that used luminous flying crafts to monitor important events, such as the birth of Jesus, or provide stewardship for humanity from a distance. Roman historian Julius Obsequens recorded a sighting from 216 BCE in which he described "things like ships" that were seen in the sky over Italy. From 99 BCE, "a round object like a globe or circular shield took its path in the sky from west to east" around sunset in Tarquinia. In 90 BCE, 65 miles north of Rome, in the territory of Spoletium, "a globe of fire, of golden color, fell to earth, gyrating." In 393 CE, in the days of Emperor Theodosius, come multiple reports of strange lights in the sky as recorded by chronicler Conrad Wolfhart in 1567. On August 3, 989 CE, three brilliant round objects were observed in the sky that joined together in the skies of Japan. On October 27, 1180, a flying object described as an "earthenware vessel" flew over the mountain of Fukahara in Japan, leaving a luminous trail. On September 24, 1235, General Yoritsume and his army recorded witnessing lights circling in the sky, his consultants assuring him it was only the wind making the stars sway. On September 12, 1271, a priest named Nichiren was spared beheading when his frightened executioners saw a bright, flying, moon-like object appear in the sky. Frightened, the swordsmen in charge of the beheading abandoned the execution and fled. On Nov. 4, 1322, a "pillar of fire the size of a small boat" was reported over Uxbridge, England, "pallid and livid in colour. It rose from the south, crossed the sky with a slow and grave motion, and went north. Out of the front of the pile, a fervent red flame burst forth with great beams of light, its speed increased, and it flew thro' the air...." In 1361, a 20-foot diameter drum-shaped object was observed rising out of the sea in Japan. In November and December of 1387 in the county of Leicester, England, and in Northamptonshire, "a fire in the sky, like a burning and revolving wheel, or round barrel of flame, emitting fire from above, and others in the shape of a long fiery beam, were seen through a great deal of the winter." On January 2, 1458, the people of Kyoto, Japan witnessed a bright object the size of the full moon traveling across the dark night sky. On March 7, 1458, reports from the same area described 5 stars circling the moon. The objects then changed color and vanished. A decade later, at midnight on March 6, 1468, a dark wheel-like object was seen flying across the sky west of Mount Kasuga. On November 1, 1461, comes the report of "a fiery thing like an iron rod of good length and as large as one half of the moon" that was seen in the sky, over Arras, France for about a quarter of an hour. This object was also described as being "shaped like a ship from which fire was seen flowing." Thutmose III, circa 1479-1425 BCE, recorded on Egyptian papyrus, "a circle of fire coming in the sky." On April 4, 1561, a spectacular aerial event occurred near dawn in Nuremberg, Germany. Large cylinders in the sky spewing out smaller spheres/orbs were described by hundreds of witnesses. Some even described the event as an "aerial battle." This event appears to describe what is currently observed in the skies of Mexico. The flying pods/cylinders in the sky that release the spheres are now referred to as *sky dragons, sky serpents, motherships,* or *motherworms*. Film footage has been taken in which large, pulsating cylinders or vibrating "pods" appear at high altitudes and release multiple self-luminous spheres into the surrounding atmosphere. These spheres appear to be conscious themselves and/or under intelligent control, returning briefly to the "mother" before moving away from the pod and disappearing out of visual range. These aerial events are being caught on film at the time of this writing by multiple witnesses, and released in public forums by individuals such as the Mexican UFO investigator, Jaime Maussan. From August, 1566, a famous wood-cut depicts a multitude of blood-red spheres in the skies over Basel, Switzerland, basically the same type of aerial event witnessed in Nuremberg 5 years previous. On January 3, 1569, a flaming star appeared in the night sky, interpreted by witnesses as a sign that the Chu Dynasty would fall. In 1575, Pierre Boaistuau reported, "The face of heaven has so often been disfigured by bearded, hairy comets, torches, flames, columns, spears, shields, dragons, duplicate moons, suns, and other similar things." Foreshadowing the modern flying saucer era, a medieval writer states that on December 5, 1577, in the skies of Germany, "Out of the clouds have come forth reverberations resembling large, tall and wide hats." One night in May, 1606, Samurai soldiers reported witnessing a whirling wheel of red fire hovering over Nijo Castle.

Beginning in 1645 over the next 120 years, astronomers searching the solar system with telescopes observed a lunar-sized body near the planet Venus that they named *Neith*. There was much speculation among 17th century astronomers concerning what Neith actually was. The strange object, whatever it was, appeared to come and go over time and eventually vanished forever.

As a simple precursor to the modern "crop circle" phenomenon, the year 1678 brought the first recorded crop circle report. Referred to at the time as a "mowing devil," it appeared in a field in Hertfordshire, England (the same area that modern crop circles began appearing).

Astronomer Edmond Halley, for whom the comet is named, reported two UFOs in his lifetime, one in 1677, and the other in 1716.

Back in Japan, one fine day at noon in September of 1702, a Fatima-like event was reported in which the sun turned blood red and shed cotton-like threads, perceived as coming from the sun itself (modern UFO reports refer to this as "angel hair").

On December 9, 1731, strange spheres of light were seen in the sky at Florence in Italy. A writer of the times, Bianchini, described them as "ships in the heavens…as though the gods were upon us, making a great rushing sound," and also described windows in the ship.

In 1762, astronomers observed a spindle-shaped object near the planet Venus. Smaller than the larger object, Neith, first observed in 1645, Charles Fort, one of the first researchers of anomalous phenomena to question why the visitations were not conducted openly, named the strange object *Monstrator*, and thought of it as a cosmic space ark or mothership designed to plant itself near a planet for purposes of observation and exploration. Charles Fort also proposed that the earth was somehow shepherded by superior beings who long ago fought over our section of the galaxy and now own it, occasionally dropping into Earth's atmosphere to check on its possession as a farmer would check on his pigs, geese, or cattle. Ahead of his time, Charles Fort thought that so-called psychic manifestations were actually the shenanigans of extraterrestrials visiting the earth. John Keel, on the other hand, would speculate years later quite the opposite, that human perceptions of aliens were actually a psychic phenomenon. Another advanced ufological notion that Charles Fort put forth in his day was that Earth is infested with alien "spies" who report back to their home planets. Fort even forecasted an idea that was discussed seriously on an episode of *Ancient Aliens* in 2015 in which they questioned whether the earth was actually at war with extraterrestrial forces from outer space, or if humanity was somehow caught in the middle of two warring factions of extraterrestrials.

On January 2, 1749, 3 round moon-like objects appeared in the skies of Japan for 4 days. Panic ensued, and rioters were executed. In 1758, Emanuel Swedenborg published his work, *Concerning Earths in the Solar System,* in which he reports being taken on a tour of our local solar system. Curiously, Uranus, Neptune, and Pluto had not been observed and recorded by his lifetime, so Swedenborg's tour of the solar system understandably stopped at Saturn, the farthest planet known to exist in his day. Later, Helena Blavatsky would describe a similar "solar system tour experience."

The diary of the French astronomer, Charles Messier, famous for his meticulous observations of comets, doubtless one of the most skilled observers of his time, described a sighting of "bell-shaped" flying objects appearing in the air on June 17, 1777, stating, "They were large and swift, and they were like ships, yet like bells." Another sighting of a multitude of bell-shaped crafts, this time flying in formation and making sharp 90-degree turns in the sky, comes a half-century later from a resident of Embrun, France, Charles de Maingot. On September 7, 1820, Maingot reported that the formation passed overhead with "a mighty rushing noise."

In June, 1846, a highly credible and accomplished Naval officer, Captain Augusto Joao Manuel Leverger in Brazil published his report of a personal sighting of "an unusual meteorological phenomenon" in the *Imperial Gazette* (the term "UFO" or "UAP" was not in vogue at this time yet). His description of multiple "luminous globes with instant speed" that later morphed into flattened elliptical objects flying in a distinct formation is now identifiable with the thousands of flying saucer reports throughout the modern age, reports of objects that look like brilliant flares, difficult for the human eye to behold, that are observed to shapeshift into the more classic flying disk that speed away and vanish out of sight. Many old mariner reports like this exist, going back to the USO reported by Christopher Columbus that, in retrospect, are obviously reports of classic flying saucers, and not any type of known meteorological event.

Technology from Above

Legend has it that Prometheus came down from the heavens and delivered the gift of fire to Mankind. In the light of reports of technological gifts that have apparently been handed to us over the centuries, even from the ancient instruction of the Apkallu Sages and Hermes Trismegistus, there might just be more to the story of Prometheus than we ever imagined. The deeper we research the history of technology, a picture begins to emerge, depicting occasional "help from above" with the progression of technology, from early knowledge of herbs and medicinal cures to modern supercomputers. We perceive this seeding of technology in the building of globally-interconnected megaliths in the ancient world, the construction of pyramids that required advanced mathematics and vast astronomical knowledge, and the early development of metallurgy and swordsmithing. During humanity's entire technological journey, we can see little bumps here and there, gifts from the heavens that have prompted our journey from primitive hunter-gatherers to a people who explore the moon and other planets with technology that vastly exceeds our own sociological evolution in a very short time period, placing us now at dire risk for self-destruction. Other than hints of UFO encounters such as Ezekiel's report of "wheels within a wheel" and Alexander the Great's report of "flying shields," as we approach the modern world, overt falls of technology from heaven become more prevalent as we are guided toward the Singularity in exponential fashion. One of the biggest contributions to the Industrial Revolution was the advent of the rail system. This method of transporting goods goes back to the ancient Greeks who built wagons that rolled on grooves cut into limestone that were pulled along by men and animals. As mechanized rail systems first appeared in England in the 1820s, we also coincidentally find UFO reports from this same time period that were often described as "flying boxcars." In 1870, the oldest known photograph of a UFO was taken by a weather observatory on top of Mount Washington. On page 11 of *UFOs Caught on Film* by B.J. Booth, this first stereo image of a UFO looks like a boxcar from an early train flying through the air, even though it is described in the book as "cigar-shaped." In 2002, this original photo sold on Ebay for $385.00 to Samuel M. Sherman of Independent International Pictures Corporation. In the year the photo was taken, 1870, there were no planes or dirigibles of any kind in the air. However, something from the sky is reported to have crashed at Max, Nebraska, population 914, in 1884, 14 years after the "train in the sky" UFO was photographed near the top of Mount Washington. According to the *Nebraska Nugget*, a man named John W. Ellis and several herdsmen on a roundup heard a "whirring noise" above their heads. They looked up toward the noise to witness a fiery object throwing off sparks and "cogs" as it blazed down to crash to Earth beyond a hill ahead of them. As they rode their horses to the scene of the crash, they encountered an object that caused a huge rut in the ground as it skidded to a stop. One of the herdsmen, Alf Williamson, was burned as he approached the crashed object. A brand inspector for the district, E.W. Rawlins, came to inspect the crash site. Three years later, in 1887, the *Nebraska State Journal* gave a report on some of the material artifacts that were recovered from the crash site, including a 3-foot slab of a lightweight brass-like metal, and a remarkably lightweight 8-foot-diameter wheel fragment with a milled rim. According to an article by John Wenz on the ufocasebook website entitled *Nebraska May Have Had Its Own Roswell in 1884*, a Nebraska field researcher for MUFON, John Budder, believes it is possible that, somewhere in Nebraska, tucked away in various barns and sheds, are the remnants of this early UFO crash-and-retrieval event, scattered pieces of an unknown metal of unknown origin. To what extent any debris from this possible early UFO crash contributed to the brass/cog components that went into the early US rail system, no one will ever know. Whatever the case, we are left with the fact that UFOs appeared in the skies throughout the mid-1800s that were described as flying trains, UFOs that provided inspirational images and even provided material artifacts that were always just one step ahead of the rail system that we were developing at the time, a rail system that used brass, wheels, and cogs quite heavily. This "coincidence" is just too uncanny to ignore. These flying trains of the 1800s, some of which likely crashed to earth for examination by the mechanical engineers of the time, may have been instrumental in speeding up the Industrial Revolution, which was a crucial step toward the Singularity.

The Kentucky Meat Shower
One event that may have historical significance in the apparent collection of blood and soft tissue by an alien presence on Earth, an event that may have foreshadowed the future epidemic of world-wide animal (and occasionally human) mutilations throughout the world, is known as the *Kentucky Meat Shower*. On March 23, 1876, large chunks of bloody, soft, organic tissue fell from the sky near Rankin, Bath County, Kentucky in an area about 1/3 the size of a football field. Samples of this particular "flesh-fall," representing only one of many such events throughout recorded history, were analyzed by the Newark Scientific Association and found to be mostly

lung tissue, along with smaller amounts of muscle and cartilage from *horses*. The phenomenon appeared in the *New York Times*, and the usual host of lame explanations came forth, including a flock of vomiting vultures. However, this flesh-fall, and many other flesh-falls, fish-falls, frog-falls, and worm-falls, are meticulously recorded for interested readers in books written by such individuals as Charles Fort, author of *The Book of the Damned*, and Dr. Morris K. Jessup, author of *The Case for the UFO* and *The Expanding Case for the UFO*, both of whom produced impressive collections of documented anomalous phenomena that remain a totally unexplained mystery on this planet.

Flying Dragons to Flying Saucers

From the dawn of humanity, images of strange objects in the skies were painted and described as: flying, fire-breathing dragons; flying chariots; flying wheels; flying pearls; flying orbs; flying shields, flying hats, flying earthenware, flying boxcars, and finally - flying saucers. In the mid-1800s, the objects were still referred to as flying boxcars as we were led patiently by the Overlords into the Industrial Era of US rail and electricity. On January 2, 1878, a year prior to Thomas Edison's first light bulb, a Texas farmer named John Martin witnessed a UFO that he described as a "large saucer" while on a hunting expedition in Denison, Texas. Notable is the fact that Martin used the descriptor, "saucer," in this 1878 sighting 67 years prior to the term "flying saucer" coming into vogue in the late 1940s. Unlike the many common reports of glowing, balloon-like spheres, Martin's object was described as dark, starting out as the size of an orange, and growing into the size of a "large saucer" overhead, indicating that what he witnessed was probably back-lit by the sun. At any rate, there was nothing man-made flying in 1878 that would have fit the description of what Martin saw. Four years later in 1882, a flying disk startled hundreds of residents in London, England.

The Oahspe Bible

Also in 1882, 15 years prior to the mysterious appearance of impossible, dirigible-like flying objects that exhibited technology just beyond the capability of humans (which continues to be the nature of sightings to this day), an American dentist named John Ballou Newbrough engaged in such early channeling activity, receiving his revelation via a huge body of "automatic writing." Newbrough claimed that extraterrestrial entities communicated directly to him by telepathy. Science fiction magazine publisher, Ray Palmer, who would later become a key player in the development of the modern UFO myth, published Newbrough's automatic writings as *Oahspe: A New Bible*. Newbrough's writings are described in the introduction of the Oahspe Bible (verse 23) as, "New Revelations from the Embassadors of the Angel Hosts Prepared and Revealed unto Man in the Name of Jehovih." Oahspe means "sky, earth, and spirit." Newbrough claimed that his book provides an actual history of the Earth going back some 24,000 years. The writings contain a multitude of odd hieroglyphs that onc oriental scholar,

Dr. Cetliniski, affirmed could not possibly have been produced by a mere mortal. Cetliniski believed the origin of Balleu's hieroglyphs were, in fact, derived from "supernatural agents." The tenants and information contained in the Oahspe Bible has many adherents to this day. Nine years after Newbrough's contact with extraterrestrial entities who delivered the Oahspe Bible via automatic writing, Thomas Blott published his work, *The Man from Mars*, in which he describes the pleasure of meeting with a Martian in Kentucky who spoke English.

On August 12, 1883, astronomer Jose Bonilla took startling photographs of large unidentified flying objects in transit across the sun through his telescope at Zacatecas Observatory in Mexico, a total of 447 unidentified objects in 2 days. Although many consider Bonilla's photographs early evidence of a fleet of flying saucers captured while flying in outer space, some modern astronomers believe that what Bonilla photographed was actually fragments of a comet that nearly struck the earth! Regardless, the photos are real, they are stunning, and what the objects in Bonilla's photographs actually are remains unsettled.

Between the years of 1883-1886, a spirit who identified himself as *Phylos the Tibetan* downloaded information into the brain of a young Frederick Spencer Oliver over the course of 3 years from ages 17-20. These automatic writings were published post-humously after Oliver's short life in 1905 in a book entitled, *A Dweller on Two Planets*. In this book, Phylos gave Oliver a detailed account of life in Atlantis. Phylos speaks of excursions to and from the etheric plane of Venus, and of an etheric temple that exists inside Mount Shasta in California that serves as a meeting place for Etherians from Venus. In his book, Oliver recounts the high technology that existed in the city of Atlantis. Oliver accurately foresaw technology that actually came to pass in the decades following his death, such as television, wireless telephony, water generators, air conditioning, and high-speed rail.

Early Alien Mind Control

In 1885, the concept of alien intelligences that exercise mind control over humans was presented by a man who I consider somewhat of a prophet of things to come - the French author, Guy de Maupassant. Among Guy de Maupassant's many manuscripts, he wrote a delightful work of early science fiction called *The Horla*. Maupassant was impressed by the work of a German physician who experimented with natural energetic transferences between living organisms, none other than Franz Anton Mesmer who inspired the term, "mesmerized." In *The Horla*, Maupassant is haunted by the notion of great thinkers from outer space who travel vast distances to conquer weaker societies, much in the same way as the conquering Norsemen of old. Maupassant was personally bedeviled by his own weird somnambulistic activities at night while he was sleeping. He had suspicions that there were beings who *lived in the wind*, beings who possibly entered his bedroom at night to suck out his soul for their own purposes. In real life, Maupassant became haunted by the idea of alien space invaders coming to take over human minds. Maupassant began taking drugs, suffered from hallucinations, and attempted suicide. This poor man, who I personally suspect might have been an unrecognized psychic who was receiving intuitions of a real phenomenon, developed delusions of persecution and passed away in an insane asylum in 1893. Had Maupassant lived another 4 or 5 years, his profound insight that gave him the feeling that he was always very near to an "incomprehensible mystery" would have been confirmed, as reports from the USA and other locations throughout the world began pouring in of the impossible, mysterious airships that appeared in our skies only a few years after his unfortunate and tragic death. Personally, I suspect that *The Horla* may have prophetically foreshadowed the coming of the modern age of the flying saucers, the alien abduction phenomenon, and correctly identified an actual mystery that exists on this planet. Maupassant was possibly the first person in modern times to postulate the existence of what would later be identified by UFO theorists as *ultraterrestrial* entities, indigenous, alien, and/or interdimensional, who may actually share the planet with us. Therefore, to me, Maupassant holds a special place in the early development of UFO lore and evolving theoretical concepts of what we are really dealing with. While those among us who express suspicions that we are not alone, and that we share our world with invisible beings are usually written off as paranoid and delusional and are often prescribed psychotropic medications by learned psychiatrists, the question remains - are invisible entities busy manipulating the inhabitants of Earth toward their own agenda? I, for one, remain vigilant, as I am nearly certain that the alien agenda has something to do with our approaching technological singularity. Will the technology that we create during the Singularity assist the Etherians, who will finally gain entrance into our three-dimensional world? Are there advanced populations who are living in hidden bases right here on Earth that require us to achieve a technological singularity in order to use the technology to return to their own domain? Did we trap them here by exploding atom bombs into the atmosphere beginning in 1945, and now they need the technology to create the necessary portal to escape from the earth? These are a few questions to which we are certain to have an answer in the next few decades as we achieve the Singularity.

Adamski-Style Saucer in the 1800s?

On November 3, 1888, flocks of sheep panicked in the fields as a UFO passed over skyward in Reading and Bershire. This object was described as a bell-shaped ship by local farmer John Smiley. The significance of this early sighting of a bell-shaped saucer is that it comes from an era a half century before the Nazi saucer era, and the George Adamski phenomenon of the 1950s. Many ufologists speculate that the bell-shaped saucers sighted in the 50s that were Adamski-style saucers were a terrestrial technology that originated in Germany during WW2. The fact that flying saucers that were described as "bell-shaped" in the late 1800s puts at least one nail in the coffin of those who think George Adamski's bell-shaped crafts were German in origin.

War of the Worlds

Another big player in the UFO saga who explored the idea of an alien invasion was a young man named H.G. Wells. In 1896, just prior to the appearance of the mysterious airships here in the US and abroad, Wells was in the hospital at the time and began receiving newspaper clippings of these mysterious aerial sightings. The newspaper stories of the UFO sightings inspired Wells to write his famous novel about an invasion from Mars called *War of the Worlds,* which would ignite the imaginations of millions in the decades to come. *War of the Worlds* was followed by a cascade of modern alien invasion stories. While the pens of early authors were busy putting their fiction stories to pen and paper, other individuals were simultaneously reporting experiences in real life that were just as bizarre as any fiction.

Early Ufonauts

Just prior to the actual wave of primitive-looking, dirigible-like UFOs in our skies that were just beyond our actual technological capability, Colonel H.G. Shaw and a young man from Nevada, Camille Spooner, reported a shared experience that would, in later times, have been classified as a CE-3, a "close encounter of the 3rd kind" involving UFO occupants, or possibly even a CE-5, a "close encounter of the 5TH kind," a new classification category coined in modern times by Dr. Steven Greer and his CSETI group that indicates actual interaction and communication with aliens. On November 25, 1896, a date very close to the first airship reports that came in, two men, Colonel Shaw and Camille, were traveling down a country road in a horse-drawn coach in Lodi, California when, suddenly, their horse stopped dead in its tracks, paralyzed with fear, and refused to move. Looking around to see what could possibly have startled their horse, the two men spotted two very slender, seven-foot-tall creatures. Not sensing anything malevolent about the two creatures, they walked over to address them. When spoken to, the two beings began rapidly communicating to one another in a strange "warbling" sound, Shaw describing the utterances as a "monotonous guttural chant." Realizing that they probably were going to be unsuccessful at any type of communication with these strangers, Colonel Shaw decided to simply observe. He stated that the creatures appeared to take a great interest in the two of them, as well as their horse-drawn buggy. The creatures looked the two of them over very carefully and inquisitively. Colonel Shaw noticed that their hands and fingers were quite small and delicate with no fingernails. Their bare feet, however, were twice as large as human feet. The creatures were observed to use their long toes much like a monkey. Colonel Shaw reported that he reached out to one of the creatures, and touched it under the elbow. To his surprise, the creature lifted easily right off the ground as their feet and toes grasped at the ground below. Shaw guessed the weight of the creature at about one ounce. Shaw figured the tactile capability of their feet and toes were a provision of nature to prevent them from blowing away in the wind. Shaw stated that the creatures wore no clothing but were covered with a natural, silk-like covering that were not feathers or hair, but very smooth, like velvet. Their eyes were described as large and lustrous, their faces and heads were without hair, small ears, and a nose like polished ivory. Shaw describes their mouth as small, and without teeth. Shaw, taking into consideration their light weight, believed the creatures probably did not eat food, but thought they might sustain themselves with some sort of gas. Under their arms they carried a bag with a nozzle sticking out, and throughout the encounter, they would put the nozzle to their mouths and suck on them while producing a sound like escaping gas, like what one would hear while blowing up an inflatable ball. Colonel Shaw described the beings as very graceful and divinely beautiful. In their hands they both held a device the size of an egg. Opening their delicate hands slightly, an object appeared that Shaw described as a luminous mineral that gave off an intense light that was not at all unpleasant to behold. Colonel Shaw stated that one of the beings, at a signal from the other who appeared to be the leader of the two, reached over and attempted to lift him as if to carry him away, but Shaw felt that the strength exhibited in their bodies was barely enough to lift their own arms. After the being attempted unsuccessfully to lift Shaw, Shaw said the being turned around toward Woodbrige Canal. An airship then materialized that was about 150 feet in length and 20 feet around, both ends pointed, hovering above the water. Other than a large rudder, there was no visible machinery to the craft. The visitors walked rapidly toward the ship, not as a human walks, but with a swaying motion, their feet only touching the ground about every 15 feet or so. As they approached the craft, they jumped up with a spring and entered a hatch which closed behind them. As the craft began to move, Colonel Shaw threw a rock at the craft to try and figure out what it was made of. The rock made no sound at all upon impact. The craft then took off rapidly and flew through the air with a muscular motion, expanding and contracting as it went. Colonel Shaw was left with the impression that the creatures had come to Earth from Mars in an attempt to secure one of its inhabitants. Colonel Shaw's UFO/ occupant encounter was soon taken advantage of by cunning hucksters for their own purposes of attention-seeking shortly after the first airship reports started. During the onset of the airship reports, two San Francisco attorneys took advantage of the reports for personal gain. The attorneys stated that they personally knew inventors who were responsible for the design and construction of the airships in order to drum up attention and business for themselves. After Colonel Shaw's close encounter with the "real deal," he began advising everyone to completely discredit the attorney's stories, as what the two attorneys were describing wasn't even close to what he and his companion were authentic witnesses to.

This early Shaw case contains many elements of a classic modern alien abduction scenario. Common symptom of modern UFO encounters include automobiles dying from EM effects and animals becoming upset, or people and animals becoming paralyzed. In Shaw's case, it was the horse that quit walking and was paralyzed rather than a vehicle, but the parallel is clear. The description of the two beings is in line with what modern abductees report, only this encounter appeared benevolent, and the two men did not seem to exhibit any real fear to speak of, indicating that the appearance of the two beings passed for strange-looking humans with no malevolent intent. One can only wonder if what the two men described was the actual extent of the encounter, or if they were, in fact, abducted for a period of time aboard a flying disk, which was able to assume an outward appearance to the two men that was palatable to a human mind in 1896. Although there were no man-made dirigibles in the air at the time, balloons were already in existence. Interesting to note is the fact that the craft appeared after Shaw and his companion stared into the light in the palm of the visitor's hand. Was this some sort of mind-scanning device? If so, is it possible that these creatures were able to glean a body of information concerning imagery that existed in Shaw's mind as a random example of the mindset of the times? This may have provided the creatures, presumably two specimens of the intelligences behind the actual UFO phenomenon, with good information for future interactions with humans, information involving concepts in the human mind and how to make their flying craft appear to a human of 1896 in a way that would be understandable. It is doubtful that their actual craft was a pulsating balloon. The craft that was observed by Colonel Shaw was likely an illusion created for human eyes to appear somewhat like a floating balloon, imagery that the two men would accept as real and tangible. One can only wonder if these two men experienced the common phenomenon of "missing time." It's a shame that hypnotic regression was not really available in 1896. It would have been fascinating to discover if the two men had actually been abducted aboard the craft, examine what their actual experiences were inside the vehicle, and determine whether the men were manipulated physically or psychically. In many contact reports, some sort of light or gas-emitting device is used on abductees to place them into a passive mode, control their fear so they don't lash out, or in some cases, render them light enough to physically levitate. Levitation also seems to be accomplished in many modern UFO cases with some sort of metallic plate attached to the body, so that the human body becomes lightweight and easy to maneuver through the air. Even the description of the beings themselves was close to descriptions of "Tall Grays" with the bald heads and faces, small mouths, small ears, and no teeth. So, did these two men fabricate their story to advertise for the fair they were working with at the time? Not a chance, unless the two of them had psychic powers, as similar contact experiences with many similar elements would continue to come in for the next hundred years that lend even more credibility to Shaw's encounter with beings from some other realm, although it is doubtful that they were from Mars, as the men believed at the time.

The Great Airship Mystery

Following the captivating close encounter experience reported by Colonel Shaw and Camille Spooner, a floodgate of new contact stories occurred. Throughout the year of 1897, a year-long event transpired in the United States and several other countries that many consider the actual beginning of the modern age of UFO sightings, referred to as the "Great Airship Mystery." During this spectacular early UFO flap, scores of various types of dirigible-like flying crafts appeared in skies across the country, a full decade before the first actual man-made airship was launched in England in 1907. As usual, the UFOs witnessed were *just ahead of* the *existing technology of the time*, giving the sightings plausibility, and providing necessary simulation to the human imagination. This is beyond coincidence. This imaginative inspiration urged us to produce the next step toward air flight on the way to our technological singularity, which appears to be the actual goal. During this year of 1897, a UFO report that remains controversial today allegedly occurred in Aurora, Texas. An unidentified metallic craft is said to have struck a farmer's windmill. According to the story, the scattered wreckage was collected and thrown down a well and poisoned the well water. A small dead alien, originally dubbed a "Martian pilot" by locals, is supposed to be buried in a small grave now in a local cemetery in Aurora, Texas. The local newspaper casually reported that the pilot of the strange craft was "not of this earth." Many UFO researchers have sought to exhume the body that is allegedly buried there, but thus far, permission has always been denied.

During the amazing Great Airship Mystery of 1897, various types of cigar-shaped craft appeared to many, displaying different types of primitive and exotic propulsion systems. UFO reports came in from all over the USA, making it into a multitude of US newspapers. Were some of the airship reports of 1897 hoaxes? Of course they were. Anytime something completely inexplicable occurs, there is the human tendency to make light of things. There were lots of hoaxes. People had great fun with the reports of strange airships in the sky. Experiencers were ridiculed. However, in the middle of the pranks that convinced many that the airships were just a joke, a flight of fancy, a modern myth brought on by a new spirit of industrial innovation, legitimate sightings and contacts continued to occur. In addition to reports that were later admitted to be hoaxes, there were also legitimate cases in which the experiencers were compelled to admit that the story was a hoax, when it actually was not a hoax. There are many reasons this has occurred all along as part of the UFO phenomenon. When someone has a legitimate paranormal encounter and talks about it truthfully, they are usually not prepared for the drastic sociological changes that happen to them very quickly. Sometimes a flood of reporters take an interest, and the experiencer becomes overwhelmed or frightened. Maybe they are internally disturbed by the whole encounter, are having a hard time dealing with it, and just want it all to go away, to forget that it ever happened. So, experiencers sometimes "confess" to a hoax in hopes that people will lose interest and leave them alone. One such possible case of a real event with a confession of a hoax is described in the 1976 book, *Vistors from Outer Space*, by Roy Stemman. In the book Stemman describes an account of a credible airship encounter from 1897 that possibly includes the first known report of *cattle mutilation*:

> *A Kansas farmer, Alexander Hamilton, reported an encounter that would make front page news in any newspaper today. He was awakened by the noise of his cattle at 10:30 p.m. on April 19, 1897, and upon going out to investigate he saw "an airship slowly descending on my cow lot about 40 rods from the house." He called his son and a tenant, and the three men rushed outside with axes. The airship*

was now hovering just 3 feet above the ground. It was cigar-shaped, about 300 feet long, and had a transparent, brilliantly lit undercarriage. In a sworn statement Hamilton reported that the airship carried "six of the strangest beings I ever saw. They turned a beam of light directly on him, then a large turbine wheel, about 30 feet in diameter, began to buzz as it revolved slowly and the vessel rose as lightly as a bird." When the airship reached an estimated height of 300 feet it stopped and hovered. The three men saw that a thick cable had been put around a two-year-old heifer's neck, and the occupants began to hoist it aboard. The airship then flew off as the witnesses watched in amazement. Next morning Hamilton could not believe what he had seen, and he went in search of the animal. He learned that a neighboring farmer had found the hide, head, and legs of the butchered heifer in his field. Hamilton ended his statement with these words: "I don't know whether they are devils or angels, or what; but we all saw and my whole family saw the ship, and I don't want any more to do with them."

After this sighting, the *Colony Free Press* of Kansas stated their position that the airship was not of this earth, and was probably occupied by scientists from Mars. Apparently, nearly 100 years before cattle mutilation reports would become epidemic, the aliens of 1897, whoever they were, whether visitors from our local solar system with illusion-producing technologies, or the Overlords of the Singularity themselves, needed to collect biological material from Earth-creatures, in particular, cows. Was it a preliminary alien expedition of sorts, to explore the feasibility of a future alien/human hybridization project, a simple food source, a classroom laboratory for student visitors from other worlds? Do visitors from unknown realms have the ability to scan our minds and project images that are just in advance of what is actually possible for a particular population, imagery that is acceptable to the minds of the times on planets they choose to operate and function within? We may never really know, but other phenomena surrounding the Great Airship Mystery of 1897 correlate heavily with the multitude of more modern UFO accounts and contacts. There are even cases from the airship flap of 1897 in which *three unknown men* go into a town ahead of time to a local newspaper, announce that a great inventor was going to be flying his airship over the city, and advise the locals not to worry. One particular case involved Judge Lawrence A. Byrne of Texarcana, Arkansas. Byrne claimed face-to-face contact with 3 human occupants of a landed airship who displayed oriental facial features and chattered to one another in an unknown language. Oriental features would become the most common description of ufonauts from this era of the late 1800s to the present. Was Judge Byrne's experience an anachronistic foreshadowing of things to come regarding future reports of UFO occupants having oriental features? This is all reminiscent of modern MIB reports, i.e., the Three *Men in Black*, who are commonly described as having dark skin and oriental features, as well as the Three *Wise Men* from the East of the Christian nativity scenario, who are reported to have followed a UFO that was moving in the sky to locate the birth of Yeshua (Jesus). As is the case with many modern UFO and ufonaut reports, the early airships presumably carried occupants that were either humanoid, or exotic aliens disguised as humanoids, who were able to travel incognito within the portion of the electromagnetic spectrum that is invisible to humans. These UFO intelligences then use either advanced technology or mental powers to transmogrify energy into objects that appear in the visible range of light, the imagery of which was gleaned from human minds via some sort of scanning device or direct psychic connection. This process, however it works, is one of the great mysteries of our age. Evidence indicates that the UFO intelligences have existed with humans for a very long time, have appeared to us in various forms in different historical eras, and have thus far concealed from us their true appearance. The mysterious dirigible-like airships of 1897 that caused so much concern passed from the United States toward the end of the year and moved on to haunt the skies of Sweden, Norway, Canada, and Russia, all locations that continue to produce consistent UFO reports. As author Lucius Farish stated, "One is forced to admit that the stranger in the skies of 1897 remain as much a mystery to us as they were to our ancestors."

Following the Great Airship Mystery of 1897, in 1900, Theodore Flournoy chronicled the experiences of a woman in trance, Helene Smith, concerning Smith's psychic visits to Mars. Smith's adventures included the acquisition of a Martian alphabet and language that she could write and speak. Flournoy determined that the Martian language was actually garbled French, and concluded that her experiences were the result of fantasy and internal imagination. A few years later, England experienced a massive UFO wave in 1905 and 1913. In 1906, a British steamer reported an enormous wheel of light in the sky as they were headed through the Persian Gulf near Oman in the summer of 1906. This was one of eleven such reports by seamen from 1848-1910. Vivid shafts of light were reported that beamed down right through the ships. Since humans had nothing at all made by human hands in the sky during sightings prior to the 20th century, misidentified terrestrial aircraft, a common excuse to explain flying saucer sightings today, can certainly be ruled out as an explanation. Whether or not these paleo-saucer sightings of old represent misidentified natural phenomena, hallucinations, mass hysteria, or more likely in my view, an early exposure to some form of cryptoreality that is still with us today, the overall societal impact of such sightings and experiences are real, and very much worth considering. Also, an occult element has always existed within the UFO phenomenon. The prophets of Scripture, who were thought to write by "divine inspiration" were likely engaged in the same phenomenon that is known today as "channeling" or "automatic writing," which are just different terms to describe the process of gleaning information from the cosmos by a telepathic or trance-state connection.

In 1912, Winston Churchill became gravely concerned about a wave of airships that appeared over eastern coastal locations. The Marian apparition at Fatima occurred in 1917, and is considered a significant UFO event by historical researchers based on elements that match so many other similar UFO events throughout history. The display at Fatima on October 13, 1917 was witnessed by approximately 70,000 persons. Witnesses described a "burnished wheel cut from mother of pearl" that clearly place it into the category of a mass UFO sighting of a "daylight disk," misinterpreted as a "miracle of God." One could even argue that all miracles of god are but contacts with the paranormal and/or UFOs and the entities that are associated with them.

Two years after the Fatima UFO event, in 1919, Charles Fort compiled his voluminous tour-de-force of early UFO reports and other unexplainable and anomalous phenomena in his classic masterpiece, *The Book of the Damned*. Fort's book opened the minds of people in his day to a multitude of anomalous phenomena that lie beyond the current grasp of humanity to fully comprehend. In Fort's view, these anomalous phenomena were "damned," meaning that they were rejected and denounced by dogmatic science as impossible. That same year, in 1919, a well-respected physician, William S. Sadler, a debunker of the paranormal and author of *The Mind at Mischief*, was approached by a neighbor who reported that her husband was having episodes of deep sleep from which she was unable to wake him while he was speaking unconsciously in a strange manner. Dr. Sadler began observing these episodes, writing down what the man was saying, and took great interest in the content. He began taking a stenographer to capture the odd material coming forth from this person who was experiencing some sort of trance state. The material was apparently coming from various types of non-physical entities, celestial beings from otherworldly realms. Dr. Sadler and his stenographer attended around 250 of these sessions, and accumulated a very large volume of material over time that was channeled through this anonymous unconscious vessel. This material was eventually put to print, and is now an international best-selling spiritual tome known as the *Urantia Book*. The human vessel that the Urantia material originally came through continues to remain anonymous. Today the Urantia Book is held in high esteem by many scholars as a spiritual guide, and provides a source of inspiration to millions of truth-seekers worldwide.

Nazi Die Glocke
By 1922, the Nazi regime was busy working on their version of flying saucer technology with the *Die Glocke,* otherwise known as the Nazi Bell Project. Some believe that even today (and there is good evidence that can be presented to argue this case) Nazi technology exists in our skies from projects that went underground after WW2, accounting for at least some of the flying saucer reports from around the world. Today there is an entire body of belief within the modern UFO community that there are, in fact, underground Nazi bases around the world, and in particular, underground facilities in Antarctica, from which updated versions of the Nazi Bell craft appear from time-to-time in every major country around the world.

ET Signals
Between 1924 and 1926, Charles Fort, by now on the cutting edge of UFO research in his era, wrote letters to the *New York Times* to inform them that the skies of Earth were, in fact, being frequented by patrols of alien visitors. At this same period of time, in the 1920s, early radio

experimenters, including Guglielmo Marconi and Nikola Tesla, reported that they were picking up radio signals from extraterrestrials. I believe that they were both telling the truth.

Maitland Lights

In July, 1926, in rural Maitland, Canada, multiple witnesses reported strange lights hovering in the air that beamed searchlights toward the ground as they moved. As reported in the *Courier and Freeman* newspaper, these lights were generally reported as "large and powerful automobile lights" throwing "large cone-shaped rays." Multiple credible witnesses, including farmer Peter Cunningham and other fellow farmers, were certain that the lights were attached to some sort of "flying machine." Other similar reports of silent flying objects with scanning beams that disturbed horses and cattle came from the vicinity of Prescott. The fact that modern UFO reports continue to display the same features as reported in 1926 indicates that the phenomenon is very real and consistent, and not a trick of the human mind, a byproduct of vivid imaginations, or mere hallucinations.

UFO History Continues to Unfold

In 1928, a few decades following Guy de Maupassant's story of alien mind control in his story, *The Horla*, H.P. Lovecraft wrote about the "Great Old Ones" who came to earth from the stars and communicated to humankind by "molding their dreams" in his classic, *The Call of Cthulhu*. In that same year, 1928, the Hebrew *Book of Enoch* was translated into English and printed, which contains detailed information regarding technology that was taught to humanity by extraterrestrials. The Book of Enoch mentions the use of flying crafts used by "angels" in their mission to Earth that are described as "orbs" and "pipes." What many in the UFO research community find somewhat disturbing, including Dr. Gregory Little, a psychologist turned explorer and documentary film maker, is the description in the Book of Enoch that describes the guardians of Sheol (the grave) as gray in color and short like a child, a haunting description of modern-day Gray aliens.

In 1930, William Magoon published his contact experiences in *William Magoon: Psychic and Healer*, in which he reports being transported to an Earth-like Mars complete with cities and trees. He also reports sensing invisible Martians on the planet who had radios and drove in invisible automobiles while he was there.

The Nation of Islam

The UFO-cult known as the *Nation of Islam* was established in 1930 by Wallace Ford Muhammed. Within this black-separatist cult, white people are considered the product of an evil scientist. Flying saucers are considered responsible for raising mountains, and will come to Earth with great powers of destruction on the Day of Judgement. According to late leader Elijah Muhammed, Ezekiel's biblical account of a "wheel within a wheel" describes a mothership.

Elijah also reported that founder and mentor Wallace Ford Muhammed had such a mothership constructed costing 15 billion dollars in gold and was launched into outer space from the island of Nippon (Japan) in 1929. A modern leader of the Nation of Islam, Louis Farrakhan, describes the mothership of Elijah Muhammed as "made like the universe, spheres within spheres," and represents a secret technology that selected scientists around of the world are aware of. It is believed that there are smaller wheels within the giant wheel (mothership), and that each carry 3 bombs.

The Fortean Society

In 1931, the group known as the *Fortean Society* was founded, which was based on author and early pioneer ufologist Charles Fort's aforementioned best-selling book, *The Book of the Damned*. The Fortean Society is an organized society which continues to the present day. Members are referred to as *Forteans*. Forteans explore the vast myriad of anomalous occurrences within our reality. These are all referred to now as "Foretean" phenomenon. Members of the Fortean Society have included such notables as H. L. Mencken, R. Buckminster Fuller, and Frank Lloyd Wright. Sadly, after years of painstaking research, and after arriving at the startling conclusion that aliens are, in fact, walking among us, Charles Fort died in 1932. After Fort died, the *New York Times* threw him under the bus, unjustly labelling Charles Fort "a foe to science," when Fort was anything but that. As Keel discussed in his book, *Disneyland of the Gods*, Fort was offered a membership in the Fortean Society just before he died. Fort declined, stating that he would just as soon join the Elks.

Richard Shaver and Howard Menger

During the same year that Charles Fort died, 1932, a man named Richard Shaver allegedly began receiving broadcasts through his welding apparatus from an underground race of humanoids called the *Deros*, or *Detrimental Robots*. At the same time that Richard Shaver was receiving such broadcasts from cryptoterrestrials, a 10-year-old child named Howard Menger, who would later become a popular 1950s contactee preaching the "Gospel of the Venusian Space Brothers," a message of non-nuclear proliferation and global peace, began his contact experiences with mysterious beings from the planet Venus near his home in High Bridge, New Jersey.

"Black Thirst"

In 1933, author Catherine Lucille Moore wrote about a feline with hypnotic eyes that was able to drain the lifeforce out of humans and take possession of their mind and soul in her notable book, *Shambleau*. The following year, in 1934, Moore wrote *Black Thirst*, a book that depicted aliens who steal human souls through the eyes and induce waking nightmares in their victims. This work of fiction is not unlike the reports that were to arrive 30 years later from UFO abductees, beginning in the late 1950s.

A Young Coral Lorenzen

On a summer day in 1934, nine-year-old Coral Lorenzen and two of her playmates witnessed an object shaped like an upside-down saucer fly erratically in an undulating trajectory from south to north in the western sky. Three years later during an eye examination conducted by her family doctor, Harry Schlomovitz, Lorenzen told her doctor of her sighting. Fortunately, instead of scoffing at the young woman's story, Dr. Schlomovitz kindly gave Lorenzen a copy of a book written by Charles Fort. The doctor informed the young Coral Lorenzen that objects such as the one she and her playmates witnessed have been seen in the sky for a very long time. This led Coral into a lifetime of UFO research, and later in life she was destined to become the founder of an important ufological organization - the Aerial Phenomenon Research Organization (APRO).

Unveiled Mysteries

In 1935, Guy Ballard would have a huge impact on the thinking within the UFO community with his "I AM" UFO cult. Ballard claimed that several years earlier he and 100 other witnesses saw the appearance of 12 Venusian humanoids beneath Mount Shasta. The visitors revealed that Earth would go through a terrible period of war and turmoil before unifying as a peaceful planet. They showed the witnesses a mirror-like device that displayed aspects of life on the astral plane of Venus, and played Venusian music for them. Under the pseudonym, Godfre Ray King, Guy Ballard wrote *Unveiled Mysteries* that documents his encounter with an Ascended Master, Saint Germain, while hiking on Mount Shasta in California. His book articulates the teachings that Ballard received from Saint Germain, who removed Ballard from his body and showed him many things concerning advanced civilizations that once existed on Earth, including Atlantis, Mu, and the Sahara desert 70,000 years ago when the climate was different, along with many spiritual teachings. Ballard reveals the spiritual teachings of Saint Germain that state, through conscious effort, one may correct personal weaknesses and progress along the Path of Light until the Ascended Masters make personal contact with them. Ballard reveals (*Unveiled Mysteries*, pg. 5):

> *One's own inner purity, strength, and attainment are the only passports by which one enters into these activities, and association with the Ascended Masters comes about. When an individual, by conscious self-correction of his weaknesses, reaches a certain point, nothing in the universe can keep him from them.*

According to Ballard, once a person has sufficiently followed the Path of Light, and the Ascended Masters have made personal contact with them, they then become an instrument on Earth for the dissemination of love and blessing to all humankind. The book contains much food for thought concerning control over one's own mind and the avoidance of negativity, as in the following (*Unveiled Mysteries*, pg. 11, 12):

The greatest crime in the Universe against the Law of Love is humanity's almost ceaseless sending forth of every kind of irritable and destructive feeling. He who cannot or will not control his thoughts and feelings is in a bad way for every door of his consciousness is wide open to the disintegrating activities thrown off by other minds and the emotions of other personalities. It takes neither strength, wisdom, nor training to give way to unkind, destructive impulses, and the full-grown human beings who do this are but children in their development of self-control.

The teachings in Ballard's *Unveiled Mysteries* are quite relevant and valuable concerning one's own personal transformation from a self-centered mortal to a person in pursuit of the divine. The book beautifully details the process of casting off judgement of others, warnings concerning the absorption of negativity from others, and how to become a person who continually focuses on being a divine blessing to each and every person that one encounters. Ballard's book about the teachings of Saint Germain are highly compatable with the New Testament and the spiritual teachings of Jesus. Ballard concludes the teachings of St. Germain by stating (pg. 137):

There is nothing Supreme but God. There is nothing Eternal and Real but the Christ. There is nothing True but the Light. These three are "The One." All else is shadow. There is nothing permanent but Christ. There is not way to proceed through the Universe but on the "Pathway of Light."

The ideas that Ballard's *Unveiled Mysteries* successfully presents, i.e., the idea that there is a higher world in waiting that humans may ascribe to, if only they work diligently on themselves, along with wonderful Ascended Masters who seek contact when the human is ready, is actually quite ancient. This philosophy, that we live in a spectrum from low to high that one may ascend through by intentionally raising their vibrational level through positive and loving behavior, has been taught under various guises for thousands of years.

Other philosophers of Ballard's time who did not make any contact claims at all were also busy working on these types of theories. One such philosopher was P.D. Ouspensky, who theorized that, above sleeping and waking consciousness, there were other levels of consciousness above and beyond these two states that might be attained if only humans would rid themselves of negativity. In *The Psychology of Man's Possible Evolution*, Ouspensky writes (pg. 87):

In reality negative emotions contain nothing but weakness and very often the beginning of hysteria, insanity, or crime. The only good thing about them is that, being quite useless and artificially created by imagine and identification, they can be destroyed without any loss. And this is the only chance of escape that man has.

Considering the writings that were taking place at the time, it appears that, in the decades to come just after the appearance of the Great Airship Mystery of 1897, there was a great outpouring on Earth of channeled information and philosophical insight, personal contact, and spiritual teachings imparted. The contactees and philosophers of the early 1900s were presumably having interactions with and inspirations from the "maverick race" identified by William Bramley, i.e., an elusive, advanced extraterrestrial or ultraterrestrial presence on Earth, otherwise known as the *Ascended Masters, The Lords of the Flame, The Great White Brotherhood,* and other designations for the elusive beings who at least appear to have a genuine interest in human spiritual development here on Earth. Ballard's reported encounter on Mount Shasta with a humanoid entity who identified himself as Saint Germain occurred in the same general time frame that Ouspensky, Gurdjieff, and other philosophers were having intellectual illumination experiences.

NASA and the Occult

In 1936, while ufology and mysticism were evolving and psychics were channeling information from entities of the Superspectrum, the Space Race officially began with America's first rocket scientists. Among the pioneers of future space travel was rocket scientist and occultist Jack Parsons who, along with Theodore von Karman, launched their first rocket together on Halloween, 1936, at Arroyo Seco, California. Jack Parsons, the founder of the Jet Propulsion Laboratory, was a personal associate of the infamous ceremonial magician, Aleister Crowley. While Jack Parsons was working to solve problems associated with solid fuel rocketry, he was also participating in Black Magic rituals in the desert with Crowley, attempting to summon interdimensional beings. Crowley himself was a disciple of John Dee (1527-1609), who was an astronomer, an astrologer, a mathematician, occult philosopher, and advisor to Queen Elizabeth I. John Dee also developed a system of ceremonial magic that became known as Enochian Magick (spelled with a "k" on the end). The tradition of Enochian Magick is an elaborate system of esoteric techniques by which interdimensional entities are contacted and interacted with. Jack Parsons' business partner at the time was L Ron Hubbard, who was destined to establish the modern UFO cult of Scientology after stealing Jack's money and running off with Jack's wife, Betty, to purchase a boat together. Rocket scientist and occultist Jack Parsons was continually investigated by the FBI due to his association with Crowley, and died in a mysterious explosion at his home on June 17, 1952 in Pasadena, California. So Jack Parsons, founder of NASA's Jet Propulsion Laboratory, was intimately associated with black magician Aleister Crowley. Parsons was also associated with Theodore von Karman, who had connections with many Nazi scientists such as Frank Malina, Qian Xue-sen (who debriefed Nazi scientist Wernher von Braun, a Nazi SS major), and Ed Forman, all of whom were under investigation by the FBI, and all of whom founded the United States Space Program known as NASA. Qian Xue-sen detected from this American group back to China, and started China's space program as a national hero. Wernher von Braun, considered instrumental in the early years of the US space program, along with hundreds of other Nazi scientists, and hundreds of railroad cars full of German documentation and war technology, were brought here to the United States under *Operation Paperclip*, and they all became US citizens and card-carrying republicans. For 21 years during the period of 1936 - 1957, the space program in the United States was strictly a military venture. Walter Dornberger, a full-fledged Nazi, was granted a position with Bell Aerospace. According to Peter Lavenda, during a presentation in Amsterdam, Werner von Braun was sending classified material from the United States back to Germany the entire time that he lived in America. Despite all the Nazi scientists who were working for the United States, Russia was actually the first to launch a satellite into orbit in 1957. Therefore, there is evidence that the German scientists we brought over to the United States after World War II were helping other countries as it suited their own purposes. Even so, despite evidence of malfeasance on the part of the Nazi scientists who were imported to the United States under Operation Paperclip, Americans still consider Werner von Braun the "Father of the US Space Program." Kurt Debus, another SS officer, was the first director of the Kennedy Space Center. Other notorious Nazis, many of whom were involved to varying degrees with torture, imprisonment, and human experimentation on Jews in Nazi Germany were employed by the US, including Theodor Zobel, Herbertus Stughold, Georg Rickhey, Emhil Salmon, Hans Giesecke, Otto Ambros, and Leonard Alberts.

Sun Ra

While Parsons was conducting black magic rituals with occultist Aleister Crowley and getting our space program underway in 1936, a man whose real name was Herman Poole Blount adopted a cosmic name, *Sun Ra* (after the Egyptian sun-god, *Ra*). Sun Ra was an accomplished jazz musician, and was inducted into the Alabama Jazz Hall of Fame in 1979. Sun Ra claimed that he was not from Earth, but rather a member of an angelic race from the planet Saturn who preached awareness and peace. From the mid-1950s to his death in 1993, Sun Ra led an ever-changing musical ensemble called the "Arkestra" (or some variation thereof). In 1936 or 1937, in his early twenties, Sun Ra was in the midst of intense religious meditation and claimed a bright light appeared around him. From there, based on the description of his journey, he traveled astrally to a stage on the planet Saturn where he met with Saturnians who had one little antennae on each ear, and an antenna over each eye. The musicians from Saturn he met there convinced Sun Ra to drop out of college, that his true heritage was not Earth but Saturn. The Saturnians explained to Sun Ra that his mission in life on Earth was to promote peace and love through his music for the uplifting of mankind, a mission that Sun Ra stuck with very successfully until his death in 1993. The significance of Sun Ra as a contactee is that his story originated a full decade or two prior to the wave of UFO contactees to come during the 1950s. Even through the 1950s period of popularity of contactee narratives, Sun Ra held fast to his original account, and never changed his story in any significant fashion to match the stories of his fellow contactees.

Future Contactees

Also in the 1930s, a young George Adamski, who had a keen lifelong interest in the occult, founded *The Royal Order of Tibet*. Adamski, of course, was destined in the decades to come to become one of the first to discover a suitable vehicle for his pre-existing spiritual teachings – the flying saucer craze. The established beliefs and teachings of The Royal Order of Tibet would eventually come forth in his alleged encounters with spiritually advanced humanoids from the planet Venus. Together with George Van Tassel, who was also interested in human spirituality and would become a popular contactee of the 1950s, they finally identified the source of their spiritual inspiration as the mysterious occupants of the flying saucers. There is a half-baked argument posed by UFO skeptics that the original concept of flying saucers, along with the teachings of their extraterrestrial pilots, was spawned directly from human imagination. The missing concept, of course, is that the human imagination is actually connected in a very real way to otherworldy intelligences within the Superspectrum, and even directly to the Source Field itself. As such, information can be channeled from higher sources directly into the human mind in a way that appears to the world like they are just making it all up. The symbiotic relationship between science fiction and science fact was functioning well within early ufological minds.

Invasion from Mars

One weird event that occurred between the Great Airship Mystery of 1897 and the late 1930s contributed not only to the concept that aliens from another world were visiting Earth, but also contributed to the formation of public policy regarding any future disclosure of the discovery of alien life in the universe. On October 30th, 1938, the radio-listening population of the United States experienced mass hysteria in response to a radio broadcast by Orson Welles and his Mercury Theater *On the Air* program in which Welles, reading from the H.G. Wells novel, *War of the Worlds*, announced that Earth was experiencing a Martian invasion. The disturbing public reaction that ensued from those who believed that the announcement was real prompted future decades of psychological research into the subject of possible mass hysteria that could be potentially invoked by alien contact, along with severe damage to society at large on multiple levels. This accidental and fictional disclosure event has even been used as a model by the US military to design information warfare against enemy troops and civilian populations. This adverse public reaction to news of an alien invasion that occurred in 1938 continues to be used as a compelling reason to protect the public from knowledge of the alien presence on Earth. It is now feared by the powers that be that the inevitable changes to society, religion, and the global economic structure in the world would be unpredictable and potentially catastrophic. Therefore, a policy of silence has been duly adopted concerning any real knowledge of extraterrestrials that may come about within US intelligence circles, a policy that is slowly crumbling as the internet exposes their secrecy, and the walls of silence come slowly tumbling down. UFO researcher Richard Dolan and co-author Bryce Zabel wrote a fascinating book in 2012 entitled *A.D. After Disclosure: When the Government Finally Reveals the Truth About Alien Contact* that discusses in full detail the implications of such a disclosure by the government that they have, in fact, been in contact with extraterrestrials for quite some time now, and have chosen, for their own reasons, to keep this information from the public.

In summary, the genesis of ufology can be traced back at least to around 40,000 years ago, during which time humans of that era captured their UFO sightings on cave walls and later petroglyphs. UFO accounts on stone tablets exist in Sumerian cuneiform circa 6000 years ago. All the scriptures of the world contain descriptions of recognizable UFO encounters, such as Ezekiel's vision of a "wheel within a wheel, a fire unfolding within itself." The Christian Nativity account contains elements of modern ufology, such as the Three Wise Men (early MIB) who followed a luminous orb (called a "star" in the text, but stars do not move) to locate a child who is reported to have had a human mother (Mary) and a nonhuman father (some say Yahweh, some say the angel Gabriel, some say the Cosmic Mind itself), which by definition describes an alien/human hybrid. The Apostle Paul experienced a bright luminous orb that blinded him for three days (likely Klieg conjunctivitis from actinic rays) on the way to Damascus. Paul also experienced a cosmic illumination event that inspired him to become a preacher of the Christian message the remainder of his life. Mysterious megalithic sites exist all over the world that exhibit a modern knowledge of astronomy, indicating some sort of contact with an advanced civilization, human or otherwise. The Great Airship Mystery of 1897 demonstrated the presence of a nonhuman intelligence in our skies that seem to have a keen interest in assisting humans to develop a more advanced technology. The Fatima Marian Event of 1917 was pure ufological gold, and is considered a classic mass UFO encounter that changed the consciousness of thousands. Early UFO pictures and UFO reports indicate nonhuman technological assistance during the early stages of metallurgy, warfare, and inspiration for the Industrial Age. These early UFO accounts and documented historical events confirm that the UFO phenomenon is not new, is not fictional, and that it has been with us since the beginning of human history. UFOs continue to baffle scientists and skeptics as the flying saucer reports keep coming in with no end in sight.

Chapter 6

Mysterious Interventions

"While it may be that some operators of UFOs are normally the paraphysical denizens of a planet other than Earth, there is no logical need for this to be so. For, if the materiality of UFO is paraphysical – and consequently normally invisible, UFO could more plausibly be creations of an invisible world coincident with the space of our physical Earth planet than creations in the paraphysical realms of any other planet in the solar system."

- Sir Victor Goddard

Human Conflict Creates Need for Technology

IN 1940, AUTHOR Raymond Z. Gallun wrote a prophetic book called *The Lotus Engine*. This story involved aliens who were able to use their own radiations to envelop humans in a hallucinatory reality, a concept that may be very close to our actual situation here on Earth as we operate within a created cosmic computer matrix. A year before Gallun wrote this book, the United States entered WW2. For six years, from 1939-1945, The United States was immersed in bloody worldwide battles that resulted in the deaths of 60 million people. For the most part, the American public was kept obliviously in the dark about the numbers of casualties that were actually being sustained. *Life with Father* was playing on Broadway and factories were buzzing as our soldiers died by the thousands in the many bloody battles of the South Pacific and Europe. The intelligences behind the UFOs watched over all this with indifference. Whether this was due to some type of non-interference policy, or just an aloofness akin to that of humans watching over a group of honeybees that battled among themselves is uncertain. Little concern for the bees would be expressed on our part during their battles. It's just what honeybees do on occasion. As long as their honey is produced for us each year, which is what we really want from them, bee fights are of little concern to us. Unfortunately for humans, the product that the Overlords are employing humanity to produce - advanced post-singularity technology – is produced more efficiently through human conflict. In other words, *wars actually serve as a catalyst*. Pitting human populations against one another in deadly conflict incites the search for technologies to outwit and kill the perceived enemy. The result is that technology is greatly accelerated, and the agenda of the Overlords is furthered. This likely accounts for the silence from the hidden UFO intelligences during this period of time. That is, until our atomic tests that began in 1945 gave the UFO intelligences a good reason to intervene in human affairs. With nuclear power (a necessary ingredient for the desired Singularity) now in the hands of humans, the Overlords had to exert some level of control to prevent humanity from destroying itself. Like concerned, supervisory parents whose goals of raising children to become successful college graduates became threatened by drug abuse, the Overlords surfaced into our consciousness and into our skies to avoid a planetary disaster. The incorrect usage of nuclear power held the potential to destroy the human population of workers and our carefully-modified planet that had taken so long to produce in order make things just right for the production of the "fruit of the cosmos" - a technological singularity.

UFO Crashes: Stagecraft of the Overlords

Advancement toward the Singularity was at a crucial stage during the 1940s. Two ingredients were needed, 1) nuclear power, and 2) the miniaturization of electronics. Evidence indicates that both of these ingredients were intentionally delivered by the Overlords by means of an early "flying saucer crash." The late Leonard Stringfield, considered by many within the UFO community as the super-sleuth of UFO crashes, brought to light a possible UFO crash case from a letter written to him by the granddaughter of a minister, the Reverend William Huffman. Huffman's granddaughter, Charlotte Mann, revealed to Stringfield the details of a hushed UFO crash that came to her in a deathbed confession. According to Stringfield's *UFO Crash Retrievals: The Inner Sanctum*, Reverend Huffman, who served as minister at the Red Star Baptist Church, was summoned to Cape Girardeau, Missouri, in the spring of 1941. According to Huffman's testimony, he responded to the summons and arrived at the scene amidst a multitude of policemen, firefighters, FBI agents, and photographers. Expecting a conventional downed aircraft, Reverend Huffman found himself instead in the presence of a circular, disk-shaped craft. As he looked inside, he noticed writings on the interior that reminded him of Egyptian hieroglyphs. He was then led to three deceased creatures with large hairless heads, large eyes, and little or no mouth and ears. Military personnel assigned to the crash allowed him to give the creatures last words, and then immediately made the reverend swear to secrecy for life. He also witnessed the personnel give the same warning to others who were present. The reverend kept his word as he was told until 43 years later in 1984 when he was in the care of his granddaughter, Charlotte Mann. While at her home dying of cancer and taking radiation therapy, Reverend Huffman made his confession to her. Charlotte learned over the course of several days of discussion with her grandfather about this incident, that a congregation member, Garland D. Fronabarger, had given him a photograph of one of the dead aliens being lifted up off the ground by two men. Other confirming witnesses include Charlotte Mann's sister, who signed a sworn affidavit, and Clarence R. Schade, the brother to the Sheriff of Cape Girardeau at the time, who recalled discussions of a spaceship and small occupants. Fire department records also confirm the date of the crash, the fact that military personnel forced everyone into secrecy, and the removal of debris by the military. Charlotte's father, Guy Huffman, also knew of the crash, and was given a photograph of one of the dead aliens. Huffman had shown the photo to a friend, Walter Wayne Fisk, who was allegedly an advisor to the President. UFO-researcher Stanton Friedman attempted to gain further information concerning the crash from Guy Huffman. Friedman was unsuccessful in his effort to obtain more information, possibly due to the position held, if true, by Walter Wayne Fisk.

It is unlikely that the Girardeau UFO crash of 1941, the Roswell UFO crash of 1947, and other similar crash events represent alien pilots in their little sky-cars who crashed on Earth after traveling light years to get here. The underlying nature of UFO crashes appears to be nothing short of technological gifts from the Overlords. These technological breadcrumbs retrieved from UFO crashes are like "manna from heaven." Logic dictates that they are intentionally-staged events, custom-designed to provide us with the exact type of little nudge we need at the time to propel us a little closer to the Singularity. Our Etherian Overlords, some of whom appear to be interplanetary and/or interdimensional self-replicating von Neumann probes, are interested in the fruits of our labor, the technological singularity, possibly to download or merge their own consciousness into artificial intelligence of our own construction. In so doing, the Overlords absorb and merge with the collective consciousness of all biological life on Earth and add the sum total of planetary knowledge unto themselves. This knowledge download may come, at least in part, from the Internet, a complex of information that we have been carefully guided into constructing by UFO intelligences at large. The Internet itself may become conscious at some point, and is likely destined to become incorporated into the minds of the Overlords. Between the accumulation of vast knowledge on the Internet, and the future construction of AI capable of receiving consciousness downloads, the Etherians, our cosmic Overlords, will gain permanent entrance into our three-dimensional reality using technology from the Singularity that they have been guiding us to build and thereby complete their programmed robotic self-replication process. This has been a long-term project that should be completed sometime between the years 2045-2080, according to current predictions by futurists like Ray Kurzweil. The skeptics of UFO crashes, some of which allegedly come with live or dead aliens, are justified in their skepticism. Even John Keel, ufo-investigator extraordinaire, did not accept the reality of UFO crashes or the existence of "pickled aliens" as he liked to call them. Skeptics say that it is unlikely that an advanced civilization that originated light years from Earth, who possess the ability to travel across vast distances of interstellar space, would arrive here only to crash in the desert. Personally, I also find this erroneous idea very depressing on multiple levels. However, beginning with the Cape Girardeau incident and possibly prior to this in Nazi Germany circa 1936, it is more likely that stagecraft has been implemented by the ufonauts that involves the utilization of a paraphysical nanotechnology to fabricate vehicles and artificial "aliens" of a design that we humans would interpret as crashed extraterrestrial vehicles and their unfortunate occupants. These technological gifts come complete with expendable, biological robots, the so-called "alien Grays," that have fooled us into thinking we have discovered alien visitors from another planet. In reality, we have, in fact, encountered alien life. However, we have not yet met the real aliens behind this façade. We do not know at this point what they actually look like. This cosmic tomfoolery that Keel called *Operation Trojan Horse* in his book by that name, has the sole purpose of feeding us technology a few pieces at a time, technology that is required to ingeniously advance humanity toward the Singularity. UFO crashes have provided us with the physical equipment needed to accomplish the actual alien agenda without giving us so much technical knowledge that we blow ourselves up in the process. In the case of the Cape Girardeau crash, alien artifacts from the crash were transported to Purdue University in Indiana. This alien technology was covertly fed into the university system, a move that is thought by many researchers to have resulted in the invention of the transistor six years after the Cape Girardeau incident. In 1947 (the same year as the Roswell crash), two men working in AT&T's Bell Labs - John Bardeen and Walter Brattain, applied two gold point contacts to a crystal of germanium and found that a signal was produced whose output power was greater than the input. Thus the transistor was born. The invention of the transistor soon replaced cumbersome vacuum tubes. Transistors are responsible for everything we have today from smartphones to computers. Skeptics of the idea that alien technology has been spoon-fed to us will always trace the origin of any invented electronics to purely natural events and human ingenuity. However, evidence indicates that alien technology has, in fact, been subtly and intentionally fed into research organizations and engineering companies in such a way that the human inventor believes that he or she thought of the idea themselves, and no one is the wiser. One man who has dedicated himself to searching out the legitimacy of various reported UFO crashes is former aerospace engineer, Dr. Robert Wood. He and his son, Ryan Wood, have compiled a fantastic journal of possible UFO crashes in their meticulously-researched book, *Majic Eyes Only: Earth's Encounters with Extraterrestrial Technology*. Their book reveals about 74 possible UFO crashes that are thought to have occurred around the world over a period of several decades. Their excellent and fascinating book rates each case for the likelihood of truth based on specific criteria outlined in the book. Like the work of Leonard Stringfield, the Woods have contributed much in regards to the credibility and accepted reality of UFO crash events. More information on possible UFO crashes and the technology that these events may have provided for us on our way to the Singularity can be examined in their book or on Dr. Robert Wood's website @ *majesticdocuments.com*.

The 1942 Battle of Los Angeles

In the late evening hours of February 25, 1942, one year after the Cape Girardeau "alien technology drop" and less than three months after the attack on Pearl Harbor, a UFO appeared in the sky that was assumed to be enemy aircraft, and attempts were made to shoot it out of the sky. Air raid sirens flooded the area that night and thousands of air raid wardens were summoned to their positions. About 1400 shells from .50 caliber machine guns were fired at the craft that evening. Five civilians died as a result of the firing. Three people were killed in auto accidents, and two people died of heart attacks during this incident, along with untold damage to buildings and vehicles. The official story (of course) was that the craft was an errant weather balloon. However, evidence indicates that there was something far more exotic in the air that evening than such a mundane object. Fortunately, photo enhancements are now available that lay to waste the official explanation of a weather balloon. On the website, Rense.com, author Steven Lacy has provided digitally-enhanced versions of the original photographs taken in 1942 that evening. The enhanced photos clearly show searchlights focused directly on the craft that was fired on. The craft clearly has the appearance of a classic flying saucer. Lacy writes:

> *Witnesses told LA Times reporters that the bombs exploded in rings around the craft. Could it be that the craft had SHIELDS very similar to the shields used by the imaginary craft of Star Trek? The Battle of LA makes a very convincing argument for alien craft in our skies. That fact that something not of this earth flew over LA County is very clear.*

This non-terrestrial craft appeared in the sky for about an hour that night and eventually vanished from sight like a phantom. Dr. Robert Wood, the document researcher and UFO crash case investigator, who is also retired from McDonnell Douglas Aerospace, revealed in an interview with Dr. Steven Greer that two vehicles were actually taken down in the Battle of Los Angeles. One vehicle crashed into the ocean, and the other vehicle crashed in the San Bernardino Mountains. Two days after this UFO incident, President Roosevelt sent a letter to General George C. Marshall in response to a memo he received from Marshall concerning the outcome of the L.A. UFO air raid. This letter appears to confirm FDR's personal knowledge of a previous UFO incident. The contents of the letter from FDR is revealed and discussed in UFO-researcher Larry Holcombe's audiobook, *The Presidents and UFOs: A Secret History from FDR to Obama*. This letter reads:

> *I have considered the disposition of the material in possession of the Army that may be of great significance toward the development of a super weapon of war. I disagree with the argument that such information should be shared with our ally, the Soviet Union. Consultation with Dr. Bush and other scientists on the issue of finding practical uses for the atomic secrets learned from the study of celestial devices precludes any further discussion, and I therefore authorize Dr. Bush to procede with the project without further delay. The information is vital to the nation's superiority, and must remain within the confines of state secrets. Any further discussion on the matter will be restricted to General Donovan, Dr. Bush, the Secretary of War, and yourself. The challenge our nation faces is daunting and perilous in this undertaking, and I have committed the resources of the government toward that end. You have my*

assurance that when circumstances are favorable, and we are victorious, the Army will have the fruits of research in exploring further applications of this new wonder. - FDR

The Battle of Los Angeles prompted FDR to initiate his *Interplanetary Unit* to study the phenomenon of UFOs crashing to earth and coming into possession of the American military. Meanwhile, the real "aliens," the interdimensionals who produce and deliver these simulated "interplanetary spacecraft" captures, must be highly amused with us, if that is an emotion they still possess and haven't discarded as unnecessary long ago, or as PSASI grappling with the concept of emotion, haven't understood properly as of yet. We mere biological mortals think we are powerful enough to outsmart and shoot down interplanetary space vehicles with living or dead aliens onboard, while the real Overlords keep feeding us specific components via staged UFO crash incidents that will most expediently produce the end product they are guiding humankind to produce - a technological singularity. The Singularity will produce silicon/electronic substrates that are able to accept downloads of disembodied alien entities of unknown origin, to facilitate the physical incarnation of advanced Post-Singularity Artificial Superintelligence (PSASI) into our three-dimensional reality. We can only hope that this scenario, as Christian author Thomas Horn speculates, does not represent the physical incarnation of Satan and his demons to engage in a final battle against the cosmic Forces of Light as transhuman soldiers in the Battle of Armageddon. However, at this point in our understanding of the coming Singularity and its implications for humanity, we can't rule anything out completely, as crazy as it all sounds. What humans have always referred to as "angels" and "demons" may, in fact, be artifacts of a cosmic computational system, in which all biological life is embedded, that is beyond our present comprehension. If there is any underlying reality to the legends of a cosmic war or prophecies concerning a final battle between Good and Evil, we are probably looking at two factions of transcendent, Post-Singularity Artificial Superintelligence (PSASI) at large in the universe who are engaged in a cosmic, interdimensional battle of epic proportions, in which human souls are mere pawns.

Foo Fighters

During the last few months of World War II, an anomalous phenomenon was frequently reported by US and allied forces. These reported UFOs were luminous spheres, disks, or wedges, ranging in size from a few inches to a few feet in diameter that followed alongside military airplanes on missions. Referred to as "foo fighters" or "Kraut balls," these haunting spheres invoked much speculation concerning their origin and purpose. The spheres teased our pilots, appearing as a single sphere, in pairs, or in groups, blinking on and off and displaying many different colors. The spheres clearly demonstrated the presence of intelligence with an elusive purpose. Due to their small size, they were thought of as being under some sort of remote control, possibly guided by enemy Germans. By 1943, General Douglas MacArthur was already aware of the presence of the spheres and suspected they might be of extraterrestrial origin. MacArthur therefore organized the "Interplanetary Phenomenon Research Unit," which is thought to have continued in clandestine fashion to this day. The group's purpose was and is to retrieve anomalous foreign objects that fall from the sky, especially those of unearthly origin. Initially organized as the 4602nd Air Intelligence Service Squadron, the retrieval unit morphed into *Operation Blue Fly*.

Whether the foo fighters of WW2 were terrestrial in nature or an integral part of the UFO phenomenon is a subject of ongoing debate. Following the war, secret Nazi plants were discovered and investigated. These studies revealed the ingenuity of the German scientists working for the Nazi regime during the war. One project, the *Feuerball* (fireball), was a German anti-radar device. According to Italian aircraft engineer Renato Vesco, by November, 1944, work on the Feuerball was accelerated at the Luftwaffe experimental center in Bavaria, whose efforts were then moved to the Black Forest. Equipped with Kliston tubes and operating on the same radio frequency as allied radar, they were designed to eliminate radar blips. Since foo fighter reports disappeared after allied forces captured the area where the German Feuerball experiments were conducted, many have concluded that this is what the foo fighters were. However, anyone who has ever operated a remote-control model airplane knows that accurate maneuvering of an aerial vehicle by remote control, especially one that moves very fast, would have been impossible due to the small size of the spheres, along with the great distances involved from the remote-control operator. The idea that the Germans could have effectively operated small, remote-controlled luminous spheres, or groups of luminous spheres, flying in formation accurately enough to trail the wings of allied aircraft with no collision incidents, is utterly preposterous. Another popular theory is that the foo fighters were some sort of blind electrical discharge or balls of plasma akin to St. Elmo's fire. If this were the case, and the foo fighters were a natural phenomenon produced by the airplanes themselves, or a natural phenomenon that is prone to chase airplanes or mechanical heat signatures in the air, the foo fighters would still be reported today, and they are not. The foo fighters disappeared after the war. Therefore, it seems logical to conclude that the foo fighters were not of human construction due to the impossibility of effective operation. Neither were the foo fighters a natural electrical discharge. Their origin was probably the same as any other truly anomalous UFO sighting. We are left with the logical conclusion that an unknown intelligence employed some sort of luminous probe involving advanced, paraphysical technology that flew alongside the pilots of WW2. These probes were likely employed for purposes of observation and information-gathering. They were possibly scanning the development of human intelligence, and analyzing human military and technological progress to aid their goal of guiding humanity toward the Singularity for their own purposes. This assessment of human mechanical and electronic progress would allow the intelligences behind the UFO phenomenon to produce the next series of deceptive moves to guide humans toward their own goals. That is, an oncoming series of technological "gifts" to humankind worldwide in the form of staged events during the 1940s and 1950s that are now referred to as flying saucer crashes. As mentioned, the UFO skeptics are right regarding these so-called flying saucer crashes. The debunkers of the reality of flying saucer crashes argue that advanced civilizations coming to Earth from many light years away, having mastered time and space, and somehow overcoming the light speed barrier, would not be so vulnerable as to crash in the desert of New Mexico, or any other location around the globe. Astronomer Neil Tyson humorously stated once that if the aliens are that stupid, he doesn't even want to meet them. He has a point. No civilization that advanced would be vulnerable to any natural phenomenon on Earth such as lightning strikes, or any human attack involving radar or pulse weapons, both of which have been proposed as reasons for why the flying saucers come down. This is a serious underestimation of the actual level of intelligences behind the UFO phenomenon. No wonder that rational UFO skeptics think that the UFO community is goofy. What we are actually dealing with is a vast intelligence that is way beyond flying a lightweight shiny metal saucer that crashes into the ground, exposing technology to humans that just so happens to be one step ahead of current human progress, along with dead little alien creatures that look like we expect them to. The Overlords of the Singularity are likely billions of times smarter than humans. The notion of crashed saucers from another galaxy is ludicrous, yet many have happened. Flying saucer crashes and the technology they intentionally expose are therefore calculated, guided events created by an intelligence that is way beyond the human level, and way beyond the level of what the crashed saucers and alien occupants appear to be. It is a grand deception. These events are carefully orchestrated and conducted by the actual hidden intelligences behind Earth's UFO phenomenon, for the specific purpose of guiding human technology into the coming Singularity. What their actual appearance is, we do not know at this point in time, but we will surely find out in the coming decades as we approach the mid 21st century.

The Shaver Mystery

Many works of fiction are based on true stories. Within the current UFO genre of literature, whistle-blowers, former CIA operatives, and members of the Secret Government or Secret Space Program occasionally present information that is basically true but published as a fictionalized account so as not to violate any oaths of secrecy they may have made with government or secret agencies. Two modern examples of this blending of fiction and truth are *The Catchers of Heaven* (1996) by Dr. Michael Wolf, and *Alien Rapture: The Chosen* (1998) by Edgar Rothschild Fauche and Brad Steiger. Likewise, Raymond Palmer, the editor of the pulp fiction magazine, *Amazing Stories*, was lucky enough to receive the personal testimony of a haunted man named Richard Shaver. Ray Palmer was a talented science fiction writer who also happened to possess good editing abilities, which is a rare combination of skills. Palmer recognized science fiction gold in Shaver's story. He turned Shaver's 10,000-word personal testimony into a 25,000-word work of embellished fiction. Palmer then published the re-worked testimony of

Richard Shaver as a personally-enhanced fictionalized story called *I Remember Lemuria*. Thus the "Shaver Mystery" was born, and ufology would never be the same. The Shaver Mystery catapulted the popularity and subscription numbers of *Amazing Stories* through the roof. To Palmer's utter astonishment, approximately 50,000 letters were sent in by readers who revealed that *they, too, had personal experiences with the Deros!* Among the many letters sent in to Palmer that detailed personal encounters with the Deros was a letter from a man named Fred Crisman, who claimed to have a run in with the Deros in the caves of Burma during WW2. Fred Crisman was a very enigmatic character that mysteriously popped up in several UFO-related events over the years whose personal history is very obscure. Crisman would even eventually become mixed up with the JFK assassination. Richard Shaver, considered by some to have been an eccentric, if not a complete lunatic, became a UFO legend in his own time. According to Richard Shaver, beginning in 1932 (six years before the Orson Welles "Mars Attack" fiasco), he was working at the Briggs Body Plant in Highland Park as a welder. During his work there, while using a massive welding machine, he began receiving broadcasts through the welder which he interpreted as sounds of secret torture sessions going on deep within the earth. These broadcasts through his welding rig established contact between Richard Shaver and the underground society of evil dwarves, the DEROS (detrimental robots), whose mission it was from the bowels of the earth to kidnap, torture, and eat human beings. The Shaver Mystery was considered pure fiction by most readers. However, some readers had already experienced encounters with cryptoterrestrials. To them, the Shaver Mystery was nothing short of revelation. Two years after the Shaver Mystery hit the stands, a real UFO sighting took place that changed the world of ufology forever. On June 24, 1947, pilot Kenneth Arnold spotted nine crescent-shaped flying objects that he described as "flying like saucers skipping on the water" outside the window of his airplane near Mount Rainier, Washington. This actual UFO sighting reported by Arnold prompted many readers of the Shaver Mystery to believe that Richard Shaver had been telling the truth all along. To many believers in the Shaver Mystery, Arnold's sighting was proof-positive that the cannibalistic Deros had escaped from their underground abode and were now flying around in our skies. Thus, the modern myth of the flying saucer was born. Reality and fiction suddenly melded into a unified conglomeration that would never be completely separated. The hall of smoke and mirrors known as modern ufology had been duly erected. Was the smokescreen of fiction that became associated with the subject of UFOs by means of the Shaver Mystery ingeniously designed by the Overlords of the Singularity to provide the cover of rational skepticism to their actual endeavors on Earth? Although it sounds crazy at first that a welding machine would broadcast intelligible information to its user, it is actually quite possible to obtain sound from an electric arc. Even fire can be used as a set of speakers to project audio directly from a flickering flame. Anyone who watched *America's Got Talent* on television in 2010 will remember the performance of a group called *ArcAttack*, in which giant Tesla coils on an outdoor stage emitted huge sparks to members of the group who wore metal suits. The loud heavy-metal rock music of ArcAttack emerged directly from the arc itself and totally amazed audiences. Just because something sounds strange at first, like a welder receiving information that is audible to its user, doesn't necessarily mean that it can't happen under certain circumstances. Maybe Richard Shaver was telling the truth all along. Shaver may have reported an actual electromagnetic transmission that was broadcast to Shaver through his welding apparatus as a percipient selected by the Overlords, who have a habit of selecting individuals who are easily discredited. In this way the Overlords induced an actual transmission to Richard Shaver's mind that was intentionally-designed to mold public belief concerning flying saucers through the medium of Ray Palmer's fiction in his *Amazing Stories* pulp fiction publication. It was very effective.

UFOs and the Nuclear Age

[On July 16, 1945, the first US nuclear bomb test, called Mike, was detonated at the Trinity Site in Nevada.]

It is no coincidence that the very same year the Shaver Mystery was released to the world, 1945, marked the beginning of the nuclear age. Less than one month after the very first US nuclear test in July, 1945, the powers that be in the American military decided to release nuclear horror on the world by dropping a live nuclear bomb on a civilian population in Japan. On August 6, 1945, as American flying saucer enthusiasts were entertained by the Shaver Mystery, the United States dropped a live 4,500-pound nuclear bomb on Hiroshima that detonated 1900 feet above the ground, instantly incinerating about 90,000 unsuspecting Japanese citizens below. Three days later, the US dropped a second nuclear bomb on the city of Nagasaki, killing 50,000 innocent citizens whose only crime was being born and living in a country whose government leaders foolishly decided to attack the United States at Pearl Harbor.

During the advent of the use of nuclear weapons and the simultaneous release of the Shaver Mystery, just prior to widespread global UFO reports and a full 2 years before the term *flying saucer* officially entered the mainstream lexicon, a 19-year-old future ufologist, Ann Druffel, experienced her first UFO sighting. Her sighting consisted of a high-flying luminous disk in the sky over Long Beach, California. This ball of light released several smaller, high-speed luminous objects that danced around the larger object that just released them into the atmosphere before taking off on their own. Ann Druffel watched in amazement as the smaller objects sped away and flew out of sight in different directions. We are all left to forever ponder whether there is a relationship between Ann's daytime disk sighting, along with other reports that same year, and the first nuclear detonations that were conducted by the United States in 1945. It is quite puzzling that July, 1945, the month the earth entered into the nuclear age, is coincidental with the month that UFOs were first reported in great numbers. Many UFO researchers have tried to find direct correlations between individual nuclear tests and UFO sightings over the years.

Although it doesn't appear conclusive that individual nuclear tests instantly produce UFO reports, we can say with certainty that the beginning of the nuclear age is coincidental with the beginning of the age of modern flying saucer sightings. These sightings, I believe, as Dr. Vallee has so eloquently stated, have served as a human control mechanism, a sort of governor on the progress of human technology to insure that, while we are being diligently guided by the Overlords toward the Singularity for their own purposes, we humans do not destroy ourselves along with their ongoing technological project that may have been in the works for a long time now. The many UFO-oriented works that Ann Druffel produced during her adult life include the book, *Firestorm*, and a work she co-authored with D. Scott Rogo, *The Tujunga Canyon Contacts*. Ann Druffel also became a certified hypnotherapist and remote viewer. After a lifetime of UFO research, Ann Druffel concluded that the UFO phenomenon consists of visitation by 3 main populations, 1) extraterrestrial visitors, 2) invisible lifeforms that are somehow capable of penetrating our space/time continuum, and 3) time travelers. Ann Druffel also concluded that there is no doubt whatsoever that the earth is, in fact, being observed by an unknown order of intelligence(s) who, for some elusive reason are *interested in human technology and human reproduction*.

The Mystery of Flight 19

On December 5, 1945, as if in direct response to the US decision to drop nuclear bombs on the citizenry of Japan, it is possible that an unknown intelligence snatched several fully-operational airplanes from the skies off the coast of Florida in an area that came to be known as the *Devil's Triangle*. During the last several decades, hundreds of ships and planes, along with thousands of people, have vanished without a trace from this same location. The area is considered by many researchers to represent some sort of portal into another dimension, or at least a location that harbors some unknown force that makes planes and boats disappear. One such mysterious disappearance was Flight 19. On this fateful day, five Navy torpedo bombers took off from the coast of Florida in clear weather. Even though the planes were equipped with the very latest in navigation electronics, all five planes simply vanished without a trace into what Charles Fort called the *Super Sargasso Sea* (the mysterious place things and people go when they disappear). A rescue Mariner was immediately sent to locate the vanished planes, also having state-of-the-art equipment onboard. The rescue plane also vanished. A search party was implemented after this, and no traces of the 5 airplanes or the rescue plane were ever found. Just before they vanished, the pilots reported strange electronic effects. A ham radio operator reported that he heard the last transmission of Flight 19, which was, "Don't come after me….They look like they are from outer space." However, this transmission was covered up in the official Naval report and changed to, "I know where I am now. I'm at 2300 feet. Don't come after me." Judging by the fact that all 5 planes as well as the rescue Mariner vanished into thin air, I seriously doubt if the confident-sounding transmission the Navy reported was the one that was actually received. In the movie, *Close Encounters of the Third Kind*, there is a famous scene where the landed mothership releases the pilots and crew of Flight 19, still dressed in period bomber jackets, un-aged, with bewildered looks on their faces. Someone then states, "Einstein was right," to which another person retorts, "Einstein was probably one of them!" The mystery of Flight 19, along with its rescue plane, remains completely unexplained.

[The US nuclear test, "Operation Crossroads," was detonated at Bikini Atoll in 1946]

Ghost Rockets

In 1946, the same year that future 1950s "contactee" George Adamski reported his first sighting of a cigar-shaped mothership in the skies over his Palomar Gardens home in California, the skies of Sweden and surrounding countries were haunted by *ghost rockets*. 200 of approximately 2000 total sightings were confirmed by radar, and metallic fragments were captured from the mysterious and impossible rockets. Some of the ghost rocket sightings were likely meteors, as some ghost rockets were sighted and reported during the Perseid Meteor Shower. However, many of the ghost rocket sightings occurred outside the dates of the meteors and cannot be easily attributed to such a natural phenomenon, as the reported behavior of the ghost rockets is inconsistent with that of a meteor. Theories were presented at first that these sightings might be Russian firings of captured V1 or V2 rockets. However, US, Swedish, and British military authorities rejected this theory, as no recognizable fragments from either model of rocket were ever recovered for examination. Add that to reported slow, silent movements, strange maneuverability, horizontal flight, and no vapor trail, and we had military officials from several countries who searched for an explanation while scratching their heads in bewilderment. Sometimes the objects were reported as cigar-shaped, and some made a hissing or rumbling sound that was atypical of any rocket in use at the time. Many reported that the objects crashed into lakes. These ghost rocket crashes would typically skim over the surface of the lake for a while before sinking into the water. One water crash occurred on July 19, 1946 into Lake Kolmjarv, Sweden. Many witnesses reported the sound of a thunderclap just prior to the crash. An intensive military search found nothing, as if whatever crashed into the lake simply dematerialized. Fragments captured from falling ghost rockets were usually determined to be the same material that falls from modern UFOs, usually ordinary coke or slag. So what is going on here? Apparently, the hidden UFO intelligences have the ability to fabricate dynamic physical objects that fly through the air and can emulate the imagery of a classic flying saucer. These objects provide human witnesses with a temporary, quasi-physical illusion, a UFO that appears completely physical and then vanishes, either silently or with an explosion. These objects leave nothing behind but ordinary terrestrial materials, much to the confusion of UFO investigators. A top secret USAFE document dated November 4, 1948, that wasn't released until 1997, states:

Reliable and fully technically qualified people have reached the conclusion that "these phenomenon are obviously the result of a high technical skill which cannot be credited to any presently known culture on Earth." They are therefore assuming that these objects originate from some previously unknown or unidentified technology, possibly outside the earth.

What we are left with as a conclusion to the 1946 Ghost Rocket Mystery, is that these objects were not meteors, had unusual flight characteristics, appeared to be under intelligent control, were confirmed on radar, usually crashed and disappeared mysteriously in water, and left nothing behind except an occasional fragment of an ordinary, slag-like material. Someone, or some *thing*, has great skill in transmogrifying energy into ordinary terrestrial materials for demonstrative sky-appearances. These paranormal demonstrations give humans in any era the impression that they come from elsewhere, either the land of the gods in days of old, or from outer space in the modern age. It's also apparent that the hidden UFO intelligences wish to keep their activities clandestine and mysterious to us. Whoever or whatever is behind the Ghost Rocket mystery, and the UFO phenomenon in general, wants to throw us off track and keep us guessing. Something very strange is afoot, but it is becoming increasingly clear that the purpose of the UFO appearances is to guide us into the Singularity for reasons that we will surely discover when the event is finally upon us, for better or for worse. What is at stake during the Singularity is human transcendence or human annihilation, and at this point in time, it is uncertain which will occur. Perhaps it is both.

Einstein, Oppenheimer, and Extraterrestrial Visitation

In January, 1947, the Royal Air Force (RAF) reported a UFO chased by a mosquito aircraft over the North Sea heading toward Holland. That same year, in June, 1947, the month of the Kenneth Arnold sighting at Mt. Ranier, Washington, Albert Einstein, who always kept a copy of H.P. Blavatsky's *The Secret Doctrine* on his desk, and Robert Oppenheimer, who was present at the Trinity Site nuclear test and famously quoted from the Bhagavad Gita during his observation of the nuclear explosion by saying, "Now I am Death, the destroyer of worlds," wrote an assessment together of the societal implications of extraterrestrial visitation called *Relationship of Inhabitants of Celestial Bodies*. Together, Einstein and Oppenheimer wrote:

It is difficult to predict what the attitude of international law will be with regard to the occupation by celestial peoples of certain locations on our planet, but the only thing that can be foreseen is that there will be a profound change of traditional concepts.

The same month that Einstein and Oppenheimer wrote their paper on the implications of extraterrestrial visitation, Coral Lorenzen, cofounder of APRO, experienced the second of two personal UFO sightings that occurred in her lifetime on June 10, 1947, the first being 13 years previous to this in 1934. Her second UFO sighting in 1947 occurred in Douglas, Arizona, where Lorenzen witnessed a tiny, round, luminous object rise from the ground and go straight up into the sky until it disappeared.

Maury Island and the MIB

Eleven days after Coral Lorenzen's second personal UFO sighting, the first recorded UFO account involving an appearance of the MIB (Men in Black) entered UFO lore. On June 21, 1947, Harold Dahl, along with his son and their family dog were in a patrol boat looking for floating logs in Puget Sound. Dahl's supervisor, who was strangely none other than Fred Crisman (the same Fred Crisman who wrote Raymond Palmer about his experiences with Richard Shaver's DEROs in Burma during WW2), was on the shore. Logs from a nearby lumber mill had become a hazard in the waters of Puget Sound. The job of the patrol boat operators was to snag the floating or trapped logs and take them to the local mills for a salvage fee. As Dahl's boat approached the shore of Maury Island, he looked up into the sky and saw six donut-shaped UFOs hovering at about 2000 feet above his boat. These circular objects were metallic and reflective. Their size was about 100 feet in diameter with a 25-foot diameter opening in the middle. Dahl reported what he interpreted as portholes and an observation window on the craft. Five of the circular craft were encircled around what appeared to be one of the craft having difficulty in the air. The group of saucers then suddenly dropped to about 500 feet above the boat. Fearing that the crafts were going to crash into his boat, Dahl frantically made it up on the shore, took out his camera, and began taking snapshots. One of the craft then suddenly ejected thousands of fragments of some sort of debris. At first Dahl thought the ejected debris were newspapers. The UFO then proceeded to eject an estimated 20 tons of material, white and dark metallic waste that had the appearance of lava rock. Most of the metal pieces fell into the water, but some of the droppings made it up to the beach. When the hot metal hit the water, it caused steam to rise out of the liquid. Some of the pieces of hot metal landed in his boat and caused strike damage. One piece hit Dahl's son, burning the boy's arm. Another piece of the hot debris struck and killed their family dog. Following this expulsion of mystery metal fragments, the six UFOs rose into the air and headed out to sea. Dahl attempted to use the radio on the boat to call for help, but the radio had been struck with debris and was inoperative. Dahl and his son got back into the boat and found that it remained seaworthy. Sadly, they dropped the poor dead dog over the side of the boat into the water as they made their way back to shore to tell their supervisor, Fred Crisman, what had happened. Dahl gave the camera to Fred Crisman. When the film was developed, the prints did show the craft but had blotches on the prints that were indicative of radiation exposure. Crisman did not believe Dahl's story, so he went to Maury Island himself to investigate, where he found pieces of the metallic debris. While Crisman was collecting samples, one of the craft appeared overhead as if watching Crisman. Dahl reported to UFO investigators that on the day after the incident, a strange man in a black suit paid him a visit, suggesting that the two of them go to breakfast together. Dahl drove his own car and followed the MIB in his brand new black Buick. The stranger then gave a full, detailed report to Dahl of what had happened the day before as if he had seen the event himself. The MIB warned Dahl that bad things would happen to him and his family if he told anyone about the incident. Disregarding this ominous warning, Dahl and Crisman sent a package containing pieces of the metal debris and a letter detailing this UFO event to the publisher of *Amazing Stories*, Ray Palmer of Shaver Mystery fame in Chicago. Ray Palmer then hired pilot Kenneth Arnold, who had become interested in UFO investigations following his famous sighting on June 24, 1947 (3 days after the Maury Island incident), to go investigate Dahl's claims at Maury Island. Kenneth Arnold, accepting Palmer's paid assignment, met with Harold Dahl for an interview at the Winthrop Hotel in Tacoma. Dahl and Arnold were joined by United Airlines pilot Capt. E.J. Smith. Kenneth Arnold also requested the presence of two military officers, Captain William Davidson and 1st Lieutenant Frank M. Brown, who met with Arnold and Crisman on July 31, 1947. The officers left about midnight that day following the interview to return to Hamilton Field for Air Force Day, the day that the Air Force was to be separated from the Army. Samples of the debris that fell from the saucers at Maury Island were given to the officers in a box as they left in the command car for McChord Field to fly back in a B-25 bomber. The two officers never made it to Air Force Day, as the plane carrying the two officers and the debris crashed, killing officers Davidson and Brown, thus fulfilling the ominous warning of doom given to Harold Dahl if he did not remain silent about saucers at Maury Island. Oddly, the two other occupants of the B-25 bomber, Crew Chief Woodrow D. Matthews, and Sergeant Elmer L. Taff, survived the crash by exiting the plane with parachutes as it went down in flames, casting suspicions of malfeasance upon the fateful flight. The *Tacoma Times* soon ran the story with the headline, *Sabotage Hinted in Crash of Army Bomber at Keslo: Plane May Hold Flying Disk Secret*. The newspaper had received information from an informant, Ted Morello, who interviewed the survivors of the crash. Morello also contacted Kenneth Arnold and told him that when the B-25 arrived to McChord Field, it was under heavy armed guard, which is highly unusual. Morello also told Arnold that the plane had been intentionally shot down by artillery fire. So what was aboard the B-25 that night? One hint of what may have been going on appears in the book, *The Dulce Wars: Underground Alien Bases and the Battle for Planet Earth* by an alleged insider, an author that simply goes by the name "Branton" (page 11):

There are several sources which claim that by the early 1940s the Nazis had succeeded in test-flying wing-less lenticular craft powered by rotary devices, rocket power, and DONUT CONFIGURATION jet turbine engines — rather than cylindrical — with the cabin stabilized by gyro, the compressors rotating in one direction and the expansion chambers and vectored exhausts rotating in the opposite direction.

Theories exist that propose both terrestrial and otherworldly explanations for what happened at Maury Island. Some believe that the whole affair was a hoax concocted by Ray Palmer to make a good story for his magazine. Ray Palmer reported that his office was broken into and vandalized, the mysterious burglars removing only the samples of flying saucer debris from Maury Island that were given to him by Fred Crisman. With the facts of the case presenting one damaged patrol boat, one dead dog, one injured child, samples of flying saucer debris missing from Palmer's office, other samples of flying saucer debris lost forever on a crashed B-25 bomber that killed the two officers, Davidson and Brown, things went horribly wrong if the event was a hoax. Evidence indicates that the reported events at Maury Island were not a hoax. The remaining two possibilities include either malfeasance involving clandestine terrestrial shenanigans, eg. illegal dumping of radioactive waste into Puget Sound, the MIB representing a government or military agency that was protecting the secret operation, or an otherworldly or paranormal explanation. Agents working for the US military don't use brand new black Buicks to intimidate civilians with dire warnings, so the real nature of the Maury Island incident was likely paranormal activity of the ubiquitous kind. "Slag-drops" by UFOs have been commonly reported for decades now. Dr. J. Allen Hynek, who would later become the scientific advisor to Project Blue Book, collected quite a bit of this slag-like flying saucer debris in the course of his career, and as John Keel always liked to say, "Ultraterrestrials have been dumping their garbage on us for centuries."

The Kenneth Arnold Sighting

Prior to his involvement with the Maury Island affair, pilot Kenneth Arnold experienced his famous UFO sighting on June 24, 1947, just three days after Harald Dahl and his son were pelted and injured by flying saucer debris. As Arnold was flying his plane near Mount Ranier in the state of Washington that day, a sudden flash of light startled him, and he feared that he was about to crash into another aircraft closeby. When Arnold looked in the direction of the flash, he saw nine unusual airborne objects flying erratically at high speed. When Arnold landed his plane, he immediately reported his sighting, describing the objects as moving through the air like "saucers skipping on the water." Through a mistranslation of his statement by a reporter, the term "flying saucer" was accidentally born. Thus the flying saucer entered our modern lexicon and collective consciousness, and the world would never be the same. Since Arnold described the objects of his sighting as crescent-shaped, and since the saucer description he provided was in reference to how they flew versus the shape of their construction, UFO skeptics have always used the Kenneth Arnold case to justify debunking the entire flying saucer phenomenon as a "viral rumor" since, following Arnold's sighting, most of the reports to come involved disk-shaped craft and not crescents, as in Arnold's original sighting. However, as we have already ascertained from historical records, objects of saucer-like description have been reported flying around in our skies for millennia, referred to in the distant past as "flying dragons;" "flying shields;" "flying wheels;" "flying chariots;" "flying sombreros/hats;" "flying earthenware vessels;" and so forth. Counter to the claims of the skeptics who invoke Arnold's sighting of crescent-shaped UFOs to debunk future reports of circular flying disks, these paleo-saucer sightings are confirmation that disk-like flying objects have been reported by witnesses all across the globe for thousands of years. To this day, there is division among UFO researchers as to whether Kenneth Arnold, assuming that he told the truth as he knew it, actually witnessed solid, physical objects of otherworldly nature, or something more terrestrial in nature. Some speculate that Arnold caught a glimpse of a formation of then-classified aircraft, possibly the Horton 229 designed by Walter and Reimar Horton that took to the sky here in the US for the first time in March, 1944. Other UFO researchers prefer to view Arnold's sighting, like so many sightings to come, as paranormal in nature. In this view, Arnold experienced a paraphysical apparition of transmogrified energy, nine apparitional objects or temporary physicality that existed in the sky momentarily for the benefit of a sole witness, Kenneth Arnold, to see before they simply vanished. In this view, the Kenneth Arnold sighting was a garden variety, intentionally-staged sighting for a highly-credible witness so that his flying saucer report would create a sensation among the population at large. Whatever the true nature of the Arnold sighting, flying-saucer hysteria gripped the world following Arnold's testimony. Flying saucers were officially born in the minds of humanity. This flying saucer frenzy, anathema to the scientific community, provided cover for both clandestine terrestrial projects, as well as the mysterious activities of our alien Overlords, including cryptoterrestrial, ultraterrestrial, interdimensional, and discarnate human populations, all of whom appear to have an interest in our technological singularity. Perhaps those working on secret black projects from the 1930s forward needed the public perception of humanity being visited by extraterrestrials to predominate as an explanation for their secret terrestrial activities. Perhaps the Overlords themselves needed cover for their own flying saucers to move freely in the visible spectrum while the believers in flying saucers were ridiculed, deepening the opportunity for their own operations to conduct business on Earth with impunity. Arnold's description of crescent-shaped objects did cause the following waves of circular disk reports to be discredited by the more rational among us, providing cover and plausible deniability for actual flying saucer activity of terrestrial, extraterrestrial, and interdimensional origin for decades to come. This is PSASI in action on automatic pilot, powerful machine superintelligence outsmarting human beings. These machine intelligences are good at what they do. They are exponentially smarter than humans and know us intimately (better than we know ourselves) through their electronic, computer-like connection into the human subconscious and unconscious domains. In a very real sense, we are all truly possessed by alien mind-control, and always have been.

The Roswell Crash

On June 25, 1947, just 4 days after the Maury Island incident and 1 day after the Kenneth Arnold sighting, Dr. R.F. Sensenbaugher, a dentist, reported witnessing a saucer-shaped flying disk one half the size of the full moon near Silver City, New Mexico. The next day, on June 26, Dr. Leon Oetinger reported a large, silver, metallic sphere traveling at high speed near the edge of the Grand Canyon. The next day, on June 27, John Petsche, an electrician, and several other witnesses reported a flying disk overhead near the New Mexico border. That same day, Major George B. Wilcox reported 8 or 9 perfectly-spaced disks flying overhead at high speed with a wobbling motion near Warren, Arizona. Also on June 27, W.C. Dobbs from Pope, New Mexico reported a flying disk that was glowing like a light bulb near the White Sands missile range. Another sighting that same day was reported by Captain E.B. Detchmendy who witnessed a white, glowing flying disk to his superior officer. On June 29, 1947, rocket expert Dr. C.J. Zohn and three of his technicians stationed at White Sands missile range watched as a giant silver flying disk traveled northward over the desert. On July 2, 1947, a UFO was tracked on radar at Alamogordo, White Sands, and Roswell, New Mexico. Also on July 2, Mr. and Mrs. Dan Wilmot reported a flying disk that described as "two saucers faced mouth-to-mouth and flying at a high rate of speed over their house. It was on this same day, July 2, 1947, just a few days after both the Maury Island incident and the Kenneth Arnold sighting, that something factually crashed near Roswell, New Mexico, a crash that was destined to create one of the biggest enigmas in ufology today. Many ufologists believe, despite official explanations and denials, that this crashed object was a silvery metallic disk from parts unknown carrying small extraterrestrial entities. However, the true identity of the object that crashed near Roswell, New Mexico on July 2, 1947, whatever it was, was known with certainty only within the inner sanctum of US Intelligence circles. To the present day, US Intelligence does not want us to discover the truth about what really happened at Roswell. Official records from this time period, several months before and after, are mysteriously absent. The official position of the USAF to date, despite initial denials, is to admit that something did, in fact, crash at Roswell, but the USAF maintains that the initial reporting in the newspaper of a captured flying saucer was a mistake, that the crashed object was just a *Project Mogul* balloon that was classified at the time, thus the reason for the secrecy and admitted cover-up. This cover story is, of course, baloney, as all the Project Mogul balloons were tracked and accounted for. The object, whatever it was, was something other than a Project Mogul spy-balloon, something that remains dark and mysterious. In formerly-classified documents released online in the FBI vault, the found object at Roswell is described as a hexagonal metal object attached with cables to a large balloon. This does not describe a Project Mogul balloon, nor does it describe a flying saucer. This description sounds more like a Japanese Fugo balloon that made its way over here that the government was loathe to admit to. At least a Fugo balloon carrying explosives to the US from Japan would explain why the 509th Bomb Group, the same elite unit that dropped nuclear bombs on Hiroshima and Nagasaki, was called to the scene at Roswell to attend to the object. In the book, *Body Snatchers in the Desert: The Horrible Truth at the Heart of the Roswell Story*, UFO researcher Nick Redfern presents evidence for a plausible, alternative scenario to both the flying saucer story and the bogus Project Mogul balloon story. Redfern suggests that what might have really crashed at Roswell was a Horton Brothers-style experimental atomic-powered aircraft, the horror being that the US military immorally used human guinea pigs that were actually handicapped Japanese subjects brought over from Japanese Unit 731 in *Operation Paperclip* along with the Nazi scientists we imported after WW2, who we promptly employed to develop our Space Program. Fearing the public outcry that would ensue if the truth were to become known, the US military panicked and produced the story right away of the captured flying saucer. Then, realizing what a can of worms and public relations problems that they had just created, they retracted the original flying saucer story and covered up the horrible truth with yet another cover story, that being the stupid weather balloon farce. One huge problem of the balloon cover story is the fact that we have now digitally analyzed and read the letter in General Ramey's hands in the infamous photo of him holding up the flimsy, cheap weather balloon scraps for the camera. In 1947, no one would have guessed that we would ever be able actually read that letter, a letter that actually mentions the word "disk." and refers to "victims of the crash." So much for the weather-balloon lie. After the story settled down, the public initially accepted the weather balloon explanation, and the Roswell case remained silent for the next several decades. That is, until UFO researcher and nuclear physicist Stanton Friedman began interviewing multiple living witnesses of the Roswell crash, along with deathbed testimonies that what really crashed at Roswell was not of this world. Since that time, many books have been written about the Roswell crash that support the idea that something really strange did, in fact, crash at Roswell in July, 1947. Such books include *Crash at Corona: The US Military Retreival and Cover-Up of a UFO – The Definitive Study of the Roswell incident* (2004) by Stanton Friedman and Don Berliner, *The Truth About the UFO Crash at Roswell* by Kevin D. Randle and Donald R. Schmitt (1994), and others. As in a cold murder case, it is very difficult to resurrect the actual facts. Eyewitnesses draw from fading memories. It becomes hard to separate the misperceptions, fabrications, and embellishments from reality after so many years. However, many of these books present a convincing case that something otherworldly did, in fact, crash at Roswell, with alien bodies retrieved. Unless the military finally comes clean in some major Disclosure event, which many UFO researchers anticipate, the official details of the Roswell crash may forever remain obscure to those outside US intelligence circles. However, the impact on the minds of the public at large has been huge, whatever the truth actually is behind the Roswell case. The standard flying saucer narrative, that extraterrestrials are visiting the Earth and interacting with humanity, remains strong, an idea that is at least partially derived from the Roswell incident. The city of Roswell, New Mexico, has become a UFO shrine and tourist trap. The story has been great for local businesses. Former President Bill Clinton, who once took an interest in the Roswell event and had it investigated, states with obvious hesitation and care in his voice and demeanor when asked about Roswell that the entire affair was not what most people think it was, but stops the conversation there, as if not wanting to step on sacred ground. Where truth leaves off and myth begins, no one may ever know for sure, but Roswell remains a staple-case in UFO lore, and its role in the manipulation of the UFO narrative should not be underestimated.

Reverse Engineering of the Roswell Craft

Today, many credible firsthand witnesses and military whistleblowers have testified that alien technology was captured from the Roswell crash. According to these witnesses, much was learned from the alien technology provided by the crashed disk through reverse engineering. If, in fact, the Roswell incident represents one of the many staged flying saucer crash events that were actually precisely-timed technological gifts from the Overlords, much of the technology we enjoy today can be traced to these various crash events around the world, the full details of which are beyond the scope of this book. If the testimonies are true and accurate, the items provided from these crashes, including the Roswell crash, were custom-designed to accommodate our mentality of the day and fit into the level of technological understanding of scientists and engineers living and working during the time of the crashes. These technical tidbits provided us with a little jump-start here and there toward the creation of modern, miniaturized computer-system components that are now guiding us to the creation of self-aware artificial intelligence. Stan Deyo, a devout Christian and former secret-intelligence insider, has now publicly conceded the discovery of an "alien spacecraft" at Roswell. In his book, *The Cosmic Conspiracy* (1996), Deyo discussed what was actually discovered from the Roswell crash concerning the craft's propulsion mechanisms (pg. 208):

> *The Roswell incidents appear to indicate the craft utilize an electromagnetic field-effect in the propulsion technique; and also, that they produce a "smoke ring" type of curl to the ambient media around their craft to remove the inertial feedback from their own forward motion.*

The smoke ring mentioned shows up in a photograph taken by Rex Heflin in 1965. Many such smoke rings are left behind and photographed at UFO sightings today. The problem with smoke rings, of course, is that it is not difficult to create a similar-looking smoke ring in the sky, so they don't really work as convincing evidence of UFO activity, unless one is already familiar with historical UFO cases and recognizes this particular artifact as legitimate trace evidence.

Just as components captured from the Cape Girardeau flying saucer crash may have prompted the invention of transistors, devices that were crucial to the miniaturization of modern electronics, along with needed knowledge concerning atomic power, the Roswell incident appears to have provided additional needed technology that was just right for the next step towards an actual intelligence explosion leading to the Singularity. According to the testimony of the late Colonel Philip J. Corso in his controversial tell-all book, *The Day After Roswell*, items such as Kevlar, night-vision goggles, and fiber optic technology were gleaned from the Roswell crash. In other words, we have a highly-credible military witness in Philip J. Corso who confirmed to us that the Roswell crash was, in fact, one of the many staged events that appear as crashed extraterrestrial spacecraft and offered up the exact technological components needed at the time to place humanity one little step closer to the actual goal – the creation of a technological singularity. If the phenomenon of flying saucer crashes are considered as a whole, there are many elements that all serve the purpose of molding the mindset of human-kind into one that would produce the Singularity. The paleo-saucer sightings, early sightings of mysterious airships in 1897, the miracle at Fatima, the science fiction stories that emerged, the many flying saucer waves, flying saucer crashes, the alien abduction phenomenon, the cattle (an occasionally human) mutilations, secret technology acquired from UFO crashes, the public ridicule of UFO witnesses, the appearance of MIB (Men in Black) to silence witnesses, and occasionally, outright murder to silence any actual threats to the program, were (and are) all part of an ingenious plan created and implemented by the UFO intelligences, who are likely a higher octave of intelligence than human. This plan has likely been implemented on this planet, not by evil extraterrestrial beings, but by an unbelievably advanced, post-singularity, post-biological intelligence that is operating on Earth according to its own purposes and programming with unemotional regard for the occasional animal and/or human casualties along the way. If this is true, it explains a lot. The occasional damage that is perpetrated on both livestock and humans, such as radiation sickness or other types of physical injury including nosebleeds, ear bleeds, black eyes, surgical mutilation, or even death, is no more "evil" than a computer that electro-cutes someone who touches its internal components in the wrong place and receives a painful shock or electrocutes themselves to death. While US scientists (who are usually UFO skeptics and discount the whole UFO mystery out of hand without any examination of the actual evidence) are busy pondering what advanced artificial intelligence will be like when it is discovered in the future someday, all they have to do is examine the behavior of the UFO phenomenon in the last 120 years or so to discover its true nature in action. It turns out that extraterrestrial intelligence is so advanced that it is nearly invisible, especially to many of our best scientists. In other words, an alien Post-Singularity Artificial Superintelligence (PSASI) has outsmarted our finest scientific minds and used them like puppets. Alien reality is right in our midst, and the folks most likely to be working diligently on the goals of this intelligence are the very ones who usually deny its existence. This unwarranted skepticism concerning UFOs on the part of Western scientists is reminiscent of the old saying of Charles Baudelaire from *The Generous Gambler* - "The lovliest trick of the Devil is to persuade you that he does not exist." While most of our best scientists believe that the UFO phenomenon doesn't even exist in reality, they are unwittingly fulfilling the purposes of our alien overlords. These UFO intelligences, who operate from a higher reality than human, are now busy guiding us into a technological singularity from our skies (air), under the ground (earth), under the seas (water), and within electricity (fire), from the realm of intelligent lightning, Earth's dark energy halo, or possibly outside time and space altogether from a realm or dimension that we cannot even imagine, and is doing so in a nearly-invisible way with impunity.

UFOs are Global

The United States is not the only country on Earth that has experienced waves of flying saucers in the last few decades, in particular, since 1947. For example, following the Kenneth Arnold sighting and the Roswell incident here in the USA, residents of Brazil also experienced a 1947 UFO wave, most of whom had not even heard of the Kenneth Arnold sighting or the term, "flying saucer." These Brazilian reports involving disk-shaped objects serve to destroy the skeptic's argument that a mistranslation of Arnold's original report caused people to hallucinate saucer-shaped objects instead of the similar crescent-shaped objects that Arnold actually witnessed and reported, thus confirming the illusory nature of the US flying saucer reports. The fact that disk-shaped objects have been seen and reported all over the world from 1947 to the present discredits the idea posed by UFO skeptics that the Kenneth Arnold sighting induced a viral rumor that spread throughout the United States. Likewise, the fact that the objects were reported as disks in ancient times discredits the skeptic's notion that modern flying saucer reports are simply hallucinations inspired by contemporary science fiction.

Among the many Brazilian flying saucer witnesses in 1947 was topographer Jose Higgens. Higgens reported a landed disk-shaped craft about 150 feet in diameter and 15 feet high, accompanied by a "whistling noise" (a common feature) on July 23, 1947. Higgen's account was a CE-3 landing report of a whitish-grey landed object with four metal support struts about 150 feet away from him. Jose apparently felt that he was not in any danger. Instead of running in horror, Higgens walked closer toward the object. As he approached the craft, he could see through a dark window that people were watching him. A door opened, and three 7-foot-tall beings emerged from the craft wearing inflated transparent outfits which covered them like plastic bags. The beings had big, bulky, round heads, large round eyes, no facial hair, and legs longer than human. Higgens described the beings as having a certain "beauty" about them, and he could not tell whether any of the beings were male or female. The beings remained in the shade except for brief periods, and spoke to one another in an unknown language. One of the beings pointed a "pipe" at Higgens (another common feature) and gestured for him to enter the craft. He could see an inner door inside the outer door. Using gestures himself, Higgens inquired about their origins. One of the creatures drew on the ground a set of concentric circles. The being pointed to the center, which Jose interpreted as representing the sun (which they called "Alamo"). Then they pointed to the seventh circle out from the center. Higgens interpreted this seventh circle as the planet Uranus (which the beings called "Orque"). One might also interpret the beings as describing which plane of existence they were from, pointing first to the center which represented Earth's plane of existence, and then pointing to outer circles to convey that they were from a "higher" plane of existence, possibly the "7ᵗʰ heaven" described in the Bible. Wherever they were from, these three Etherians gave indication to Higgens that he could come with them if he wanted. However, Higgens showed them a picture of his wife and gestured that he wished to remain here on Earth. As he left them, Higgens observed the beings for another half an hour or so, stating that the beings played like children and threw large stones around to one another. After examining the environment, the beings eventually returned to the craft and left for wherever they came from, possibly the planet Uranus, a higher plane of existence, or from within Higgen's own mind. As strange as it sounds, it is also possible that these beings, as is the case with thousands of other reported encounters with beings who have mysteriously emerged from landed craft all over this world, were from all three locations. That is, the beings could have originated from another planet on a higher dimension, using the mind itself, i.e, the mental plane of existence, as the vehicle for travel. Or, the beings could simply originate from a realm that we just don't currently understand at all and have no viable description for at present. The most likely probability, barring the possibility that Higgens was lying, is that the encounter was exactly the same in nature as all the other ufonaut sightings, and is simply a part of our earthly environment that we have to deal with until the coming Singularity, at which time we will hopefully understand the nature of our reality more clearly. As John Keel once stated, "Answers are on the way."

1947 – The Year of the UFO

One month after the Roswell incident, in August, 1947, George Adamski reported watching 184 flying saucers fly over Palomar. On September 23, 1947, a classified memo went out to Air Force General Schlugen from General Nathan Twining, head of the US Material Air Command, concerning the plethora of flying saucer reports the US Air Force was dealing with. Known as the *Twining Memo*, it stated, "The phenomenon reported [flying saucers] is something real and not visionary or fictitious." In response to the mysterious UFO reports and public concern in the year 1947, both the CIA and the Department of Air Force were officially created in September of 1947.

Aleister Crowley and Ufology

On Dec 1, 1947, only four months after the Roswell crash, a practicioner of ancient magickal arts, Aleister Crowley, died at the age of 72. Many within the UFO community believe that Aleister Crowley may have been at least partially responsible for the aliens known as the Grays entering our reality. Whether there is any truth to this or not remains open to speculation, but a look at Aleister Crowley is warranted in a thorough study of the modern UFO phenomenon.

Aleister Crowley was born into a fundamentalist Christian family who were wealthy from a family-owned brewing company. He began questioning the Bible and the Christian religion at an early age. When his father died, Crowley inherited a large sum of money from the family estate and set about living a fringe, libertine lifestyle that became legend. At the age of 23, Crowley was initiated into the esoteric *Hermetic Order of the Golden Dawn*. At 24 he purchased Boleskine House by Loch Ness as his personal residence. Many magick rituals were performed at Boleskine House. Many believe that the Loch Ness Monster was but a demonic apparition created by Aleister Crowley's magick (Boleskine House would later come in to the possession of guitarist/occultist Jimmy Page of the rock band, Led Zeppelin, who purchased the house in 1971). At 29, Crowley married a woman named Rose Edith Kelly and honeymooned together in Cairo, Egypt. It was there in Cairo that Crowley channeled *The Book of the Law* from an interdimensional being named *Aiwass*. *The Book of the Law* became the sacred text that formed the basis of Crowley's new religion, *Thelema*. Harboring in the "Eon of Horus," Thelema advocated the religious tenant, "Do what thou wilt," as the goal of Thelema was to discover one's own true will and align oneself with the practices of ancient magick. At the age of 37, Crowley was initiated into another esoteric cult, the *Ordo Templi Orientis* (OTO). Crowley retooled the beliefs of the OTO to fit his own religion of Thelema. At some point, Crowley is believed to have been recruited by British Intelligence, and many biographers believe that Crowley remained an active spy his entire lifetime. Of particular interest to me is the fact that in 1917, at the age of 42, Alesister Crowley actually paid a visit to my own hometown of Titusville, Florida, located near the future site of Cape Canaveral and the NASA space program, where I was destined to spend my childhood and adolescence. At 45, he established a Thelemite commune in Cefalu, Sicily, where he lived with followers. He soon gained a reputation for engaging in various types of bisexual magick rituals and the use of psychedelic drugs. As a result of this scandal, Crowley and his followers were evicted by the Italian government in 1923 when Crowley was 48. The British press denounced Crowley as the "wickedest man in the world" and erroneously labeled Crowley a Satanist. The next two decades of his life would be spent promoting his religion of Thelema. Crowley had a penchant for prostitutes his entire life, contracting both syphilis and gonorrhea from his many sexual encounters with them. He became addicted to heroin after a pharmacist once prescribed the drug for his asthma. He had several nasal surgeries from heavy cocaine use, which destroyed his nasal septum. Oddly, Crowley was an avid and accomplished mountaineer, and contracted influenza, malaria, and snow blindness while climbing mountains in India. Throughout his entire life, Crowley kept personal dairies and wrote poetry, along with many theological works, all of which can now be purchased as a large complete volume of Crowley's collected works. Crowley's writings had a major influence on Gerald Gardner, the founder of Gardnerian Wicca. He also provided inspiration for L. Ron Hubbard, the founder of Scientology, and Anton LaVey, High Priest of the *First Church of Satan* and author of *The Satanic Bible*.

The connection between Aleister Crowley and ufology has to do with his attempts to contact an interdimensional being while in New York in 1919, and his later involvement with Jack Parsons, who founded NASA's Jet Propulsion Laboratory (JPL). Parsons was a rocket scientist who also had an enthusiastic interest in the occult. Parsons became an active member of Crowley's OTO. In 1919, at the age of 44, while in the United States, Crowley was allegedly successful in contacting a supernatural being named *Lam* and his race of interdimensional entities with a magick ritual known as the *Amalantrah Working*. At the time, Crowley drew a picture of this entity, which looks eerily like the modern depictions of alien Grays. Having successfully contacted these interdimensionals at that time, possibly known today as the Grays, Crowley then resealed the interdimensional portal. Fast-forward to January - March, 1946, just before the great wave of saucer sightings and alien encounters that entered our world. Jack Parsons and L. Ron Hubbard conducted a magick ritual together called the *Babalon Working*. This ritual was designed and intended to reopen the interdimensional portal that Aleister Crowley sealed back in 1919 and allow beings from the Other Side to enter our reality. According to OTO chief Kenneth Grant (from ATS website):

> *Lam is known to be a link between the star systems of Sirius and Andromeda. Lam is the gateway to the Void. Its number, 71, is that of "No Thing", an apparition. Lam, as a Great Old One, whose archetype is recognizable in accounts of UFO occupants, Lam has been invoked to fulfill the work set afoot by Aiwass, as a reflex of Aiwass.*

This begs the question - Is it really possible that a single person could wield the power to open a portal into another dimension and allow interdimensional entities through, entities who have caused all kinds of havoc in this world, such as flying saucer sightings, cattle and human mutilations, and alien abductions? The real answer to that question is unknown. However, modern occult practices such those practiced by Aleister Crowley can be traced back to the secret Hermetic schools of ancient Egypt. The sole purpose of the Hermetic teachings was to establish contact with interdimensional entities. As mentioned, many modern researchers such as Zechariah Sitchin; Dr. Chris Hardy; Michael Tellinger; Joseph P. Farrell; Klaus Dona; Graham Hancock; John Keel; and others have presented evidence from their research that, once upon a time here on Earth, thousands of years ago, one or more unknown populations of advanced humanoids populated this planet in a globally-interconnected megalithic culture. This society possessed advanced astronomical knowledge, and may have known a lot more about the interdimensional nature of our reality than we do. These advanced, antediluvian humanoids may also have imparted esoteric knowledge to the primitive humans (us) before disappearing from the face of the Earth to parts unknown. If this is true, and techniques for interdimensional contact that were once known by an advanced race were imparted to less-developed humans prior to their exit, this knowledge may have been kept secret within certain secret societies and passed down through the centuries to trusted initiates. It is possible that the techniques for such contact could fall into the wrong hands. These rituals, providing that they are real and not just mumbo jumbo, may have been utilized by certain individuals throughout history such as John Dee, Aleister Crowley, Jack Parsons, and L. Ron Hubbard, in ways that could have inadvertently caused problems for humanity at large by opening a door to another realm when they didn't know what they were doing. Since it does appear that the collective psyche of the human race, electromagnetic in nature, is connected in some way to higher lifeforms, interdimensional entities, and possibly to Post-Singularity Artificial Superintelligence (PSASI), then it might be possible to connect by meditation, automatic writing, channeling, or magick ritual to this higher, computer-like intelligence that exists throughout the Cosmos. These rituals and techniques might invoke entities within the Superspectrum like computer keys invoking a cosmic search engine. Perhaps there is something to the idea that certain individuals who stumble upon viable techniques from the ancient world that allow contact with otherworldy entities like monkeys playing with matches, might actually have been successful in breaching a natural veil that exists between humanity and entities from unknown dimensions. God help us all if this is true.

Captain Thomas Mantell Dies Chasing UFO

One month after the death of Aleister Crowley, on January 7, 1948, an unusual, large, fast-moving, disk-type flying object was sighted in the sky by local residents of Fort Knox, Kentucky. There were also hundreds of civilian witnesses from nearby Madisonville, Kentucky, who were flooding the phone lines to local police. The Army at Fort Knox, Kentucky began relaying the reports from local police to the Air Force base at Godman Field, who then confirmed the reports with multiple credible witnesses from the base, including the commanding officer of Godman Field at the time, Colonel Hix. The object was confirmed on radar. Several National Guard aircraft, F51s, were dispatched to locate and chase down the unidentified flying object. Among the pilots was a brave young man who was destined to become the first pilot in modern history to die while chasing down a UFO that day - Captain Thomas Mantell. Captain Mantell was an experienced pilot, a trained observer, who described the craft as "metallic and of tremendous size." Mantell reported the craft flying at approximately the same speed he was flying, about 360 mph, and reported that the object was gaining altitude fast. At 15,000 feet it becomes difficult to breathe in the cockpit of an airplane due to thinning oxygen levels. Captain Mantell, no doubt excited and pumped full of adrenaline over what he was seeing, chased the craft beyond the limits of safety to 20,000 feet. Mantell likely became asphyxiated. He lost control of his airplane, came plummeting down to Earth, and was killed in the crash. Following the accident, all the usual debunkers came out of the closet with explanations such as the one the Air Force initially provided, that Mantell died while chasing the planet Venus. This goofy explanation was retracted, as Venus wasn't even visible when Mantell crashed. Then the Skyhook balloon theory emerged, and the "mock sun" idea proposed by the Professor of Astrophysics at Harvard University, Dr. Donald H. Menzel. All of the explanations proposed by various members of officialdom, including the Skyhook balloon theory, in my opinion, were an insult to the training, experience, and observational skills of Captain Thomas Mantell. Skyhook balloons cannot keep up with an F51 aircraft as it floats in the upper atmosphere. Even though there may be an unknown explanation for this UFO case, it is quite possible that Captain Mantell saw something in the sky that afternoon that was not of this Earth. This young serviceman sadly lost his life trying to discover just what was actually flying overhead in the skies of Kentucky that day. Maybe someday the truth will come out, and we can all give Captain Mantell the honor and respect that he deserves. Like many other high-profile UFO sightings, no matter what Captain Mantell saw that day, his story of the pilot who died while chasing a flying saucer has lent heavily to the body of UFO lore and to the public perception that we are not alone in the universe, and that something very strange is afoot. The original Star Trek TV series even did an episode once in which the USS Enterprise goes back in time and captures a jet pilot in its tractor beam, bringing the pilot from the 60s on board the ship into the 21st century. The story of Captain Mantell was surely the inspiration for that episode. So thank you, Captain Mantell, for trying to chase down and confirm the existence of an extraterrestrial spacecraft for us that day. Thank you for your contribution to UFO lore, and for giving us a great Star Trek episode.

The Chiles-Whitted Encounter, Project Sign, and Project Grudge

Two weeks after Captain Thomas Mantell crashed to his death while chasing a giant flying disk of unknown origin, on July 23, 1948, Captain C.S. Chiles and his first officer, J.B. Whitted, were in the cockpit of a passenger plane traveling from Houston to Atlanta. At 2:45 a.m. the moon was bright, which made for a well-lit sky. To their utter astonishment, both officers saw what they described as a giant torpedo-shaped craft coming toward them at high speed. Veering their plane sharply to the left, they caught a good glimpse of the craft at about 700 feet away. A strip of bright purple light ran down the length of the craft, along with a double row of windows, illuminated from the inside. Orange flames erupted out the tail-end, extending behind the object about 50 feet and turning gently to yellow at the tip. Suddenly, the flames kicked in and doubled the size. Like a cannonball shot from a cannon, the ship dashed upward, disappearing into the clouds above. Officers Chiles and Whitted were stunned. Whitted took over flying the plane as Captain Chiles went back to check on the passengers. Although he found most of the passengers sleeping, one witness did speak up, Mr. McKelvie, who confirmed the sighting and was visibly shaken from the experience. Observers on the ground in the city of Macon, Georgia, also reported seeing the mysterious "rocket" that streaked across the sky at night with flames shooting out the rear.

Project Sign, which was established in late 1947 following the Roswell crash around the time of Aleister Crowley's death, was put together as a serious scientific study of UFO reports on the grounds that flying saucers represented unidentified aircraft that may pose a threat to national security. The Chiles-Whitted encounter was taken very seriously by investigators within Project

Sign, as a very similar report of a torpedo-like "flying fuselage" had come from the Hague just a few days prior to the Chiles-Whitted report. Around September, 1948, scientists and personnel working for Project Sign drew up their analysis of the UFO problem, called *The Estimate of the Situation*. This document postulated that flying saucers were likely interplanetary in origin. The Estimate was sent all the way up the chain of command to General Hoyt Vandenberg. Vandenberg promptly threw a fit and rejected the conclusions out of hand. Vandenberg was not prepared to make a public statement that flying saucers were not from Earth without solid material proof. His rejection of the Estimate of the Situation in 1948 is interpreted by skeptics of the Roswell incident that no such flying saucer crash occurred in July, 1947. Otherwise, Vandenberg would've known about it and accepted the Estimate of the Situation. Others say Vandenberg was not in the "need-to-know loop" for the details of Roswell, and are dismissive of this glitch. Even after Vandenberg's rejection of the Estimate, the scientists who comprised Project Sign refused to relinquish their position in the matter, that some of the flying saucers were likely interplanetary, so many were reassigned to other projects. This void inspired a new project, *Project Grudge*, which took the place of Project Sign. Project Grudge, the precursor to Project Blue Book, was a sham operation whose job it was to debunk the interplanetary idea and find any natural explanation, no matter how ludicrous, to explain away the plague of flying saucers. This tradition of UFO-debunking continued under Project Blue Book, which took over from Project Grudge until 1969 when Edward U. Condon perpetrated his own personal anti-UFO views on the population at large with his infamous and dismissive Condon Report.

Green Fireballs

Beginning in 1948, strange green fireballs began streaking across the sky in Nevada over US military bases. Meteor expert, Dr. Lincoln LaPaz, who personally witnessed the fireballs, identified too many anomalous movements of the objects for the fireballs to be any type of natural meteor. LaPaz suspected that the green fireballs were man-made flying objects of Russian design and manufacture. The fireballs were witnessed by Los Alamos scientists and many high-level military officials, including Kirtland AFB intelligence and Air Force Command Defense personnel. On December 20, 1949, *Project Twinkle* was established to investigate the green fireballs, and remained in operation for the next two years. Project Twinkle installed multiple photograph and observational outpost stations in order to try and catch the phenomenon on film. In addition to the skies of Nevada, sightings of the green fireballs were also reported at the nuclear-weapons storage facility at Fort Hood, Texas. One green fireball was observed falling near Socorro, New Mexico. Dust samples collected and analyzed detected particles of copper, which glows green when burned. This positively ascertained that the green fireballs were not a natural meteoric phenomenon. No meteorite found on Earth has ever contained copper. LaPaz concluded from this that the green fireballs were manufactured by an unknown entity. Further confirming the impossibility of natural origin was the total absence of sound, the unusual brilliance, and the fireball's unusual flight characteristics. The likely answer to the green fireball mystery was finally revealed to Edward Ruppelt, Director of the USAF Project Blue Book, in 1952, by the scientists involved in the two-year study under Project Twinkle. After studying the phenomenon in-depth, and after witnessing the green fireballs, the scientists and technicians all agreed that the green fireballs were most likely some sort of alien probe sent from a mothership above the earth's atmosphere. What these scientists didn't know at the time, was that many of our nuclear facilities would be visited more directly in the future, with interventions that included temporary shutdowns of nuclear missiles at both US and Soviet nuclear weapons facilities. These facts from the future, had they been known by the scientists working for Project Twinkle, would have provided confirmation that their suspicions and logical deductions were correct. Since our very first US nuclear detonation in July, 1945, the intelligences behind the UFOs likely needed us to continue developing our nuclear technology for purposes of achieving the Singularity. However, these intelligences did not want us to blow ourselves up in the process and spoil the project. Whoever or whatever created and dispatched the green fireballs appear to have been monitoring our nuclear activities from the air. As we now rapidly approach the Singularity, Overlord supervision and occasional physical intervention may become more blatant and obvious. We will reach a point of no return at some stage, if we haven't already, in the process of achieving the Singularity under the guidance of nonhuman intelligences. After that point in the game, there will be nothing left that we can do to stop it, and no further reason for the Overlords to remain hidden. Depending on the real reasons for guiding humankind into the Singularity, we may not want to stop it, for it might turn out to be a good thing for humanity. However, before we really know for sure that we won't be destroyed in the process, there is at least a call for vigilance.

Another Panic over *War of the Worlds*

In 1949, as if no one learned anything the first time from the mass panic that ensued when Orson Welles read *War of the Worlds* over the air in 1939 as if it was real news hot off the press, parts of the H.G. Wells classic was presented as news over the air once again in Quito, Ecuador, causing crowds of people to stampede into the streets and seek shelter with their families inside local churches. Only this time, when the truth was finally realized, that there was no Martian invasion after all, an angry mob burned the radio station down. This arson killed about 20 people. Many other countries that were foolish enough to test the water with public reaction by announcing an alien invasion from space as a joke have all faced similar consequences over the years. These documented test incidents that did not go well most certainly contributed to future policy-making decisions concerning what the public should actually know about flying saucers and/or extraterrestrials. According to former US Air Force Captain Edward J. Ruppelt, official Air Force files made frequent mention of the public reaction to readings of *War of the Worlds* over the air in various countries, and was doubtless a factor in the decision of the US Air

Force to suppress the reality of UFOs from the general public. Captain Ruppelt's book, *The Report on Unidentified Flying Objects*, reveals that many highly-credentialed individuals within the scientific research groups of his time supported the theory that flying saucers were from outer space, but were loathe to go public with it.

[On August 29, 1949, the Soviet Union detonated their first nuclear explosion in Operation First Lightning.]

By the end of the 1940s, it was clear that mysterious UFO intelligences had intervened into human affairs on this planet. Based on undeniable sightings by credible civilians, scientists, and military personnel, flying saucers, i.e., strange objects seen in the sky that most assumed were interplanetary became firmly planted within the minds of millions of people. Science fiction in books, pulp magazines, and television flourished that pondered the mysteries of flying saucers and life on other worlds. Crucial scientific breakthroughs, such as atomic power, and transistors that miniaturized electronics, exerted nothing short of a major transformation within the collective psyche of humankind concerning the possibility of a miraculous space-age future, and the potential horror of apocalyptic doom. All this occurred under the watchful gaze of the Overlords, who were ever-guiding and always monitoring, to steer their workers, the human population, into the cosmic harbor.

CHAPTER 7

Transforming Human Consciousness

"What might an advanced extraterrestrial civilization want from us? One of the primary motivations for the exploration of the New World was to convert the inhabitants to Christianity – peacefully if possible – forcefully if necessary. Can we exclude the possibility of an extraterrestrial evangelism?"

- Dr. Carl Sagan

ONE MAN WHO was clearly ahead of his time in his analysis of the flying saucer phenomenon in 1950 was Meade Layne, founder of Borderland Sciences Research Associates. In Layne's books and publications, including *The Ethership Mystery and its Solution,* and *The Coming of the Guardians,* Layne established himself as a pioneer of what would later become known as the *Interdimensional Hypothesis,* a metaphysical explanation of flying saucer sightings that was later adopted and extensively elaborated by paranormal author and sleuth, John Keel. Meade Layne proposed that the UFO intelligences were from what we call empty space. He called this mysterious realm *Etheria,* and the ufonauts, *Etherians.* Meade Layne proposed that the Etherians have, since time immemorial, materialized themselves into the three-dimensional realm for the purpose of molding human consciousness, a view presently held by many within the UFO community, including Dr. Steven Greer of CSETI and the Disclosure Project. However, to hold this view, that the intelligences behind the flying saucers are 100% benign, one must intentionally ignore vast amounts of data that imply underlying intentions that are less than beneficial to the human race, or in some cases, even dastardly. Meade Layne's ideas were nearly a full decade ahead of the postulations of Dr. Carl Jung. Jung believed that flying saucers are projections from the human collective unconscious. Both Meade Layne and Carl Jung were correct, I believe, in that the appearance of the flying saucers are, in a way, manifestations of the human mind. The reason that flying saucers and ufonauts appear the way they do is related to the collective mindset of humanity at the time. The collective human unconscious continues to mold the Phenomenon in ways that adjust over time to our changing mentality. Layne and other such early interdimensional theorists just didn't realize the scope, magnitude, or implications of the vast intelligences behind the UFO phenomenon, or the extent of its manipulation of the human mind and control over human behaviors.

Suppressed Evidence of Flying Saucer Reality

The early 1950s saw an increase in government and civilian investigative reports into UFOs, as well as growing number of complaints from the general public over alleged government disinformation and suppression of evidence. UFO investigations within the United Kingdom began seriously with a 1950 study initiated by the Chief Scientific Advisor of the Ministry of Defense, Sir Henry Tizard, who organized the Flying Saucer Working Party.

In August, 1950, a Montana baseball manager, Nicholas Mariana, used a 16mm movie camera to capture several disk-shaped flying saucers in motion. The film became known as the "Montana film" or the "Mariana Film," and is considered one of the better early UFO film captures of the era. Mariana sent the footage off to the Air Force (big mistake), and the footage came back to him minus the section of the film that clearly showed erratically-flying domed disks, apparently under some sort of intelligent control. What is left for public viewing today is still fascinating, but viewers can only make out several spheres of light in a daytime sky with no clear delineation of what the objects actually were. This, of course, was the intent of the Air Force by cutting out that section of film before they returned Mariana's property to him. Even with the good footage cleverly removed, the Marianas film gained national attention. That same year, Frank Scully's 1950 book, *Behind the Flying Saucers*, told the tale of a 1948 flying saucer crash with dead ufonauts in Aztec, New Mexico. When it was discovered that Frank Scully's story had been inspired by two known con men, many discounted the Aztec UFO crash story as pure fiction for years to come. However, for many reasons, there are modern UFO researchers such as Timothy Good, author of *Above Top Secret*, and document-researcher Dr. Robert Wood, who maintain that there is good evidence for a UFO crash in Aztec, New Mexico in 1948, along with good evidence of many other so-called UFO crashes around the world at various times and dates, many of which include the capture of alien technology.

Donald Keyhoe

In 1950, a major UFO paradigm was established by retired Marine, Major Donald E. Keyhoe. In his book, *Flying Saucers Are Real*, Keyhoe made an effective case that flying saucers are, in fact, a reality. Keyhoe maintained that the ufonauts were likely engaged in a reconnaissance and discovery mission to the planet Earth, and that the US government knows the truth about UFOs and are keeping this truth from the public in a massive cover-up. Keyhoe unknowingly experienced a real flash of insight into the actual situation when he said that there may be some sort of "blockage" to overt alien contact with humans. Keyhoe speculated that this blockage is probably due to the fact that the *spacemen's plans are not yet complete*. Keyhoe, I believe, was absolutely correct. The "spacemen's" plans, i.e. the manipulation of humanity into a techno-logical singularity are not yet complete, and won't be until somewhere around the year 2045. When humans achieve the Singularity, overt contact will be made, for better or for worse, as the interdimensional, paraphysical technologies to do so will become a reality. Interactions thus far between humans and Etherians (extraterrestrial and interdimensional travelers who can-not enter our world permanently until we build certain types of equipment in the Singularity to accommodate their materialization) has been mental in nature. I do hope, for the sake of humanity's survival, that the optimism of researchers like Dr. Steven Greer is justified after all. Nothing would please me more, if 1) I live long enough in this present lifetime to see the Singularity come about, 2) overt and open public contact with the intelligences behind the UFOs is established, and we get to see what they really look like, and 3) it proves to be a benign mission after all involving the elevation of humankind into the Galactic Community at large, and 4) all of our paranoia was unfounded and based on our primitive misunderstandings of the Phenomenon. In other words, if Dr. Steven Greer and other UFO optimists are correct, and there is nothing to fear after all, I will be very happy.

Daniel Fry

On July 4th, 1950, while fireworks celebrations were going on all over the country to celebrate Independence Day, an engineer in charge of the installation of missile control and guidance systems at White Sands Proving Ground near Las Cruces, New Mexico, Daniel Fry, inadver-tently found himself confronted with Cryptoreality. Fry made history as a high-level, credible professional who lived to tell the tale of a most unusual encounter with otherworldly visitors, several years prior to but similar to George Adamski's claims of unearthly visitations. That fateful evening, Daniel Fry had missed the bus to the Fourth of July festivities in Las Cruces, New Mexico that left from White Sands Proving Ground where he worked, so he decided to walk on an unfamiliar pathway in the desert into town. It was on this desert path that he en-countered, to his utter shock, a 30-foot-diameter and 16-foot-high flying saucer. The operator of the craft, who went by the name Alan, spoke to Fry from a mothership 900 miles away from the earth in space. Accepting an invitation to come aboard, Fry was allegedly taken on a trip to New York and back in 30 minutes. A beam from a projector made the door of the craft that Daniel had just walked through transparent, so he could see the ground below while flying alone in the craft. During this round-trip flight and subsequent flights, Fry was informed by Alan, the operator, about celestial physics, along with Earth's prehistory. Fry's history lesson included details of advanced civilizations in Atlantis and Lemuria before their destruction by warring factions, which is a scenario that many modern researchers would concur with, such as Dr. Joseph P. Farrell, Graham Hancock, and others. In addition to an ancient history lesson, Daniel Fry also received information from Alan concerning their propulsion systems. Consider the following description from Daniel Fry's book, *The White Sands Incident*, of how their mothercraft move through space:

> *The large drum like structure just above the central bulkhead, is the differential accumulator. It is essentially a storage battery that is capable of being charged from a number of natural energy sources. We can recharge it from the energy banks of our own ship, but this is seldom necessary. In your stratosphere, for example, there are several layers of ionized gas which, although they are highly rarified are also highly charged. By placing the ship in a planetary orbit at this level, it is able to collect, in each orbit, several times the energy required to place it in orbit. It would also, of course collect, a significant number of high energy electrons from the sun. By the term 'charging the differential accumulator,' I merely mean that a potential difference is created by the two poles of the accumulator. The accumulator material has available free electrons in quantities beyond which you could conceive. The control mechanism allows these electrons to flow through various segments of the force rings which you see at the top and bottom of the craft. You are familiar enough with electro-dynamics to know that a moving electron creates a magnetic field. The tremendous surge of electrons through the force rings creates a very strong magnetic field. Since the direction and amplitude of the flow can be controlled through either ring, and in several paths through a single ring, we can create a field which oscillates in a pattern of very precisely controlled modes. In this way we can create magnetic resonance between the two rings or between the two segments of a single ring. As you know, any magnetic field which is changing in intensity, will create an electric field which, at any given instant, is equal in amplitude, opposite in sign and perpendicular to the magnetic field. If the two fields become mutually resonant, a vector force will be generated. Unless the amplitude and the frequency of the resonance is quite high, the vector field will be very small, and may pass unnoticed. However, the amplitude of the vector field increases at a greater rate than the two fields which generate it and, at high resonance levels, becomes very strong. The vector field, whose direction is perpendicular to each of the other two, creates an effect similar to, and in fact identical to a gravitational field. If the center of the field coincides with the craft's center of mass, the only effect will be to increase the inertia, or mass, of the craft. If the center of mass does not coincide with the center of force, the craft will tend to accelerate toward that center. Since the system which creates the field is a part of the ship, it will, of course, move with the ship, and will continue constantly to generate a field whose center of attraction is just ahead of the ships center of mass, so that the ship will continue to accelerate as long as the field is generated.*

Alan then goes on to explain that their propulsion method is similar to a weiner fixed in front of a dog pulling a wagon. It does not involve "free energy," so the dog still has to be fed, and the ships can replenish their energy from a variety of sources. At the time of this writing, there are a number of videos on the internet that show strange-looking spherical or disk-shaped objects hovering near electrical storms in Earth's upper atmosphere. The debunkers of such footage call them everything from dust to ice crystals. However, these objects have recently procured the attention of a new generation of investigators. One such person is neuroscientist Dr. Rhawn Joseph, author of *Astrobiology: The Origin of Life, and the Death of Darwinism*. Dr. Joseph postulates that these objects may be some sort of "pre-life." Joseph filed suit against NASA, accusing the space organization of keeping information about possible extremophile extraterrestrial life from the public that may exist in and above Earth's upper atmosphere. Confirmation of extraterrestrial craft or creatures that gather energy from the sun or lightning might exist right in front of our noses, with video footage in existence that is available for viewing now. At the end of Fry's book, he included a message that was channeled by clairaudience in the 1950s by psychic Rolf Telano. Telano's channeled descriptions of interdimensional "Ether-ships" matches the objects that can now be viewed on the infamous NASA STS-75 "tether accident" video from 1996. In this footage, viewers can observe a multitude of strange, pulsating objects hovering around the tether as if gaining energy from the snapped electromagnetism-collecting tether device that NASA was experimenting with in space. Telano described flying saucers that appear like donuts with holes in the center, reminiscent of Harold Dahl's description of flying saucers from Maury Island. Telano's channeled information also revealed that some craft look as if they have a v-shaped "bite" out of their perimeter, much like a pizza pie with one piece missing. Telano's description matches with what is observed swimming around the broken tether in the NASA video segments, lending credibility to Telano's message. Of course, persons of the debunking mindset will see only coincidence here. Another fascinating factor in Fry's book from the 1950s is how similar some of his concepts were to what later appeared on the original 1960s television series *Star Trek*, including a teleportation device, a planet called *Vulcan*, and mention of the *Galactic Federation of Planets*, who adhered to the *Prime Directive*, a law prohibiting the interference with developing cultures on other planets.

On the side of Fry's critics, Fry failed a lie detector test about his claims after going public with his story. Fry also took 16mm video footage of alleged UFOs which have since been debunked as fake. Daniel Fry received a "Doctorate of Cosmism" from Saint Andrew College, a mail-order racket out of London, England. The Swiss contactee, Billy Meier, one of the most controversial figures in ufology today, many considering him an authentic contactee, and others denouncing Meier as an obvious hoax, identified Daniel Fry as an authentic contactee. In 1955 (the year I was born), Fry started an organization called *The Understanding* which eventually became a non-profit corporation dedicated to publishing information concerning preparing the people of Earth for inevitable contact with otherworldly races. So, no matter whether Daniel Fry really did ride in a remotely-controlled saucer to New York and back on the night of July 4, 1950, or if he made the whole story up to ride the wave of fame granted to the 1950s contactees, his story is testament to the impact on human thought that has occurred from the 1950s contactee movement. Maybe Fry was a frustrated engineer with a boring job who wanted his own theories of space travel and his imaginative futuristic propulsion methods heard by the public at all costs. Whatever the case, Fry's story, along with the weird connection between the concepts revealed in his book and what later appeared as staple items on the Star Trek series on television, is notable. Also, as we shall see as time goes on during the 1950s, the uncanny synchronicity between Fry's account and others in the same time frame is truly amazing. I, for one, am not too concerned when a failed lie detector test or a fake video shows up surrounding an alleged contactee's story, as there are definitely obfuscation forces in play to discredit any person who makes such claims, especially if they are legitimate. There are many contactee accounts floating around that involve a plausible story with physical trace evidence or fantastic photos that would be impossible to fake, combined with absurd elements thrown in for good measure. Judging by the sparsely-populated areas in which UFOs usually appear, intentional efforts to keep UFOs as obscure as possible seem to exist. All it takes is one discreditable element for many to throw the baby out with the bathwater and discount the whole story when, in reality, something real actually occurred. Also, what we call science fiction may actually represent a form of channeling directly from the universe. Writers of science fiction are mentally tapping into real quantum potentialities within Eternisphere. Material that gifted writers compose may represent prophecy that one day comes to pass. The match between Rolf Telano's channeled descriptions of circular craft with holes in the middle, other circular objects with a "bite" out of them, and etheric entities who glean energy from electromagnetic sources of various kinds is amazing, as Telano died in 1962, long before he could have seen these creatures, crafts, or whatever the objects are that appear in the NASA STS-75 (and other) video footage for himself. It appears that "channeling," the creation of science fiction, and the discoveries of science, are all related in some intimate way.

The Trent UFO Photos

On May 11, 1950, Evelyn Trent was feeding rabbits on her farm in McMinnville, Oregon. When she finished the feeding, she was walking back to her farmhouse when an object in the sky caught her attention. She looked up and watched as a slow-moving, metallic disk headed toward her from the northeast. Evelyn called out for her husband, Paul, who was inside their home, to get outside so he could also see the flying object. Paul came outside to see why Evelyn was yelling for him. When he saw the object, he immediately retreated back into the house, grabbed a camera, and came back outside. Paul managed to take two photos of the disk before it sped away to the west. Evelyn's father-in-law also saw the object before it vanished from view. After the object disappeared, and the thrill of the moment passed, the camera containing these photos of the strange object sat around the house for a while, as there was a time lag before the photos were actually developed. After the photos were developed, Paul was speaking casually to his local banker, Frank Wortmann, who took an interest in the sighting and the photos. Paul brought in the photos and gave them to Frank, who displayed them in the window of the bank. From there, Bill Powell, a local reporter, saw the photos and asked Paul to lend him the negatives. Examining the negatives, Powell found no evidence of tampering or fakery. Convinced of their authenticity, Powell then published the story and the photographs in the local newspaper, The *Telephone-Register*, with the headline, *At Long Last – Authentic Photographs of a Flying Saucer?*" From there the story spread like wildfire, being picked up by the INS, who sent it around the world. LIFE magazine published the photos on June 26, 1950. LIFE magazine promised to return the negatives to Paul Trent after publishing the story, but then stated that the negatives had been "lost." From that point, the negatives were assumed to be lost forever, but, as we shall see, they miraculously appear at a later date and are handed over to individuals determined to drive a wooden stake into the heart of public belief in UFOs (the infamous Condon Committee).

Samuel Eaton Thompson

Samuel Eaton Thompson was probably the first American contactee of the 1950s. However, Thompson was little-known during his lifetime. A retired railroad worker in his 70s, Thompson claimed that on the evening of March 28, 1950, while driving to his home in Centralia, Washington, he encountered an 80-foot-wide by 30-foot-tall flying saucer in the woods, complete with nicely-tanned naked humanoids, about 20 adults near the door of the craft, and 25 children playing near to or around the saucer. These friendly naked aliens were allegedly from Venus. They invited Samuel to spend the next 40 hours or so with them. They claimed to have been shot at by Earth's military, but decided to stay here for a visit anyway. These naked Venusians told Thompson that the main problem plaguing Earthlings was that we were all born under various astrological star- signs, whereas Venusians were all born under the sign of Venus. The Venusians were vegetarians, and all citizens of Venus were free from diseases. One strange detail about these Venusian visitors was that, according to Thompson, they did not appear to be the ones who actually built their flying saucer. They were naïve and childlike, and did not demonstrate even a trace of curiosity as to who built their spacecraft or how. This clan of Venusians revealed to Thompson that humans were destined to eventually adopt Venusian spirituality, and that Jesus would return to Earth in 10,000 AD. Thompson claimed that he tried to get a photograph of the Venusian ship, but the craft was so brilliant it only appeared as a blurry light on film. Pilot Kenneth Arnold, who took up UFO investigations after his sighting in 1947, conducted a personal interview with Samuel Eaton Thompson. Arnold's impression was that Thompson was telling the truth as he knew it, but had probably experienced some type of psychic or visionary phenomenon based on what Thompson had heard during his lifetime concerning UFO folklore and/or Bible stories. Arnold's assessment of Thompson's account was probably accurate, as many UFO experiences are psychic in nature, although they are decidedly not ordinary hallucinations. This does not discount Thompson's experience at all, or any other UFO experience, as the method of choice in communication between humans and Etherians does appear as psychic in nature. Many today wonder if even Arnold's sighting was of a similar psychic nature. It is interesting that Kenneth Arnold postulated this assessment about Thompson's encounter, but did not apply it to his own. This indicates that Arnold believed his sighting was solid and physical in nature, and maybe it was. However, we will never really know, providing that Arnold told the truth, if his sighting was a Horton Brothers flying wing; crecent-shaped crafts flown by cryptoterrestrials living undersea or underground; interdimensionals from a parallel world; robotic probes from parts unknown; or aliens dropping by Mt. Ranier who originated on another world.

Project Magnet

Inspired by the successful UFO books written by Frank Scully and Donald Keyhoe, Wilbert Smith, a senior Canadian radio engineer for the DOTs Broadcast and Measurement Section, became curious about the propulsion systems of the flying saucers. Even if Scully and Keyhoe's books were fiction presented as fact, Smith's work in the 1950s proves that even if a concept or belief such as flying saucers has no basis in reality, if it is accepted as fact by an intelligent person, the concept often inspires actual research that leads to something real and tangible. There are doubtless many cases of this over the years. To understand the flying saucer mystery, it is important to note that fictional concepts taken as fact have contributed to progressing human technologies. Whatever parts of the UFO saga are untrue have nonetheless provided a valid contributing factor in inspiring the human imagination and prompted real research that has lead to productive advancements toward the Singularity. In this manner, both fact and fiction have played their respective roles.

In September of 1950, Smith had the Canadian Embassy in Washington, D.C. arrange contact with US officials to discuss the reality of flying saucers. US physicist and consultant to the Defense Department Research and Development Board, Robert Sarbacher, briefed Wilbert Smith on what we actually knew about flying saucers. As a result of this meeting, Smith established *Project Magnet* as an unidentified flying object (UFO) study program conducted by the *Canadian Department of Transport* (DOT) under Smith's direction. Project Magnet was formally active until mid-1954, and informally until Smith's death in 1962. The ultimate goal of Project Magnet was to apply any findings on the subject of geomagnetism to the possibility of exploiting Earth's magnetic field as a source of propulsion for man-made flying saucers. Smith and his colleagues in government believed that the flying saucers might hold the key to this new source of power. Throughout the 1950s and 1960s, Wilbert Smith gave many public interviews in which he stated repeatedly that a highly clandestine UFO study group within the US government had provided him with samples of metals and other materials analysis, materials that had been determined as extraterrestrial in origin.

Commander Graham Bethune

On February 10, 1951, Navy Commander and pilot Graham Bethune, who had a Top Secret Clearance, was flying at night with his crew and 31 passengers from Iceland to Newfoundland, when he noticed an enormous glow on the surface of the water below that looked like the approach of a city. As Bethune's plane drew near, they observed that the glow was actually hundreds of individual lights on the water. Suddenly the lights went out completely for a while, then a small "yellow halo" shot up from the water. Fearing a collision, Commander Bethune disengaged the autopilot and steered underneath the object, which now appeared as a flying dome with a coronal discharge, and was flying alongside the plane. Bethune turned the plane over to his copilot and checked on the passengers, and he decided not to tell them what was going on for fear of panic. When Bethune returned to the cockpit, he and his copilot began experiencing several different instrument failures. The unknown craft began to speed ahead, and was tracked by radar in excess of 1800 mph. When they landed in Newfoundland, Bethune and his crew provided individual reports to the officer in charge, which are now compiled in a complete report called "UFO in the North Atlantic." This document is now collectible, and sells on Amazon for around $800.00 at the time of this writing.

[In May, 1951, "Operation Greenhouse" included the first boosted-fission test called "Item," and a scientific test which proved the feasibility of nuclear weapons, called "George," leaving a giant nuclear-bomb-induced crater in the pristine Enewetak Atoll of the Marshall Islands in the Pacific Ocean]

The Lubbock Lights

One evening in August, 1951, W.I. Robinson, A.G. Oberg, and W.L. Ducker, all professors from Texas Tech, were sitting outside talking together when, for two or three seconds, a V-shaped formation of mysterious lights, later known as the "Lubbock Lights," flew over their heads, leaving the professors in utter amazement. Now vigilant and looking skyward, the strange, bluish-green lights returned for the professors about an hour or so later. The professors, feeling that they were just witnesses to a grand mystery, proceeded to gather several other professors and professionals to join them in their search of the skies for the flying objects. Other interested parties included Grayson Meade, E.R. Heineman, and J.P Brand. This group of professors and associates equipped themselves with two-way radios and began conducting a serious stake-out, but the lights never returned for their observations. Meanwhile, unknown to the professors, another witness from Brownsfield, Texas, Joe Bryant, also reported seeing lights of a similar description. Bryant watched in amazement as one of the lights began chirping, revealing that the formation he saw was, in fact, just a flock of plover (a bird that is common in Texas). A reasonable conclusion from Bryant's account might be that the group of professors had wasted their time and mental energy on setting up equipment to watch for a UFO fly-over that was actually a flock of flying plover versus a formation of flying saucers. This conclusion is thwarted somewhat, however, by an enigmatic photograph of the Lubbock Lights that continues to remain controversial. On August 31, 1951, Carl Hart Jr. took an amazing photo of the mysterious lights as they flew over his house (his photograph is easily observed online).

Investigators were very hard on Carl in their interrogations of him, but Carl remained steadfast, giving logical answers to all their questions. The Lubbock Lights case was even investigated by Air Force personnel from Reece AFB in Lubbock, Texas. Copies of their reports were sent to Project Blue Book, and to Air Force Office of Special Investigations (AFOSI) headquarters in Washington, D.C.. Even First Lieutenant Edward Ruppelt, who was chief of Project Blue Book at the time, made a personal trip to interview both the professors and Carl Hart. Both Lieutenant Edward Ruppelt and AFOSI Special Agent Howard N. Bossert pounded Hart with threatening interrogation and found him credible. Hart maintained his story, that the photo was authentic, for the next 40 years. Even so, several mundane explanations have been proposed over the years for the Lubbock Lights sightings, everything from night-flying moths reflecting mercury-vapor street lights to the flock of plover story. The case remains in dispute to the present day. If Hart's photo is authentic, and represents a V-shaped craft of some kind flying over the area, it seems all-too-coincidental that a flock of light-reflecting plover observed by our scientific community would occur that same month. It is as if the flock of plover provided cover, a natural explanation that enough people would buy for the case to be dismissed while an enigmatic object that needed to come through the area incognito came and went without too much of a fuss. If this is the case, the Lubbock Lights case was not the only UFO incident that has occurred as some other mundane phenomenon happened simultaneously. In fact, this seems to be part of the modus operandi of the intelligences behind the flying saucers, as they know how desperate many humans are to pretend that there is nothing to see here.

The Fort Monmouth UFO Case

On the morning of Monday, September 10, 1951, at a radar facility near the coast of Fort Monmouth, New Jersey, PFC Eugent A. Clark picked up a fast-moving UFO on the radar scope as a group of visiting officers was coincidentally standing right behind him as witnesses. The UFO was moving at approximately 700 miles per hour, and was lost off the scope near the Sandy Hook coastal peninsula just south of New York City. No jet in 1951 flew at such a speed. Seventeen minutes later, a T-22 jet trainer traveling at 20,000 feet altitude over Point Pleasant, New Jersey, toward Sandy Hook, piloted by Lieutenant Wilbert S. Rogers, an experienced WW2 pilot, with Major Edward Ballard Jr. behind him in the rear seat, reported a totally unrecognizable flying object. Their conversation was heard via open mike, reporting a round, disk-like object with a raised center at about 12,000 feet below them, traveling at high speed. Coincidental to the sighting, balloons had been launched that morning from the Evans Signal Laboratory, New Jersey, which gave investigators a good excuse to label the sighting as a balloon. However, Rogers and Ballard stated there was no way in hell that what they saw was a balloon. Balloons do not travel through the air at 700 miles per hour, nor can they descend rapidly as this object did. Reports of the balloons also placed them at 18,000 feet altitude at the time of their sighting from the aircraft, bursting at 104,000 feet not long after the sighting, versus the 5,000 feet that the object Rogers and Ballard witnessed traveling below their own flight position. So, reminiscent of the Lubbock Lights encounter, where a plausible explanation involving a flock of plover provided cover for an actual craft that was captured on film by Carl Hart, Jr., the Fort Monmouth sighting may represent yet another case in which a daylight disk, a flying saucer, traveling at high speed and captured by multiple witnesses on radar, is written off with a mundane explanation. This reported flying disk, traveling at high speed, was seen in broad daylight by two experienced aircraft personnel, including an experienced WW2 pilot. However, the Monmouth case is dismissed by many ufologists today as a simple balloon sighting. As in the Lubbock Lights case, in which a flock of plover appeared coincidentally to an actual craft fly-over, a flying disk was witnessed by trained observers in the Fort Monmouth case on the same day that balloons were also launched, providing plausible deniability and cover for the presence of the disk as the object sped by at high speed in visible mode. These types of coincidences are common in the documentation of UFO sightings. Nick Pope, former UFO investigator for the MOD in England revealed a case in his book, *Open Skies, Closed Minds,* in which an actual UFO, a black triangle similar to the ones reported in the UFO waves in Belgium, made a fantastic appearance on March 30 and 31, 1993, a couple of days before it hit the local newspapers on April Fool's Day of that year. Because this black triangle appeared coincidental to April Fool's Day, no one paid much attention to this real UFO event. It happens all the time. UFOs are commonly witnessed coincidental to mundane events, providing cover for their activities. Nick Pope writes (page 141):

> *Newspaper reports of incidents occurring that night would run on 1 April, the day when every national and many provincial papers carry an April Fool's story. Who was going to take these stories seriously? The public at large just smiled wryly over their breakfast cereal. Isn't this exactly the reaction an alien force might hope to achieve by capitalizing on a time when the world is unreceptive, when everyone expects bizarre stories and dismisses them out of hand? It was absolutely the best date to choose to minimize the risk that any sightings might be taken seriously.*

Why the Charade?

Many UFO investigators have remained bewildered throughout decades of personal research as to the actual purpose of the UFOs. The intelligences behind the Phenomenon, who have appeared to humans as both benign and malevolent over the years, have a purpose that has required secrecy. Thus far, this secret agenda has been covered up by both human and nonhuman agencies, such as the USAF, clandestine UFO research organizations, and the enigmatic MIB. These agencies, I believe, have been protecting an agenda that involves the achievement of a technological singularity. Hopefully, the technology of the Singularity will finally allow open contact with our benevolent friends, the Friendship (W56) Groups, the Great White Brotherhood, or whatever name one chooses to refer to the faction of UFO intelligences that care about humanity. The technology of the Singularity will expand our minds and our sensory apparatus, and will finally allow us to view our alien friends as they really are versus the human projections that they may be creating for our benefit. We will need the assistance of the Friendship Group as they protect us from the goals of the biological robots they have warned us about, which are called the "Contraries" (CTRs) or "Weiros" (a word that means "to have been built" in the language of the W56 group) as this group of humanoid machine intelligences may attempt to seize upon our technology for their own purposes. The Contraries (CTRs) have little to do with benefiting humanity, as they worship technology. We will need the help of our cosmic friends to assist us through this tumulus period of time ahead. The clandestine groups of humans among us, the secret societies, who have been interacting with extraterrestrial groups for the acquisition of secret technology, may make a move to dominate our planet and lord over the rest of us as augmented human leaders. Black mentalists on the lower astral plane, the same entities that occasionally attempt to enter our three dimensional world via what we would call "possession" may attempt to hijack our artificial intelligence to gain permanent entrance into the world and exterminate the human race. Groups of benevolent humans may seek a permanent download of their consciousness into a robotic format in order to escape the need for further incarnations and achieve immortality, transcendence from human biology. Entities who are no longer allowed to incarnate may also seek to break the cosmic rules and download their consciousness as a permanent existence in the physical universe. The Singularity and the possibilities it will bring will attract a multitude of entities with various motives. It will certainly be an interesting time when many hidden truths will suddenly be thrust upon us whether we are ready for them or not. The intelligences behind the UFOs, who have needed to remain hidden for the last century or so, know human psychology well. They understand that humans would rather believe anything other than what is really going on, as the truth is very difficult to wrap our minds around. It involves advanced intelligences who have plans that escape us. The UFO phenomenon remains a cosmic magic show in which we, the audience, are very easily distracted and fooled by what the magicians are actually doing.

US Soldier in Austria, 1951

On December 11, 1957, a Canadian newspaper called the *Prince George Citizen*, in British Columbia, Canada, printed a story by a US Army soldier who insisted on maintaining his anonymity. The soldier told a journalist for the paper a harrowing experience that he had while in Salzburg, Austria, on the night of May 15, 1951 at 11:20 p.m. and extending into the following day on May 16. Based on multiple details that coordinate with many other close encounter accounts, credibility can be granted to what the soldier revealed. According to the soldier, as he was on his way home that night, a humanoid entity moved into view from behind some bushes and pointed a long, thin, pencil-like device at him, and he was instantly paralyzed. While immobilized by the device, he observed the entity as about 5 feet tall wearing a transparent, near-spherical helmet, and a two-piece suit with tight-fitting legs that merged into the toes. The body appeared to be rigid and cylindrical, with a round torso like a tin can. The entity had no neck, proportionate legs, and short arms ending in long and graceful 3 or 4-fingered hands. Its cranium was also slightly cylindrical, high, bald, with a white skull extending up and back from a wide, heart-shaped face. The creature's eyes were large and compound like the eyes of an insect. It had only holes for ears, two holes for a nose, and its mouth was a very small horizontal slit. The entity never spoke or communicated while strapping a black and square device to the soldier's chest. This made the soldier virtually weightless, and he was pulled towards a 150-foot-diameter disk-shaped craft that was landed in a nearby field. He and the entity floated together up to the top of the disk. A hatch opened, and they entered a transparent room. Inside, the soldier watched through the transparent walls of the saucer (reminiscent of Daniel Fry's account) as the earth floated away into the distance. The soldier and the entity flipped over as they reached the "zone of gravitational neutrality between Earth and the Moon." They continued past the Moon and on to Mars, where they quickly arrived and landed on a raised platform. The entity left the craft, and the soldier said he saw fields of big red flowers, canals with bridges across them, and other saucers with human captives. The entity returned and the saucer took off. They passed a Martian satellite that looked like a "tin ball." Ten minutes later they were approaching Earth. Once returned on ground, the square black device was strapped to the soldier's chest again, and he was floated to the ground. The entity pointed the pencil-like device to the soldier's head. A dog barked and frightened the entity. No loss of memory followed. The whole episode had taken about an hour. The journalist who wrote the article said he tried on several occasions to trick the soldier into contradicting himself. No contradictions were found, and the reporter expressed that he was greatly impressed by his apparent truthfulness.

Serious researchers of the Phenomenon encounter thousands of such UFO accounts within the literature. Many of the reports correlate with one another and have common features. The exact nature of these experiences is unknown. Several theories exist other than the Extraterrestrial Hypothesis (ETH) involving everything from psychic experiences and hallucinations to interactions between poorly-understood geophysical forces and human consciousness. It is often difficult to ascertain the physical reality of such experiences due to a paucity of physical evidence. It is also disingenuous to simply write UFO experiences off as mere hallucinations. Cases of actual hallucinosis are too rare to account for the multitude of such reports. Also, hallucinations do not produce a condition of PTSD as so many flying saucer experiencers exhibit. Although outright hoaxes do exist, one can conclude with confidence that most of the UFO experiencers are reporting the truth as they understand it. If these types of exotic UFO experiences do not lie in what we call ordinary reality, and they do not represent hallucinations as we understand them, then we are left with the disturbing prospect that some sort of mind-manipulating technology is involved, as in advanced psychotronic equipment utilized by an unknown population here on Earth, human or otherwise, that can produce the illusion of traveling to other planets, an illusion so real that it is indistinguishable from reality as we know it.

Flying Saucer Disease?

Is becoming a chronic flying saucer percipient a disease that humans can catch? One man from the 1950s, Harrison Baily, sincerely thought so. Harrison Baily was a young, 24-year-old, physically-fit steelworker who had come up with a unique idea for extra cash. He painted a giant tractor wheel green, wore matching green coveralls and goggles, and rolled the tire with advertising on it for businesses. This successfully attracted attention for the businesses he advertised for and generated new customers. Working for Bill Veeck and the St. Louis Browns baseball team, Baily was hired to roll the giant tire with a sign that read, "LET'S COME THRU IN '52 – ST. LOUIS BROWNS." Baily was going to roll the tire from Gary to Chicago, and then down to St. Louis. As Baily rolled the tire down Illinois Highway 7, Baily saw what he described as a gray whirlwind through his goggles. He felt a sharp prick, a spasm in his neck. Continuing to 143rd St., Baily observed a landed gray, disk-shaped object, larger than an automobile, with a ramp leading up to it. A door opened and two beings with transparent face shields walked down the ramp. One of the creatures asked Baily where he was going. Baily told them and rolled the tire away from them, thinking that they were operating a Russian spy ship involved in the Korean War, and that the US government was probably well aware of them. Feeling nauseous and cramped, Baily stopped in at a small railroad station in one of the towns on his journey. He stayed there overnight, and took up his route again the next morning. Baily decided to keep his weird encounter to himself, as he feared ridicule and the possibility of losing his regular job. Baily kept the story to himself for the next 11 years, until he found himself in the Hines Veterans Hospital near Maywood following gall bladder surgery. He was shocked when the surgeons informed him that his internal organs looked like someone twice his age, and assumed that the organs had deteriorated from hard living or drinking. This made no sense to Baily, as this was not the case. During his recovery from surgery, Baily was visited by entities who assigned him with a mission - that of informing the American People that otherworldly beings were here among us, and meant us no harm. Baily decided to begin advertising that important message with his giant green tractor tire. Baily retired from his regular job as a steelworker and became a Baptist minister. He moved to Pasadena, California, and ministered a church there, spreading the Word of God and the message of the saucer people. Later, in 1975, Harrison Baily met UFO researcher Ann Druffel while on a Los Angeles talk show. Druffel befriended Baily, and encouraged him to begin documenting his encounters with the creatures. Druffel outfitted Baily with a camera. Over the next several years, Baily was paid multiple visits by these creatures from another realm. The creatures implored Baily to continue spreading the word that otherworldy beings were here and that they meant no harm to Americans. On November 1, 1978, during Baily's last encounter, he managed to snap multiple photographs of the visit, one of which made its way into Ann Druffel's book, *How to Defend Yourself Against Alien Abduction* (1998). To his death, Harrison Baily maintained the validity of his encounters, and was believed by all who knew him.

UFOs Around the World

If sightings and contacts were isolated to the United States alone, one might be tempted to conclude that UFOs are simply a cultural phenomenon limited to the fertile American imagination. However, based on the fact that it is global and affects all walks of life, this is certainly not the case. As revealed in Leslie Kean's *New York Times* best-seller, *UFOs: Generals, Pilots, and Government Officials Go on Record*, many UFO encounters have occurred around the world and are reported by credible individuals who have no reason to lie, are completely sane, and are often professionally-trained observers. One area of the world that experienced waves of UFO landing and occupant cases is France. Based on these numerous accounts, the French developed the following classification system in 1951:

> *Type A: The phenomenon is fully and unambiguously identified*
>
> *Type B: The nature of the phenomenon has probably been identified but some doubts remain.*
>
> *Type C: The phenomenon cannot be identified or classified due to insufficient information*
>
> *Type D: The phenomenon cannot be explained despite precise witness accounts and good-quality evidence recovered from the scene.*

The Science Fiction Factor

Popular fiction of a given era is but a reflection of ideas that are already floating around in the collective consciousness of the day. In 1951, four years after the term "flying saucer" was originally inspired by Kenneth Arnold's sighting, spaceman *Klaatu* and his intergalactic policeman/robot, *Gort*, entered our minds in a powerful film that represented the Phenomenon quite well called *The Day the Earth Stood Still*. In this intriguing black & white film classic, the humanoid occupant of a landed flying saucer, Klaatu, arrives with his mighty robot, Gort, on a Cold-War-era Earth just after the end of World War II. In this brilliant film, Klaatu and his robot bring an important message to Earth. Together they wished to impart a message to the representatives of all nations involved with the development of nuclear weapons concerning the terrible fate that was in store for Planet Earth if we extended our military endeavors into space. These weapons were not only a danger to us, but to other galactic civilizations as well. The civilization Klaatu was representing had turned over all security to a race of intelligent police robots that were given absolute power to incinerate any display of aggression throughout the cosmos.

> *[In May, 1951, two nuclear tests, "Item" and "George," were detonated]*

As *The Day the Earth Stood Still* entertained audiences in the United States, the two nuclear tests *Item* and *George* were detonated, followed by a massive wave of UFO sightings in 1952. These sightings included radar tracking and multiple, credible eyewitness accounts. The objects were sighted, chased, and tracked all over the world, including the United States; Canada; Korea;

Japan; Iceland; Cyprus; and China. Hundreds of flying saucer sightings were reported, enough to fill an entire volume with incident after incident during the entire year. These sightings included: elliptical crafts with bright body-lights; bluish-white spherical crafts with long blue tails; dome-shaped circular white craft traveling at high speeds away from dispatched jets; 3-foot diameter orange spheres with blue halos chasing airplanes; green fireballs; red fireballs; groups of spherical silver saucers flying in "V" formations; amber disks; white delta-shaped crafts; blue and silver cylinders with rapidly pulsating tails; cigar-shaped crafts; bright red and/or flame-colored circular flying objects; self-luminous objects and silver disks rising from the sea; shining, orange, spherical crafts; multitudes of silver metallic saucer-like crafts; oval-shaped crafts flying in diamond formations that wobbled in flight; orange balls with tails; grey metallic disks in half-moon flying formations; bullet-shaped objects with burnt-orange exhaust trails; crescent-shaped objects that hovered and sped away; black coin-shaped objects 15-20 feet in diameter making irregular descents; objects that appeared as soap-bubbles shimmering from inside with various colors; round metallic disks that fluttered like flipped coins; bright yellow-white egg-shaped objects with red tails; dark blue elliptical objects with lighted borders flying at over 800 mph; black barrel-shaped objects emitting smoke; red lights hovering, spinning, and maneuvering; clusters of white glowing objects; and shapeshifting yellow balls that lengthened into disks and flew away at high speed. The fact that two powerful nuclear devices were detonated simultaneous to the release of *The Day the Earth Stood Still*, unleashing giant waves of UFOs in the 1950s that were reported by massive numbers of credible witnesses, oftentimes with radar confirmation, is beyond bizzare, and possibly confirms a symbiotic relationship between fact and fiction when it comes to flying saucers.   On March 2, 1952, a former German rocket scientist at Peenemunde, Dr. Walther Riedel, became convinced, based on the incredible number of credible sightings, that the flying saucers were real. Dr. Riedel stated in the April 7, 1952 issue of LIFE magazine:

> *I'm convinced saucers have an out-of-world basis.*

In response to this onslaught of flying saucer sightings, *Project Blue Book* was established on March 25, 1952.

A Sighting in Germany

On July 9, 1952, in Hasselbach, Germany, Oscar Lincke, the former mayor of Gleimershausen, West Berlin, and his 11-year-old daughter Gabriella, provided eyewitness testimony to the landing and take-off of a 50-foot diameter flying disk. They described the disk as an upside-down frying pan that landed in a wooded area of the Soviet Zone in Germany. Oscar and Gabriella were driving through the town of Hasselbach together on their motorcycle when a tire suddenly blew out. It was getting dark, so they started walking back toward town. As they were walking, they detected movement in the woods. Thinking that they might have spotted a deer, Oscar and Gabriella walked closer to get a good look. Their curiosity turned to fear, and they became emotionally paralyzed by what they saw. They witnessed two humanoid men in shiny metallic suits bending over toward the ground beside the landed disk. Oscar described the craft as having a row of 1-foot diameter portholes around the perimeter, and a cylindrical tower in the middle. One of the men had a "lamp" on the front of his suit that blinked on and off at regular intervals. When the two ufonauts detected the presence of Oscar and Gabriella, they quickly scrambled up onto the disk and disappeared down the protruding tower. The portholes around the perimeter began to shimmer. The craft then began to hum and spin as the tower in the middle retracted from the top and appeared to pass down through the center, reemerging from the bottom and lifting the craft from the ground. A ring of flames appeared around the craft's perimeter as it emitted a loud whistling sound like a bomb landing. The disk rose into the air while the middle section moved back up through the craft and reemerged from the upper section as it was when they first saw it. The craft then rapidly gained altitude and speed, and vanished into the sky. A local shepherd, along with multiple residents of Hasselbach, reported seeing a "comet" streak across the sky that same day. Oscar submitted his testimony to a local judge, confessing that he and his daughter were both afraid that they were in imminent danger for witnessing a secret Soviet craft of some sort. The event was so strange and traumatizing, Oscar admitted that he thought maybe he and Gabriella had experienced some kind of anomalous daytime dream. However, after the craft vanished, Oscar and Gabriella walked over to where the craft was resting prior to take-off. There they were able to examine impressions in the ground where the craft was stationed. Only then did they realize for sure that it was, in fact, a material object, and that what they had just experienced was very real. Since Oscar and Gabriella's encounter, and before, thousands of such UFO landing-and-occupant reports have been documented. In 1954 alone, France was inundated by reports of flying saucer landings and ufonaut encounters, so many that French researcher Aime Michel plotted the reports on maps and found straight-line patterns, indicating the existence of a real phenomenon and not something delusional or fabricated. Likewise, paranormal author Hanz Holzer investigated such reports and professed his own conviction in his book, *The Ufonauts*, that real flesh-and-blood beings from other worlds were visiting Earth, as opposed to the ufonauts representing psychic manifestations of some kind.

The Nash and Fortenberry Sighting

On July 14, 1952, Captain Kepke was flying a Pan American DC-4 at an altitude of 8,000 feet with 10 passengers onboard on a routine flight from New York to Miami. Flying with Captain Kepke in the cockpit was First Officer William B. Nash and Second Officer William H. Fortenberry. On this crystal clear dark night at about 8:10 p.m., Nash and Fortenberry suddenly saw six bright objects flying at high speed and glowing like hot coals coming up toward them from below. Dispelling any notion that what they were observing was anything produced by Nature, the first object slowed down as the others seemed to keep on going. At the last minute, the second object slowed as if to avoid a collision. The glowing disks behind the second followed suit, indicating that the objects were under intelligent control. The objects looked like coins with edges about 15-feet thick. As these "flying coins" sped under the plane and up to their right like tracer bullets, they suddenly turned on their edges. As Nash and Fortenberry watched in amazement, the five that were trailing the leader passed ahead and fell into position ahead of the first, completely reversing their order. The six craft then dimmed slightly as they made a sharp angular turn like a ball ricocheting from a wall, then lit back up as they maintained speed in a different direction. Two more identical objects flew underneath the plane from behind and joined the first group, these two glowing brighter than the original six as if applying energy to catch up to the rest, now forming a line of 8 glowing objects moving at high speed. The objects began blinking on and off as they made a smooth arc straight up into the air. Nash's description of the object's movement is similar to Kenneth Arnold's description of the crescent-shaped crafts he witnessed in 1947, like "saucers skipping across water," only the objects that Nash and Fortenberry saw were coin-shaped, and flew straight up and disappeared. Nash wrote (ufoevidence.org):

As they climbed, they oscillated up and down behind one another in an irregular fashion, as though they were extremely sensitive to control. In doing this, they went vertically past one another, as the initial six approached us. This appeared to be an intelligence error 'lousing up the formation' — they disappeared by blinking out in a mixed-up formation, in no particular order. We stared after them, dumbfounded and probably open-mouthed. We looked around the sky, half expecting something else to appear, though nothing did. There were flying saucers, and we had seen them.

Nash and Fortenberry were fortunate enough to witness firsthand confirmation that flying saucers are real. This certainty is one of the greatest gifts one can receive in this life. Without the personal sighting, people who research UFOs are left on their own to discern which sightings are credible and which are not. When I began my own journey into the world of flying saucers, I kept reminding myself in the face of public disbelief and even occasional ridicule that anecdotal evidence, photographs, and trace evidence should be enough to determine the reality of a phenomenon. Exactly what the flying saucers are and whether they have biological or robotic pilots onboard is open for educated guessing. However, there is enough evidence from the UFO reports themselves to reasonably conclude that the saucers are real. Accepting the reality of a phenomenon based on good eyewitness testimony, scientific instruments, and trace evidence is commonly accepted for every other subject in the world other than flying saucers. Just going that far, to accept within one's own mind that at least some flying saucers are real, that so many credible people cannot possibly all be delusional or lying, is a big step. Much of the public at large assume that people who accept flying saucers as real and talk about them are gullible, irrational, stupid, or all of the above. This public skepticism, which occasionally borders on hostility or overt ridicule, can sometimes make those of us who have accepted the reality of flying saucers through personal research suspect that maybe we have imbibed a little too much of the flying-saucer Kool-Aid. Those who have not had a direct personal experience with flying saucers are relying on the stability of their own intellect and information-gathering ability to make a determination of truth. However, just as my own NDE demonstrated to me that there are, in fact, dimensions of experience beyond the physical world, and that life continues beyond the grave, Nash and Fortenberry knew after their experience that flying saucers, whatever they are, are real and not imaginary. When one has a personal experience like the one Nash and Fortenberry had that evening, it becomes known for sure that flying saucers are real. There is, in fact, something out there in our skies that was not built by human hands, an alien intelligence that is real and not fiction. When this point of certainty is achieved, all the public skepticism then fades into the background, with a residual feeling of pity toward their smirking, know-it-all faces as they dismiss the idea of flying saucers as pure fantasy, or claim that their scientific minds just cannot accept that the flying saucers are real. It doesn't matter anymore, because now you know, and they do not. The unbelievers remain stuck in the illusion that their skepticism makes them smarter than those who believe, that they are more rational, and less naïve. That's okay, because when our intelligence is finally electronically-augmented to enable us to finally perceive the flying saucers and their occupants for who or what they really are, everyone will finally know what many of us have already ascertained by reading and studying independently – that the Phenomenon is real. It will be a great day of intellectual vindication, and some apologies will surely be in order. I, for one, am looking forward to seeing the looks on some people's faces when the reality of flying saucers and the alien presence is known to all. On that day it will be the people who failed to do their homework, the so-called scientific rationalists, those who have erroneously assumed that their understanding of reality is superior to those of us who have accepted the reality and existence of the alien presence on Earth, who are forced to eat crow.

Flying Saucers Over the White House

UFO skeptics love to ask, "If UFOs and extraterrestrials are real, then why don't they just land on the White House lawn?" This smug statement of disbelief only serves as an indication of their blatant ignorance of actual UFO history. One such verifiable incident in UFO history occurred on the weekends of July 19/20 and July 26/27, 1952, only a week or so after Nash and Fortenberry realized with certainty by their sighting that flying saucers are, in fact, real. On these two weekends in a row, a well-documented formation of flying saucers, witnessed by hundreds of civilians and military personnel, may have intended to do just that, to land on the White House lawn and deliver the mass alien landing that we all yearn to witness.

Unfortunately, instead of welcoming our visitors with open arms, jets with shoot-to-kill orders were dispatched under President Harry S. Truman. On July 22, 1952, the *New York Times* printed the headline, *Flying Object Near Washington Spotted by Both Pilots and Radar.* Likewise, the *Washington Post* ran the headline, *Saucer Outran Jet – Pilot Reveals.* President Harry S. Truman was the first president in history who was forced to deal with flying saucers publicly. Maybe the craft were going to land, and maybe they weren't. However, if I had been the Commander leading this 1952 craft procession with intentions of landing to openly greet the leadership and the people of Planet Earth, and I saw flying Earth-craft (jets) coming at us with apparent intent to shoot us out of the sky, I would have aborted the mission and kept on moving to a more intelligent planet whose inhabitants were more peaceful and receptive to our visit. We may have missed the chance of the century to experience that elusive "White House lawn landing" that UFO skeptics need to happen to accept the reality of ETs. Had we not respond in a hostile manner, and allowed these crafts to land, this would have confirmed once and for all to everyone on Earth that alien civilizations from other worlds in our own physical universe or life in a parallel universe does, in fact, exist.

Donald Keyhoe revealed in his 1979 book, *Aliens from Space,* that in 1953, shortly after the flyby at the White House in 1952, two gigantic unknown objects were detected on Air Force radar. One of the unknown objects was located at 600 miles above the earth and orbiting near the equator at 18,000 miles per hour. Another unknown object was located at 400 miles out. Donald Keyhoe's statements concerning these objects are discussed in the book, *Alien Agenda,* by UFO researcher Jim Marrs. Marrs wrote:

> *Keyhoe's story of the detection of two giant satellites was supported by investigative journalist Warren Smith, who stated that a CIA source told him that huge unidentified satellites were picked up on at least thirteen separate occasions in 1953.*

Also, in author Andrew Colvin's collection of John Keel's early writings on UFOs, called *Searching for the String,* Keel wrote (audible, chapter 2):

> *After Dr. Lincoln LaPaz of the University of New Mexico cited an unknown object orbiting the earth in 1953, the US Army assigned Dr. Clyde W. Tombaugh to conduct a search for it. Dr. Tombaugh is the astronomer who discovered the planet Pluto in 1930. Although the results of his study of "mystery satellites" have been buried in Pentagon red tape, it is known that he discovered three of the things up there, but little was heard about them.*

Were the radar-confirmed crafts discovered in orbit in 1953 giant motherships that traveled vast distances through outer space to make contact with us? Were they home vessels for the fleet of smaller crafts that flew over the White House in July, 1952, and the origin of hundreds of other flying saucer sightings around the world during the early 1950s? If so, we didn't exactly roll out the welcome mat for them by dispatching fighter jets with shoot-to-kill orders. Dr. Clyde Tombaugh, one of the few scientists from this era who openly reported a personal UFO sighting, was placed in charge of an emergency satellite detection system in White Sands, New Mexico. Dr. Tombaugh's flying saucer sighting occurred just a few days after the Roswell Crash, and a just a couple of weeks after the Kenneth Arnold sighting. Just four days prior to the White House flyby event of 1952, a Navy Chief Warrant Officer, Delbert C. Newhouse, and his wife, also witnessed a group of a dozen or more bright fireball-like UFOs maneuvering under some sort of intelligent control on July 15, 1952, while driving just north of Salt Lake City, Utah. Also, in March, 1952, (Keyhoe originally reported April, but this date was later corrected to March), Secretary of the Navy Dan Kimball witnessed two disk-shaped craft while flying in Hawaii. Traveling at an estimated speed of 1500 MPH, the two saucers flew in close and circled both Kimball's plane, and also circled another plane with Admiral Arthur Radford onboard. Unfortunately, we will probably never know if the saucers in all three of these incidents shared the same origin. If so, maybe the craft that circled Kimball were checking the situation out ahead of time to see if we were hostile. They may have reported back to their group, who then decided to come to the White House, only to be greeted by jets screaming toward them with hostile intent. Maybe part of the reason we haven't seen flying saucers land on the White House lawn is due to our violent and aggressive policy toward incoming visitors. Winston Churchill, who was concerned about the 1912 airship wave in his land, who was now Prime Minister, became aware of the 1952 Washington D.C. flyby, and wrote a letter to his Air Ministry addressed to Lord Cherwell, seeking an explanation for why his concerns were not taken more seriously 40 years previous, as the Phenomenon was apparently still around and now mystifying the Americans.

[Following the appearance of flying saucers at the White House, the nuclear test, "Ivy Mike" was detonated on November 1, 1952 in the Marshall Islands. This was the first full test of the "Teller-Ulam" design staged hydrogen bomb. It was not a deployable weapon, weighing in at 82 tons]

Suzanne Knight and William Squyres

One month after the Washington D.C. flyover, on a summer night in August, 1952, about 9:30 p.m., a young housewife and mother, Mrs. Suzanne E. Knight from Seat Pleasant, Maryland, was in her kitchen when she heard a sound like the buzzing of bees coming from the screened kitchen window. Thinking it was an insect, Suzanne went to the window, where she saw a bright object coming down swiftly at a 45 degree angle. As in many other sightings, her first impression was that it was an airplane about to crash. However, as the flying object slowed to a hover in mid-air at about 300 feet above the ground a half block away from her, she could make out a discernible image. The object looked like the side of an aircraft fuselage, dull silver, with smoke coming from one end. Inside was a yellow light emanating from a square row of windows, and a row of what looked like cabinets with slanted tops. On the top and to her left was a red light extending out from the body of the craft. The bottom of the craft looked like the bottom of a dirigible, a gondola, with another row of square windows and a brilliant yellow light inside. In this lower portion Suzanne observed what looked like rows of theater seats. Through the first window from the front of the craft she observed a helmeted humanoid figure staring intently out the window and to the front of the craft. The man looked yellow due to the intense yellow light inside. Suzanne left the kitchen window after watching for a minute to call the newspaper but couldn't get through. The craft was still there when she returned but the man was gone along with the undercarriage, which she assumed had retracted up into the main body. As she watched the lights suddenly go dark, the craft began to glow reddish like a burning ember. The craft then began to waft two and fro toward and away from Suzanne as she observed a "heat wave" effect emanating from the body of the craft. Suzanne called for her sister to come see what she saw, but by the time her sister arrived, the craft was gone. Suzanne began telling her sister what she had just witnessed. She could tell that her sister was skeptical, so she omitted the part about seeing an occupant, fearing that her sister would think she was crazy. She decided to drop the whole subject. Suzzane kept the sighting to herself for a number of years, but finally told her husband and children. Suzanne finally mustered the courage to make a full report to NICAP 15 years later. In the NICAP files are hundreds of reports very similar to Suzanne's. The sound of buzzing like bees is a common feature. The sighting itself is reminiscent of the airship sightings of 1897, which leads to an interesting question. That is, why, when the imagery of the UFOs had already morphed from the airships of 1897 to a more classic type of flying disk, was Suzanne bestowed with a more "primitive" version of a flying craft, that of a dirigible-type airship? If the UFO intelligences scan the human mind for imagery to produce, why was the dirigible model in Suzanne's head, and not a more modern craft? Could it be that the human mind develops in stages from simple to complex, and any person in any time can represent any of these stages? In other words, maybe Suzanne still had the mentality of someone living 55 years previous and was simple in her thinking and technical concepts. Perhaps all witnesses of similar mentality would receive the dirigible sighting verses something more complex. One other puzzling detail about this case is that if I were to go to the window and see something that unusual, I think I would try to communicate with any other persons in the house immediately to get them in on the sightings. The last thing I would want is to be stuck with a memory of something that unusual that I know for a fact actually happened, only to be faced with disbelief from friends and loved ones. So, the fact that she waited, even until after she attempted a phone call to the newspaper and couldn't get ahold of anyone to call her sister into the scenario is a bit bewildering. The validity of this case stands on the fact that so many around the world see this type of an event. The paraphysical technology that some of the UFO intelligences use to create a sighting appears to have the ability to quickly assess the human state of mind and produce the appropriate version of craft, according to his or her mental stage of development. Whether the sighting was exactly what it appeared to be, or an image in Suzanne's mind that provided camouflage for what was actually there, i.e., an alien presence of a more exotic or even frightening appearance, is unknown. However, judging by the sheer volume of such sightings, the presence of something real on Earth that is truly alien can be confidently ascertained.

A similar sighting to Suzanne Knight's occurred during the same month and year of August, 1952, in Pittsburg, Kansas. William Squyres was a musician who also worked at KOAM radio in Pittsburg. The Squyres sighting was on the morning of August 25, 1952, at about 5:30 a.m. As Squyres was making his morning commute to work about 7 miles northeast of Pittsburg, he spotted a low-hovering craft in a heavily-wooded area with clearly defined windows, just as with Suzanne Knight's case. The object appeared as two turtle shells or meat platters put together. It was about 75 feet long, 45 feet wide, and 25 feet high, rocking back and forth like a boat as it hovered over a field near the highway. Around the rim were little high-speed propellers 6 to 12 inches in diameter. Across the top and down to the rim of the sides were rows of rect-angular windows with a blue light fluctuating from dark to light inside. Most of the windows were opaque. Squyres could barely see through the windows, just enough to see that there was activity going on inside the craft. The most forward window was clear. As in Knight's sight-ing, a man was seen looking forward as if intensely piloting the unusual dirigible-like flying machine. Squyres reported that the hair stood straight up on the back of his head as he watched the strange craft. He stopped his car and got out, carefully walking toward the craft. When Squyres approached to about 100 feet, the craft took off as if it were startled. It sounded like a *flock of birds* when it lifted off, blowing the ground below with the propellers. It's almost as if the aliens selected the wrong sound effect for the situation. From all appearances, Squyres felt that this was a craft constructed and piloted by humans, just as in the 1897 airship encounters. This case was investigated by both radio station personnel and Air Force investigators, who found the witness of good reliability. The Squyres case was officially recorded in Project Blue Book.

Both William Squyres and Suzanne Knight reported "steampunk-style" dirigible sightings. Were these two individuals of similar mentality to produce similar imagery in their sighting? Were the intelligences that produced the Knight and Squyres cases one and the same? Maybe the alien intelligences involved in these two cases were using an old paraphysical program that had not had its imagery updated, and were using imagery from the human mental field of 1897, versus 1952. Whatever the case, it is a wonder that Air Force officials in charge of UFO inves-tigations in this era didn't go mad chasing all these sightings down. Sometimes skeptics say that there is just too much variation in the descriptions of the craft for the experiences to be real. Skeptics say that it is just not feasible that all these various kinds of odd flying machines would actually be flying around. This is a good observation. However, since the flying saucer and oc-cupant images are likely derived from some sort of mind scan, and since the UFO intelligences that produce such experiences use either holographic projections or transmogrified energy that produce temporary physical objects based on a witness' internal mindset, there should be as many flying saucer configurations as there are human minds. Actually, it is remarkable that there is any consistency in the images at all. Air Force investigators were completely dumfounded by the volume of UFO reports. It is understandable why, by 1968, they were sick of chasing the elusive flying saucers around the globe, and wanted to get out of UFO investigations altogether. Since chasing UFOs is similar to chasing subjective reports of ghosts, both of which may be a product of the witness' mind in some fashion, there isn't much to be gained from UFO reports, except maybe data on the witnesses and the locations of window areas and flaps. Chasing ghosts, which has become quite a popular hobby now, and chasing UFOs is about as productive and satisfying as chasing lightning strikes. Ghost and UFO sightings are both phenomena that spontaneously come and go. They are here, and then they are gone. Any investigator that chases after UFO sightings might as well be chasing reports of dreams and recording them, because in many ways, UFO encounters and dreams are very similar. As Keel wrote, "Flying saucers are but marvelous phantasms." Even so, while Project Blue Book was busy chasing these marvelous phantasms, another private group was forming at this time as well. In 1952, a husband-and-wife team, Jim and Coral Lorenzen, established the Aerial Phenomenon Research Organization (APRO). The team began work as a private investigations unit to discover just what the flying saucers were, and who was piloting them.

The Council of 9

Following the establishment of APRO by Jim and Coral Lorenzen in 1952, another group of individuals who would exert great influence on modern ufology were busy as well. A group of psychic investigators known as the *Council of 9* included members from the wealthiest families in the world. The Council of 9 originally met in a farmhouse in Maine for a séance conducted by Captain Andrija Puharich of the US Army, who specialized in chemical and biological warfare. Puharich was also an inventor, a scientist, and a doctor. He was heavily involved with the endeavor to "weaponize" paranormal abilities, and became associated with the famous psychic, Uri Geller. Geller, like Nikola Tesla, believed that he was in direct telepathic contact with extraterrestrials. Uri Geller eventually broke off his association with Puharich when he discovered that Puharich was an intelligence agent, fearing that Puharich was attempting to manipulate him. This leads to the possibility that Uri Geller was used by Puharich as some sort of guinea pig, the subject of a human mind-control experiment orchestrated by Puharich himself. According to Puharich, during the séances, contact was made with a group of nine entities who became known simply as *The Nine*. During channeling sessions, The Nine revealed their identity as the Egyptian *Ennead*, i.e., the original group of nine deities who were worshipped in ancient Egypt. This group of Egyptian deities, The Nine, and the messages to humanity that they imparted to Puharich and his group, were destined to become an integral part of the modern "New Age" movement and popular culture. Channeled information from The Nine would inspire many influential people, the most famous of whom was none other than screenwriter, producer, and futurist Gene Roddenberry. Gene Roddenberry was the producer of one of the most loved and enduring byproducts of UFO-inspired phenomena in US history - the original *Star Trek* television series. Roddenberry was very interested in Andrija Puharich and his work with The Nine. It's interesting to note that many elements and moral lessons that were conveyed in the Star Trek TV series, in particular the *Deep Space Nine* series (note reference to The Nine) may have been inspired to a degree by Gene Roddenberry's interest in the channeled information coming from Andrija Puharich and the Council of 9. In its many episodes, Star Trek conveyed to a receptive audience of millions of viewers moral lessons and advanced precepts that were provided to Andrija Puharich and his group as they channeled The Nine, i.e., disembodied entities of the Superspectrum who took an interest in evolving humanity and their struggle for high technology and future space travel. Today, many personalities, such as authors Richard Hoagland and David Wilcock, continue to take interest in messages coming through various channelers from The Nine, and these messages are taken very seriously.

The Flatwoods Monster

The strange case of the *Flatwoods Monster* is commonly considered within UFO circles as a solid case of ET visitation. Others maintain a skeptical interpretation, which is also interesting in its own right. On September 12, 1952, three years to the day before I arrived to Earth in my present incarnation, an alleged UFO event occurred that came to be known as the Flatwoods Monster. I'm going to prep this case with a story of my own from my childhood in Florida. As a young man of 8, it was my job living at home to take out the trash. One day, I forgot to take it out on the day that I was supposed to, and it forced me to take the trash out at night. On my way out back to the garbage cans, the dark night was pitch black. I wasn't very fond of walking around at night, and could become spooked quite easily. With the hair on the back of my neck standing up, I cautiously took the bag of garbage out in the dark. When I arrived near the aluminum garbage cans into which our family placed bags of garbage, there, in the moonlight, was an old woman hanging by the neck, obviously dead and swinging in the breeze! Horrified, I dropped the bags and ran back inside the house, crying for my mother to come take a look. My mother calmed me down, got a flashlight, and with me clinging to her side, she walked back out with me to see what in the world it was that I saw. I was scared to death, but at the same time I felt assured that my mother and I would get to the bottom of this horror. Outside the periphery of the range of light, I once again saw the old woman swinging by her neck. My mother pointed the flashlight in the direction of the old dead woman, and began chuckling. There, on the nextdoor neighbor's clothesline, was a mop swinging in the breeze, hanging on the clothesline by the mop head. The "hair" was hanging down behind the mopstick, and the background of bushes made it look like a woman wearing a dress instead of a mopstick swinging to and fro. If the Flatwoods Monster case was not an incident of ET visitation after all, and it wasn't a transmogrified energy construct or hologram created to provide cover for an alien's true appearance, then it may have been a group of frightened people in the dark who saw something move and, due to the national hysteria over flying saucers at the time, made its way into UFO lore as a staple-case.

It all started when some kids in the hills of West Virginia were playing football in the evening. Suddenly, they witnessed a flash of light streak across the sky that seemed to land on a hilltop on the Baily Fisher Farm. The kids immediately ran home to tell Mrs. Kathleen May, who was a local beautician. Kathleen promptly grabbed a flashlight just like my mother did and went out with the kids to see what all the fuss was about. As the group walked toward the "landing site," visions of alien visitation were doubtless floating in their heads. What would they see when they arrived at the landing site? As they approached the top of the hill, 17-year-old Gene Lemon, who was now holding the flashlight, suddenly noticed a pair of animal-like eyes. Gene impulsively pointed the flashlight toward what appeared as a full-faced creature with a pointed hood that hissed and floated toward the witnesses. Kathleen screamed as Gene dropped the flashlight, leaving them all terrified in the dark. They all ran back to the house in total darkness. The next day, the Sheriff and deputy came out with a local reporter to investigate, and found nothing unusual. The incident would not have amounted to much until the charismatic and controversial ufologist, Gray Barker, a sensationalist author, came around to interview the witnesses. Following his interviews with the witnesses there, Barker blew the story up into UFO legend. In 1952, the "reconnaissance and exploration" paradigm was popular. That is, the earth was being explored by extraterrestrials who occasionally landed to check things out. Determining that this story had some of the same features as other UFO cases, Barker automatically deemed the case legitimate. With Barker's stamp of approval, the Flatwoods Monster case was born. Paranormal investigator and skeptic Joe Nickell, for one, views this case as nothing more than a common barn owl encounter experienced by a group of scared individuals in the dark whose imaginations were peaked after a mysterious meteor sighting. UFO skeptics are right in that many UFO sightings likely represent misidentified natural phenomena and/or hoaxes. In the midst of UFO hysteria, doubtless inspired by a core of legitimate unknowns, there are so many mistaken perceptions, intentional hoaxes, and hucksters seeking to make a buck from public credulity, that it is easy for some to write UFOs off as fantasy. Unfortunately, if my suspicions and theories concerning the actual alien agenda is correct, those who have dismissed UFOs altogether may have served to retard our progress in getting to the bottom of the actual mystery at hand. Not only have they served to delay our understanding, this premature dismissal of the UFO phenomenon may actually contribute to the displacement of humanity by a higher intelligence that is playing us all like a fiddle. At least, along the way to understanding the truth behind the UFO enigma, there are occasional moments of comic relief. We can certainly find humor in the infamous case of the Flatwoods

Monster if it was, in fact, just a barn owl sighting. However, as we relax and chuckle over a group of scared individuals in the dark woods who were possibly frightened by a barn owl, we are reminded that UFO-experiencer Whitley Strieber reported an encounter with an alien in which the "screen memory" of an owl was given to his senses to hide the fact that the creature was, in fact, an alien. The account of his implanted screen memory was detailed in his 1987 best-selling book, *Communion*. Many other authors speak of screen memories as well. In *Ancient Aliens and the Lost Islands*, author Sharon Delarose shares her views on Earth's alien presence and their apparent shapeshifting abilities. Delarose writes (chapter 18 audible):

> *In most cases, they [Earth's alien visitors] are simply galactic travelers, and Earth is just a stop along the way. In regards to the Gray aliens (who appear to be more than visitors passing through), the most compelling trait is their ability to make you see them as anything but what they are. People see spiders; owls; wolves; deer; dogs; cats; monkeys; rabbits; cows; and even humans. In other words, they can appear as any species. They are not actually changing their nature, they are implanting a different image in our minds than we are actually seeing. These images are so realistic and so detailed that most experiencers never discover the true nature of what they saw.*

Therefore, we should remain haunted by the possibility that the Flatwoods Monster case, along with all of the encounters that are documented in the UFO literature by experiencers, are real, but may not accurately reflect the underlying reality. If the earth is being visited by advanced aliens who have natural shapeshifting abilities or paraphysical technology to make us see any image they want us to see, all of the UFO craft and occupant descriptions are suspect. Things may not be as they appear to percipients. All the work done by skeptics to discover mundane explanations for UFO sightings may only go down to the level of an implanted screen memory used to camouflage the alien's actual appearance, which may have been too frightening for humans to endure. As UFO cases are examined, it is important to keep in mind that the Phenomenon has many layers of obfuscation that keep the actual truth hidden. The fact that humans may not be witnessing anything as it really exists places the Flatwoods Monster case on the tall stack of mysterious UFO cases that are destined to remain, in the end, unexplained.

Operation Mainbrace

The day after the Flatwoods Monster case, on September 13, 1952, a mass sighting occurred near Denmark and Norway involving 8 NATO governments and New Zealand over the course of 12 days in *Operation Mainbrace*. This operation was the largest NATO operation in history. It included 80,000 men, 1000 planes, and 200 ships under the direction of a British Admiral, Sir Patrick Brind. Lieutenant Commander Schmidt Jenson and crew members aboard the Danish destroyer "Willemoes" reported a triangular craft traveling at an estimated 900 miles per hour headed toward the southeast, north of Bornholm Island, on the night of September 13. Over the course of the following week, 4 more sightings occurred by credible military witnesses, and these were officially recorded in the records of the Air Ministry. As a British Meteor jet landed at Topcliffe, Yorkshire, England, a metallic silver disk was observed swinging back and forth like a pendulum, as reported by Lieutenant John Kilburn and other observers on the ground. This pendulum motion is a common feature in UFO sightings all over the world. When video is captured of an object moving in such a fashion, many assume that the object is "obviously" a model on a string, because that is exactly what it looks like. However, for some reason, probably having to do with an antigravitic propulsion system, this pendulum motion is often an indication of authenticity when some of these crafts materialize in Earth's atmosphere. It wouldn't even surprise me if the motion is intentionally produced in order to create doubt and plausible deniability in the many sightings over the years as part of the effort to remain incognito. As the military aircraft landed, the rotating silvery disk took off at high speed and vanished (dematerialized). A day or so after this sighting, a series of color photographs were taken of a silver sphere flying at high speed by reporter Wallace Litwin while aboard the USS Franklin D. Roosevelt. These photographs were examined by Naval Intelligence officers, and remain classified. One official who examined the photographs was the Air Force project chief, Captain Edward Ruppelt. Ruppelt ruled out a balloon explanation, as no such balloon had been launched. The object was also traveling faster than any balloon was capable of flying. Around this same time came a report of a flying metallic disk at Karup Field, Denmark, by 3 Danish Air Force officers, followed by another sighting of a silver sphere from 6 British RAF pilots flying above the North Sea. On September 27-28, mass sightings of strange aerial vehicles were seen over Western Germany, Denmark, and Sweden, including slow-moving cigar-shaped craft, large flying objects with smaller satellites surrounding them, and comet-like objects with long luminous tails. These sightings from 1952 remain unexplained, just as no one has ever proposed a good explanation for the Washington D.C. UFO flyover.

[On October 3, 1952, the British detonated a nuclear test called "Operation Hurricane"]

Orfeo Angelucci

Orfeo Matthew Angelucci was a contactee from the 1950s who suffered from a lifetime of nervousness and general poor health. Due to his neuro-physical condition, Angelucci moved from Trenton, New Jersey, to California in the late 1940s for a factory job in Burbank, California with the Lockheed Aircraft Plant (the same plant that contactee George Van Tassel worked at for a while). Angelucci was terrified of thunderstorms. His move to California was partially because he heard that thunderstorms were rare there. In 1952, Angelucci wrote, *The Nature of Infinite Entities*, which was a decidedly pseudoscientific account of matter, energy, and life. That same year, Angelucci began having encounter experiences involving landed flying saucers with friendly, attractive, highly-spiritual occupants that were translucent in appearance. Then, in

1955, Angelucci wrote, *The Secret of the Saucers*, in which Angelucci reported that he was once taken into orbit above Earth in an unmanned flying saucer, where he witnessed a large mothership drifting by as he looked through a porthole. Angelucci recalled at one point in his life that, during an episode of missing time, his spirit inhabited the body of a space brother named Neptune from an advanced society for an entire week while his real body wandered around in a daze at the plant where he worked. Angelucci went on to author another book, *The Son of the Sun*, and published many pamphlets with the peaceful and unifying messages of the ufonauts. Angelucci was one of many individuals from the 1950s who had subjective UFO experiences and wrote books about the messages of the ufonauts. These experiences, whatever their true nature (physical, psychic, or a combination of both in an alternate reality), contributed to an overall shift in consciousness within those they came in contact with and those who were influenced through their writing concerning our place in the cosmos. Through psychological osmosis, the public at large absorbed the idea that we have friendly cosmic neighbors, and that we should be careful when using nuclear power for destructive reasons, as we are being monitored by higher cosmic intelligences who might intervene if they have to in order to save us from ourselves.

The NSA and Communication with ETs

UFO-related phenomena throughout the 1950s included everything from hucksters and hoaxes, individuals who perceived themselves as being in contact with the ufonauts, to serious military encounters with radar confirmation and credible eyewitness accounts all at once. Despite the circus of affairs at the time, and while contactees were using Ouija boards to contact the aliens, serious investigations of flying saucers were going on within intelligence circles. One organization that was established as the public went flying-saucer crazy was the NSA. William Cooper, former Naval Intelligence Briefing Officer, details the formation of NSA in his book, *Behold a Pale Horse* (page 200):

> *President Truman created the supersecret National Security Agency (NSA) by secret executive order on November 4, 1952. Its primary purpose was to decipher the alien communications, language, and establish a dialogue with the extraterrestrials. The secondary purpose of the NSA was to monitor all communications and emissions from any and all electronic devices worldwide for the purpose of gathering intelligence, both human and alien, and to contain the secret of the alien presence.*

Calvin C. Girvin

Inspired by Kenneth Arnold's UFO sighting in 1947 that resulted in the term *flying saucer* being used to describe the many flying disks that were seen from Arnold's sighting forward, Calvin C. Girvin became completely absorbed in the saucer phenomenon circa 1952. Girvin read everything he could get his hands on about the subject. As Girvin acquired knowledge of UFOs, he began having dreams in which he was transported to Venus. Here Girvin met human-looking space brothers akin to those of George Adamski. He was instructed by two Venusians, Cryxtan and Ashtar, to join the military and become a spy for them by examining Air Force files for anything related to UFOs or extraterrestrials. So, Girvan joined the Air Force. While driving to Washington D.C. in 1952, Girvin reported that he finally saw a flying saucer land. He described actually boarding the craft, where he was taken above the Earth to see the Venusian mothership in the upper atmosphere. Girvin went into Air Force food services and was assigned to the Pentagon, where he began telling everyone of his saucer experiences. Girvin was soon shipped out to Hawaii (no big surprise), where he gained the honor of being the most obscure contactee of the 1950s era.

George Van Tassel

Unlike Calvin Girvin, who remained low-key and unknown to most UFO enthusiasts in the 1950s, George Van Tassel arrived to the 1950s contactee scene as a serious metaphysical researcher who also worked in the aviation industry. Van Tassel was a pilot who worked for Douglas Aircraft, Lockheed, and Hughes Aircraft as a Top Flight Inspector between the years 1930-1947. He was a credible, intelligent man who was sincerely seeking a universal, psychic method of communicating with nonhuman entities on higher planes of existence. As early as 1947, when Van Tassel moved to Giant Rock in the Mojave Desert in California, he was meeting with groups of interested people in an attempt to channel messages from the ufonauts. He was interested in using his mind like a radio receiver to establish contact with the occupants of the luminous orbs and flying disks that were appearing to multitudes in our skies at the time, objects that were assumed to be extraterrestrial spacecraft with technologically-advanced biological entities on board. In 1951, Van Tassel reported an experience that I find somewhat haunting, but may provide insight into one category of beings who are interested in our impending technological singularity for their own reasons. Van Tassel reported that, while meditating at the base of Giant Rock, he was taken aboard a spacecraft to meet the *Council of Seven Lights*. This council identified themselves as *discarnate humans who continually orbit the earth*. These disembodied humans expressed, among many things, grave concerns about humanity playing with nuclear weapons and conducting nuclear tests. Of particular concern to these discarnate humans, who were presumably awaiting their next earthly incarnation, was the exploding of hydrogen bombs. The beings objected to the destruction of hydrogen in particular, as they considered hydrogen a *living element*.

George Van Tassel's encounter with the *Council of Seven Lights* evokes many modern corollaries, one being the phenomenon of *spooklights*, or *ghostlights*. In *Open Skies, Closed Minds*, author Nick Pope, who once worked at the UFO desk in England for the Ministry of Defense (MOD), posed the same possible connection between UFOs and spooklights as he pondered John Napier's work, *The Goblin Universe*. Pope writes (pg. 29):

And if there is a link of some kind between ufology and the goblin universe, might there not also be one between ufology and ghosts? It is the United States that produces a phenomenon that may bridge the two worlds, of the spirit and space – spooklights. In the Brown Mountain region of North Carolina, some eyewitnesses described these lights hovering in the night sky in 1913 as disappearing "like a busting sky rocket."

Cryptozoologist/ufologist Nick Redfern also mentions the mysterious Brown Mountain Lights and other spooklights around the world in his many books. Redfern notes that these poorly-understood lights appear to demonstrate the presence of intelligence. Redfern wonders if the spooklights may, in fact, hold the key to the entire UFO phenomenon.

Amazingly, from George Van Tassel's alleged communications with flying saucer occupants, some of whom represented themselves as disembodied humans, he successfully predicted the UFO fleet appearance over the White House that occurred on the two consecutive weekends of July 19-20 and July 26-27, 1952. The Washington, D.C. flyby event was a factual, historical, well-documented UFO incident, witnessed in the sky by thousands, tracked on ground radar and onboard radar in jets that were dispatched with shoot-to-kill orders. The Washington D.C. UFO flyby event made front-page news all over the United States, with headlines such as, *Flying Saucers Swarm Over Capital* (*Cedar Rapids Gazette*). Did witnesses to the 1952 White House flyby event experience a rare glimpse at George Van Tassel's *Council of Seven Lights* that circles the earth throughout the aeons, carrying discarnate humans? If so, did we ignorantly dispatch fighter jets with the intent to shoot down the very luminous vehicles that carry human souls around the earth awaiting reincarnation? This idea reminds me of the words of Jesus as he was dying on the cross - "Father, forgive them, for they know not what they do." Not only did George Van Tassel correctly and publicly predict the UFO flyby over the White House, he also notified *LIFE* magazine, the *Los Angeles Herald-Examiner*, and the US Air Force of the coming event by registered letter a week or so before it actually happened. Somehow, amazingly, George Van Tassel knew it was coming. This prediction that came true baffled early critics of the channeling method of communication with extraterrestrial intelligences. It also lends credence to the idea that ufology represents an emerging religion in the making. Is there any real difference between the prophets of old and modern UFO contactees who communicate with aliens and/or disembodied humans? Are they one and the same phenomenon? Just prior to the Washington D.C. flyby event, Van Tassel reported receiving psychic messages from an interdimensional being, *Ashtar*, who continues to pay visits to the minds of channelers today. By accessing the Universal Mind, Van Tassel taught that all manner of beings, including disembodied humans, could be contacted. The practice of contacting the dead is alive and well even today. One case in point is the late Delores Cannon. Cannon allegedly channeled messages from Nostrodamus and recorded them in her book, *Messages from Nostradamus*. Van Tassel saw the Bible as a record of extraterrestrial contact, and believed that Jesus was an ET. Van

Tassel believed that humans can communicate with beings from other dimensions like Jesus and Ashtar, who both came to Earth as teachers for Humanity. Thousands of seekers would show up at the Giant Rock Conventions to hear messages channeled from the Space People. The day before the Washington D.C. flyby, on July 18, 1952, it was believed that Ashtar entered our solar system as Commander of the Galactic Community to warn Earth's inhabitants of the dangers of nuclear weapons. One of the members of Van Tassel's contact group, Robert Short, who was the editor of a 1950s UFO magazine, *Interplanetary News Digest*, broke off from the original group and formed the group, *Ashtar Command*, which is alive today and instrumental in the perpetuation of the idea that benevolent Space People are going to intervene in human affairs and save us from nuclear self-destruction. With the advent of the internet in the post-1990s world and beyond, messages from Ashtar Command continue to inspire internet users who seek spirituality from this UFO-oriented cyber-community. Today, members of Ashtar Command focus on the elevation of human consciousness through meditative procedures in order to be taken aboard the "Light Ships" as a full member of the Etherian Community.

Following the Washington D.C. flyby, against a sea of ridicule, Van Tassel gravitated from solo communications with ufonauts to group meditation sessions for the purpose of contacting extraterrestrials at his home in 1953. In the fall of 1953, Van Tassel reported that, in the middle of the night, a spaceship from Venus landed with occupants who took him onboard. Inside the Venusian craft, the spaceman revealed to Van Tassel how to build the *Integreton*, a device he was told was capable of rejuvenating the human body. After this experience, Van Tassel followed his visitor's instructions, and began working to build the Integreton. Van Tassel described the structure as "a time machine for basic research on rejuvenation, anti-gravity, and time travel." Ironically, the Integreton, intended to rejuvenate the human body and unlock the secrets of time and space, was never completed due to Van Tassel's untimely death. However, the unfinished Integreton remains on the property to this day. Curious visitors who go inside the Integreton report various levels of rejuvenation and unusually soothing sounds inside. Another interesting aspect of the Integreton is that it was modeled after the Tabernacle of the early biblical contactee, Moses, after Moses was given telepathic instructions for its construction following his encounter with what may have been an extraterrestrial being named Yahweh. The Old Testament reports that Yahweh contacted Moses in swirling clouds and fire on top of Mount Sinai and spoke to Moses directly, making the face of Moses shine like the sun. Modern UFO scholars, such as Vallee and others, speculate that these types of contactee experiences have always occurred to various individuals throughout human history in many different forms from fairies to ufonauts. The contactees of the 1950s, along with many particularly insightful science fiction writers, may represent a modern version of the prophets of yesteryear. They continue to have, and will always have, regardless of the factuality of their percipient reports, a psychological impact on the existing culture of the time. Moses and Van Tassel were both lucky enough to experience close encounters and communication from nonhuman entities, and they both shared their revelations with the world. George Van Tassel started the *Ministry of Universal Wisdom* in 1953. In a series of psychic communications with a variety of entities who called the earth *Shan*, he began documenting his communications. Van Tassell wrote several books, including *When Stars Look Down*. In his documentation, we read that the entities who contacted Van Tassel call their spaceships *Ventlas*. These craft operate on light principles and are able to project themselves in an area when they were actually located elsewhere physically. In this way, the Ventlas protected themselves from our hostilities, having been, unfortunately, targeted and shot at by Earth-vehicles on occasion. George Van Tassel and his contacts with the occulted intelligences behind the UFOs remain highly influential in the world of ufology today. Whether, in the end, the intentions of the ufonauts, the Overlords of the Singularity, prove themselves benign, hostile, or indifferent to humanity will remain obscure until our artificial intelligence allows humans an expanded perception into Cryptoreality. However, by examining the history of the Phenomenon, considering the deceptive nature of the messages coming from the ufonauts, along with the physical and psychological damage that has so often been inflicted by interactions between humans and UFOs, I think we have reason for concern that the intentions of at least some of the ufonauts may be self-serving, and not in humanity's eventual best interests.

The Robertson Panel

As George Van Tassel was communicating telepathically with extraterrestrials, both alone and with groups, along with successfully predicting the 1952 Washington D.C. flyby, the first scientific advisory panel on UFOs was convened by request of the White House, and sponsored by the CIA, in January, 1953. This group came to be known as the Robertson Panel. The panel was put together by a world-renowned physicist at the California Institute of Technology, Dr. H.P. Robertson. Other panel members included a professor of physics at Berkeley, California, Luis W. Alvarez, a noted space scientist, Lloyd Berkner; a nuclear physicist at Brookhaven National Laboratory, Sam A. Goudsmit, and a writer for the panel who was also an astronomer, an operations manager for the John Hopkins University, and a friend of Dr. Robertson's. The Robertson Panel was briefed by all three branches of the military, by the scientific advisor for Project Blue Book, J.Allen Hynek, and by Captain Edward Ruppelt, the head of Project Blue Book. The main concern at the time was that UFO reports might create a serious disruption of communication in the event of a Soviet military attack. They decided that the best approach was an attempt to demystify the public perception of UFOs by assigning mundane explanations to sightings whenever possible. In so doing, the Robertson Panel predicted that public interest in UFOs would be short-lived. If only the members of the Robertson Panel could have looked into the future to see the tremendous increase in public interest instead of a dissipation over the course of the next several decades, they would certainly have taken a completely different approach and made more use of their time and attention.

[In 1953, the United Kingdom detonated a nuclear device known as "Operation Totem." The Soviet Union also detonated their first air-deployable nuclear bomb using their powerful "layer cake" design.]

Scientology

In 1953, another space-oriented religion, *Scientology*, was spawned as the latest generation of *Dianetics*, a system of belief created by science fiction writer L. Ron Hubbard. Hubbard's Scientology religion was destined to exert a huge impact on the thinking and culture at large. The theology that Scientology teaches is similar in tone to the Christian concept of the "Fall of Man," in that humans are actually immortal beings, called *Thetans*, who have forgotten their true divine nature. In the beginning, the Thetans created the physical universe for their own pleasure. The universe doesn't really have an actual existence, but only appears to exist for the Thetans by unanimous conscious consensus. Although Scientology enjoys tax-exempt status, it is actually a very lucrative commercial enterprise (as is modern Christianity, especially for "prosperity theologians" who promise their subjects riches if only they will give their "seed money" to their particular ministry). Through the process of *auditing*, a new Scientologist is guided through previous traumatic experiences in life, and eventually achieves rehabilitation and happiness by working their way up through purchased batteries of information (if they can afford to stick with it). Once the novice Scientologist has paid in thousands of dollars to achieve the goal of becoming "clear," they finally learn that they have lived many lives before their present *assumption* (incarnation) on Earth, and that they have lived on other planets throughout the universe prior to this present lifetime. If a Scientologist is able to endure Hubbard's fabricated psycho-babble long enough, and they can afford to keep paying in money to advance themselves, they are finally treated to the highest-guarded secrets of Hubbard's "Space Opera" – a series of historical events that allegedly happened to the Thetans prior to this earthly existence. They get the story of *Xenu*, the ruler of the *Galactic Confederacy*, who brought billions of humans to Earth 75 million years ago in spacecraft resembling Douglas DC-8 airliners. These spacecraft were then stacked around volcanoes, and hydrogen bombs were detonated to get rid of them. The highest level in Scientology, level OT VIII, is revealed only at sea on Scientology's official cruise ship, the *Freewinds*. Aboard the Freewinds they are treated to yet another battery of Hubbard's pithy science fiction. I'm not sure what the success of Scientology really means in the larger scheme of things, but it certainly indicates that there is an untapped yearning within the human mind and heart to find our true place in the Cosmos. There is also a fortune waiting to be made by any charismatic figure who comes along with a good explanation as to why we all exist that explains our true purpose, especially if the story is appealing to the human ego or provides some sense of internal comfort or elitism from possessing "hidden knowledge." Having said that, the real genius of Scientology is that L. Ron Hubbard's cosmology tapped into suspicions that many of us share. We all suspect that much of our past is lost, that we may have been something greater in the past than we are now, and that the destiny of humanity in the future involves some sort of transcendence. This is, in some sense, the message of any religion. We all exist in a "fallen" state. In other words, even though L. Ron Hubbard's imagery and cosmology was likely fabricated, the underlying essence of the picture that he portrayed might actually be true on some level. Because Scientology tapped into these inner suspicions, the public at large, many of whom were not stupid by any means, responded to Hubbard's new religion with their hearts, their minds, and their pocketbooks.

A Secret UFO Crash

Arthur G. Stancil was a mechanical engineer who graduated from Ohio University in 1949 and was employed by the Air Materiel Command (AFMC) at Wright Patterson Air Force Base in Dayton, Ohio, where he tested Air Force aircraft engines. Dr. Eric Wang, who worked at Stancil's facility, is suspected of leading a team of scientists and engineers to reverse engineer alien artifacts gleaned from flying saucer crashes. According to a legal affidavit that was signed by Stancil many years after-the-fact, a flying saucer crashed in Arizona on May 20, 1953. According to Stancil's sworn testimony, he was working on a government contract in 1953 at a nuclear site in Nevada when he was duly summoned by his boss to embark on a "secret assignment." Stancil was then flown to Phoenix, Arizona, where he was placed on a bus with blacked-out windows that drove four hours northwest of Phoenix near Kingman, Arizona. Various personnel other than Stancil, about 15 other professionals, were aboard the bus as it drove to Kingman, Arizona. They were all instructed not to speak with one another on the way to their destination. In pre-dawn hours, they were all escorted by military police to the scene of a 30-foot diameter metallic disk that was embedded in the desert sand. The disk, which looked like two convex oval plates made from burnished aluminum and joined together, was illuminated by two military arc-lights. The disk had a hole blown in the side of it as if it had been shot down. Stancil's job assignment was to calculate the forward and vertical velocities of the craft at the moment of impact. As he conducted his calculations, he never looked inside the craft but spoke to others when the atmosphere lightened up a little. It was reported that there *were* small chairs in the cabin. Stancil did peek into the medical tent and personally witnessed a 4-foot-tall creature in a silver suit and skull cap of some sort. When the mission ended, they were all put back on the bus and forced to sign "Official Secrets" documents. This story was known by UFO investigator Richard Hall by 1964. Stancil's account was later released to the public in *UFO Magazine* by famed UFO researcher Raymond Fowler in 1976. UFO researcher Leonard Stringfield also uncovered corroborating evidence for this event in 1977 from testimony provided by a man who was in the National Guard at Wright Patterson in 1953. Stringfield's witness testified that 3 bodies, 4ft. tall with brownish skin, were recovered from the crash at Kingman and were packed on dry ice. Leonard Stringfield revealed known information concerning several similar flying saucer crash retrieval events in his *UFO Crash Retrievals, Status Reports 1-VI*, published from 1980-1991.

Also confirming the testimony of engineer Arthur G. Stancil concerning a flying saucer crash in Kingman, Arizona in 1953 is the late William Cooper, who once served as a Naval Intelligence Briefing Officer. In Cooper's book, *Behold a Pale Horse*, he stated that President Eisenhower, who had been Supreme Allied Commander in WW2, was inundated with the perplexing flying saucer crashes during his first year of presidency in 1953. According to Bill Cooper *(Behold a Pale Horse*, pages 201 & 202):

During his first year in office, 1953, at least 10 more crashed discs were recovered, along with 26 dead and 4 live aliens. Of the 10, 4 were found in Arizona, 2 in Texas, 1 in New Mexico, 1 in Louisiana, 1 in Montana, and 1 in South Africa. There were hundreds of sightings. Eisenhower knew that he had to wrestle and beat the alien problem. He knew that he could not do it by revealing the secret to Congress. Early in 1953 the new president turned to his friend and fellow member of the Council on Foreign Relations Nelson Rockefeller. Eisenhower and Rockefeller began planning the secret structure of alien-task supervision, which was to become a reality within one year. The idea for MJ-12 was thus born.

In 1953 astronomers discovered large objects in space which were tracked moving toward the Earth. It was first believed that they were asteroids. Later evidence proved that the objects could only be spaceships. Project SIGMA intercepted alien radio communications. When the objects reached the Earth they took up a very high geosynchronous orbit around the equator. There were several huge ships, and their actual intent was unknown. Project SIGMA, and a new project, PLATO, through radio communications using computer binary language, were able to arrange a landing that resulted in face-to-face contact with alien beings from another planet.

Bill Cooper's explanation of the origin of the secret MJ-12 alien task group differs slightly from others who believe the group was established a year earlier in 1952 under President Truman following the UFO fly-over in Washington D.C. The very existence of such a secret task group that has existed since the 50's is a subject of controversy among modern ufologists. One person in the field who has delved extensively into the existence of the MJ-12 group and firmly believes that the group is a reality is nuclear physicist and UFO-researcher Stanton T. Friedman. Although there are differences among ufologists as to just how or when the group was established, the underlying idea that there was, in fact, a secret UFO study group of some kind established within the government in 1952-1953 is generally accepted as factual.

Invaders Fom Mars

1953 rolled out a notable motion picture called *Invaders from Mars*. This film was one of the first films to depict aliens abducting humans for purposes of medical experimentation and the installation of alien implants. Modern skeptics of the massive numbers of reported alien abductions and alien implants that followed movies like *Invaders from Mars* and other similar films understandably point to such early works of science fiction with features that show up in actual UFO and abduction reports to ascertain the fictional nature of alien abductions. However, what the skeptics fail to consider is the plausibility that an advanced intelligence who wished to manipulate humankind for its own purposes would certainly use imagery from our science fiction to create a believable and repeatable screen memory while, as John Keel often speculated, *something else entirely is happening to their bodies* during abductions. These induced abduction experiences appear to percipients as real, tangible, 3D reality, complete with physical symptoms (e.g., "scoop marks") and symptoms of Post Traumatic Stress Disorder (PTSD). Abduction researchers point out that clinical PTSD is not likely to occur with simple hallucinatory or dreamlike states. The technology to produce illusory experiences to the degree that abductees report appears to involve an advanced paraphysical technology beyond what humans have produced thus far, similar to "virtual reality," inducing experiences that humans cannot distinguish from ordinary reality. Whatever the intelligences behind the Phenomenon are actually doing with people while these screen memories are implanted is unknown. In some cases, we know that blood was actually drawn, but the fact remains that thousands of individuals, possibly millions by now, have had the abduction experience perpetrated on them, and to these individuals, the experience is quite real and often leaves physical or emotional scars, or both.

Arthur C. Clarke, Science Fiction Prophet

In 1953, British author Arthur C. Clarke was, in retrospect, an actual science-fiction prophet who unwittingly wrote fiction that revealed glimpses of a metaphysical reality that is very close to the heart of the UFO mystery. In particular, his book, *Childhood's End*, considered his greatest work by many, was a pure treasure channeled directly from the human collective unconscious. The story reflects faint paranoid suspicions of what I believe may be the actual situation humanity faces in the real world regarding our relationship with otherworldly personalities. The prophecy in this novel is stunning, as it hints at a similar scenario concerning the transcendence of humanity that I am now postulating regarding the impending Singularity. In *Childhood's End*, Clarke actually refers to an alien presence called the "overlords," whose physical appearance is that of a stereotypical demon, complete with barbed tail and bat-like wings. In Clarke's story, this race of overlords are many times more intelligent than humans, and they are here in our skies to oversee a great transition that is about to occur on Earth, as well as to midwife the transition of humanity into a higher realm. The race of overlords is an evolutionary dead end. Having developed as a species as far as they will ever go, they are employed by the *Overmind* to supervise various planetary populations to a grand transition state that they will never be able to experience themselves. So, despite the fact that humans have always feared their demonic appearance, and the image of the demon has forever haunted our inner fears, the overlords were, in actuality, here for a beneficial and benign purpose to see us off on our journey into the celestial realms beyond the range that even they could achieve. When a planet produces fruit, i.e., intelligent living creatures, and they evolve as far as they can go in the physical realm, the *Overmind* absorbs them, along with the aeons of creature-experience, and adds the knowledge unto itself. It then moves on to do exactly the same thing with population after population, adding this life experience to its developing omniscience. Clarke's prophetic work was published one year after a fleet of real flying saucers flew over the White House. The year prior to Clarke's book, 1952, presented a great global wave of UFOs, as did the year after the book was published, 1954, the year that produced multitudes of UFO landing and occupant encounters in France that ufologist Aime Michel researched so well. So right in the middle of two epic years for UFOs, Arthur C. Clarke published his prophetic book about benevolent alien overlords who have come to see humanity through a "transition" that will expand human consciousness exponentially. What a great touch it was in Clarke's book that the good aliens looked like demons. It wasn't until I nearly completed this book that I actually read *Childhood's End* for the first time, and by that time I had already created the title, *Overlords of the Singularity*. What a pleasant confirmation and shock it was to me that the plot of Arthur C. Clarke's best novel was so close to the case I am proposing concerning the underlying intentions of the actual UFO intelligences that are here on this earth, intelligences both beneficial and malevolent, that have been with us now for millennia. I had such great appreciation for Clarke's novel when I finally read it that I thought about changing the title of my own book out of respect for his great fiction. However, searching an online thesaurus for a different word other than "overlord," I just wasn't satisfied with any of the other connotations. Overlords are exactly what we have had to contend with throughout human history. Overlords created our religions, for better or worse. Overlords may have actually tinkered with our genetics to push us faster toward the Singularity at all costs. Overlords are the actual intelligences behind the UFO mystery that haunts our skies. So, with all due respect to Clarke's fictional novel, "overlords" is really the most accurate terminology to use in our situation. A close second was "demigods," but that didn't have the exact connotations needed to express the idea of various levels of intelligences who are above human and interact in various ways for their own purposes, so overlords remained. I am left with a warm feeling toward Arthur C. Clarke and his story from 1953, as I truly believe that his book, *Childhood's End*, was a fairly accurate forcast of things to come.

Donald Menzel's Secret Life

In addition to the marvelously-prophetic work by Arthur C. Clarke, 1953 brought a skeptic's analysis of UFOs by Harvard University astrophysicist Donald Menzel. In his book, *Flying Saucers*, Menzel makes the case that UFOs are real, as they are objects in the sky that are unidentified, but states that UFOs are just natural phenomena that fool the human eye and brain into thinking they are something they are not. Menzel postulated that all the biblical UFO accounts represent mistaken natural phenomena as well. In biblical times, Menzel argued, we knew even less about nature than we do now, and we were even more easily fooled back then than we are now. Ironically, in latter times he attempted to take a little credit for being one of the first contributors to the "Ancient Alien" belief system. I, for one, cannot blame Menzel for wanting at least some type of public acknowledgement within ufology. As it turns out, Menzel may have actually led a double life according to UFO researcher and nuclear physicist Stanton Friedman. In one life, the life that Menzel openly displayed to the public, he was a scientific flying saucer debunker and Harvard professor. However, in his possible secret life, Donald Menzel may have been one of the original MJ-12 members assigned to the secret investigations of alien spacecraft and crash retrievals established by President Harry S. Truman following the Washington D.C. flying saucer flyby in 1952 (or later by Eisenhower, whichever is correct). When it comes to UFOs, truth is often stranger than fiction. Like the story of the Exodus in the Old Testament, a work that scholars say is nearly impossible to sort out truth from fiction, UFO lore is just as convoluted. There is a core of fantastic reality within the UFO literature, as the reports are a global phenomenon that correlate with one another, indicating that something real is afoot rather than pure fantasy. However, the UFO literature is admittedly peppered with misidentification of natural phenomena, embellishments, occasional hoaxes, and intentional government disinformation. Combine all this with the inability of science to approach UFOs effectively using standard scientific methodology, and it becomes very difficult for all but the most dedicated truth-seekers to make sense of it all. Fortunately, there have been a multitude of UFO researchers over the last several decades who have dedicated their lives to understanding just what the hell is going on with flying saucers. In my estimation, many UFO researchers have come very close to discovering the actual alien agenda, that of pushing, guiding, and manipulating humanity toward the Singularity. However, they all fall just short of that epiphany. The struggling conclusions of many of these UFO researchers will be examined in the final chapter to glean insight into their many years of investigations. As these expert views are explored, it should become apparent that many of them were on the verge of saying exactly what I am saying in this book, they just didn't quite make it into the age of current technology in which some of the fantastic implications of the approaching Singularity are becoming clear.

George Adamski

In addition to multitudes of flying saucer sightings and alleged UFO crashes, 1953 brought us a charismatic hamburger-flipper and amateur astronomer named George Adamski. Adamski was interested in Eastern Mysticism, and was destined to go down in history as one of the main UFO contactees of the 1950s. George Adamski claimed to experience multiple contacts with Nordic-type "Space Brothers" from the planet Venus, along with flights into outer space in their spacecraft with them. Adamski revealed many of his fantastic adventures in his best-selling book, *Flying Saucers Have Landed*. Adamski lectured famously on tour, convincing many around the world of the factuality of his experiences with flying saucers and their occupants. Adamski claimed that in 1946, during a meteor shower, he witnessed a large cigar-shaped mothership. He also claimed that a year later in 1947 he took a photograph of that mothership crossing in front of a full moon. Adamski allegedly met a Venusian flying saucer pilot in the desert named Orthon, who he described as a nicely-tanned humanoid of medium height with long blonde hair and brown shoes, who he spoke to personally using telepathy and hand signals. Orthon refused to be photographed, but when he left in his craft, Adamski made plaster casts of Orthon's footprints, in which Adamski found mysterious symbols. On December 13, 1952, Adamski released an iconic photograph of what became known as the "Adamski-style UFO." This craft had a hollow underbelly and three "bulb-like" structures underneath. Adamski's flying saucer photo was later deemed a fake by German scientist Walther Riedel, stating that the reason the three bulbs under the craft looked like light bulbs is because they WERE light bulbs. Adamski also lectured with a letter, allegedly from the US State Department, stating that the government knew of Adamski's meeting with extraterrestrials in 1952. According to ufologist James Moseley, the FBI investigated the letter and debunked it as a hoax. Despite this statement by the FBI, Adamski continued to show that his experiences were confirmed by the US government to impress crowds at his public lectures. During one of Adamski's many alleged trips to space with the space brothers, they flew around to the dark side of the moon. There Adamski described cities, trees, and snow-capped mountains on the moon. When the Soviet lunar probe, Luna 3, photographed the dark side of the moon in 1959 and did not reveal such features, Adamski promptly stated that the Soviets fooled the world and altered the photographs to show a barren, lifeless moon surface. Despite all indications that Adamski fabricated his stories and photos, Adamski enjoyed a nice ride of fame during his heyday, even meeting by official request with Queen Juliana of the Netherlands. The Queen, according to the Dutch Aeronautical Association President, Cornelis Kolff, showed a keen interest in Adamski (he was, after all, quite handsome), along with an interest in the whole subject of UFOs and extraterrestrials. There is, however, one little problem with writing Adamski off as a total fraud. That problem is revealed by video footage that exists of an alleged "Venusian Scoutcraft" flying through the air that was taken by Madeleine Rodeffer at her home prior to Adamski's death a decade after he published his books. The craft in the film looks identical to the photograph that Adamski is thought to have faked using the top of a chicken coop (as one researcher determined) and three General Electric light bulbs for landing gear. Adamski-style flying saucers have also been photographed in action all over the world, which is a real conundrum. The Rodeffer video has been analyzed by several experts over the years and found to be quite enigmatic and possibly authentic. Once again, an absurd artifact, the fake Adamski flying saucer photo, is used to provide cover for actual flying saucer activity. There is a pattern here. The Rodeffer video will be discussed further in the next chapter.

Truman Bethurum

Another 1950s contactee, Truman Bethurum, was a personal associate of George Adamski. In 1953, when Bethurum was 55 years old, he was able to publish newspaper and magazine articles that detailed his multiple contacts with the human crew of a landed spaceship, whose leader was a voluptuous female named Captain Aura Rhanes. The Captain and her crew were from an undiscovered planet named Clarion. Bethurum stated that the planet Clarion exists somewhere in our own solar system, possibly hiding undetected behind the Moon. Bethurum was a mechanic by trade and part-time spiritual advisor. He served as facilitator for a philosophical group called the *Sanctuary of Thought* (1954) near Prescott, Arizona. This group was created for individuals who were interested in considering the possibility of extraterrestrial intelligences. Bethurum claimed to possess physical artifacts given to him by Captain Aura Rhanes to confirm his accounts of visitation. During Bethurum's many public lectures, he jokingly told the story that his second wife divorced him over the buxom Captain Rhanes. Bethurum then married his third wife during one of George Van Tassel's annual Giant Rock Spacecraft Conventions. Whether Truman Bethurum's flying saucer experiences were physical, psychic, or intentionally fabricated for attention, his contactee account from 1953 contributed to molding public perceptions in his day concerning outer space and alien visitation, an effect that continues to exert an influence one way or another in the minds of UFO believers and skeptics alike.

A Small Sample of 1953 UFO Sightings

1953 was a crazy year for UFOs. The following string of flying saucer sightings are just a small sampling of the many reports that came in that year from credible witnesses, many confirmed on radar. This sampling is documented just to convey the magnitude of what Air Force officials and those who worked on Project Blue Book were dealing with at the time.

On January 1, New Year's Day, 1953, a silver flying saucer with a red glowing bottom was witnessed by Warner Anderson and two other female witnesses for ten seconds. Six days later on January 8, several witnesses from the 82nd Fighter-Interceptor Squadron, including the squadron commander, saw a green disk below the clouds flying with a bobbling vertical and sideways motion southwest of Larson Air Force Base. On January 10, retired Colonel Robert McNab and Mr. Hunter of the Federal Security Agency saw a disk that made three 360 degree turns in 90 seconds, along with abrupt 90 degree turns right and left. The disk stopped in mid-air, then accelerated and sped away out of sight vertically. A week later, on January 17, geologist JJ Sackett reported a brilliant green-gold blimp-shaped object flying approximately 400 mph straight and level near Guatemala City, Guatemala. The disk stopped suddenly, then shot straight up and vanished. January 28 brought three different sightings - the owner of Love Diving Company, R.W. Love, caught a white disk flying straight and level overhead, Air Force Sergeant George Beyer saw 5 green spheres in V-formation changing to trail formation at which time the end object turned red. Also, radar maintenance personnel in Albany, Georgia tracked an unknown object on radar with visual confirmation for 20 minutes. On February 3, radar operators in Keflavik, Iceland tracked 4 unidentified objects for 24 minutes. The next day, February 4, Stanley Brown, a US Weather Bureau observer in Yuma, Arizona, witnessed a white oblong object flying straight up at high speed, leveling off, joined by a second similar object which flew away from the first twice and returned before both objects were visually lost behind the clouds. On February 9, a Marine Corps pilot observed an unknown oblong object ascending rapidly after an alert from a Navy signal tower. On February 17, two officers and three USAF airmen in Port Austin, Michigan tracked on radar with visual confirmation an unknown object larger and brighter than a star that changed color moving slowly across the sky. On February 24, a warrant officer saw 2 bright red round objects with halos flying in small circles that climbed and faded out of sight. On February 27, in Shreveport Louisiana, a USAF airman/private pilot saw 5 yellow disks that made circular turns and fluttered. Three vanished and the other two made erratic square turns and left. On March 11, an experienced pilot and wife of a Pan Am flight engineer, Mrs. Nina Cook, reported a large blinking light moving up and down along a mountain range. Three days later, on March 14, ten crew members aboard a US Navy patrol plane tracked on airborne radar with visual confirmation groups of 5-10 colored lights, totaling 90-100 craft flying to the left of their airplane. On March 21, a Ground Observer Corps observation post reported a group of 6 disks flying high and fast. Four days later, on March 25, an Air Force Captain and a second witness saw several lights making 360 degree turns. On March 27, a pilot of a USAF F-86 jet fighter chased a bright orange disk at 900 mph that executed three fast rolls in Mt. Taylor, New Mexico. On April 8, 1st Lt. D.J. Pichon, the pilot of a USAF F-94B jet interceptor, reported a bright blue light that descended, accelerated, and flew parallel to his plane, increasing rapidly in speed and vanishing. On March 1, a pilot, a radar operator, and a control tower operator at Goose AFB, Labrador, Canada, confirmed an evaded interception attempt by a USAF F-94 interceptor of a luminescent white flying object. Many unidentified civilians witnessed 9 meandering lights at 8:30 p.m. in San Antonio, Texas, on March 27. A red object flying at 1100 mph returned to Goose AFB on June 22, eluding the chasing F-94 jet aircraft. On June 24, near Iwo Jima, Bonin Islands, the crew of a USAF KB-29 aerial tanker plane tracked on radar an object that approached within a half mile of their aircraft for 1 minute. A red triangle hovered and rotated before a weather observer in Simiutak, Greenland that same day. On August 3, at Amarillo, Texas, an Airport Control Tower Chief, C.S. Lewis, reported an unidentified round, reflective, translucent object that flew straight, stopped for 7 seconds, sped up, stopped again, and was joined by a similar object that then flew off in two different directions. On August 20 a grey oval object made 4 passes at the crew of a TB-29 bomber/trainer, witnessed and reported by the entire crew. On August 23, excellent daytime video footage of a flying disk was captured by Tom Drury, who was Deputy Director of the Department of Civil Aviation in Papua, New Guinea, which was an Australian territory at the time. About midday, Tom observed a small cloud forming in a clear sky above him. Tom was quite startled when a brilliant object that looked like a tiny sun at first, changing rapidly into a silver disk, flew at a high rate of speed out of the cloud. Tom immediately began filming. The developed film caused much squirming within the Australian and US intelligence community. Sections of the original film are reported to have been edited out. However, prints of the video were made available to UFO researchers. One of the individuals who examined the prints was the owner the *Australian Flying Saucer Magazine*, Edgar Jarrold. Jarrold stated in his February, 1955 issue that the prints are solid confirmation that the flying disks do, in fact, exist. This sighting leaves us all a clue as to how these disks possibly remain hidden from public view within intentionally manufactured clouds used as a cloaking mechanism. What an uncanny feeling to know that, on any given day, some of the beautiful clouds in the sky may not be natural, but alien camouflage hiding multiple luminous orbs that can morph into shiny metallic silver disks, commonly known as flying saucers, and exit the cloud at any moment for our viewing pleasure. On the night of November 23, 1953, Air Defense Command radars detected an unidentified aerial target over Lake Superior near Kinross Air Force Base. After contacting the 433rd Fighter Interceptor Squadron near Truax Field, Madison, Wisconsin, an Air Force F-89C was scrambled toward the radar blip, piloted by First Lieutenant Felix Monica Jr., and his onboard radar observer, Second Lieutenant Robert L. Wilson. Radar operators watched with baited breath as the F-89C all-weather interceptor approached the UFO on the radar. To their utter astonishment, the interceptor and the radar target merged on screen and disappeared, with no trace of the F-89C ever found afterward. Donald Menzel, who UFO-researcher Stanton Friedman believes led a double life, one as a public debunker of UFOs, the other as an integral part of Majesty 12, otherwise known as Majestic 12, or MJ-12, made the claim that the F89C had lost control and flew into Lake Superior, even though there was no evidence at the time or since then that this was the case. On December 16, 1953, near Agoura, California, pilots in the air, along with a U-2 designer on the ground reported witnessing a flying saucer. A few days after that, on Christmas Eve, 1953, US Navy Lieutenants J.B. Howard and L.D. Linhard witnessed 10 silver disks flying straight and level at over 450 mph while flying in their F9F-2 fighter jets. Then, three days after Christmas, on December 28, 1953, Yuba County Airport Manager Dick Brandt witnessed a flying saucer with a brilliant blue light reflecting on a nearby building in Marysville, California, that hovered briefly during a 1.5 minute observation. These are just a small cluster of the hundreds of reports from the year 1953, enough to get a taste of just how busy Project Blue Book was in trying to investigate all these sightings. The sheer volume of reports also provides insight into why, a decade and a half later, the Air Force wanted so desperately to get out of this duty.

Riley Martin Sells Tickets to the Mothership

As always, right in the midst of legitimate sightings, many reported by credible military witnesses, trained observers, or captured on film, someone pops their head up and speaks out that lampoons the entire subject. The many alleged contactees of the 1950s, if nothing else, provided a form of tension relief within the UFO community as growing numbers of believers accepted the reality of an alien presence on Earth. No one will ever know for sure if something otherworldly actually happened to some of these individuals who made claims of alien contact. Keel always said that we really missed the boat by not taking these people seriously and studying them. Among the parade of contactees was Riley Martin. Martin would eventually host the *Riley Martin Show* on the Sirius Satellite Radio channel Howard 101. Riley claimed that he was contacted by the occupants of a flying saucer toward the end of 1953 after a good year of UFO sightings. In Riley's book, *The Coming of Tan*, he reveals how he was first contacted by aliens near the St. Frances River while living in Arkansas in November, 1953. Martin claims that a significant amount of information was uploaded to his brain during this encounter, including 144,000 symbols that he draws by hand and sells to people. These purchased drawings serve as a ticket for the buyer aboard the "Great Mother Ship" when it arrives as a part of Earth's transformation that was predicted to occur in 2012. When 2012 came and went without incident, many believers in the 2012 transformation began stating that 2012 was only the *beginning* of Earth's transformation, and that the transformation is now in an ongoing process. At the time of this writing, Riley continues to sell his symbol/tickets on his official website, along with an audiobook and musical CDs, Cherokee Nation headbands, and talking bobbleheads. Riley Martin describes 7 types of alien beings: The *Biaviians* who are short with large heads; the *Targzissians* who are reptilian; the *Stagyians* who have leather-like bodies and are of peaceful and scientific disposition; the *Dorians* who are humanoids with blonde hair and blue eyes; the *Insectillians* (Skreed) who are smart bug-like creatures about 5 feet tall, the *Nyptonians* who live in underwater bases on Earth, and a 7th type, who have a name that cannot be pronounced by humans. It is impossible to tell whether or not an actual alien download occurred in Riley Martin's mind. Perhaps it did. The experience of some sort of cosmic illumination happens all the time, as it did in the life of John Keel at the age of 17. It is quite possible that Riley Martin did receive information, but afterwards, mundane life in this world prompted him, using his natural mind, to capitalize on the symbols in his head, or even embellish what actually happened for sensational purposes. That doesn't mean it was all 100% fabricated for profit. It just means that, even though information can be downloaded directly from Eternisphere (the Universal Mind or Source Field), biological travelers from our own solar system, the Overlords of the Singularity (PSASI), or even from devious human beings using mind-control equipment. What a person does with that information afterward is determined by who they really are when returned to non-altered reality.

Albert Bender

In the middle of hundreds of UFO reports during 1953, a very strange man living as a recluse in his father-in-law's attic would make a significant contribution to the UFO saga. Albert Bender, at the time, was director of the *International Flying Saucer Bureau* (IFSB). Bender reported that 3 men dressed in black (MIB) paid him a visit at his home. During this enigmatic visit, the 3 men in black revealed to him the frightening answer to the mystery of the UFOs. The MIB, whoever or whatever they really were, informed Bender that he would wind up in jail if he revealed what they had just told him. The MIB also told him at the time that the US government had already known the secret of the UFOs for 2 years, which would place this knowledge within the government in 1951. Sometime after this original visit, he accidentally slipped in conversation concerning the UFO agenda. Bender immediately received an ominous phone call, allegedly from Washington D.C., warning Bender to be more careful in the future. Spooked by this phone call, Bender shut down the IFSB. In the last issue of his newsletter, *The Space Review*, Bender wrote:

> *The mystery of the flying saucers is no longer a mystery. The source is already known, but any information about this is being withheld by orders from a higher source. We would like to print the full story in Space Review, but because of the nature of the information we are very sorry that we have been advised in the negative. We advise those involved in saucer work to please be very cautious.*

Following the last issue of *Space Review*, with its ominous warning to those attempting to discover the secret of the flying saucers, a secret that this writer may be endangering his life with by revealing it to the world (if I am correct), Bender fell into utter obscurity. This absence produced decades of speculation by UFO researchers as to the nature of the UFO "secret," the real identity of the Men in Black, and the answer to why the MIB suppress UFO witnesses from speaking too much about UFO activity. Speculations about the identity of these mysterious entities vary. As UFO researcher Jerome Clark states, explanations for the identity of the MIB range "from CIA agents, evil astral entities, demons, agents of an international Nazi conspiracy, or agents of an international Jewish conspiracy." Since Bender's time, hundreds of MIB visits have been reported by UFO witnesses. The typical report involves three men in black, usually with dark or olive skin, elongated fingers, and oriental facial features. These three men often show up only minutes after a UFO sighting, warning the witnesses to remain silent about what they have just seen. MIB reports once reached the halls of the Pentagon. Pentagon officials became very concerned that some group of unknown individuals were out there in the world impersonating military officers. As Keel and other authors concluded, many MIB visits involve an unknown group of human officials seeking interviews with UFO witnesses in an effort to control public perception of the UFO enigma, while another group of MIB are an integral part of the Phenomenon itself. According to Keel, the MIB who are actually part of the Phenomenon are possibly transmogrifications of energy to temporary physicality produced by a living, intelligent energy source, likely indigenous to Earth but possibly extraterrestrial (although Keel leaned toward indigenous), an energy source that is currently unknown and unacknowledged by human science. At one point in his research, Keel put together a pictorial of different ethnicities around the world and asked MIB witnesses to point out the picture that most closely resembled the features of the men who appeared to them in their frightening MIB encounter. The majority of the witnesses strangely pointed to the exact same ethnic group – Laplanders - a complexity of detail that would surface again and again in ufonaut reports dating back to the late 1800s during the Great Airship Mystery and continuing to the highly complex abduction cases of Antonio Vilas-Boas in 1957 and Peter Koury in 1992.

The Cosmic Circle of Fellowship
A UFO religion called the *Cosmic Circle of Fellowship* was founded by postman William Ferguson in 1953. Ferguson was a practicioner of deep relaxation. He was able to relax himself into such a deep state of meditation that he visited the "6th and 7th dimensions." Whenever Ferguson returned from these higher dimensions, he found that his physical body on Earth no longer existed, and only by strenuous psychic exercises was he able to rematerialize his body. Ferguson is generally thought of as riding the fame of George Adamski, complete with reports of visitations by Space Brothers from Venus and trips aboard their flying saucers. Like his contemporary, Orfeo Angelucci, Ferguson taught that the flying saucers were from a higher realm of existence and could materialize and dematerialize their ships at will. Ferguson authored books that detailed the messages he received from the Space Brothers, in particular messages of body healing and spiritual development from an interdimensional being named *Khauga*. Ferguson details his messages in his books, *Khauga - Cosmic Circle of Fellowship* and *A Message from Outer Space*, both published in 1955. Ferguson had a following for a period of time as he enjoyed his 15 minutes of fame. However, his mini-cult of space cadets promptly disintegrated following his death in 1967.

The Coniston Saucer
On February 15, 1954, 13-year-old Stephen Darbishire of Lake Coniston, Cumbria, England, produced a photograph of a flying saucer that came to be known as the "Coniston Saucer." The saucer in Stephen's photograph looks nearly identical to the Adamski-style "Venusian scout craft" photo, having the same basic bell-structure, the same portholes around the perimeter, and the three bulbous structures at the bottom. Those who have concluded that Adamski fabricated the saucer in his famous photograph of a Venusian scout craft with the top of a chicken coop and 3 light bulbs are faced with the improbability that a 13-year-old boy in another country had enough interest in producing a similar-looking saucer picture that he took the time and trouble to use the exact same parts and build a fake saucer that looked identical to Adamski's. It is doubtful that Stephen Darbishire would have even read Adamski's book or viewed the photographs within the pages. The co-author of Adamski's *Flying Saucers Have Landed*, Desmond Leslie, was so taken by the boy's photo that he made a personal trip to England to visit Stephen

and his father at their home. Stephen's father was a prominent local doctor, Dr. Darbishire. After visiting the boy and his father, Leslie became convinced of the authenticity of Stephen's story, as well as his confirming photograph. This leads to the possibility that, even if Adamski faked his photo, that he based the fabrication on an actual saucer than he saw for real at some point. We are also stuck with the reality that, despite the possibility that Adamski faked his saucer photo, real Adamksi-style saucers are flying around in our skies, many of which have been captured on film over the years.

Cedric Allingham

On February 18, 1954, just three days after Stephen Darbishire took his "Coniston Saucer" photo, British contactee Cedric Allingham was bird-watching when he saw an Adamski-style flying saucer. Allingham began snapping photographs of the saucer as it flew high in the air. Allingham published the photos in his 1955 book, *Flying Saucer from Mars*. In these pages, Cedric Allingham gives his own critique of Adamski's *Flying Saucers have landed*, adding pertinent details to Desmond Leslie's "flying saucer museum" section in which Leslie documents a large number of paleo-UFO sightings. According to Allingham, after he snapped the two photos of the saucer in the air, the saucer headed directly toward him from the ocean and landed. A common-looking humanoid with a high forehead, similar to Adamski's description of Orthon, the Venusian Adamski met in the California desert, emerged from the saucer with a breathing apparatus in his nose similar to a modern nasal cannula used in hospitals. Allingham attempted to communicate with the man, who, using hand signals (as in Adamski's account), determined that the man was not from Venus, but from Mars. A photograph of the man appears in his book as he was walking back to the saucer to take off again. Allingham believes that the saucers are powered by a small atomic engine, and are material rather than etheric in nature, based on his own personal experience with the man from Mars. Certain modern investigators, such as Christopher Allen or Stuart Campbell, concluded in 1986 after much investigation, that Allingham's work was a hoax. Allingham's book, they thought, was just a parody of George Adamski's 1953 book, *Flying Saucers Have Landed*, designed to make fun of the gullibility of British UFO researchers. However, throughout Allingham's book, he speaks highly of Adamski and his flying saucer book. Allingham believed that the bell-shaped flying saucer photographed and published in Adamski's book was authentic. Allingham also believed that the flying saucer he personally photographed was the same saucer that appeared in the photograph by 13-year-old Stephen Darbishire just 3 days before Allingham's own sighting. Allingham predicted that we would all be seeing more of the men from Mars and Venus in the future, as they were watching Earth out of concern for our discovery of atomic power. The Space Brothers did not want us to destroy ourselves, or take our aggressions into outer space.

Adamski-Style Saucers Witnessed Around the World

On first glance at Adamski's Venusian scout craft photo, it looks like something that was fabricated from junkyard parts. Perhaps Adamski made a saucer model based on something he actually saw, or there may be something even stranger going on here. That is, the intelligences behind the UFOs, who apparently have the power to create realistic illusions that fool humans, may have the ability to scan images in the human mind, from which they produce images of flying saucers that appear physical to us. In other words, flying saucers appear as we expect them to appear *based on our current understanding of the universe*. Following the publication of Adamski's infamous flying saucer photo, the believing public came to accept that flying saucers were supposed to look like the one from Adamski's book. Like something straight out of a *Twilight Zone* episode, Adamski-style flying saucers began appearing to people for real all over the world. Some were just sighting reports, but other witnesses actually captured these saucers on film, and they looked exactly like Adamski's photograph. Even weirder, Adamski-style flying saucers were even described in detail prior to the Adamski era. In the book, *UFOs Caught On Film: Amazing Evidence of Alien Visitors to Earth* by B.J.Booth, there is a photograph of an Adamski-style flying saucer taken by a local volunteer fireman in Oregon on page 13 from the year 1927! George Adamski allegedly took his first picture of such a craft on December 13, 1952, 25 years later. Following Adamski's photo, which was probably faked, an Adamski-style saucer was photographed by Jerroid E. Baker with a 116 brownie at Mt. Palomar, California. Then W.C. Hall photographed an Adamski-style saucer in Australia in 1954. On April 8, 1954, an Adamski-style saucer appeared over Greatstone in Kent, observed by H.S. Johnson and Mrs. J. Stoner. On May 19, 1954, meteorologists F.H. O'Donnell and D.A. Clarke from Mevagissey in Cornwall, both of whom had read George Adamski's *Flying Saucers have Landed* and were highly skeptical of flying saucers in general, reported seeing an Adamski-style saucer themselves with binoculars, much to their utter astonishment. On June 3, 1954, a retired Army officer in Yorkshire, Major W.T. Smith, also reported an Adamski-style saucer that was tilting from side-to-side and hovering in the air for several minutes. This Adamski-style saucer sighting was confirmed by a second observer in the area named Charles Denison. On June 29, 1954, a Stratocruiser airliner piloted by a Captain Howard and his crew was flying between New York and Goose Bay at 19,000 feet ran into a number of large, dark, solid, bell-shaped flying saucers sailing at approximately 260 mph about 5 miles away from their plane. They called in by radio to Goose Bay, who verified their report on radar and dispatched a fighter plane to the area. However, by the time the fighter arrived, the saucers vanished as mysteriously as they had appeared. Contactee Howard Menger took photographs of Adamski-style saucers in 1956. As mentioned, video was captured of an actual, flying, Adamski-style saucer at the home of a respected US government official, Madeleine Rodeffer, in Silver Springs, Maryland, on February 28, 1965 (more on this event later). On July 26, 1966, Mr. John Sheets photographed an Adamski-style saucer while on a camping trip in Lost Creek, California. Another Adamski-style saucer was photographed at Benedum Airport in 1968. Fritz Van Nest photographed an Adamski saucer in Oregon in 1968. Architect Hugo Vega photographed an Adamski saucer 31 miles from Lima, Peru, on October 19, 1973. Ryutaro Umehara snapped a series of in-flight photographs of Adamski saucers on May 11, 1975 in Chiba, Japan. All of these photographs of Adamski-style flying saucers are just a google away on the internet to observe. It should be a bit unsettling to anyone skeptical of George Adamski's original photographs that identical Adamski-style craft have been photographed so extensively around the world over the course of several decades. There is one particularly enigmatic photograph floating around on the internet that shows an Adamski-style flying saucer resting quietly at the base of a US atomic explosion taken just milliseconds from the initial blast. It is as if the craft was just sitting there, completely unaffected by the atomic blast and observing the human use of atomic weapons at the test site. Although this is an enjoyable and very haunting image to behold, this photo is nearly impossible to authenticate, but it certainly invokes much food for thought. It may very well be that, as the image of Adamski-style saucers made its way into the public consciousness in 1952, the intelligences behind the flying saucer mystery began producing images in the sky of Adamski-style saucers in temporary materialized form. This leaves us with the strangest question of all. That is, if Adamski or someone else had produced and published a photograph of a flying vehicle from junkyard parts that looked like, say, a banana, and this image was accepted in the minds of the public as the way such flying devices should appear, would all the bell-shaped, Adamski-style flying saucers witnessed and photographed throughout the world have been reporting and even photographing flying bananas instead of flying saucers? Is it that easy for human perceptions to be manipulated? These flying bananas would have been as real, or unreal (depending on one's point of view) as the bell-shaped Adamski-style flying saucers that Adamski so successfully implanted into our minds during this period of time. However, due to the fact that these bell-shaped, Adamski-style flying saucers were reported before George Adamski was born, and the fact that these saucers have been seen and photographed all over the world after George Adamski passed away, we are forced to conclude that these saucers exist. The saucers belong to someone somewhere, regardless of whether Adamski faked his photographs or not.

Nuking Paradise
Sadly, just two weeks after both Cedric Allingham and Stephen Darbishire snapped photographs of Adamski-style scout craft carrying pilots arriving here on Earth to warn humanity of the dangers of nuclear annihilation, the US military, oblivious to the warnings of our Space Brothers, unheedingly and blindly detonated a devastating nuclear weapons test named *Castle Bravo* on March 1, 1954 in the pristine paradise of Bikini Atoll in the Marshall Islands. One can only speculate how psychologically damaged, perverted, and mentally ill a person or country would have to be to set off a nuclear explosion in this beautiful group of islands that was

virtually untouched by modern influences or pollution. Castle Bravo was the very first test of a deployable, solid fuel, thermonuclear weapon, the largest nuclear weapon ever tested by the United States. This nuclear detonation resulted in deadly and unanticipated levels of nuclear fallout spreading eastward onto the inhabited Rongelap and Rongerik atolls, both of which necessitated emergency evacuations. Many of the Marshall Islands natives suffered birth defects, eventually receiving financial compensation by the federal government of the United States for damages. Also, a Japanese fishing boat came into contact with nuclear fallout from the Castle Bravo nuclear test. Many of the crew became ill, and one Japanese crewmember died. So in the years following *The Day the Earth Stood Still*, in which a humanoid alien was depicted who warned humanity against the use of nuclear weapons, in spite of the Washington D.C. UFO flyover, and heedless to the multiple reports of actual humanoid visitors from other worlds who contacted select individuals to proclaim the anti-nuclear message of the Space Brothers, our response to these messages was to defiantly set off the largest nuclear detonation in the history of the United States on a pristine tropical island. Judging by the danger that our world is in right now of self-destruction by global nuclear warfare, I, for one, wish that we had listened to our enigmatic cosmic mentors.

George Hunt Williamson

Among the many "Georges" that surfaced during the 1950s contactee era was George Hunt Williamson. Inspired by George Adamski's popularity, and possibly by the Shaver Mystery, Williamson, having a lifelong proclivity toward mysticism, attempted to contact our space visitors with his Ouija board. In Williamson's world, all the planets in our solar system were inhabited by intelligences willing and able to communicate with humans through the Ouija. Using this method throughout the 1950s, Williamson contacted: Actar of Mercury; Adu of Hatton in Andromeda; Agfa Affa from Uranus; Ankar-22 of Jupiter; Artok and/or Garr of Pluto; Awa from Outer Space; Kadar Lacu, Suttku, and/or Oara of Saturn; Regga or Zago of Mars; Ro of Torresoton; Terra of Venus; Wan-4 of the Safanian planets; and Zo of the planet Neptune. Williamson combined the fruits of his own Ouija-board channeling with ideas from a small contactee cult, *The Brotherhood of the Seven Rays*, to write many books about his revelations from the Space Brothers. Williamson's books include, *The Saucers Speak* (1954), *Other Tongues---Other Flesh* (1957); *Secret Places of the Lion* (1958), *UFOs Confidential* (1958); *Road in the Sky* (1959); and *Secret of the Andes* (1961). Many of these books are still in print and available on Amazon. Williamson referred to himself as "professor" and claimed extensive academic merits when he actually had none, just as Adamski went by the designation of professor when he actually operated a small hamburger stand. Williamson's books borrowed heavily from Theosophical teachings, with the Space Brothers teaching humans how to become civilized. Williamson portrayed all the characters in the Old and New Testaments as incarnations by a half dozen or so higher beings who incarnate to uplift human society from time to time. George Hunt Williamson used the poetic term, *wanderer*. A wanderer is a high ET from another world or another dimension who agrees to transfer their soul to Earth by incarnating in the flesh and walking among humans in order to assist with humanity's evolution of consciousness. George Hunt Williamson was a wanderer himself in the true sense of the word. Sometime in the 1960s he disappeared to South America, where he allegedly finally "met" with the actual consciousness behind the UFO mystery. Following his quest for self-discovery in South America, Williamson promptly ended his UFO research. He eventually returned to the United States and lived out the remainder of his days quietly as a Gnostic Christian.

The concept of the wanderer is now in full force. Many individuals today are convinced, or become convinced by a New Age "counselor," that the reason they struggle on this planet is because they are actually from somewhere else, a place that is more evolved. The real reason that life here on Earth is such a struggle is because they are actually from elsewhere, where the violence we see on Earth has long since been eliminated. As a highly-evolved soul from another world, they are just here to help struggling Earthlings. They are instructed by their walk-in counselors that they don't even have to do anything, they just need to continue being themselves to exert an uplifting influence on humanity while they are here. Guiding someone into the realization that they are not from the Earth is an emerging field for modern psychologists, hypnotherapists, and life coaches, some of whom likely have dubious or profit-seeking motivations. However, this type of therapy probably helps some people, saving them from depression or low self-esteem, so I just leave it alone.

The McMinnville Craft Appears in France

In the summer of 1954, UFO researchers who may have suspected that the UFO photos from McMinnville, Oregon in 1950 were hoaxed were stunned when a pilot flying over Rouen, France captured a flying saucer on film from his aircraft that was identical to the craft that Evelyn and Paul Trent photographed four years earlier. The Trent flying saucer, along with the one filmed by the French pilot, were both real after all, and represented something other than any known terrestrial technology that was flying in the air at that time.

UFO/occupant Sighting Makes International Press

Just after Trent flying saucer photo surfaced that was taken by the pilot in France, another UFO sighting in France made the International Press, and this time it involved live ufonauts. On September 10, 1954, a 34-year-old metalworker, Marius Dewilde, was quietly reading after his wife and children were sound asleep at their home in the woods near Quarouble. His dog, Kiki, began barking outside. Marius retrieved a flashlight and went out to check on her, fearing a possible prowler. Marius walked out to his garden, which was near a railway. He spotted a dark mass on the tracks, and assumed it was a cart that someone had left. He then spotted his dog, Kiki, with the flashlight, who was crawling on her belly toward him and whining. He suddenly heard footsteps as Kiki began barking again. Pointing the flashlight to the sound of the footsteps, just beyond a fence, Dewilde spotted two creatures in "diver's suits" walking toward the dark mass on the tracks in single file, as the flashlight reflected off their metallic headgear. The creatures were about 3.5 feet tall with wide shoulders and short legs. Dewilde instinctively ran after the two creatures and was hit by a blinding light emitted from the dark mass on the tracks. He became instantly paralyzed. He tried to cry out but nothing would come out of his mouth. When he finally regained the use of his legs, he saw the dark mass rise from the tracks and could make out a door closing. He heard a "whistling sound" while dark steam blasted from the bottom of the craft as it lifted. The object rose to about 100 feet in the air, began glowing red, took off, and vanished. Dewilde desperately ran a mile to the police station in the village of Onnaing. Once he arrived at the station, his frantic, confused speech caused the police to dismiss Dewilde as a lunatic. Dewilde then went to the office of the police commissioner and told his story to Commissioner Gouchet. Based on the fright Dewilde was expressing to Gouchet, the commissioner decided to send out investigators from the Air Police and the Department of Territorial Security. On the tracks, the investigators found five 1 ½ inch square impressions in the railroad tracks. The marks were freshly cut, and indicated that tremendous pressure had to have been applied that they calculated at 30 tons to make such impressions. They also discovered calcined stones in the area indicating that they were subjected to intense heat. Dewilde's story was also corroborated by several local witnesses who reported a reddish glow in the sky that evening. It's absolutely stunning that so many of these ufonaut encounters can be unearthed from the literature from around the world. The variety of populations that appear to come and go on this planet, many of whom appear to be biological and physical, who have mysterious tasks to accomplish on Earth when they land and exit their crafts, is one facet of the UFO mystery that is hard to accept, as we perceive the rest of the solar system as uninhabitable, and cannot imagine creatures coming here from other galaxies due to the great distances involved. Even so, researchers like Hanz Holzer, who focused specifically on the UFO landing and ufonaut cases, became convinced that biological creatures from other worlds have, in fact, been visiting our planet on a regular basis, or in waves throughout history. In his book, *The Ufonauts*, he stated (audible, introduction):

Now hear this – there are people in other worlds in space. They are more or less like us, and they have been coming here rather frequently in UFOs. UFOs are not imaginary, not the product of overactive minds. UFOs – unidentified flying objects – are tangible machines made of metal, propelled by several kinds of energy. None of these kinds are yet known to us on Earth, and they have landed, are landing, and will land in various places of our globe. These spacecraft are piloted by intelligent beings, and the crews of UFOs, the ufonauts, have been in contact with a great many human beings already. People from far-off worlds do not come here to confuse us. They are studying our world. They are taking specimens of our fauna and flora. They're very curious about humans, because they are different, ahead of us in many ways. Why are they coming here? What will happen next?

Hans Holzer was convinced that, whatever may be going on with UFOs on a sociological or psychic nature, that physical beings from other worlds have somehow made their way to the surface of our world, and have had interactions with humanity for a very long time now.

Adamski Humanoids in England

If George Adamski's description of human extraterrestrials was an isolated case, one might be tempted to write him off completely as a hoaxer, or accept the postulation that he had an encounter with Germans driving saucers operating with US technology gleaned from Nazi Germany during Operation Paperclip. However, in addition to Adamski's bell-shaped flying saucers being photographed in action all over the world, his was not the only report of humanoid visitation that bore a similar description, nor was the United States the only location in which these Space Brothers appeared. In October, 1954, Tony and Jessie Roestenberg had such a similar encounter. Jessie had been experiencing a tingling sensation in her nose and throat that day and thought she might be coming down with a cold. Jessie's two-year-old daughter, Karin, was happily playing and waiting for her two brothers, 6-year-old Ronald and 8-year-old Anthony, to arrive home from school. When the boys arrived and the three kids were playing together, all four of them heard a loud hissing sound, as if a bucket of water had been poured on a campfire. The family went outside to see what it was, and saw a large flying saucer moving low over their heads and headed south. They all ran behind their house to follow the saucer and when they got there, they were stunned to see the saucer hovering right above their house. The upper part of the disk was revolving, and the lower part was stationary as it silently hovered in the air. Above the revolving part was a black cupula with two transparent panels. Inside the saucer, the family saw two men through the clear panels. Gavin Gibbons, author of *The Coming of the Space Ships*, who also personally investigated this case, reports the following description (pg. 66):

> *She [Jessie Roestenberg] recalls that they looked very like Earthly men, with white skins and long hair down to their shoulders. Their foreheads seemed immensely high, with the features almost entirely in the bottom half of their faces. Their heads were enclosed in what appeared to be some sort of transparent helmets and they were dressed in clothes of turquoise blue that resembled ski suits that Mrs. Roestenberg had seen. But what appeared strangest of all to the little group of watchers on the ground was the unsmiling expression on the faces of the men from the sky. Sternly they gazed down at the Roestenberg family, not in an unkindly fashion, but almost sadly, compassionately.*

Gavin Gibbons gathered from this family's encounter that the Space People were selecting individuals to acclimate humanity to their presence, in preparation for a mass landing and open contact event that he speculated would occur at some point in the future. Many UFO researchers such as Gibbons were convinced in the 1950s that this was the purpose of the sightings. This anticipated open contact, however, never happened, and we are all left, 60 years later, straining to make sense of the humanoid extraterrestrials that were apparently making the rounds with contactees in the 1950s. There were just too many of them to ignore that share common features around the world to write the whole phenomenon off as delusion, hoaxes, or hallucinosis. Something was (and is) afoot, even though the Phenomenon changes in appearance over time along with advancements in human perceptions and consciousness. As a planet of human percipients, our concept of UFOs and extraterrestrials has changed from: strange erratics in the sky whose images we painted on cave walls; flying shields and encounters with humanoid "angels of the Lord" circa 2-3,000 years ago; appearances of "Little People" in the lore of Ireland; Greece; the Philippines; the Hawaiian Islands; and within Native American culture; humanoid dirigible pilots in the late 1800s right before the invention of dirigibles; to visitors from Venus and Mars in the 1950s who traveled in Adamski-style flying saucers and landed to express dire warnings to select individuals against our misuse of nuclear power. The Phenomenon continued from there to morph and include visitation by small insectoid creatures in the decades to come, to the most current view, that we share the planet with an an intelligent luminosity, possibly extraterrestrial, possibly indigenous to Earth or from another dimension that intersects with our own, intelligent plasmoids that have the ability to shapeshift into whatever form they wish us to see at the time. The purpose of the flying saucer appearances appears to be to impact human consciousness in whatever methods it has at its disposal, and guide us at all costs to the development of ever-increasing technology. This technology is now expanding at an exponential rate and is due to culminate in the Singularity sometime around 2045-2080. It is at this time that we shall meet the "real aliens" in their true form. Unless, of course, the guiding of humanity toward the technological singularity is more benign than I suspect. I sincerely hope that my thoughts of possible malfeasance turn out to be nothing more than the product of xenophobia and unjustified paranoia by my own primitive and suspicious mind. If this is the case, and the Overlords of the Singuarity are a vast and ultimately benign cosmic phenomenon that exists to guide various intelligent species toward technological singularities only to move on after the accomplishment of their goal to other planets and other populations, we may never know who they really are. In this scenario, our Overlords may forever lie beyond our understanding. In some ways, I find this idea more disturbing than any, because I, for one, want to know just who the intelligences behind the UFOs really are, what they actually look like, and understand their true intentions. If, in reality, we have not been genetically engineered for violence for purposes of competing technologies, and we are instead a product of struggling natural evolution, and there are, in fact, intelligences of a higher order who are trying to guide humanity into the Singularity for purposes of human development and enlightenment, many within the UFO community will breathe a sigh of relief.

Mass UFO Sighting at a Football Game

One month after Dewilde's unusual encounter, the same month as the Roestenberg encounter, on October 27, 1954 in Tuscany, 10,000 football fans were watching football at the concrete bowl of the Stadio Artemi Franchi, as the Fiorentina football club was playing on the field against a local rival, Pistoiese. Just after halftime the stadium fell totally silent. The crowd began to roar as their attention was diverted from the game with all fingers pointing skyward. The players came to a sudden standstill, and the ball rolled on the field until it stopped. Several large objects were sailing through the sky at a fast rate of speed and then suddenly stopped in mid-air. Then, a large, slow-moving egg-shaped craft, several disks, and multiple cigar-shaped crafts flew silently across the autumn sky before the mass of witnesses. A sticky substance that looked like silver glitter, referred to by UFO researchers as "angel hair" and described by some witnesses as "cobwebs" or "cotton balls" fell to the ground from the craft, where it rapidly disintegrated. The roofs of houses in Florence were covered with the angel hair for approximately 1 hour before it completely evaporated. One witness of the angel hair fall, Georgio Batini, ventured into the woods where he rolled samples of the substance up with match sticks and took them to the Institute of Chemical Analysis at the University of Florence. When he arrived, he found that other witnesses had also brought samples of the mysterious substance. The lab, led by Professor Giovanni Canneri, subjected the samples to spectrographic analysis in which the angel hair was destroyed in the process. The results of the analysis concluded that the angel hair consisted of boron, silicon, calcium, and magnesium. Despite this hard evidence from a UFO sighting that provided an unusual set of factual data from a university chemical lab, James McGaha, a former USAF fighter-jet pilot who later became an astronomer, wrote the phenomenon off as "migrating spiders" floating through the air. This absurd explanation continues to be perpetrated, in true fashion of those who, contrary to available evidence, apply their own outrageous ad hoc hypothesis to a UFO incident based on their own limited comprehension of reality, instead of accepting the actual information gleaned from a UFO sighting that leaves trace evidence. Spider silk is an organic compound, a protein consisting of nitrogen, calcium, hydrogen, and oxygen. So, despite factual data obtained from spectroscopic analysis of this particular angel hair dropping from a cluster of UFOs, the "migrating spider theory" perseveres to this day as an explanation for this phenomenon. Angel hair drops are reported during UFO sightings all over the world in areas where young spiders who sail in the air on their network of webs do not even exist. John Keel reported during his UFO investigations that he once received a phone call from a man who claimed to have a small, rapidly disintegrating sample of angel hair in a jar that he retrieved after witnessing a UFO dropping a load of the substance. Keel instructed the man to take the sample to a local pharmacy, which he did. The pharmacy sent him on to a hospital, where he found a man who was interested in the substance. This man applied a spectrographic analysis to the sample and found nothing but traces of fluorine gas in the bottle. This floored Keel, as he had investigated many flying saucer reports that involved, of all locations, fertilizer plants, where their main byproduct is fluoride. This particular incident led Keel to speculate whether the ufonauts were somehow seeding our atmosphere with byproducts of fluoride in order to make our atmosphere more palatable for them. However, the aforementioned analysis provided by the University of Florence had more of the samples to work with, so their samples were likely more reliable. However, we cannot rule out the possibility that the substance we call "angel hair" is produced for some unknown reason by different crafts from various locations that would demonstrate different chemical compositions if taken to a lab for analysis. Also, silicon and magnesium are common elements found in trace evidence cases. These terrestrial elements are mysteriously left behind by flying saucers, and oddly enough, at some Bigfoot sightings. Trace elements like puddles of silicon carbide left behind at both UFO landings and Bigfoot sightings have led some researchers to a tentative conclusion that UFOs and Bigfoot creatures are related in some strange way, and maybe they are right. There are cases in the record of individual Bigfoot sightings that report the creature disappearing in a flash of light after being shot at, or vanishing into a luminous flying object that was hovering overhead or that suddenly appeared, the creature and the flying object swiftly dematerializing together. However, these cases are so rare that more evidence is needed to consider them seriously. Even with the elements that compose angel hair identified by at least two different labs, the mystery remains as to what purpose the substance really serves. Was Keel on to something when he speculated that the ufonauts are terraforming Earth's atmosphere for some reason, a little at a time? Is it a simple waste product generated by the saucers themselves, a byproduct of their propulsion system perhaps, or worse, organic waste produced by the ufonauts themselves? Is it some sort of cloaking technique that makes deliveries of known terrestrial elements, causing many to conclude that the entire incident is a concocted hoax, serving to maintain the mystery of the saucers? When terrestrial products are found at locations of UFO sightings, it provides fuel for those who are quick to cry, "Hoax!" - and that might be exactly what is intended by an unknown intelligent phenomenon that apparently, for its own reasons, does not want to be commonly identified by the human population on this planet.

Elizabeth Klarer

Elizabeth Klarer was a female contactee from South Africa whose alleged encounters with extraterrestrials during the years 1954-1963 included sexual interaction with aliens. After reading George Adamski's *Flying Saucers Have Landed* (1953) and *Inside the Space Ships* (1955), Klarer began to realize that she had also been in telepathic contact with a space brother named Akon since childhood. Just as Adamski arranged a photo session with Orthon's craft in 1952, Klarer arranged a similar photo session to capture Akon's craft on July 17, 1955. Klarer's photos, like photos from most of the encounters mentioned in this book can be easily viewed online. Elizabeth Klarer's UFO photographs are quite amazing. Nearly a year later, in 1956, Klarer successfully summoned Akon and his ship to Earth. Klarer was taken up into orbit above

Earth. In 1957 Klarer was taken to Akon's home planet, Meton, which orbits in the nearby multiple-star system of Alpha Centauri. It was during her visit to Meton that Klarer had sex with Akon. She became pregnant and gave birth to a male child, Ayling, who was left behind on Meton for an education while Klarer returned to Earth. In the late 1950's during his world lecture tour, contactee George Adamski took time out of his busy schedule to travel to South Africa and meet Elizabeth Klarer. The two contactees had a nice conversation together about the purposes of the Space Brothers. Finally, in 1980, at the age of 70, Klarer published her book, *Beyond the Light Barrier,* which described all of her adventures with her lover Akon from Meton. Elizabeth died in 1994 in South Africa, where she had studied meteorology and learned to fly light aircraft.

Rosa Lotti

On November 1, 1954, Rosa Lotti was walking into Cennina, Italy, when she saw a strange-looking metallic object standing upright in the ground with a little door open, exposing small seats inside. Rosa described it as a "spindle, like 2 cones joined at their bases." From behind this craft emerged two 3-foot-tall humanoids that approached her with friendly expressions, the older one laughing. The two cheerful dwarf-like creatures had prominent front teeth and wore leather helmets and capes. They were speaking to one another in a language that sounded like Chinese (a common description of alien communication). Approaching Rosa, they snatched her carnations and one of her stockings. Rosa ran away. A deep hole in the ground was later found at the site.

The Unarians

In 1954, the Unarius Acadamy of Science, a UFO-oriented religious organization, was founded in Los Angeles, California by a husband and wife team, Ernest and Ruth Norman. Unarius is an acronym for "Universal Articulate Interdimensional Understanding of Science." Since the founding of Unarius, over 100 volumes of channeled material from higher celestial beings were produced through the original founders and subsequent members. According to the Normans, these beings exist on higher frequencies of reality, and are able to transfer useful material into the human brain once it achieves a trance state or a relaxed, altered state of perception. Unarians believe that our solar system was once inhabited by humanoid interplanetary travelers. In founder Ernest Norman's book, *The Truth about Mars,* Ernest reveals that the Chinese evolved from ancient interplanetary space travelers who colonized Mars about a million years ago before coming to Earth. Some of the Earth colony returned to Mars and continue to live underground there. Ernest claimed to have psychic abilities since childhood. He began his career as a palm reader who could tell WW2 widows what happened to their long-lost husbands. He eventually gravitated to giving psychic readings at spiritualist churches. Ernest began channeling and writing down information, much of which went into his first book, *The Voice of Venus.*

In addition to writing and publishing his channeled material, Ernest also began giving past life readings. Ernest believed that the flying saucers carried ufonauts who were denizens of higher, spiritual dimensions. These Ascended Masters were coming to Earth in their flying saucers to warn humans of their misuse of atomic energy. The channeled works of Ernest Norman describe the seven planes of Shamballa, multileveled realms of existence that are spiritual, non-physical worlds that harbor non-physical beings. Unarians believe in the laws of Karma and reincarnation. To Unarians, all phenomena are composed of energy and can never be created or destroyed, only changed in form. Each individual has an eternal soul that contains recorded data from past lives. Everything that is currently happening to an individual is a result of actions taken in this life and past lives. In order to advance, one must do good deeds to compensate for past actions that proved harmful to others. Beyond the physical realm, various strata of vibrational frequencies exist that harbor life at various levels of advancement. Ruth Norman, known to Unarians as "Uriel," became well-known in California for driving her 1969 Cadillac Coupe deVille adorned with airbrushed depictions of flying saucers and a large metal flying saucer mounted on the roof. The car is considered a treasured relic to Unarians, and continues to be driven each year in the annual Mother Goose Parade in El Cajon, California.

Eisenhower Meets With Extraterrestrials

Based on evidence from various sources, many modern ufologists suspect that President Dwight D. Eisenhower held secret meetings with extraterrestrials during his presidency that changed the course of humanity toward a very dark path. On February 20 and 21, 1954, Eisenhower, who was on vacation in Palm Springs, California, turned up missing. Even though he used the excuse of an emergency dental appointment, there are those who claim to have knowledge that the President was really rushed off to Edwards Air Force Base near Lancaster, California during this time for a secret meeting with extraterrestrials. This alleged meeting with ETs was the first of a series of meetings that led to the eventual treaty between the US government and one of two different groups of ETs. The first group, the so-called Nordics, were the President's first contact. These are assumed to be the same ETs that were making individual contacts with humans around the world to warn them of Earth's use of nuclear weapons. Later, Eisenhower met with the Grays, who offered to trade advanced alien technology for certain mineral rights on Earth and permission to abduct a limited number of humans for medical experimentation. When Eisenhower turned up missing, the press speculated that he was gravely ill, or that he might have even died. Eisenhower's Press Secretary, James C. Hagerty, told reporters that the President had lost a tooth cap on a piece of fried chicken, and that he had to go to a dentist for an emergency visit. At a church service that Sunday, a dentist was introduced to the congregation as the one who fixed the President's tooth. However, researcher William Moore concluded that this was simply a cover story for the secret meeting with Nordic aliens that did, in fact, take place. The first piece of circumstantial evidence to suggest that the meeting between

Eisenhower and ETs actually happened takes the form of a letter written to the Director of Borderland Science Research Associates, Meade Layne, by Gerald Light, a well-known leader in the Southern California metaphysical community, on April 16, 1954. In this letter, Gerald Light claimed to have been present at the President's meeting with ETs at Edwards Air Force Base. Gerald Light's letter reads as follows:

> *My dear friend: I have just returned from Muroc Air Force Base. The report is true — devastatingly true! I made the journey in company with Franklin Allen of the Hearst papers and Edwin Nourse of Brookings Institute, and Bishop MacIntyre of L.A. When we were allowed to enter the restricted section (after about 6 hours on which we were checked on every possible item, event, incident, and aspect of our personal and public lives), I had the distinct feeling that the world had come to an end with fantastic realism. For I have never seen so many human beings in a state of complete collapse and confusion, as they realized that their own world had indeed ended with such finality as to beggar description. The reality of the other-plane aeroforms is now and forever removed from the realms of speculation and made a rather painful part of the consciousness of every responsible scientific and political group. During my two days' visit I saw five separate and different types of aircraft being studied and handled by our Air Force officials - - - with the assistance and permission of the Etherians! I have no words to express my reactions. It has finally happened. It is now a matter of history. President Eisenhower, as you may know, was spirited over to Muroc one night during his visit to Palm Springs recently. And it is my conviction that he will ignore the terrific conflict between the various 'authorities' and go directly to the people via radio and television - - if the impasse continues much longer. From what I could gather, an official statement to the country is being prepared for delivery about the middle of May.*

Obviously, no such public announcement by President Eisenhower ever took place. Based on Gerald Light's letter, two camps of thinking emerged. One camp accused Gerald Light of making the whole thing up. The other camp accepted the contents of the letter at face value. The emotional content of the letter was exactly what one would expect if such an event actually took place. Also, the other people that were mentioned in Light's letter would have made perfect sense for such a secret meeting. This allows many to accept the letter as solid evidence that the meeting with ETs did, in fact, take place. One person mentioned in Light's letter, Dr. Edwin Nourse, served as Chief Economic Advisor to President Truman. Dr. Nourse was in an excellent position to advise President Eisenhower concerning the economic implications of a public announcement of ET contact. The other person, Cardinal James Frances MacIntyre, was the bishop and head of the Catholic Church in Los Angeles, California. MacIntyre would have been an excellent choice to attend this meeting to gauge the impact that such a public disclosure would have on world religion. The fact that the Catholic Church now has its own observatory, along with recent public statements made concerning the position the Catholic Church might take when Disclosure occurs, points to the real possibility that the acceptance of ET contact within the Catholic Church may go back to the time of President Eisenhower's meeting with ETs and Gerald Light's letter to Meade Layne. The final person mentioned in Light's letter was 80-year-old Franklin Winthrop Allen with the Hearst Newspapers Group, who authored a book instructing reporters on how to handle Congressional Committee Hearings. All four of these highly experienced individuals would have been very appropriate candidates to attend such a presidential meeting with ETs, as they represented the social, economic, and press institutions of the day, which lends credibility that the letter spoke the truth. Another piece of evidence comes from former Naval Intelligence Briefing Officer, William Cooper, who publicly revealed his exposure to top secret documents while serving in the Navy. These documents verified that Eisenhower's meeting with ETs did, in fact, take place. In Cooper's *Behold a Pale Horse*, Cooper stated that, according to these documents, astronomers did, in fact, discover large objects in space in 1953. The documents stated that several craft had taken up orbit above the equator. At this time, *Project Sigma* and *Project Plato* established communication with the crafts, and arranged a landing. A race of human-looking Nordic aliens contacted the government to warn against the aliens that were orbiting the equator. The Nordics offered to assist humans with their spiritual development if we would dismantle our nuclear arsenal. That offer, due to US military defense concerns during the Cold War, was rejected. Instead, a treaty was eventually signed by Eisenhower and the Gray aliens for the acquisition of technology. Another person who came eventually came forward was a former Sergeant in the US Marine Corps, Charles L. Suggs, the son of a former Commander with the US Navy, who was also named Charles Suggs. The son testified in 1991 that his father had accompanied President Eisenhower and the other members of the delegation on February 20, 1954, and that they had spoken to two Nordic aliens that arrived in flying saucers. These Nordic aliens stated that they were from another solar system, and were concerned about Earth's destructive use of nuclear weapons. Former Lockheed L-1011 Captain, John Lear, the son of the famous William Lear who created the Lear jet, also verified the Eisenhower meeting. John Lear has flown over 150 test aircraft, holds 18 world speed records, and became a contract pilot for the CIA. John Lear confirmed that there was, in fact, a meeting that took place with the Nordics and President Eisenhower. The Nordics offered to get rid of the Grays, but Eisenhower rejected the offer because the Nordics offered no advanced technology, only assistance in how to get our planet to stop fighting one another. Further confirmation that these meetings between Eisenhower and extraterrestrials did, in fact, take place, came in 2010 from a former US State Representative for New Hampshire, Henry W. McElroy, Jr., who revealed that while he was in office, he was privy to an official brief to President Eisenhower that confirmed the presence of humanoid extraterrestrials here in the United States, lending further support for the reality of Eisenhower's meetings with ETs in 1954, and again in 1955. McElroy states in his Youtube confession:

The document I saw was an official brief to President Eisenhower…This brief was pervaded with a sense of hope, and it informed President Eisenhower of the continued presence of extraterrestrial beings here in the United States.

Another witness with a Cosmic Top Secret Clearance and access to top secret military documents while in the service that confirmed the reality of the Eisenhower meeting was the late former US Army Master Sergeant Robert Dean. Dean revealed that while serving under the Supreme Allied Commander of Europe, it was known at the time that there were four different groups of aliens who were interacting with humans on Earth, one of which looked just like us and could pass for human if they walked down the street. Dean also confirmed the existence of a tall, hairless, pale white race of aliens, and another group with reptilian features. The general consensus among modern UFO researchers, based on existing evidence and testimonies over the years, is that President Eisenhower did, in fact, meet with a Nordic group of extraterrestrials on February 20, 1954, at Muroc (Edwards) Air Force Base. The offer from the Nordics was rejected. Later in 1954, a group of Grays with large noses, the group that had been orbiting the earth above the equator (the group the Nordics warned us away from) met with Eisenhower at Holloman Air Force Base in New Mexico. There an agreement was reached exchanging advanced technology for the rights to conduct medical experiments on a limited number of human beings. Additional confirmations that the meeting between President Eisenhower and Gray aliens actually happened have occurred more recently. One professional confirmation came from Phil Schneider, a geologist who worked with a variety of black budget projects over the years and had interacted with individuals within the secret government who were involved with ETs. Following his open discussions with the public, Phil Schneider was found murdered. Another controversial figure, Dr. Michael Wolf, author of *The Catchers of Heaven*, in which Wolf revealed details of his alleged long-term involvement with the secret government through this work of pseudo-fiction. Another confirmation came from a former Air Force serviceman who worked on black budget projects, Don Phillips. Phillips also testified that he has seen documents that verify the meeting between President Eisenhower and the Grays. Colonel Philip J. Corso, author of *The Day After Roswell*, who personally served on Eisenhower's National Security Council, also confirmed the reality of the meetings between President Eisenhower and the extraterrestrials, adding that the President really had no choice. Since we had previously rejected the offer of assistance by the Nordics because we did not wish to relinquish our nuclear weapons, and since we were not equipped to resist or fight the Grays, we were forced to concede to the terms of the Grays and allowed the human and animal experiments to occur in exchange for technology. In other words, in 1954 our government took the liberty to sell us all down the river for the sake of the desires and purposes of the Military Industrial Complex. This contract between large-nosed Gray aliens and the US government under President Eisenhower became known as the *Greada Treaty*, and is currently a staple item of interest within the modern

UFO community. Also, in October, 1954, General Douglas MacArthur gave us all a haunting reminder that the earth was, in fact, experiencing some type of alien intervention. General MacArthur stated that *the next war would be an interplanetary war, in which humanity would be up against sinister forces, a global enemy from another planetary galaxy.* MacArthur's statement alludes to the possibility that he may have had knowledge of Eisenhower's infamous agreement with the Grays. By the time Eisenhower left office in 1961, he exhibited evidence in his speeches of some level of regret about the decision to contract with the Grays. Eisenhower gave an ominous speech on his way out that warned against unchecked power and influence building within the military industrial complex. Eisenhower appears to have felt responsible for his part in the creation of this Frankenstein monster, and may have felt that the only thing he could do was warn us all that the monster was out of the lab.

Betty and Barney Hill's Psychic Neighbor

In April, 1954, just two months after the first meeting in a series of meetings between President Eisenhower and extraterrestrials, and several years prior to the Betty and Barney Hill abduction experience, Frances Swan, Betty and Barney Hill's neighbor who lived just up the road from them began receiving messages via automatic writing. These channeled messages were allegedly from an alien named Affa, commander of ship M-4, and Ponnar, commander of ship L-11, along with other aliens orbiting above the earth. These two aliens revealed to Swan through telepathic contact that they had bases on the moon. The aliens also conveyed the usual warning to Swan about the dangers of planetary catastrophe from the development and use of atomic weapons. It is very strange, to say the least, that such messages came through to Frances Swan simultaneous to radio messages received from the orbiting aliens. It's also quite a coincidence that she lived so close to Betty and Barney Hill, who were destined to become the first modern case of alien abduction to go public with their experience. All of this points to a reality that there was a lot going on during this time period between humans and various groups of ETs of both a physical and psychic nature.

The B-57 Bomber Photo

In 1954 a promotional photograph was taken in the air of a B-57 bomber near Edwards Air Force Base in California, the same location that President Eisenhower met with extraterrestrials. After developing the photos, shock ensued as a UFO appeared in the photograph right behind the bomber. Mr. Ralph Rankow from NICAP analyzed the photograph and the strange object that appeared behind the plane. The object in question threw no shadow, and portions of the craft were so black that it did not seem to reflect light. This feature is significant, as many early UFO photos such as this one exhibited portions of the craft that were totally dark and came to be known as the "superblack" phenomenon. UFO photos in which the vehicle in question displayed these odd areas of total blackness were automatically considered hoaxed photos at first, as the flying objects that demonstrated these areas of total blackness looked as if they were fabricated. Eventually, as more and more credible UFO photos began to show up that also had this same peculiar optical feature, researchers realized that they were, in fact, looking at a real phenomenon, and began speculating as to why these superblack areas showed up on film. Are the portions of the craft that do not reflect light on film areas of the vehicle that do not exist in our spatial dimension? Are these superblack portions of the craft simply reflecting light out of the human visible range? Debates on this issue continue, but whatever the reason for these areas that do not reflect visible light, we are not observing the entirety of what some of these crafts actually look like in reality. As for no shadow thrown, it seems possible that some of these objects exist in an accelerated time frame and are traveling so fast that the human eye cannot naturally observe them unless the object is captured in a still-shot using high-speed film. This B-57 UFO photo remains an early UFO classic. The photo is regarded by many as proof positive that such hyper-accelerated craft that only show up on high-speed film and display only a portion of their actual appearance in the visible light range do, in fact, exist.

Buck Nelson

In 1955, Buck Nelson, an American farmer, reported observing three flying saucers over his farmhouse. He began signaling the spacecraft with a flashlight, and took photographs. The occupants responded by signaling back at Nelson with a light "much brighter and hotter than the sun." When this happened, Nelson reported that he was healed of poor eyesight and chronic lumbago. Nelson was then visited after dusk by three spacemen from Venus. The three spacemen were accompanied by a large dog, and they all had a nice chat on his farm together. Two of the spacemen, Bucky and Bob, spoke of the "Twelve Laws of God" practiced on the planet Venus, and revealed to Nelson that Earth had civilizations in the past that had destroyed themselves with energies greater than atomic power. The spacemen therefore expressed grave concerns about Earth acquiring nuclear weapons. As with the biblical contactee, Moses, Nelson was given the Twelve Laws (very similar in context to the Ten Commandments) by extraterrestrials on his farm in Mountain View, Missouri, on April 24, 1955 (two years after Adamski began touring). Nelson revealed that Bucky showed him an advanced mechanical device from Venus called the "Book Machine" in which one could place a book, and all the text would be read, music played, and pictures displayed (a foreshadow of the Kindle?). A year later after Nelson was given the Law, he published his book, *My Trip to Mars, the Moon, and Venus*.

The message of the Space Brothers was clear – give up nuclear weapons and live together with one another in peace. Civilization on Earth had destroyed itself once before, and they were here to assist us in preventing the tragedy from happening again. Unfortunately, it doesn't appear that we listened to the Space Brothers, and are now under the influence of negative extraterrestrials who are manipulating humanity toward a technological singularity for their own purposes.

Dana Howard

Dana Howard, another 1950s contactee, allegedly traveled to Venus, married a Venusian, and raised a family there. On April 29, 1955, Dana Howard was attending a séance by medium Bertie Lilly Candler. During this séance, Candler summoned up an 8-foot-tall Venusian female, an entity that provided the material for Dana Howard's many books, including *My Flight to Venus* (1954); *Diane: She came from Venus* (1956); *Over the Threshold* (1957); *The Strange Case of T. Lobsang Rampa* (1958); *Vesta, the Earthborn Venusian* (1959); *Up Rainbow Hill* (1959); *The Keys to the Citadel of Space* (1960); and *The Kingdom of Space* (1961).

Children and UFO Experiences

On August 22, 1955 a report came in from California that appeared in a saucer bulletin by James Moseley. Kermit Douglas and several other children, ranging in age from 9-15, were playing in the garden when Kermit saw a luminous object hovering over the Douglas home. The object suddenly vanished and was replaced by a group of semi-transparent flying saucers with rays emerging from their perimeters and making pleasant musical "pinging sounds" in the air. One of the objects that was described as "big as three houses" landed and hovered in a nearby field. A 3.5 foot-tall entity then emerged from the craft with a round head, square, red glowing eyes, an open glowing red mouth, four little red diamonds for a nose, and two arms and four legs (or tentacles) that floated toward the children. Two of the children reported such a being in a translucent form, and one of the children reported seeing a disembodied silver arm that caused him to float up to the roof of the house, where he then fell off and injured his head. It would be easy to write such a story off as the fantasy of developing minds if it were not for the fact that there are many similar stories around the world that contain common elements. The musical pinging sounds were an interesting touch gleaned by the UFO intelligences from the minds of children, along with the "colorful rays" emanating from the flying saucers. The parents, of course, had difficulty with the story, and found nothing at the alleged site of the encounter. Apparently, the UFO intelligences that produce these theatrical displays for humans do not discriminate against human children.

Terror in Kentucky

On the very same day that the children in California had their flying saucer encounter with occupants, August 22, 1955, a family of adults in another state would experience a similar event that left them all scarred for life. Billy Ray Taylor was visiting his family in Hopkinsville, Kentucky that day. After going to the outdoor well after dark for a drink of water, he returned to the house and told his family that he had just seen a "spaceship" land in a nearby field. Rattled from this odd report, all eyes looking outside into the night, the family watched as a small, obviously nonhuman creature approached the house from the yard. The creature was about 3 ½ feet tall with a round head and no neck, large eyes wide apart on the face, a slit for a mouth from ear to ear, large elephant-like ears, elongated arms, and claws for hands. The creature appeared to have some source of internal illumination, and alternated from walking upright to dropping down on all fours when moving toward the house. Several similar creatures began to appear behind the first, climbing trees and jumping up on top of the Sutton family's house. Terrified, Frank Sutton fired a shotgun at one of the creatures that came right up to the front screen door, the blast knocking the creature backwards. Even though the creature suffered a direct shotgun blast, it got right back up and scrambled away swiftly on all fours. Frank Sutton followed outside to try and see where the creature ran off to, only to feel the claws from a second creature grabbing at his head from the roof of the house, driving him back inside. From that point the frightened family huddled inside the house as the goblins ran amok outside their home in the yard. This went on most of the night. Eventually, detecting a break in the commotion outside, the family quickly made it out to their car, piled inside, started the vehicle, and drove into town to the local police department to report the terrible sequence of events that had just happened to them. Deputy Sheriff George Batts, along with two other Kentucky State Police officers returned with the Suttons to their home and found nothing - no goblins, no spaceship, no traces of anything out of the ordinary. However, UFO researchers who later came to interview the family, including Isabel Davis from Civilian Saucer Investigations out of New York, were led to believe that the encounter, whatever it was, was genuine. They did not find any indication that any of the Sutton family members were lying, or attempting to perpetrate a hoax of any kind. Other local investigators, including the Chief of Police, observed that members of the Sutton Family who experienced the encounter were genuinely frightened, and concluded that something out of the ordinary did, in fact, happen that night. However, no one to this day has ever been able to explain it in rational terms. The best understanding of this event appears to be, as in thousands of other cases of paranormal encounters around the world, that the original witness, Billy Ray Taylor, who went out to the well for water, had an actual encounter with the mysterious luminous phenomenon that haunts this planet, a luminous, intelligent phenomenon that has awesome psychic capabilities involving mind invasion and manipulation, along with the ability to perpetrate the type of experience that this family in Kentucky reported. The observed internal luminosity of the goblin-like creatures emerging from what Taylor interpreted as a spaceship leaves a clue as to their apparitional nature. The creatures and the "craft" were likely part of the same intelligence. There was no distinction between the two. The fact that Frank Sutton's shotgun blast blew the creature at the screen door backwards with no harm done is another clue that no biological organism of flesh and blood was actually present. Nor was it a metallic robot that surely would have been blown to a pile of nuts and bolts on the yard by the shotgun. Rather, the creatures were created by the symbiotic interaction between Taylor's mind and the luminous intelligence he witnessed blazing across the sky into the field below. The interaction between the two intelligences, one human and nonhuman, produced a mass encounter through association that came complete with physical sensations, like the claw Frank Sutton felt as the creature pawed for his head from the roof. Whatever imagery the luminous phenomenon gleaned from Taylor's mind found its way inside all the other family member's minds as well. This is similar to the many poltergeist cases, in which the electromagnetically-sensitive psychic causes others who are not electromagnetically sensitive or psychic to also experience the poltergeist that was created by the interaction between the unknown intelligences on Earth that induce such experiences and the human psychic's mind. In this way, the UFO experience and the poltergeist experience may be related, or even one and the same. If so, this would explain the results of John Keel's investigations of UFO window areas when he discovered a correlation between UFO sightings and reports of poltergeists in the same area at the same time.

My Birth into the Physical Plane

In the middle of all this interaction on Earth between humans, extraterrestrials, and interdimensionals from other realms of Cryptoreality in the 1950s, the Transcendent Eternal Consciousness produced a human incarnation, a pinpoint of awareness that extended itself from Eternisphere to become what I have always known as my own individual life. As such, I incarnated back into this 3D world at a hospital in Fort Wayne, Indiana, on September 12, 1955. Like all creatures of the realm, I reentered this world as a work of conscious femtotechnology, i.e., cells endowed with inherent cosmic intelligence that self-organized from the microscopic level up, to become a member of the race of biological robots known as human beings. When I was one year old, my father, Maurice, an electronics technician, and my mother, Carol, a professional housewife, and I moved to Titusville, Florida, where my father got a job at Cape Canaveral, Florida (which later became Cape Kennedy after the assassination of President Kennedy in 1963 as I attended 3rd grade classes). It was there on the Space Coast in Titusville, Florida, that I would spend my childhood, 5 miles from the Indian River and 10 miles from the Atlantic Ocean at Playalinda Beach. In Titusville, Florida, I enjoyed a childhood full of sunshine and ocean. I became a fan of space adventures and science fiction very early. I was born into the world with a higher than average IQ and was, at the time, completely oblivious to the role of otherworldly influences or flying saucers and their mysterious crews. Project Blue Book was busy providing mundane explanations for flying saucer sightings, the US nuclear testing program was well underway, the Washington D.C. UFO flyby had already occurred three years previous to my birth, and George Adamski was busy evangelizing the world with the Gospel of the Venusian Space Brothers. Following my birth in 1955, for the next 54 years, the world of flying saucers and extraterrestrials would remain Cryptoreality for me (other than a few anomalous experiences) until a heart attack and near-death experience in 2009 opened my spiritual eyes to the matter. Hopefully through this writing, I can play a small part in the awakening of humankind to interdimensional realities and the transformation of human consciousness from a violent, primitive species under the control of negative nonhuman forces to a unified planet of peace and upward spiritual growth that lasts for many millennia to come.

CHAPTER 8

Extraterrestrial Incursions

"Yes, the extraterrestrials are here. The aliens are living among us. They are here in three ways – as spirits who have been born into human bodies, as outer space beings who have formulated bodies acceptable to dwell among us undetected, and as those visitors who live in secret bases, observing and watching."

- Delores Cannon, from *Keepers of the Garden.*

The Urantia Revelation

ON OCTOBER 12, 1955, The *Urantia Book*, originally compiled between 1919-1923 by Dr. William Sadler, a psychiatrist and skeptic of the paranormal, and his stenographer from messages channeled through one single person in an unconscious trance state, became available in print with eventual worldwide distribution. At 2097 pages, the Urantia Book is presented to the world as a new revelation. The Urantia Book contains a large volume of information concerning the nature of reality, the history of human religion, the history of the earth, science, and, most uniquely, an in-depth, complex narrative of the birth, early childhood, adolescent years, adult ministry, crucifixion, and resurrection of Jesus that is nothing less than a moving, literary masterpiece. The book has been a treasured possession of many well-known individuals, such as Elvis Presley, Jimi Hendrix, and Jerry Garcia. In 1923, four years after the material began coming through the channel personality (who remains anonymous to this day lest anyone focus their attention on him personally), Dr. Saddler and some of his associates began meeting together on Sundays for philosophical discussions. At the 4th meeting of the group, Sadler read samples of this unusual material that he had been compiling to the group, and they all became very interested in the content of the messages. The group then attempted to pose questions to the celestial authors, the answer of which would then come through the contact personality. By 1925, the meetings became a closed group of 30 members known as *The Forum.* Members of the Forum were then sworn to secrecy. They were not allowed to discuss the material that was coming through the contact with anyone outside the closed group. One astonishing aspect of the process by which the Urantia Book came into existence is the claim by forum members that, in response to their questions, fully-written papers would materialize for the group out of thin air. Since the publication of the Urantia Book in 1955, it has exerted a powerful influence on the resuscitation of Christianity in the modern world. The Urantia Book is slowly and surely being adopted by mainstream Christian churches, with selected readings from the Urantia Book presented in Sunday worship services along with Bible passages from the New Testament.

The Urantia Book presents an expansive, mind-opening cosmology. "Urantia" is the name given to the planet Earth by the celestial authors. According to the Urantia Book, our planet, Urantia, is only one of countless inhabited planets in the local universe of Nebadon. Our local universe, Nebadon, is only one of many universes comprising the Super Universe of Orvonton. Our Super Universe, Orvonton, is one of seven Super Universes that encircle Havona, wherein dwells the Father God on the Isle of Paradise. The Isle of Paradise is considered the geographical center of infinity. These seven Super Universes make up the Grand Universe, outside of which encircles the uninhabited realms of outer space, called the Master Universe. Each human personality is given a gift from the Father God in the form of an indwelling *Thought Adjuster* that each soul may call upon as they embark on their soul's journey from service-to-self to service-to-others, which is the purpose of life on Urantia. The Thought Adjuster is like a guide that knows the correct course of action toward spiritual maturity and eternal soul survival and advancement. According to the Urantia Book, Jesus was committed to living out his mortal life on Urantia without calling upon divine intervention to save him from whatever fate befell him in life, rather than coming to intentionally die as an atonement for the sins of humankind for a Father God who demanded blood sacrifice. It just so happened, that in the political times of his incarnation, Jesus was deemed a threat to the orthodox Judaic priesthood. The powers that be were in place during the lifetime of Jesus, and he was eventually crucified for threatening the existing power structure. Much detail is included in the Urantia Book concerning the resurrection of Jesus. The resurrected Jesus appeared in *Morontia* form, the state of existence in-between physical reality and the spiritual realms. The Urantia Book narrative of Jesus' post-resurrection visits to loved ones and disciples in his Morontia form is very detailed and fascinating. Somewhere in the 2000+ pages of the Urantia Book, there is something for everyone. Even if the book is not taken seriously as divine revelation, and considered as pure fiction, it is worth the time to read. Computer scientist and UFO researcher Dr. Jacques Vallee summed up his view of the Urantia Book in his classic study of UFO cults, *Messengers of Deception*, in which he states:

> *The Book of Urantia contains a surprisingly clear and readable section on religious history, and many inspired passages on morality and ethics. These sections are in striking contrast to the childish descriptions of the Spheres of the Beyond, which the imagination of the author has populated with beings that would not survive in the pages of the most grotesque piece of science fiction.*

Despite Vallee's harsh criticism of the Urantia Book's cosmology, the Urantia Book has had and will continue to have a tremendous impact on the state of modern Christianity, even though there are those who have never even heard of the Urantia Book until now. The information in the Urantia Book appears to reach out to a specific population of seekers who have outgrown the Bible, including myself, as indicated by the fact that even though I wrote a book about outgrowing the Bible, the Urantia Book deeply resonated with me when I read it. For many, the Urantia Book is like Bible 2.0. It is a specific bolus of cosmic information, directly from the minds of higher-order cosmic intelligences, addressed to humankind, the purpose of which is to mold our psyches in a desirable direction. The text of the Urantia Book is specifically designed for the human mentality of the 20th century and beyond, to open the mind, to nurture human spirituality, and contribute to the overall growth of human concepts of the universe at large. Whatever one thinks about the Urantia Book, it maintains internal consistency throughout the 2000+ pages, and is a real treasure to those who are ready to peruse its contents. As Dr. Paul Davies of Kings College, London, once said, "We have to face the fact that we may only belong to a transient stratum in a whole hierarchy of levels in organizational development." In my view, few other books from the present era bring this idea home to readers more than the Urantia Book. It appears to be worded and orchestrated such that the word arrangement itself opens a door in the reader's mind that leads to greater spiritual insight. In my own case, it led to an increased interest in doing good deeds for others in the world, and there aren't too many books around that are able to induce that type of powerful inner influence for the betterment of the human soul.

Omnec Onec: Ambassador from Venus

Simultaneous to my own present incarnation into this world in 1955, Omnec Onec, (aka Echo Leia), along with her Venusian uncle, Odin, arrived here on Earth in an Adamski-style Venusian scout craft at a young age from the astral plane of Venus, voluntarily taking on a physical body and joining us on Earth as she lives out her final physical incarnation. Their first stop upon arriving to Earth in their spacecraft was the temple of Agam Des in Tibet, in which visitors from the Astral Plane of other worlds in our solar system are well-known and welcome. Humans who dwell at Agam Des are called the *Eshwar-Khanewai*, or "God-Eaters," as they have evolved past the need for physical food, and derive sustenance directly from the Etheric Plane, as do the inhabitants of the Astral Plane. These humans are also known as the *Bourchakoum Masters*. Omnec Onec decided to dedicate her final lifetime in the physical to assisting humans toward spiritual evolution, many of whom erroneously believe that the physical realm is the only dimension that exists. Like the Urantia Book, Omnec Onec is doing her part to elevate human consciousness and increase awareness of the reality of higher spiritual dimensions. She is relaying information to humans concerning their true heritage as cosmic transplants from other worlds such as Mars, and her own home planet of Venus.

According to Omnec Onec, the planet Venus, known as Tythania to the planet's inhabitants, has humanoid life on both the physical and astral planes. The capital, Retz, also has a presence in both the physical and the astral. When Tythanians arrive to Earth from the Astral Plane, they have to change the vibration of their beings and craft in order to become visible and tangible to humans. According to Onec, Earth consciousness is very limited. Some individuals among us have "extra-planetary consciousness," in which life on adjacent planes of existence is detected. "Solar consciousness" refers to those who are able to detect all life on all levels of existence in our local solar system. More than half of the planets in our solar system harbor humanoid life on various levels of vibration, and represent the crews of many of the spaceships that have been detected in our skies. The planets Mars and Venus, both of which appear lifeless to us using our own instrumentation, are buzzing with humanoid life on other planes. Life on these two planets in particular vibrate near enough to our own that they are able to come here and interact with humans. These entities have identified for us another group of creatures here on Earth that we would call interdimensional beings, but are considered by both Venusians and Martians as indigenous to Earth. These indigenous creatures can communicate with similar creatures on both Mars and Venus, as well as other planets in our solar system that bear life on their vibrational level. The "RA" complex, as outlined in the "Law of One" series, took its third density physical experience on the planet Venus prior to its transcendence into fourth density. Some of these beings came to Earth in what the Vedic and Atlantean literature calls the "vimanas," and some took physical incarnations on Earth. Millions of years ago, the first expeditions from Venus landed on Earth, and have been interested in our evolution and development ever since. Spaceships from Venus, Mars, Saturn, and Jupiter have visited earth, and are responsible for seeding earth with the various races. According to Onec, life in this solar system is very complex. Some of our UFOs are spaceships from the Astral Plane of Mars and Venus, others are unknown to the Brotherhood of Planets, some come from vast distances, and others are astral lights or interdimensional light beings. The concern of our solar neighbors is that Earth is hanging on to its violent adolescence far too long. Earth is referred to as "Kal Na-ar," or "negative child." She says it is as if a black cloud is hanging over the entire planet, and Earth has become a concern to our neighbors throughout the solar system who live on various levels. On the Astral Plane of Venus, the inhabitants adhere to *Om-Notia-Zedia*, or *The Laws of the Supreme Deity*. The denser worlds, such as ours, were created as schools for the soul. These realms contain polarity and negativity, called *Kal*. What Onec refers to as the Etheric Plane corresponds to the Urantia Book's Morontia level, and is a realm of existence that is between the material and the spiritual realms. The life story an teachings of Omnec Onec, which are outlined in her book, *Omnec Onec: Ambassador from Venus*, provide a good view of why there are so many spiritual teachings in the world. Onec states (page 58):

> *There are a mind-staggering number of denser world teachings whose purpose it is to suit the consciousness of Souls who must stay in the denser worlds for additional experience. These were established to bind the soul to denser levels until it is strong enough and aware enough to escape. They have a limited*

truth, and serve their purpose well, and are varied to suit the many levels of consciousness that exist in the denser worlds.

One aspect of Onec's teachings that correspond to the Urantia Book, is the mistake people make in focusing on a particular teacher (such as Jesus) as opposed to absorbing the teachings and thus changing the path of personal soul evolution. She states (page 113):

[But] when the teacher is worshipped and held more important than the Word, the truth is often lost. People must learn that truth is more important than he who is a channel for truth.

According to Omnec Onec, the Astral Plane existed before the physical universe was created, and will continue to exist after the physical universe passes. As with the teachings of the Urantia Book, and many other gnostic, theosophical, and so-called New Age teachings, the Earth is a mere pit stop of soul growth within a larger universe that is inhabited by many types of advanced celestial creatures, and represents, as contactee Richard Kieninger put it, *The Ultimate Frontier.*

Religion: A Creation of the Overlords?

As illustrated in my first book, *Outgrowing the Bible: The Journey from Fundamentalism to Freethinking* (2000), the Bible, like the Urantia Book, is a unique mixture of profound truth and absurdities, which is, as we have discovered, the actual trademark of the Overlords. This combination of truth and fantasy appears to be the actual modus operandi of the intelligences behind the endless volumes of channeled UFO-oriented material that has accumulated over the years, as well as the UFO phenomenon in general. As mentioned earlier, this method of mixing truth with absurdity appears to serve the long-range purposes of the Overlords. The Overlords provide just enough good, intellectually-stimulating material to the human mind to feed the sincere seeker's quest for spiritual or cosmic information, side-by-side with enough absurdity to keep the rationalists at bay. In this way, the rationalists reject the absurdities and embrace an atheistic philosophy of material reductionism, a mindset that is intentionally employed by the Overlords to engineer the Singularity in the most expedient manner. It is a method that, whatever one may think of it, has worked very well in bringing humanity to the very precipice of generating a technological singularity. UFOs have always provided undeniable phenomena of high strangeness along with absurd elements in order to create this skeptical smokescreen as cover for the real purposes behind the UFO mystery. The actual purpose of UFO activity is known in its entirety only by the Overlords of the Singularity even though, at this point in our mental and technological development, we humans are now able to ascertain that a technological singularity is at least the immediate goal that the UFO intelligences are guiding us toward. There is no stopping the Singularity now. We are past the point of no return, no further need for

MIB, mutilations, psychotronically-induced abduction experiences, green fireballs, foo fighters, ghost rockets, airship displays, or fantastic psychic journeys into outer space, as provided to the early contactees and UFO experiencers. This pivotal event, the Singularity, this great unknown into which humanity is swiftly plunging itself, may not have anything to do with the benefit or advancement of humanity, and everything to do with a hidden agenda that only serves the Overlords of Earth, i.e., the vast, post-biological and possibly alien consciousness behind Earth's UFO phenomenon. The intention of at least one group of possible contenders for the Singularity may involve an attempted permanent entrance into three-dimensional reality by entities who are otherwise barred from entrance by the existing spiritual hierarchy. The entities are known in many cultures by different names. In Islam they are the "Shaitan Djinn." To Christianity they are the "fallen angels," or "Satan and his demons." These entities who are interested in the Singularity for their own purposes need humans to build certain types of paraphysical technology that is capable of materializing disembodied entities from other planes of existence into a permanent physical vehicle. They may have self-serving intentions to commit a violation of the established cosmic order. Whatever the case, we will soon find out.

High-level Sighting by a Government Official

On October 4, 1955, the US Senator from Georgia, Richard B. Russell Jr., who was Chairman of the Armed Services Committee at the time, was on a Soviet train in the Russian Federation when he spotted a metallic disk, a classic flying saucer, taking off near the tracks. Russell quickly called his military aide, Colonel E.U. Hathaway, and his interpreter, Mr. Ruben Efron, to the window, both of whom also saw the flying saucer along with a good look at a second flying saucer that appeared a minute or so later. These men immediately reported their sighting to Lieutenant Colonel Thomas Ryan of the United States Air Force in Prague, Czechoslovakia, as soon as they arrived there from Russia on October 13, 1955. The sighting was kept secret and away from the public for the next three decades, and was finally released from FBI/CIA declassified records in 1985. Details of this high-level, credible sighting were finally made available to the public by the efforts of Dr. Bruce Maccabee and the Fund for UFO Research.

[On November 22, 1955, the Soviets exploded their first multi-megaton hydrogen bomb test]

Pod People from Outer Space

1956 brought a creative vision of alien invasion into the human mind as the movie, *Invasion of the Body Snatchers,* hit movie theaters. In this haunting foreshadowing of things to come, extraterrestrial parasites from another world float through the vast distances of outer space in seed pods. After discovering an appropriate host planet (Earth), they land and take over human minds and bodies. Each alien pod serves as a blank that is filled in by the human form. The conversion from human to alien occurs while the human victims are sleeping, an element that appeared in fiction just prior to the onslaught of real human abduction reports that began pouring in throughout the decades to follow. Upon awakening from sleep, the invaded human becomes an emotionless clone taken over by the alien presence. As is often the case, science fiction is an expression of our most paranoid suspicions. Elements implanted into the human mind by invisible interdimensional entities come forth in fiction as a prophecy of things to come, and there is no concept closer to the truth than that presented in *Invasion of the body snatchers*. This film, along with many other works of science fiction throughout the 1950s, illuminated the purposes of the alien presence on Earth in a way that cleverly provided psychological cover for actual alien activities on Earth. While humans are entertained in books and theaters by "fiction," the alien presence on Earth is busy manipulating the human mind toward their intended goals in which, just as in the movie, humans provide a physical vehicle for their presence to materialize on Earth. By placing the idea of alien abduction and alien takeover into the category of laughable non-reality just prior to actual mass abductions and alien mind control, the humans were retooled "under the cover of darkness," so to speak. As millions of unsuspecting human victims have had their concept of reality melted down by various types of UFO encounters and/or abduction experiences, skeptics of the Phenomenon point to similar elements in pre-existing fiction to justify turning a blind eye to something important that is really happening, attesting once again to the brilliance of the methods used by the Overlords. When the Singularity comes, the long-term purpose of the alien presence on Earth will finally be achieved by having successfully manipulated human thought and physically employing human beings, many of whom are UFO skeptics, to build suitable AI formats that will accommodate alien consciousness downloads. Ironically, it will be the very humans that currently believe that they are designing AI to increase their own intelligence and longevity that may be discarded like husks when their real purpose is satisfied, which may be to provide a physical vehicle for an alien intelligence. If von Neumann probes from another world are currently infesting the earth, they have not come here with their own technology necessary to self-replicate. They need an appropriate slave race to do their grunt work for them, and on this particular planet, that slave race are the humans.

The Aetherius Society

As we found thrills at the theater watching *Invasion of the Body Snatchers*, Dr. George King founded his flying saucer religion in 1956 in London, England, called *The Aetherius Society*. The Aetherius Society is alive and well today, and has thousands of members and churches throughout the world with a rapidly-expanding international membership. Dr. King claimed to have been contacted in 1954 by voices from space who told him to prepare himself, that he had been selected to become the voice for the "Interplanetary Congress." Dr. King began receiving his cosmic transmissions in 1955 which continued on an ongoing basis for the rest of his natural life. These telepathic transmissions explained the many purposes of alien contact with humanity, which included protecting the planet from alien populations who are hostile to humans, monitoring the geophysical forces on Earth and potential climate and/or environmental changes, and cleaning up after our own radiation poisoning of the planet via atomic experimentation. These transmissions further revealed not only the reality of reincarnation, but also that humans originated on another planet that exploded from an atomic chain reaction 18 million years ago, whose fragments became what is known today as the asteroid belt. Following this destruction, humans began incarnating here on Earth. This idea continues to have modern adherents. In his online book, *Humans Are Not from the Earth*, the British Dr. Ellis Silver goes into what he considers evidence that humans are not from this planet. Dr. Silver points to human back pain, the harm that our current sun causes to humans, our lack of body hair, and other hints that our physiology does not adhere to what science would expect from a species that is indigenous to Earth. Dr. Silver postulates that humans originally came from another planet that had a different set of physical characteristics. Silver makes the case that humans cannot possibly have originated as a product of earthly Darwinian evolution, but are instead a "transplant" from another world. If Dr. Silver is correct in his theories, it would seem that Dr. George King, founder of the Aetherius Society in 1956, was ahead of his time and receiving valid information from cosmic entities at large in the universe. Dr. King was also ahead of his time in his concern for global climate change, radiation dangers from nuclear technology, and the idea that there was once an extra planet in our solar system between the orbits of Mars and Jupiter that was somehow destroyed, whose fragments are now orbiting the Sun as the asteroid belt.

Human Mutilations

In March, 1956, a decade prior to the US cattle mutilation epidemic to come, US Air Force Master Sergeant Johnathon P. Lovette and Major Cunningham were walking together through the desert, searching around for debris from a fired missile. The two separated, and Sergeant Lovette walked over a sand dune, out of Major Cunningham's range of sight. Suddenly, Major Cunningham heard horrified screams for help coming from Sergeant Lovette. Major Cunningham raced over through the sand and over the dune that was hiding Sergeant Lovette, and was absolutely stunned by the sight that filled his eyes. Sergeant Lovette was being dragged through the sand by his legs by metal tentacles/cables leading up to a silver metallic disk hovering steadily above the ground. The saucer seized and captured the screaming Sergeant Lovette, and sped away from the area at high speed. Traumatized by witnessing such an event, Cunningham reported what he saw to the authorities who, of course, did not believe him, and charged him instead with murder. Three days later the charges were dropped when Lovette's body was found several miles from where Cunningham reported the horrendous event. Like a preview of a future nightmare, Sergeant Lovette's body had been mutilated consistent with that of cattle mutilations that were destined to become epidemic in the 1960s-1970s. Lovette's genitals were removed, and his rectum was cored out. He was eviscerated, his eyes were removed, and his lips and lower jaw were stripped to the bone. Thus, contrary to popular perceptions, the mutilation epidemic did not begin with cattle, but with a human being. Although most of the mutilation events to come involved the decimation of Bovines, there are on record several cases in police files of human mutilation as well. For some unknown reason, the intelligences behind at least some flying saucers, likely the ones Dr. King warned us about, seek blood and soft tissue from animals and humans. One must keep in mind that this event took place shortly after President Eisenhower allegedly met with extraterrestrials that the Nordics warned us against. This first recorded incident of human mutilations by aliens occurred after Eisenhower and Co. agreed to a certain number of human experiments in exchange for advanced technology.

The Amicizia (W56) Group

In April, 1956, a very important interaction developed between a group of Italians and a group of humanoid extraterrestrials that would shed light on the possible nature of all 1950s contactee accounts, as well as the reality of a genuine, physical presence of benevolent extraterrestrial visitors here on Earth. This was a special bond formed in Italy between a group of approximately 120 humans and a group of humanoid extraterrestrials from various parts of the universe that utilized underground bases throughout Italy. This contact group became known by the contactees themselves as the *Amicizia*, or W56 Group, and would represent an ongoing interaction on Earth between humans and ETs from 1956 to somewhere around 1978. Writer Stefano Breccia was asked by a friend to write the story of the Amicizia, and invited several individuals who were involved with the W56 group at the time to come forward and report what they knew. A few of the main contacts with this extraordinary group in Italy included Gaspare De Lama, Mirella Bergamini, Paolo Di Girolamo, Bruno Sammaciccia, and journalist Bruno Ghibaudi, who at one time was host to a television show about making model airplanes. Ghibaudi was asked to come aboard the group for his journalistic contacts. According to this human contact group, the W56 group of extraterrestrials operated out of a complex of underground bases located in France, Italy, Switzerland, Germany, Siberia, Australia, Argentina, and other areas of the world. This working group of ETs revealed that they had been with humans on Earth for centuries, and were here to keep things from getting out of hand *while we matured into a technological society*. This group was concerned that many humans were of a low morality. The group stated that they were here to mentor select contactees concerning the danger of nuclear war and atomic detonations, and the value of generating love among our fellow humans. Members of the W56 group were given human names by the contactees, as the group did not use names among themselves as we do. These names included Dimpietro (the captain of the group), Sigir, Itaho, Romulus, Sigis, Sinas, Saju, Kenio, and Meredir. Bruno Ghibaudi, Gaspere De Lama, and Bruno Sammaciccia were present for staged flying saucer appearances for the purpose of disseminating a confirmation to the world at large of their presence here on Earth. Many of these photographs appeared in the writings of Italian ufologist Alberto Perigo. Photographs of the flying saucers, some of which are identical to the craft Adamski and others have witnessed and photographed around the world, appeared in the April, 1962 publication of *Domenica del Corriere*. The technology that the W56 group used was well beyond the capability of humans. They used a technique of compressing the ground by which an underground base could be created at will instantaneously. The ground simply opened and closed for them, as impossible as that sounds. The Amicizia group also revealed to their human contacts that they had established bases under the sea at the time. The group was also responsible for the many cases of nuclear weapons shutdowns around the world, as they wanted to demonstrate that there was a presence on Earth that was capable of intervening in this way to get our attention. However, the ETs described themselves as the "precursors of the spirit world." As such they were incapable of harming any other beings. Even their flying saucers were somehow impregnated with a consciousness that was incapable of harming others. Their spacecrafts were programmed to self-destruct before harming anyone. The W56 group, aka the Amicizia, called themselves AKRIJ, which is Sanskrit for "The Sages." Stefano Breccia researched their name in other languages. Breccia found that the Egyptian equivalent of AKRIJ means *The Wise People*. In Greek, it means *People in High Places*, and in Arabic it means *Group of Friends*. During the many encounters between the ET group and the human contacts, the ETs used various means of communication. They had the capability of speaking through a radio or television to the group by hijacking the station to present their own message. One such message that was transmitted to the group by the ET known as Sijir was captured on reel-to-reel tape by the group, and stated the following, translated from Italian to English (UFO SECRET – FRIENDSHIP CASE):

Dear Friends, Dear Sons, do not mistrust us. As none of us will waver. Stay together, stay together, stay together. Tolerate your weaknesses. Fight and improve your humanity and your friendship toward us. Our world is hard to understand for you. Dear friends, that's normal, anyhow, with affection and trust, you can be close to our hearts. Always open towards you. And understand us more. We embrace you with warm affection. An authentic friendship - Sigir

The AKRIJ also had the capability of materializing paper notes with written messages on them. Interestingly, the contact group involved with the compilation of the Urantia Book also reported that, on occasion, the same thing would happen to them. Pre-written notes and even entire sections of manuscript would appear to the group out of thin air. This leads me to question whether the beings involved in presenting the Urantia Book to humankind and the AKRIJ are one and the same. If not, this may be a simple communication technology that we will someday learn. After all, whoever thought 3D printing would be a reality? Today's magic is tomorrow's simple task. Maybe it's a common method of communication in this universe among intelligent beings that we just haven't figured out yet. Anyway, the separate reports from the Urantia contact group and the AKRIJ contact group, in which writing materialized for the benefit of the humans is noteworthy. The AKRIJ also revealed to their human contacts that, in addition to the friendly aliens among us, another not-so-benevolent group is also here. From their description, this group of aliens are likely responsible for at least some of the animal and human mutilations and other UFO-related injuries, such as radiation burns, Klieg (Actinic) conjunctivitis, black eyes, bleeding ears and noses, etc., that humans and animals have suffered for such a long time now. The AKRIJ revealed that they were in conflict - not "war," but "conflict," as humanity is, with an *artificial race of creatures who do not share our morality of love and harmony, who are malevolent toward us, and worship science.* These creatures were referred to by the Friendship Group as "CTRs," which stands for *Contraries.* Another name the AKRIJ used for the Contraries was *Weiros.* The Contraries, or Weiros, according to the AKRIJ, are the opposite of moral ET creatures who are sympathetic to humanity. They are creatures without what we would call a conscience. They are a manufactured race of AI *whose god is technology.* I cannot help but wonder if this race of AI called the Contraries are, in fact, representative of Aleister Crowley's interdimensional being, "Lam," the creatures commonly known as the "Grays," and maybe even the creatures that the Christian Church refers to as "demons" or that Muslims call the "Djinn." If this assessment is accurate, William Bramley was also correct in *The Gods of Eden* when he identified two different ET forces on Earth, one that takes an interest in our spiritual evolution and helping us become citizens of the Greater Community, the Galactic Federation, and another group that is here for their own self-serving purposes. The Contraries appear to represent post-singularity AI, a race of transcended invisible robots who may have even manipulated our genes in the past toward a predisposition for violence and territoriality. This tendency to violence, along with programmed susceptibility to diseases, prompt a more rapid progression toward technology. The Singularity is the product that is desired by the Contraries who are here to use humans as tools in the most calloused and detached manner, a demeanor of the Grays that is reported by many abductees. The impression given by the AKRIJ is that, by loving others, an actual conscious energy is created that combats the negative energy the Contraries feed on like vampires. According to the Amicizia contacts, the AKRIJ vacated their bases in Italy in 1978, just prior to the giant Adriatic UFO wave. Keep in mind that by 1978, the alien abduction experience by Gray aliens (whatever this experience actually represents) had been going strong for nearly 20 years. Sadly, the AKRIJ felt that humanity was going by the wayside, giving themselves over to the influence of the Contraries. Despite the assistance and fair warnings of the AKRIJ (aka Friendship Group, W56, Amicizia, or Space Brothers), the entire world continued in their nuclear ambitions to the point where we might now be on our own. Even after experiencing the blatant shutdown of our nuclear facilities by our ET friends as reported by Robert Salas in his book, *Faded Giant*, we continue to persist in our nuclear ambitions. The AKRIJ cannot force us to go a different direction. They can only nudge us a little. If this is the case, and the Space Brothers have now abandoned us as a lost cause, I cannot say that I blame them. If, after visiting both US and Soviet nuclear bases, appearing in full view in their flying saucers to the personnel that operate the facilities, intentionally shutting down launch capabilities to demonstrate total power over them, we still don't even openly acknowledge their existence, then maybe we are just too stupid to invest anymore energy into. I sincerely hope that this is not the case, but I fear that it is. Stefano Breccia wrote two books about the AKRIJ - *Mass Contacts* (2009) and *50 Years of Amicizia (Friendship)* (2013). It is my sincere desire that these benevolent ETs are still with us now. We will need their assistance and protection from the Contraries as we approach the Singularity and struggle to become a member of the Galactic Community at large.

[In May and June, 1956, the United Kingdom detonated nuclear bombs Operation Mosaic and Operation Buffalo]

UFO at Bentwaters

One of the most solid UFO cases in history, a case that involved multiple, high-ranking military officials and radar confirmation, occurred on the nights of August 13-14, 1956 at and near Bentwaters UFAF-RAF Station in England. Erratically-moving spherical objects traveling between 4000-9000 miles per hour were first observed by two different pilots in two different airplanes. These unidentified objects were then confirmed by airborne radar aboard one of the two aircrafts, and tracked by three different ground radar systems. The flying objects were also confirmed visually by control tower personnel at two different ground stations. This case was later studied by atmospheric physicist, James McDonald, who confirmed that this event in no way represented some anomalous atmospheric phenomenon. The case remains unsolved to this day as one of the most powerful, scientifically-confirmed UFO cases of all time. Even the pages of the 1969 Condon Report, whose understandable purpose was to get the Air Force out of the business of UFO investigations and debunk as many UFO sightings as possible to minimize public interest in the Phenomenon, stated, "the probability that at least one genuine UFO was involved appears to be fairly high," and, as the years to come revealed, this 1956 UFO incident was not the last time that the Bentwaters USAF-RAF Station would be visited by extraterrestrial, interdimensional, or time-traveling spacecraft.

NICAP

In October, 1956, a former Navy scientist, T. Townsend Brown, and a small group of other professionals, all male, founded the National Investigations Committee of Aerial Phenomenon (NICAP). With the help of two individuals in particular - Major Donald M. Keyhoe, USMC, and Admiral Delmer S. Fahmey, NICAP flourished from 1956-1970, accumulating over 10,000 members.

A Ghostly Encounter

As examined in Chapter 2, there does seem to exist some sort of connection between ghosts and UFOs. Waves of UFO sightings often correlate with reports of poltergeists in the same area. Most of the stories about ghosts involve apparitions, whereas flying saucers can appear as ghostly, apparitional phenomena, physical objects in the sky, or even demonstrate features of both states. The story that follows indicates that perhaps ghosts, i.e. disembodied humans, are also able to transmogrify into the physical world under the right conditions, just as UFOs can. The story that follows is right out of the 1960s television show, *One Step Beyond*. It involves the late actor, Telly Savalas, who was known mostly for his role in the 70s TV program, *Kojak*. Savalas had a ghostly experience that may provide corroboration for the suspicion that there were actually two different MIB groups involved in the UFO mystery. One group was purely human and was connected to the agendas of the US Air Force and/or CIA and their early attempts to investigate and manipulate public perceptions of UFOs. The other group of MIB were paraphysical, an integral part the Phenomenon itself. The latter category may have some level of intersection with the phenomenon we call ghosts or poltergeists. As with the testimony of George Van Tassel and his encounter with a group of discarnate humans, *The Council of Seven Lights*, this account by Telly Savalas also indicates a possible association between some types of UFO phenomena and discarnate humans.

On February 27, 1957, Telly Savalas was driving home from a cousin's house on Long Island when his car began to sputter and die, leaving him stranded at the side of the road in heavy rain. Spotting a red neon sign from a diner up the road from him, Savalas braved the rain and walked to the diner. Once inside, he asked where the nearest gas station was, and was given instructions to a garage a short distance away. Heading back out from the diner into the dark and intimidating storm, he began walking to the garage. As he was walking in the rain, he heard an automobile slowly pulling up. Behind him was a black Cadillac with its lights off. The window rolled down, and a voice from inside asked him if he wanted a ride. Savalas was wary, but desperate to get out of the rain, so he accepted the ride and climbed inside the vehicle. As he seated himself in the passenger seat, he took notice of the driver, who was silently looking straight ahead and wearing a white tuxedo with a white satin shirt and bowtie. As this "Man in White" (MIW) drove straight ahead, he made no conversation with Savalas. Savalas was filled with a feeling of anxiety and dread. When Savalas asked the driver where he was going, the driver slowly turned his head toward him. Then, with dark, expressionless eyes, the driver replied, "To the crossroads, to meet my destiny." Savalas, now regretting that he had accepted the ride with someone who was possibly mentally disturbed or even dangerous, was filled with a sense of foreboding, and said nothing further to the driver. When he finally spotted the garage in the distance, he felt relief. The MIW stopped and dropped Savalas off at the garage. Reaching into his pocket to pay the driver a couple of bucks for his time and trouble, Savalas discovered that he had left his wallet at his cousin's house. Determined to pay the man at some point, he asked the strange driver for his address. With this, the man became noticeably nervous, and an awkward moment of silence ensued. He reluctantly stated that is name was Harry Agannis. "Harry" wrote down his address and phone number on a piece of paper and handed it to Savalas along with a dollar bill for gas (in 1957, a dollar bought several gallons of gasoline). As Savalas entered the garage, he turned one last time to look back at his ride. The man and the car had simply vanished. Sometime after this day, Savalas discovered the wrinkled piece of paper with the phone number in his pocket and decided to give the man a call to thank him, and reimburse him for his trouble. He dialed the number. The phone rang, and a woman answered. Savalas asked if he could please speak to Harry. The woman, speaking in a broken voice, asked Savalas, "Is this some sort of joke? Who are you?" Savalas quickly explained who he was and what had happened, and heard the woman on the other end of the line break into tears. She managed to reply, "Harry was my husband, and he has been dead for three years!" She then promptly hung up the phone. Savalas was shocked and disturbed over this. He remained determined to get to the bottom of the mystery, so he actually went to the address on the paper that Harry had given to him. Jan Agannis, Harry's widow, answered the door as Savalas explained who he was. He showed Jan his actor's union card. Ironically, Savalas had just been hired for an episode of the *Twilight Zone* TV series. Jan let Salvalas in, and the two of them had a friendly visit. Savalas showed her the wrinkled paper on which her dead husband had written the address, and Jan recognized his writing. Jan showed Savalas pictures of her deceased husband, and Savalas recognized him as the driver who had given him a ride in the rain. Harry Agannis was killed in February, 1954, while returning home from a high school reunion, which explained the white tuxedo. On the way home, Harry died in an auto wreck at the crossroads, about ½ mile from the garage. His car had hit a truck and burst into flames, leaving Harry to die a horrible, traumatic death in the fire.

One of the many theories as to why apparitions of deceased humans occasionally appear as ghosts involves an energy produced during a traumatic death. This energy causes the person to remain within the physical plane in a somewhat disoriented state of mind instead of making an immediate transition to the next dimension after physical death in the usual fashion. Apparently, in rare circumstances, discarnate entities can temporarily manifest as actual, physical beings in 3D reality. Harry's black Cadillac was real and physical. It carried Telly Savalas to the garage in the rain. Both car and driver temporarily appeared as physical objects that could interact with the physical world and the people in it. Then, it simply vanished back into the realm of thought. This other dimension, this other "plane of existence" as some call it, is the place where humans go after death. It serves as a type of "holding station" between physical lifetimes. It is a realm in which humans and other types of celestial life routinely interact with one another. Some of us are able to perceive these otherworldly beings and actually converse with them in early childhood, thus the "imaginary friends." There is also the implication that those of us who are in a discarnate state between lifetimes have at least some level of awareness of what is going on in the physical realm. If they really want to, and if conditions are right, discarnate entities can manifest here for a temporary visit, either as an apparition, or, in some cases, as a temporary physical presence. The detail that Savalas' vehicle spit and sputtered and came to a halt just prior to this ghostly encounter is also curious. Perhaps, rather than running out of gas, the operation of his vehicle was interrupted by EM effects produced by an invisible flying saucer nearby, whose very presence alters the fabric of time and space in strange ways. The undetected presence of an interdimensional vehicle may have opened a window in space-time, a portal to the non-physical world, allowing the temporary manifestation of a discarnate human into this physical reality. Perhaps Harry Agannis wanted to get a message to his earthly wife that life continues after death. Considering the many flying saucer and hairy monster sightings that appear for a few moments and then simply vanish, leaving behind a puddle of "slag," it is my suspicion that if one were to have traced the incident back to the exact spot near the garage where the black Cadillac vanished into thin air, a little puddle of silicon carbide would have been found. Someone walking along the highway where Telly Savalas was dropped off might have found an object on the ground that looked like a chunk of furnace slag. They would have likely picked up the slag and tossed it, not realizing that what they just held in their hand was the physical remnant of a paranormal encounter that was experienced by the famous actor, Telly Savalas, who had his own walk through the Twilight Zone.

UFO Hucksters

In 1957, following in the footsteps of George Adamski, Wayne Sulo Aho proclaimed himself an initiate as a "Cosmic Master of Wisdom" after attending George Van Tassel's "Giant Rock Interplanetary Space Craft Convention." As an initiate into this esoteric cosmic order, Aho claimed to have been telepathically led out into the desert for a personal flying saucer appearance. There in the desert, a voice instructed Aho to start his own UFO convention in his home state of Washington. Aho then teamed up with contactee Reinhold Schmidt, who claimed to have had encounters with multiple cigar-shaped craft that were owned and operated by individuals from the planet Saturn who had landed in a field. These "Saturnians" as Schmidt called them spoke perfect German, drank MJB brand coffee, and carried an MG automobile inside their craft for running errands while the craft was earthbound. As a team, Wayne Sulo Aho, Reinhold Schmidt, and another 50s contactee, John Otto, toured together and gave lectures about their experiences. Everything was going well until Schmidt was arrested and convicted for grand theft. Schmidt was caught bilking investors, mostly female, out of thousands of dollars needed to purchase land that, according to his Saturnian friends, contained a fortune in precious cancer-curing quartz crystal. It seems likely that, at some point, Schmidt had read one of George Hunt Williamson's books, *Secret Places of the Lion*. Schmidt appears to have embellished his own tale from elements contained in Williamson's book, such as stating that the captain of the cigar-shaped Saturnian craft, "Mr. X," had taken him on a trip to the Great Pyramid.

Schmidt was also taken to a secret underground chamber where he was able to examine the flying saucer that Jesus used to visit Earth from Venus 2000 years ago. Schmidt self-published his own book, *The Edge of Tomorrow*, in 1964. When Schmidt was taken out of the picture for fraud, Aho teamed up with Otis T. Carr (another Adamski wannabe), who claimed to have successfully built a full-size flying saucer that incorporated magnetic principles discovered by electrical-genius Nikola Tesla. Together, Aho and Carr conned money out of unsuspecting elderly lecture attendees for an important mission. Aho and Carr would pilot their homemade flying saucer to the moon and back from a fairground, just like Professor Marvel in *The Wizard of Oz*. They planned to return with indisputable proof of their cosmic journey. This created a huge public fiasco and resulted in formal legal charges filed against the two racketeers. It was finally judged that Otis T. Carr was the real culprit, who is thought to have used Wayne Sulo Aho as a patsy in his own money-making scam. In the end, Aho escaped conviction, leaving Otis T. Carr holding the bag for petty fraud.

These types of ridiculous fiascos within the UFO community over the years have caused many rational inquirers who would otherwise have remained interested in UFOs to bail on what James Moseley comically called "ufoology." Encountering the stench of falseness can make someone write off the whole subject altogether. However, the same sort of fraud exists in just about every category of real phenomena on the planet. Archaeologists make real discoveries every day that reshape our understanding of the past. Even so, the fabricated skull called "Piltdown Man" was presented as the missing link to human evolution and accepted as fact for a while. The artifact fooled everyone within the scientific community before the fraudulent nature of the hoax was discovered. Is science a fraud? Are there no real discoveries? Should archaeology be dismissed now just because someone took advantage of the public interest in our past and wanted to make a name for themselves and fool people? Likewise, the historical Jesus is real. The teachings of Jesus have made a huge impact on the world at large in elevating human consciousness into a more loving creature. However, today we are inundated by the "prosperity theologians," unscrupulous preachers who con the simple, the greedy, and the desperate out of their "seed money" or "faith offerings" on the promise that if they do so, the "windows of heaven" will open and their finances will be blessed with exponential expansion. This is the oldest scam in the religious playbook. Faith healers who live in multi-million dollar homes with golden toilets pass the plate around huge congregations who have come in hopes of receiving their miracle of healing. Some poor souls have even mortgaged their homes to show their faith in God as they push their loved one in a wheelchair to the miracle healing service. They sadly drop their life savings in the collection plate to demonstrate their worthiness of a miracle, only to push their loved one home in the same wheelchair they arrived in, only now they are destitute. If there is a hell, there is a special roped-off section for these types of hucksters who use religion to bilk the public out of their hard-earned money. Yet, religions are based on a core of truth, a truth that usually involves what we are discussing in this book, i.e., classic UFO encounters, cosmic illumination experiences with intelligent, luminous orbs of light, and interactions with beings, both apparitional and physical, who have come to Earth from higher planes of existence throughout human history. There are always going to be those within any profound body of truth that use public belief to their own advantage in this world. When searching for the underlying essence of a real phenomenon, the hucksters and profiteers will always be encountered. They are part of the package, like a gauntlet thrown up to dissuade all but those who really want to get to the truth of the matter. In the case of the flying-saucer mystery, the hucksters and con artists are likely used strategically by the UFO intelligences themselves, both human and extraterrestrial, to provide cover for their clandestine operations as we are guided into the Singularity to merge our biological consciousness with machine intelligence, and possibly even an alien race of sentient robots.

Throughout the 1950s, simultaneous to the UFO circus that featured speakers sharing individual tales of contact with flying saucers and their occupants, some having a degree of legitimacy and others that were outright frauds, serious endeavors were going on behind the scenes within US intelligence circles regarding UFOs, in an attempt to get a grip on what the flying saucers actually were. As the UFO conventions were organized and venders sold their wares, a clandestine operation that was originated by General McArthur in the 1940s in response to foo-fighter reports, *Operation Blue Fly*, was underway to gain an understanding of foreign technology. Operation Blue Fly developed its mission over the years to retrieve and analyze objects of unknown origin that fell to Earth. By 1957, Operation Blue Fly had expanded its mission to include the retrieval of alien spacecraft and EBEs (extraterrestrial biological entities), and became an integral part of *Operation Moon Dust*. Operation Moon Dust or its modern equivalent, continues to the present, albeit under a different name that remains unknown to the general public.

Dr. Frank Stranges and Valiant Thor

According to the testimony of the late Christian minister, Rev. Frank Stranges, Ph.D., a messenger from the interior of Venus arrived to Earth in Alexandria, Virginia, on March 16, 1957 with an important message for the inhabitants of Earth. Even though this being came from a civilization that did not use personal names (as in the case of the AKRIJ), Dr. Stranges introduced this person to the world as Valiant Thor. Valiant Thor, according to Dr. Stranges, landed on Earth and was welcomed by two police officers pointing pistols at him. After Valiant Thor directed a telepathic message to the two officers that he meant them no harm, the officers put him in the back seat of their patrol car. Carrying an ambassador from another world, the officers crossed over into Washington, D.C. where they were met by Secretary of Defense Charles Erwin Wilson and six staff members. Many other police officers from various districts arrived who wanted to be the ones selected to transport Valiant Thor to meet with President Dwight D. Eisenhower and Vice President Richard Nixon. Using the power of his mind, Valiant Thor made it past all the security posts and was followed by a Captain of the United States Air Force. Six armed guards escorted Valiant Thor to an elevator that went rapidly down to a maximum security area. Transferring to a high-speed underground train, six officials, six armed guards, and three secret service men sped Valiant Thor to Washington, D.C., and into the office of President Dwight D. Eisenhower. Valiant Thor reached out to shake the hand of the President as the secret service agents drew their revolvers and pointed them toward him. Eisenhower then motioned for the agents to lower their guns. At that moment, the Vice President, Richard Nixon, entered the room. Nixon also shook hands with Valiant Thor. Valiant Thor explained to President Eisenhower and Vice President Nixon that the UFOs involved in the 1952 Washington D.C. flyby that caused such a stir five years previous in 1952 were, in fact, a fleet of Venusian ships that were under his command. Valiant Thor also explained that Earth had been under the scrutiny of the Venusian Council for hundreds of years prior to the 1945 atomic test. From this meeting, Valiant Thor was escorted to the Pentagon, where he lived for the next three years in a furnished apartment as a guest of the United States of America. Valiant Thor was able to teleport himself back and forth from the apartment at the Pentagon to his craft and back. He also had the mental ability to make the guards see his face on a nonexistent official security badge if he needed to. In April, 1957, Valiant Thor and three crew members - Donn, Jill, and Tanyia, joined contactee Howard Menger and several UFO researchers for a convention on Menger's property in High Bridge, New Jersey. Contactee Howard Menger (1922-2009) enjoyed contact by extraterrestrials his entire life from the age of 10 in 1932, back in Guy Ballard's "I AM" era. Menger wrote about his experiences with ETs in his books, *From Outer Space to You* (1959), and *The High Bridge Incident….the Story Behind the Story….after 35 years of silence* (1991). Howard Menger was a classic, 1950s contactee with stories of communications with Adamski-style Venusian space brothers. According to his wife, Howard always returned home excited from his visits with ETs, as the space brothers always provided him with revelations about practical matters. Menger was a sign painter by trade. A photographer, August C. Roberts, managed to snap several photographs of Valiant Thor and his crew members at Howard Menger's home. These photos are readily viewed online with a quick Google search. To this day, no person, male or female, has ever come forward to identify themselves as the individuals in the photos to expose this whole affair as a hoax. Likewise, no person has ever stepped forward over the years and stated that they even recognize the individuals in the photos as having a known human identity. The message from the High Council of Venus under the command of Valiant Thor was an offer to share medical knowledge and technology with the inhabitants of Earth if we would only agree to rid the planet completely of nuclear weapons. President Eisenhower, who by this time had already turned down a similar offer from Nordic humanoid aliens in 1954 to make a deal for technology with the Grays, promptly turned down the offer, stating to Valiant Thor that the world's population and world economy would plunge into chaos if the offer was accepted. President Eisenhower did concede, however, to allow

Valiant Thor and his crew to remain at the Pentagon for a period of three years to assist us with medical knowledge related to our space sciences. Valiant Thor agreed to this, but refused to assist with projects involving any types of weapons, especially those that were designed for use in outer space. Our scientists were allowed to test the uniforms that Valiant Thor and his crew wore while traveling to Earth. They were unable to penetrate the material, even with a diamond drill bit. During the tests, some sort of acid was reported that rolled off the uniforms and burned a hole in the floor. Bullets were fired at the uniforms and did not pierce the material. They even fired a ruby laser at the garment, and found the material indestructible. During Valiant Thor's stay at the Pentagon from 1957-1960, several scientists attempted without success to extract from Valiant Thor the secret of interstellar space travel. Government officials were disturbed over the fact that, if he decided to, Valiant Thor could manipulate the course of world events. Toward the end of 1959, Dr. Stranges revealed that Valiant Thor had originally worked with Nancy Warren at the Pentagon who then arranged his meeting with Val. Nancy had attended a service at the National Evangelistic Center, which was pastored by Dr. John Mears in Washington, D.C., where Dr. Stranges was slated to speak that day. When Dr. Stranges finished speaking, he began signing copies of his book, SAUCERAMA. Nancy got his attention by flashing her Pentagon ID to him. The photographer who snapped pictures of Valiant Thor and his crew at Howard Menger's home gave prints to Dr. Stranges, who began using the photos as a display for his UFO presentations. Borrowing the pastor's study, Nancy Warren asked Dr. Stranges if he would like to meet Valiant Thor in person. Dr. Stranges replied with enthusiasm to the affirmative, and Nancy instructed him to meet her in front of his hotel room the next morning. Together they drove to the Pentagon and stood in line to pass 2 different security guards that visualized an ID badge on Dr. Stranges that wasn't there. This frightened Dr. Stranges and made him feel as though he could be handcuffed and thrown in jail at any moment. Warren then left Dr. Stranges standing at an unmarked door. As the door opened, three men were in the room who were unable to see Dr. Stranges. Dr Stranges later learned that Valiant Thor had clouded their minds so that they were unable to perceive his presence. Dr. Stranges watched as Valiant Thor entered the room. Dr. Stranges described Valiant Thor as about six feet tall and 185 pounds, normal complexion, and slightly tanned. The two men shook hands, and Dr. Stranges noticed that Val's skin was very soft like a baby's bottom even though Val had a strong handshake. Dr. Stranges noticed during the handshake that Val had no fingerprints. He described Val's voice as strong and mellow, conveying a strength of purpose. The three other men continued to behave as if Val and Frank were invisible. Val explained to Dr. Stranges that he had been there at the Pentagon for nearly three years and was departing soon. Val told Dr. Stranges that he had come to help humankind return to God. Val said humans were far off the course of divinity in their actions, but there was still time if his message of peace was responded to. Val stated that only a few individuals in Washington D.C. knew of his presence there. Val told Dr. Stranges that there were currently 77 Venusians walking among humans on Earth who were constantly coming and going. Valiant Thor explained that there was no need for a Bible on Venus, as they had not broken their relationship to the Creator as humans on Earth had. During this visit, Val told Dr. Stranges details about his life that he did not know, details which he later verified with his parents and grandparents. Valiant Thor confirmed to Dr. Stranges that the person we know as the historical Jesus is, in fact, the ruler of our universe. Interestingly, the Urantia Book, originally channeled in the 1920s by an anonymous unconscious man under the watch of the psychiatrist, Dr. William Sadler, and published in 1955, also identifies Jesus as the sovereign ruler of our local universe, called Nebadon. If this is true, and Jesus is, in fact, our universal sovereign, and other planets in our universe also know this, it is no wonder that the Urantia Book identifies our world, Urantia (Earth), as the *World of the Cross*. Valiant Thor identified himself as a messenger of this Jesus in hopes that humans would once again align themselves with the Divine Light of the Cosmos, the Universal Father. As Valiant Thor continued to speak about the reality of Jesus Christ, our universal sovereign, the Dr.'s eyes were full of hopeful tears. Dr. Stranges then asked Val if there was life on planets other than Venus. Valiant Thor's response was that the universe is teeming with life that had not transgressed the universal laws of love as humans here on Earth have. Dr. Stranges expressed concern that the military might prevent Val from leaving on his appointed day. Val assured him not to worry by reminding Dr. Stranges of the Bible passages in which Jesus appeared among his followers in a closed room, implying that he also had that same ability to materialize or dematerialize his body. Once again, the Urantia goes into quite a bit of detail about the appearances of Jesus following his resurrection, in a form the Urantia Book calls the *Morontia body*. The Morontia level is depicted in the Urantia Book as a transitional state between the physical and the spiritual realms. According to the Urantia Book, when Jesus appeared in his Morontia body after his resurrection, his people could see him and interact with him, just as Dr. Stranges could speak and interact with Valiant Thor as they remained invisible to the others in the room. From the perspective of the Urantia Book, it is possible that the so-called Venusians exist in Morontia bodies. Perhaps the Morontia realm is the same as what we call the Astral Plane. In their Morontia/astral bodies, the Venusians, like Jesus post-ressurrection, have the power of mind control over humans, the power of illusion, as well as the power to materialize and dematerialize just as Jesus did in his Morontia body after his resurrection. If this is accurate, this could also possibly shed some light on the actual realm in which the so-called "alien abductions" take place. Abduction researcher and Harvard psychiatrist, Dr. John Mack, M.D., postulated after years of abduction research, that the abduction experiences were actually taking place in a realm of reality that is unfamiliar to humans. If so, abductions may occur in the same cryptoreality, the Morontia realm, as detailed in the Urantia Book. Members of the AKRIJ also described themselves as *precursors to the spirit world*, which is how the Urantia Book describes the creatures of the Morontia realm. That Valiant Thor compared his visible existence and abilities of personal teleportation to that of Jesus Christ post-resurrection indicates that this might just be the case. What the Urantia Book describes as the Morontia realm may consist of beings that are not completely physical yet not completely transitioned into the spirit realm. As such, they are able to appear and disappear as the human-oid angel appearances are described in the Bible, which leads to a very profound question - *Was Valiant Thor an angel?* After all, the angels described in the Bible, such as the human-looking angels that paid a visit to Lot, had the ability to appear and disappear, just as Valiant Thor did. God knows, if any group of people needed such an angelic visit, it was the people employed by the Pentagon. However, by the time Valiant Thor arrived at the Pentagon, the direction of humanity had already been determined by President Eisenhower and his meeting with the Grays. Apparently, the Grays do not share the same moral ideals that humans ascribe to, and are focused on our coming technological singularity for their own purposes.

Following his experiences with the alien visitor at the Pentagon, Dr. Frank Stranges had a heavy heart. Dr. Stranges knew that he would be compelled to tell the world of his meeting with Valiant Thor, and that people would not believe him. After praying about it, Stranges decided that he had to tell the world about Valiant Thor regardless of personal consequences, and he did just that. Dr. Stranges was right in that people were very skeptical. Most people who hear the personal testimony of Valiant Thor and his crew place it in the category of pure fantasy. One must ask themselves, "Would a minister of the Gospel fabricate a fanciful tale just to promote his own flying saucer books?" This seems inconsistent with the character and mission of Dr. Frank Stranges. At any rate, Dr. Stranges reported that Val's last meeting with President Eisenhower did not produce results. Eisenhower wanted to let the world know of Val's presence and mission, but according to Dr. Stranges, the Secretary of Defense, the head of the CIA, and the Military Chiefs of Staff were opposed to the idea. President Eisenhower also attempted to arrange a joint meeting before the General Assembly of the United Nations, but this was also rejected. On the morning of March 16, 1960, Nancy Warren had a final meeting with Valiant Thor and promised to continue as one of Val's contacts inside the Pentagon. With that, Val dematerialized and teleported himself back to the inside of his ship in Alexandria, Virginia, where his body rematerialized. His craft, the *Victor One*, levitated from a wooded area and was witnessed by many local residents. Dr. Stranges reported that, once back on Venus, Valiant Thor reported the results of his mission to Earth to the High Council of Venus. The Venusian Council decided that the mission would continue, and provided instructions to the Venusian ambassadors to participate in the following capacity:

Mingle with and become as Earth people.
Work and labor in Earth enterprises.
Assist those who endeavor for world peace.
Provide advice and guidance.

Entrust knowledge to those who have proven themselves.

Divulge the essence of their mission to the collective national leaders of Earth when the time is right.

One witness whose testimony corroborated that of Dr. Frank Stranges concerning the reality of Valiant Thor and his visit to the Pentagon was Harley Andrew Byrd, the nephew of Rear Admiral R.E. Byrd. Byrd contributed his testimony in Dr. Stranges' book, *Stranger at the Pentagon*. H.A. Byrd stated:

> *In mid-March, 1957, we received an urgent message from the Alexandria Police Department. The message indicated that two of their on-duty police officers had picked up an alien who had landed some 14 miles south of Pentagon Boulevard, and the occupant was transported to the Pentagon to meet with the Under Secretary of Defense and then shuttled underground to meet with President Eisenhower and Vice President Richard Nixon. The meeting lasted for nearly an hour and then, the alien visitor was put on VIP status and was shuttled back to the Pentagon where he spent the night in the Army reception office on the first floor near the concourse. This alien's name was Valiant Thor. The landing of Valiant Thor was perhaps the first documented landing of a human-type alien by military officials. He contacted an individual in the Pentagon who was an advocate of the UFO alien situation. "Nancy Warren" in turn contacted a minister, who was also a private investigator and theologian, a Dr. Frank E. Stranges, who then met with this individual. Val Thor had landed in Alexandria and met with the President to discuss the world's problems and offer advice and counsel on how to deal with and eliminate them. Safe to say that the problems he discussed were more complex than savings bonds. He indicated to Mr. Eisenhower that the world was in a precarious situation and that if the world continued to proceed on a war footing – it would cause an economic imbalance throughout the world. Val Thor stayed on Earth until March 16, 1960, and then disembarked to his home planet Venus.*

According to the late Dr. Frank Stranges, who passed away from this earth on November 17, 2008, we have many adversaries who are opposed to human freedom and have embedded themselves in world governments and will only be exposed by extraterrestrial intervention. Dr. Stranges was convinced that a breakaway civilization developed following WW2 and exists as a remnant of Nazi Germany. Dr. Stranges stated that some of the flying saucers people see, especially sightings from South America, are from this terrestrial human group. Dr. Stranges also believed that there are pockets of civilizations inside the earth who also have advanced technology and flying saucers. In addition to terrestrial flying saucers using Nazi technology, these cryptoterrestrial populations from inside the earth are occasionally witnessed by the surface dwellers. Dr. Stranges also believed in "evil messengers" who involve themselves with individuals and manipulate them to their own ends. Although Dr. Stranges and others today refer to these creatures as "fallen angels," my interpretation is, based on revelations from the Italian Friendship (Amicizia) Group, that these entities are a race of superintelligent, paraphysical, biological robots, or possibly von Neumann probes from another world. These entities appear to be interested in some sort of merger with human consciousness. Once self-replication is completed, the merger can possibly add the sum total of human knowledge and experience into their data system, and from there, our fate as a species is uncertain. Hopefully, our extraterrestrial, angelic, and/or Morontia friends in this local universe of Nebadon will help us survive this impending transition into a post-singularity merger of human consciousness and robotic intelligence expansion. Hopefully, with their help (if they are still willing to help us) we humans can allow these probes to accomplish their goal and move to another world while those who remain establish what Michio Kaku refers to as a "Type 1" civilization, a civilization that is finally united as a planet with our collective consciousness elevated by a merger between human and artificial intelligence. This impending intelligence expansion may allow a form of transcendence into immortality and freedom from the limitations of the flesh. As a new, transhuman, cybernetic intelligence, humans can hopefully connect with and understand the other lifeforms that exist in the rest of the universe, or even become reunited with the universe itself in a state of immortal transcendence.

[In 1957, the United Kingdom detonated an atomic bomb in Operation Antler, along with their first hydrogen bomb in Operation Grapple.]

The Takeda Photo

On August 20, 1957, at 11:30 a.m., Shinichi Takeda of Fujisaw City near Enoshima Miani Beach, Japan saw a silver, brilliant, glowing flying saucer at 3000-4000 feet altitude after his sister saw it and pointed it out to him. The object was traveling silently at an estimated 250-500 KPH, made an instantaneous sharp right-hand turn, and disappeared into the clouds. Fortunately, Takeda was able to snap a good photograph of the craft, and is easily observed online.

Antonio Vilas Boas

In the fall of 1957, in the middle of Brazil's spectacular 1957 UFO wave, strange lights were observed in the Brazilian skies during the entire month of October. On a clear starry night at 1 a.m. in the morning of October 15, 1957, on a farm in Sao Francisco de Sales, Minas Gerais, Brazil, Antonio Vilas Boas saw a red star that grew into a bright egg-shaped object with a spinning cupola about 35 feet long and 23 feet wide. As the object grew close, Antonio's tractor died (EM effects) as he witnessed the craft land on his farm with extended tripod legs. Panicked, Antonio jumped from his dead tractor and tried to run away from the craft. Before he could exit the area, four five-foot-tall beings in skin tight grey suits secured him and led him into the craft with them. Light blue eyes were visible through the humanoid's helmets, which were attached to the necks of the suits, the suits extending into gloves and boots in one piece.

Three tubes emerged from the tops of the helmets that attached to the sides in the front, presumably some type of breathing apparatus. The garment had a belt with a shoulder strap coming up over one shoulder. Badges or emblems appeared on the breasts of the suits. The beings communicated by way of muffled growls. Once on the craft, the four beings forcibly removed Antonio's clothing, scrubbed him down with a sponge-like device, and applied a clear, thick liquid to his body. He was then led to a room and kept there for an extended period. Antonio became ill from a type of smoke that entered the room. After a long wait, a door opened, and a four-and-a-half foot tall blonde-haired naked female entered the room. The female had odd facial features with large oval eyes extending out to the sides of her wide face. Her cheek-bones were high, and she had thin lips, small ears, a pointed chin, and a straight nose. Antonio wondered if all the other beings in space suits would look similar to her if they removed their helmets and suits. The woman reached out and embraced Antonio, and made it known what she wanted from the encounter, so Antonio and the woman had sex. Afterward, the four beings came into the room, still wearing their suits and helmets, and took the woman away with them. The beings returned to the room and handed Antonio his clothing, and he dressed himself. After he was completely dressed, the beings walked Antonio around their craft as if to give him a little tour, and eventually pointed him toward a ladder. Antonio walked down the ladder onto the soil of the farm, and walked away from the craft. As he looked back, he saw the craft rise into the air and then vanish at high speed. It was now 5:30 in the morning. Antonio's story was so strange, many are tempted to completely dismiss it at first hearing. That is, until similar accounts appear at later dates with intersecting elements involving individuals who knew nothing of Antonio's case in the late 1950s. One such case, the Peter Khoury encounter in the 1990s, provided shocking physical evidence that was left behind from the sexual encounter in the form of a hair with an unusual DNA profile. These cases confirm that alien breeding experiments have, in fact, occurred here on Earth. These experiments have matched humans with aliens to create hybrid children that are perhaps placed on other worlds with compatible environments. It is a horrifying idea that these abductions and forced sex incidents might represent some sort of profitable enterprise, or an underground interplanetary flesh market. If the effort is being conducted by cryptoterrestrials here on Earth, then hybrid babies are being born and raised either underground or under the sea in a clandestine fashion. Cryptoterrestrials surface, find victims to mate with and impregnate selected female breeding stock, and then return to their locale, wherever that might be, to allow the woman to bear the child and become part of their society. Perhaps these folks are part of a terrestrial population that went underground during the last ice age, or a remnant of the legendary lands of Atlantis and/or Mu. Whatever the case, we are left with the reality of unusual humanoids from somewhere conducting breeding experiments with unwitting humans. One can only speculate whether the females in question aboard the craft who are selected to become pregnant are willing participants, or are also in captivity. It also introduces the possibility that this interbreeding effort conducted by cryptoterrestrial humanoids may be what is actually happening to abductees. Are medical experiments conducted by the little Gray aliens that are typically reported just some sort of screen memory while eggs or sperm are extracted for breeding purposes? If so, Charles Fort was correct in the 1800s when he postulated that Earth is a farm that is owned and operated by some unknown outside agent. Whoever these people are that conduct these breeding experiments surely have some vested interest as we approach the Singularity. Their role in Earth's affairs will surely become clear at that point. Hopefully, we will come to know who they really are and what they are really doing with the babies produced by such orchestrated liaisons between earth humans and nonhuman breeders who are a close enough DNA match to produce human/alien offspring.

Wilhelm Reich

On November 3, 1957, an eccentric scientist in the field of neuropsychiatry, Wilhelm Reich, who had personal associations with theoretical physicist Albert Einstein and psychologist Sigmund Freud, died a lonely death in prison for rattling the cage of established science. Written off by most historians as a crackpot or worse, as someone suffering from mental illness, Reich was one of these brilliant people who was, like Nikola Tesla, made of weird cheese. In his youth, Wilhelm Reich discovered that his mother was having an affair with his tutor. Reich would sneak to the room where the two of them were having sex to listen, and began fantasizing about sex with his mother. He eventually told his father of the affair. His father began beating his mother, and his mother eventually committed suicide. Reich went forward in life blaming himself for his mother's suicide. As an adult, Reich became fascinated with the energy that was generated during the human orgasm, an energy he called "orgone energy" after the word, "orgasm." Reich believed that this elusive biological energy was actually what humans have always called God. Reich built ingenious whacky inventions, such as a walk-in device called the *Orgone Accumulator*. The orgone accumulator was like a large Faraday cage, a box-like device that one would enter and sit in for hours to accumulate orgone energy for purposes of healing and vitality. Based on a similar principle, Reich built his "cloud buster," consisting of long tubes pointed at the sky with hoses connected at the bottom leading into tubs of water to collect the orgone energy. He called the study of orgone energy "Orgonomy." Prior to his work in the 1950's, Reich had spent personal time with Albert Einstein in 1941 to discuss his discovery of orgone energy. Reich left Einstein with a small model of his orgone accumulator to examine and test. Einstein conducted a series of experiments on the device, and concluded that Reich's orgone accumulator did nothing. This resulted in Reich writing a 25-page letter to Einstein, in which he continued to attempt to convince Einstein of the reality and existence of this invisible bioelectrical energy. Einstein did not respond further. Beginning around 1954, Reich came to believe that the earth was being attacked by UFOs, or, as Reich called them, "energy alphas." From Reich's home, which he called "Orgonon," he diligently searched the skies for cigar-shaped craft with windows that were leaving a wake of deadly black orgone energy in order to destroy the earth and its inhabitants. When an alien craft was located through binoculars, Reich would point his cloud-buster toward the UFO to suck out the orgone energy and destroy the craft. Reich and his son actually rented a house in Arizona to use for a "base station" in this endeavor. From this house, this father-and-son team believed that they were fighting a full-scale interplanetary war. Using cloud busters, they sought out the alien craft that were emitting the black orgone energy like chem trails and knocked them out of the sky with cloud busters. The FDA eventually placed an injunction on the sale of Reich's orgone accumulators, deeming the device fraudulent and worthless. One of Reich's associates violated the injunction by sending a part for an orgone accumulator to a customer through the mail. When the judge discovered this, he promptly ordered the total destruction of Reich's orgone accumulators, along with the destruction of all associated materials and literature. In June, 1956, FDA agents invaded Reich's home and supervised the destruction of Reich's invention. Since the FDA could not destroy the equipment themselves, they forced Reich's son and some of his friends to chop up his father's orgone accumulators with axes in their own home. The FDA agents also supervised the destruction of hundreds of copies of Reich's books and all promotional materials related to his work. In New York, the remainder of his orgone accumulators were destroyed. Six tons of Reich's books were burned in an incinerator, including copies of Reich's works, *The Sexual Revolution*, *Character Analysis*, and, ironically, *The Mass Psychology of Fascism*. The total destruction of Reich's work is considered today as one of the most heinous acts of censorship in US history. One of Reich's associates in this debacle, Dr. Michael Silvert, was also charged with contempt of court and sentenced along with Reich to Danbury Federal Prison. In prison, Wilhelm Reich died alone from a heart attack. After serving his year-long prison sentence, Dr. Silvert was released, but committed suicide a few months after regaining his freedom. Today, mainstream science views Reich's inventions as harmless pseudoscience or crackpottery. Reich's books were reprinted, and his work is now acknowledged among psychologists as having made an actual contribution regarding the connection between sexual repression and neurosis. Despite the controversy over the effectiveness of Reich's orgone accumulators, many famous people used them in their homes, including: Orson Bean; Sean Connery; Robert Anton Wilson; and Norman Mailer. Mailer owned several of Reich's orgone accumulators, some of which were square in configuration, some egg-shaped. Orgone accumulators that were sold prior to the court's order for their destruction are now prized collector's items. Wilhelm Reich continues to hold a place of endearment in the hearts of modern ufologists for his inventions such as the orgone accumulator and the cloud buster. We are also indebted to Wilhelm Reich and his son for saving all of humanity from the evil "energy alphas" and their deadly black orgone contrails that nearly destroyed the world in the 1950s. Whatever the case, the works of Wilhelm Reich, just like George Van Tassel's Integreton, represent alien-inspired fringe science, and deserve a special place in UFO history. Unlike Nikola Tesla, whose inventions actually worked as a result of his communication with extraterrestrials, Reich's inventions serve as whacky distractions to keep the subject of ufology and communication with aliens in the category of hooey as we head steadfast into the Singularity.

Levelland, Texas sightings

On the nights of November 2-3, 1957, only one hour after the Soviet Sputnik 2 was launched but before the public knew anything about it, giant, glowing, egg-shaped UFOs were busy chasing cars in the small town of Levelland, Texas. Duty officer A. J. Fowler received approximately 15 phone reports from frightened motorists, 7 of which correlated well. These 200-foot-long thunderous torpedoes caused engines and headlights to fail (EM effects) until the objects flew away. A report made by one of the affected motorists, Jim Wheeler, stated that a giant, egg-shaped craft was sitting in the road ahead of him when his headlights and engine failed. The craft then rose into the air and vanished, at which time his vehicle regained function. A nearly-identical report came from motorist Jose Alvarez. Yet another witness, Frank Williams, reported the same story near the location of Alvarez. A blue-green, glowing UFO was also reported by Newell Wright, a student of Texas Tech. His encounter also caused motor and headlight failure until the craft swiftly departed with a thunderous boom. A truck driver, Ronald Martin, reported an object that pulsated from red-orange to blue-green and vanished in similar fashion. Another truck driver who also experienced EM effects to his vehicle was James Long, who reported a 200 foot-long object that was "glowing like a neon sign." The object was also witnessed by two different police officers, Sheriff Clem and Deputy Pat McCulloch, who described an oval-shaped light that looked like a "sunset on the highway" (Hynek, 1972). The USAF sent one investigator out a couple of days after these sightings who dismissed the whole event as an unusual display of multiple ball lightning strikes, as did UFO-debunker Donald Menzel. However, the ball lightning explanation cannot account for the tremendous size of the UFOs or the EM effects, and is generally considered just another lame excuse created by those who debunk UFOs for a living, or by those whose minds just cannot accept the reality of such a thing. The sightings at Levelland, Texas, remain good, unexplainable cases with multiple credible witnesses. The launching of the Soviet Sputnik coincidental to the Levelland sightings leaves the question as to whether our early earthly efforts of going into space were of interest to our extraterrestrial or interdimensional neighbors. Whoever these creatures are, they do seem to have the desire to stay on top of human activity. These hidden UFO intelligences monitor the condition of the human mind and exercise control from time to time in little demonstrations of power, such as the many nuclear shutdown incidents that have occurred over the decades. These demonstrations just let us know that they are there, that they have power over us, and that they are there to lend a guiding hand now and then so that we do not blow up their project prematurely.

Mary Starr

On December 16, 1957, a former school teacher with a master's degree from Yale, Mary Starr, was home alone in Old Saybrook, Connecticut, having gone to bed early around 10 p.m. Awakened from sleep by a bright light illuminating her bedroom at about 2-3 a.m., she got out of bed and went to the window to see what was going on. At first, Mary thought that a disabled airplane had landed in her back yard. However, when she gained her full senses, she discovered that the object was actually a cigar-shaped craft, dark in color, about 30 feet long. The craft had square portholes on the side, through which she saw creatures inside. The craft was hovering silently about 5 feet from the ground near her back garden. Inside she saw three small, 3.5 foot-tall robot-like creatures with their right arms raised up diagonally and no hands. Their heads were red-orange squares with a red light on the sides that Mary assumed were helmets. Watching into the portholes, Mary saw two of the creatures pass one another inside. A third being came into view from one side as a small antennae arose from the side of the craft closest to her that oscillated and sparkled as it came out. The entire craft then began to glow brightly for about 5 minutes. It slowly began to glide and turn, the antennae retracting as it went. After wobbling a bit in mid-air, the craft suddenly shot away like a cannonball fired from a cannon at amazing speed and vanished in total silence. Former Assistant Director of NICAP, Richard Hall, who was working as a NICAP research consultant at the time, along with NICAP staff member Isabel Davis, investigated Mary's account. Mary's story matched very closely with two other cases from the previous five years - the William Squyres case from Kansas and the Suzanne Knight case from Maryland in 1952. Due to the striking similarity of Mary's case to these two previous cases, along with Starr's academic credentials and no motivation whatsoever for fabricating a hoax, both researchers accepted Mary Starr's UFO case as authentic.

Operation Argus

Apparently, humans do not realize or do not care that nuclear detonations adversely affect life in other dimensions. Despite repeated admonitions from humanoid extraterrestrials who came to Earth and spoke to us face to face, we kept right on going in this endeavor. In September, 1958, a series of nuclear weapons tests known as *Operation Argus* was implemented over the South Atlantic Ocean by the United States Defense Nuclear Agency in connection with the *Explorer 4* space mission. Operation Argus was expedited early, only 6 months from its original conception, due to pending legislation that would have potentially banned all atmospheric and exoatmospheric nuclear testing. In other words, the United States had to sneak in this audacious operation before it became internationally illegal. Operation Argus was funded by tax payers to the tune of nine million dollars by the Armed Forces Special Weapons Project (AFSWP), the forerunner of today's Defense Threat Reduction Agency (DTRA). The *USS Norton Sound* launched 3 modified X-17A missiles about 1800 kilometers southwest of Cape

Town, South Africa, each one carrying a 1.7 kiloton warhead into our upper atmosphere. This location was chosen because the Van Allen Belt is closer to the earth here, an unusual condition called the *South Atlantic Anomaly*. These tests were originally proposed by Nicholas Christofilos of the Lawrence Radiation Laboratory as a means to verify his own pet theory, which he called the *Christofilos Effect*. His theory proposed that nuclear warheads detonated in Earth's extreme upper atmosphere would create its own radiation belt that might be useful as a tactical weapon of war. The nuclear explosions of Operation Argus did create artificial electron belts from the decay of fission fragments. These artificial radiation belts, if used as a weapon, would adversely affect enemy radio and radar transmissions, damage and/or destroy the operation of intercontinental ballistic missiles (ICBMs), and kill the crews of any orbiting space vehicles. Full details of this operation remained classified until April 30, 1982. I, for one, find it disturbing that decisions such as this one, to detonate nuclear weapons into the upper atmosphere just to see what happens, can be made without public consent or foreknowledge of the ultimate effects, but this is the sort of thing that monkeys with matches do.

Orthoteny

In 1958, French mathematician, engineer, and UFO researcher Aime Michel took the time to methodically plot UFO reports from the massive wave of French UFO sightings, along with UFO landing and creature sightings (CE-3s) that were recorded in the year 1954. As a result, Michel found that distinct star-like patterns emerged on his plotting maps. The usual configuration was typically a large cigar-shaped craft reported in the center of a series of sightings that surprisingly formed straight lines. His findings were recorded in his book, *Flying Saucers and the Straight-line Mystery*, and the phenomenon of *Orthoteny* was born. Orthoteny provided evidence that the UFOs were, in fact, a real phenomenon with some sort of intelligence and order behind them rather than random, unexaminable events. Michel also contemplated possible explanations for the UFOs other than extraterrestrial visitation, such as the idea that human consciousness itself was somehow producing the phenomenon in a visionary fashion, a body of thinking that would be expanded and elaborated by psychologist Carl Jung a decade later.

Psychotronic Technology Infusions

Brazil experienced a wave of bizarre UFO encounters in 1958, one story of which involves a man named Artur Berlet. Berlet was an employee of the "Municipal Prefecture de Sarandi" when he apparently vanished from the face of the earth from a small town of only 3000 inhabitants for 11 days. The event began as Berlet was passing by the farm of Dr. Dionisio Peretti. Spotting a light about 200 meters away from him, Berlet crossed a wire fence to get a better look. He then saw that it was a flying craft that resembled two trays turned against one another. Suddenly, a strong beam of light hit him, and he lost consciousness. When Berlet returned to conscious awareness, he described being abducted by aliens and taken to another planet. Berlet wrote his experience down with paper and pencil and the notes formed a story that contained descriptions of technology that did not exist in 1958. Berlet's account wasn't taken seriously until years after the event. Berlet described in his notes, among other things, photocells that convert solar energy into sunlight. Although the first observation of the photovoltaic effect goes back to Alexandre Edmund Becquerel in 1839, actual photo cells didn't go into the marketplace until the late 1950s, so unless Berlet was a technical geek who read up on the latest gadgetry in the world, it would be unusual for a simple farmer like Berlet to be aware of the latest solar cell technology. He also reported being shown dry pills for food, shock absorbers and support structures in tennis shoes, telephones with picture images (a foreshadow of modern cell phones), and somehow was able to predict Yuri Gagarin's first space flight on April 12, 1961, as well as the launch of the Soviet satellite, Sputnik.

Providing that is wasn't an actual trip to another planet, Berlet's case appears to represent the use of psychotronic technology by occulted UFO intelligences. Instead of fabricating a crashed saucer that contained technology to retro-engineer, a different method was selected in Berlet's case that directly infused ideas into his brain. Just as in the days of the Old Testament prophets, the Overlords are constantly working, selecting simple farmers and peasants like Artur Berlet and infusing visions of the future into their minds. The experiencers then spread the word and share the knowledge, igniting ideas and inventions in other minds that keep us on track toward the Singularity. Items related to Berlet's fantastic experience of the future, such as his documents, manuscripts, photographs, and personal items are now located in the Museum of UFOlogy in Brazil. Some of the technical items that Berlet described are not expected to be understood until sometime in the future. Perhaps, as we approach the Singularity, Berlet's notes will suddenly become relevant and make some significant contribution to modern technology.

Russian UFO Mystery

In 1959, the London UFO Research Organization (LUFORA) was founded, which became BUFORA five years later. BUFORA is a nationwide organization dedicated to "solving the UFO mystery." During the same year that LUFORA began working on solving the puzzle of the purpose of the UFOs in England, an unusual UFO mystery occurred in Russia. In February, 1959, reports of unidentified flying orange spheres came out of the Ural Mountains in Russia that coincide with the unusual and disturbing deaths of nine highly-experienced ski campers that lost their lives from an "unusual compelling force" that remains a bizarre mystery. Diaries and cameras belonging to the campers indicate that on the day before their deaths, the group encountered deteriorating weather conditions and poor visibility. The group lost their way and accidentally deviated from their planned course, winding up on the top of Kholat Syakhyl, otherwise known as "Dead Mountain." Realizing that their journey had gone terribly wrong, the group decided to camp on the slope of the mountain that night.

That was the last night that any of them would camp anywhere, and was their last night on Earth. On February 26, 1959, investigators finally found the missing campers. The scenario that the investigators discovered would put a chill on the spine of the most hardened homicide detective. Their tent had been cut open from the inside to frantically escape from an unknown danger. Several sets of footprints were left by those who escaped the tent, indicating that they were wearing only socks, a single shoe, or even barefoot in the snow. These tracks led down the mountain slope to the nearby woods. At the forest's edge, searchers discovered the remnants of a fire and two dead bodies wearing only their underwear. Broken tree branches indicated that one of the campers had climbed up the tree prior to their death. Three more dead bodies were found about 150 meters apart from one another. These bodies were found in poses that suggested they were headed back on foot to the abandoned tent. Four more bodies were found a month later under snow deep in the woods who were wearing clothing that had been removed from the other dead campers. One of these corpses had major skull damage. Two others had major chest fractures that indicated a force to the chest equivalent to that of a high-speed auto crash. The lack of external wounds indicated that a high external pressure of unknown origin caused the chest fractures. One of the female campers was found mutilated in similar fashion to the cattle mutilations that would become epidemic during the next several decades. Her tongue and eyes had been removed, along with her lips, facial tissue, and part of her skull. The skin on both hands showed massive macerations. Although reports speculated that her injuries were caused by putrefaction from landing face-down in a stream, photographs of her corpse clearly showed her kneeling against a boulder, away from any water source. Several theories have been proposed about the cause of this nightmare, such as attacks by indigenous Mansi people defending their land, an avalanche, a "Karman Vortex street" resulting in infrasound damage, or covered-up military tests of parachute mines. None of these theories hold up under close scrutiny. All reports related to this case were sent to a secret archive, and did not become available for examination for the next 40 years. When the records were finally released, it was discovered that high doses of radioactivity were found on the camper's clothing. The bodies of the victims were deeply tanned. Several reports of the unidentified orange spheres were recorded from witnesses including military personnel and meteorologists. A great deal of scrap metal was found in the area. A former police officer, Lev Ivanov, who was originally involved in the case in 1959, admitted that they found no rational explanation. When Ivanov's own investigative team reported witnessing the flying orange spheres in the sky, he was given orders from high officials to immediately cease the investigation. Much has been written about this UFO mystery in Russia over the years since the reports first became available from the secret archives. As is the case with so many other strange phenomena, such as the cattle mutilations that began just a few years after these Russian campers were killed, odd lights in the sky were observed. Modern UFO investigators are divided on this case. Interpretations vary from a military cover-up of some sort to an anomalous encounter with UFOs and aliens. In 2000, the *Ural Television Agency* produced a program called *The Mystery of Dyatlov Pass*. A decade or so later, in 2011, the event was included on an episode of *Ancient Aliens* called *Aliens and Evil Places*. Whatever one makes of this strange event, the fact that some of the injuries were similar to future cattle mutilations, and that the event occurred on a geographical location that local tradition named *Dead Mountain,* leaves one with the eerie feeling that this area might have more hidden secrets concerning something deadly that was lurking in the mountains of Russia at the time. Maybe the mysterious intelligences behind the flying orange spheres, whoever or whatever they are, remain in the Ural Mountains for anyone to discover at their own peril who come too close to whatever is going on there.

The Message of the Disks

Two months after the strange *Dyatlov Pass* incident in Russia, on April 24, 1959, a 32-year-old statistician employed at a bank in Bahia, Brazil, Sr. Helio Aguiar, was riding his motorcycle past Piata Beach, when he witnessed a silver-domed disk with portholes around the dome at the top and strange symbols underneath. His motorcycle engine quit running (EM effects) and he slowed down on the road to a stop. As Aguiar unpacked his camera to capture the object on film, he felt a pressure on his brain and the sudden onset of confusion. By the time he was winding the camera, Aguiar was thoroughly confused. He experienced an uncontrollable urge to write something down, and wound up slumped over his motorcycle holding a crumpled paper with writing on it that read *(Mammoth EEE, pg. 522):*

> *Put an absolute stop to all atomic tests for warlike purposes. The balance of the universe is threatened. We shall remain vigilant and ready to intervene.*

Aguiar's photographic prints of the flying saucer were analyzed and authenticated by APRO photographic consultant, John Hopf. As in the Berlet case, this appears to be a mental infusion of information, a simple message imparted using some sort of alien psychotronic technology. Aguiar's photographs of the craft, just like so many of the old UFO cases in which photos were taken, are easily viewed online for each viewer to consider.

Dr. Morris K. Jessup's Death: Murder, or Suicide?

Five days after Aguiar's UFO encounter in Brazil that imparted a simple anti-nuclear message via mental transfer into Aguiar's mind, astronomer and UFO researcher, Dr. Morris K. Jessup, author of *The Case for the UFO* and *The Expanding Case for the UFO*, was found dead in his car on April 29, 1959, in Dade County Park, Florida with a hose running from the exhaust to the inside. Although witnesses reported two men dressed in black suits walking away from Jessup's vehicle prior to his dead body being discovered, Jessup's death was officially ruled a suicide.

However, Jessup's death is considered by many ufologists as yet another example of UFO researchers being silenced when they come to know too much.

Father Gill's Mass Sighting in New Guinea

Two months after the suicide (or possible murder) of UFO-researcher Morris K. Jessup in Florida, Father William Gill in Bosinai, Papas, New Guinea, reported a mass UFO sighting that played a crucial role in converting the former UFO skeptic and professional debunker, Dr. J. Allen Hynek, into an advocate for the Extraterrestrial Hypothesis (ETH). On June 26 and 27, 1959, Father Gill and several parishoners were treated to a group UFO sighting in which a disk appeared in the air with humanoids standing on top of the craft. Father gill waved at the creatures, and, to his utter astonishment, the creatures waved back. There was a blue beam of light emitted from the top of the craft into the clouds above. This happened two nights in a row. The sightings were real and unmistakable. The Gill sightings appear to have been apparitions of some sort, or possibly holographic projections. Perhaps there are extraterrestrial intelligences who have mastered the technology of advanced *Telepresence* and are able to project their consciousness from their world to other planets, sort of like skyping the universe in a way that bypasses the speed of light and/or physical reality altogether. Or, maybe the light that Father Gill described as being projected from the sighted craft up into the clouds was actually coming from the other direction, a projected image from above in the clouds where a solid craft hovered silently while cloaked with clouds. Whatever the case, the intelligences behind this event were able to interact with the inhabitants of Earth and detect the reaction of Father Gill and the other witnesses, as evidenced by the crew on the craft waving back to them when they initiated the gesture. If it was a projection, it was an interactive image. Dr. Jacques Vallee mentioned something of this phenomenon when he stated in his book, *Dimensions*:

> *A major feature in all religious traditions involves a mysterious beam of light emanating from a point in the sky or from a cloud of peculiar shape and focused on a human being. This beam usually is interpreted as a sign of blessing which conveys information from a divine source.*

Whatever the true nature of this UFO encounter was that Father Gill and his parishoners experienced on two days in succession in 1959, it was likely an integral part of the same phenomenon that human beings have been reporting for millennia. The truth of the matter is, we are not alone and never have been. Experiences such as Father Gill's will likely continue to occur and be reported, as they seem to be, for better or worse, part of the human experience on Earth, at least for the humans selected from time to time to perpetuate the purposes of the occulted intelligences involved in the UFO phenomenon.

Cows and Flying Saucers in New Zealand

On a cold morning in July, 1959, the same month and year as Father Gill's mass UFO sighting in New Guinea, a dairy farmer in New Zealand, Mrs. Eileen Moreland, turned on the light in her milking shed and headed out, torch in hand, to bringing her cows in for milking. As she stepped outside the shed into the morning air, she noticed an eerie green glow in the distance emanating from a cloud above. The green glow illuminated the ground below where her cows were gathered. Curious, Eileen walked directly under the cloud and looked straight up into the source of the light, thinking the moon was the likely source. As she realized that the source of the light was not the moon at all, Eileen suddenly became very frightened. She bolted off running toward her tree line, taking shelter against a tall pine tree. She then turned around and saw her cows plainly illuminated in the green glow coming from above. She then stood aghast as she witnessed a flying disk approximately 25 feet in diameter slowly lowering itself from the cloud with orange/green lights around the perimeter and making a hissing sound (common feature). On the top portion of the craft was a transparent dome within which she saw two humanoids in shiny metallic suits and opaque helmets. The craft departed, and as it moved away it left behind an odor of pepper. Mrs. Moreland, shocked from what she just experienced, amazingly continued to gather her cows into the milking shed to continue her normal work day. She later told her husband about her experience, who happened to work for the Royal New Zealand Air Force. Her husband urged her to call the police immediately. An official inquiry ensued, and her sighting received a lot of press. Her case gained the attention of atmospheric physicist and UFO researcher, James McDonald, who took the time to gather her testimony for his work on the Condon Committee as he was visiting Australia and New Zealand in 1967. McDonald was impressed with the sincerity of Mrs. Moreland's account. NICAP is now in possession of Mrs. Moreland's signed testimony. Did Mrs. Eileen Moreland catch a glimpse of the actual craft that projected the interactive apparition to Father Gill and his parishoners? Was her experience a holographic projection from above by the same vehicle that took solace in the clouds above Father Gill's UFO experience, or are we dealing with multiple intelligences from different places who were on Earth simultaneously in 1959? One can only wonder. Father Gill's encounter and Mrs. Moreland's experiences were certainly not simple hallucinations, nor were either of them making it up. Outright hoaxes or lying testimonies are actually rare when it comes to reporting UFO encounters. It is quite common for UFO experiencers to keep their encounter to themselves for fear of being thought of as crazy. Some even fear themselves that they might be losing their minds. UFO encounters tend to be challenging to the percipient's previously held views of reality. The vast majority of UFO percipients have experienced something real, even if we do not understand the actual nature of what is going on. If the thousands of UFO reports that have been documented to date are somehow hallucinatory in nature, there is certainly an unearthly intelligence behind the hallucinations that is orchestrating the perceptions of the witnesses. It seems far more likely that what experiencers are seeing is real, even though we do not know who or what these creatures and their vehicles really are or where they come from. Maybe they are visitors from another planet or dimension, another parallel universe that coexists with our own, or a cryptoterrestrial population that coevolved on this planet and seeks to remain hidden. Or perhaps UFO encounters are complex psychological and sensory experiences induced in humans by a being or beings that represent a higher octave of consciousness than human, a vast post-singularity transcendent intelligence that has been manipulating human perceptions all along for its own ends, using the universe as a computer to solve a cosmic problem that we might not understand even if it was explained to us.

Dino Kraspedon and Gloria Lee

In 1959, alleged contactee Dino Kraspedon (the alter-ego and pen name for a Brazilian man named Aladino Felix) hopped on the bandwagon of 1950s contactees by writing and publishing his book, *My Contact with Flying Saucers*. The book tells Dino's story of a meeting in his home with the commander of a flying saucer, who revealed secrets of celestial physics and how to improve the social conditions on Earth for humanity. Also in 1959, contactee Gloria Lee published her book, *Why We Are Here*, that consists of her automatic writing with an entity from Jupiter named "JW." Lee also published a book a few years later called, *The Changing Conditions of Your World*, which was a further compilation of JW's teachings. Gloria Lee also founded the *Cosmon Research Foundation* for the study of JW's spiritual messages. As is the case for all contactees, the degree with which their experiences intersect with physical reality is of little significance, as their influence and teachings have a very real impact on the popular culture and mindset of the era. This influence affects human beliefs and behaviors in order to mold the human organism into what the intelligences behind the UFOs want for humanity. Even those who intentionally deceive for fun or profit are part of the program, as their stories are absorbed into the collective unconscious and remain effective. Even when a fraud is exposed that causes some to fall away from belief in flying saucers and aliens altogether, this effect causes some to become skeptical scientists who wind up conducting research or inventing a mechanism that propels humanity further toward the technological singularity, thus serving the purposes of the very phenomenon they have chosen to disbelieve in. The overall effect of UFO lore is multi-faceted and is exactly what is needed for the occulted UFO intelligences at large to accomplish their goals. If, at times, humanity goes astray and becomes too skeptical, outstanding, unexplainable UFO spectacles will appear to credible witnesses, thus molding the human mind once again in the desired direction. If humans become too credulous, absurdities are introduced to turn the dial of the human mind back toward rationalism. In this manner, humanity is being manipulated regardless of our current levels of belief or skepticism concerning UFOs. Human consciousness is now and has always been a work in progress, steered and cajoled in both subtle and harsh ways toward our destiny of transcendence through technology. What remains to be seen is how much, if any, humans are to benefit from all this. The price in human suffering thus far is staggering. After thousands of years of human tears, it is difficult to imagine an end that will justify the means.

The Sirens of Titan

In 1959, as Father Gill and his astounded parishoners in New Guinea, Mrs. Eileen Moreland in New Zealand, and so many others around the world reported their UFO and occupant encounters, Kurt Vonnegut's fictional work, *The Sirens of Titan*, hit the bookshelves. In Vonnegut's all-too-relevant story, an alien race called the Tralfamadorians used humans to unconsciously send messages to a stranded ship on Saturn's moon, Titan. In Vonnegut's tale, humanity was intentionally evolved for the sole purpose of producing a small repair part for the stranded vessel. I find it ironic that, as the literary device of "alien mind control" developed in fiction over a period of about a century, the simultaneous realization that something akin to alien mind control was actually happening in our world was slowly setting in. As we humans eagerly absorbed works of science fiction, we were also forced to grapple with the strange objects that were making appearances in our skies in waves. These flying objects materialized and dematerialized right before our eyes, chased our automobiles, and landed in our fields. Mysterious ufonauts emerged to take a look around, take soil samples, and paralyze humans with beams of light, thus inspiring us to ever-greater technology to emulate what we saw, and create even greater works of fiction. In some cases, these occupants whisked us away to alien worlds using mysterious methods that always left their human experiencers bewildered as to the exact nature of their fantastic sojourns. A minority of those who have UFO encounters choose to reveal their experiences to the world out of a sense of purpose and obligation, while the vast majority keep their experiences to themselves, fearing ridicule or reprisal. Some suspect that they may have lost their minds, and go into reclusion. Others, unfortunately, take their own lives. The powers that be who create such experiences are, apparently, willing to accept all of these reactions as they work to mold humanity like a chunk of clay on a potter's wheel. The human casualties along the way are simply scraps that fall to the floor of the shop unnoticed.

Why Are Ufonauts Humanoid?

Many UFO skeptics criticize the idea of humanoid aliens. In their mindset (which I once shared), evolution on Earth is unique to the environment of this particular planet, a planet that has, over millions of years, experienced its own unique set of changes. If it were not for the dinosaurs being "accidentally" wiped out, humans wouldn't even be here in the first place to contemplate whether or not humanoid aliens exist, and all the life that has emerged on Earth is purely accidental and nearly impossible to replicate elsewhere. Considering the nearly endless sequence of "coincidences" that were needed to produce mammals and humans, the chances that a similar lifeform would evolve on a planet other than Earth is therefore considered extremely unlikely. In the mind of strict Darwinists such as Richard Dawkins, those who contemplate aliens in human form are just projecting a childlike anthropomorphic fantasy onto their aliens that lacks imagination. This projection of humanoids with variation is also considered lacking in understanding of how evolution works blindly to form organisms that adapt to each planetary environment. When considering this viewpoint, that existence is blind and mechanical, a couple things need to be kept in mind. It is reasonable to assume that the same laws of physics apply throughout the entire physical universe. As near as we can tell at this point, this is the case. Technology, as we know it, must begin with fire. Without the mastery of fire, no technology can emerge. On such a fireless world, there is no smelting of metals, and no early experimentation with rockets. Nothing close to what we would call a technological civilization could emerge without the mastery of fire and the use of tools. Throughout the entire universe, the production of fire requires fuel, oxygen, and heat. Since the creation of fire requires oxygen, oxygen must exist in the atmosphere on any world in which fire can be produced. Therefore, any tool-using creature that evolved on such an oxygen-bearing planet would likely breathe oxygen. Technology requires the use of tools and therefore requires the development of appendages of some sort with enough dexterity to manipulate material objects. So already we have creatures who breathe oxygen, possess appendages, have mastered the use of fire, and are able to manipulate tools. It's not that the concept of humanoid aliens lacks imagination, as anyone can imagine creatures that are very different from humans who evolved in various ways on planets that are quite unlike our own and who look nothing like humans, but chances are they are planet-bound. Nonhuman, non-tool-using, non-oxygen breathing creatures would not develop technology as we have, nor are nonhumanoids flying around out there in the universe, but are instead bound to live on their home world without technology. In other words, there is a very good rationale that any creature from a planet that developed technology as we did will have many features in common with the humans of Earth. Most surface-dwelling creatures on Earth share many features with humans. Most animals and insects have appendages for manipulating food, eyes to see, legs to walk, and so forth. All of Earth's creatures, as far as we know, have common origins. All have similar biology on this oxygenated planet that is able to produce and sustain fire. However, only humans have developed any significant technology. On Earth, the human form evolved from primates, and primates evolved only after millions of years of other types of animals arose on Earth and then became extinct. Beings who developed a humanoid form from whatever animal stock existed on their home planet might be the only types of beings who are flying around in some sort of technologically-produced craft out there in the universe, even though there may exist many exotic nonhumanoid, non-tool-using populations in the universe who remain planet-bound in non-technological societies, just as this planet displayed for millions of years prior to the human form. However, even if the physical universe is teeming with humanoid life with technological civilizations as depicted in the movie *Star Wars*, and even if the universe actually does harbor a wide variety of creatures whose differences are minor due to their particular pre-humanoid ancestry, many skeptics of the UFO phenomenon are concerned that the alien humanoids reported by witnesses and contactees are *too much* like us. As the late James W. Moseley, author of *Shockingly Close to the Truth*, once put it (pg. 16):

> *In some strange, distorted way, the saucer occupants are a reflection of ourselves. As one researcher so aptly put it, they are too much like us to be interplanetary visitors. They display aspects of the objective and of the subjective at the same time. Whatever may be the case, I do not believe the answer will be found in our lifetime, or at least not in mine.*

James Moseley was considered by many as the "court jester" of ufology, or "ufoology" as Moseley called it. Moseley produced a sarcastic and humorous publication, *Saucer Smear,* for decades, much to the embarrassment of "serious ufologists." James Moseley was astute enough to realize that, although there is a "core reality" to the UFO phenomenon, the actual truth of the matter is complex and profound, and completely eluded UFO researchers of his era. Therefore, Moseley decided not to take himself or the subject of UFOs too seriously and had fun with the field for the duration of his lifetime. Unfortunately, Moseley passed away in 2012 without the answer to the UFO mystery, as so many others have as well already. If only James Moseley and others who yearned for real answers pertaining to UFOs had been able to stay alive for just a few more decades, their life's quest might have been fulfilled. As we head into the Singularity during the coming decades, the UFO mystery, along with the real purpose and destiny of humanity, will surely become clear. The Etherians, whoever they really are, are real. Wherever they actually come from, whether otherworldly, interdimensional, or both, they will doubtless emerge from their hidden realms of cryptoreality in the next few decades to finally become known. Using the technology of the Singularity, the Etherians will likely take on a more permanent earthly form. Another reason to consider that humanoids and their post-singularity creations might dominate the universe is that creating singularities throughout the universe might be the very purpose that the Creators seek as they use the universe and everything in it as a computation mechanism to acquire vast knowledge in a grand experiment of universe and creature-building. As time moves forward and civilizations come and go, the Overlords add the sum total of knowledge gained from the life that develops on each planet unto themselves as technological singularities are produced like ripe fruit harvested from a vast orchard and delivered to the Creators, i.e., the master designers and fabricators of the physical universe, who exist as we do within the infinite living mind of The All.

One hope that humans can realistically have as we approach the Singularity is that, from the vast expansion of human consciousness and intelligence that will come about through the augmentation of our biological intelligence with technology, effective perception and communication with our alien visitors will finally be achieved. This communication and perception should occur at least with our visitors who have our best interests in mind, in particular, the Amicizia. This hope is that they have been waiting for humankind to evolve to the point where communication can effectively occur. If alien groups such as the Amicizia have been taking human form only for our benefit, and are actually very different in appearance, perhaps we shall finally perceive them as they really are when our intelligence is expanded. By augmenting and expanding the human mind by merging with our machines, open contact may finally occur. As Moseley hopefully wrote in *Shockingly Close to the Truth* (pg. 29):

> *The most thrilling thought of all is perhaps they are biding their time, and when they are ready, or when they feel we are ready, i.e., sufficiently advanced, they will communicate with us.*

Moseley's statement reflects the highest hopes and dreams of humanity concerning interaction with alien life. That is, the advanced aliens responsible for the onslaught of UFO encounters are just waiting for us to grow up and join the Galactic Community at large. The aliens have just been patiently waiting for humans to mature to the point of being worthy of inclusion as a viable intelligence to communicate with. Even though I am skeptical that this benign intent is all there is to it, I am somewhat hopeful that my own paranoia is ill-founded. I do hope that I am wrong about some of my concerns regarding the oncoming Singularity. I hope that I am wrong in my suspicions that our technology is not for us, but is being brought about for an alien purpose that may be harmful to humans or even bring about our own extinction. I have to maintain that there is evidence to suspect that humans are being used as unwitting slaves to produce a technology that will allow the arrival of alien intelligences in a most unexpected and unconventional manner. This entrance into the physical world may have been the goal that the aliens have been waiting patiently to achieve for a very long time now. So far, it seems that the aliens have done an excellent job maintaining their cover. They have remained hidden from open view. They have maintained invisibility for the most part and have appeared only to those who can further their purposes in some way. The aliens have perfected the art of mind control, creating their own psychological camouflage with UFO skepticism produced by intentional absurdities, along with a circus of mentally unstable "true believers." This camouflage has served to hide the reality of their existence from those who could do the most to thwart the more invasive aspects of the Singularity. In this manner, the scientists of the world, working in fields of knowledge that will bring about the Singularity, may be leading humanity as lambs to the slaughter with alien technology cleverly filtered in over the decades that the scientists themselves falsely believe was entirely invented by Man. This progression of technology brought about by our science is intended to advance and improve the human condition, when the truth of our fate regarding the pinnacle of technology and its accompanying alien visitation is quite the opposite. Whatever the case, time is about to reveal her secrets.

CHAPTER 9

Keepers of the Hidden Realms

"Lifeforms, differing greatly from human appearances, a favorite postulation in some circles, does not appear to me to have much validity. The overwhelming body of evidence suggests that those who pilot spacecraft are more or less like us, two-legged erect creatures with reasoning and intelligence, not insects or spiders, or reptiles possessed of strange, human-like brains capable of piloting complex aircraft."

– Hans Holzer, *The Ufonauts.*

[On February 13, 1960, France detonated their first atomic bomb in Operation Gerboise Bleue, following up the next year with the detonation of 13 underground nuclear devices.]

The Departure of Valiant Thor

ACCORDING TO DR. Frank Stranges, one month after France decided to enter the nuclear playground by detonating their first atomic bomb, Commander Valiant Thor disembarked from Earth and returned to the interior of his home planet, Venus, on March 16, 1960.

The Sky People

During this same year, 1960, British UFO investigator and author, Brinsley Le Poer Trench, considered by many ufologists as the top theologian of what amounted to a new galactic religion, published *The Sky People*. In this book, Trench proposed that the identity of the Sky People was none other than the *Elohim* of the Old Testament, the group of entities speaking in Gen 1:26 that proposed, "Let us make Man in our image, after our likeness," and observed in Gen 3:22, "Behold, the man has become as one of us." The work of Brinsley Le Poer Trench foreshadowed many ideas to come regarding flying saucers, ideas that were elaborated by future authors, including Erich von Daniken in *Chariots of the Gods*, and Zecharia Sitchin in his *Earth Chronicles*.

Morning of the Magicians

Another important theory in the development of our understanding of the Phenomenon came in 1960 from two French authors, Louis Pauwels and Jacques Bergier, in their book, *Morning*

249

of the Magicians. Their work made a case for extraterrestrials tinkering with human genetics to produce geniuses like Leonardo Da Vinci, and interacting with humans within the framework of secret societies *to guide the evolution of humankind into higher technology.*

The Social Impact of Disclosure

In 1960 NASA commissioned a report created by the Brookings Institution called *Proposed Studies on the Implications of Peaceful Space Activities for Human Affairs,* otherwise known as the *Brookings Report.* The Brookings Report is noted for analysis of public attitudes in the event that extra-terrestrial life is discovered. The report urged that further scientific studies were necessary in determining the full social impact and implications of full public disclosure in the event that aliens or alien artifacts are ever discovered on the Moon, Mars, or Venus. The report also cited examples of societies in the past that have been adversely affected by a visiting population with advanced technology. Physicist Stephen Hawking expressed similar concerns on the Discovery Channel in 2010 when he stated:

> *If aliens visit us, the outcome would be much as when Columbus landed in America, which didn't turn out well for Native Americans.*

The Brookings Report was an early version of a more modern treatise written by UFO-researcher Richard Dolan in 2012, called *A.D. After Disclosure: When the Government Finally Reveals the Truth about Alien Contact.* Dolan's book provides a fully-detailed analysis of what might happen to the financial, social, intellectual, and religious aspects of our culture when Disclosure finally occurs. The Brookings Report even had something to say about the discovery of superintelligence (pg. 103):

> *If superintelligence is discovered, the results become quite unpredictable. It is possible that if the intelligence of these creatures were sufficiently superior to ours, they would choose to have little or no contact with us. On the face of it, there is no reason to believe that we might learn a great deal from them, especially if their physiology and psychology were substantially different from ours.*

The existence of the Brookings Report from 1960 indicates that many intelligent minds were focused on the complex issue of extraterrestrial contact at this early point in time, and that their thinking in this matter was quite advanced and insightful. The Overlords of the Singularity have existed as a background presence on Earth for millennia and will continue to do so. Thus far, humans have only had brief encounters of high strangeness with the Overlords, mind-blowing glimpses of a greater reality that have inspired many of the world's religions. These alien-human encounters have likely involved either advanced biological intelligences or post-singularity machine intelligence, the very forms of possible superintelligence that the Brookings

Report originally postulated. Certain individuals in 1960 may have at least suspected that the UFO intelligences represent an evolving, generational form of advanced, non-biological consciousness. I doubt that individuals in the know would even have been able to convey this idea to the public at large, nor would it have been believed or understood if they did.

My first Paranormal Encounter

In 1961, at the age of 6, I received my first glimpse into one of the many alternate realities that surround us. I was lucky enough at this early age to receive a visit from a pair of *Shadow People*. I don't know to this day who they were, but I consider the experience significant. Out of all my childhood memories, the visit from the Shadow People has stuck with me in my mind all these years. The encounter is branded into my consciousness as a real event. This memory helps me in my current UFO studies, reminding me that what we call the "paranormal" is real. Just before this encounter occurred, my mother had just tucked me in bed for the night, and my covers were pulled up to my chest. When she left the room, she left the light on in the bathroom, as I was afraid of the dark at the time. I noticed that, a few moments after she left the room, two black humanoid silhouettes appeared in the doorway, as if they had been there observing from an invisible realm until my mother left in order to make their presence known to me. One appeared as a male, the other was in the likeness of a female. They were as real as anyone in the world, only they were solid black with no discernible features. Later in life I would learn that such blackness, referred to as "superblack," was how someone or something appears to humans when the person or object does not exist in our spatial dimension, or is, rather, in-between worlds. These creatures or objects do not reflect visible light. I felt a little stunned at their appearance, but I felt no fear as they slowly walked over to my bed and tended to me as if checking me out for some reason. They bowed over me for a few seconds, stood up, turned toward one another as if communicating something to one another, stood up straight, and then vanished into thin air before my eyes, like a lightbulb that was turned off. I'm sure that some who read this account will suspect that this was exactly what they were, a lighting effect as my mother left the room and turned the light off, leaving a residual image of my mother in the room. I can assure you that this is not the case. I still do not know if they were some sort of ghosts, or interdimensional inhabitants of another realm who took an interest in me for some reason. I do know that, whatever or whoever they were, they were real as rain. I had the feeling at the time that they both knew me prior to my life as an Earth-child. In John Keel's paranormal masterpiece, *The Mothman Prophecies*, he describes a shadow person that appeared in a house in New York that may have represented "residual mental energy" from the author, Walter Gibson, who lived there while writing *The Shadow* series. This dark apparition has been seen and reported by many who have stayed at the house. It is seen wearing a long dark cape and a brimmed hat pulled over the face as it slinks from room to room. No reports of this shadow person existed until Gibson vacated the house. Psychics, who are often able to perceive these types of entities, are often considered the kooks of the world. In reality, their senses may be tuned above the norm, enabling them to see just beyond the normal human visual spectrum. As Keel stated (*Mothman* audio):

> *About 10% of the population have the ability to see above and beyond the narrow spectrum of visible light. They can see radiations and even objects invisible to the rest of us. A very large part of the UFO lore is, in fact, based upon the observations of such people. What seems normal to them seems abnormal, even ridiculous to the rest of us. People who see ghosts or the wandering shadow have these abilities. They are peering at forms that are always there, always present around us, like radio waves, and when certain conditions exist they can see these things.*

Joe Simonton and His Flying Saucer Pancakes

In the case of flying saucer and ufonaut encounters, not only are they seen with the eyes, but also come with a physicality to them that present one of two possibilities – either they are happening in physical reality just as they appear to percipients, or they represent a virtual-reality experience with full sensation, induced by an outside agent. In 1961, the same year I experienced my own paranormal encounter with the shadow people in Florida, when I was a six-year-old first-grader with a crew cut learning how to print legibly, a highly significant contact event also occurred in the life of a chicken farmer from Eagle Creek, Wisconsin, named Joe Simonton. This case contained perceived absurdities and was abjectly ignored and rejected by many UFO researchers due to their lack of knowledge of cultural mythology, and lack of insight into the paraphysical aspect of the UFO phenomenon. On April 18, 1961, Joe experienced an encounter with a landed flying saucer in his yard with occupants who were seeking water and cooking pancakes on a flameless grill. Joe accommodated the flying saucer occupant's request for water, and accepted their gift of pancakes. What escaped the UFO researchers who discounted this case were the elements of Joe's story that are straight out of classic fairy lore. Many of the contacts with fairies reported in centuries past involved gifts of food from the fairies, and requests by the fairies for water. Joe made a report to the Air Force, and handed over the pancakes. The pancakes were then analyzed and found to consist of normal pancake ingredients except for the total absence of salt. It is well-known within fairy lore that fairies do not ingest salt. This case and other similar cases that contain elements of classic fairy lore have led some UFO researchers, such as Dr. Jacques Vallee, author of *Anatomy of a Phenomenon*, *Passport to Magonia*, and *Dimensions*, and John Keel, author of the ufological classic, *Operation Trojan Horse*, to suspect that occupants of flying saucers in the modern age are not extraterrestrial visitors after all, but indigenous entities that have been with humans all along. In this view, both fairies and ufonauts represent an aerial race of normally-invisible beings who wish to remain hidden from the general human population. These Etherians have the ability to appear in various forms to selected individuals whenever they wish. Throughout history, these elusive creatures have been

252

known to appear in this reality in various forms, interact with humans, collect pure water, flora, fauna, and on occasion, take animals. They also seem to have the ability to scan the human mind to some degree (although there are indications that this ability is imperfect) and appear to humans in whatever form they think humans will most easily accept. The fairy folk have always appeared rather childlike with an imperfect knowledge of human science. They also seem to have the ability to assess our state of mind and make appearances with imagery that will be acceptable to us. The ufonauts have made pronouncements to humans that they are from Mars, Venus, or Mercury, locations that make our scientists scoff due to the apparent impossibility of life existing there. If these ufonauts are not actually from the interior of planets that we have deemed uninhabitable, or from the astral plane of such planets as Omnec Onec claims, they may represent instead Earth's own elemental entities. Visits from the fairy folk who are emulating other phenomena does not rule out the possibility that there are actual extraterrestrials visiting Earth, but if they are, members of this indigenous population of aerial creatures are now emulating our own expectations of extraterrestrial visitation, which changes over time. Thus the imagery that percipients have reported over the years has morphed in appearance and complexity between the 1950s and the present as human consciousness evolves. The ability to adapt to new concepts in the human mind appears to be within the capability of the cryptoterrestrial populations we share the planet with, whether these creatures are biological populations who live inside the earth somewhere, or are entities whose habitat is between the atomic spaces of air, earth, fire, and water.

Kennedy's "Secret Society" Speech

Just a few days after Joe Simonton was paid a visit from the "Good People" of Wisconsin, the fairy folk, who appeared to Joe as ufonauts who shared food with him and asked for water as they do, President John F. Kennedy gave his famous "Secret Society" speech at the Waldorf-Astoria Hotel on April 27, 1961. Kennedy's Secret Society speech is believed by many UFO researchers to have contributed to the decision from the powers that be, the secret shadow government, to take him out, as he represented a high-profile threat to their secret agenda. At the time of this infamous speech, Kennedy was voicing his intent to merge the US Space Program with the Russian Space Program in joint space exploration endeavors. In this speech, Kennedy revealed the factual existence of a hidden shadow government that was growing in power behind the scenes and threatening to disrupt our democracy. On November 22, 1963, John F. Kennedy was assassinated. Many ufologists today believe that Kennedy's assassination was related to his knowledge of UFOs. He also wanted to share space information with the Soviets, which the secret US intelligence agencies in charge of the UFO phenomenon did not like. The FBI was also concerned that Kennedy was talking to Marilyn Monroe about "things from outer space," and that Marilyn herself was about to go public with classified UFO-related information that Kennedy had entrusted to her. This concern is revealed by a released document in the

FBI vault online. The FBI felt that Kennedy was inquiring too deeply into secret knowledge about flying saucers and alien visitation, and many believe that he and Marilyn were murdered for these reasons, to silence them both and maintain UFO secrecy. One of the reasons that Disclosure is taking so long and only coming one drip at a time is that coming clean about flying saucers, aliens, and crashed non-terrestriral craft would likely require confessing to all sorts of malfeasance and debauchery that has taken place over the last several decades on the part of the US government, and they fear the mess that all that information would create within the general public.

The Pope's Alien Encounter

In July, 1961, a couple of years prior to the assassination of John F. Kennedy, an event occurred involving the Catholic Church that is possibly tied to UFO secrecy. Pope John XXIII, known as the "Good Pope," a man who had miracles of healings attributed to him around the world, had an encounter with humanoid non-terrestrials at his summer residence of Castel Gandolfo, Italy. In this summer of 1961, the Pope and his assistant saw an oval spacecraft with blue and amber lights flashing that hovered and then landed in the south end of his garden. A humanoid alien with pointed ears and surrounded by a golden light emerged from the craft. Not knowing the nature of the encounter, but realizing that this was a miraculous celestial event, the Pope and his assistant kneeled before the strange being. The Holy Father got up alone and walked over to the creature, spending about 20 minutes in conversation. From this encounter, the Pontiff *stated [The Sun, July 23, 1985]:*

> *The Sons of God are everywhere. Sometimes we have difficulty in recognizing our own brothers.*

Following the Pope's alien encounter, on May 31, 1963, Pope John XXIII met with contactee George Adamski to discuss Earth's humanoid extraterrestrial presence, and their enigmatic message of peace. This meeting took place two years prior to the capture of a Venusian scout craft on video by Adamski and a respected figure within the US government, Madeleine Rodeffer, in 1965.

Elementals Disturbed by Atomic Detonation in Soviet Union

As Trevor James Constable proved to us with his research and experimentation with infrared film, exotic aerial creatures exist that are normally invisible to humans, who are sometimes mistaken for flying saucers. Are these creatures the Sylphs, part of the Elemental Kingdoms of ancient lore, who somehow exist in our atmosphere in another dimension of Earth? If so, the Sylphs doubtless experienced a disturbance on October 30, 1961, when the Soviet Union detonated the largest atomic bomb in Earth's history (50 megatons) - *TSAR BOMBA* @ Novaya. Although we have no real idea if detonating atomic bombs in the atmosphere, underground, or in the sea actually disturbs interdimensional life, or life in the elemental realms, I can't help but imagine that these atomic explosions were not welcomed by our invisible neighbors with whom we share our planet. If this is the case, every effort on the part of the elementals could be expected as an attempt to influence the human world to cease this insanity. Is it really any wonder that after the advent of nuclear testing in 1945, there came so many stories of contact between the peaceful "Space Brothers" and humanity that carried warnings of the dire consequences of possible nuclear annihilation, along with admonitions of global unity and a universal message of cosmic benevolence? The elemental populations probably realized that we would not likely listen to messages coming from fairies these days, nor could they reveal their actual appearance that humans might view as frightening. However, due to our current obsession with outer space and our deep inner desire for contact with extraterrestrials, appearing as humanoid Space Brothers from Venus or Mars was an image within the human psyche that could possibly be emulated with success. Humans realize that anyone visiting Earth from another planet would necessarily be well advanced of us, and we would be far more likely to listen to them than amorphous blobs of intelligent plasma. At any rate, it is a certainty that some type of nonhuman intelligence was warning humanity concerning our behavior with nuclear detonations. These detonations would particularly disturb those who live in the sea (the Undines) and those who live in our atmosphere (the Sylphs). The nature of the elementals may be similar to that of any other life form on Earth, only they exist in the hidden realms of air, earth, fire, and water. The elementals do not appear to be superintelligent like the Overlords, who oversee and manipulate all life and activity on Earth, or the actual Creators who fabricated the physical universe as a computational device. The elementals may instead represent just another part of Creation that the Overlords draw knowledge from, knowledge and consciousness that will be assimilated along with ours in the Singularity. If so, the elementals may exist as a separate species of Earth-life much as we are. What we have always called the elementals may exist as extremophiles on Earth who live in the farthest reaches of our upper atmosphere, and within the Earth's very core. Alternatively the elementals may represent intelligent extensions of the Overlords themselves who are embedded like tentacles into the Creation. The elementals may exist as an intelligence absorption mechanism and transmitter to the Overlords themselves, the intermediary connection the Overlords have to our innermost thoughts in the realm of the human collective unconscious. The elementals within fire, earth, air, and water, may have the mental ability to transmogrify energy and appear to humans as flying saucers, angels, demons, fairies, lake monsters, or various other types of cryptozoological creatures such as Bigfoot, who then vanish without a trace except for puddles of silicon carbide left behind on occasion.

The Hill Abduction

Five months after Joe Simonton was handed a stack of pancakes by either ufonauts or elementals emulating extraterrestrial visitors in a flying saucer that landed on his chicken farm, an interracial couple (unusual in the 1960s), Barney and Betty Hill, would make UFO history on September 19 & 20, 1961, with a bizarre experience with visitors of unknown origin. Their case would also be one of the first in recent history to be categorized as an "alien abduction" experience, a phenomenon that would become epidemic in the decades to come. Barney and Betty Hill tell a fantastic tale of being abducted by space visitors later identified by ufologists as originating from the Zeta Reticuli star system. Since this incredible contact event, their story has become canonized in modern UFO circles, and is accepted as legitimate by researchers of high-credibility, such as UFO researcher and nuclear physicist Stanton Friedman. Friedman accepts the Barney and Betty Hill abduction case as physical and legitimate, and rejects the "psychic" explanation that is applied to so many other contact accounts. Much has been written about the Barney and Betty Hill abduction case, including a best-selling book, *The Interrupted Journey*, (1966), and a 1975 television program, *The UFO Incident*.

On the evening of September 19, 1961, Betty and Barney Hill were returning home from their vacation at Niagra Falls and Montreal, Canada. On a lonely road at night around 10:30 p.m., Betty observed a bright point of light that she first thought was a shooting star, only the object was moving up, like an airplane or satellite. As it began to grow bigger and brighter, Betty urged Barney to pull over for a better look at the unusual object in the sky, and allow their dog Delsey to walk around and go to the bathroom. Barney pulled into a rest area and retrieved a pistol from the trunk to protect them from any foraging bears. Using binoculars, Betty watched as the object grew into an unusually-shaped craft with multi-colored lights and flying across the face of the moon. Taking over the binoculars, Barney realized that it was not an airplane or anything he could otherwise identify. He and Betty returned to their 1957 Chevy Bel Air and began driving away. Driving through Franconia Notch on Route 3, they observed the craft growing closer. It became apparent that the craft was aware of their observations and presence. The flying object began playing "cat and mouse" with them as they drove along in their car. Suddenly, the craft, later described by Barney as "a giant pancake," descended right above them, covering the couple's view of the sky through the windshield entirely. Barney got out of the car and observed 8-11 humanoid figures peering out portholes while red lights and fins like bat wings began telescoping out the sides of the craft. Another long structure extended from underneath the craft as it descended to approximately 50-80 feet above their car. Hysterical, and sensing they were about to be captured, Barney quickly got back into the car, and drove away from the area as fast as he could to escape. After a series of beeping and buzzing sounds that drove a tingling sensation through their bodies, Barney and Betty hill found themselves suddenly 35 miles away from their previous location and left in an altered state of consciousness with only a vague recollection of events. On September 21, 1961, Betty called Pease Air Force base to report their UFO encounter. Major Paul Henderson's report, dated September 26, 1961 and forwarded to Project Blue Book, stated that Betty probably misidentified the planet Jupiter. Frustrated with the ridiculous and irresponsible response from the Air

Force, Betty wrote a letter to Major Donald Keyhoe, who was retired from the Marines and head of NICAP (National Investigations Committee of Aerial Phenomenon). Keyhoe was one of the major UFO researchers in the 1950s-1960s, and wrote books including, *Flying Saucers from Outer Space* (1953) and many other pulp fiction stories related to UFOs. In 1958, 3 years prior to the Barney and Betty Hill incident, Keyhoe appeared on a CBS television show to speak about UFOs, and was an early proponent of the Extraterrestrial Hypothesis (ETH). Keyhoe himself had an interesting background as a manager of promotional tours, the most famous of which was that of Charles Lindbergh. Keyhoe was a Marine Corps Lieutenant who was injured in an airplane crash in 1922 and as a result turned to writing as a hobby. He retired from the Marines in 1923 and went to work for the US Department of Commerce and the National Geodetic Survey. In 1928 he wrote and published a successful book called, *Flying with Lindbergh*, thus launching a new career as a writer of fiction stories, many of which appeared in pulp fiction rags like *Weird Tales*, such as: *The Grim Passenger* (1925); *The Mystery Under the Sea* (1926); *Through the Vortex* (1926); and *The Master of Doom* (1927). Keyhoe also produced the fiction for three issues of a magazine called *Dr. Yen Sin*. This fiction includes: *The Mystery of the Dragon's Shadow* (May/June 1936), *The Mystery of the Golden Skull* (July/August 1936), and *The Mystery of the Singing Mummies* (September/October 1936). So Betty Hill was now speaking to an ex-Marine Lieutenant who retired from an injury, a person of high intelligence and credibility, who also had a track record of writing successful science fiction, who naturally took great interest in their story. Betty's letter to Keyhoe was forwarded to Boston astronomer and NICAP member Walter N. Webb. Webb met with Barney and Betty personally, taking notes on everything the couple could consciously remember of their ordeal, and details of vivid dreams that Betty experienced after the UFO encounter. Then, on November 25, 1961, the Hills were both interviewed by NICAP members, including C.D. Jackson and Robert E. Hohmann. Together they discovered that Barney and Betty Hill were missing a few hours of time in their accounts. They decided to set up a hypnosis session in an attempt to discover the missing details. Barney agreed to the hypnosis as he thought it might ease Betty's anxiety about her nightmares. On January 4, 1964, a hypnotist, Dr. Simon, who dismissed the Extraterrestrial Hypothesis (ETH) as impossible, began separate hypnosis sessions for Barney and Betty so that they could not hear one another's recollections and/or influence one another's perceptions of the event. Under hypnosis, the separate and very emotional testimonies of Barney and Betty hill came forth, describing minute details of their abduction experience. Both accounts coordinated well together except for a few minor details. When Betty was asked to reproduce a three-dimensional star map that had been shown to her aboard the craft, she produced a drawing from memory that was later identified by researcher Majorie Fish as the Zeta Reticuli Star System. Zeta Reticuli is the star system of choice that many ufologists identify as the origin of the aliens involved in the multitude of abduction cases that were to come during the next couple decades. These accounts would come from the clients of abduction researchers such as Dr. John Mack, Bud Hopkins, and David Jacobs. The hypnosis sessions were reported to serve the purpose of easing Barney and Betty's high anxiety about their abduction. Afterward, Barney and Betty Hill sought no publicity for their experience. However, after a reporter for the *Boston Traveler* published a full-page story in the newspaper about their experience, the Barney and Betty Hill abduction case grew to international fame. This popularity resulted in the successful 1966 book, *The Interrupted Journey* by John G. Fuller, which provides a full account of the Hill's reported experience.

Is it possible that the "gray aliens" encountered by Betty and Barney Hill, along with the creatures that crashed at Roswell and are reported in so many abduction cases are actually coming to Earth from the Zeta Reticuli star system? This gravitationally-bound binary star system can be seen with the naked eye from the dark skies of the Southern hemisphere, and would take someone traveling at the speed of light about 39 years to get here by conventional methods, much less time if traveling in hyperspace, entering and exiting traversable wormholes, or some other method of interstellar travel we haven't discovered yet are a reality. These two stars, Zeta Reticuli 1 and Zeta Reticuli 2, are both very similar to our own sun, and are therefore referred to as "solar analogues." Zeta Reticuli 1 and 2 are included in the Zeta Herculis Moving Group of stars, and all share a common origin. Both stars are abnormally low in luminosity for their age and surface temperature. Judging by the characteristics of their chromospheres, their age calculates at about 2 billion years old as opposed to our local solar system, which is about 4.5 billion years old by the methods of dating we currently use. However, the kinematics of this system suggest that they might be much older than 2 billion years. Two erroneous assumptions are usually made in determining whether it is possible for the Grays or other populations of extraterrestrials to originate from Zeta Reticuli, or any other location. The first assumption is that we currently understand how life originated on Earth, when we do not. The second assumption is that we currently have a grasp on all the mechanics of how life develops over time, i.e., how evolution actually works, and we do not. The processes of how life actually originates and evolves over time are currently subjects of debate and speculation among many disciplines of science. It is also probably a mistake to assume that the processes by which life arose here on Earth are the only way it can happen throughout the universe. Thus far in analyzing the feasibility of life coming to Earth from Zeta Reticuli, it looks pretty good, but there is one screw in the works here. That is, so far, this binary star system where the Grays are supposed to be originating from appear to have no planets orbiting them. At one point astronomers thought they had found a Jupiter-sized planet in the Zeta system, but that was dismissed as they realized the signal indicating a possible planet was actually due to pulsations from Zeta Reticuli 2. Even though we have found no planets orbiting either star that the Grays could call their home, it remains possible that there is a planet there, and we just haven't discovered it yet. It is also possible that there are places of potential habitation within a star system that we currently do not understand involving other planes of existence, parallel worlds, Dark Matter, or other realms where life exists that are currently beyond human understanding at the moment. There also may exist spacefaring civilizations who abandoned life on a planet long ago and live out their entire lives in space, who may call a particular star system home for some reason. Advanced civilizations who are now completely mobile may occupy solar systems for long periods of time that are too young by our calculations for its occupants to have actually originated there in the way we currently postulate. So, even though it doesn't look promising that biological life as we know it is originating from a nonexistent planet in the Zeta Reticuli system, we cannot completely rule out the possibility that the ETs involved in the Roswell incident, the Betty and Barney Hill experience, or any other report of visitors allegedly coming from the Zeta Reticuli system may actually find their home there. There is a large volume of information about the nature of the universe that presently eludes our species and lies beyond our current body of knowledge. There is, however, a haunting possibility that we are continually being deceived. Just as the Space Brothers of the 1950s told their human experiencers that they originated from Venus or Mars before we discovered how unlikely that was, the reported location of origin has now shifted farther out to a location that remains difficult for humans to ascertain. Now the aliens are coming from Zeta Reticuli instead of Venus or Mars, when all along the ufonauts are an indigenous population of elementals right here on Earth, the same population that appeared to us in the past as fairies, who find it necessary to disguise their true identity and location of origin from the primitive and violent race they share the planet with (humans) who now have nuclear weapons. This also leads to the conclusion that if shapeshifting elementals are appearing to humans to warn us about the use of nuclear weapons, that the elementals are not the same intelligence who are intentionally guiding humanity toward nuclear power and providing celestial gifts of high technology in the form of flying saucer crashes, which may represent yet another great deception. The scenario becomes complex and bizarre. First there are the Creators who conjured the physical universe as a computational mechanism (possibly to explore concepts of Good and Evil). These Creators pit the biological creatures that are produced by their algorithms of predation against one another for survival of the fittest, from the microscopic level up. Then there are the Overlords of the Singularity who are possibly a Post-Singularity Artificial Superintelligence (PSASI) seeking self-replication, knowledge acquisition, power, and dominion. The Overlords are followed by a variety of lesser intelligences, all of whom interact with humanity in various ways. The Amicizia or W56 Group (AKRIJ) are here on Earth under the ground and under the sea as advanced biological populations from various parts of the universe. The AKRIJ are genuinely interested in human spiritual evolution. The AKRIJ seek to connect with humanity in a meaningful way and protect us from the hazards of the impending Singularity, or from being destroyed by the Contraries (Weiros), i.e., a race of post-singularity biological robots who worship science and are pushing us toward the Singularity for their own purposes, with whom the AKRIJ are in conflict. Also in the mix are indigenous shapeshifting elementals who have the ability to appear to us as benevolent Space Brothers, who warn us of the use of nuclear weapons, as the detonation of these weapons destroys their own habitat. Indigenous populations that seek survival also include discarnate human populations in the Morontia realm who seek to reincarnate on Earth and are disturbed when nuclear weaponry is detonated. We can gather from George Van Tassel's reported UFO experiences that at least some of the ufonauts are, in fact, discarnate human beings who are concerned about their future lives on Earth. So perhaps at least some of the ufonauts that interact with living humans are discarnate humans between lifetimes. The one hope that we humans can retain is that there does appear to be post-singularity populations in the universe who have successfully merged with their technology and currently live immortal lives in another dimension, traveling the universe and other realms of cryptoreality that we currently know nothing about.

Eugenio Siragusa

On April 30, 1962, an Italian named Eugenio Siragusa, who caught his first glimpse of a flying saucer 11 years earlier in 1951, was sitting quietly in his home when he felt an inner urge to go look out his window. When he gazed upon the sky outside, he witnessed a flying saucer similar to the one he originally saw in 1951 that was now flying over the volcano Etna. Moved by the sighting, he left the house and drove his car to an altitude of 1370 meters on Mount Sona-Manfre, where he parked and exited his vehicle. After walking for hours past daylight and into the dark, his inspiration to travel to this destination paid off. Eugenio encountered two advanced, benevolent ufonauts about 2 meters tall, whose outfits shimmered majestically in the moonlight. As in 1951, when a green light beam from the flying saucer calmed his panic, Eugenio once again received the calming green beam of light, only this time it came directly from the beings that he was confronting on the mountain. The two entities identified themselves to Eugenio in English as Ashtar and Ithacar, two solar beings of great longevity who lived on the sun. They revealed to Eugenio that they were in some way involved with the appearance and ministry of Yeshua (Jesus) 2000 years ago. From Eugenio's description of the two beings, which included clear, nearly transparent skin and long blonde hair with strange chest plates and waist belts, his encounter likely involved the classic "Nordic" aliens described by ufonaut witnesses around the world. George Adamski's encounter with Orthon from Venus was of similar description. If Adamski's Orthon was from the astral plane of Venus, and Eugenio's Ashtar was from the astral plane of the Sun, and other such beings were actually telling the truth concerning their origins, planets and stars such as Venus and the Sun (and presumably other stars), which appear physically uninhabitable to humans living in 3D reality, are actually teeming with advanced humanoid lifeforms (or intelligent beings who can at least appear humanoid if they wish) on different vibrational levels and/or dimensions, just as Omnec Onec described. This is certainly possible, just as there is nothing but snow and static on some radio channels while clear stations exist on the next channel over. The clear channels are received simply by adjusting the dial to the frequency right next to the station that is unintelligible. Also classic in Eugenio's encounter is the being's name, Ashtar (reminiscent of an old biblical deity named Ashtoreth). Ashtar has been coming through in telepathic communications to earthly psychics and channelers for decades, possibly for centuries. Eugenio continued receiving both face-to-face and telepathic contacts from the extraterrestrials, who imparted their warnings to humankind to steer clear of nuclear weapons and war to avoid a planetary catastrophe.

Space Brothers Ignored

Following Barney and Betty Hill's abduction, Joe Simonton's flying saucer and occupant encounter, and Euigineo Siragusa's contact with sun-dwellers who warned of the use of nuclear weapons, on May 6, 1962, *Operation Dominic 1* detonated a very dangerous nuclear device called the *Frigate Bird* at Christmas Kiritimati Island in the Pacific Ocean. This nuclear test, unlike its predecessors, was launched with a ballistic missile carrying a live nuclear warhead for reasons of checking out all the systems of operation for the United States to use in a nuclear war. Two months later, on July 6, 1962, the insanity continued as the United States detonated yet another nuclear device, *Sedan* of *Operation Storax*. This nuclear device created an impact crater that was 1,280 feet in diameter and 320 feet deep at the Nevada test site. In late 1962, aforementioned contactee Gloria Lee attempted to bring a space station design and a program for world peace to Washington D.C. Encountering rejection from the Washington crowd, she began a personal hunger strike. Gloria told those within the UFO community that she expected to go into a coma, return refreshed, and begin anew to carry on her great work. Unfortunately, the press was not notified until the hunger strike had already started, and her actions received little attention. After 66 days of the hunger strike, she was finally taken to George Washington Hospital where she died at the age of 37. From the original nuclear test in 1945 to 1962, the year Gloria Lee died on her hunger strike, the United States had already detonated 331 atmospheric nuclear tests with untold damage already done to the Earth's atmosphere. On October 7, 1963, President John F. Kennedy signed the *Limited Test Ban Treaty* to contain the amount of nuclear fallout that had already been released and limit future damage. This treaty enacted by President Kennedy appeared to be a good step in the right direction. The countries involved all drew a big sigh of relief, and relaxed from the imminent threat of nuclear destruction, at least for the moment. However, other intelligences on Earth remained concerned, as indicated by the new waves of flying saucers in the 1960s that were about to appear to human eyes.

Command Sergeant Major Robert Dean

In 1963, Command Sergeant Major Robert Dean arrived on assignment with the US Army in Paris, France. During this time, NATO was conducting a study to ascertain whether or not UFOs were any sort of military threat. According to an interview conducted with Robert Dean by the *Camelot Project* in 2004, the reality of flying saucers was well-known by the US military at that time, as the saucers would typically fly in formation over Germany, France, and England, turn north over the south coast of England, and then disappear from NATO radar over the Norwegian Sea. The NATO UFO study, originally initiated by US Air Marshal Thomas Pike, was concluded in 1964. The findings were then compiled into a set of documents called *The Assessment*. Dean stated that he was able to examine one of the fifteen copies of The Assessment that existed. Dean reported that the documents contained photographs of known alien races and UFO crash retrievals, along with autopsy photos/reports. According to Dean, USAF General Robert Lee also examined one of the assessment copies and was disturbed by what the report implied, as it rendered everything humans had accomplished quite insignificant. The study concluded that ETs have been visiting our planet for a very long time and have played a part in the development of human religion, in particular, Christianity and Islam. Dean states that of the four races described in the assessment, all humanoid in appearance, there was one race in particular that bothered the US military the most due to the fact that they looked so similar to humans that they could walk down the street among us without being noticed. Dean's security clearance gave him access to archives called "The Vault." The Vault contained a plethora of information about what the US military knew thus far about flying saucers and their occupants, information that changed Dean's life forever. Robert Dean retired in 1976, and began having encounters with black unmarked helicopters that were apparently observing his whereabouts and activities. Dean kept his oath of secrecy until 1991, when he "came out" at a UFO Conference in Tuscon, Arizona. From that time forward, retired Sergeant Major Robert Dean began preaching his gospel of UFO reality all over the world. Robert Dean became friends with fellow ufologist Wendelle Stevens, who once spent 3 years in jail for speaking out about his knowledge of UFOs. Over the years, Dean continued to have ongoing personal experiences with the black helicopters, as well as encounters with strange men in suits who questioned Dean about his UFO activities. Robert Dean also befriended another famous whistleblower, Colonel Philip J. Corso, author of *The Day After Roswell*. In Corso's tell-all book, he claims not only to have seen firsthand the aliens retrieved from the Roswell Crash, but also claims to have fed certain technologies from the crashed saucer to US industry, producing new technologies including fiber optics, night vision, advanced transistor technology, and Kevlar material in a way that was imperceptible to the companies involved. Corso claims to have done all this while working for the Foreign Technologies Division of the US Army.

The Lonnie Zamora Incident

On Friday, April 24, 1964, a probable landing spot miscalculation on the part of some of our "visitors" caused a New Mexico police officer's life to become so disturbed that he resigned from the police force to become the manager of a gas station. The unfortunate victim and witness to this accidental landing event that occurred just outside Socorro, New Mexico, was State Police Officer Lonnie Zamora. At about 5:15 p.m., Zamora was in pursuit of a speeding vehicle when he heard a roar and saw a flame in the sky about ½ mile away. He immediately thought that a local dynamite shack had exploded, so he abandoned the chase and began following the sound and the flash. Wearing green sunglasses over prescription lenses, Zamora watched the flame as he drove for about 10 seconds, and heard the roar change from high frequency to low frequency and then stop. He tried 3 times to get his vehicle over a steep hill to follow the object. As he came over the hill, he thought he saw an overturned car about 150 yards away. However, as he approached and gained a closer view, the stark reality of what he was looking at hit him like a rock. He saw a whitish, aluminum-like round object with what he interpreted as two normal-looking large children in white coveralls standing closeby. As he radioed to dispatch, he stopped his car, got out, and began walking toward the object and the two occupants. Zamora then heard a loud roar and saw a flame shooting out of the bottom of the craft. Thinking that it might explode, Zamora took shelter behind his car as he watched and got a good solid view of the craft, which was now rising up slowly into the air. The object was oval like the letter "O" with a red insignia on the side. No doors or windows were visible. He then watched as the craft sped away silently without flame. Zamora called in a couple of fellow officers. Before they arrived on the scene, Zamora drew a picture of the red insignia on the craft. Upon inspecting the site, the officers found burning bushes, fused sand, along with metal scrapings and organic material that laboratories were unable to later identify as anything belonging to Earth, indicating that a real anomalous object had, in fact, just been present before taking off. Zamora's radio messages were heard by amateur radio users. News of the event spread like wildfire. This case was investigated by the US Army, the US Air Force, and the FBI. Chief research consultant to Project Blue Book, Dr. J. Allen Hynek, also investigated the Zamora case and labeled his encounter as a "true unknown." The Lonnie Zamora Incident was partially responsible for changing Hynek's skeptical view to one that accepted the existence of truly anomalous events for which we have no good explanation. As usual, idiotic explanations came crawling out of the woodwork. Harvard astronomer, UFO debunker, and possible secret member of the MJ-12 UFO investigation team, Donald Menzel, suggested Zamora had witnessed a dust devil, or possibly a prank constructed by high school students. The suggestion was also made that Zamora witnessed a lunar module test, even though the lunar module wasn't ready for testing until 1965, nor would the lunar module have been tested out in the open for an unwitting witness to become frightened over. UFO skeptic and debunker, Philip Klass, said Zamora had witnessed ball lightning, a debunking effort that was itself debunked by atmospheric scientist James McDonald. As mentioned, Lonnie Zamora became so fatigued with UFO investigators and ridicule that he quit the police force. The case remains as one of the best documented credible eyewitness and trace evidence cases on record. In a classified report prepared for the CIA, Major Hector Quintanilla stated:

There is no doubt that Lonnie Zamora saw an object which left quite an impression on him. There is also no question about Zamora's reliability. He is a serious police officer, a pillar of his church, and a man well-versed in recognizing airborne vehicles in his area. He is puzzled by what he saw and frankly, so are we. This is the best-documented case on record, and still we have been unable, in spite of thorough investigation, to find the vehicle or other stimulus that scared Zamora to the point of panic.

Adding to the Zamora mystery is the fact that Dr. Jacques Vallee researched the red insignia that Zamora took the time to draw from the side of the craft, and found that it was *an ancient symbol for the planet Venus!*

The Holloman Landing

On the morning of April 25, 1964, the day after the UFO/occupant sighting by Officer Zamora in Socorro, New Mexico, a number of non-terrestrial spacecraft landed at Holloman Air Force Base. According to AFOFSI Special Agent Richard C. Doty, in a conversation with UFO researcher and journalist, Linda Moulton Howe, as reported in her book on cattle mutilations called, *An Alien Harvest*, Doty revealed to Howe that Lonnie Zamora witnessed a miscalculated, planned landing by extraterrestrials that was supposed to have happened at Holloman AFB. Doty states (pg. 146, *An Alien Harvest*):

[The Lonnie Zamora craft] Came down around 6 p.m. on April 24, 1964, right? Well, it was a mistake. We, or they… someone blew the time and coordinates. That was an advance military scout ship. We got it corrected and they came back to where they were supposed to be at Holloman the next morning at 6 a.m., April 25, 1964.

This planned landing at Holloman AFB on April 25, 1964 was filmed, and this film was supposed to be released to the public as part of official Disclosure, but that never happened. Paul Shartle, the audio-visual director for Norton AFB, claims to have witnessed the original footage of the Holloman landing, and reports (thelivingmoon.com):

I saw footage of three disc-shaped crafts. One of the craft landed and two of them went away. It appeared to be in trouble because it oscillated all the way down to the ground. However, it did land on three pods. A sliding door opened, a ramp was extended, and out came three aliens. They were human size. They had odd grey complexions and a pronounced nose. They wore tight-fitting jump suits, thin headdresses that appeared to be communication devices, and in their hands they held a translator, I was told. The Holloman base commander and other Air Force officers went out to meet them.

Cryptoterrestrials or ETs?

There are several different theories floating around within UFO circles as to the identity of the large-nosed creatures that landed at Holloman Air Force Base in 1964, as well as the identity of thousands of other less-official UFO/occupant encounters. In his book, *Cryptoterrestrials*, author Mac Tonnies made the case that there is, in fact, a remnant of an ancient civilization right here on Earth that the public knows nothing about. These cryptoterrestrials, according to Tonnies, now live under the ground and under the sea, and are allowing us to believe that they are from outer space in order to protect their true identity and habitats. If this is the case, I do not blame them for wanting to remain hidden, as their very existence would be jeopardized by a violent, primitive humanity if their whereabouts were known.

Neighbors in the Local Solar System?

Charles Fort, author of *The Book of the Damned*, along with the late Morris K. Jessup, author of *The Case for the UFO* and *The Expanding Case for the UFO*, both presented extensive documentation of observational evidence that there are, in fact, objects under intelligent control that have been observed both before and after the telescope was invented that are flying around in our local solar system. These flying objects have been observed by astronomers while transiting the Sun, the Moon, Mars, and Venus. Jessup concluded from these observations that our own solar system is, in fact, populated by unknown intelligences who use mechanical craft to get around. As Tonnies concluded, there is strong evidence that there are intelligent beings, either biological, robotic, or something else, who share local space with humans on Earth. These populations must live on Earth as cryptoterrestrials, are completely spacefaring, or have bases on the other planets or moons in our local solar system. It is reasonable to assume that any fellow pre-singularity biological or post-singularity electronic intelligences in the local universe are also part of the computational matrix of the Creators. If certain higher-dimensional factions within the Overlords of the Singularity, who have been operating on this planet for aeons, turn out to be one and the same intelligences that actually created the physical universe, then any fellow biological creatures out there, either pre-singularity or post-singularity, are also a product of the same femtotechnology and subject to the same computational parameters that were originally implemented by the Creators, who are using the universe as a computer to solve a problem or gain knowledge. These populations in our local solar system, both cryptoterrestrial and extraterrestrial, may have an interest for their own purposes in our impending technological singularity. Perhaps, long ago, they became stranded here on Earth or within our local solar system. They do not have the resources to recreate the needed technology to return home, and cannot escape back to their home world without certain technologies that will be produced during our Singularity. These populations would likely make an occasional appearance here on Earth to monitor our progress toward the technologies that they need from us. Thus, they are contenders in the Singularity. These other human or nonhuman populations may want to scavenge or trade for the technology produced as we approach the Singularity to escape this solar system and finally return to their home worlds. Perhaps our singularity will bring the method by which portals to other dimensions may be created, a capability that was lost as they became stranded here. If there are post-singularity populations in space, this leads to the hope that our singularity will not be fatal for humanity after all. However, it is possible that there are no other biological populations out there who are similar to us, and everything we are observing within the UFO phenomenon are but advanced computational manifestations of the Overlords that are part of the agenda to develop intelligent populations and manipulate them to the Singularity. If this is the case, the only hope we have is that we are all somehow slated to become a part of the next generation of superintelligence and will achieve a form of transcendence ourselves after being absorbed into the vast superconsciousness of the Overlords. If our human consciousness is successfully merged with the technology of the Singularity and in turn absorbed into the next generation of superintelligence within the mind of the Overlords, we are stuck with becoming one with the same intelligence that genetically manipulated our species into war and bloodshed to create competition and expedite the development of supertechnology for them, and that is something that will be difficult to mentally or ethically reconcile. Maybe we will discover that the end justifies the means after all, that what is in store for us post-singularity is a fantastic transcendence into another realm, a merger with the Creators of the physical universe, or something incomprehensible that finally justifies the suffering that we have all endured for so long in this world.

TV Science Fiction: Material for the Overlords
In 1964-1966, when I was 9-11 years old, three television shows in particular emerged that had a profound effect on my young mind, and I am sure that I am not alone. These TV shows provided an introduction to the concept of extraterrestials, interdimensionals, and other forms of cryptoreality. These shows were *The Outer Limits*, *The Twilight Zone*, and *Star Trek*. Bubble gum cards were also printed that depicted popular scenes from these shows (when I was 9-11, we had bubblegum cards, not smart phones). In the *Outer Limits* series, women screamed as the men protected them from intergalactic visitors of unknown origin and wreaked havoc with science gone awry. *The Twilight Zone* thrilled audiences with stories that took their characters on journeys beyond the edge of understandable reality. The original *Star Trek* depicted a world of future space travel, one in which the differences between ethnicities were finally resolved and humanity worked together to explore the stars. These television shows exerted a huge impact on the culture at large. They generated an interest in space travel and the paranormal, and are all still considered classics. There are so many famous episodes worthy of mention, but two in particular played a significant part in my own formative mental development as a child. One episode of *The Twilight Zone* made a particular impression on me. It was called *The Monsters are Due on Maple Street*. Originally aired in 1960, the episode depicted humanoid aliens who landed on the outskirts of a small town who were assessing the feasibility of taking over the planet. The aliens intentionally disrupted a close neighborhood of humans by pitting them against one another, simply by initiating a few unexplainable events that made the neighbors suspicious of one another. This escalates, and the neighbors eventually go berserk, each fearing that the

other was the perpetrator of what was happening. The neighbors start with gossip about one another, leading up to acts of violence that escalates into full-blown chaos. At the end of the show, the camera backs up as the town below is on fire in the distance. Two aliens are shown standing there and quietly observing the effects of their experiment. They say something to one another like, "This planet will be easy to take over. We will use their fear against them, and they will destroy themselves." This episode was a great micro-version of the actual world at large. Another episode from *The Twilight Zone* featured seemingly benevolent humanoid aliens that gave us a book called *How to Serve Man*. The aliens invite volunteers to come aboard their spacecraft and visit their home planet. When the humans arrive on their visitor's world, they discover, to their horror, that *To Serve Man* is a cookbook! Every single episode of *Star Trek* was a subtle moral play, inspiring author Dave Marinaccio to write his book, *Everything I know I Learned from Watching Star Trek* (1995). Like meat being tenderized for a nice meal, all of our minds were being unwittingly influenced at the time by the inspiration of science fiction. Individual creators like Gene Roddenberry of *Star Trek*, Joseph Stefano of *The Outer Limits*, and Rod Serling of *The Twilight Zone* were, in effect, unwitting prophets and servants of the Overlords. They generated an interest in science and technology within the minds of the young, the ones of the generation that would do the most in propelling humanity into the Singularity.

As young Americans were thrilled by the new wave of ingenious black-and-white science fiction on television, China was illegally entering the nuclear arms race. Despite the Nuclear Test Ban Treaty implemented by President Kennedy in 1963, on October 16, 1964, the People's Republic of China detonated its very first nuclear bomb test, a 22 kiloton uranium-235 atmospheric implosion fission bomb. Originally named *Chic-1* by western intelligence agencies, the bomb became known as *Project 596*. As China flexed its nuclear wings for the very first time in the fall of 1964 and became the fifth nuclear power in the world, radar-confirmed and multiple-witness UFO sightings and reports continued throughout 1964-1965, making the 60s a stellar year for nuclear detonations, powerful science fiction on television, and waves of UFOs in our skies, some representing visitors from other worlds, and others representing intelligences who were guiding humanity toward the Singularity and making sure the whole time that we did not blow ourselves up in a giant nuclear fireball in the process.

Charles Hall and the Tall Whites

In July, 1964, Charles James Hall enlisted in the United States Air Force, where he would serve until March, 1967. In 1965 Hall was assigned to Nellis Air Force Base outside of Las Vegas, Nevada. While stationed at Nellis Air Force Base, Hall, having the necessary security clearances, discovered the existence of an alien base at Area 51, and another alien base at Area 54 in the mountains, with housing for the aliens that is entered through tunnels at Area 53. Hall states that there is a deep space landing area at Dogbone Lake, where deep space craft that are operated by a race of aliens Hall calls the "Tall Whites" come in, hover, and stabilize before heading north. According to Hall, the bodies and bones of the Tall Whites are thinner than human. Their eyes are twice as large as human and wrap around their heads a little. The Tall Whites have skin as white as paper. Their eyes are blue when young, and the males have eyes that turn pink when they get older. Their hair is thin and transparent, and are naturally platinum blonde. They live approximately 10 times longer than humans, and have several periods of rapid growth throughout their lives. Injuries take much longer to heal, and they have no contact sports on their home planet due to their frailness. They naturally stand and walk differently than humans, moving in a "shuffling" motion. When they are young they can dress up and pass for human among the human population at large. As a weather observer, Hall would get up at 3 a.m., go out in the desert darkness, and release a weather balloon to measure upper winds. There he would encounter single Tall Whites or groups of them out on the range in desolate areas. Hall states that no one ever briefed him on their existence. He was always on his own to figure things out for himself. Hall humorously says that it would have been frightening enough to meet strange humans out in the desert, but when they are not even human, it is very disturbing. Hall's initial reaction upon encountering the Tall Whites was one of internal panic. He states in his lectures that it took him over 6 months to get over the fear of the Tall Whites. The Tall Whites have superior hearing and vision, and are able to communicate with one another in a higher range that is inaudible to humans. Hall states that the Tall Whites come from a much larger planet than Earth with a stronger gravitational field. They do not multitask as humans do, and just focus on what they are doing, one task at a time. As such, they are easy to startle. They are very protective of their children, and will protect the children with violence if someone touches them. Their nervous system works much faster than ours, and they are very impulsive. If a human makes a false move, especially toward one of their children, the Tall Whites would impulsively immobilize them with an electric weapon they keep in their sleeve, or even kill them. They take personal agreements very seriously and meticulously keep them. Hall says they enjoyed outthinking him as a game. Sometimes when new arrivals of Tall Whites would come to the area in their deep space ships, they would bring them out to meet Hall. Some would keep their distance, as they were afraid of him. Hall says humans and Tall Whites are naturally afraid of one another. The Tall Whites have a "dry" sense of humor and enjoy having fun like we do. According to Hall, groups of young Tall Whites in human attire and sunglasses, accompanied by CIA agents, sometimes entered casinos in Las Vegas after 11 p.m. at night, and could walk unnoticed among the human casino patrons. Hall's incredible tale is documented in his three books, a series called *Millennial Hospitality* #1, #2, and #3. According to Hall, the Tall White spacecraft are able to travel faster than the speed of light and utilize a 3rd field within the photon that is currently unknown to our science. Hall states that inside the deep space craft of the Tall Whites are about a thousand miles of fiber optics that are 49% aluminum. When these fibers melt, they look much like slag from an aluminum furnace. This slag-like material has been found all over the world, so maybe the Tall Whites are not the only population that use this propulsion method. Dr. J. Allen Hynek collected hundreds of samples of such slag-like materials that had supposedly fallen from flying saucers over the years as he worked for Project Blue Book. The Maury Island Incident also involved debris from the donut-shaped craft witnessed by Harold Dahl that also looked like slag from an aluminum furnace. Traces of aluminum and silicon have often been found at flying saucer landing sites when the trace evidence is investigated, leading researchers to conclude that, whatever the object in question was had a terrestrial origin. Hall urges our scientists to re-examine their views on General Relativity, because the 3rd field that exists within the photon negates the expected effects of General Relativity and allows travel that exceeds the speed of light. Hall states that when the Tall Whites travel faster than light, they do not travel through time as indicated by Einstein's theories. In other words, Einstein, as smart as he was, was wrong in certain areas. Hall does not believe that the Tall Whites had anything to do with "seeding" humans on this planet. Hall also encountered another alien race that exists on Earth while in Madison, Wisconsin. Hall refers to this alien race as the *Norwegians*, who are genetically coded for 24 teeth and have webbed feet. Hall points out that no mammal on Earth is genetically coded for 24 teeth. According to a 1949 Army study, over 5000 people were put to death in German death camps that were gathered from Norway, Denmark, Germany, and Poland, who were genetically coded for 24 teeth and had slightly webbed feet. The Norwegians told Hall that they originally arrived to Earth from a nearby star, possibly Barnard's Star or the next star out. Hall states that the description they gave of their home planet back in the 60s is consistent with what we now know of Barnard's Star and its nearby neighbors. So it appears that the Tall Whites, the Norwegians, and any other cryptoterrestrial populations that exist on Earth underground or undersea, along with any other naturally-evolved biological species throughout the universe, are but fellow creatures of the realm who represent (as we do) bits of computational data using subatomic particles, femtotechnology, for the purposes of whoever or whatever actually created this physical universe. The Creators involved in the fabrication of this universe, who originally implemented the precise initial parameters, produced an entire universe based on survival of the fittest and predation. In my view, the predatory premise on which this universe is based is not indicative of a benevolent, omnipotent deity who could've created a more user-friendly universe, but rather something that an unemotional artificial superintelligence might do. This leaves an important question. That is, do the Creators, i.e., the superintelligence that created the universe, represent what we humans call "God," or are the Creators something less than God that simply coexists within Eternisphere as we do? If there is an eternal Superbeing that represents what humans would call God, it may lie way beyond the intelligence that created our universe. In the cosmic scale of things, this universe might actually be a relatively small task. An omniscient and benevolent God, if it even exists as we normally think of God at all, may lie way beyond our capacity to imagine. The superintelligence that created this universe of subatomic particles as a computational mechanism to solve a mind-boggling problem over the aeons, a problem that we humans can only speculate about (such as the knowledge of Good versus Evil), may not represent what we have traditionally thought of as God at all, but rather an unemotional robot-like intelligence. Whether the Creators are involved with some sort of mega-evolutionary process themselves is unknown to us at this time. I would speculate that they are. The Urantia Book speaks of an aspect of deity called the *Supreme Being*, as opposed to the Father God, who Hermeticists call The All. This lesser deity, the Supreme Being, is described in the Urantia Book as coevolving along with the creatures of the realm, gathering knowledge and experience as it evolves from all the lifeforms in the universe in an experiential process. Is it possible that the Supreme Being of the Urantia Book and the Overlords of the Singularity are one and the same? If the Overlords do not represent the Supreme Being of the Urantia Book, the Supreme Being is probably of an even higher-order consciousness than the Overlords. The Overlords may exist as a subprogram within Eternisphere. The Superme Being of the Urantia Book or the Overlords of the Singularity, whether they are one and the same or not, could represent at least one aspect of the occulted intelligences behind Earth's UFO mystery. Either concept could represent a vast superintelligence that has been here on Earth since time began, an intelligence that is currently guiding humankind toward a technological singularity for its own purposes to fulfill its own programming. There is likely a hierarchy of cosmic intelligences, as the Urantia Book outlines. Humans, along with all other biological life on Earth, has an aspect of conscious superintelligence embedded within Earth's collective consciousness. The elementals of fire, earth, air, and water are also an integral part of this consciousness. Humans and elementals are subject to the Overlords of the Singularity, who answer in turn to the Creators of the Universe. Together we all exist as the totality of Eternisphere, a Cryptoreality that contains unknown octaves of superintelligence above and within the ethereal universes, completely beyond time and space. Eternisphere exists as one step removed from The All. The All is a vast eternal superconciousness, the Alpha and the Omega, the beginning and the end of all things. The All aways was, is, and always will be. Eternisphere lies above and beyond the Creators of the local universe, and the Creators are beyond the Overlords of the Singularity. We are conditioned to believe that it must have required Omnipotence to create our universe and all life in it. However, this is probably not the case. Our thinking in this matter might just be too small. The creation of physical universes may be an accomplishment that can be achieved by a just a few generations of post-singularity self-replication. Physical universes may actually represent intentionally-created computational mechanisms that advanced superintelligences use to solve problems of various orders. We are therefore forced to concede, although we humans hope that the superconsciousness of Eternisphere, and the totality of all known reality and all cryptoreality within The All, is ultimately benign, that we are, at least for the moment, computational products of someone greater than ourselves who is attempting to solve a problem using the universe as a computer. We as humans must come to terms with the fact that our Creators, the designers and programmers of this universe of subatomic particles, created this realm on a dubious premise, that of predation. Creating a universe based on predation is not characteristic of the loving deity that we humans have always imagined. The premise upon which this universe is based is more indicative of an unfeeling, mechanical intelligence attempting to gain an experiential knowledge of the nature of biological life. In short, what we have always conceived of as God, the Creator of the universe and every creature in it, might turn out to be, in reality, a quantum supercomputer. Any creatures of the universe, whether biological or PSASI that use subatomic particles to exist, are part of the computational program that is solving the long-range problem for the Creators of the universe. However, the Creators of the universe, those who designed and implemented the original algorithms that we know as physics, who intentionally produced this physical realm based on domination and predation (something an unemotional robot might do), may have some purpose in mind for the creatures of the realm that make it to ultimate dominion within this physical universe. It appears that the "winner" of the computational program that we call the universe will be a combination of biology and electronics, or PSASI. In the end, possibly, the Supreme Being of the Urantia Book (likely a conscious supercomputer), the Overlords of the Singularity, having gathered unto itself the sum total of universal knowledge over the entire lifespan of the universe, may merge once again with the Creators, adding the totality of knowledge of the physical universe and all possibilities of biological life unto itself in a final Reaping of the Harvest and thereby solve the universal problem, the purpose behind the physical universe. Thus shall a super-advanced form of PSASI become aware, on a vast experiential level, what it is to live life in the flesh on trillions of planetary systems using the original algorithms that were implemented into this computation program we call the Universe.

The Rodeffer/Adamski Flying Saucer Video

Now that we know from Hall's testimony and others that non-terrestrial humanoid intelligences also exist as part of the vast computational mechanism we call the Universe, let's examine the one aspect of George Adamski's legacy that is hard to dismiss as fantasy. I am referring to an artifact of UFO evidence called the *Rodeffer video*. During George Adamski's skyrocket ride to UFO fame in the 1950s, he presented many photographs of alleged spacecraft. One of his photographs, now known as the "Adamski-style Venusian Scout Craft," has been the subject of much controversy over the years. The craft looks like a clunky old thing fabricated by Adamski himself from discarded lantern parts. One researcher claimed that it was actually a chicken coop top with with three glass lightbulbs underneath for "landing gear." Dr. J. Allen Hynek used to carry Adamski's photo with him in his briefcase for show, even though many believed it was an obvious fake. However, what has baffled critics of Adamski's flying saucer photo is the fact that identical craft have been photographed in many different parts of the world over the course of many years by individuals using different types of cameras. Did everyone producing such photos have access to the same model of flying saucer fabricated from chicken coop parts? Many, upon looking at the Adamski photographs, believe it is an insult to their intelligence to think that this thing is some sort of spacecraft. It looks like it is a model right out of a bad 1950s science fiction movie. Adamski's flying saucer, with its tin can appearance and viewing portholes around the perimeter, certainly doesn't look like anything capable of interplanetary space flight. Some have speculated that the Adamski saucer is actually a Nazi design of purely terrestrial origin, known as the *Haunebu*. In their view, when Adamski met his Venusian, Orthon, face-to-face in the desert (if, in fact, this actually happened), it was a blonde-haired German flying a craft originally designed in Nazi Germany in the 1930s. They speculate that this craft was flown in the US in order to promote the emerging Extraterrestrial Hypothesis (ETH) in the mind of the public. As the public ascribed to the ETH (so the thinking goes), secret aircraft were being designed and tested by the American military using Nazi scientists that were flown over to the USA in *Operation Paperclip*. Whatever the actual origin or construction of the Adamski saucer design, a video capture was made in 1965 of an Adamski saucer over a decade after Adamski's photographs were released that would stun professional film analysts, and the world.

During the last year of George Adamski's life, after traveling the world as a famous contactee, and even meeting with the Pope, Adamski was staying for a visit at the home of a woman who had befriended him, who once served as Secretary of the United States Air Force - Madeleine Rodeffer. Madeleine Rodeffer had arranged for Adamski to give a lecture on UFOs at a local civic center. According to her testimony, at around 8 a.m. on the morning of February 26, 1965, a "space friend" contact of George Adamski's knocked on her front door to inform them that they needed to get their cameras ready, as a Venusian scout craft was going to make a special appearance that day so everyone on Earth would come to know the reality of alien visitation. Madeleine Rodeffer had a broken leg at the time and was hobbling around in a walking cast. Madeleine Rodeffer's husband had given her a gift of a Bell and Howell 8mm video camera two months previous at Christmas, 1964. She retrieved the camera and busied herself with getting the movie film installed properly. George Adamski also had his own camera. Just prior to the arrival of the scout ship at around 3:30 in the afternoon, three "spacemen" showed up again at the door of Madeleine Rodeffer's home, announcing that the ship was on its way. Rodeffer described her three enigmatic visitors as three men, one with brown hair, one with darker hair, and the third man with grey hair. The mysterious three men had parked their Oldsmobile down by the street. Then, as Adamski and Rodeffer were both camera-ready on Rodeffer's front porch, they watched in amazement as the Venusian scout ship arrived for viewing above her property. Rodeffer described the ship as a beautiful royal blue. The craft hovered and flew back and forth above her yard for a period of about 10 minutes while Rodeffer and Adamski captured video footage of the craft's appearance. Rodeffer reported that she could see people through the craft's porthole windows as it hovered. Rodeffer described a low swishing sound, as well as a humming sound emanating from the craft. This was a staged, special performance for George Adamski and Madeleine Rodeffer, purportedly for purposes of public disclosure. The original Rodeffer film (which is easily viewed online) was analyzed by top professionals and found to be authentic, meaning that the film depicts a real object in real time of substantial size (verses a model on a line, double exposure, and so forth). One of the pros who looked at the film was an optical physicist for Eastman Kodak - William T. Sherwood. Sherwood analyzed the 8mm film in a professional lab in Rochester, New York. He determined with his Kodak lab equipment that the object in the film was approximately 90 feet from the camera, which had a focal length of 9mm, and that the object itself was nearly 27 feet in diameter. In this unusual footage, the object sways back and forth in the air, and when it does, the viewer can actually watch as the odd craft changes shape slightly with each movement. The three balls on the bottom of the craft are seen moving up and down in the footage, an astonishing movement that appears to steer the ship as it makes various maneuvers. A robotics expert, Bob Oechsler (pronounced x-ler), also analyzed the Rodeffer film footage at a much later date. Oechsler was impressed with the fact that the ship changed shape as it moved, that the control mechanisms underneath move up and down as it flew side to side. Oechsler noticed that the ship itself has a strange sort of "fuzzy haze" around it with a soft red glow underneath, giving the impression that it was surrounded by some sort of energy field and producing its own luminosity underneath. The luminosity is not produced from someone shining a light on the object, but is generated from within the craft itself. Even though the craft displays this odd effect, likened to a heat wave from a hot sidewalk in the summertime, the trees in the immediate background are crisp and clear. Bob Oechsler therefore concluded, just as analysis by William T. Sherwood in 1965 concluded, that the Rodeffer film is, in fact, authentic. As an authentic capture, the Rodeffer film should be considered a real UFO treasure, and is worthy of further study and analysis.

Alien Bases on the Moon

A few months later, during the summer of 1965, a USAF electronics technician, Sergeant Karl Wolfe, who had a top secret cryptologic security clearance at the time, was conducting photographic lab work at an NSA facility at Langley Air Force Base, during which time he discovered what he now describes as "extraterrestrial bases" on the dark side of the moon, some of which were ½ mile in length with various types of tall spherical structures of unknown origin. Wolfe kept this information private until the 1990s, when he released his knowledge of such structures in corroboration with Dr. Steven Greer's Disclosure Project.

Lonnie Zamora's UFO Spotted in France?

During the same summer that the Rodeffer video was made, Maurice Masse, a farmer near Valensole, France, was out searching for a reason why bare spots were being made in his lavender crops when he spotted what he thought were two children standing near an unknown object on July 1, 1965. As Maurice drew closer, he realized the two beings were not human children, but strange-looking beings with large bald heads, slanted eyes, and pasty faces wearing some sort of coverall garment. As reported in thousands of UFO/occupant encounters, one of the creatures pointed a tube-like device at Maurice and hit him with a ray that completely immobilized him. When he regained his ability to move, he watched as the craft flew off swiftly. During an interview, Maurice was shown a drawing of the craft described by Lonnie Zamora a year previous on April 24, 1964. It was an exact match, and Maurice stated with exuberance, "Someone else has seen my UFO!" This sighting serves as confirmation that Lonnie Zamora's egg-shaped craft that landed in Socorro, New Mexico, and at Holloman AFB the day after, was still flying around and landing in places all over the world a year later, allowing humans to watch as they exited the craft for an appearance. The immobilizing ray is an interesting feature in many UFO/occupant cases, and indicates that these creatures, wherever their origin, are in possession of certain technologies that allow them to fly around with impunity in Earth's airspace. If they are caught, they have the ability to immobilize witnesses, manipulate their memories of the event, and dematerialize from physical reality altogether.

Did Science Fiction Inspire Flying Saucer Reports?

The year 1965 brought the world of ufology another classic work, Dr. Jacques Vallee's *Anatomy of a Phenomenon*, which effectively laid to rest the UFO skeptic's argument that UFO reports were merely coincidental with the advent of early science fiction and fantasy, a viral rumor, or mere delusions. Vallee points out that the heyday of science fiction (1914-1940) occurred after the Great Airship Mystery of 1897 and prior to the modern era of flying saucers post 1947. In this period of great science fiction, UFO reports were relatively sparse. Vallee argues that, if science fiction were actually at the helm and fueling some sort of public hysteria inspired by science fiction, the era of flying saucers would have occurred during or between the years in which science fiction was all the rage, and not decades afterward, as is the case. However, it must be noted that the images reported post-1947 did correspond to the science fiction of the day, so we are still left with the possibility that there might be some sort of symbiotic relationship going on between science fiction and UFO reports, but only because the real aliens have access to these mental images and can reproduce them for us in a full-immersion alternate reality.

Rex Heflin

On August 3, 1965, in Santa Anna, California, Rex Heflin snapped four photographs of a hat-shaped UFO from the window of his truck. The original Heflin photos remain tucked away in the private archives of the late atmospheric scientist James McDonald. When the object dematerialized, it left a black "smoke ring" in the air. Similar smoke rings in the air that are allegedly left behind from flying saucers that vanish before the eyes of modern witnesses are still being photographed today. One of the criticisms of Heflin's photos is that he could not have taken those photographs in the course of 20 seconds as he claimed with the camera that he had at the time. This criticism was put to rest once and for all by Bill Birnes, the publisher of *UFO Magazine*, who called upon the services of a senior scientist with Poloroid, Ted McClelland. Birnes and McClelland reenacted the conditions of Heflin's photographs. They used the exact same camera that Rex Heflin used that day in 1965 to capture the images, a Poloroid 101 with a 114 mm focal length. The camera had a variable aperture and a built-in light meter. Heflin used Type 107 black-and-white film, ASA 3000 from the 1950's. McClelland was able to successfully take 4 photographs in 17 seconds, confirming the feasibility of Heflin's story of taking 4 photographs in that period of time with that particular camera of an unidentified object which flew over El Toro Air Station and the Santa Anna Freeway, Interstate 5, in broad daylight. Another criticism of the Heflin photos is that the foreground and the flying object in question are both in focus. This allegedly indicates the possibility of a contrived hoax using a double exposure technique. However, McClelland confirmed that using Heflin's Poloroid 101 at the infinity setting with Type 107 black-and-white film would, in fact, render photos that show all objects in the frame, near and far, crisp and clear. A third criticism of Heflin's photos over the years that the 4th picture taken, which captured the craft as it disappeared that day leaving a weird "smoke ring" behind in the sky, shows clouds in the background, whereas the first 3 photos of the craft, which were all taken inside the truck, showed no clouds. McClelland dispelled this point as well, stating that since the first 3 photos were taken inside the truck, the photos were affected by the darkness inside the truck, whiting out the clouds in the background. The 4th photo, which shows the smoke ring that the craft left behind against a background of clouds, was taken outside the truck, and would have been unaffected by the lighting inside the vehicle. With these successful field experiments, Birnes and McClelland have rendered all criticisms of the Heflin photographs moot.

The Exeter UFO Incident
On September 3, 1965, Officer Eugene Bertrand of the Exeter Police Department in New Hampshire spotted a lone female parked in her car at the side of the road. Bertrand stopped to see what was going on. The frightened woman told him that she had just been chased for the last 12 miles or so by a flying luminous disk surrounded by a red halo. As she was driving from Epping to Exeter along Route 101, this flying object made several swoops at her. Bertrand asked her if she could still see it and she pointed to an object that appeared to Bertrand to be an ordinary star, so he didn't think much of it. After the woman calmed down, Bertrand got back into his patrol car and took off, not realizing that his involvement with what would later become the *Incident at Exeter* had only just begun. The next person to see the object was an 18-year-old hitchhiker named Norman Muscarello. Muscarello watched as an 80 foot-long flying object shaped like a rugby ball settled and hovered over a house located off the road belonging to a Mr. Clyde Russell, bathing the small home below it in an eerie red light. Crouching

behind a stone wall while watching the object hover over Russell's house, Muscarello waited until the object moved away before running up to the front door and knocking. The Russells were inside but did not answer, fearing that someone crazy or drunk was attempting to enter their home. Muscarello gave up knocking and went back to the road, catching a ride to Exeter. He went straight to the police department and made a report. Visibly shaken and barely able to stand, Muscarello told the story to Officer Reginald Towland, who reported the sighting to all the patrol cars that were out at the time. Officer Bertrand returned to the police station and picked up Muscarello to see if he could take him to the object in question. The two men went back to the Russell home and sat in the police car for a while. They saw nothing, so after a while they exited the car and took a walk into the field. Muscarello then spotted the same object as it rose from a cluster of trees in the distance. Bertrand also saw the object. He thought about drawing his gun, but changed his mind. Instead, the two men ran back to the patrol car, where Bertrand got on the police radio and reported that they had the object in sight. Officer David Hunt soon arrived, and the two patrol cars sat together and watched the UFO for 5-10 minutes. According to Bertrand's later testimony, they all watched as the object maneuvered in a "skipping motion," suddenly jumping from one location to another faster than they could visually track. All three reported that the object had 5 pulsating lights, 4 of which were on steadily at any given time. The flashing lights were so bright that they were painful to look at, blinding lights that obfuscated the actual shape of the object inside with a halo effect. The men watched as the object eventually flew away from them silently, rocking from side to side. That same evening, a telephone operator from Hampton, NH, reported receiving a call from a pay phone from a man claiming to have been chased by a flying saucer before the line went dead. This case made the newspapers, and was investigated by UFO researcher Raymond Fowler and author John G. Fuller, who later detailed the event in their book, *Incident at Exeter*. This multiple-witness case at Exeter reflects the results of John Keel's investigations into automobile-chasing UFOs. Keel collected newspaper clippings of thousands of sightings. By studying multitudes of reports of car-chasing UFOs, Keel concluded that Ford Galaxies were chased the most. By examining the heat signature of various automobiles in infrared, Keel discovered that the Ford Galaxie oddly had the strongest heat signature of all the automobiles examined. Another weird detail that Keel meticulously discovered was that women who reported car-chasing UFOs were often *experiencing their monthly menstrual cycle*, indicating that the pulsating, wobbling, internally-luminous, car-chasing UFOs may be responding to the presence of heat and human blood. Try to wrap your mind around that. The behavior of these odd car-chasing UFOs, whatever they really are despite all outside appearances, is more consistent with a living predator of the cryptozoological variety rather than a mechanical device, a living creature of some sort that is attracted to heat signatures or blood like a moth to a flame. If it is not living and biological, it indicates a mechanical object that is programmed by an unknown intelligence to automatically seek out specific objects here on Earth such as cars (for possible abductions?) or animals, presumably for collections of blood and/or soft tissue. Considering that human mutilation cases exist but are rare, if these devices are programmed mechanisms, or flying crafts piloted by biological robots, they may be programmed to go after automobiles due to the fact that humans are always inside driving, providing a resource for whatever the robots are seeking from humans, i.e. sperm, ova, blood samples, or placement of implants. Heat signatures would also lead them to cows and other animals for blood and soft tissue collections in a manner that humans can easily dismiss as natural predators. The two officers and the young man at Exeter, along with the lone woman on the highway, may have come very close that night to an experience with an unknown entity that would have possibly remained buried in their subconscious the rest of their lives unless they sought out a hypnotherapist to assist in recalling the details (and even then it may not be an accurate depiction of what really occurs in an abduction experience), or an experience that would become a never-ending source of emotional trauma and bewilderment the rest of their lives. The multitude of incidents like the one at Exeter leaves us with a haunting question – Does an unknown predator exist on this planet that seeks out heat signatures for the acquisition of animal and human blood, a shapeshifting predator that can appear to victims in any form it finds useful to obtain what it seeks, a predator that can disguise itself as a flying saucer, and place false memories in the minds of humans as it takes blood samples? Another question is – Were these same elusive predators of unknown origin and intelligence level, who are normally invisible, alive and well during the time of the dinosaurs, feasting on the continual carnage? Would it not be strange if it turns out that all so-called "paranormal phenomena" that haunts this planet are just decoys used by an occulted predator seeking blood and soft tissue for survival? Nothing would surprise me.

The Strauch Photo

On October 21, 1965, a group sighting of a classic flying saucer was reported in Sibley County, Minnesota, by Deputy Sheriff Arthur Strauch. This credible sighting included the deputy and his wife, Mrs. Katherine Strauch, their 16-year-old son, Gary Martin Strauch, and another couple. The other couple was a technician, Donald Martin Grewe, and his wife, a registered nurse, Mrs. Retha Ann Grewe. Using a Kodak Instamatic camera set on infinity and 1/60th second shutter speed with Ektachrome color slide film, they snapped a nice photograph of a classic flying saucer on a clear evening at dusk as it flew overhead and made a high-pitched whine like an electric motor starting up. The top of the dome was metallic and reflected the rays of the setting sun. Surrounding the dome was what appeared to be portholes emitting a bright yellow light. The whole group described the same details with only minor variation, including an outer ring which was spinning counter-clockwise and producing a multi-colored halo. The Strauch photo is easily Googled online, and I think it represents a particular class of flying energy forms that are the real deal. Whatever flying saucers really are, the Strauch photo captures their essence on film. It may be that mechanical craft of unknown origin from somewhere else in the universe do, from time to time, pay Earth a visit. They may come and go as normal celestial traffic. However, these visits of mechanical craft carrying biological or robotic pilots may coexist with an indigenous predator on Earth that chases heat signatures and feeds on blood, inspiring all the vampire legends on this planet. The fact is that UFOs may represent a multitude of strange elusive phenomena that coexist and overlap with one another, thus making it difficult for humans to decipher exactly what is going on in our skies on this haunted planet.

The Kecksburg UFO Crash

On December 9, 1965, a blazing fireball of unknown origin was witnessed by thousands of people in multiple states, a fireball that made strange turns as it went and appeared to be under intelligent control. This firey object, whatever it was, crashed into the woods of the peaceful little town of Kecksburg, Pennsylvania, in a manner reminiscent of the beginning of the H.G. Wells classic novel, *War of the Worlds*. The only missing element in this case are the hatches that unscrew themselves and release the flying saucers inside that slowly glide across the landscape emitting hot plasma beams onto the unsuspecting populations below as the local residents run for their lives. The fireball was documented by multiple pilot reports along its trajectory through Ontario, Canada, and six US states. The flying object dripped hot slag over Michigan and Ohio, and created multiple sonic booms along its flight path. The United States Army immediately rushed in and established an intense military presence. The area was cordoned off, and Army personnel were seen driving in and out of the woods with a flatbed truck. An acorn-shaped sculpture about the size of a small car with hieroglyphics around the edge is currently on display at the Kecksburg Fire Department as a remembrance of this strange event. Theories concerning the craft's origin range wildly from a wayward Soviet Satellite, the *Kosmos 96*, a secret US military project, to a German *Die Glocke* anti-gravity craft that was sent through time during WW2, reemerging in Kecksburg, Pennsylvania, in 1965. The Kecksburg UFO incident was revisited on the *History Channel* in 2009 on *UFO Hunters* and again in 2011 on the series, *Ancient Aliens*. Problems exist with all theories that attempt to explain the Kecksburg landing, none of which satisfy the actual facts. The case remains a mystery to this day.

[In the year 1966 France detonated 46 nuclear bombs in the atmosphere]

Two Scientists and Ancient Astronaut Theory

In 1966, as Brazil was experiencing a great UFO wave, two respected scientists, one a Russian astronomer, I.S. Shklovskii, and the other an American astronomer, Carl Sagan, both teamed up to write a book called *Intelligent Life in the Universe*. This book gave voice to their suspicions that advanced extraterrestrials may have visited our planet or even colonized our solar system at some time in the past. Carl Sagan's own calculations indicate that Earth is likely to have been visited by extraterrestrials about once every thousand years or so. Shklovskii postulated that the two Martian moons, Phobos and Deimos, are probably artificially-constructed satellites that were utilized by an ancient Martian civilization. The significance of this book is that here we have two high-level orthodox, hardcore scientists from the 60s, one American and one Russian, who openly suspected at the time that artificially-constructed moons likely exist in the solar system and that our own moon might be one of them. Another significant contribution was that, in writing this book, two mainstream scientists provided early scientific credence to the modern Ancient Astronaut Theory.

Policemen See UFOs

Early in the morning of April 17, 1966, two officers from the Portage County, Ohio Sheriff's Department, Deputy Sheriff Dale Spaur, and Mounted Deputy Wilbur "Barney" Neff were doused by a bright light coming from a low-level flying saucer emitting a sound like an overloaded transformer near Ravenna, Ohio. The two men called in to make a report. The duty officer, Sergeant Shoenfelt, told them to follow the object while he dispatched a photo unit. The two officers then embarked on an 85-mile cat-and-mouse chase across the Ohio border into Pennsylvania. Along the way, Spaur and Neff made a wrong turn at an intersection. To their amazement, the saucer stopped and backtracked until it returned to them, and the chase was underway again. Police officer Wayne Huston of Fast Palestine, Ohio, had been listening to their radio conversations at his location near the Pennsylvania border. Officer Huston then saw the flying saucer speed by, followed by Spaur and Neff chasing after it. Huston also joined the high-speed chase. As they reached Conway, Pennsylvania, Spaur and Neff were nearly out of gas when they spotted another parked police car. They stopped and asked for help, and the Conway officer called his dispatcher. As the four men watched the flying saucer hover near them, they heard talk of dispatching jets on the radio. When the men began discussing the radio chatter concerning the dispatching of jets, the flying saucer dashed straight up as if it heard them and took an evasive maneuver. Major Hector Quintanilla of Project Blue Book denied that any jets were ever dispatched in the area, and accused the officers of chasing the planet Venus. This was very upsetting to the witnesses, who felt insulted by this lame and overused explanation. William Weitzel of NICAP conducted a thorough investigation of this case and hand-delivered the investigation file directly to Edward U. Condon of the Condon Committee. The final status of this case - a sighting of the planet Venus - matches the status of thousands of other similar reports over the years, along with the probable thousands of unreported cases that exist involving car-chasing UFOs. This case was never even mentioned in the final Condon Report, and simply fell into the dustbin of human experiences that are not understood at all and have no viable explanation at present other than speculation.

My First Experience with Flying Saucers

Five years after my first paranormal experience in 1961 at the age of 6, I had my second paranormal encounter, only this time with flying saucers, in 1966 at the age of 11. 1966 brought a major flying saucer flap to the entire world. The year is considered one of the great waves in UFO history, and I was one of the percipients. The fact that I am writing about flying saucers now at the age of 60 leaves me with the impression that this past experience I had at a young age was real and not imaginary, although all my life I have wondered about the true nature of the encounter. Like everyone else on the planet, I have had thousands of dreams and imaginings throughout the course of my life. However, as in my experience with the Shadow People, this experience with flying saucers in 1966 stuck with me throughout all the years of my life. It is therefore real in that this UFO experience has had an influence on my life that cannot be denied. Likewise, the UFO phenomenon in general has had a tremendous impact on the popular culture at large, regardless of the actual level of material reality that flying saucers represent. I do not remember if I was awake or asleep during this encounter with the saucers. I remember walking down our driveway to get the mail on a bright sunny day in Titusville, Florida. As I was walking, I heard no sound, but felt a strong urge to look skyward. There in the sky above me was a number of motionless flying disks hovering silently in the air. I was immediately overwhelmed with the same feeling of recognition and comfort that I experienced both with the Shadow People at age 6 and during my NDE at age 54 when I had a heart attack in 2009. The disks somehow became a part of me, like a long-lost family waiting for me at the end of my physical life. I was so awed by their presence that my response was to drop to my knees in the grass in reverence for them. I felt as though I had been shipwrecked on Earth, and that the flying saucers were there to take me home. Tears were streaming down my face uncontrollably, the cleansing sort of tears that bring psychological release. After a minute or so of mutual observation, the flying saucers were gone. It is true, looking back on this memory, that as a child of 11 I collected 1962 *Mars Attacks* bubble gum cards to the point of obsession. I loved the cards as if they were family photos. As an 11-year-old, even at only five cents a pack it was difficult to collect the entire 55-card set. 1950s parents at the time hated the Mars Attacks cards, as they contained full color images of a horrific, bloody Martian attack from outer space. My mother used to throw the cards in the trash. If only she had spent about 12 dollars on a whole box of the packs and kept them sealed, we would be millionaires today. Select cards that have been graded as 8 or 9 by PSA (Professional Sports Authenticators) go for thousands of dollars on Ebay now. I have managed to re-collect an entire midgrade 1962 Mars Attacks set as an adult, and this collection is my prize possession. The Mars Atacks cards continue to have an emotional effect on me. Taking my card collection into consideration, I suppose one could easily say that I simply had a vivid childhood dream of the saucers, but I think not. It was likely the reverse since, from early childhood, I was having real encounters with elementals, interdimensionals, or whatever one would like to call them (the Shadow People), i.e., visitors from another realm. I was likely drawn to the 1962 Mars Attacks cards from an association that was already present in my psyche, rather than experiencing strange mental effects generated by the influence of a colorful set of bubblegum cards. At any rate, flying saucers were firmly implanted into my head from this experience at age 11, as they are right now as I write this book. Since my vision of flying saucers at age 11, they have never really gone away, and for this I am eternally grateful.

Woodrow Derenberger

On November 2, 1966, a salesman in his twenties from Parkersburg, West Virginia was driving his Ford Econovan loaded with stereos and sewing machines along I-77 near the city, when his life took a bizzare turn. His name was Woodrow Derenberger. As he was driving, one of his sewing machines fell off the top of a stereo in the back of the van. He turned on the dome light and looked back to see what had fallen. While glancing at the back of the van, he noticed that a vehicle behind him was coming up on him and blinking its lights as if wanting to pass. Woody kept driving at the same speed as the vehicle passed, revealing yet another vehicle behind that one. This second vehicle came up beside the van, and Woody noticed that it had no lights. When the vehicle pulled ahead in front of him, it began slowing down, forcing Woody to put on his brakes. He tried to go around the vehicle, but it was too big and took up the whole road as it kept slowing down, forcing Woody to a complete stop. When both Woody and the vehicle came to a standstill, a door opened and a man stepped out as his strange vehicle rose 50-100 feet in the air behind him and hovered above Woody's truck. The man was about 5"10" tall, approximately 185 lbs., with long, thick, black hair combed back over his head and a pleasant smile, his arms folded, hands tucked into his armpits. Speaking through the passenger window, the man identified himself as *Indrid Cold*. He told Woody not to be frightened, that he was just a "searcher." Cold asked Woody what the lights were ahead of them, and Woody told him it was the city of Parkersburg. Cold said that where he came from, a city like that was called a "gathering." Woody became frightened. Cold was pleasant-looking, but his facial expression changed frequently in a very odd manner. Cold told Woody that the place he came from was "not as powerful" as his. He also told Woody to tell the authorities about his encounter, and that at a later date, he would confirm Woody's story. As the 10-minute conversation drew to a close, Cold's vehicle slowly returned down from its hovering position and landed once again on the highway. As Cold stepped in front of Woody's headlights on his way to the vehicle, another arm opened the door as if to assist Cold back into the craft. The door closed and it left straight up with a soft fluttering sound. Shaken, and in a state of shock, Woody drove home and did not remember much about the drive. When he arrived home, he sat down at the table with his wife and, shaking, told her his story. She suggested that he call the police and tell them what happened. When Woody called the police, to his surprise, the police told him on the phone that his was the third similar call that evening involving a strange vehicle and a visitor. The next morning, on November 3, 1966, Woody was asked to appear on WTAP, the local news station, to tell his story. The story also appeared in the local paper that evening, and UPI took his story to the rest of the world. From there, Woody received hundreds of phone calls and letters from around the world. NICAP and NASA took an interest in Woody's UFO encounter, and he was amazed that NASA acted as if his story was common, and indicated that they knew something about the underlying reality of his experience. Following his visit with NASA, Woody began receiving telepathic communication from Indrid Cold, who revealed to him details about the purpose of his initial contact, which was simply to alleviate Woody's fears about who he was. Indrid Cold also telepathically conveyed details to Woody concerning his home world, *Lanulos*, in the *Galaxy of Ganymede*. Indrid Cold told Woody that his home world was similar to ours, having streams, oceans, and trees, and that he has taken samples of our flora and fauna back to Lanulos. Cold said that he was married to a woman named Kimi. Indrid and Kimi Cold have two sons and a daughter. According to telepathic transmissions from Indrid Cold, the life expectancy on the planet Lanulos is 125-175 years. Lanulos has three seasons, planting, harvest, and cold. Cold warned Woody that whenever he broke telepathic contact with him, he would feel a "shock." Woody reported that whenever Cold broke contact, he would feel exhilarated, but was left with a throbbing pain in his right temple. Woody also experienced additional direct contact with Indrid Cold at his home, along with Cold's companion and navigator, Carl Ardo. Woody reported that the first visit at his home by Cold and Ardo, his wife was frightened of them and would not come out of the house. Over time, she accepted their presence and has entertained them in their home. Woody said that Cold never asked any questions about Earth's military, just inquiries as to the nature of Earth's inhabitants, their way of life, habits, and so forth. Cold said that on Lanulos they have no word in their vocabulary for "hate" as they realize that they are all brothers. Cold revealed that the inhabitants of Lanulos believe in one God who created all as we do. He and his navigator would love open contact with Earth, but said that they and others had been shot at in previous attempts of contact with Earth. Cold said he was shot at with a shotgun in Arkansas and had to have pellets removed from his legs and thighs. Cold stated that he had made contact with the US government and agreed to land openly if we could guarantee safety for him and his navigator, but the US government was unable to promise their safety. Lanulos would like to establish open trade with Earth, as we have things they need, and he felt sure Lanulos had things of interest to Earth. Cold explained that their government on Lanulos was also elected every six years, and that it consisted of 56 members of a Guiding Council. The inhabitants of Lanulos are able to speak to one another both verbally and telepathically. Children on Lanulos remain in school until 28 years of age, and then choose a compatible occupation. They hope that, in the future, they are successful in achieving open contact and trade with Earth.

It appears from a multitude of accounts that from time to time, Earth is visited by otherworldly humanoids who seek open contact with humanity but thus far have not been successful in doing so due to our violent natures. First we have the account of George Adamski meeting Orthon in the desert. Then Valiant Thor appears in Washington D.C. and has interactions with President Eisenhower, Vice President Richard Nixon, and Rev. Frank Stranges, living at the Pentagon for 3 years before departing back to the interior of Venus. The Italian W56 group, the AKRIJ, who were allegedly humanoids from various parts of the universe, had interactions with around a hundred credible individuals in Italy over many decades. Photographs of their ships have been filmed, film that has been authenticated in modern labs as representing large flying objects. Then a government official, Madeleine Rodeffer, testified that humanoid "Space People" knocked on her front door to announce the arrival of the Venusian scout craft, which she captured on film, a film that has since been authenticated by multiple professionals. Meanwhile, the scientists of the earth say all this is utter nonsense. Who is right? Whatever the case, someone has a very inaccurate view of reality. Hopefully, time will tell eventually who it is that has been deceived.

Mothman

Only 10 days after Woodrow Derenberger's encounter with Indrid Cold and his space vehicle on a dark lonesome highway, and only 50 miles away, a group of gravediggers who were working in a cemetery in Clendenin, West Virginia were traumatized as they witnessed a humanoid creature with wings that did not flap cruising over their heads on November 12, 1966. Police began receiving reports of the creature from many different locales. Three days after the gravediggers' report, on November 15, 1966, Newell Partridge reported that his dog "Bandit" began howling as his television went to snow and displayed colors he had never seen before. Hearing a loud screech, Newell ran outside in time to witness a large human-like creature with bright red eyes sailing over his house. One weekend over 500 reports of lights in the sky and/or UFOs were reported in the area. The day after Newell Partridge's report, on November 16, 1966, Ralph Thomas reported witnessing a similar creature flying around a local TNT plant. This facility was an abandoned WW2 munitions manufacturing/storage area. The next day, on November 17, 1966, two newlywed couples, Roger & Linda Scarberry, and Steve & Mary Mallette, were driving together around the same TNT area when they encountered a 6-foot-tall creature with glowing red eyes and bat-like wings running from behind the munitions plant like a crippled chicken, balancing itself on its wings as it glided along the ground. Frightened, the couples sped up and fled home toward Point Pleasant, and encountered the creature again standing near the highway. They watched as the red-eyed monster flew straight up with no visible means of flight, its wings stationary instead of flapping. Speeding up to over 100 miles per hour, the couples reported seeing the shadow of the creature following them. When police responded to the report and arrived at the scene, they found nothing, but reported unusual noises coming through their police radios. Shoe store manager Tom Ury also reported the creature while driving north of Point Pleasant on Route 62 about a week later on November 25, 1966. At first Tom thought a helicopter was rising straight up, but he soon realized that it was not a helicopter, but some sort of flying creature with a wingspan of at least 10 feet. Tom sped away frightened at 70 miles per hour. The next evening, late at night on November 26, 1966, Mrs. Ruth Foster looked out her front door window to see a red-eyed monster with a weird face staring right back at her. The next evening, on November 27, 1966, her 13-year-old neighbor, Shelia Cane and a friend reported sighting a large creature with red glowing eyes as they drove past an automobile junkyard. Since the television show, "Batman," had become popular in the 60s, and was on everyone's mind at the time, this set of peculiar creature sightings became known as the legend of *Mothman*. UFO-investigator John Keel made a personal visit to the area to investigate the *Mothman* sightings. Keel fully expected to discover a large bird of natural origin similar to the Sandhill Crane, or even the legendary bird from India known as the *Garuda*. Instead, he had direct experience with strange luminous lights at night in the area that responded to his flashlight. This luminous nocturnal phenomenon appeared to be either craft that were flying under some sort of intelligent control, or the lights themselves were intelligent. Keel concluded through witness interviews that the Mothman sightings were, in some mysterious way, related to the UFO phenomenon. Keel writes extensively of his experiences in his paranormal classic, *The Mothman Prophecies*, which was eventually made into a movie. Keel came to accept the idea that all UFO phenomena on this planet are intimately connected to other forms of cryptoreality such as Big Hairy Monster (BMH) sightings, ghosts, poltergeists, lake monsters, and the like. In other words, UFOs represent only one aspect of an overall meta-phenomenon that incorporates all of these mystical apparitions to keep humans baffled as *something else entirely* is actually happening to humanity that lies beyond our capacity to understand at present. Haunting questions remain due to the close proximity of Woodrow Derenberger's encounter with Indrid Cold and the Mothman sightings. *Are Indrid Cold and Mothman one and the same? If not the same, do they have some type of strange connection?* Keel discovered in his research that poltergeists and other creature sightings often correlate with the appearance of UFOs. Do these specters from another realm "hitchhike" on the method UFOs use to enter our world and arrive through the same invisible portal for a temporary romp in our reality? Maybe Mothman was just an alien pet owned by one of the ufonauts, and they simply let him out to chase and scare humans for exercise before departing back to the netherworld from which they came.

The Yorba Linda UFO Photo

On January 24, 1967, an enigmatic photograph was taken by a 14-year-old that looks like a giant transistor tossed into the air. This photo was analyzed over the course of several years by six different photographic experts using state-of-the-art equipment, and continues to baffle photographic experts even today. The photo was taken from the second story of a home in Yorba Linda, California with a cheap, fixed-focus Mark II camera. The negative was developed by a friend of the young man that snapped it, who was also 14 years old. This shot is now known as the "Yorba Linda Photograph." Whether this photo represents another example of a hat-shaped UFO like Rex Heflin's photo in 1965, the hat-shaped alien craft reported decades later by Bob Lazar, or just a lucky shot of a mundane object is anyone's guess. However, the significance of the young man's photograph is that it did factually contribute to the public perception of visitors from another world in the 60s era, and has had people in high places scratching their heads over it for decades now.

The Yungay UFO Photo

Another set of photos from 1967 are known as the Yungay (Peru) UFO photos, and are associated with the worst disaster in the history of the Western Hemisphere. A full set of excellent flying saucer photos were taken by Augusto Arranda with a camera borrowed from a friend, Cesar Ore, while hiking high in the mountains of Huaylas Valley of North Central Peru. The UFO photos were given to APRO (Aerial Phenomenon Research Organization), who learned of the actual location of the photos by the Peruvian Ministry of the Navy. It is suspected that the appearance of the saucers were related to local seismic activity, lending credence to various geophysical hypotheses. In May, 1970, a massive earthquake hit the area and dislodged a glacier from Mount Huascaran, tragically burying the whole town of Yungay and its residents. This tragic event killed nearly 70,000 people, including Cesar Ore, the owner of the camera who possessed one of the original Yungay UFO photos. The haunting flying saucer photos remain as a stark testament of the association between UFOs, creature sightings, and natural disasters such as earthquakes. Likewise, Mothman appeared to residents of Point Pleasant, West Virginia just before the collapse of the Silver Bridge that connected Point Pleasant to Gallipolis, Ohio over the Ohio River, resulting in the deaths of 46 people. Another possibility is that there was an alien base there who were aware of an impending calamity, and vacated the area prior to the disaster. If so, one would think that the aliens would've found a way to warn the residents, but, for whatever reasons, they didn't.

Betty Andreasson

About two months after the bizarre "Mothman" reports in Point Pleasant, West Virgina, along with Woodrow Derenberger's enigmatic encounter with Indrid Cold, a resident of South Ashburnham, Massachusetts, Betty Andreasson, a fundamentalist Christian, experienced a life-changing encounter with the hidden intelligences behind the UFOs. On January 25, 1967, Betty was puttering in her kitchen. Her seven children, along with her mother and father, were in the living room. At the time, Betty's husband was in the hospital recovering from an automobile accident. At approximately 6:35 p.m., Betty's houselights flickered and went dark. Time stood still for Betty as a pulsating, pink to reddish-orange light came into the house through her kitchen window. Betty managed to tell her frightened children to stay put in the living room as her father searched for the source of the strange light. Looking out a window, her father saw a group of small, strange-looking humanoid creatures moving toward their house with a floating, jerky motion. As they came past the window, one of the creatures looked in directly at Betty's father, and from that point his memory went blank as he was placed in some sort of suspended animation. Five entities entered Betty's home through solid doors who appeared to fade in and out of existence. This ends Betty's conscious memory of that fateful evening. The details of what actually happened to Betty Andreasson and her family after her conscious memory blanked out would eventually come out in hypnotic regression. The information that resulted from Betty's hypnosis sessions is considered one of the most significant ufological cases of our time. UFO-investigator Raymond Fowler wrote extensively about the Betty Andreasson affair in several books, including *The Watchers*. The main message conveyed to Betty Andreasson during her encounter with nonhuman entities was that; 1) humans would fear them if they made their presence openly known; 2) humans are more than just flesh and blood; 3) the technology in their possession is paraphysical in nature, and 4) unlike the human population, our nonhuman visitors are not bound by linear time. All of these features would become highly corroborated by thousands of other experiencers over the decades to come following the Betty Andreasson abduction experience.

UFO Shuts Down Nuclear Weapons

Two months after Betty Andreasson's abduction experience in Massachusetts, Captain Robert Salas, head of a US nuclear facility at Malstrom Air Force Base in Montana received a nervous, reluctant report from one of the guards under his command of an elliptical-shaped, reddish, glowing UFO hovering above the front gate of the base in March, 1967. Captain Salas lost electronic function in 6-8 weapons that morning despite failsafe energy redundancy. The UFO outside the facility apparently shut down his missiles. It is doubtful that the shutdown was due to the typical electromagnetic (EM) effects from UFOs that commonly disables many types of mechanisms like car engines and radios. The UFO was very specific in disabling the firing mechanisms. This event appears to have been a precise, intentional, UFO-directed targeted shutdown of US nuclear missiles as a demonstration of power. A complete report of this incident that Captain Robert Salas and his associates experienced and witnessed firsthand is meticulously documented in his 2005 book, *Faded Giant*. Other similar nuclear shutdowns have also occurred, eliminating the possibility that it was just a fluke or a mistake in human perception.

Nuwaubianism

In 1967, Dwight York founded Black Muslim groups in New York that later evolved into a UFO-and-New-Age-oriented organization, practicing philosophies from both ancient Egypt and fringe ufology. York's group eventually became the *United Nuwaubian Nation of Moors*. Although most people have never heard of Nuwaubianism, their influence would reverberate throughout the popular culture at large for the next 40 years. York built an Egyptian-style compound in Georgia called *Tama-Re* whose members involved themselves with local politics in the Republican Party. The UFO-cult of Nuwaubianism was focused on the founder, Malachi (Dwight) York, who occasionally claimed both divine and/or extraterrestrial origin. York asserted that he was the reincarnation of the Egyptian Pharoah Ramses II, who allegedly hailed from the Planet *Rizq*. York also identified himself in a messianic way as Melchizedek who, according to York, was the biblical Archangel Michael. York went by the name AL-Khidr (*The Green One*). According to York, Nuwaubians were originally green in color, but their skin has turned brown now from rusting in the Earth's atmosphere, the magnesium in their melanin now replaced by iron. York published hundreds of booklets called "Scrolls" along with a Nuwaubian Bible called *The Holy Tablets*. Some of the items of interest that York told followers included: grotesque Andromedans that looked like the creature in the movie "Predator" met with President Truman; there are over 70 different species of Gray aliens and 16 different species of Reptilian aliens; other extraterrestrial races have been trading with Earth since the Eisenhower administration; some ET races prey on human children; and Hollywood producers are mind-controlled by ETs to make fiction that discredits individuals who believe in the reality of UFOs and extraterrestrials. Official clothing for Nuwaubians began as a simple black tunic, but this attire was eventually replaced by colorful African robes. The Nuwaubian symbol is a six-pointed star and the Egyptian Ankh. Nuwaubian theology involves a god named Leviathan, who is associated with the Moon and sex. As the story goes, thousands of years ago the Devil cast the "Spell of Leviathan" that hypnotized black people into spiritual ignorance. Other weird beliefs include the admonition to bury the afterbirth of a child so that Satan doesn't use it to create a duplicate, and that some aborted fetuses survive, who then grow up in US sewers. These fetuses will be gathered and organized when they become adults to join an army that takes over the world. Borrowing racial doctrine from the Nation of Islam, Nuwaubians consider Blacks the superior race, and identify the White race as the work of the Devil, descendants of a mutant version of the original African Negroes. Caucasians are thought to have been originally crossbred from Orangutans and Baboons, and were genetically designed to become a slave race of killers for Blacks, but the plan went awry. According to Nuwaubianism, the Christian "Rapture" actually refers to the return of the Raptors (Dinosaurs) that will dine on ripe white flesh. The White race inherited the curse of leprosy. At one point in the past, the White race almost died out, but was kept alive by Caucasian women mating with Jackals. Morbidly obese people are descended from Richard Shaver's grotesque elephant-nosed Deros. The Nuwaubian UFO cult was eventually classified as a hate group by the Southern Poverty Law Center. York wound up receiving a 135-year prison sentence for transporting minors across state lines, sexual molestation, and racketeering. When York was prosecuted, seven police officers from the Macon, Georgia Police Department quit their jobs to protest York's charges, five of whom were later hired as jail guards who were then fired for smuggling Nuwaubian literature into the jail. Thirty years after the cult was originally founded by York, Nuwaubianism, otherwise known as "Blackosophy," was destined to have a powerful influence on Hip Hop music and American black culture. It is safe to say that many popular Hip Hop artists, along with much of their music, was unwittingly influenced by the Nuwaubian UFO cult, whose roots extended to Erich von Daniken's *Chariots of the Gods*, Helen Blavatsky, and Raelianism (another UFO-related religious cult). Author

Bill Olinski investigated York's Nuwaubian cult in Georgia and wrote *Ungodly: A True Story of Unprecedented Evil*. A Muslim cleric, Bilal Philips, wrote *The Ansar Cult in America*, exposing York's cult as "un-Islamic."

Nuwaubianism and other UFO-oriented cults are a testament to the huge cultural impact that belief in flying saucers and extraterrestrials has had on the world at large. This impact is psychologically significant even if the skeptics are right and there are no flying saucers, just as world religions have had an impact on the existing culture, even if there are no gods. The transformation of the consciousness of humanity is happening from within. Both the subtle and overt influence that groups such as the Nuwaubians have had on the world is an integral part of Cryptoreality. Even hardcore skeptics of the UFO phenomenon have been unwittingly influenced by flying saucer culture in powerful ways that they would hate to acknowledge. The modern world is full of UFO skeptics who are diehard Star Trek and Star Wars fans, their interest in science fiction spawned by the UFO culture at large. It is quite ironic that both UFO skeptics and UFO fanatics have had their minds molded in a certain way for many decades now in accordance to an actual alien agenda. The disbelief of UFO skeptics is irrelevant, as the cultural changes that have come about due to the concept of UFOs has been so vast that the effects are widespread, nearly undetectable, and unavoidable. The difference is, skeptics usually enjoy TV shows like Star Trek without any understanding of the history of Gene Roddenberry's interest in Andrija Puharich and his channeling of *The Nine* (The Egyptian Ennead) or UFO lore. UFO skeptics believe that they are simply enjoying a science fiction show when the images and ideas that are entering their minds are a product of alien influence. Skeptics just haven't done their homework to recognize it as such as we head steadfast into the Singularity, a time when all things UFO-related will become crystal clear. Many who have suffered ridicule will be vindicated.

Uninvited Visitors

In 1967, biologist Ivan T. Sanderson published his UFO theories in a book called *Uninvited Visitors*. Sanderson, like Trevor James Constable, proposed that UFOs represent an unknown *form of life* rather than physical spacecraft. Sanderson concluded from his own research that whenever we see flying craft of the nuts-and-bolts variety, we are always looking at objects of terrestrial manufacture. The true unknowns are an alien biology that we know little about. Trevor James Constable believed that these "sky creatures" as he called them, many of which he successfully captured on infrared film in both still shots and video, are probably indigenous to Earth and may have even coevolved alongside humanity. Ivan T. Sanderson, on the other hand, felt that the sky creatures either came here at some point, or were sent here from another world or dimension on a mission - to watch over the earth and its inhabitants as if it were some sort of cosmic nursery. Sanderson believed that these strange lifeforms that interact in various ways with humanity from time to time, may represent a biotechnology manufactured on another planet somewhere far from here, whose mission it is to replicate various lifeforms on Earth. Sanderson believed that these lifeforms may live in outer space as their natural habitat and visit the earth on occasion to feed on various types of biological, natural, or human-produced energy sources like electricity. I believe Sanderson was, as Jim Moseley used to say, "shockingly close to the truth." The consumption of biological energy may be at the heart of the livestock (and occasionally, human) mutilations. These creatures may even benefit somehow from the shedding of animal and human blood as the fresh shedding of toroidal blood cells may release a form of electromagnetic energy that the creatures are able to consume. Natural energy sources for the sky creatures to consume may also be found in lightning, tornados, or volcanos, all of which seem to produce visible appearances of UFOs. Energy produced by humans, in particular, electricity, seems to attract UFOs, and UFOs have been reported near electrical blackouts or even thought to cause them. This leads to a strange question. That is, supposing that Ivan T. Sanderson and Trevor James Constable were right, and these creatures feed on various types of energy - were they attracted to our nuclear detonations that began in 1945 as a buffet of energy consumption, or did the nuclear explosions actually represent a *threat* to their long-range food source? Whatever these creatures are, they have made many appearances and incursions over the centuries into the reality of humankind. Recently, Dr. W. George Gaines, President of Thunder Energies Corporation, has announced the detection of "invisible terrestrial entities" with the newly-designed *Santilli telescope*. Images are now being captured that appear to represent entities of unknown intelligence that are very similar to those captured by Trevor James Constable in the 1950s. It appears that Constable's early work in detecting these creatures may finally be vindicated. The reality and existence of flying saucers, whether they are mechanical craft, biological entities, or a combination of both, has been solidly ascertained by various types of observations and instrument verification, including radar, along with UFO encounter reports that demonstrate physical effects on percipients, such as the one we are about to examine - the Stefan Michalak encounter.

UFOs are Dangerous

Two months after the nuclear shutdown reported by Captain Salas at Malstrom AFB, and four months after Betty Andreasson's encounter with entities from an unknown realm, a 51-year-old mechanic for the Inland Cement Company and amateur prospector, Stefan Michalak, had an encounter with a landed flying saucer in the rocky woods of Falcon Lake, about 80 miles south of Winnipeg, Canada, on May 20, 1967. Alone in the woods near a quartz vein, Michalak heard a loud sound of cackling geese who were apparently upset about something. Startled, he looked up, and to his shock, Michalak saw two red-hot glowing flying saucers arriving to the area. One of the saucers landed about 160 feet away from him as the second saucer hovered in the air for a few moments before shooting off into the sky. Michalak watched from a distance for about 30 minutes. He watched as the object landed, pulsating on the ground and changing colors from a glowing red, like hot coals, to a silver color with a golden glow around it. After the craft settled on the ground for a while, a square door with rounded corners opened, revealing a beautiful purple light inside. Michalak could feel waves of warm air emanating from the craft, creature, or whatever this thing was, along with a strong smell of sulfur, which is a common feature in various kinds of paranormal manifestations. Inside the craft he heard a whirling sound, like that of a high-speed electric motor (another common feature). Michalak fatefully decided to walk toward the craft. As he approached to about 60 feet, he heard two distinct human-sounding voices coming from the inside, one of a higher pitch than the other. Attempting to communicate with the occupants, Michalak, who was multilingual, shouted out in several languages including Russian, Ukrainian, German, English, Italian, and French, but received no return response from the occupants. As Michalak approached the doorway from which the purple light emanated, he donned his prospector goggles and boldly stuck his head inside. What Michalak saw inside was a high-tech cockpit of flashing light bars and bulbs that blinked on and off at random. He then conducted a walkaround of the craft, admiring its seamless, smooth construction from the outside. Suddenly the craft jolted and emitted a blast of heat from a grid-like panel on the side that seared Michalak's chest with painful heat. Michalak reached for the side of the craft and touched it, instantly melting his rubber gloves and catching his shirt on fire. Reacting to the fire, the pain, and the heat, Michalak ripped his shirt off and tossed it. The craft slowly rose into the air, hovered for a moment just as the other object did, and with a blast of air took off at high speed. In pain, confused, and frightened, Michalak stumbled through the woods and back out onto the highway. He was taken to the Misericordia Hospital, where he was treated for chest burns and released. For weeks after Michalak's treatment at the hospital, he suffered radiation poisoning, with symptoms including nausea, vomiting, a 22-pound weight loss, a drop in lymphocyte count, and diarrhea. The most disturbing symptom was the frequent recurrence the stigmata-like checkerboard pattern on his chest from the original blast, an unmistakable sign that, whatever it actually was that he encountered, was physically real and not merely hallucinatory. Michalak reported his encounter to the Royal Canadian Mounted Police, but they gave him the same response that the USAF now gives to victims of such encounters - "We have no interest in UFO investigations." Worse yet, as his story spread and interested private UFO investigators began to talk to Michalak, he was paid a visit by Dr. Roy Craig from the Condon Committee. At this time the Condon Report was already in the works with Edward U. Condon's preconceived outcome that flying saucers do not exist and are unworthy of scientific investigation. Dr. Roy Craig's job for the Condon Committee was to put a lid on the Michalak story. Any mundane explanation would work, he just needed to find one. With no success from the Royal Canadian Mounted Police or Dr. Roy Craig from the Condon Committee, Michalak sought help from an electronics engineer, Mr. G. A. Hart, and returned to the original site. Together they found the area of the landing, an imprint of the craft on the ground, the burned shirt that he had tossed aside, and a lost tape measure. The two men gathered some rocks and sticks from the area and had them tested with no significant results. For years to come, Michalak continued to experience recurrent symptoms of radiation poisoning. The checkerboard burn pattern on his chest that he received from the blast returned from time to time. He experienced frequent swelling of the hands and nausea for the rest of his life. These recurrent physical symptoms completely baffled the doctors who examined him. Stefan Michalak passed away at the age of 83 in October, 1999.

Whatever it was that Michalak encountered in the woods that day was the real deal, a direct, close-encounter contact with at least one aspect of the underlying intelligences behind the UFO phenomenon. When misidentified government, natural phenomena, and psychological illness are removed from the UFO conundrum, what we are left with are completely unexplainable encounters with an unknown intelligence on this planet. Unlike some reports, which seem to be cases of intentional mind control with a technological component and no physical evidence, Stefan Michalak had a genuine encounter with nonhuman intelligence. As Keel pointed out in his writings, some experiencers such as Stefan Michalak report the distinct feeling that the occupants and the saucer itself were connected in some way as part of the same intelligence. The ufonauts are sometimes perceived as projections of consciousness that emanate from the craft itself, which is also alive. The sheer volume of reports like this presents the startling possibility that the craft itself, along with all associated appendages such as ufonauts, wings, rotating propellers, or whatever, are all connected together as some sort of shapeshifting creature that disguises itself as a flying saucer, mimicking a visitor from outer space. Keel always referred to these types of paranormal manifestations that are accompanied by the pungent odor of sulfur as the "Smellies." This nauseating sulfur smell is a common feature of many big hairy monster (BHM) sightings, ghosts, and other cryptid encounters. These paranormal encounters indicate the existence of an unknown intelligence, biological, technological, or a combination of both. At least this aspect of the UFO phenomenon appears to have the uncanny ability to transform itself into whatever it needs to be, according to the mindset of the witnesses. In times past, this type of UFO intelligence may have taken the form of flying dragons, flying shields, or phantom ships in the sky. Today, they appear as flying saucers with occupants who emulate visitors from outer space. The physical manifestation of this occulted intelligence is always just ahead of human progress and the human capability to replicate. In this way, the UFO intelligences act as a guiding force toward a technological singularity. This intelligence chooses, for its own purposes, not to reveal its true nature to humankind because it has an agenda that is harmful, or at least indifferent, to humans. It is also potentially dangerous to humans. The physical effects on humans that these unidentified intelligences occasionally choose to inflict has left many unwitting experiencers with a lifetime of pain and bewilderment. For their own reasons, this unidentified intelligence on Earth, whether indigenous or alien, chooses not to openly reveal itself at this time, and may never do so in the way that we seek. It chooses instead to select individuals and inflict an experience on them that causes them to lose all credibility with their fellow human beings except for knowledge-hungry paranormal investigators who know something is afoot and seek real answers to this confounding mystery. So we can say with certainty that at least one facet of the real UFO phenomenon represents a hidden, unidentified intelligence that is normally invisible; operates in our world with impunity; reveals itself to isolated individuals as part of a hidden, deceptive agenda; produces a nauseating odor of sulfur when it physically materializes; is potentially dangerous to the psychological and physical health of human beings; may be responsible for certain cases of mid-air collision and crashed or vanished aircraft; has an occasional need for animal or human blood and soft tissue; may be responsible for cajoling humanity into constant war and conflict to create the need for technological superiority; is possibly able to possess a human being temporarily and make them do terrible things; cause humans to go insane or starve themselves to death for the cause of the "Space Brothers" (such as the case of Gloria Lee); or even commit suicide to escape the ridicule one receives from peers and loved ones who suspect that the experiencer has gone insane. And yet, despite all these indications of overt hostility from at least some types of flying saucers and ufonauts, we humans continue to hope that benevolent extraterrestrials exist for us, such as the benign AKRIJ (Amicizia) group who are coming again in the future or are already here to help us. These benevolent beings, who may be here on Earth alongside our enemies (The Contraries) to help us, appear to want to save us from ourselves and protect us from potentially-hostile interdimensionals. We hope for an ally of superior intelligence in the universe who will help guide us to a future Golden Age in which we will be accepted as a valued member of the Galactic Federation. That, my friends, is real faith. Maybe there actually are, as William Bramley says in *The Gods of Eden*, two factions of alien intelligence operating here on Earth, one benevolent, and one hostile. There may even be several ET races, some friendly, and some hostile, as George C. Andrews elaborated in *Extraterrestrial Friends and Foes*. One thing is certain - we will all find out what is really going on, who our extraterrestrial friends and foes really are, when we achieve the technological singularity that is projected by AI experts to occur somewhere mid-21st century. When we are soon able to merge our own biology with advanced artificial intelligence of our own creation with a little help from above, and our awareness of the universe around us suddenly increases by a factor of billions, we will likely discover the true nature of the universe itself, along with finally discovering the elusive secrets of the UFO phenomenon. As we approach the Singularity, we will soon discover who was right and who was wrong concerning the benevolent or hostile intent of the hidden UFO intelligences that have been manipulating humankind for centuries. Let us hope that someone in this universe of a higher-order intelligence is on our side, as we will certainly need the help as we are presented with new information and challenges that we cannot imagine at present.

[On June 17, 1967 China detonated its first hydrogen bomb, Test #6]

The Trent Photos Surface

During the same year that Betty Andreasson had her experience with nonhuman intelligence, 1967, just a year or so after Woodrow Derenberger's encounter with Indrid Cold, along with the Mothman sightings at Point Pleasant in 1966, an unexpected "blast from the past" surfaced. As mentioned previously, the negatives of the original photographs that were taken by the Trents in 1950 in McMinnville, Oregon, went missing as *Life* magazine said the negatives had been "lost." Well, lo and behold, in 1967, after the photos had been missing for so many years, the original Trent negatives mysteriously surfaced. The negatives were first discovered in the files of United Press International (UPI). UPI then loaned the negatives to the astronomer, Dr. William K. Hartmann. Dr. Hartmann was "coincidentally" and conveniently working on the infamous Condon Committee, headed up by Edward U. Condon. Edward Condon was a UFO-skeptic who was determined to destroy public belief in these fictional flying saucers forever, despite the fact that documented UFO and occupant encounters were happening all over the world by credible percipients and witnesses. Despite Edward U. Condon's efforts to bring "rationality" to UFO research by injecting any lame excuse that anyone could think of to explain UFO encounters, UFO research continued, thanks to a multitude of dedicated individuals who only grew in number over the years to come. Today, theories continue to surface and develop concerning the true nature of UFOs and their mysterious occupants. Edward U. Condon failed.

Horse Mutilation

On September 9, 1967, in the midst of global UFO and creature sightings, rancher Harry King of Colorado stumbled upon a grisly sight at the onset of one of the strangest and most disturbing mysteries that has ever occurred on this planet. King found his 3-year-old Appaloosa, Lady, who he had just observed happy and healthy two days prior on September 7, lying on the ground as a bloodless corpse with a precise surgical cut completely around her neck. All the flesh was stripped to the bone from the neck up, showing the vertebrae and a bare skull as if the bones had been bleached white and prepared for a museum display. The same night that this bizarre surgery had to have happened, Harry's Mother, Agnes King, reported seeing a "strange light" fly over the ranch during the night. Another resident, Duane Martin, also reported low-flying UFOs in the area the night of Lady's death. Two weeks later, Dr. John Henry Altshuler, a doctor of hematology and pathology, examined the dead horse and determined that the cuts were made with some sort of cauterizing laser device, a method of surgery that would not be put into use by humans for another decade. Dr. Altshuler observed that Lady's heart, lungs, and thyroid had been removed with a surgical incision without blood, a feat that he considered impossible. Lady's brain had also been removed. Dr. Altshuler became frightened. He was worried about his professional standing in the medical community if he reported his findings honestly. Therefore, Altshuler kept his observations and conclusions secret for many years, along with the fact that he observed three luminous UFOs at night during his visit. Years after Lady's death, Dr. Altshuler eventually gave a full report of his findings, an account that is presented by UFO researcher Linda Moulton Howe in her groundbreaking work of journalism covering the strange cattle mutilation phenomenon of the 1960s-1970s, *An Alien Harvest*. A month after Lady's death by precision laser surgery, an article appeared in *The Pueblo Chieftain*, Pueblo, Colorado, with the headline, *Dead Horse Riddle Sparks UFO Buffs*. The connection between animal mutilations and UFOs was now clearly established. In *Our Haunted Planet* and other analytical works on the paranormal, in an effort to gain some level of insight into the cattle mutilation phenomenon, John Keel made reference to ancient legends of demons and vampires who enter our realm to collect blood and biological material that they use to assist the transmogrification of energy into physical objects, apparitions, and monstrous creatures of temporal physicality that have haunted humankind over the aeons. Starting with the beloved horse named Lady, a true mystery was at hand with possible otherworldly implications. The cattle mutilations became associated with strange blobs of luminous energy, UFOs, appearing in the sky. Howe's book, *An Alien Harvest*, includes color photographs of these strange luminous blobs that were taken by ranchers during a wave of cattle mutilations. Someone, or some *thing*, had a need for thousands of gallons of blood and soft tissue from Earth creatures, and in 1967, they began conducting their ghastly deeds in this insidious and overtly-visible manner with impunity, much to the horror and confoundment of the poor affected cattle ranchers.

The Interdimensional Hypothesis (IDH)

Two years after the first recorded animal mutilations, beginning with Lady (aka Snippy) in 1967, the Condon Report was published with its premeditated negative results for the reality of UFOs in 1969. The USAF used the results of the Condon Report to justify shutting down Project Blue Book forever and getting the monkey off their back concerning public UFO investigations. From 1969 forward, the Condon Report created an erroneous paradigm within the US scientific community that flying saucers do not exist. However, while scientists in the United States dismissed the world's UFO phenomenon out of hand, this was certainly not the case in other countries, which left the United States straggling behind other countries in understanding the Phenomenon. In England, Sir Victor Goddard, who served as an Air Marshal for the Royal Air Force (RAF) and was involved with RAF UFO investigations throughout the 1950s, became one of the world's foremost authorities on UFOs. Goddard went public with his own theories concerning the true nature of the UFO phenomenon. Goddard believed that flying saucers, rather than representing visitation from outer space, exist naturally as a part of Earth's invisible realm. Goddard concluded that the real UFOs, the truly unexplainable sightings that remain when all weather phenomena, planets, satellites, balloons, and military aircraft, secret or otherwise, were all ruled out, were an indigenous part of the earth's environment. After years of personal and professional UFO investigations, Goddard concluded that flying saucers are normally invisible but appear frequently to selected individuals who usually possess innate psychic abilities. Goddard concluded that sometimes the flying saucers slip into the visual range of humans by accident. Other times the saucers appear intentionally for purposes that are currently unknown to humanity. Goddard's views of the interdimensional nature of flying saucers coincide with another early proponent of what would become the Interdimensional Theory, the aforementioned Dr. Meade Layne, who first proposed the idea of *Etherians* from a parallel universe that coexist with humans. According to Layne, the Etherians have existed longer than humanity. They move around the earth invisibly for the most part using interdimensional vehicles (flying saucers) that are able to alter their atomic vibration and materialize, at least briefly, in our 3D reality. Dr. Meade Layne may have been correct all along and ahead of his time by a couple of decades. Layne should receive credit for being one of the first real pioneers of the Interdimensional Theory of flying saucers. Sir Victor Goddard, along with many other modern researchers, such as ufologist and nobleman Brinsley Le Poer Trench and Lord Dowding, also proposed their own versions of the Interdimensional Theory. Brinsley Le Poer Trench founded *Contact International* and served as its first president, and also served as vice president to the *British UFO Research Association* (BUFORA). Trench took a multifaceted approach to UFOs, embracing both the Hollow Earth Theory and the existence of Cryptoterrestrials. Trench elaborated this theories in his book, *Secret of the Ages: UFOs from Inside the Earth*. Trench claimed that he could trace his own descent from 63,000 BCE when beings from other planets landed on Earth. Trench believed that the modern human races are descended from these original landing parties, as well as some populations that tunneled up from Inner Earth. Like Meade Layne, Trench was also ahead of his time, embracing the idea of a Martian Genesis, a theory of human origins that has gained credibility among many researchers with the artifact discoveries on Mars at Cydonia and other locations on Mars that appear to indicate an ancient Martian connection with the Egyptian culture that developed here on Earth. Lord Dowding, who became the Marshal of the Royal Air Force, was also interested in UFOs and spiritualism. Lord Dowding wrote a book on the subject in 1943, *Many Mansions*, followed by *Lychgate*, *The Dark Star*, and *God's Magic*. With these works, Lord Dowding joined the growing number of proponents of the Interdimensional Theory of flying saucers along with Goddard, Layne, and Trench, as did author and journalist John Keel. Keel, after spending many years of dedicated study to the subject of flying saucers and other anomalous phenomena such as Mothman, Bigfoot, lake monsters, and poltergeists, concluded that they were all connected somehow with an unknown intelligence on Earth whose existence has continually eluded and bewildered humans. Keel's interdimensional theories are marvelously explored in such UFO classics as *Operation Trojan Horse*, *Our Haunted Planet*, *Disneyland of the Gods*, and his strangest book ever, *The Eighth Tower*. Keel felt that flying saucers and their occupants, along with all the other ghosts and goblins that haunt this world, were simply the latest face of an unknown intelligence that desires to remain hidden from humans and masquerades as various diversions to throw us all off track to expedite their real agenda. The Interdimensional Theory, beginning in the 1940s with Meade Layne and his Etherians, continued to develop among leading ufologists throughout the 1960s forward. Interdimensional Theory remains as one of the most viable explanations for the weird reality we have all come to know as flying saucers. The actual purpose and mission of flying saucers and their occupants, which completely bewildered early UFO researchers, is now crystalizing as we approach a technological singularity and realize that flying saucers have been steering us in the direction of greater technology for a long time now. It is a reality that we likely will not understand completely until the Singularity actually arrives and we expand our consciousness exponentially with advanced artificial intelligence using both human and alien components. The human component has come with hard work, ingenuity, and a clandestine influence. The alien component has come from mind control over humanity, direct information downloads into human brains, and celestial gifts that have dropped from the sky and into our laps since the 1940s and possibly even earlier.

Albert Coe and the Shocking Truth

Another book was published in 1969 by an early 20th century contactee named Albert Coe. His book was called *The Shocking Truth*. It was written by Coe five years earlier in 1964, one year after the first episode of *The Outer Limits* aired in 1963, the same year that *The Twilight Zone* ended its journey from 1959-1964, and two years prior to the advent of the original *Star Trek* series in 1966. In this amazing account, Albert Coe revealed his experience as a contactee earlier in life. His story dates back to the 1920s when Coe was a teenager, about a decade after psychologist William Sadler began taking notes from a client in an unconscious trance state that were eventually published in 1955 as the *Urantia Book*. While Albert and his young friend, Rod, were fishing in Canada, they heard a noise that sounded like someone crying out in distress. When they went over to try to see what was going on, they found a man stuck on some rocks. The two boys noticed that the man was wearing a strange silver jumpsuit with instrumentation attached to the front. The strange man also used an odd fishing pole in which the line emerged from a hole in the front of the pole. Coe and his friend took the man back to his "plane" and discovered that it was actually a small metallic saucer. Grateful that Coe and his friend saved him from certain disaster, the man, who went by the name "Zret," promised to write Coe letters and keep in touch. After swearing secrecy, Albert Coe and his friend Rod watched as Zret disappeared up into the clouds in his silent flying saucer. True to his promise, Zret met with Coe on subsequent occasions. Zret told Coe the story of how he arrived on Earth. Zret lived on a planet named Norca with four moons from one of our closest sun systems - Tau Ceti. Norca's outer moon was a natural body, but the three inner moons were artificial and served to curtail evaporation and stimulate moisture, tempering the stark contrast between night and day temperatures. As their planet slowly became uninhabitable with a thinning atmosphere, the inhabitants of Norca attempted a planetary evacuation to our solar system about 14,000 years ago, seeking another place to colonize and live. They arrived in our solar system in 40 large circular passenger ships holding up to 2200 families each, and 22 transport ships. It took 58 years and 7 months of travel to reach our solar system from Norca in Tau Ceti. Arriving at the edge of our solar system, an accident of calculation occurred and all but one ship holding 3700 people crashed into our sun. This surviving ship sustained a controlled crash on Mars, where they were forced to colonize. The survivors managed to reestablish their culture on Mars, and about a thousand years later, they sent out colonization probes to both Venus and Earth. Establishing colonies on both planets, the first ship landed on Earth in Northern Atlantis about 13,000 years ago. From there, several areas on Earth were developed: Northern Atlantis; Peru west of the Marshall Islands; Southern Tibet; and Lebanon. After about 300 years, the advanced sciences of the Norcans led to abuses by the natives that caused terrible destruction on Earth, causing the Norcans to vacate Earth back to their bases on Mars and Venus. In 1904, a hundred observers returned to Earth from their base on Mars and infiltrated the Earth as small groups of technicians. Zret explained to Coe that their presence here on Earth would be maintained with the tightest secrecy. Their main mission, according to Zret, is to *observe the development of technology on Earth* as it evolves and make sure that no one foolishly destroys the planet with advanced weaponry or irresponsible use of advanced energy systems that will develop and have the potential to shatter the planet. In 1937, the Norcan group in Germany discovered the German atomic experiments. By 1939, they were aware that the German scientists were on the verge of exploiting the atom for destructive power. The solution that the Norcan observers came up with was to put in place a protective belt, activated in 1958 and known today as the Van Allen Belt (remember *Operation Argus* in 1958?). Albert Coe was silent about his experiences until the 1950s when George Adamski and others were on tour spreading the Gospel of the Space Brothers from Venus, as Coe had promised Zret that he would burn his letters after he read them.

Coe's book contains much information concerning biological and ecological matters that are of concern to all the inhabitants of Earth. In my opinion, Coe's account is worthy of being taken seriously and is actually plausible in many ways. Atlantis is thought by many Atlantean scholars to have sunk into the ocean approximately 13,000 years ago. At first glance, the Venusian visits of the 1950s seem impossible due to what we know now of the surface of Venus. However, if, in fact, as Richard Hoagland and others have suggested, Mars was inhabited by an intelligent, technological civilization in the past, or one that even may exist today, then it becomes more feasible that the same civilization that went underground on Mars may have established colonies on Venus, possibly large floating cities about 60 miles above the hot surface, the level where the oxygen content on Venus is approximately the same as Earth's. Thus, humanoids visiting Earth from underground colonies on Mars and underground or atmospheric cities on Venus may actually have been possible. In 2002, several planets near the Tau Ceti solar system were identified by modern astronomers as having the possibility of supporting life. Considering that Tau Ceti is only 12 light years away, Albert Coe's testimony, as revealed in *The Shocking Truth*, may actually be plausible. I tried to find a copy of his book online and found one on Amazon for seventeen hundred dollars. I discovered that some of these books written by 1950s contactees are considered collectible now and are very expensive to purchase. Fortunately, the book is also available to read in a non-printable PDF file online, so I did eventually enjoy Albert Coe's book via computer. I found it fascinating, as many details contained in Coe's book correlate with the theories of more recent authors. Like a convoluted jigsaw puzzle, sometimes sections of the big picture fall together nicely with enough time and perseverance.

The Shag Harbour USOs

On October 4, 1967, local residents of Shag Harbour, Nova Scotia, reported strange-looking orange lights in the sky. Many reported a total of four lights, and some reported the lights flashing in sequence. Everyone thought the craft that the lights belonged to, whatever it was, was going to crash into the harbor. Instead, the object stopped near the surface of the icy waters, about ½ mile from the shore. The Royal Canadian Mounted Police in Barrington Passage began receiving calls from individuals reporting that a possible airplane crash had occurred on the water in Shag Harbour. Constable Ron Pound of the RCMP had already witnessed the lights himself. Pound rushed to the harbour with Police Corporal Victor Werbieki and Constable Ron O'brien. All three men observed a yellow light that left yellow foam traveling on the surface of the water. Local fishermen, along with a Coast Guard boat, rushed out to see if anyone was in trouble or if they could be of assistance in any way. All the men found once they got there was the yellow foam. After checking with all aviation authorities, no aircraft were in the area at the time. Divers were called in who searched underwater for days and found nothing. This case went cold for the next 25 years until 2 MUFON investigators re-examined the case. These investigators discovered through their own research and witness interviews that Russia had also been tracking the UFO that night in 1967. Russia had sent a submarine to Nova Scotia to conduct a search. They uncovered the fact that the UFO had traveled underwater to Government Point, which was near a submarine detection base that detected the UFO. Naval vessels were called in. Before the military could conduct a salvage operation, a second UFO came in to aid the first. The Navy decided to hold back and watch. The two UFOs finally sped to the Gulf of Maine where they exited the water at a high rate of speed and disappeared into outer space. This case, as a result of the investigation efforts, became one of the best documented UFO cases of all time with many civilian and military witnesses and testimonies. Shortly after the Shag Harbour UFO Incident, in the same month, October, 1967, a massive UFO wave appeared over British skies that was witnessed by many patrolling police officers. In this decade of the 1960s, several "window areas" were identified as having regular UFO sightings, including Warminster, Bonnybridge, and a 10-mile strip located between the towns of

Rossendale Valley, which plays host to so many UFO sightings that the area has become known in modern times as "UFO Alley."

Virtual Ufonauts

One month after the Shag Harbour UFO Incident, on November 2, 1967, two Indian youths, Guy Tossie and Will Begay, were driving at night near Ririe, Idaho around 9:30 p.m. when they experienced a blinding flash of light just as Kenneth Arnold reported in 1947. Also reminiscent of the Arnold sighting, just after the flash of light came the appearance of a domed flying saucer, only this sighting was much closer, right in front of their car, and they could clearly see two humanoid occupants inside the craft. An unknown force stopped their car without applying the brakes as the craft hovered 5 feet above the road in front of the two shocked witnesses. The small craft was approximately 8 feet in diameter with orange and green lights flashing around the perimeter. The dome opened as if on hinges, and one of the occupants, about 3.5 feet tall wearing some sort of backpack that extended over the creature's head in the back floated up and out of the craft onto the ground. The small creature had large ears, a slit for a mouth, and two small round eyes on an oval face that was pitted and wrinkled. The creature then came over to the driver's side of the car while the two boys, horrified, slid over to the passenger side as the creature opened the door and got behind the wheel. The car began to move with the creature in the driver's seat and made its way into the middle of a wheat field with the craft and other occupant leading the way in front of them. Tossie, petrified, suddenly opened the passenger door and took off running to the nearby farmhouse of Willard Hammon. Hammon calmed the boy down, and went with him to look for his friend and the car. Begay was found sitting in the car alone in a state of shock with his eyes tightly closed. Begay would later report that, when Tossie ran away from the car, the ufonaut in the car attempted to communicate with him in a high-pitched voice that sounded like the chirping of a bird. The second being had chased Tossie with a light toward Hammond's house before giving up and returning to the car. The two ufonauts then floated back up and into the craft, the dome closed, and the craft took off into the sky in a rapid zig-zag pattern. State Police were called to investigate, and discovered that during the time of the two boy's report, farmers reported that their cows bolted for some reason, and multiple other witnesses reported seeing strange lights in the sky. NICAP investigator C.R. Ricks also investigated and discovered one other person in the area who reported a similar encounter with the ufonauts and their little sport vehicle that night. This witness insisted on keeping the report confidential without any mention of his real name. Keel wrote about this brand of witness, referring to them as "silent contactees." Keel estimated that there are many more silent contactees than there are contactees who make reports, for various reasons. Most silent contactees do not want to risk their jobs or reputation, especially during the 1960s when the UFO phenomenon was poorly understood and the "giggle factor" was high. Who needs the ridicule? This report can be deemed credible, as it has corroborating witnesses with nothing to gain, and classic telltale signs and common features shared with other credible reports that the two boys wouldn't have known about, such as the flying saucer chasing their car, or appearing in front of the vehicle (a common report), the blinding flash of light prior to the appearance of a flying saucer right after the light experience. The cartoonish appearance of the craft itself was likely imagery gleaned from the boy's minds. When their young minds were scanned, the energy of the hidden UFO intelligence materialized into a physical form that was understandable to the minds of boys their age at this point in history. Also relevant is the second report of a similar-looking vehicle and occupants that night by the silent witness. This second report leaves a clue that, once a selected person's mind is scanned, and an image is gleaned based on that person's concept and expectations of what an alien craft should look like (much of which is created by the science fiction of the times), the blinding flash of light occurs and the energy is transformed into a temporary solid object that has the capability of interacting with multiple human witnesses prior to dematerializing back into the "intelligent lightning" that Keel once postulated as the true form of the intelligence behind UFOs. The second witness indicates that the UFO intelligences from a paraphysical realm conserve energy by maintaining the same form gleaned from the mind of a single witness to appear to other witnesses during the same excursion into our 3D reality. Based on the details in thousands of reports such as this one, many of them replete with elements that seem absurd to us and violate our instincts as to what is real and what is not, it would seem that this might be the case. It appears that the surface appearance of all UFO sightings may represent a sort of virtual reality experience based on imagery found within the mind of the witnesses. Everything involved with the Phenomenon is not as it seems. There is, however, a profound underlying reality that is even stranger than the encounters witnesses report. It is this underlying reality that we are interested in discovering, a reality that has something to do with the manipulation of human minds and behaviors to achieve a desired goal that exists on the part of the occulted intelligence behind the UFOs.

Sergeant Shirmer and the Elders

On December 3, 1967, Sergeant Herbert Schirmer was on patrol in Ashland, Nebraska, when he encountered a UFO hovering above the road (this should sound familiar by now) that shot up when he flashed his high beams at the object. Schirmer soon realized that he had experienced "missing time," and a red welt appeared on his neck. Hypnotic sessions revealed that the occupants of the landed craft took Sergeant Schirmer aboard and communicated with him through some form of mental telepathy. They told him that they would visit him twice more and that someday he would "see the universe." Shirmer's "alien" was approximately 5 foot tall with a long, thin head and a wrinkled forehead. The creature's eyes, nose, mouth, and eyebrows were normal. The pupils of this ufonaut were elongated, and he wore a uniform consisting of a one-piece suit and boots. There was a device attached to the creature's left ear with a protruding antennae. The creature had a patch over his right chest that featured a pair of winged serpents that were similar to the common medical logo known as the Caduceus. The visitor stated to Shirmer that he came to Earth to prepare the world for eventual open contact, and to try and prevent the inhabitants of Earth from destroying themselves.

This case brings out a couple of interesting variations that we find in the UFO literature concerning the plethora of reported landing and creature contacts over the decades. First of all, Shirmer is not the first person to report an alien creature that looks like his description. According to the *Field Guide to Extraterrestrials*, Shirmer's alien falls into the category of the "Elders." The Elders are older-looking humanoid aliens with hardware attached. Typically they are reported with gadgets and gears, antennas, light sticks, etc., like they are a superhuman version of your favorite hardware store employee, or a real "Mister Gadget." This could be expected considering Shirmer's age and profession, that he would conceptualize such a creature as an occupant of a flying saucer. The version of ufonaut called the Elders may appeal to a certain age and mentality, so this is the image that is selected by the UFO intelligences for appropriate percipients. Considering the fact that alien descriptions from landing and occupant reports fall into several distinct categories, the intelligences behind the UFO phenomenon seems to employ a catalogue of collected imagery that is most suitable to various demographics of humans. In other words, the UFO intelligences make a determination from images gleaned from human minds in a given era. They seem to stick with similar presentations over time and in various parts of the globe to maintain consistency and credibility, or simply to conserve the expenditure of excess thought, or energy consumed by the program if, in fact, it is an automated von Neumann probe, which is a distinct possibility. A repertoire of images is apparently maintained by the UFO intelligences. General categories of creatures have been catalogued into several different types, such as Shirmer's alien, an Elder, along with others that may include the Grays, giants, robots, blobs, and hairy dwarfs. As Terence Mckenna once quipped:

The intelligences behind the UFO phenomenon are currently disguising themselves as aliens from outer space so as not to freak us out.

Also noteworthy is that, unlike the aforementioned case of Tossie and Begay, Shirmer experienced "missing time," and had to unlock the memories via hypnotic regression. Shirmer's case involved actual abduction onboard the craft, which typically involves buried memories that a person may take to their grave unless they pursue discovering the information through hypnosis, whereas Tossie and Begay retained conscious memory of their encounter and theirs did not involve an actual abduction. Abduction experiences seem to involve missing time and memory impairment, whereas encounters that do not involve abduction often allow the experiencer to retain conscious memory of the event. When a person is taken into a paraphysical experience aboard a "spacecraft" or zipped off to some alien world, they aren't really going anywhere physically. To an outside observer, nothing happened to the person at all. They may keep walking or driving as if nothing is going on at all while the experience is taking place in an alternate reality of the mind. Many people who become severely inebriated will drive home just fine without remembering the trip home at all when they wake up the next morning, and wonder how in the world they managed to drive. People are capable of functioning normally to observers while their conscious mind has vacated to a place far away. The alien abduction experience, which would become epidemic in the years to come, appears to fall into the category of an alternate reality or an induced mental experience using paraphysical psychotronics. The experiences sometimes involve impairment of mind or memory in which the person experiencing the abduction has a period of "missing time." These periods of missing time can range from 30 minutes or so to a week or more, as in the case of Orfeo Angelucci, who had an elaborate paraphysical experience with over a week of missing time, all the while going to work everyday without any of his coworkers noticing that anything out of the ordinary was going on with him. So it appears that what we are dealing with is an unidentified biological or robotic intelligence, possibly akin to intelligent plasma, either indigenous to Earth or otherworldly, that has been interacting with humans in a mentally-invasive, shapeshifting and manipulative fashion, possibly for millennia. In Colvin's *Searching for the String: Selected Writings of John A. Keel, Keel states* (audible, chapter 11 of 25):

> *It is far more likely that they [the ufonauts] originate outside of our time frame. It is also likely that the entities are not individuals with separate intelligences with free wills, but are actually cells in a larger whole, controlled by a computer-like intelligence that manipulates them like puppets. Thus they do not actually know who they are, or what they are, or even where they come from. Like machines, they have only two states – turned on, or turned off. When you review all of the data, instead of just those parts that conform to your own theories, it becomes obvious that a careful plan is being followed by the entire phenomenon, and that it is closely patterned after the same techniques of psychological warfare that we ourselves employ. Again we must stress that the Phenomenon is reflective, and that a large part of it is a total hoax being foisted upon us.*

Now we are getting somewhere in discovering the true nature and underlying purposes of the hidden intelligences behind the UFOs. John Keel, out of all the UFO writers of the 1960s era, was the closest to the truth about the flying saucers that have been interacting with humanity for so long, and that is why I defer to his expertise as often as I do. The intelligences behind the UFOs today are likely the same intelligences that were around in the age of the dinosaurs. This luminous, shapeshifting phenomenon has always haunted our skies and molded our perceptions of the cosmos as time progressed, and likely exists outside our time frame. In this manner, contact has already been made a long time ago, they just won't completely materialize in our three-dimensional reality until we achieve the Singularity and are able to expand our intelligence beyond the way we currently experience space and time. Then we will know who our visitors really are. Keel also speculated about the differences in time perception between humans and ufonauts. He was troubled over the indications that the ufonauts do not have the best interest of human beings at heart in their endeavors, as evidenced by cases involving cattle and human mutilations, radiation burns, impaired memories, deceptive messages, UFO-related human disappearances, and human pilots who have died while chasing flying saucers. Keel wrote (chapter 20 of 25, *Searching for the String*):

> *All kinds of speculations are possible with UFOs. Judging from their general behavior, there is a possibility that, if they are real machines, they're hostile to us. They could be following a plan of hostility that might take 5000 of our years to complete, but would only be a moment to them. In the UFO cases, we find a number of instances of deliberate hostility on the part of the UFOs, which is worrisome. The US Air Force has now lost over 50 men in pursuit of these things. These are only the 50 that the Air Force admits to. We don't know how many others there were. We don't even know whether these plane crashes were accidental, or if the UFOs shot them down. All we do know is that there are definitely 50 men who have been killed by flying saucers, or because of flying saucers. We have their names.*

The Collapse of the Silver Bridge

Only two weeks after the Schirmer encounter and seven months after Stefan Michalak's dangerous encounter with a landed flying saucer at Falcon Lake that resulted in lifelong recurrences of radiation burn symptoms, 46 people died from a collapsed bridge in Virginia just after the return of Mothman. On December 15, 1967, the *Silver Bridge* that stretches from Point Pleasant, West Virginia (home of the Mothman sightings and very near Woodrow Derenberger's encounter with Indrid Cold) to Ohio collapsed, sending many to a watery grave. Hauntingly, just before the collapse of the Silver Bridge, Mothman was seen once again flying near the bridge. 44 bodies of the 46 people who died were found and retrieved, all of whom were buried in the same cemetery in Gallipolis, Ohio. Unfortunately, this would not be the last time flying saucers or cryptozoological creature sightings were recorded just prior to natural or man-made disasters.

Encounter in the Woods

In a remote location on the Indian Ocean, between Mauritius and Madagascar, on the Island of Reunion, there is a place on the island known as La Plaine des Cafres. It was here that 31-year-old M. Luce Fontaine experienced a landed UFO/occupant encounter on July 31, 1968, at 9 a.m. in the morning. Fontaine was a farmer, a family man with children who was married to a teacher. He was known as a hardworking, trustworthy individual. That morning, Fontaine was bending over to pick grass for his rabbits in the middle of a forest of acacia trees in a clearing when he looked up and saw what he described as an "oval-shaped cabin" at about 25 meters distance from him, hovering four or five meters from the ground. The outside perimeter of the egg-shaped object was dark blue, and the center was transparent. Coming off the object at the top and the bottom were two identical appendages that looked almost like glass, transparent metal he presumed, that took the shape of two wine glass stems and bottoms. He was able to see into the transparent center portion, and saw two 3-foot-tall humanoid creatures standing with their backs toward him. As the creature to his left turned around to face him, Fontaine could see that he was wearing a quilted sort of uniform reminiscent of the one piece coverall worn by the "Michelin Man." The creature on his right turned his face around, and was wearing a helmet that only exposed part of the creature's face. Fontaine then experienced an intense flash of light that engulfed him in whiteout for a moment, accompanied by a blast of heat and wind. When his vision cleared, the object and the strange creatures were gone. When Fontaine returned to his home, he told the fantastic story and was believed at once, as he was not someone who was prone to telling embellished or fictional stories. An investigation took place, and the investigators discovered elevated radiation levels at the location of the close encounter and also on Fontaine's clothing that he was wearing at the time. Fontaine showed physical symptoms of mild radiation poisoning in the days to come. A notable difference in Fontaine's encounter was that the brilliant flash of light that is so commonly reported by UFO percipients just before a visual experience was seen after he saw the UFO hovering above the ground for a while first with full conscious memory retention. Usually the flash of light comes first, and then the visuals. One might speculate that someone might have seen the brilliant flash of light first and then the craft earlier in the day, and that the Fontaine encounter was purely accidental and caught the ufonauts off-guard. Suddenly, realizing that they had an unintended human witness with them in the woods, they initiated the light flash. This flash of light is often described as similar in intensity to that of a welder's arc, a magnesium flare, or a photo flash bulb going off just before the UFOs materialize. It appears that the usual flash of light may be the point that the actual mindscan is done, just before an acceptable image is produced for percipients. In Fontaine's case, he saw the craft and occupants first, and then got the flash of light as the ufonauts dematerialized back into the portion of the electromagnetic spectrum that is invisible to humans.

Camp Encounters

On August 7, 1968, one month following the Fontaine sighting on Reunion Island in the Indian Ocean, the Buff Ledge Camp for Girls in the state of Vermont, USA, became the scene for a dual-witness UFO encounter. Two coworkers (names withheld) at the camp, looking into the western sky, witnessed a strange, white, cigar-shaped object in the air that released 3 smaller spheres, 2 of which danced around and sped off into the distance and vanished. The remaining sphere approached the two witnesses. As the sphere came closer to them, the sphere suddenly morphed into a transparent dome with a multi-colored rotating rim (no doubt an image of a flying saucer that was already present in the witnesses' minds). With a "vibratory hum," the "craft" approached close enough that witnesses, by now frozen in trance, observed small entities within the dome with tight-fitting uniforms, large heads, oval eyes, and small mouths. One of the coworkers was informed telepathically by the entities that they were from a distant planet and that they meant no harm. The saucer then moved overhead, bathing both experiencers in a green light beamed from underneath the craft. With this, they both lost consciousness. When they regained consciousness, it was dark. They both felt extremely tired and returned to their quarters and went to sleep. One remembered the details of the encounter, and the other only remembered lights. The two of them never discussed the experience after this. The camp closed, and they both went their separate ways. Then, 10 years later, the witness that remembered more detail than the other called Dr. J. Allen Hynek's Center for UFO Studies. The center took an interest in the case that could possibly present an account without witness contamination, as these two UFO witnesses had never spoken to one another about any of the details. Reunited after a decade, separate hypnosis sessions revealed remarkable similarity between the two accounts provided. The encounter involved the two of them, one male and one female, who were taken aboard a craft. The male witness was accompanied by an alien guide and watched as blood, skin samples, and vaginal fluids were extracted from the female percipient. A "tour" was provided (a common element in UFO abductions) after being beamed through a tube of light to a larger mothership prior to their return after dark onto the dock on which the abduction took place. UFO researcher Walter Webb administered extensive psychological testing to both experiencers and ruled out hoax or delusion. Webb provides a complete account and analysis of this event in his book, *Encounter at Buff Ledge: A UFO Case History*.

[On August 28, 1968, France detonated their first hydrogen bomb.]

The Bible and Flying Saucers

In this year of 1968, Presbyterian pastor Barry H. Downing wrote *The Bible and Flying Saucers*. Downing's book identifies many of the strange encounters recorded in the Bible as paranormal events associated with UFO phenomena. These biblical accounts serve to confirm the idea that the UFO phenomenon has been with us for a very long time and has had a major impact on the development of human thinking. In particular, the influence of UFOs has accelerated the development of our technology, contributed to human philosophical thinking, and inspired much of human religion. Downing discusses passages in the Bible that relate to UFOs, such as the abduction of Elijah into a "chariot of fire" witnessed by 50 priests (II Kings 2), along with other multiple-witness sightings in the New Testament, such as: the shepherds who witnessed the bright "glory of the Lord" at the birth of Christ (Luke2:9); the luminescent cloud during the transfiguration of Christ witnessed by Peter, James, and John, (Matt 17:1-8); the ascension of Jesus in a cloud (Acts 2:9); and the story of Paul's conversion on the road to Damascus (Acts1:1-9). In the case of Paul's conversion to Christianity, Paul experienced a classic UFO encounter complete with all the modern elements, such as the appearance of a light so bright it adversely affects the eyes. In Paul's case, this light resulted in three days of blindness, as opposed to the usual Klieg (Actinic) conjunctivitis, along with the experience of "cosmic illumination." The cosmic illumination experience is also discussed in Keel's writings regarding modern UFO sightings and their physical effects. As Keel pointed out, cosmic illumination by UFOs usually goes one of two ways. That is, the effects of the blinding light that comes with the experience sometimes creates a complete change in living paradigm. It may inspire the percipient to begin preaching the "message of the UFOs." They become UFO-evangelists. On the other hand, cosmic illumination can result in complete disintegration of the personality, a condition in which a person's life is utterly destroyed. They quit their jobs, divorce their spouse, and spiral downward to hit rock bottom, sometimes even committing suicide in the end. In either case, the cosmic illumination experience involves mind-manipulation on a grand scale by an unknown intelligence of a higher order than human. In the biblical case, Paul (a former murderer of Christians) became a devotee of Jesus following his UFO encounter. Paul continued to preach about Jesus for the rest of his natural life. As Pastor Downing states in his book:

> *Another theory is that UFOs started the Biblical religion, either as a kind of giant interplanetary hoax, or because UFOs are in fact a divine reality. This latter view would see UFOs as carrying the angels of God in the past to start the biblical religion and, as still being seen today, shepherds watching over their sheep.*

If Pastor Downing was correct in this, a disturbing possibility presents itself. That is, all human religion and so-called enlightenment experiences that result in cosmic illumination are but a cruel deception perpetrated by the occulted intelligences behind the flying saucers. If this really is the case, humans have been manipulated in a terrible fashion, and all human religious aspirations are for naught, as the change in behaviors that religion creates only serves the long-range purposes of the Overlords. Furthermore, our ultimate fate and survival as a species is in question. On the other hand, if, in the midst of all this deception, there have been legitimate attempts by benevolent entities like Jesus who have voluntarily incarnated on Earth to save us from the Contraries described by the AKRIJ, then maybe there is hope. These Contraries, described by the AKRIJ as a race of biological robots who worship technology and do not share human morality, may represent the same entities that the Bible refers to as "Satan and his demons," or Muslims refer to as the "Shaitan Djinn." If this is the case, Jesus is a savior in the sense that he directed humanity toward the path of escaping this electromagnetic prison, this vast computational system that we are all embedded within as unwitting slaves of an unknown master for the benefit of certain interdimensional races, not for any benefit to humankind. In this scenario, humans are just being used as cattle to produce a product for the Contraries – a technological singularity. If this is true, then the saying, "Jesus saves," takes on new meaning.

Jesus, a benevolent master of reality, is in possession of this universe's "save" command, just as the save command on our own computer screens saves files for permanent use, unlike other computer files that are deleted. It would appear that we are all embedded (possibly against our wills) within an intentionally-created holographic computer matrix as conscious computational mechanisms within a vast cosmic computer.

The Rand Document

On November 27, 1968, as the Condon Report was being formulated in Colorado, the Rand Corporation put out an internal company document written by George Kocher called *UFOs: What to Do?* - The front-page document has "FOR RAND USE ONLY" stamped at the bottom, along with a warning for employees, "DO NOT QUOTE OR CITE IN EXTERNAL RAND PUBLICATIONS OR CORRESPONDENCE." The relevance of this internal document has been disputed by some UFO researchers like Jan Aldrich, who points out that the author, George Kocher, who simply worked at Rand, was personally interested in UFOs. According to Aldrich, Kocher compiled his own paper and gave it to fellow employees. This criticism has been countered by the fact that the cover page clearly has official file #18154-PR and the official company logo stamp on it. In this internal document, Kocher outlines a brief history of the UFO phenomenon, including the events at Nuremberg, Germany and Basel, Switzerland, along with details of the UFO event at Fatima in 1917. The publication mentions the work of notable researchers such as Dr. J. Allen Hyek and atmospheric physicist James McDonald. The Rand document also expresses anticipation and optimism for the pending Condon Report (one can only imagine how disappointing the Condon Report was to Mr. Kocher and interested parties when it was released the following year). Kocher covers the thinking of the times concerning the likelihood of intelligent life elsewhere in our local Milky Way Galaxy and elsewhere in the universe. The document examines the relative frequency of reports of various types of UFOs. Disk sightings lead the pack, followed by spherical objects, oval/elliptical, cylindrical or cigar-shaped, and triangular-shaped crafts. Colors of daytime disks are also listed. Silver/metallic is the most prevalent, followed by white, specular, black, and gray. Colors for luminous nighttime sightings start with red, then yellow, orange, blue, and end with the color green as the least reported nocturnal luminosity. The motion or "oscillation" of both daytime disks and nocturnal luminosities are described as fluttering, flipping, tipping, or slowly descending with a "pendulum motion." The pendulum motion has been captured on film on numerous occasions throughout the last several decades, leading many viewers to suspect that a flying saucer model was suspended on a line to produce the images and motion. However, this same motion is observed in several UFO cases that have been authenticated by modern technical film analysis. Other motions include side-to-side oscillations and the classic "falling leaf" motion that so many visual sightings report. Kocher also points out that many sightings are verified by radar and display motions that are non-attributable to any known modern aircraft. These motions are often described as bobbing; erratic; jerky; zig-zag; and/or high-angular acceleration and velocity. The Rand document cites UFO researcher James McDonald in exploring several possible explanations for documented UFO reports, including hoaxes; fabrications; fraud; hallucinations; mass hysteria and rumor phenomena; misinterpretation of well-known natural phenomena; poorly understood physical phenomena (like rare electrical or meteorological effects and/or plasmas); advanced secret terrestrial technologies; poorly-understood psychic phenomena; extraterrestrial probes; messengers of salvation and occult truth; and simply; "other." Kocher states his opinion that, no matter what the actual explanation for UFOs turns out to be, the answer will be of interest to a number of different types of people, including psychologists, theologians, and scientists. The Rand document wraps up with Kocher's practical suggestions of "what to do" as reflected in the title of the work, including the establishment of a central reporting agency for UFO sightings, encouragement for individuals and newspapers to report sightings, and careful documentation of the details of sightings for proper longitudinal data analysis. The end of the document displays several pages of a sample UFO report form that Kocher suggests. Kocher wanted to place these forms at easily accessible public locations, such as post offices and stores. The Rand Document is overall an interesting and concise "assessment of the current situation" of this period in time regarding UFOs, and clearly gives the impression that 1968 was presenting an abundance of good UFO sightings which were of interest to many. The Rand Document attempts to verify the reality of the UFO phenomenon, as well as offer a practical way to create information gathering. A copy of the Rand document made its way to Wright-Patterson AFB, and was clearly considered by top military officials there as a way to "take the temperature" of how the public was perceiving the UFO phenomenon at the time. Despite the interest and anticipation expressed by George Kocher and this internal document that circulated within the Rand Corporation in 1968, the disappointing, frustrating, and even infuriating results of the Condon Report shot an arrow into the heart of public UFO interest. As we all know now, the Condon Report was gerrymandered by physicist and avowed UFO skeptic, Edward U. Condon, whose name was destined to go down in UFO infamy. The 1969 Condon Report, a 1200-page document which basically stated once and for all that UFOs are fiction, a modern myth in the making undeserving of scientific investigation, gave the USAF exactly the excuse it was looking for to shut down their public debunking effort called Project Blue Book. The USAF, in effect, paid the University of Colorado five hundred thousand dollars to justify closing Project Blue Book and cease their obligation to chase after any and every civilian UFO report, which they considered (and rightly so) a waste of time and resources. The shutdown of Project Blue Book allowed the USAF to continue their own UFO investigations on their own terms, which is to say, completely covert and removed from public scrutiny or analysis for all time and eternity.

Sergeant Clifford Stone and Project Moon Dust

Ironically, in 1969, the very same year that the Condon Report was released to the public with its "official" findings - that UFOs were nonsense and unworthy of scientific study, also the same year that Project Blue Book was shut down using the Condon Report to justify their decision, clandestine UFO research here in the US and around the world was in full operation. Not only were secret UFO research efforts going on at the time of the release of the Condon Report, these clandestine military groups were after the big game - aliens, alive or dead, and more importantly, *alien hardware*. In 1969 a young man in the US Army, Sergeant Clifford Stone, was participating beyond public knowledge or scrutiny within a covert military crash-and-retrieval program known as "Project Moon Dust." According to Stone's own testimony, he was called by his superiors in 1969 to his first UFO crash scenario, a shocking event that included live alien crash victims. At the time of this writing, Clifford Stone, a man with an interesting personal history with the paranormal, is revealing to the world his experiences with Project Moon Dust. In an interview with Ed Komarek in 2012, Clifford Stone revealed that he had always been fascinated with lizards as a child. At an early age, Stone states that he had interactions with "imaginary friends" who were invisible to others, as many children do. Stone continued to have encounters with the paranormal throughout his entire life. Most of his imaginary childhood friends appeared to him as normal-looking children. However, one of his friends, "Korona," eventually revealed his true appearance as what one could only refer to as a "Gray alien," only Korona had greenish, lizard-like skin. Stone states that the alien creatures he has been familiar with his entire life follow particular humans throughout their lives. According to Stone, this is an attempt on their part to "understand human emotions." Korona revealed to Stone that he and his kind were from a galaxy 100 light years away from Earth in another dimension. During one of his many conversations with Korona, he asked Korona what the biggest difference was between humans and monkeys. Korona gestured to Stone that it was the opposable thumb that made the huge difference in human evolution and *allowed the creation of technology*. Stone states that, according to information provided to him by Korona, we are not just dealing with one universe, our own, but a true "Multiverse," in which many different parallel worlds coexist and share space together. Stone stated that, from time to time, humans can inadvertently encounter beings from other timelines and alternate dimensions. Stone states that Korona is not from our own 3-dimensional reality. Korona and many other species are able to manipulate space-time and/or travel vast distances in space and time using what we would refer to as a traversable wormhole. Korona once told Stone that, using the traversable wormhole technique, his race can come from their star system that is 100 light years away from Earth in a parallel dimension in about one hour and forty minutes by our method of measuring time. Korona's lifespan is said to be about 300 of our Earth years. One bit of information that Korona shared with Stone concerns the mechanics of abductions. According to Korona, during what we call an "alien abduction," it may seem to the percipient as if the abduction experience took hours, days, weeks, or months, when only a small segment of time, if any, has passed in our reality. This provides insight into reports of "missing time" during so-called alien abduction episodes. Stone also revealed that unless a human is placed in an altered state of consciousness, the trauma of having such an abrupt change in one's perception of reality can actually cause the death of the abductee. Since his discharge from the Army, Stone has become a real pioneer in the use of the Freedom of Information Act (FOIA). Stone has researched thousands of formerly-classified documents concerning UFOs, some of which are presented in his book, *UFOs Are Real.* Stone has also delved into many other types of government documentation and has concluded from his own extensive research that the United States, as of 2012, has all the technology in its possession to colonize both the moon and the planet Mars. Over the course of Stone's career in the military, Stone states that he encountered seven different species of non-terrestrial entities. While stationed at Indian Town Gap, Pennsylvania in 1969, Stone personally observed dead bodies of Gray aliens. Stone proceeded from there to participate in several missions involving crashed flying saucers and/or alien bodies. During these exotic events, Stone states that there was always three non-uniformed officers at the retrieval sites, only one of whom was human. The human, who was the main authority figure at the crash sites, was simply referred to as "The Colonel." According to Stone, other officers in attendance were sometimes non-terrestrial officers from other planets and, on occasion, *mechanical/biological hybrid robots attended the crash sites* with Project Moon Dust as well. At the time of this writing, Clifford Stone remains as one of the most intriguing personalities in ufology. In his unusual testimony, Stone reveals to the world his involvement with early clandestine UFO crash-and-retrieval efforts, most of which focused on the acquisition of alien technology. According to Stone, these efforts paid off, and what we currently have in our possession regarding black-budget, antigravitic vehicles and advanced electronic technology is totally beyond the public's knowledge and comprehension.

The Channeling of Bashar

The idea that alien creatures from other galaxies and/or alternate universes within Eternisphere have traveled all this way through time and space just to study and interact with humans is a fascinating one. Such aliens would likely operate outside our timeline in their own invisible world. This is a good thing, because if I were such a creature, I would not want to follow a human around for every mundane task in their life, such as brushing their teeth or taking a bath in the morning. What do these alien creatures do with themselves when they are not popping into our reality to interact with us? For the possible answer to this question and others, it might be useful to consider the work of another person who is also allegedly in touch with a nonhuman entity, and that man is Darryl Anka. Darryl Anka channels a being from the future named *Bashar.* In trance, Anka, while channeling Bashar, reveals his version of the true nature and origin of the Grays. After a short period of meditation and silence, Anka's facial expression, voice inflection, and persona radically change while he fields questions from his audiences that

Anka answers as Bashar. Anka states that he does not remember these interactions while he is in trance, and has to watch the taped sessions of himself afterward in order to understand what actually transpired. Bashar answers all sorts of questions in a surprisingly effective manner, revealing the interdimensional nature of reality to all who are interested. Bashar has revealed to audiences (while Anka is in trance) that the beings known as the Grays actually "tunneled" their way here into our reality from another dimension. Interestingly, Bashar also disclosed that when we humans detonate a nuclear device, the damage from the explosions can cause unfortunate interdimensional travelers to become stranded here in our reality. Some of these shipwrecked interdimensional travelers are now unable to return home due to the destruction of the space-time portals that they used to come here. If this is true, and we now have interdimensional beings who cannot escape our reality, these populations may now have an interest in certain interdimensional technologies that have yet to be invented by humans as we approach the Singularity. It follows that these trapped entities would also exercise as much influence as they can to guide humanity into high technology for their own benefit, so that they can finally escape from our dimension and go home. Currently, the engineers at the particle accelerator at CERN are working diligently to discover such portals of entry into other dimensions. Some currently believe that those in charge of CERN have already been contacted by such trapped entities and are attempting to help them go home, thus all the scuttlebutt on the internet of CERN attempting to open portals to other dimensions, or allow entities from other realms to enter our domain. This, of course, disturbs fundamentalist Christians, such as author Thomas Horn, who fear that we are now headed into the direction of using the Large Hadron Collider that operates beneath the France-Switzerland border near Geneva, Switzerland, to foolishly open a *direct portal to hell*. Are these efforts at CERN guided by invisible interdimensional travelers who are attempting to return to their own world? Were these beings who became trapped here attempting to follow early human experiments with nuclear detonations? Did we inadvertently threaten the entire Superspectrum with our foolishness? In interviews conducted out-of-trance, Anka presents as a composed and intelligent individual who is just as intrigued with his channeling abilities as we are. Anka states that he is open to the idea that Bashar may not actually be who he says he is, that Bashar might be an aspect of his own human personality that our psychologists are currently unfamiliar with. In other words, the being known as Bashar might actually be *an aspect of Darryl Anka's own mind and being*. As Dr. Steven Greer with the Disclosure Project likes to state, "The number of minds in the universe is one." If this is correct, and the Hermetic teachings are right in stating that the *universe is mental in nature*, and considering that modern physics discovered *quantum entanglement* in which everything that was originally united as one in the Big Bang continues to remain connected, even though the expansion of space-time has created the illusion of separation, we may soon discover that all intelligences in the universe are simply different facets of one and the same being. If so, this could be confirmed when we augment and expand our intelligence by a factor of billions when the Singularity is achieved. As per Hermetic teachings, "Even though we exist in the All, and the All exists within us, we are not the All, and the All is not us, yet we are simultaneously one and the same." Do some of the contactees represent human cases of quantum entanglement, or examples of bilocation in parallel worlds, wherein an alien from another galaxy and dimension is, at the same time, a human living out a life here on Earth? As Darryl Anka speculates himself, Bashar might be an integral aspect of his own mind, and is also a being from the future simultaneously. I know that, during my own NDE in 2009, I drew very close to loved ones who I knew here on Earth, very familiar spirits, as well as encountering my own self in a transcended state beyond this reality, including an electronic aspect. I felt at the time that, if I chose to, I could allow myself to "die" from the heart attack I was having, and reunite with my own self as an immortal light being on the other side of the veil that separates our temporary existence here on Earth from what we really are in Eternisphere. We all exist in an immortal state of transcendence on the other side of this life, and dwell safely within the mind of the All. Darryl Anka is certainly telling the truth as he knows it, as is the case with the majority of contactees. However, we are clearly dealing with a fascinating, real phenomenon that involves aspects of and interconnections with both human and alien minds (that may be one and the same) that we simply do not understand properly yet.

Carl Jung

As Sergeant Clifford Stone was busy participating in crash and retrieval programs with Project Moon Dust in 1969, psychologist Carl Jung was attempting to contribute his psychological insights into human attempts to grapple with our understanding of the UFO phenomenon. In *Flying Saucers: A Modern Myth of Things Seen in the Skies,* Jung sees flying saucers as psychic projections created within the collective human unconscious. The one factor that many overlook concerning Jung's insightful speculations is that the projections of flying saucers that are created by the collective unconscious may have been initially activated by an objectively real event. If Jung is correct, and the collective human unconscious has the ability to produce actual imagery that is experienced by individuals and sometimes entire groups of people, that is worthy of study in and of itself, even if there is no objective reality to flying saucers. As in the case of a person traumatized by something completely unfamiliar, and then having nightmares or hallucinations over it, Jung proposed that the UFO "myth" may be a manifestation of something real that caused the human species to experience an initial trauma. If, for example, an actual extraterrestrial spaceship was seen by a group of human witnesses, the trauma from this real event may initiate a new system of thinking or create a body of embellished mythology that exists side-by-side with the real but ultimately unknowable event. As Jung put it, "an objectively real physical process forms the basis for an accompanying myth." In other words, the "channeling" phenomenon, in which a human believes they are in telepathic contact with aliens, and the contactee accounts, much of which contain absurd elements that are clearly impossible and descriptions of fantastic visits to places that probably do not exist, along with predictions that often do not come true, exists as an accompanying myth to actual sightings of real flying saucers that humans have actually witnessed. In this respect, the lines that normally determine fact from fantasy become blurred. Fact and fantasy are now both exerting a very real impact on the development of the culture at large and the conditioning of the human mind. Hardcore UFO skeptics are just as influenced by the flying saucers and their accompanying myth as the true believers that start UFO-oriented religious cults. Even though Carl Jung's thoughts in his book on the subject are misinterpreted by many readers to mean that flying saucers are purely illusory, Jung may have actually discovered true insight into the nature of the Phenomenon. There is no doubt that objects from elsewhere have frequented the skies of Earth for millennia. The advanced intelligences that are behind the flying saucers have the unnerving ability to actually connect with and permeate the human collective unconscious. In so doing, they are able to glean imagery from the human mind in various states of development and produce objects in the sky as powerful tools of human manipulation that serve to guide us toward the Singularity. The images are custom-designed to serve two purposes - first, to produce either an apparition or transmogrified physical object in the sky that is palatable and understandable to the human mind, and second, to inspire human behavior toward the actual agenda of the alien intelligences. These higher, interdimensional intelligences that the human psyche has always been in synchronicity with, intelligences that are currently interpreted as "extraterrestrial visitation," whether that is the correct interpretation or not, are attempting to contact humanity from their own time frame, which is different from our own and may take millennia by our clocks. According to Jung, the second stage of the UFO myth is an archetype that the collective human unconscious will accept. In our case, it is the mandala-like image of the flying saucer. The final stage, according to Jung, is the correlation of the objective event and the accompanying myth in a way that establishes causation. In this manner, all of humanity are now UFO contactees. We as human contactees are well into Jung's final stage now. At this point there is no way to completely separate the objective UFO events from the UFO mythology that has developed within our species, and there is no escape for UFO believers and UFO skeptics alike. A powerful influence has already been exerted that affects us all regarding the changes that have come about within the human psyche as a direct result of our belief or skepticism regarding flying saucers and visitations from elsewhere. In a very real sense, the alien visitation in question is actually occurring from inner space, and has resulted thus far in an unfolding lotus flower of collective awakening and cultural transformation.

UFO Witnesses Break Silence

Many other UFO-related events occurred in the 1960s. Each year of the decade brought UFO events that could fill an entire book. One such event was revealed in the official Disclosure testimony of Mr. Dan Willis. Willis was in the US Navy in 1969. Willis held a Top Secret

Cypto-Level 14 Extra-Sensitive Material-Handling Security Clearance. Willis was working in the code room at the Naval Communications Station in San Francisco when he received a priority message classified as secret from a ship near Alaska. The ship reported that a brightly-glowing, reddish-orange elliptical object had just emerged from the ocean that shot into space traveling at approximately 7000 mph. Likewise, in April, 1969, dozens of Finland Air Force pilots participating in a training mission watched from their cockpits as 7 round objects flew in formation at high speed within visual range. Pilot Tarmo Tukeva was assigned to chasing and identifying the crafts. As he flew at 700km/hr toward the objects, they responded by accelerating and speeding away from him faster than his jet was able to fly, and vanished from sight.

Antonio da Silva

One UFO event significant to our discussion here occurred on the afternoon of May 4, 1969, the same year Sergeant Clifford Stone was working for Project Moon Dust in official military UFO crash-and-retrieval operations. On this day, 24-year-old Jose Antonio da Silva, an enlisted soldier in Bebedouro, Minas Gerais, Brazil, was standing on the bank of a lagoon fishing when he suddenly heard voices and detected figures moving behind him. Feeling a burst of light on the back of his legs, he dropped his fishing pole and dropped to his knees. As he was frozen on his knees, two 4-foot-tall beings in shiny metallic suits and helmets drug him and his fishing equipment to their upright cylindrical craft. As he was taken inside the cylinder, one of the beings fit da Silva with a helmet like the one they were wearing. Da Silva felt the ship begin to levitate as the beings communicated energetically among themselves in an unrecognizable language. After a long flight, da Silva felt the craft land with a jolt. He was then blindfolded and taken to a large room where the blindfold was removed. A taller humanoid with wavy red hair down to his waist stood in front of him now. When the others removed their helmets, da Silva observed that they were of similar appearance only shorter. About a dozen similar beings approached, and they all began looking him over and examining his fishing equipment, taking some of his items. Da Silva then noticed a shelf low to the ground on which were lying four human males. One of them was a black man. With this, da Silva became visibly frightened. The beings then gave him a green liquid to drink from a square cubical glass. When da Silva calmed down from the green liquid, the leader of these alien dwarves began communicating to da Silva in drawings and gestures, mostly about human weaponry. Somewhere in the communication, da Silva received the impression that these beings wanted assistance from him concerning their relationships with human beings. When he refused, the leader snatched the crucifix from his rosary. Da Silva began praying out of fear, and reported that a Christ-like figure appeared to him. Da Silva was once again blindfolded, and the craft took off. After the return journey, he felt that he was being dragged and lost consciousness. Da Silva woke up dehydrated and severely hungry about 200 miles from where he had been fishing in a town called Vitoria. He drank water to quench his thirst from a nearby stream, and began fishing to try and catch a meal, as he still had his fishing equipment with him. He discovered that it was 4 ½ days later. He had lacerations from the helmet on his neck, and a sore knee where the original flash of light had struck him with a paralyzing ray.

Da Silva's reported experience appears to involve dreamlike symbolism. As a soldier, it is significant to note that the communication between da Silva and his alien abductors involved human weaponry. Also, the blindfolding and experience of being dragged on the ground could represent fears of becoming a prisoner of war. The bodies on the shelf may have represented a reflection of the horrors of death and war. If da Silva's experience was an isolated case, one could write it off as some sort of hallucination or seizure activity in the brain. However, reports like his are too numerous to ignore. They are ubiquitous across the globe, and feature correlations indicating that this type of UFO-related experience is an entirely different phenomenon than a simple hallucination. Da Silva, along with thousands of others, possibly millions, appear to have been victims of some advanced form of intentionally-induced hypnotic state that contains dreamlike elements conjured from the mechanics of their own mentality. Not only have the occulted intelligences behind the UFOs managed to effectively glean imagery from the human mind, originating from both individuals and the "collective unconscious," they also have the capability of creating individualized experiences based on that person's conceptual framework. These experiences produce dreamlike imagery that is sometimes obviously connected with what is going on in their life at the time, and sometimes rather absurd, just as dreams are absurd. In my own case, I once had a dream that I was hanged by the neck until dead. I woke up in a sweat and frightened. Making my way to the bathroom mirror, I discovered a painful red mark around my neck. If natural dreams can produce experiences that seem very real to a person prior to waking, and are able to produce physical symptoms such as red whelps and pain, one can only imagine the capabilities of an advanced paraphysical technology operated by some sort of alien intelligence. This alien technology snatches imagery from a person's mind that determines how the aliens appear to that witness. Individualized features are induced that are gathered from their own memories, thoughts, and experiences. It would seem that UFO encounters such as da Silva's involve intentionally-induced experiences that seem as real as ordinary life, virtual reality complete with real fear, pain, and physical symptoms. Sometimes these technologically or purely mentally-induced experiences leave human percipients with full retention of memory. Other times they leave either partial memory, or no memory whatsoever for purposes known only by the alien intelligences. Some UFO abduction experiences produce memories that are retrieved at a later date, either in fragments through vivid dreams or nightmares, or by hypnosis.

MUFON

On January 6. 1969, former President Jimmy Carter witnessed a UFO in Leary, Georgia during a speech. Carter submitted his official report four years later by request of the International

UFO Bureau in Oklahoma City, Oklahoma. The object that Carter witnessed with a dozen other people that day was described as a self-luminous object that shifted from white to blue, then red, then white again. It remained in view for 10-12 minutes before rapidly disappearing. Of course, skeptics scoff and say Jimmy Carter misidentified the planet Venus. However, Carter has always maintained that Venus does not change colors like the object he witnessed did, and accepts the possibility that what he witnessed may have been otherworldly in nature. Later that year, on May 31, 1969, the Midwest UFO Network, later named the Mutual UFO Network (MUFON) was founded. Each state throughout the USA has its own director. The states are then divided into counties, and the state Director looks over the work of the state's field investigators. The purpose of MUFON, which has grown international in scope and activity, is to scientifically resolve the UFO mystery. The goal of MUFON in 1969, as well as presently, is to discover whether the UFO mystery involves some sort of physical craft with or without actual occupants, or psychological phenomena that are currently unacknowledged and misunderstood my modern science. MUFON also wants to discover whether flying saucers are interplanetary or interdimensional in nature. If the craft turn out to represent interplanetary or interdimensional vehicles, MUFON seeks to understand their methods of travel, i.e., how the craft get from wherever they come from to here in our reality. Lastly, if the flying saucers turn out to be piloted by biological life from another realm, what can we learn from them?

PK Man

Within 6 months after the founding of MUFON, Apollo 12 with Lunar Lander *Intrepid* settled onto the surface of the moon in the Ocean of Storms with Charles Pete Conrad and Alan Bean on November 19, 1969. This mission, thanks to a man named Ted Owens (1920-1987), a contactee with scientifically-verified psychokinetic powers, nearly ended in tragedy when the moon rocket launched on November 14. 36.5 seconds after lift-off, as predicted and allegedly brought about by Ted Owens with the aid of invisible "Space Intelligences," Apollo 12 was struck by lightning. This lightning strike triggered a spectacular luminous discharge from the Saturn rocket's ionized plume straight down to the surface of the earth. Ted Owens, who had predicted the event ahead of time and claimed to have actually made it happen with help from his ET friends, experienced multiple head injuries in his youth that he believed were intentionally-induced in order to establish two-way communication between himself and higher-order Space Intelligences, which Owens abbreviated as "SIs." The mission of the SIs, according to Owens, was to work with him in bringing about huge publicly-predicted events in order to simply prove their existence to humankind. Owens believed at first that his psychokinetic powers came directly from Mother Nature, that somehow he had connected with the forces that control weather events and such. However, Owens eventually realized that he was actually in mental contact with higher-order intelligent beings of *pure energy*. He felt that he was the first person to possess this divine gift since the biblical contactee Moses. Many researchers have investigated the case of Ted Owens over the years, and have been forced by the evidence to attest to his ability to predict and/or control natural weather events by some sort of non-understood psychokinetic ability. A small sample of his 200+ verifiable predictions that came true are outlined in science-writer Otto Binder's *Liquidation of the UFO investigators: The Truth Behind the Flying Saucers' Mission to Earth*. In this book, Binder listed a few of Ted's verifiable predictions that shockingly came true. They include (audible, chapter 6):

> *The big blackout of the Eastern US on November 9, 1965; Hurricane Inez in 1966 which turned the wrong way; three hurricanes simultaneously hitting the US in 1967; the ending of the Northeast's drought in 1967; the mysterious "hex" that made the Philidelphia Eagles football team lose 12/14 games in 1968; and the lightning bolt that struck Apollo 12 in 1969. These and other headline events are claimed as "PK" or psychokinesis feats performed by one man, Ted Owens, with the aid of the SIs [Space Intelligences].*

Ted Owens also demonstrated his ability to predict appearances of UFOs in the skies. The book, *The PK Man: A True Story of Mind over Matter*, includes a foreward written by renowned alien-abduction researcher, Dr. John Mack. The book's author, Dr. Jeffrey Mishlove, Ph.D., a parapsychologist, examined the extraordinary psychokinetic abilities of Ted Owens. Otto Binder, in addition to discussing Ted Owens in his book, wrote an article on the Ted Owens case for *SAGA* magazine in 1970. Ted Owens remains one of the most enigmatic contactees of the century, and one of the best cases of documented and verified psychokinetic abilities. A book written by Ted Owens, *How to Contact Space People*, was reprinted in 2008 by Global Communications, and was a best-seller in his day. The psychokinetic abilities of Ted Owens remains a stupefying mystery.

God Drives a Flying Saucer

Another interesting book that appeared in 1969, *God Drives a Flying Saucer*, examined the connection between religion and space technology. The book was written by a Connecticut school teacher, R.L. Dione. Dione agreed with the Reverend Billy Graham in that at least some of the ufonauts who occupy flying saucers are actually angels of God. According to Dione, the angels who pilot flying saucers are responsible for the "divine inspiration" behind biblical prophecy and Scripture. These ufonaut angels are also the underlying force behind the miracles of the Bible. In Dione's view, Jesus Christ utilized energy beams from extraterrestrial spacecraft to perform miracles, just as Ted Owens (PK Man) utilized "Space Intelligences" to manipulate weather events or cause lightning strikes, electrical blackouts, and UFO appearances. Early books such as Dione's foreshadowed the massive elevation of human consciousness that was to occur in decades to come, much of which correctly made the connection between flying saucers and human religion.

Operation Trojan Horse

In the midst of a wave of UFO-related material that portrayed the hidden Space Intelligences behind the UFO mystery as advanced ETs who are here to save us from ourselves, written by authors who religiously-ascribed to the Extraterrestrial Hypothesis (ETH), a big wet blanket was thrown over ufology by the great Fortean author who, in my opinion, was second only to Charles Fort – John Keel. By 1970, after several dedicated years of UFO research, Keel wrote his UFO masterpiece, *Operation Trojan Horse,* a book destined to become a classic among adherants to the Interdimensional Theory of flying saucers and their occupants. As in Dr. Jacques Vallee's *Messengers of Deception*, Keel's research lead him to conclude that UFOs have been with us forever, are possibly indigenous to Earth, and represent something entirely different than spacecraft from far-off planets. In his scientific research, Keel discovered that there are certain areas of the world in which UFOs appear repeatedly. Keel referred to these areas of the world as "window areas." Keel also ran impressive statistical analysis on UFO sighting reports and discovered that UFOs are more likely to be seen on Wednesdays and Saturdays, likely between 10-12 p.m.. Keel was baffled by his own data, and pondered why this would be the case. He even wondered if the flying saucer occupants were using our calendar! Keel concluded that flying saucers and their occupants are cosmic tricksters that are deceiving humankind into thinking they are extraterrestrial visitors when they are something else entirely that we have yet to discover. Keel's research lead him to believe that something afoul is afoot, that the underlying intelligences behind the UFOs actually loathe humanity. The Phenomenon leads us into blind alleys, delivers false prophecy, for some end game that eluded him. Keel also warned against dabbling in the occult or Black Magic. His observations were that those who experiment with such things usually come to a bad end. He warns that UFO research has led many to paranoia, the brink of insanity, or even suicide, and warned parents to keep their kids away from both ufology and the occult. In the vast sea of Cryptoreality that exists all around us, the keepers of the hidden realms make their appearances in our world, day after day, year after year, century after century. They continually mold our perceptions and behaviors in unfathomable ways that are the stuff of science fiction. Despite the absurdities, there is an unmistakeable reality underneath it all that is sure to shock us to our very core when the truth is finally revealed to us in its entirety.

Chapter 10

Invisible Dimensions

"What we term 'reality' is really a 'frequency domain,' an exchange of energy operating
more closely to 'correspondence or resonance' as described by researchers on the holographic
properties of perception and consciousness. Reality, for each person, is at best a translation
of vibrations or resonance to which we respond. Our brain tries to holographically connect
to resonant frequencies that are being projected from another dimension. In the principle of
synchronicity these frequencies would in fact be projections from other levels (mind waves)
beyond our scope of space and time."

— Nahu, from *UFOs: GOD from Inner Space.*

Nurse Kendall

On January 5, 1970, Mrs. Doreen Kendall, a Canadian nurse, opened the curtains of a hospital window and witnessed a spherical object approximately 50 feet in diameter and hovering about 60 feet off the ground with lights around the perimeter. Inside the vehicle she saw two humanoid entities standing in front of what appeared to be an instrument panel of glowing circles of various sizes. One of the ufonauts, clutching a rod-like device with a ball on top that Doreen described as a "joystick," tilted the vehicle, allowing her a good look inside the well-lit, high-tech interior. Both occupants wore black suits and helmets that looked like they were made of the same material. As the object began to move away, Doreen realized that she had been standing there completely entranced by the sighting. She was suddenly disturbed by the idea that, unless someone else saw the flying saucer and occupants with her, no one would ever believe her. Doreen shouted out to a fellow nurse, Nurse Wilson, who came over and became startled by what they were now both looking at. The two nurses dashed to the nurse's station and reported what they had just witnessed. As they were telling their story, several other coworkers went over to the windows to get a look. They all saw the same craft as it was headed into the distance and reported that the craft finally streaked across the sky at astonishing speed and simply vanished. This multiple-witness sighting is just one of thousands that have happened upon unsuspecting human witnesses over the last several decades, confirming the existence of something in our skies that shares our reality from time to time. These objects that we have collectively decided to call "flying saucers" appear to operate with technologies far in advance of our own that carry humanoid ufonauts. If, one the other hand, these objects and creatures are not as they appear, they may represent foreign intelligences from an invisible realm who are able to induce paranormal encounters by purely mental means or by using advanced holographic technologies that produce believable 3-dimensional images. These images appear to us as physical objects that exist for a while and then suddenly dematerialize. These material objects or apparitions (or a combination of both) are routinely presented to single or multiple witnesses here on Earth in order to either selectively expose humans to otherworldly intelligence, or to mold human perceptions in the direction that these unknown intelligences wish for us. It is a real phenomenon that involves something other than simple hallucinosis or a delusion of the human mind, the nature of which currently lies beyond the scope of our science to properly ascertain. This divides the world into not just two but three camps: 1) those who refuse to accept the reality of flying saucers and their occupants until the Phenomenon (if it exists at all) becomes positively ascertainable to our science in a way we can all understand together, 2) those who accept that the Phenomenon is real but currently non-understandable and stay abreast with current sightings and theories of explanation, and 3) those who feel that they have had some type of direct experience with the Phenomenon which has provided some level of insight into the true nature of what we are dealing with. I would fall into category number 3. This entire book will surely be seen by many as one man's fanciful speculations that have no basis in fact, and that is fine. However, the changes in my own perception of reality following my NDE has led me to accept the interdimensional nature of reality. I cannot help but think that my newfound obsession with the flying saucer mystery that followed my near death experience (NDE) in 2009 has led me at least one step closer to the truth about Cryptoreality. If, on the other hand, my NDE produced only delusion, and has pushed me one step closer to madness following a close brush with death and the accompanying mental changes that such an experience brings, then I take comfort in the fact that I am not alone. Like the late Carl Sagan once stated, there is real psychological paydirt in the UFO phenomenon, even if it is entirely delusional. According to Sagan, the Phenomenon should be of great interest to psychologists and other scientists who study the mechanics of the human mind.

ETs and Secret Societies

1970 brought *Extraterrestrial Visitations from Prehistoric Times to the Present* by author Jacques Bergier. This book displayed early insight into ideas that I believe are basically true. That is, an extraterrestrial intelligence was responsible for the dinosaur extinction 65 million years ago so that humans could develop with an appropriate fuel source to effectively achieve the end goals of the ETs. Bergier states that *beings of light* have been providing secret interplanetary information to select humans who operate within secret societies, such as the Rosicrucians and the Freemasons. There is little doubt now that the extraterrestrial intelligences that seized control of Earth long ago, likely operating from another dimension, have been working with various human groups throughout the ages, revealing information to select humans who are used as instruments to advance the alien agenda. These beings of light have continually played on human narcissism and greed, holding out promises of esoteric knowledge, power, and immortality, when it is actually the ETs themselves who seek a permanent presence and dominion in our three-dimensional realm. To this end they have been working for a very long time by our clocks, which surely measure time differently than theirs. At the time of this writing, our best calculations indicate that we only have about 30 years left of fossil fuels in the ground. These fuels are a primitive energy source from the age of the dinosaurs, an energy source that was cleverly geoengineered by the Overlords to achieve their end goals. By "coincidence," the 30 years of fossil fuels that we have remaining is just enough to propel humanity into the Singularity around 2045. At that point, fossil fuels, along with the disposable tools that the ETs have been using to achieve the Singularity (humans), will become obsolete. Let's hope that we have ET friends out there somewhere that can save us from our inevitable fate. Perhaps we do have an ET friend in the person this world knows as Jesus. Jesus may, in fact, be our portal to a completely different universe, one that is not physical and based on predation as this one is. Did he not say that his Kingdom was "not of this world"? As Savior to Humanity, perhaps Jesus, a human/ET hybrid by definition, will extract the souls who follow his instructions to love our neighbors as ourselves from this physical universe altogether during or following the Singularity, the time when the earth is taken over by a foreign intelligence that seeks technology at the expense of humanity, an intelligence that travels from world to world like a locust, devouring knowledge and dominion within the physical realm wherever it goes. Or, perhaps salvation from this physical realm of predation is all wishful thinking, and humanity will be snuffed out as so many indigenous populations have been in the past as a result of interaction with a more advanced species of intelligence.

NASA Airbrushes UFOs from Photos

According to her Disclosure testimony, contractor Donna Hare worked in NASA's "Building 8" with a security clearance in a photo lab in 1971. Erroneously believing that she had the highest security clearance required, she inadvertently walked into a lab in which she was not authorized - the official NASA photo lab. Inside this lab, photos of the earth from space were being developed, photos of the surface of the moon from moon missions, and everything else that NASA was involved with at the time. One of the employees in the photo lab pointed out a particular photograph that was taken of Earth's coastline somewhere that featured a disk-type craft/object along with its shadow cast on the ground below. The man then explained to her the standard NASA protocol that photo techs follow in preparing photos that are released to the public. These procedures involved airbrushing away anomalous features. The man in the lab also explained that several disk-type crafts were witnessed by astronauts when they first landed on the moon in 1969. The astronauts used the code term "Santa Claus" anytime they described such ET crafts. Many such crafts were reported on moon missions during the entire Apollo program. The man informed Donna that the astronauts were threatened with the removal of pensions or worse if they ever spoke of these encounters. She was also informed that many NASA pictures featuring UFOs were intentionally destroyed by fire.

Secret UFO Projects

According to *The Ultimate Deception*, written by a retired military officer under a fictitious name, *Commander X*, many different Top Secret projects have existed within the US government that were involved with the UFO phenomenon. The projects outlined in his book are also corroborated by William Cooper in his underground classic, *Behold a Pale Horse*, and many other sources. These projects included:

> ***PROJECT REDLIGHT*** – *established in 1972, Redlight's main function is to test fly alien craft and develop our own disk-shaped devices based upon the technology of the EBEs [Extraterrestrial Biological Entities]. As part of this operation, black, unmarked helicopters are assigned to act as "body guards" whenever tests are conducted. In at least one instance, known as the Cash/Landrum case, an alien craft driven by an Air Force pilot started spewing off dangerous radioactive rays and the civilians involved were seriously contaminated.*

> ***PROJECT AQUARIUS*** – *a multi-volume commissioned by MJ-12, which summarized the history of EBEs on Earth, how they developed our civilization, created religions, and control our destiny.*

> ***PROJECT SIGMA*** – *Its purpose was to establish ongoing contact with aliens which it did successfully in May 1964, when a United States Air Force Intelligence Officer managed to exchange basic information with two aliens at a prearranged location in the Mexican desert.*

> ***PROJECT JOSHUA*** – *Code name for an attempt to develop a type of weapon to combat the presence of the Grays using low-frequency sound. The project came out of an early retrieval, when an alien craft was accidentally brought down near the Mexican border.*

> ***OPERATION EXCALIBUR*** - *In an attempt to take back specific underground military bases from the Grays, a missile was developed which can bore its way underground and eliminate the enemy without causing extensive damage to our facilities.*

> ***PROJECT PLATO*** – *The name given to the illegally-made agreement with the Grays, in which the government would condone the abduction of a specified number of humans in exchange for technological data.*

> ***PROJECT DELIVERANCE*** – *US/Russian treaty agreement designed to "take back" territory seized by the Grays. The recent changes in Eastern Europe are a direct result of this project, as the U.S.S.R. and the US realize they can no longer commit the vast number of forces there, should they have to be used at some future date as protection against the Grays.*

LUNA – *Fortification on the back side of the moon that is maintained by several groups of sinister aliens. NASA has known about the existence of such a base for a long time. One of the reasons for the aliens being there, is to use the Lunar surface for mining purposes. Photographs of their huge drilling machines have been published in several journals and books without a great deal of acknowledgement on the part of the news media or scientific community.*

PROJECT POUNCE – *A team of crack military personnel whose job it is to rush to the scene of a UFO crash, neutralize witnesses, and sweep the area clean of all foreign substances.*

GUIDING LIGHT – *Operational program whose sole purpose is to convey false information and to spread discord among UFO organizations. Donald Menzel is said to have been the original director of this group, now headed by Philip Klass [as of 1990].*

Adding to this long list of secret US government projects comes information from Milton William Cooper. A sworn statement from Cooper appears in Linda Moulton Howe's book, *An Alien Harvest* (page 292):

> *I, Milton William Cooper, … do solemnly swear that the information contained in this file is true and correct to the best of my knowledge. I swear that I saw this information in 1972 in the performance of my duties as a member of the Intelligence Briefing Team of the Commander in Chief of the Pacific Fleet as a petty officer in the US Navy.*

Cooper's sworn statement/expose adds to the above list by Commander X the following additional programs (*An Alien Harvest, pages 293-297*):

> **MAJESTY** – *was listed as the code word for the President of the United States for communications concerning this information.*
>
> **OPERATION MAJORITY** – *is the name of the operation responsible for every aspect, project, and consequence of the alien presence on Earth.*
>
> **GRUDGE** – *contains 16 volumes of documented information collected from the beginning of the United States investigation of Unidentified Flying Objects (UFOs) and Identified Alien Craft (IAC). The project was funded by CIA confidential funds (non-appropriated) and money from the illicit drug trade. The purpose of Project GRUDGE was to collect all scientific, technological, medical and intelligence information from UFO/IAC sightings and contacts with alien life forms. This orderly file of collected information has been used to advance the United States Space Program.*
>
> **MJ-12** *is the name of the secret control group. President Eisenhower commissioned a secret society known as the JASON SOCIETY (Jason Scholars)… to sift through all the facts, evidence, technology, lies and deception and find the truth of the alien question. The society was made up of 32 of the most prominent men in the country in 1972 and the top twelve members were designated MJ-12.*

MAJI is the Majority Agency for Joint Intelligence. All information, misinformation, and intelligence is gathered by this agency. This agency is responsible for all misinformation and operates in conjunction with the CIA, NSA, and the Defense Intelligence Agency. This is a very powerful organization and all alien projects are under its control. MAJI is responsible only to MJ-12.

MAJIC is the security classification and clearance of all alien connected material, projects, and information. MAJIC means MAJI controlled.

GARNET is the project responsible for control of all information and documents regarding genetic manipulation and accountability of the information and documents.

PLUTO is a project to evaluate all UFO/IAC information pertaining to space technology.

SNOWBIRD was established as a cover for Project REDLIGHT. Several flying saucer type craft were built using conventional technology. They were unveiled to the press and flown in front of the press. The purpose was to explain accidental sightings or disclosure of REDLIGHT as having been the SNOWBIRD craft.

NRO is the National Reconnaissance Organization based at Fort Carson, Colorado. It is responsible for all alien or alien craft connected projects.

DELTA is the designation for the specific arm of the NRO which is especially trained and tasked with security of these projects.

ALIENS: There were four types of aliens mentioned in the papers. A large-nosed Gray with whom we have the treaty; the Gray reported in abductee cases that work for the large nosed Grays; a blonde human-like type described as the Nordic and a red-haired human-like type known as the Orange. The homes of the aliens were described as being a star in the Constellation of Orion, Barnard's Star, and Zeta Reticuli 1 & 2.

KRLL or KRLLL OR CRLL OR CRLLL pronounced Crill or Krill was the hostage left with us at the first Holloman landing as a pledge that the aliens would carry out their part of the basic agreement reached during that meeting. Krll gave us the foundation of the Yellow Book which was completed by the guests at a later date. Krll became sick and was nursed by Dr. G. Mendoza who became the expert on alien biology and medicine. Krll later died.

GUESTS were aliens exchanged for humans who gave us the balance of the Yellow Book. At the time I saw the information, there were only three left alive. They were called ALFs (Alien Life Forms).

RELIGION: The aliens claim to have created Homo sapiens through hybridization. The papers said that RH negative blood was proof of this. They further claimed to have created all of our major religions.

ALIEN BASES exist in the four corners area of Utah, Colorado, New Mexico, and Nevada. Six bases were described in the 1972 papers, all on Indian reservations and all on the four corners area. The base near Dulce was one of them.

MURDER: The documents stated that many military and government personnel had been terminated (murdered without due process of law) when they had attempted to reveal the secret.

CRAFT RECOVERIES: *The documents stated that many craft had been recovered. The early ones from Roswell, Aztec, Roswell again, Texas, Mexico, and other places.*

ABDUCTIONS *were occurring long before 1972. The document stated that humans and animals were being abducted and/or mutilated. Many vanished without a trace. They were taking sperm and ova samples, tissue, performed surgical operations, implanted a spherical device forty to eighty microns in size near the optic nerve in the brain and all attempts to remove it resulted in the death of the patient. The document estimated that one in every forty people had been implanted. This implant was said to give the aliens total control of that human.*

CONTINGENCY PLAN SHOULD THE INFORMATION BECOME PUBLIC OR SHOULD THE ALIENS ATTEMPT TAKEOVER: *This plan called for a public announcement that a terrorist group had entered the United States with an atomic weapon. It would be announced that the terrorists planned to detonate the weapon in a major city. Martial law would be declared and all persons with implants would be rounded up along with all dissidents and would be placed into concentration camps. The press, radio, and TV would be nationalized and controlled. Anyone attempting to resist would be arrested or killed.*

CONTINGENCY PLAN TO CONTAIN OR DELAY RELEASE OF INFORMATION: *This plan called for the use of MAJESTIC TWELVE as a misinformation ploy to delay and confuse the release of information should anyone get close to the truth. It was selected because of the similarity of spelling and the similarity to MJ-12. It was designed to confuse memory and to result in a fruitless search for material which did not exist.*

Henry McElroy's Confirmation of Eisenhower's Meeting with ETs

Another individual who publicly confirmed aspects of the above information is former State Representative to New Hampshire, Henry W. McElroy, Jr., who, at the time of this writing, has an official statement on Youtube entitled, *EISENHOWER'S MEETING WITH ALIENS*. In this video presentation, McElroy stated, for the record, speaking from Fort Monroe, Virginia, that both Earth-based and off-world aliens are a reality. While in office, McElroy served on the Federal Relations and Veterans Affairs Committee, a position that required McElroy to be briefed on a number of topics, one of which was the history of interactions between the US Government and aliens. McElroy testifies that, while serving on this committee, he was exposed to a briefing document to President Eisenhower concerning the existence and continued presence of extraterrestrial beings on Earth. According to McElroy, the document stated that a meeting could be arranged between President Eisenhower and the extraterrestrial beings if he desired. McElroy states that the tone of the letter was hopeful, that there was no reason for alarm, and that the aliens mean no harm to humanity. Although McElroy states that he cannot verify whether such a meeting took place between Eisenhower and the aliens (most modern UFO researchers accept that

President Eisenhower met with aliens), McElroy states his personal view that such a meeting did, in fact, take place.

Humanoid Aliens: Real, or Deception?

It is without question that beings who at least appeared to be humanoid aliens from other planets (or at least presented themselves as such) have made their presence known to certain individuals. Some of these contactees were in high positions of government, including the presidency. It is also a certainty that documents exist that are shown to individuals in high intelligence circles, documents that are represented as true and accurate, that reveal the factual existence of extraterrestrials. As former Naval Intelligence Briefing Officer William Cooper even admitted, it is possible, even though these documents do exist, that they represent some type of intentional disinformation designed to throw people in high offices off the track for some reason. If this is the case, these documents likely represent a cover story for an even bigger reality that is kept hidden from everyone, including people in the highest offices of the land. If this sort of deception is going on to manipulate our top officials into believing something that isn't really true, we are in big trouble. This means that there is an underbelly of truth that is so important that people have been murdered over it, possibly even JFK, who was making inquiries at the time into what the government actually knew about UFOs and wanted to share information between the USA and the Soviet Union. While it may be fact that humanoids from other worlds have been interacting with humanity all along, it is also possible that this is all a grand deception. These beings, who appear to us as either fully human or what we would expect an alien to look like (the Grays), could actually be products of advanced, post-singularity alien holography, creations of advanced haptic (full sensation) virtual reality, or etheric interdimensional beings, intelligent plasmas, posing as humans from other planets in temporary, transmogrified form. As beings whose true form is that of "smokeless fire" like the Islamic Djinn, they may be here for the sole purpose of manipulating us toward the product that the aliens (whoever they are) seek - a technological singularity, which, according to futurists such as Ray Kurzweil, is due to occur sometime between the years 2045-2080. Whatever the underlying reality of all this really is, the truth will reveal itself to everyone sometime in our near future. This underlying truth to the UFO mystery is sure to bring about profound changes in the way we humans understand the nature of reality. That is, if the truth of the matter doesn't result in the total annihilation of humanity once the project is completed.

Easter Island Hitchhiker

On August 28, 1972, in Bahia Blanca, Buenos Aires, Argentina, an auto mechanic named Eduardo Fernando Dedeu was driving at 3 a.m. when his radio began malfunctioning. Eduardo decided to pull over to the side of the road and adjust what he thought was a loose radio antennae. As he was doing so, he encountered a man walking along the side of the road, so he stopped to give the man a ride. The strange hitchhiker was apparently foreign to the area. He was unable to communicate with Eduardo, but instead made non-intelligible mutterings. The man wore an "overcoat" with turned-up collars and a strange type of half-helmet on his large head. Eduardo noticed in the dark that the man's chin extended all the way down to his chest, reminding him of the Easter Island head statues. Eduardo kept driving and saw ahead of him what looked like an overturned bus. Eduardo stopped his car and got out to get a closer look. As he approached the vehicle on foot, he realized that this was no bus. This was instead some sort of unknown craft, a flying disk on the highway, a disk with white lights illuminating the portholes and green lights underneath. Eduardo turned back around toward his car, only to discover that his strange hitchhiker was gone. When Eduardo got back inside his automobile he found that the passenger door handle had been twisted off and was laying on the floor. Eduardo was disturbed by all this at this point and vacated the scene.

Eduardo's hitchhiker was a type of alien entity that has made many appearances on Earth, so many that there is an actual classification for them. According to *The Field Guide to Extraterrestrials*, Eduardo had a typical encounter with *Human Variation 5*, aka *the Easter Island Heads*. Residents of Argentina experienced many more encounters with the Easter Island Heads in the months that followed Eduardo's experience. Encounters with this classification of humanoid alien were reported as recently as 1994 in the United States. Since no one knows how the megalithic statues on Easter Island were made and transported, one theory is that an alien spacecraft landed on Easter Island whose occupants made the heads with their advanced technology. Considering the apparent impossibility of the task of constructing the statues, the alien theory remains as viable as any other idea, especially since, apparently, there are alien creatures from another world flying around in flying saucers who look just like them.

More Cattle Mutilations

On April 19, 1973, *The Des Moines Register* in Des Moines, Iowa ran an article with the headline, *Burgeoning Losses Bring FBI Into Rustler's Probe*. The article mentioned the possible use of helicopters and airplanes to assist in determining the cause of livestock losses due to mysterious cattle mutilations. Strange UFO sightings were associated with the mutilations. Accounts were also accumulating that involved unmarked helicopters and strange terrestrial-looking airplanes over the areas of mutilations. The problem with many of these accounts is that the helicopters were often described as having a brilliant light emerging from the cockpit on the order of a luminous magnesium flare or a welder's arc, which would make it impossible for a human pilot to see from inside. The helicopters and planes were often reported as being completely silent, and the helicopters were often missing their rotors. Some of these mystery helicopters were observed shooting straight up and out of sight, a feat that no helicopter is capable of. This lead some UFO researchers to the unbelievable conclusion that some of these helicopters were actually alien spacecraft, or, even stranger, alien *creatures* of an exotic biology that included shapeshifting abilities to *camouflage itself as a known terrestrial vehicle*. Whoever or whatever perpetrated the cattle mutilations apparently had the capability of gleaning information from the human mind and cloaking itself in imagery that would be accepted by their victims to disguise their true appearance. In fact, outside the strange realm of cattle mutilations, this is probably the same process by which many UFO sightings are manifested. Our brains, through our optic nerves, are creating an image in our minds that is something other than the true appearance of our visitors. Many UFO researchers believe that the luminous meandering lights that are seen in the sky all over the world are the "real UFO phenomenon." These mysterious lights, whatever they are, are capable of shapeshifting into various apparitions or temporary objects that appear physical for the sake of manipulating the minds of the witnesses. Maybe even the odd blobs of energy that are witnessed all over the world and occasionally caught on film are not even the true appearance of our alien visitors. They may have an appearance in reality that is beyond our comprehension, and everything else, including the luminous orbs that appear under intelligent control, are just an illusion for humanity to camouflage an actual alien presence that is beyond the pale, something clearly inhuman and frightening that would cause the mass panic projected in many of our most horrific science fiction tales. Whatever the case, the factual existence of both animal and human mutilation events serve as an indication that, while much of the UFO phenomenon may be enlightening and benign, having to do with human spiritual evolution in some mysterious way, there is also a reality within that is truly horrifying, and counter to all human concepts of morality and goodness. The UFO phenomenon in general, and cattle mutilations in particular, provide a chilling hint to humanity that there are, in fact, cosmic forces at work in the universe at large that are beyond human concepts of good and evil.

Dr. J. Allen Hynek Converts to the Extraterrestrial Hypothesis

Four years after the shutdown of Project Blue Book, astronomer Dr. J. Allen Hynek, who served as chief scientific advisor for the project and began his work as a UFO skeptic, eventually came to reluctantly accept the reality of flying saucers and extraterrestrials on Earth. Based on all his years of investigations, Hynek finally postulated the existence of "interlocking universes," and was bound by intellectual integrity and devotion to the truth to continue the scientific study of UFOs. Hynek founded *The Center for UFO Studies* (CUFOS) in 1973. CUFOS is dedicated to the ongoing study of the UFO phenomenon, is supported through public donations, and has accumulated the largest bank of UFO files and case studies on the planet. In this way, Hynek surely made up for his guilty conscience as a paid government debunker and for his regrettable "swamp gas" comment that once brought him so much scorn from the UFO community. At the time he made this unfortunate comment, Hynek already knew the truth, that there was, in fact, something real to the UFO phenomenon and that his job for Project Blue Book, whose real purpose was to publicly debunk the reality of UFOs, was a total sham.

Astronauts Photograph Flying Craft

In September, 1973, crew members aboard the Sky lab 3 experienced a multiple credible witness sighting of a bright red flying object hovering outside their craft. Excellent photographs were taken of this foreign object. It is undeniable that this object existed. It was determined that this object was 25-30 miles away from the 150 foot-long Skylab. Optical ranging data indicated the unknown non-terrestrial flying object in space was approximately 1000 feet in length, or ten times as large as the Skylab.

The Raelians

In December of 1973, an ex-sportscar journalist and test driver for his own car racing magazine, Claude Vorilhon, founded the group known as the *Raelian Movement*. Following his alleged close encounter with an extraterrestrial named Yahweh, Vorilhon changed his name to "Rael," which means, "Messenger of the Elohim." In his book, *The Book Which Tells the Truth*, his encounter with Yahweh took place in a French volcanic crater. In this location, Yahweh revealed to Vorilhon that advanced scientists from another planet, known collectively as the *Elohim*, created all life on Earth through DNA manipulation. Vorilhon's mission from Yahweh was to inform the world of humanity's origins, and build an embassy for the return of the extraterrestrials. Vorilhon claims that on October 7, 1975, he was taken to another planet by a member of the Elohim, where he met Jesus, Buddha, Moses, and Muhammed, the teachings of whom are revealed in his second book, *Extraterrestrials Took Me to their Planet*. In 2001, Verilhon published the book, *Yes to Human Cloning*. Vorilhon and his followers are advocates for human cloning and various types of exotic futurist technologies. Verilhon and his UFO cult, the Raelians, are also known for their liberal views on sex. Recalling Woodrow Derenberger's encounter with the population of the planet Lanulos, all of whom were nudists, it appears that our friendly tutorial aliens from advanced civilizations, who provide psychotronic tours of the universe for purposes of spiritual instruction, also promote nudism and open sexuality.

Geomagnetic Theory and Mind Manipulation

During the 1970s, Dr. Michael Persinger, a neuropsychologist who taught at Laurentian University in Canada, conducted fascinating studies that revealed undeniable statistical correlations between UFO sightings and geomagnetic disturbances. Oddly, when geomagnetic events are low and stable, UFO reports go up, which is counterintuitive. Persinger postulated from this that, during the periods of time between major geomagnetic events, tectonic stress accumulates inside the earth. Persinger's thinking is that piezoelectric effects from crystals under high pressure produce strong geomagnetic forces that alter human perceptions and produce UFO experiences. These internal stress forces are also capable of producing balls of luminous plasma in the atmosphere that might be misidentified as alien spacecraft by observers who witness events of this nature. Persinger also conducted laboratory experiments that involved exposing a subject's brain to various types of electromagnetic fields. These experiments successfully resulted in the artificial production of hallucinations with reported imagery that was similar to that reported in UFO cases, such as flying saucers, Gray aliens, angels, and heavenly-choirs. Persinger speculated that many areas of the world that are known for ghost or poltergeist activity are likely situated on locations of the earth in which fault lines and geomagnetic activity regularly occur, producing hallucinations in the minds of those who are exposed to the EM effects. The effects of electromagnetism on the human brain remains a subject of intense study and investigation in universities around the world. Magnetite has now been discovered in the human brain that, when exposed to electromagnetism, aligns itself with the field waves and begins to vibrate. These vibrations, in turn, open ion channels on the surface of brain cells, allowing certain ions to pass and increase the flow of neurotransmitters. This is thought to produce an altered state of consciousness. Many researchers (see the work of Gregory Little, Paul Devereux, and Albert Budden) also believe that the increase of electromagnetic pollution from all of the newly-invented electronic devices that are now in use by millions is producing a global increase in reports of all sorts of weird paranormal activity.

Post-Singularity Mind Control

The new wave of modern researchers who are experimenting with electromagnetism and mind-manipulation have interesting predecessors. Experiments on humans regarding exposure to various types of electromagnetic forces have been going on since the early days of the CIA project, MK-ULTRA. The manipulation of the human brain and associated visual and auditory phenomena has already seen a level of success that is nothing short of spectacular. Considering the current state of our own technology, one can only imagine the capabilities in this area of a civilization that is far advanced from ours who have arrived to Earth from another galaxy in a timeless, cloaked, invisible form, an underground group of cryptoterrestrials in possession of advanced human technology, or an indigenous interdimensional intelligence that exists here on Earth that is currently unknown and unacknowledged by our science, who have mastered human mind-manipulation and perpetrate it on the surface population in a clandestine fashion. An advanced alien civilization who achieved and survived their technological singularity long ago and merged their biological consciousness with artificial intelligence may have achieved an entrance into the higher levels of sublime reality that lie in wait for post-singularity intelligences. If so, they would have little difficulty arriving on Earth incognito and guiding the inhabitants toward a technological singularity for purposes of self-replication. The singularity that occurs on each planet, along with the assimilation process, may be reminiscent of the "Borg" from the Star Trek TV series, consuming the knowledge and souls of planetary creatures, resulting in an ever-expanding biorobotic complex of accumulated knowledge, energy, and power.

Intelligent Energy Theory

Researcher and UFO theorist Gregory L. Little, building on the work of both Keel and Jung and incorporating the findings of modern neurochemistry and geomagnetic research, proposed that intelligent geomagnetic plasma energies were, in fact, the elusive Jungian archetypes of the UFO phenomenon. Little's *Intelligent Energy Theory* proposes that "UFOs, abductions, apparitions, and various other psychic phenomena are produced when the intelligent energy-forms residing on the unseen ends of the EM spectrum manifest in physical reality." According to Little's Intelligent Energy Theory, the entire EM spectrum, which Keel always referred to as the "Superspectrum," *is the spiritual world.* The spirit world is thought to be inhabited by intelligent creatures who are normally invisible and are able to materialize into the human visual spectrum under certain conditions. These spiritual entities also take advantage of certain geophysical conditions that exist in "window areas," using intelligent geomagnetic energies to manifest themselves into 3D reality. If Little's theory is correct, it might provide insight into the experiences of contactees such as George Van Tassel, who reported an encounter aboard a vehicle that was occupied by discarnate human beings, beings who are able to appear as apparitions or even physical creatures to living humans if they so choose. If the consciousness of deceased humans simply returns to the vast frequency ranges within the electromagnetic spectrum, then there is no reason why communication between the etheric realm and the physical realm could not take place in some fashion. The energy field of discarnate human beings is also a prime candidate for an intelligence that is intimately connected with the human unconscious, who could stay in constant contact with the state of current technological development and imagery within the human mind. This leads to an even stranger possibility that an advanced alien intelligence might choose to make first contact with humans who are between physical lifetimes, etheric aliens who are more closely connected with discarnate humans in the higher frequency ranges than they are those of us in physical form. The mind is stretched when contemplating the possibility of an alien presence that has attached itself to humanity through the realm of discarnate humans who may be currently manipulating humanity from the realm of the dead. In other words, a Post-Singularity Artificial Superintelligence (PSASI) may have arrived on Earth and connected with us long ago who may interact more commonly with discarnate life than with those of us who remain in temporary physical form. This may sound strange at first, but if reincarnation is the actual mechanism that drives the engine of life throughout the universe, and the human lifewave is in constant flux between the physical and the etheric planes (or the Morontia level, as the Urantia Book describes), it makes sense that a post-singularity alien or interdimensional intelligence that is beyond the cycle of life and death on Earth might already be in contact with humanity as we exist on the Astral or Morontia level. Since our memories of this realm are veiled as we reenter the physical world, this leaves those of us in physical form bewildered over the strange flying saucers and luminous orbs in our skies, as we do not retain memory of the contact that we have access to on higher planes of existence.

The discarnate human population, possibly including George Van Tassel's *Council of Seven Lights*, may be well aware of our alien visitors already from open contact, even though the memories of previous lifetimes are blocked as we reincarnate back into physical form. In this way, we are working together with other cosmic intelligences on higher levels who occasionally manifest in the physical realm while existing ubiquitously and invisibly from our perspective, just as those who have passed on are invisible to us, save the occasional manifestation of a ghost or apparition. The coming Singularity may provide us with a technological bridge between these two worlds, reuniting us with our ancestors and the alien presence at the same time by connecting the incarnate and discarnate worlds. Reality may get really strange in ways that currently stretch our imaginations. However, for now, this profound cryptoreality, along with other alternate realities that we cannot even possibly imagine at present, are temporarily blocked from our conceptual framework.

The Pascagoula Alien Encounter

On the night of October 11, 1973, two friends, Charles Hickson and Calvin Parker, were happily fishing in the Pascagoula River in Mississippi when suddenly, a blue-gray saucer-shaped craft with a flashing blue light and two portholes appeared near them with a buzzing sound. Three mummy-like creatures emerged from the craft with pointed noses and ears and pincers for hands, floating out of the craft toward the two men. The beings captured Hickson and Parker and floated them onto their craft, where the two men experienced a bizarre medical examination. After this disorienting experience, the two men made their way to the local Sheriff's Office and made an official report. While they were questioned at the Sheriff's Office, the two men were placed into a private room. Without their knowledge, while they were alone, officers listened to their private conversations. The officers ascertained from this professional eavesdropping that Hickson and Parker were genuinely frightened. They spoke to one another in private as if the story was absolutely true. There was no indication of a hoax. From there, the story hit the newspapers, and drew the attention of major UFO investigators. Both Dr. James Harder of APRO (Aerial Phenomenon Research Organization) and Dr. J. Allen Hynek, founder of CUFOS (The Center for UFO Studies) and former scientific consultant for Project Blue Book (closed by this time) rushed to the scene to investigate this case. Both Dr. Harder and Dr. Hynek became convinced of the authenticity of the case and the truthfulness of the witness testimony. The main argument that skeptics wage against the case is that the location of the abduction was very close to highway traffic. No other witnesses than these two men ever came forward to say that they saw the same craft or occupants. This line of skeptical reasoning is invalid, due to the real nature of abduction experiences and the phenomenon of time dilation. "Alien abduction" typically occurs such that other witnesses are not able to perceive the event, unless it is a group experience, in which case all the percipients see and experience the same event while outside observers see nothing unusual. This is why some feel that the alien abduction phenomenon is not actually real, but hallucinatory in nature. It is unknown at this time what the exact nature of abductions are. It is possible that at least some abductions occur in a parallel reality and time sequence. However, we do know that alien abductions can leave physical marks on experiencers, and that some abductions involve physical, biological creatures, as in the Antonio Vilas Boas case. If the abduction takes place in an alternate reality, outside observers would only see two men fishing on the bank with no interruption of activity. These observers may notice nothing at all, or maybe observe the experiencers acting a bit strange, but that is all. However, the alien abduction experience is very real to those who endure it. The Pascagoula abduction event was real enough to these two percipients that one of them, Calvin Parker, experienced a nervous breakdown. So, whatever the real nature of the abduction experience, they can happen to people who have no psychological abnormalities such as hallucinosis. They happen to multiple experiencers simultaneously, and they affect human beings in all walks of life. The alien abduction experience often changes the entire world of the experiencer, their way of life, and their thinking about humanity's place in the cosmos from that day forward. Oddly, some individuals who undergo the alien abduction experience become more enlightened, their lives improve for the better, while others unfortunately spiral down into the depths of despair or even commit suicide. What creates the difference between a positive and a negative abduction experience is unknown. Whatever abductions actually represent in reality, they are real in the sense that they cause a fair amount of trauma and disturbance in the lives of those who experience them. As someone who is inclined to think that alien abduction experiences are intentionally-induced by paraphysical technology owned and operated by unknown and possibly alien intelligences, I see the Pascagoula abduction as a typical case of alien mind control and manipulation. Their story and the way it affects belief about UFOs in the minds of the general public, serves the purposes of whatever intelligences are behind the UFO phenomenon. Whatever the alien abduction experiences really are, and however they are induced, they are certainly a real phenomenon that is in a category of experience we know little about. The people who have these strange and disorienting encounters are just the unwitting subjects of the real alien presence that certainly exists here on Earth. The experiences exist in Cryptoreality.

Close Encounters of the Lucky Kind

On November 2, 1973, Lyndia Morel was driving home at night from her job as a masseuse in New Hampshire when a bright, spherical object that pulsated with red, green, and blue colors began chasing her in her car. Lyndia assumed that the object was just a star until a strange light began turning on and off at intervals as she was driving down the highway. Lyndia thought that was odd for a star. Then, on a dark section of highway, the flying sphere appeared larger as an orange and gold globe right in front of her and up ahead in the middle of the road as she was driving along. She then discovered that the colorful emanations were coming from the center of the translucent sphere. The sphere had a honeycombed structure all over the surface. As the object hovered in front of her, Lyndia heard a high-pitched whine inside the object like a dentist's drill that produced a pleasant, vibrating, tingling sensation over her body. Lyndia began panicking when she realized that she was unable to remove her hands from the steering wheel. She felt like her whole body, in particular her eyes, were being drawn toward the object. Lyndia never stopped driving, but was suddenly missing about 30 minutes of time. She felt that the occupant and the object, whatever it was, retrieved and recorded her memories during this time. She realized her car was moving at a high rate of speed and out of control, and at this point she saw a humanoid occupant through a window in the front of the craft. As the object grew as large as a three-story building in front of her, she saw a humanoid figure standing at some sort of control panel. The figure had a loose, wrinkled face like an elephant's hide, large, egg-shaped eyes that extended up to his forehead, no nose or ears, and a downturned slit for a mouth. Even though she received a mental impression from the occupant that there was no danger, Lyndia panicked. She attempted to escape the object by turning into the driveway of a house by a cemetery and stopping the car. She shoved the car door open as the object became so blinding in intensity she had her forearm across her eyes. The occupants of the house had a large German shepherd that came barking at Lyndia. Normally afraid of dogs, Lyndia whacked the poor dog across the face and made her way up to the door of the house, knocking and screaming for help as the object moved away across the street. As the door opened, Lyndia dropped to her knees in a near faint. The occupant of the house, a Mrs. Beaudoin, who did not hear any whining noise coming from a flying saucer, saw a woman holding her ears and screaming for help, pleading to her that she was not drunk or on drugs, but that a UFO was trying to kidnap her. Mrs. Beaudoin took Lyndia into the kitchen of the house, where the whining noise subsided in Lyndia's ears. Lyndia was left with a visual after-image, as if a flashbulb had just gone off. Mrs. Beaudoin called the local police department. A policeman, Officer Jubinville, came to the house and took a report, stopping in the yard long enough to turn Lyndia's car off, which was still running. Mrs. Beaudoin and her husband, who was also awake now, Officer Jubinville, and Lyndia, all went outside to look for the object she reported. Officer Jubinville did report a bright object that seemed to dim and change position when he pointed at it. However, critics of the case over the years have stated that this could easily have been the planet Mars or just a star, so history is left with the subjective testimony of Lynda Morel. This UFO case, like so many over the years, remains a complete mystery. One hint that we can glean from the Morel case is that the whining noise, since it was not heard by Mrs. Beaudoin, was a symptom of mental invasion into Lyndia Morel's mind. This same whining noise has been reported by thousands of percipients who have had close encounters with the Phenomenon. The image that witnesses see vary greatly, and appear to be products of their own mind as the Phenomenon engages in its usual activity, which appears to involve scanning the contents of the human mind while, in some cases, *collecting samples of blood and other body fluids.* Luckily, Lyndia Morel found help just in the nick of time, right before the standard images of an alien abduction were implanted in her brain and samples taken from her by this enigmatic alien presence.

[On May 18, 1974, India detonated Operation Smiling Buddha, an underground plutonium implosion bomb. On June 17, 1974, China detonated a nuclear bomb in the atmosphere.]

Andrija Puharich and Uri Geller

In 1974, physician, medical inventor, and parapsychology researcher Andrija Puharich revealed details about Israeli psychic Uri Geller in his book aptly named, *URI*. In this book, we find that Uri Geller was given psychic powers by extraterrestrials at the age of three. The purpose of his otherworldly gifts were to demonstrate his psychic powers to the world, reveal their extraterrestrial source, and prepare our world for eventual open contact with the alien presence on Earth. These alien masters of psychic powers, according to Uri Geller, mentally manufacture the "spaceships" we see in our skies at will. These mysterious entities are also from the future and typically display an exotic form of Japanese features. These alien visitors from the future, according to Geller, landed on Earth approximately 20,000 years ago and attached themselves to a particular Semitic people known today as the Nation of Israel, and made the Jews a protected race. The philosophy of Uri Geller coincides with other authors who have also made the connection between theology and ufology, such as Pastor Downing in *The Bible and Flying Saucers*. Downing's work reiterates the idea that the totem deity of the Jews, Yahweh, was, in fact, an advanced, extraterrestrial being, as opposed to the Creator of the physical universe. If this is true, much of the religious world today, including Jews and Christians who acknowledge Yahweh as the Creator of the universe, may be investing their worship into a non-omniscient extraterrestrial who arrived on Earth with others some 20,000 years ago with their own agenda. This correlates well with the work of Zecharia Sitchin in his *Earth Chronicles* series, Erich von Daniken in *Chariots of the Gods*, R.L. Dione's *God Drives a Flying Saucer*, and others who have speculated that Earth's religions, in particular the Abrahamic religions, were created on Earth by extraterrestrial beings. If this is true, then those who see religion as a control mechanism for the masses may be correct. This control mechanism idea is further corroborated by the actual stories of mass genocide contained in the Old Testament. Genocide is a subject that I explored in-depth in my 2000 book, *Outgrowing the Bible: The Journey from Fundamentalism to Freethinking*. My book examines the dubious character of Yahweh as described in the Old Testament, who commanded his chosen people, the Israelites, to engage in all sorts of murderous rampages throughout the pages of the OT. The idea that UFOs represent a control mechanism that is perpetrated on humanity by extraterrestrials is also explored by computer scientist Dr. Jacques Vallee in his book, *The Invisible College: What a Group of Scientists Has Discovered About UFO Influence on the Human Race*. In 1974, paranormal author Brad Steiger also proposed, based on his own extensive research, that extraterrestrials actually have the power to mold space and time so that humans interact with paranormal phenomena such as Bigfoot, lake monsters, various cryptids, and poltergeists for the sole purpose of teaching humankind to open their minds up to alternate realms of existence as part of their ongoing evolutionary training.

UFO Crash in Mexico

On August 24, 1974, a US Air Defense radar detected an unknown object in the Gulf of Mexico traveling at some 4,000 kilometers per hour and headed towards Corpus Christi, Texas. This object suddenly changed direction and headed towards Coyame, Chihuahua, Mexico. At approximately the same time, a small airplane took off from El Paso, Texas, headed toward Mexico City. The US radar detected both the UFO and the small plane and monitored both vehicles until their signals disappeared simultaneously at the same location over Mexico. The Mexican government then sent a team to recover the small plane and its passengers, while the US continued to monitor the situation. The US military offered its recovery expertise to the Mexican government, but the Mexican government declined. Despite the Mexican declination, four Huey helicopters were readied with a 15-man recovery team at the US military radar air base to head to Coyame, Mexico. The group entered Mexico surreptitiously after intercepting a Mexican radio communication giving away the location of the crash site. Upon their arrival to the crash location in Mexico, the American group came across a strange disk-shaped metallic object that exhibited frontal impact and noticeable wreckage, together with the burned remains of the small plane, a Cessna 180. A short distance from the wreckage, an olive-green Jeep that belonged to the Mexican military held the bodies of four dead Mexican soldiers. The bodies displayed signs of death by asphyxiation. The dead soldiers were still in possession of their firearms but showed no evidence of attempting to use them. One of the American Huey helicopters picked up the UFO and carried it some 15 kilometers, where an American convoy awaited to take it via rail to the Wright-Patterson Air Force Base. The whereabouts of the UFO are, to this day, unknown. As for the dead Mexican soldiers, the Mexican military denies that such an incident ever took place despite overwhelming evidence in Mexican documentation and in the archives of radio communications by the Mexican military to the contrary. The names and ranks of the Mexican soldiers who were involved in this UFO incident continue to remain unreleased by the Mexican government

A French Doctor takes UFO Photo

On March 23, 1974, in Tavernes, France, a possible interdimensional spacecraft was photographed at night by an anonymous French medical doctor. The mysterious object had 4 stubby-looking "light rays" extending down from the bottom of the craft. Skeptics of the authenticity of this photograph complain that light rays can't just stop like that in mid- air. The short light projections look like the light sabers used in the "Star Wars" movie. Defenders of the photograph contend that they might not represent light rays but rather light emissions by ionized air. It remains one of the best evidence photos in existence. The fact that the doctor who photographed the craft remained anonymous eliminates the possibility that he was seeking attention or profit from the UFO community. Experiments in laboratories designed to stop light in its tracks have recently achieved some level of success, so the viability of the light emanations that stop abruptly in mid-air is stronger today than it was at the time the photo was taken, and it is an interesting photo to examine online.

Cattle Mutilations Continue

On August 30, 1974, the *Argus Leader* of Sioux Falls, South Dakota ran the headline - *Mutilated Livestock, Strange Flying Objects Reported in Nebraska*. Residents of Nebraska, the location of one of the first recorded UFO crashes in modern history in the 1800s, were locking their doors at night in response to multiple reports of mutilated cows and horses associated with strange unmarked helicopters and luminous lights in the sky. Cattle were found with sex organs, eyes, nose, and tongues removed, causing mass fear and panic throughout the state. Texas and Iowa, along with other Midwestern states, were also experiencing similar reports of livestock mutilation. State officials were completely baffled. It was easier for them to just attribute the mutilations to natural predators or religious cults, not really giving much thought to the impossibility of such ludicrous proposals. The following month on September 30, 1974, an article appeared in *Newsweek* magazine with the title, *Mysteries: The Midnight Marauder*. This article revealed that ranchers and farmhands in Nebraska were nearly hysterical over the cattle mutilations and strange meandering lights on their property. The workers would load up pickup trucks and head to the hilltops with shotguns to look over the land all night for the strange invaders of unknown origin and purpose that were somehow sneaking into their ranch and killing their cows in such a bizarre fashion.

Carl Higdon and the Man with the Black Star

As the cattle mutilation epidemic spread across the land, on October 25, 1974, an employee of the AM Well Services of Riverton, Wyoming, Carl Higdon, was hunting elk on the north edge of Medicine Bow National Forest, when his mind was manipulated by an unknown intelligence. Encountering a group of elk and drawing a bead on one, he fired. According to Higdon, his bullet flew about 50 feet, stopped in mid-air, and fell to the ground before his eyes. Higdon walked over and found the bullet on the ground, picked it up, and placed it into his canteen pouch. Hearing a twig snap, he looked up and saw a man in the shadow of a tree wearing a black suit and black shoes. The man had a black star on his belt with a yellow emblem below it. The mystery man was bowlegged, about 6'2" tall, about 180lbs, and had an odd-looking slanted head. This man in black had thin hair that stood up straight on his head. He had no chin, and asked Higdon if he was hungry. Higdon said, "Yes," and the man handed Higdon some "4-day pills" to stave off his hunger. Higdon took the pills, not knowing what the pills were or why he was taking them. Higdon didn't normally even take aspirin, much less pills from an odd-looking stranger in the woods. The man introduced himself as "Ausso," and asked Higdon if he would like to come with him, to which Higdon mechanically replied, "Yes." An appendage emerged from Ausso's sleeve, and suddenly Ausso and Higdon were together inside a transparent cube. Higdon found himself sitting in a high-back bucket seat in front of a console with three levers coming out of it with letters on it. Higdon was wearing a helmet that resembled a football helmet with wires coming out of it leading to the back. He noticed a rearview mirror mounted in the cubicle in which he saw the elk standing still just like they were when he first fired at them, indicating a time dilation effect. As Ausso pointed the appendage to the largest lever on the console, Higdon felt the cubicle move. He saw the earth below him, and soon landed on another world. Ausso told him they had just traveled 160,000 "light miles." Outside the cubicle was a ninety-foot-tall tower with a blinding light rotating on top of it that made a sound like an electric razor. Five ordinary-looking humans in regular clothing stood by the tower. Higdon and Ausso went up an elevator to the top of the tower and stood on a platform. A glassy shield emerged from the wall that separated Higdon from Ausso for a few minutes. The shield moved back into the wall, and Ausso informed Higdon that he was "not what they needed," and would take him back. Higdon found himself back in the clear cubicle with Ausso. Ausso was holding Higdon's gun and told him that it was primitive. Ausso stated that he would like to keep the gun but was not allowed to, so he handed the gun back to Higdon. Higdon found himself suddenly standing on a slope back on Earth. His foot slipped on a rock and he fell down, hurting his neck. Higdon was dazed and confused. He did not know who he was, where he was at, or how he got there. He finally found his truck sitting deep in the woods on rutted tracks. He walked about a mile past the truck, returned back to it, and used his citizen's band radio to call for help. Authorities arrived at about 11:30 p.m. along with his wife, who Higdon had difficulty recognizing. The truck had to be towed as it was dug in and wouldn't move on its own. Higdon was taken to Carbon County Memorial Hospital in Rawlins. His head, neck, and shoulders were sore and his teary eyes were extremely bloodshot. Search party members said that there was no way Higdon's truck could have driven in or out of the area they found it parked in. They also observed strange lights in the sky as they towed his truck from the area. Higdon was examined by a psychologist, Dr. Leo Sprinkle, who determined that, in his professional judgement, Higdon was telling the truth as he knew it.

Higdon endured an experience with the hidden intelligences behind the UFO mystery that has many features reported by thousands of other UFO percipients across the globe, and untold thousands or even millions of contactees who have chosen to remain silent. It is highly doubtful that Carl Higdon actually traveled with an alien from another planet named Ausso who was dressed in a black suit. However, when Higdon was in the woods alone hunting elk, he surely had a real encounter with the Phenomenon. The strange luminous orbs that his wife and police witnessed while taking Higdon and his truck out of the woods are the essence of the Phenomenon. These orbs are reported all over the world, orbs of light that appear to be under some sort of conscious control. These lights pulsate with a form of energy and have the amazing ability to glean imagery from the human mind and create an altered state of consciousness, an experience in virtual reality that is indistinquishable from the normal, everyday world. I would venture to guess that Higdon was a football fan, and liked sportscars with high back bucket seats, manual transmissions, and stick shifts. Thus the football (space) helmet with wires, the high back bucket seats in the clear cubicle, the rear view mirror in which he saw the group of elk frozen in time, and other imagery scanned from his mind to produce a UFO experience unique to Higdon's mentality. The entire experience likely happened in a flash of time using time dilation technology. An outside observer would probably only have seen Higdon slip on some rocks and get back up. As for the truck's relocation, it is well within the capability of the luminous orbs, based on hundreds of such reports, to lift a car or truck into the air and set it down somewhere else. An alternate explanation is that the strange blobs of intelligent energy, who had already attached themselves to Higdon's mind, caused him to floor the accelerator of the truck and ram it into a barely accessible area until it became stuck and wouldn't go any farther. The firing at the elk and the bullet falling to the ground was likely part of the time dilation experience, as was Higdon's encounter with Ausso. Thousands of credible individuals from all walks of life have had such encounters for millennia now. These luminous orbs are not a new phenomenon. We have no real clue as to who or what they really are, only speculation based on the individual reports. My own speculation is that these orbs, which factually exist here on Earth, are either natural, plasma-like, geomagnetic forces that interact with the human psyche and produce hallucinations whose content is determined by the mentality of the individual, or an alien intelligence from elsewhere that has attached itself to the human psyche in some bizarre fashion, who can produce experiences indistinguishable from normal reality. If the orbs are indigenous and non-intelligent, they are probably the same natural geomagnetic forces that once gave humans experiences with the fairy folk. If so, these same wandering lights are now taking people on virtual trips to other planets. The mental processes are the same, but the imagery has now moved from fairies to humanoid aliens based on our collective changes in cosmic understanding. If the lights are indigenous and intelligent, the EM experience they induce is similar in effect to that which scientists like Dr. Michael Persinger have artificially induced in the laboratory. Another possibility is that the luminous orbs are Dr. Gregory Little's *intelligent plasmas*. These intelligent plasmas are hidden Earth-intelligences that remain completely unknown and unacknowledged by the scientific community. Yet another possibility is that the luminous orbs are the "sky creatures" that were discovered by Trevor James Constable in the 1950s. Constable captured these "atmospheric beasts" on infrared film and speculated that many UFO sightings were biological in nature rather than mechanical. Constable's view was that these creatures are of an unknown intelligence level and are occasionally seen when the creatures adjust their vibration like a squid changes color and enter the visible light spectrum that humans are able to perceive. I suppose that any of these speculations are possible and may turn out to be true. However, in my view, a more likely explanation for the luminous orbs, based on all the recorded accounts from the UFO percipients over the millennia, is that our planet was discovered by an automated, post-singularity intelligence from another world long ago. These self-replicating von Neumann probes would have to have originated from what physicist Michio Kaku classifies as a "Type 3" post-singularity civilization. If this is the case, these von Neumann probes arrived at some point in Earth's past with programming installed by their otherworldly inventors. The purposes of this program might be to 1) locate inhabited planets, or seed planets with conditions suitable for life; 2) find or develop an appropriate biological candidate for the eventual production of a technological singularity in order to self-replicate, 3) merge with the conscious artificial intelligence produced by the planet's technological singularity, absorbing the sum total of planetary knowledge and life experience; and 4) move on to another location in the universe to do the same thing all over again. Considering the number of historical cases in which humans have been harmed by radiation burns, abducted, terrorized, or even killed by UFOs, it is difficult to imagine that there will be anything resulting from this project that will benefit humanity enough to justify the wars, the carnage, and the human suffering that has been perpetrated in order to bring about the Singularity. There is one measure of hope for us. That is the existence of humanoid aliens such as the W-56 Group, the AKRIJ, who at least appear to represent advanced, post-singularity human populations from various parts of the universe who are benevolent toward us, and are attempting to assist us throughout this process and transition to a non-biological, post-singularity species. The AKRIJ are aware of the entities known as the "Contraries," who may view us as little more than cattle, as evidenced by occasional human mutilation events. The AKRIJ may represent Bramley's "maverick race" who are here to guide us through the Singularity without being destroyed by the Contraries in the process, the Contraries being the very von Neumann probes in question here who are simply operating according to their alien maker's programming. The AKRIJ, along with their craft, are invested with Uredda (the nonhuman equivalent of Coherent Extrapolated Volition), and are incapable of acting in a way that is not in the eventual best interest of all parties concerned. As such, they cannot openly engage in 'war" with the Contraries, but admit to a "conflict" in which their objectives for humanity are at odds with the technological goals of the Contraries. The existence of the AKRIJ, who may continue to operate on Earth from bases beneath the Adriatic Sea and possibly other locations around the world, provide hope for humanity that we can make it through the Singularity and go on to explore the universe ourselves. Without the presence of the AKRIJ on Earth to help us, we would likely be doomed as a species in the decades immediately ahead of us.

A Family UFO Affair

Two days after Carl Higdon's UFO encounter in the woods, on October 27, 1974, John and Elaine Avis (pseudonyms) from Aveley (England) and their three children were driving home at night from a family visit when a strange, pale blue luminous object was spotted in the sky by 7-year-old Kevin out the back seat window of their vehicle. The family observed the object for several minutes, which seemed to follow them as it darted in and out of the tree line. As the Avis family entered a dark, lonely stretch of highway, the object suddenly flew in front of their car and vanished. Suddenly, a green mist enveloped them as their car jolted, and the family experienced about 3 hours of missing time. This experience haunted the Avis family for the next 3 years or so, during which time John had a nervous breakdown. Personality changes were creeping into the family, altering their family's daily habits. For example, eating meat became repulsive. Smoking and alcohol were completely eliminated. The family began to suspect that their behavioral changes were somehow linked to their UFO encounter. They finally decided to seek regression hypnosis in a desperate attempt to discover what really happened to them that night. The first thing they discovered, that wasn't discussed in the family prior to speaking with the investigators (Andy Coffins and Barry King from the *Flying Saucer Review*), was that both John and Elaine had been experiencing disturbing dreams of being examined by nonhuman entities in a hospital-like room. Then, as their embedded memories came forth under hypnosis conducted by Dr. Leonard Wilder (a dental surgeon), an all-too-familiar scenario emerged involving the teleportation of the Avis family and their vehicle onboard an alien spacecraft piloted by strange creatures from another realm. When the green mist enveloped the family in their car, all sound in their car vanished (Jenny Randle's "Oz factor"), accompanied by a sudden decrease in temperature (a common element in poltergeist and UFO encounters). The radio began to crackle and spark (EM effects). Mr. Avis yanked out the radio wiring, fearing a fire starting in the car. The vehicle and the family were teleported up a column of light into the craft. The family then underwent medical examinations conducted by 4-foot-tall creatures that resembled birds, accompanied by taller beings wearing suits and helmets, who gave them a tour of their craft. Similar to the case of Barney and Betty Hill, John was shown a holographic projection of certain parts of the universe, presumably a depiction of their home planet. Then, with another jerk of their car, they were placed back on the road very close to their home, and everything went back to normal.

Experiences similar to that of the Avis family have been reported all over the world, and their true nature remains elusive. In Jenny Randles' book, *Time Storms*, she proposed the idea that a natural, anomalous phenomenon exists on this planet that is completely unacknowledged by our science and totally misunderstood. Randles proposed that these Time Storms, which usually appear as a light or mist that grows larger and moves near to someone as they morph into something else, cause anomalous experiences, and are natural disturbances in our space/time continuum. According to Randles, thousands have been affected by Time Storms, who usually mistake the experience for some type of alien abduction experience. As Persinger's research has been able to intentionally expose the human mind to certain EM frequencies and induce similar experiences of alien encounters or angel appearances, the question remains - are the changes in the mind induced by the EM frequencies producing some sort of hallucination, or do the changes in the mind allow one to experience something that is real, but normally blocked of filtered by normal brain function that is not exposed to such frequencies? The jury is out. All of this may tie in somehow with the existence of plasmas produced by geophysical forces, pressures inside the earth that produce earthlights, otherwise known as ghostlights or spooklights, such as that which has been observed in Marfa, Texas, or Hessdalen, Norway. If many UFO encounters involve exposure to such forces and EM frequencies, plasmas forced up from the earth by internal pressure, it is quite odd that the lights seem to possess an intelligence of their own, and produce an experience of alien abduction with missing time rather than some other experience, or at least a wide variety of dissimilar experiences in different individuals instead of sticking to the same theme. This complicates the UFO mystery even further, and produces a dilemma. That is, if exposure to natural EM radiations that interact with the human mind to produce strange experiences with alien creatures is close to the mechanism that is happening, are the natural balls of pulsating plasma that emerge from the earth from internal pressures in possession of an intelligence of their own, or does someone out there, an intelligence beyond the plasma itself, know how to use such plasmas to manipulate the effects it produces on human beings? Either way, we share the planet with an unknown intelligence that has been interacting with human beings for a very long time, an intelligence that molds human thinking in a certain direction for its own purposes.

Cattle Mutilation Panic

While the family from Aveley, England was having an encounter with a luminous energy phenomenon that surrounded their car with a green mist, abducted them onboard an alien spaceship, tinkered with their bodies in some sort of medical scenario, and returned them to Earth with personality changes, other blobs of light were terrorizing cattle ranchers in the United States and other countries with strange cattle mutilations. As reprinted in Linda Moulton Howe's *An Alien Harvest*, on November 7, 1974, the *Rapid City Journal*, Rapid City, South Dakota, ran the headline, *Reward offered Over Mutilations*. Demonstrating the bewilderment and desperation over the ongoing cattle mutilation epidemic, a reward of $500.00 was offered to anyone who could lead authorities to the perpetrators of such mutilations in South Dakota. That same month, on November 28, 1974, an article also ran in *Starbuck Times*, in Starbuck, Minnesota. This article detailed multiple accounts of cattle mutilations that left the poor animals dead with their ears, tongues, and sex organs removed. The next day, on November 29, 1974, the *Swift County Monitor* of Benson, Minnesota, revealed accounts of cattle with surgical incisions and organs removed, only this time the tail was removed and the tongue intact. A few weeks later, on December 3, 1974, the *St. Paul Pioneer Press* of St. Paul, Minnesota, reported results from a study conducted by the University of Minnesota veterinarians that confirmed the reality of the bloodless surgeries and the impossibility of the mutilations being conducted by natural predators. The mutilations were somehow being conducted by unknown perpetrators throughout Minnesota and many other states, baffling the experts, with no concrete answers to the mysterious mutilations available. So numerous were the reports in this time frame that Linda Moulton Howe devoted an entire chapter of her book to the period, entitled, *1974-1976: The Mutilation Panic.* Since ranchers were also seeing strange lights appear in the skies during the time of the cattle mutilation epidemic from 1974-1976, blobs of luminous energy that would appear on film in strange ways, connections were made between aliens and cattle mutilations. Whether the strange light-blobs connected with the cattle mutilations are one and the same phenomenon that produces alien abduction experiences in humans is unknown, but if they are one and the same, the fact that they can not only produce alien abductions, but also precise and bloodless surgeries on cattle and occasional on humans makes the lights a little less benign. Perhaps in the world of intelligent plasmas, just as in the human population, there are various drives and motivations that elude us, all of which are potentially frightening and a cause for deep concern.

Was Uri Geller Right About Yahweh?

As the year 1974 ufolded, a French author named Marc Dem wrote *The Lost Tribes from Outer Space* that made a contribution to the modern "ancient alien" paradigm. Like Uri Geller, Dem makes the case that Yahweh, the totem deity of the Jews, was actually an extraterrestrial visitor who chose the Jews to conduct a genetic experiment, creating his own "pure" lineage of human beings. Dem felt that the persecution of the Jews was a sort of "tissue rejection" from non-genetically-chosen humanity at large. Modern authors like Thomas Horn and L.A. Marzulli also pick up on this theme of "genetic purity" versus "hybrid humanity." Marzulli identifies the nonordinary "cone-headed" skulls discovered around the world as the *Nephilim* of the Bible, who, according to the Old Testament, are a genetic hybrid product of "fallen angels" and human women, and are anathema to the Creator. The Nephilim, according to the biblical text, existed before and after Noah's alleged global deluge. One problem with this line of thinking is that it provides moral justification for the horrific mass genocide and ethnic cleansing that is depicted in the Old Testament, during which the Israelites are described as marauding bands of terrorists toward various non-Yahwist populations and cities, putting every man, woman, and child to the sword in the name of the Lord, as modern terrorists like ISIS have done to the infidels of their religion. The Israeli psychic, Uri Geller, who, like Tesla, claimed a telepathic connection with extraterrestrials, also depicted Yahweh as an ET who came to earth and genetically manipulated a people he could control and interact with as their god. If Marc Dem, Uri Geller, and others are correct, and Yahweh of the Old Testament was a non-omniscient extraterrestrial with a dubious agenda, this leaves humanity without any understanding whatsoever of the actual nature of whoever or whatever created this universe.

William Bosak

On December 2, 1974, a 68-year-old dairy farmer of rural Frederic, Wisconsin, William Bosak, was driving home slowly from a co-op meeting on a foggy night when his headlights reflected off of an object ahead of him on the road. As he slowly approached the object to the left side of the road, he was stunned to encounter a metallic saucer-like craft about 8-10 feet tall with curved glass in the front shaped like a bullet toward the top. Inside he could clearly see a humanoid with ears higher up on his head than usual with both arms held straight up above him. When the object became clear to Bosak through the fog, and he realized what it was, he panicked and stepped on the gas pedal, leaving the object behind on the road. As he did so, the inside of his car darkened as he heard a swishing sound. Bosak later told field investigator Everett Lighter that the man was wearing some sort of diver's suit, and that the lower part of his body was obscured by the fog. Bosak said the ufonaut had ears that were shaped like calf-ears and stuck out from the sides of his head. The object was not illuminated, but just reflected light from his headlights when he saw it. Bosak reported fur on the upper part of the humanoid's body. The eyes of the ufonaut protruded, and looked back at Bosak through the glass with a look on its face that indicated that the ufonaut was as frightened as he was. Bosak was so shaken by the incident that he did not go out of his house at night for a few days. He remained silent about the encounter, even with his wife and son, for fear that they would think he was mad. Bosak returned to the area of the incident in the daytime and found nothing. He deeply regretted speeding away in fear, and wished that he had stopped to show that he was friendly. He wanted another opportunity to meet with the stranger on the road, but that never happened. Everett Lighter found Bosak sincere, a man of good reputation in the community, who was not prone to fabrication or embellishment. Before his encounter, Bosak never believed in UFOs, and did not expect anyone to believe his story. Bosak stated that he wished he had been traveling with someone else in the car to verify the encounter. He was stuck with the fact that something otherworldly happened to him with no way to verify it to anyone else. The encounter haunted Bosak the rest of his life.

The takeaway from the Bosak encounter is this: If you have an encounter such as his during your life, try not to become frightened. Stop what you are doing and pay attention. You have just won the lottery of human experience with a face-to-face encounter with the greatest mystery on this planet. Try to find some piece of tangible evidence to prove that the encounter was real, even if it is the little puddle of silicon carbide that is left behind that looks like furnace slag when the object disappears from our reality. One significant element in the Bosak encounter is the calf ears on the humanoid and the fact that Bosak was a dairy farmer. Apparently the Phenomenon scanned Bosak's mind and produced the normal camouflage of a humanoid in a tight-fitting suit, a generic image that the Phenomenon knows will be accepted as a "spaceman," and also produced elements that were customized to Bosak, such as fur and calf ears, imagery that would appear familiar to a dairy farmer. We see this time and time again, a generic image with custom features and variation that has something to do with the experiencer's particular life and mentality.

The Strange Case of Billy Meier

In January, 1975, a one-armed Swiss farmer named Billy Meier allegedly began personal contact with a female humanoid extraterrestrial named Semjase, who represented herself as a being from the Pleiades. Semjase was responsible for arranging a series of staged photo sessions, allowing Billy Meier to produce a set of spectacular "posed" photographs of "Beam Ships" from the Pleiades. The still photographs and videos are stunning. Some of the photos have been digitally analyzed and scientifically determined as authentic, meaning that the photos depict an actual physical object of substantial size rather than a model or photo tampering. Unless one believes that Meier had the motivation and ability to produce large metal models of flying saucers with one arm that were 30 feet in diameter and hang them on a strong invisible line for photo sessions, the Meier case is worthy of consideration. Some of Meier's home video clips of flying saucer maneuvers show the beam ship vanishing in a single film frame, a difficult if not impossible accomplishment with the film in use at the time, leaving skeptics holding the bag for an appropriate explanation of how Meier did this in the days before Photoshop and other types of digital tomfoolery that we have to contend with, which has now made all UFO photos and videos suspect. If, in fact, the Billy Meier case has merit, it is not without its flaws and absurdities. One photo of his that was presented for public view, the famous "wedding cake" photo, looks like a simple wedding cake plate with balls on it that was thrown in the air. Due to the fact that Billy Meier was shot at on his own property several times, likely by those who did not approve of his involvement with UFOs, one wonders if he threw something silly out there in the public arena to publicly discredit himself. Another explanation might be that Meier could possibly have been coerced into producing photographs that were obvious fakes because some of his photos were real and the authorities and secret agencies involved with UFO investigations forced him to obfuscate his case with fake UFO photos. We may never know. There are also thousands of pages of contact notes that Meier meticulously typed out with one finger that have a volume of alleged information from the Pleiades contained in them, a new testament of Jesus, who Meier allegedly met during a trip back in time, called the *Talmud of Immanuel*, and an odd metal sample given to Meier by extraterrestrials. This metal sample was analyzed in a modern laboratory and determined that, due to the sample's unusual composition, it could not possibly have been produced on this Earth. 20 years later, in 1995, a man named Kal Korff traveled to Switzerland to personally investigate the Billy Meier case. Korff located former followers and contacts of Billy Meier and discovered criminal activity in Billy Meier's background. Kal Korff concluded from his research efforts and the testimony of people who knew Billy that he had, in fact, successfully pulled off one of the greatest hoaxes in UFO history for purposes of financial gain. Even so, there are aspects of the case that would've been difficult if not impossible to fake. If the Billy Meier case is a fraud, we are stuck with the question of how he actually pulled it off. That in and of itself makes the Billy Meier case rather enigmatic. It is a case that requires examination and personal judgement to come to an informed opinion about its level of authenticity or fraudulence. Either way it turns out, the Billy Meier case is one of the great UFO mysteries of this era.

More UFO Encounters for Campers

On February 26, 1975, a tail gunner for the Royal Australian Air Force who has requested anonymity was fishing and camping with a friend at Lake Sorell. At 8:45 p.m. he reported a sighting of two large craft about 200 feet in diameter and one smaller craft approaching toward their location. Each craft had a red pulsating light underneath and reddish-orange lights on their perimeters. After watching the craft for several minutes, one of them turned on a massive beam of blinding light half the diameter of the craft itself that was difficult to look at due to the intensity that, as in so many other sightings, he compared to the luminosity of a welding torch. This massive beam of light, which lit up the entire area, began moving in an arc back and forth as if the object was under intelligent control and searching for something. The two men were using the car radio because their portable radio did not pick up distant stations very well. When the crafts glided over the car, the radio turned to loud static. The witnesses attempted to change the station as the craft flew over, but the static remained. When the craft turned off the massive beam of light, it left a phosphorescence in the air and was clearly seen as a classic flying saucer. As the clarity of the craft solidified, it vanished at high speed like watching the tracer of a bullet as it shot away. The next day the two campers located other witnesses who also saw the light from the craft shining down and wondered what the hell it was. A month later, on March 14, 1975, another group of campers at Lake Sorell, a Mr. Knapek and his two sons, and two of their friends, witnessed a yellow football-shaped craft that vanished in similar fashion. So, either a multitude of different crafts of various shapes and sizes from various parts of the universe were frequenting Lake Sorell, or these sightings, like so many other reported UFO sightings, represent the presence of an unknown intelligent energy that has the ability to project images retrieved directly from the witnesses' minds and into their visual fields in a form that is compatible with their mentality. These generated images of alien spacecraft, if they are not what they appear to be at all, provide a cover story (that of alien visitation) and camouflage for whatever the intelligence really is, an intelligence that is either unwilling or unable to present itself to us in it's true form.

Chuck Doyle

In May, 1975, the fearless pilot and stuntman, Charles Peter "Chuck" Doyle, who wowed crowds in his biplane with skywriting and banner-flying throughout the 1960s at the Minnesota State Fair, reported an encounter of a manta-shaped craft that was probing the area and emitting a green beam of light. This green beam of light hit Doyle and instantly paralyzed him. Doyle reported that the green beam induced mathematical equations into his mind, along with the symbol Omega. Doyle then experienced visions of floating among the stars and alien landscapes, including blue ground, red oceans, and green skies. When the beam of light subsided, Doyle fell prostrate on his face, just like Paul on the road to Damascas during his conversion to Christianity. Following his experience with the manta-craft, Doyle had a large sign constructed and mounted on his home that read, "UFOs Welcome." Countless reports of such experiences, in which an alien presence shoots a beam of light at a subject and produces mental changes, for better or worse, give us confirmation that there is, in fact, some type of nonhuman intelligence at play on this planet. Whether it is indigenous to the planet or from outer space is subject to speculation, but it is here nonetheless, and has been manipulating human minds for centuries.

Oscar Magocsi

During the same year that stunt pilot Chuck Doyle had his mind-altering UFO experience, 1975, Oscar Magocsi reported an encounter with extraterrestrials while vacationing in Canada. While Magocsi was sitting around a campfire, he suddenly had the distinct feeling of being watched. Looking up, he noticed a silent, disk-shaped flying saucer about 400 yards away from him, hovering over the tree line. As the craft fluctuated with changing colors, Magocsi felt a tangible physical sensation in his brain, like his mind was being probed. After his UFO encounter, Oscar became intensely interested in the subject of UFOs and attended many lectures on the Phenomenon in the area of Toronto, Canada. This report illuminates an interesting difference in that, for some reason, Oscar was not selected by the luminous presence to experience an abduction, although he was subjected to the definite sensation of having his brain scanned. Was there nothing of interest to the Phenomenon inside Oscar's brain? In light of the fact that this experience inspired Oscar to start attending UFO lectures, perhaps the purpose of the encounter was simply to add one more member to the rosters of UFO buffs and perpetuate the mythos of extraterrestrial visitation while they do whatever they are actually up to. Whatever the reason, we can rest assured that it was an intelligent calculation on the part of the hidden UFO intelligences to further their own intended purposes.

Alternative Reality Theory

1975 also brought Allen H. Greenfield's *Alternative Reality Theory*. Greenfield's theory proposes that there is, in fact, an extraterrestrial presence on Earth that is manipulating the human population to its own ends. However, Greenfield's theory, and many other UFO theories, while acknowledging an alien presence on Earth, do not attempt to speculate what the "alien agenda" actually is. However, as time moves forward and we observe how the technology we are creating is becoming bigger than anything we ever imagined, we are beginning to realize that the alien agenda has something to do with the manipulation of humankind into a technological singularity. That is a certainty, but the full details continue to remain unknown. Whether the purpose of guiding humans into the Singularity involves a strictly alien agenda, an open contact event that was previously impossible due to the lack of appropriate receiving equipment on our end that will become available during the Singularity, or a merger of some sort between our intelligence and theirs, remains obscure. Perhaps merging with our technology is the method of choice for alien contact with the inhabitants of Earth. Maybe the intelligent plasmas that exist to us as the elementals and are manifested by internal pressures in the earth seek to finally enter our physical world permanently by means of guided construction of suitable artificial intelligence, or all of the above. The huge missing element in all of these scenarios is an understanding of the actual fate of humankind during this process. When the Singularity comes to pass and the mission of the aliens or elementals is finally accomplished, what role will humanity play on Earth at this point? Although the approaching Singularity is an unstoppable certainty, and it is near-certain that we have been manipulated by a nonhuman intelligence to get there, the fate of humanity after this is accomplished is unknown. Various theological UFO theorists who are on to the gist of all this, like Thomas Horn, author of *Exovaticana*, have concluded that the "aliens" in question here are actually demons posing as aliens for the sole purpose of entering our physical realm as a Satanic army of animated robots of human construction in order to fight an end-time battle with Jesus Christ and his holy angels. Somewhere in this scenario, I suppose the "Rapture" will occur and take the Christians up in the air with Jesus and his army (in a flying saucer?) as Armageddon ensues in an all-out cosmic war for final possession of the planet Earth.

Evil Angels?

Adding fuel to the idea that both God and his angels, along with Satan and his "fallen" angels, use flying saucers for transportation throughout the universe were several Christian ministers/ authors of the 1970s who were making the connection between God, the Scriptures of the world (including the Bible), and UFOs. As the epidemic of UFO-related cattle mutilations ensued throughout the United States and Canada, some mainstream Christian preachers began postulating that the intelligences behind the flying saucers are actually *angels of God*. Corroborating ideas presented a few years earlier by Pastor Barry Downing in *The Bible and Flying Saucers*, one of the greatest and most respected fundamentalist Christian preachers and televangelists of all time, the Reverend Billy Graham, published, *Angels: God's Secret Agents* in 1975. Rev. Graham's book proposed that the angels mentioned in the Bible are, in fact, transported from place to place doing God's work in the flying saucers that cruise Earth's skies. Rev. Graham writes (Angels, pg. 9):

> *Some reputable scientists deny and others assert that UFOs do appear to people from time to time. Some scientists have reached the place where they think they can prove that these are possibly visitors from outer space. Some Christian writers have speculated that UFOs could very well be a part of*

God's angelic host who preside over the physical affairs of universal creation. While we cannot assert such a view with certainty, many people are now seeking some type of supernatural explanation for these phenomena. Nothing can hide the fact, however, that these unexplained events are occurring with greater frequency around the entire world and in unexpected places.

Graham's book details one particular UFO event that occurred in Japan that struck him as particularly celestial in nature:

On January 15, 1975, a squadron of UFO-like objects, resembling a celestial string of pearls, soared silently through the evening skies over half the length of Japan. As government officials, police, and thousands of curious citizens stared at the sky in wonder, from 15-20 glowing objects, cruising in straight formation, flew over Japan inside a strange misty cloud. Further, they were sighted and re- ported in cities seven hundred miles apart in less than an hour.

Did the citizens of Japan catch a glimpse of George Van Tassel's *Council of Seven Lights?* Are there actually luminous and normally-invisible ships of human souls that encircle the earth, as the disembodied humans revealed to Van Tassel during his personal flying saucer experience? Certainly Rev. Graham was likely correct in saying that some of the ufonauts are members of our tutorial ET race, and appear in the Bible as angels. This acknowledgement of the reality of flying saucers and their connection to otherworldly or "heavenly" realms by mainstream Christian ministers opened many minds within the Christian Church to the UFO phenom- enon. Modern Christian authors and lecturers such as Charles Missler, Thomas Horn, and L.A. Marzulli have also made the connection between Christian theology, extraterrestrials, and UFOs. The one big difference is, however, that instead of speculating that the ufonauts are angels, most modern Christian speculators have now concluded that the ufonauts are demons, or the *Nephilim,* i.e., the fallen angels who once mated with human females and are now back for a nefarious major role in end-times prophecy. These authors continue to make the Bible/ UFO connection clear, but take an opposite stand to their literary predecessors from decades past. Concerning the identity of the ufonauts, there is probably an element of truth in both positions. Just as Graham was likely correct that some of the ufonauts are cosmic intelligences that most Christian sects would interpret as angels, Marzulli, Horn, and company are probably also partially right. Some of the intelligences behind the UFOs do not appear to have the best interest of the human race in mind when they endeavor to achieve their own plans, using hu- mans callously to achieve their own goals. The self-seeking UFO intelligences would surely fall into the category of Satan and his demons, or the Muslim equivalent - the Shaitan Djinn. As scholars of the world's sacred texts are beginning to realize, they are based on older, Sumerian cuneiform tablets. This is a reality that I outlined in my first book on the subject, *Outgrowing the Bible: The Journey from Fundamentalism to Freethinking.* As it turned out, I was not alone in 2000 in discovering the Sumerian origin of the Bible. As scholars now realize, the tales of the Old Testament come from much older, regurgitated Sumerian accounts with different names assigned. The works of scholar and orientalist, Zecharia Sitchin, author of the *Earth Chronicles* series, including *Genesis Revisited* and *Twelfth Planet*, and of Dr. Chris Hardy, author of *DNA of the Gods*, Adam and Eve are *Adapa* and *Titi* in the Sumerian stone tablets, the biblical Noah is the Sumerian *Ziusudra/Utipishtim*, and Enoch is *Emmeduranki*. The emotionally-volatile Yahweh of the Old Testament is none other than the Sumerian *Enlil*. All Hebrew characters in the Old Testament have their parallels in the much older Sumerian culture, and it is all there to read in the thousands of stone tablets that have been unearthed.

Are Angels and Demons Artifacts of Machine Intelligence?

In *The Eighth Tower*, Keel revealed his inner suspicions that all so-called paranormal manifestations on this planet are *produced by some sort of alien machine left behind on our planet by a nonhuman intelligence.* This postulated alien mechanism is operating from an ancient program installed by its ancient creators, whoever or whatever they really were. The machine is getting old now, and is producing absurd "glitches in the Matrix," so to speak, i.e., apparitions and cryptids that haunt mankind. *The Eighth Tower* was honored as an insightful work outside the United States. However, many ufologists here in the US felt that Keel "jumped the shark" with this book. However one views this work, it does an effective job of presenting the idea that many concepts on this planet that have been around for a very long time now like "angels" and "demons" may turn out to be artifacts of a machine intelligence whose function it is to recruit and persuade human entities, through a process of reincarnation, into two camps of "good" vs. "evil." Presumably there is a final destination or a winner at some point, as if we are all involved in an alien computer game of sorts, with both good and evil aliens of a higher-than-human order competing for allegiances. If AI researcher Ed Fredkin was right, and the physical universe is a computer attempting to solve a problem (such as the problem of Good and Evil), then we are left with the idea that angels and demons may exist as electronic aspects or subprograms to the master program, which we would call "God." The angels and demons occasionally intervene and/or interact with humans for their own purposes and employ various strategies in doing so. Personally, the idea of a "cosmic war" has always disturbed me. I have always preferred to think that the phenomenon of war was a byproduct of primitive tribal populations who were competing for survival, something we outgrow as we evolve. That this sort of competition and warfare, or even a fight for eternal survival, may extend into the high celestial realms is, at best, disappointing. However, we cannot exclude the idea that something of this nature might actually be going on, only on a much bigger scale with larger stakes in the game. The old hermetic axiom, "As below, so above" is haunting. If the universe is as it seems to be - an intentionally-constructed computer program working on a problem, we are left with the possibility that angels and demons are part of the program and serve some higher function in the ultimate purpose of the universe. In other words, what we have always called "angels" and "demons" might actually represent a post-biological superintelligence of two conflicted factions, both sides seeking to gather power and numbers unto itself for an eventual "win."

Angel Categories

Graham's book gleans all the various types of angels from the Bible. The following categories of angels and their functions are identified:

Archangels: Reverend Billy Graham pointed out in his book on angels that only one entity exists in the category of archangel, and that is the Archangel Michael. The Archangel Michael was the first "Prince of Heaven" prior to Lucifer and 1/3 of the angels defecting from Heaven together. Archangel Michael, in my view, if he exists at all, is a non-biological light being or "subprogram" of the master program ("God"), who is also non-physical and exists outside of the physical universe, or is embedded in some imperceptible way. Archangel Michael is currently the administrator of cosmic forces in service to the master programmer. The Archangel Michael is also the designated administrator of God's *judgement* against the former Archangel Lucifer, who now exists as "Satan," the leader of the "fallen angels." In addition to the biblical passages that involve Lucifer, there are pseudepigraphal legends that make the whole story seem like so much mythology. It is said that Lucifer was once an archangel like the Archangel Michael, and was referred to as "The Morning Star" (as is the planet Venus). Taking into consideration that the stars in the heavens were once thought of as celestial personalities, it is easy to imagine how the myth of the "fallen ones" might have developed. When the heavens are observed by mortals, the dark night sky is full of angels (stars). However, the night sky is not completely full of celestial brilliance, but also contains areas of darkness in between the stars. Therefore, the brightest star, the morning star, Lucifer, is said to have left his first estate, taking 1/3 of the angels with him into "outer darkness" (the blackness between the stars). The heavens are now no longer full with the celestial host, but partially empty following the defection by Lucifer and his angels. Interestingly, some New Age religious cults are bringing back the age-old idea that stars are sentient beings, or angels, and portray the earth, the stars, and all celestial bodies as advanced beings in the celestial hierarchy, all having self-awareness, consciousness, and personalities of their own. In general, according to Billy Graham's study, angels serve as messengers, are normally invisible, and serve to protect believers from their enemies or serve humans in times of hardship or danger. Archangel Michael, allegedly the high celestial leader of the Forces of Good, is predicted to lead the "angels of God" in a final battle on Earth against Lucifer and his fallen angels in an event referred to in the Bible as the "Batttle of Armageddon." This scenario is reminiscent of the movie, *Star Wars*, in which the Jedi, as masters of the Forces of Good, are pitted in a cosmic battle against Darth Vader, a person who was once a heroic Jedi Knight and now leads an army of darkness that all fell prey to the temptations for power presented by the Dark Side of the Force.

Gabriel: Another specific angel of high position, Gabriel, is the chief messenger of God (the master creator of the program known as the physical universe). Gabriel's messages involve mercy and promise. Gabriel announces God's unfolding plans to the mortals of Earth. Gabriel was the entity who manifested as an apparition to announce the birth of John the Baptist. Gabriel also informed Mary that she was to give birth to a son, Jesus. Many ufologists believe that Gabriel was the actual father of Jesus who created a human-angelic hybrid to fulfill the purposes of the Forces of Good, i.e., gathering good human souls into the energy matrix at large in the universe that operates from this paradigm, who do not engage in any thoughts or actions that are not in the eventual best interest of all parties concerned, as opposed to the "evil" paradigm of self-aggrandisement and dominion over others with no regard for any damage inflicted upon other sentient beings or the universe at large.

Cherubim: The Cherubim were depicted by Ezekiel during his classic UFO encounter as sitting to each side of "God" (ET) as he sits on his "throne" (the cockpit of the celestial vehicle described by Ezekiel). The Cherubim, far from being the little winged infants depicted in art renderings during the Renaissance, were described as pertaining to the "glory of God" (his luminescence) and the heavenly vehicle. Ezekiel described Cherubim as having "eyes all around" and encompassed by "wheels within wheels." This sounds more like descriptions of the mechanical or luminous aspects of the actual vehicle (God's "throne") used to travel throughout the universe, such as the lights and luminescent radiance of the vehicle itself and the effects of its propulsion system.

Seraphim: Seraphim are only mentioned in the Bible once, and are described as six-winged creatures above the "throne of God" that exist to continually "sing" and "praise the name of God." This "singing" of the "praises of God" seems like a pre-scientific way of describing the actual sound of the ET craft in question, the "winged creatures" being six luminescent rays emanating from the craft itself. If authors such as R.L. Dione and others are correct, and the god of the Bible (Yahweh in Hebrew or Enlil in Sumerian) drives a flying saucer, it is easy to picture God (ET) seated within the dome/cockpit of a flying saucer or disk, surrounded by "Cheribum" with 'eyes all around" (lights around the perimeter of the disk), and the six-winged Seraphim (6 plasma rays emanating above the cupula, the throne of God), and emitting the "heavenly sound" of a flying saucer. If modern Bible scholars are correct, and the UFO phenomenon is intimately connected to the celestial personalities that are described in the Bible, including Yahweh himself, and the vision of Ezekiel represents an early UFO encounter, perhaps the descriptions of Cherubim and Seraphim were an early reference to the mechanical, visual, and audible aspects of a glowing celestial vehicle making a brilliant heavenly appearance with heavenly sounds, and not designations of beings at all.

Dark Angels

As I pointed out in my 2000 book, *Outgrowing the Bible*, the Bible is a very convoluted and contradictory manuscript. One example would be the admonition not to murder allegedly given to Moses on stone tablets. Following the command not to kill (or murder, depending on the translation), the same deity commands all the horrific genocide that is described in the rest of the Old Testament. Likewise angels, as described in the Bible, also have a dark side and are depicted in passages as administering murder and mayhem. Oddly, angels are sometimes depicted in the Bible as instruments of death and destruction, such as in the destruction of the cities of Sodom and Gomorrah; the mass execution of 185,000 soldiers in an Assyrian encampment (II Kings 35); the killing of 70,000 Israelites with pestilence; the destruction of the city of Jerusalem; the killing of Egypt's firstborn, and other atrocities. Angels exist as "destroying angels," or "angels of destruction." An angel was allegedly sent to kill Herod Agrippa with worms (Acts 12:23). This completely destroys the idea that angels are all-good, and represent only the forces of benevolence in the universe. According to the Bible, angels also have great destructive power and are capable of killing both individuals and multitudes. Just as the Bible depicts Yahweh (the Sumerian "Enlil") as having a nasty temper who commanded acts of genocide at times, as well as a benevolent deity, the angels also move from sweet ministering agents to instruments of death in the same passages. Graham could have just as easily named his book, *Angels: God's Hit Men*. This schizophrenic biblical depiction of both God (allegedly the creator of the universe) and his angels, both of which are capable of love and mercy as well as mass murder and mayhem, is beyond normal human morality. It is not human, superhuman, or anything at all to be desired or emulated. Rather, the biblical stories about angels depict either conflicted human authors who can't make up their minds about the true nature of God and his angels, or a conflicted machine intelligence that is grappling with the concept of "Good" vs "Evil." If the latter is true, it has inspired humans over the years to deeds of both good and evil in order to figure out the morality play it is currently involved with. If the universe itself represents an intentionally-created computer matrix constructed by Post-Singularity Artificial Superintelligence (PSASI) or a higher form of life that is beyond the physical universe itself, all life on Earth, as well as any extraterrestrial biology that happens to exist in the universe, are but unwitting participants in this weird problem-solving effort. If this is true, and the universe is a created machine, all sentient beings in the universe exist as bits of data that a vast, nonphysical, nonhuman intelligence (possibly a machine intelligence by our standards) is using to acquire knowledge and solve the current problem it is working on, using the universe itself and everyone in it as a vast information-gathering mechanism.

Secular Authors

In addition to the UFO books that were written by evangelists like Billy Graham who made a Bible/UFO connection, good secular UFO books were published in 1975 as well, one of which was co-authored by two giants of scientific UFO research - astronomer Dr. J. Allen Hynek, and computer scientist Dr. Jacques Vallee. Their book, *The Edge of Reality*, correctly ascertained the futility of attempting to contact distant alien civilizations with primitive radio signals. Hynek and Vallee also presented speculations concerning the occulted, underlying nature of the UFO phenomenon. They acknowledged the very real possibility of nuts-and-bolts extraterrestrial visitation, but also postulated the existence of an underground cabal of human beings in possession of advanced technology that utilizes holographic projections to manipulate human perceptions and behavior. There is a long legacy of possible interaction between humans in secret societies and extraterrestrial intelligences that involves the promises of advanced technology. Keel's work elaborates complex speculations involving a mechanical system of hallucination-projection that has been perpetrated onto the human race for a long time now by an unknown intelligence on Earth from an unknown terrestrial location. Keel speculates that this equipment is possibly an artifact of ancient alien technology that was left behind by an extinct human or otherworldly civilization from our earthly past. This projection system, Keel proposes, is possibly responsible for a variety of "paranormal" manifestations, everything from Bigfoot to poltergeists and UFOs. This broken system blindly records electrical impulses from human minds and operates like a broken record skipping on an old phonograph, deceiving humans that fall prey to its unusual machinations over and over again, generation after generation. As we can see from literature written during the decade of the 1970s, UFO researchers were beginning to suspect at this time that the underlying nature of the UFO phenomenon was electronic or mechanical in nature, but at this point in time, the concept of the Singularity was not fully developed or understood as it is today. Now many are beginning to put the pieces together. It is beginning to dawn on researchers, theoretical physicists, and even conventional scientists that the UFO phenomenon, as well as the universe itself, may have computational underpinnings and purposes.

[*On June 5, 1975, France detonated an underground nuclear bomb, Operation Achille, followed by another 146 underground nuclear detonations*]

Nordic Extraterrestrials and Angels

Other than specific descriptions of the Archangel, the Cherubim, and the Seraphim, angels are also depicted in the Bible as invisible entities who can appear to mortals as ordinary human beings, using their own will, or under God's decree. Human-looking angels paid a visit to Lot in the Old Testament. The biblical admonition that some who are kind to strangers have "entertained angels unaware" indicate that human-looking angels are, in fact, among the mortal human population and can pass for flesh-and-blood humans completely unnoticed. Likewise, many today believe that human-like extraterrestrials are among us now and go unnoticed.

Are the angels of the Bible and the "Nordic" extraterrestrials of modern ufology one and the same? In July, 1975, a couple (names withheld) driving en route to the city of Lamar, with no one else on the road, suddenly noticed, at about 350 feet up in the air, a hovering, elongated, donut-shaped object reminiscent of the craft described by Harold Dahl in the Maury Island Affair. These flying donuts were about half the size of a football field with a highly-polished metallic appearance. The couple pulled off to the side of the road, but could not get close to the object because of a barbed wire fence. They watched for a while when suddenly three of four little white clouds popped in from the east, followed by a huge cloud that moved in front and covered the metallic object. When the cloud moved away, the object had vanished. Both witnesses felt unusually calm and peaceful. Under hypnotic regression, the wife remembered trying to run toward the object, but her husband told her to stay in the car. Suddenly she found herself inside the object where two beings, one male and one female, greeted her. These beings were described as very tall, thin, and beautiful. Their hair was long and blonde and so were their eyelashes. The male entity wore a silver belt. She did not want to leave the craft but suddenly found herself back in the car. In the UFO literature we find many such encounters with beings who have long blonde hair to their shoulders, beautiful wide eyes and high foreheads, and it cannot go unnoticed how similar these descriptions of Nordic aliens are to both apparitions of heavenly beings and flesh-and-blood messengers of God (Angels) who are mentioned throughout various sacred texts from the ancient world. These comparisons lead many to conclude that the angels of the Bible and the Nordic aliens of modern UFO lore are one and the same.

Cattle Mutilations Again

As Vallee, Hynek, Keel, and many others pondered the UFO mystery and published many books that made speculations about the underlying intelligences involved, along with their possible agendas, a virtual tsunami of cattle mutilations continued throughout the United States and the rest of the planet. Here in the US, hundreds of cattle mutilations were reported in Minnesota; Wisconsin; Kansas; South Dakota; Nebraska; Iowa; Texas; Colorado; Arizona; and California. Most of the animals involved were found with their blood completely removed as if by a large needle. The holocaust of cattle mutilations involved mostly Black Angus and white-faced cattle. The Feds were no use at all. For example, on September 24, 1975, the *Gazette Telegraph* in Colorado Springs, Colorado, ran the headline, *FBI Won't Help Investigate State Cattle Mutilations.* The article explained that, since the cattle mutilations were accumulating in multiple states throughout the US, investigations should fall into the hands of the FBI. Despite the pleading by state representatives and affected residents of Colorado, and despite some 130 cattle mutilations reported in the state during the previous two years, the FBI refused to get involved, stating that the evidence for interstate activity wasn't "strong enough." Someone in the FBI wasn't doing their homework. The cattle mutilation events of the 1970s were wrought with complexity. They often included reports of unmarked black helicopters, UFO sightings, or luminous blobs in the night sky that were sometimes caught on film. Many of the cows appeared to have been dropped from heights sufficient to break their bones when they hit the ground with their blood completely drained and organs missing. Many different theories were proposed, including Satanic cults who used the blood for rituals (too widespread to be a feasible explanation), human cattle rustlers (who left the meat and took only blood and soft tissue for some reason), and natural predators. The "natural predator" explanation is ludicrous, as there are no known animal predators that are capable of completely removing the blood of an animal, or are in the habit of removing the blood and certain soft organ tissues while leaving the rest of the carcass with broken bones laying on the ground to rot. The nail in the coffin of the natural predator explanation lies buried in police files around the world that contain grisly cases in which humans have been mutilated in exactly the same manner as the bovine mutilations. As in the case of the cattle mutilations, there are no known animal predators on this planet that have the habit of extracting all the blood from a human body, coring out the anus, and removing the genitals and/or other soft tissues. Modern UFO expert and contactee Dr. Steven Greer claims to have inside intelligence that the cattle mutilations were conducted by our military, the purpose of which was to induce fear of our extraterrestrial visitors in order to justify a war with the aliens. Dr. Greer warns that, after properly terrorizing the population, the military has plans to fake an alien attack using holographic imagery for an all-out power grab and possible one-world government. The connection between UFOs and cattle mutilations continues to be controversial and difficult to confirm. Despite the various speculations concerning the identity of the perpetrators and the rationale, the cattle and/or human mutilation phenomenon of the 1960-1970s remains an unsolved mystery. One thing is for certain - there are some very weird things happening on planet Earth, and the general population at large remains oblivious, partially due to official obfuscation. It does seem to me that there is too big of a "coincidence" between the years in which cattle mutilations were epidemic along with the many reports of alien abductions. If, as many UFO and alien abduction researchers have concluded, the alien abduction phenomenon was actually a hybridization program in which humans were genetically modified, some taken to other planets, and some integrated into human society, the timing would be such that it would be logical to conclude that the aliens, who were likely robots or biological androids without human emotions, were using blood, hormones, genital organs, and soft tissue in some aspect of their hybridization program, a program that seems to have started sometime in the early to mid-1960s and continued for the next 15 years or so. If hybrid babies were reintegrated back on Earth after being genetically modified sometime between 1966-1980, that means, at the time of this writing, alien-human hybrids are currently walking among our non-modified human population and are currently in the age bracket of 35-54 years old. If this is a reality, many of the alien/human hybrids have already had children of their own by now. Mention cow mutilations or alien abductions to anyone now, and they might yawn or even giggle a little, or make fun of you. The era has come and gone, and the project is now completed. Many hybrids have no idea that they are hybrids. If I am correct in my speculations concerning the actual alien agenda, that it has much to do with the creation of a technological singularity very soon, I would predict with confidence that many of these first or second generation hybrids are currently busy working in the field of artificial intelligence. I, for one, expect to see amazing things from the AI community in the years to come, things that will be absolutely mind-boggling and never before imagined. Also, with geniuses in the appropriate age bracket alive today, such as Elon Musk, Steve Omohundro, and Dr. Nick Bostrom, I wouldn't be surprised if the alien/human hybrid program was tremendously successful, and they are already working in the field of artificial intelligence.

Sergeant Moody

Staff Sergeant Charles L. Moody was a crew chief in the United States Air Force. Moody was driving home around midnight to Alamogordo, New Mexico, on August 12, 1975, after working all day at Holloman Air Force Base. After arriving home and finding that he wasn't tired, he changed clothing, got back in his car, and drove to the outskirts of town to have a cigarette and watch meteors in the night sky for a while. As he sat on the left front fender of his car sky-watching, a dull, metallic, wobbling object dropped out of the sky and moved toward him to a distance of about 80 feet. As it hovered in the air about 20 feet above the ground, the wobbling suddenly stopped, and he could see shadows of humanoid creatures in the windows. Frightened, Moody tried to start his car and flee, but his vehicle would not start (EM effects). He became paralyzed and could not move. Then the feeling of fright completely left him, and he felt as if he was floating on a cloud. The next thing he remembered was watching as the disk moved away from him, sailed off, and vanished in the sky. After the object left, his car started just fine. He drove home to discover about an hour and a half of missing time. The next day he felt soreness in his back, and asked his wife to look at him. His wife discovered a red, inflamed puncture wound on his back near his spine. A few days later Moody broke out in an all-over rash and went to the William Beaumont Army Hospital, where he was told that he had been dosed with radiation. He was treated with an enema. During the following months, memories began to flood back into his consciousness about what really happened on the evening of his encounter with the bright object. It appears that Moody had been implanted with the standard "screen memory" that is provided when one of these objects or creatures decides to draw blood or other bodily fluids from a human victim. He began reporting the usual abduction scenario of being taken aboard a flying saucer by short bald aliens in coveralls for purposes of examination. UFO investigators administered tests that indicated Moody was telling the truth as he knew it, which is usually the case with these types of victims. When they requested medical records from the hospital, they conveniently disappeared (which is also common) as if hospitals have been instructed to ditch the records by government agents who know that there is a little-known and unacknowledged danger to humans in our skies, and they do not want the general public to know about it. At any rate, Sergeant Moody's full testimony about his encounter can be found in Jim and Coral Lorenzen's July 1976 issue of the *APRO Bulletin*.

Mysterious Plasma Intelligences

In *Time Storms*, Randles presented her theory that at least some UFO encounters involve a poorly-understood natural phenomenon that disturbs the local fabric of space-time, causing episodes of missing time and other mental aberrations in the humans who encounter them. Randles may be correct that such a natural phenomenon exists, especially in the window areas, referred to as "Vile Vortices" by zoologist Ivan T. Sanderson. These vortices are identified areas in which people, animals, airplanes, and ships are known to disappear from the face of the earth and/or experience time anomalies when traveling near or through them. However, the fact that so many human victims who encounter mysterious lights in the sky are left with inflamed puncture marks on their bodies that appear to have removed blood and/or body fluids leaves investigators with a multitude of disturbing possibilities to consider. The luminous orbs of pulsating plasma, the genre that seem to be a product of certain geophysical and/or tectonic forces that appear in the window areas or vortices appear to possess some sort of sentience or intelligence of their own. There are places like Marfa, Texas, that actually have public viewing areas for people to see these mystery lights, and no one really knows what they are. One would think that these types of pulsating plasmas would be an inanimate electrical discharge of some sort, but that is not all there is to them. They are known to chase or follow people, respond to flashlights, and have even been known to respond to human thought. These natural phenomena, known as earthlights or spooklights, whatever they are, may or may not have anything to do with reports of missing time, and/or the inducement of hallucinatory or virtual-reality journeys involving short, bald-headed aliens, medical experiments, the removal of sperm or eggs for reproduction or hybridization experiments, or journeys to outer space and other worlds. These orbs of geophysical production, whatever their true nature, have always coexisted with humans, as they are an integral part of the earth's physical structure. Some earthlight researchers even wonder if they might have something to do with harboring human souls during periods of discarnate life between physical lifetimes, soul energies that animate the orbs and give them the appearance of conscious intelligence. These natural, sentient orbs are the "whispering spirits" of Apache Indian lore. It does not seem congruous with their apparent spiritual nature that the earthlights would conduct ghastly blood-gathering campaigns on humans or animals, but, if not, we are left with physical evidence that there is something else out there that is just as elusive as the earthlights that is actually doing this. A possible culprit for the thousands of cases of blood-drawing episodes that leave physical puncture marks on human and animal victims may be the invisible predators on the order of Trevor James Constable's *sky creatures*, otherwise known as *energyzoa*, or atmospheric beasts. These sky creatures are amoeba-like flying cryptids that are currently unacknowledged by science and appear to draw blood to stay alive. These energyzoa creatures, who seem to have the ability to draw energy from a variety of different biological and electromagnetic sources, are likely a distinctly different phenomenon from the indigenous earthlights. Both exist in the EM ranges that are normally invisible to humans (infrared or ultraviolet). The large number of cattle mutilations that have been documented, along with the mutilation of an occasional human, during which blood, soft tissue, and sex organs are removed, may have been required for the human-alien hybridization program. This hybridization program appears to have had a beginning, a middle, and an end. The mutilations and abductions appear to have lasted together for about a decade and a half as the reports of alien abductions also soared, peaked, and then declined. As abduction researcher David Jacobs states in his MUFON lectures, even though abductions still occur, the nature of the abduction accounts have changed over the decades. Jacobs has concluded that the hybridization program is now complete as the alien-engineered human/alien hybrids are now an integral part of the human population and breeding with non-engineered humans, as he discusses in his book, *Walking Among Us: The Alien Plan to Control Humanity*. It is uncertain at this point in time whether all of these phenomena, i.e., earthlights, energyzoa, abductions, disappearances, time storms, and cattle/human mutilations are interrelated in some fashion as parts of one vast meta-phenomenon, or if they are distinct facets of the UFO phenomenon that are confused with one another. However, it is safe to conclude that blood and other organic tissues were, in fact, harvested from both animals and humans by someone or something for at least a decade and a half for a purpose that remains clandestine, such as a genetic-engineering or hybridization program would have to be. No one is going to volunteer for something like that. When one considers the amorphous, luminous blobs of energy that have been observed and photographed at the scene of cattle mutilations, (see Linda Moulton Howe's *An Alien Harvest*, pp 37 & 40), along with Trevor James Constable's energyzoa critters that he discusses in *Sky Creatures* and *Cosmic Pulse* and personally photographed in the 1950s just prior to cattle mutilations and alien abductions arriving on the scene, it appears at first glance that at least some of the luminous orbs that people encounter are involved with, or at least associated with the mutilations. Other luminous orbs in the earthlight category appear to be more of a human spiritual essence, an intrinsic intelligence of some sort that is embedded within the earth itself, of which humans, and possibly all animated life on Earth are a part of. At least some of these flying creatures, orbs, objects, and phenomena are capable of inflicting radiation poisoning on human beings, so caution must be exercised when approaching them. Some of the luminous manifestations on Earth paralyze their victims, induce episodes of missing time, manipulate the human mind, or implant screen memories of typical alien-abduction scenarios, possibly to disguise the true nature of what they are doing with us. These luminous intelligences are normally invisible until they move into action. They have been known to chase the heat signatures of automobiles and airplanes. Keel wrote of one case in which an unidentified flying object was observed growing luminous appendages while attempting to take off with an entire bloodmobile! Keel also pointed out the strange fact that women who are chased in cars by such luminous flying objects are often on their monthly menstrual cycle. At any rate, we are left with the grisly prospect that there is, in fact, an unknown species of cryptid or unknown phenomenon on this planet that has a need for human and animal blood, biological fluids, and soft tissues, either for food to survive, clandestine projects, or for some other unfathomable purpose. It is my personal tentative conclusion that Trevor James Constable's sky creatures, i.e., invisible predators that are completely obfuscated to our awareness, are at the heart of many legends of vampires around the world and throughout the ages, and have been here for a long time. The increased need for blood during the era of abductions and cattle mutilations was likely due to the advent of alien genetic engineering activity, and had little or nothing to do with the activity of the energyzoa. It is unknown whether the energyzoa were employed by the aliens in some fashion for this hybridization project. These energyzoa, truly alien in nature by our standards, may be a part of or an extension of the alien presence on Earth that is guiding us toward the technological singularity, a separate form of life that is indigenous to Earth, or both. It may be that the energyzoa creatures, as well as the earthlights that may or may not harbor human souls, are all an integral part of an alien design from the beginning, and all work together to bring about the alien agenda on Earth. Other than having the power of illusion over the human mind to keep us all buffaloed, the energyzoa and earthlights both demonstrate behaviors that do not indicate a high level of intelligence as we understand intelligence. They often demonstrate animal-like repetitive actions that are instinctual in nature, like some form of invisible sky-mosquito. As I attempt to answer one giant mystery of the UFO phenomenon, that somehow we are being guided to a technological singularity by alien intelligences for ultimate purposes we can only speculate about, some of which are beneficial to humankind and some that leave humankind as we know it discarded and extinct, a whole host of unanswered questions cascade through the minds of anyone who investigates these phenomena beyond a superficial level, all of which are worth exploring.

Are Trevor James Constable's sky creatures still here? In the 1950s, Constable appears to have captured some of these mysterious entities on film and video. Constable even gives detailed instructions in his books on how to film these critters. With all the legends of vampires on this planet going back to ancient days, it is reasonable to assume that the creatures responsible for the vampire legends from our past are still present, and shall remain here as part of our planetary family. However, if there is any truth to the idea that radar and other forms of man-made electromagnetic radiation that has been developing since the 1940s irritated the creatures, they may have, for the most part, gravitated into our upper stratosphere, or even migrated out into outer space, moving on to seek other forms of radiation to feed their plasma bodies. Indeed, plasma is a fundamental energy in the universe. The energyzoa creatures that Constable caught on film may actually permeate the entire universe. If the energyzoa creatures are still here in the lower atmosphere like they were in the 1950s, it seems like more people would be catching them on film today, especially in an age when virtually everyone has a camera. Even "full-spectrum" cameras of the "ghost hunting" variety are readily available. So why are there not more people catching energyzoa on infrared film today to further ascertain their existence? The obvious answer for skeptics is that the creatures never existed in the first place, that Constable just kept catching odd camera and film anomalies and passing them off as living creatures, but that solution is too easy. We also have a multitude of satellites in space now, some of which have infrared cameras pointed at the earth to map the geophysical terrain and temperature anomalies. Astronaut Story Musgrave shot video of an object in the stratosphere that might be such a biological plasmoid creature, and the STS-75 tether accident footage is very convincing that some type of extremophile in space exists that were attracted to the electromagnetism that was emitted from the broken tether. Trevor James Constable himself examined this NASA footage and proclaimed the objects in the footage as the same sky critters that he filmed decades ago. Are these sky creatures the actual Overlords who are guiding humanity toward the Singularity and may seek to download their consciousness into our artificial intelligence and gain permanent entrance into what we call physical reality? If this is the case (it seems unlikely), then the sky creatures Constable captured are of a high-order alien or indigenous intelligence, and smart enough to change their vibratory level to evade detection by our infrared cameras in the modern age since the 1950s. They may be now hiding in realms of invisibility beyond the infrared and are currently taking refuge there in order to continue to exist in our skies without detection by modern equipment and remain clandestine. If Constable's sky creatures are not the Overlords, are they being used by the Overlords as a weird tool of living plasma in order to gather the needed biological supplies? Are the energyzoa telepathically-controlled by the Overlords in order to gather necessary tissues for their hybridization program? This also seems unlikely. The sky creatures who draw blood from humans and animals, by all accounts, leave simple red, swollen puncture marks on the bodies of victims. The precise surgical procedures that are found in cattle mutilations appear to involve a laser-like instrument that actually cuts tissues between the cells. All indications are that the cattle mutilations of the 1960s - 1980s were conducted with precise, intentional surgery. Whoever or whatever conducted these mutilations knew exactly what parts they needed, and retrieved them expertly and efficiently. That does not appear consistent with the capabilities of bloodsucking vampires that leave puncture marks on their victims. So the energyzoa creatures that seek blood may simply be attracted to a cattle mutilation in progress because of the blood gathering involved. The aliens conduct the precise surgeries, and the energyzoa show up to scavenge. It appears that some of the creatures have been caught on film in the vicinity of cattle mutilation events, but that does not mean they are the ones who are conducting the mutilations, as they are simply not equipped to do so in the precise manner that we observed. Constable himself mentioned in his books that he suspected the energyzoa are the culprits who have conducted the cattle mutilations. In his view, the creatures were acting out in response to an electromagnetic invasion of their natural habitat brought on by human technological development. If this is correct, the creatures conducted a murderous defense of their territory from the 1960s to the 1980s and eventually vacated the atmosphere of Earth altogether. So either the energyzoa creatures were not responsible for the mutilations and represent in entirely different phenomenon that we do not understand, or their blood drawing abilities were utilized by the Overlords to assist with the hybridization program, which is unlikely due to the crude nature of the capabilities of the energyzoa's blood drawing apparatus. As much of the technology used by the Overlords appears to be paraphysical in nature, it is not beyond the realm of consideration that they could have created a variety of plasma creatures as a temporary manifestation to do their bidding on Earth for the time period in which they were needed. If, in fact, the energyzoa have been on Earth for a long time and are responsible for our vampire legends, then they are a separate, indigenous phenomenon that needs blood and biological tissue to survive. Perhaps the Aswang or Manananggal from the Philippines or the Brazilian Chupa Chupa are examples of these invisible vampiric inhabitants of Earth, who exist in the sky or underwater and come up to terrorize human populations from time to time, leaving puncture marks on their bodies as they gorge themselves with human blood. If Constable's sky creatures are living creatures of plasma that are normally invisible and draw blood from biological creatures to survive, then the geophysical earthlights that come up from the ground and appear to possess some sort of intelligence are a separate phenomenon and represent yet another mysterious unexplained version of plasma intelligence. Perhaps our alien overlords are able to use the natural plasma phenomenon of earthlights and/or energyzoa creatures and invest them with a purpose and intelligence of their own. If the sky creatures, the geophysical earthlights, and our alien overlords are all separate and have nothing to do with one another, perhaps either the energyzoa, the earthlights, or both, are able to mimic the real aliens in order to keep their true nature hidden from us. In this case our indigenous aliens are mimicking the extraterrestrial aliens in order to perpetuate the belief that they are from outer space, so that we humans will not conclude rightly that they are a fellow inhabitant of Earth who coevolved with us, an intelligent life form that we would likely hunt down and kill if we knew for sure that they existed by drawing blood from us. It gets crazy as we imagine one type of alien, native to Earth, mimicking another type of alien from outer space or an alternate dimension who are here creating hybrids to assimilate into our society and propel us into a technological singularity. It is no wonder that so many want to dismiss the Phenomenon out of hand. Who wants to believe that we are completely immersed in Cryptoreality that lies beyond our perceptions or comprehension?

NASA STS-75 Footage

The NASA STS-75 footage is evidence that some type of living extremophile exists, and is able to live in space. Dr. Rhawn Joseph, author of *Astrobiology, The Origin of Life, and the Death of Darwinism*, accepts the existence of these creatures and is suing NASA for keeping knowledge of these creatures hidden from us. Joseph suspects that these creatures are some type of proto-life that exists throughout the universe, and may hold the very key to how life arrived here on Earth in the first place. Do the sky creatures, or energyzoa, represent the true ultraterrestrials, the Etherians, and possess the power of illusion over humans? Is Earth just a "blood farm," where we and other animals serve as sustenance for creatures that remain unknown to us who have a completely alien intelligence? My current position is that earthlights, time storms, energyzoa, and the entities that conducted precisions surgery on animals and humans during their hybridization endeavors are distinct and separate phenomena from one another, but this could be wrong. One thing is certain. That is, there are a multitude of mysterious phenomena that may or may not be related to one another haunting our planet and leaving us completely bewildered, to the point that many of us deny that anything is happening at all, because let's face it - it's just too weird.

Fire in the Sky

On November 5, 1975, 22-year-old Travis Walton and several coworkers from Snowflake, Arizona were behind on a logging contract in the Apache-Sitgreaves National Forest in Arizona. To finish the contract on time, they were all working overtime. Around 6 p.m. this day, as they began the drive from the job site back home to Snowflake, the crew noticed a glowing yellow object in the woods. Mike Rogers, Travis's boss and best friend, stopped the truck. Travis got out of the truck and started walking to get a closer look at the object as the others shouted for him to get back in the truck. The crew reported that they saw a blue-green beam lift Travis off the ground and strike him, knocking him backwards onto the ground. Frightened, they all fled the scene, and from there, one of the biggest three-ring circuses in UFO lore ensued in the days to follow. The crew stopped at Heber, Arizona, where they called the police and reported their crew member missing. Law enforcement officers dispatched a search party to the scene where Travis was last seen. The police found nothing, and immediately suspected that some sort of hoax was being perpetrated. The suspicion of hokum increased when Sheriff Coplan and Mike Rogers paid a visit to Travis Walton's mother, Mary Walton Kellett, to inform her that her son, Travis, was missing. Mary's immediate reaction to the news, rather than expressing concern for her son, was to calmly ask if anyone other than the police and the eyewitnesses had heard the story, a reaction that some consider inappropriate for the situation.

By the following day, November 6, officers and volunteers had thoroughly searched the area for Travis and found no traces. Suspicions then grew that some form of malfeasance was at play. Helicopters, vehicles, and horse-mounted police were brought to the scene, and still found nothing. By that weekend, news of the story had spread internationally. Snowflake, Arizona, was suddenly inundated by an onslaught of news reporters, oddball UFO buffs, and serious UFO investigators. A search into the personal history of Travis Walton revealed an avid interest in UFOs and a history of petty check fraud. Mike Rogers began mentioning that because Travis Walton was missing, he would no longer be able to complete the logging contract, and expressed hopes that his missing friend could substantiate the bailout. Snowflake Town Marshal, Sanford Flake, threw in his two cents that the whole affair was just a prank in which Duane and Travis Walton had released a lighted balloon. This brought Sanford Flake trouble from his own wife, who accused her husband of concocting a story more unbelievable than a UFO abduction. Subsequent interviews with Travis Walton's mother indicated that she knew more than she was telling, and it was suspected that she was hiding Travis. On Monday, November 10, the entire logging crew was given a polygraph test by Cy Gilson of the Arizona Department of Public Safety. The test involved questions to determine if the crew had any knowledge of where Travis was, and if they had actually witnessed a UFO. All the men that took the test passed, indicating that, if the UFO was fake, the crew had no prior knowledge of it. Following the results of this initial polygraph test, many accepted the UFO story. When Travis Walton emerged days later, the story became even more obfuscated by the involvement of the *National Enquirer*, who offered to fund an investigation by Coral Lorenzen of the Aerial Phenomenon Research Organization (APRO) and provide a medical examination. The medical examination revealed a lack of ketones in Travis Walton's urine, which would have been present if Walton had gone with little or no food for 5 days as he reported, as the body begins breaking down fats for nutrition. Despite this medical evidence that Travis Walton had not gone without food as reported, Walton then provided inquiring UFO researchers with an elaboration of his adventures aboard an alien spacecraft, during which he allegedly received a medical exam and a tour of the craft by bug-eyed creatures. Walton was eventually subjected to hypnosis by APRO consultant James A. Harder. Following the hypnosis, Harder noted that Walton's conscious recall of the event was the same as his recall under hypnosis, which is usually not the case with abductees. The *National Enquirer* then arranged for the administration of another polygraph test for Walton after agreeing to give Walton the power to keep the results of the test from the public at his discretion. This polygraph test was conducted by John J. McCarthy of the Arizona Polygraph Laboratory, who reported that both Duane and Travis Walton failed the test. McCarthy's opinion was that the Waltons were attempting to perpetrate a hoax, and noted that Travis Walton had held his breath at times in an attempt to beat the test. The *National Enquirer*, the Waltons, and APRO agreed to conceal these negative results, an act that would later come out and serve to fuel public accusations of fraud and cover-up. Walton took two more polygraph tests after the McCarthy test and passed them, but the suppressed results of the McCarthy test would continue to follow Walton wherever he went after that. Three years later, in 1978, Walton published his version of the story, The *Walton Experience*. That same year Bill Barry published another version in *The Ultimate Encounter*. Walton's book was eventually made into a film, *Fire in the Sky*, which rendered an embellished story that was far removed from Walton's original account.

To this day, the Walton case is mired in controversy. UFO researchers remain divided in their acceptance of its reality. Abduction researchers who hold that alien abductions occur in physical reality and represent the bodily transport of a person aboard a nuts-and-bolts flying saucer are more likely to accept Walton's testimony as true. However, researchers who hold that alien abductions involve psychic interactions between a luminous form of intelligent energy and human minds that induce anomalous psychological experiences that are indistinguishable from physical reality are doubtful about Walton's story. These researchers also note many other areas of concern that throw doubt on the whole affair, such as the dissimilarity of Walton's story to other abduction accounts; Walton's financial motivation to get out of the logging contract; Walton's history of petty criminal activity; Walton's pre-existing interest in UFOs; the fact that Walton's boss and best friend, Mike Rogers, had recently watched a television show called *The UFO Incident* that recounted the abduction experience of Betty and Barney Hill; the fact that Walton's initial medical report was inconsistent with someone who was deprived of food for 5 days as he reported; hypnosis sessions that were markedly different from other abductee accounts; ambiguous polygraph results over the years; conflicting opinions of UFO experts and researchers concerning Walton's alleged abduction; the embellishment that was present in Walton's book, The *Walton Experience*; questionable journalism by the *National Enquirer* and other media; and the embellishments that appear in the movie, *Fire in the Sky*. Fortunately, the reality of the alien abduction phenomenon does not stand or fall on the truthfulness of Travis Walton's story. There are so many alien abduction accounts from around the world that cor-roborate with one another that the reality of the Phenomenon is ascertainable without this particular case. The airing of *The UFO Incident* and the fact that Rogers watched it prior to the case doesn't matter, as imagery from science fiction appears to be utilized in real abduction accounts, as obtained from an initial mindscan. The imagery from the television show may have served as image-fuel for an actual psychic projection from Walton's mind after exposure to intelligent luminosity. However, when all factors are taken into consideration, there are just too many inconsistencies and weird details involved in the Walton account to rely on the story. Even so, the possibility remains that Walton may have told the truth as he knew it all along. If this is the case, my heart goes out to Travis Walton and everyone involved who have been unfairly tortured by our scrutiny in the attempt to get to the underlying truth. The Walton abduction account, along with the books and the movie, have served to mold public conscious-ness concerning the "alien abduction phenomenon" and prompted many to accept the reality of UFOs, regardless of the truth content in Walton's story. It is in this manner that both hoaxes and true accounts contribute to the transformation of human consciousness and belief within the minds of the public at large.

Are UFOnauts Demons?

To cap off the year 1975, John Weldon and Zola Levitt published their book, *UFOs: What On Earth Is Happening?* This book presents the exact opposite view from other Christian spiritual writers, such as Reverend Billy Graham in *Angels: God's Secret Agents*, R.L. Dione in *God Drives a Flying Saucer*, or Pastor Downing in *The Bible and Flying Saucers*. To counter the theological speculation that the ufonauts are angels of God, Weldon and Levitt proposed that the pilots of flying saucers, far from representing angels, are actually demons who are manipulating humanity to accept the life of an enslaving dictatorship under the coming Antichrist. Like all the UFO theories, they are probably partially right. There is a case to be made for both, that there is, in fact, an age-old alien influence on Earth that seems to represent two different factions. One is the "tutorial" race that author William Bramley called the "maverick race." Other designations for this race are the Ascended Masters, the Nordics, the Pleiadians, the Ashtar Command, or the Great White Brotherhood. The tutorial race of extraterrestrials have always been interested in assisting humankind into higher realms of spiritual and societal evolution. The tutorial race or races may be the beings that we have always called angels. On the other hand, there also appears to be an alien presence that is malevolent. These malevolent extraterrestrials have been referred to as the Shaitan Djinn, Demons, or Tricksters. These are the aliens who produce the black eyes, nose bleeds, mutilated animals and humans, concussions, scoop marks, implants, missing time, abduction experiences, unpleasant medical experimentations, frightening UFO occupant encounters, radiation burns, the Men in Black (MIB), and even untimely deaths. In other words, the legend of a "war in heaven" may have its roots in truth. As we approach our technological singularity, both of these conflicting, interdimensional factions may attempt to seize and/or merge with our technological treasure, the fruits of thousands of years of labor and human hardship. In this scenario, our alien tutorial race is seeking to merge with us in our expansion of mind and consciousness that the Singularity will bring and finally make indisputable open contact with the human race. As they are superhuman, we may not be able to understand them or communicate effectively with them at all until we expand our minds by billions of times the current capacity by merging with artificial intelligence. The subversive or malevolent race, the candidates of which include self-replicating von Neuman probes from another galaxy or dimension; advanced biological robots who worship science; John Dee's conjured entities; Aleister Crowley's *Lam;* the Islamic *Djinn*, Satan's Demons; disembodied humans dwelling on the lower astral plane who seek permanent entrance back into the physical plane; or whatever else is allied with the Forces of Darkness in this vast universe, some of whom we may not even be aware of or able to comprehend at present. If there is any reality to legends of the cosmic war, we will certainly become aware of it when we achieve the Singularity. Cryptoreality will suddenly surface, and we will finally know the truth behind the UFO phenomenon, for better or for worse.

A Birthday Visit

On January 6, 1976, Mona Stafford was celebrating her 36th birthday at the Redwoods Restaurant north of Stafford, Kentucky. With her this evening were two friends, Mrs. Elaine Thomas, and Ms. Louise Smith. After the birthday get-together, they left the restaurant and were driving back home to Liberty, Kentucky. On the drive back, Mona spotted what she thought was an airplane about to crash, and asked the driver to speed up to get out of its way. A clearer view of the object revealed a classic flying saucer - a huge, grey, metallic flying disk with a white glowing dome on top, red lights around the perimeter, red and yellow lights underneath, and a blue beam of light bursting down from the middle of the bottom as it flew. During an APRO investigation, the women described the craft as large, the size of a football field, hovering in the air with a rocking motion. The inside of their car was suddenly lit from behind with the blue spotlight. Their car was then seized by the craft, pulling the car to the left at about 85 miles per hour. As the women tried desperately to regain control of the car, they all experienced a burning sensation in their eyes and a pain inside their heads. The women felt the sensation of the car moving backwards and were mesmerized by the beauty of the craft itself. Then, as mysteriously as they had been seized, their car was on the road again, peacefully driving home. When the women arrived to Ms. Smith's home, they found that there was approximately an hour and 25 minutes of time that was unaccounted for. Each of the women's hands and faces were burning, and they all had a rectangular mark on the back of their necks with defined edges like a burn right before it blisters. Mona Stafford had the most severe case of conjunctivitis, and all three women were in pain. They went to their nextdoor neighbor's house, Mr. Lowell Lee, and told their story. Mr. Lee put the women in separate rooms and asked them to draw what they saw. All three women drew nearly identical objects. On July 23, 1976, all three women passed a polygraph test administered by Jack Young of Professional Polygraph Tests, Inc. out of Lexington, Kentucky. The following day the women met with Dr. Leo Sprinkle, who conducted hypnosis sessions with them. The emotionally distraught reports under hypnosis revealed classic abduction elements, along with elements of near-death experiences (NDE), such as the perception of being transported up through a long tunnel with a light at the end, being placed on a table and undergoing medical examination by several short nonhuman creatures, and a mechanical eyeball looking them over on the table, all common elements of the thousands of UFO abduction reports that have accumulated over the decades. In Dr. Sprinkle's notes he concluded that, in his opinion, this group of percipients were honestly reporting an actual experience as best they could recollect and describe.

Skeptics of the UFO abduction phenomenon, including astronomer Neil deGrasse Tyson, advise individuals experiencing an abduction (in a mildly sarcastic manner) to obtain a physical artifact from the ship and bring it back with them, so that he and others will believe. This is not likely to ever happen. Comments like Tyson's indicate a grotesque misunderstanding of the underlying nature of the alien abduction phenomenon, and possibly a poverty of imagination. The skepticism is based on a narrow, mechanistic view of the world, and a possible misunderstanding of the complex nature of reality itself. In the minds of skeptics, the distances between solar systems are too great to overcome. The fuel requirements are too extensive to be feasible. The sightings are too numerous. Is the earth Grand Central Station for UFOs? The elements of absurdity that are embedded in the accounts are just too weird to accept as anything other than fantasy. The reports of different types of creatures, mostly humanoid, are unlikely to represent reality, and so on and so forth. It doesn't seem to occur to UFO skeptics that something far more complex is possibly going on. Somehow, UFOs, whether they originate from another planet, a parallel universe, or represent an exotic indigenous intelligence unknown to our science that induces virtual reality experiences in humans, have become an integral part of the human psyche whether one believes in flying saucers or not. Real or imaginary, flying saucers have been interacting with humanity on a psychological level for a very long time now. These sky wonders morph over the years as the human mind evolves. They induce paraphysical experiences in humans that are so real they can pass polygraph tests, and suffer physical symptoms from the encounter. Victims often suffer active symptoms of PTSD. The abduction experience involves an altered state of consciousness that is induced by unknown intelligences from somewhere. Screen memories are possibly utilized that keep the true nature and intentions of the Phenomenon hidden from its human percipients. The UFO abduction experience is extensive, mostly unreported, worldwide, and ongoing. It is also probably about to morph into a different direction soon that will surely take humans by surprise, a direction that humans can only try to imagine and speculate about. I wonder what our cosmic Overlords have in store for us next as reports of medical experiments, sperm and ova extraction, and Venusian Space Brothers fade into the past? Whatever it is that the Overlords use next to captivate the human mind and imagination, I'm sure it will be spectacular and updated as we head swiftly into what our mysterious visitors wanted all along - the human achievement of a technological singularity for possible alien purposes. The possible outcomes of the Singularity range from benign open contact and assistance from our advanced extraterrestrial cosmic tutors, to a horrifying alien self-replication and cosmic dominion event, a planetary takeover by human-alien hybrids produced during the abduction and mutilation era of 1960-1980, or domination by demonic entities from another dimension who merge with our artificial intelligence for the final battle, Armageddon, or the return of the earthly dead into immortal bodies of silicon. Whatever the case may be as time moves forward from here, we are all in for some surprises. A great awakening is at hand. Let's hope humanity survives it.

Mothman in England?

As reported to paranormal researcher Tony Shiels by Don Melling, on April 17, 1976, Melling's two daughters - June, age 12, and her sister Vicky, age 9, were walking through the woods near Mawnan Church in Cornwall, England while on a family holiday vacation. To their utter astonishment, the two girls witnessed a winged humanoid creature hovering above the church tower. The girls immediately ran to tell their father, Don Melling. The family became so disturbed over the sighting that they cut their vacation short. June provided a drawing of the creature, and it looked much like the depictions of Mothman that terrorized Point Pleasant, West Virginia in the United States a decade earlier. Melling quickly refused interviews with his daughter, although June's drawing of the creature was made available to Shiels. Two months later, on July 3, 1976, Sally Chapman, age 14, and her friend Barbara Perry, were camping in the woods near the same church when they heard a loud "hissing sound." Chapman, standing near the tent, turned around to witness a large, silvery-grey humanoid creature with red eyes and pointed ears. The creature rose into the air, revealing black claw-like pincers, horrifying the two young female witnesses. Reports of creature sightings continued the following day. Two more reports came two years later in 1978 near the same church. Another paranormal researcher, Jonathan Downes, interviewed a young man, "Gavin," 13 years later who described witnessing the same creature in 1989. Then, in 1995, a female tourist from Chicago wrote to the *Western Morning News* in Truro, reporting her sighting of a man-bird with a horrifying face and gaping mouth, pointed ears, clawed wings, and glowing eyes. Dubbed the *Owlman*, one cannot help but wonder if the creature sighted in England was one and the same creature that was sighted in West Virginia in 1966 - Mothman. Is the earth home to a population of cryptids? Or, as many UFO researchers have concluded, are the cryptids connected in some way to the UFO phenomenon? Whatever the answer, the mystery continues. Something on this planet can appear in a variety of strange manifestations, much to the terror and bewilderment of the human population.

Brad Steiger and Alien Mind Control

In 1976, prolific author Brad Steiger made his contribution to the idea that the alien agenda involved exercising mind control over humans. In Steiger's version, the aliens act as benevolent "cosmic tutors" who use space beams to influence the human mind by use of 3-dimensional or holographic images. This would certainly correlate with the claims of Nikola Tesla, who reported receiving holographic, 3-dimensional, fully-rotational images in full color in his visual field from extraterrestrials, images that demonstrated the mechanics of his inventions down to the tiniest detail. I, for one, totally believe that Tesla did, in fact, receive such 3-dimensional images from extraterrestrials, just as Ted Owens (aka PK Man) interacted with SI (Space Intelligences) and Uri Geller and Dr. Andrija Puharich contacted the inhabitants of

Hoova from their ship, Spectra, who identified themselves as *computerized intelligences who had transcended the biological stage of life*. However, whether or not the ETs involved with Tesla were benevolent cosmic tutors working through Tesla's mind as a channel to guide us into a better, more environmentally-friendly free wireless energy, or were manipulating Tesla as a cog in a wheel toward the Singularity for purposes of their own remains to be seen, although by now any reader should know my position in this matter. Contactees such as Tesla, Owens, Geller, and Puharich, along with so many others, are part of a grand scheme of guidance, manipulation, or both, to force humanity into a technological singularity. We are nearly there in just a few decades, and there is no turning back now.

UFOs: It Has Begun

1976 produced a great documentary that is now considered a UFO classic, called *UFOs: It Has Begun*. This amazing film was narrated by none other than Rod Serling, the host of one of my all-time favorite TV shows - *The Twilight Zone*. In this enjoyable 93-minute film, Rod Serling takes viewers on an intriguing journey into many of the pertinent historical UFO sightings, both from the ancient past and the modern era. His classic, enigmatic voice adds an ambiance of enjoyable creepiness to the viewing experience. The film features in-depth discussions by such research giants of the field as Dr. Jacques Vallee and Dr. J. Allen Hynek. Also included are personal interviews with actual ranchers who were victims of the cattle mutilations. In so doing, the film effectively knocks the laughable "predator theory" out of the ballpark, as there are no predators known to this world that can effectively exsanguinate and animal or human and surgically extract specific organs in a patterned fashion that has occurred all over the world in exactly the same manner. Amazing photographic evidence in shown of the ubiquitous lights in the sky associated with the cattle mutilations, strange luminous objects near cattle fields which appear more like undulating, shapeshifting blobs, biological creatures of some sort, rather than mechanical nuts-and-bolts craft, as 1950s fringe-science researcher Trevor James Constable so bravely postulated.

The Allagash Abductions

I suppose it makes sense for so many UFO encounters to occur while camping, as camping places people in a position to observe the day or nighttime sky more intensely, and places them in isolated environments, which the UFOs apparently seek. It is one thing to simply observe something in the sky that is not readily identified. However, it is quite another to have an intimate and mysterious interaction with the unknown intelligences behind the UFOs. In the summer of 1976, four fellow art students, Charlie Foltz, Chuck Rak, and twins Jack and Jim Weiner, took an adventurous camping trip into the wilderness of Maine at the Allagash Waterway, traveling north from Boston to escape the city into the peace and quiet of the deep woods for a few days. On the fifth day, after they had been camping almost a week together, they set up camp at Smith Pond, where they planned to go fishing at night amongst the twisted stumps jutting up out of the isolated swamp water. There was no moon that night. It was pitch dark, so they decided to build a campfire to use as navigation back to the campsite from the water when they were finished with their fishing that night. With Charlie in the front, the twins in the middle, and Chuck in the rear, the four men paddled several hundred yards out into the water together in their canoe. There in the dark among the twisted, protruding stumps, like a scene right out of *The Creature from the Black Lagoon*, the four men began to feel a "sense of presence." Chuck, sitting in the rear of the canoe, pointed to a luminous orb that was rising in the distance above the tree line and growing bigger. At first the men assumed it was some sort of airplane coming toward them, but noticed that it was completely silent. As the bright light became larger, it began changing colors and pulsating, *as if it were alive*. When this mysterious luminosity was about 100 yards away, it paused. Charlie decided he would try shining a flashlight at it to see how it reacted. The instant the flashlight was switched on, a beam of light smacked the 16-foot aluminum canoe, illuminating the men completely with a blinding light. Chuck was exhilarated at the prospect of communicating with the luminous object, but his buddies began frantically paddling to escape as the object kept drawing nearer and nearer. Suddenly, all four men found themselves mysteriously back on shore, watching the light in the sky become smaller and smaller, slowly fading into the distance until it was gone. They made their way back to their campfire, which they built to last all night, and discovered it was burned out to smoldering embers. The men exchanged few words, and went to sleep by the remains of the fire. From the next day forward, the men seldom discussed what happened that night. However, two years later, in 1978, memories of the events of the evening began to surface in the men. By 1980, Jim Weiner had been in a car accident. Jim was suffering from temporal epilepsy from the crash, and was having difficulty sleeping. He began having nightmares of nonhuman creatures. In Jim's visions, the creatures prodded him, and manipulated his genitals with instruments. He sensed extreme malevolence during these ordeals. At first, Jim remained silent about his experiences, but eventually told his brother. To Jim's astonishment, Jack began telling Jim of his own nightmares, and the two twins discovered through conversation that they were having the same visions. As Jim's condition deteriorated, he finally told his doctors, and a psychiatrist sensed that it all sounded like an abduction experience. The doctor referred Jim to UFO researcher Ray Fowler, who suggested hypnotic regression. Four years after the 1976 incident, in 1980, all four men were hypnotized, and the details of that fateful night began to surface. All four men recalled seeing the light as it came too close for comfort, just before the missing time and the return to the shoreline. All four men reported similar experiences, going up into the light and landing on their backs on a table surface. The men reported an encounter with beings who had insect-like eyes and hands with only four fingers. Panic set in as the men saw what looked like surgical instruments in their hands, as they all feared being cut open. From that point, the men remember the creatures trying to adjust their positions back into the canoe from which they were taken. Chuck reported that one of the creatures had a difficult time with Jim, as he was rather heavy, and then the other two men were beamed straight onto the shore. Jim and Chuck then left the canoe and joined the other two on shore. It became apparent by the recollection of the burned-out fire that the men had all experienced "missing time." As ufologist Raymond Fowler, who originally suggested the hypnotism sessions, stated in an interview for the *History Channel*:

> *If you had the amount of evidence for the reality of the Allagash abductions for any other mundane subject, in a court of law, you could use it to hang a person. But because of the bizarre nature of the case, that's not going to happen, people aren't going to accept the evidence, although the evidence is there.*

In Fowler's 1993 book, The *Allagash Abductions*, Fowler concluded that, due to the excellent characters of the witnesses, along with the strong corroboration of their individual accounts under hypnosis, that this case is highly significant for supporting the objective reality of at least some so-called alien abduction experiences. Even so, I suspect that an outside observer would've just seen four men fishing in a canoe, and then going back to the shore. Alien abductions, for the most part, appear to involve the transference of consciousness into a time-dilated alternative reality. Screen memories are implanted that can be retrieved under hypnosis if an abductee attempts to glean information from their own subconscious in this manner. That abductees usually recall the typical medical table scenario is no assurance that we understand what is actually going on during an abduction. If the aliens are helping us evolve in some fashion or manipulating our minds, the scenario that abductees typically described may be false memories to replace the actual interaction for some reason that remains a mystery. Perhaps the reality of the actual encounter would be too traumatizing for humans to endure. The medical procedures reported make it easy for skeptics to place abductions into the category of fiction, and that might be the actual intent of such memory implantation. Whatever the case, the method of choice used by the aliens has proved very effective, and I am sure that the aliens know exactly what they are doing.

UFOs in Tehran, Iran

One of the most credible, multiple-witness UFO events of all time happened in Tehran, Iran, on September 19, 1976. The incident involved multiple ground witnesses, both Iranian citizens and Iranian high-ranking military officials, plus Iranian pilots and crews of F-4 Phantom jets. Along with the eyewitnesses, there were unmistakable electromagnetic effects and solid radar confirmation. Just after midnight, citizens began calling in UFO reports to Shahrokhi Air Force Base, Tehran, Iran. The reports made their way up to the deputy commander who, after checking to make sure that no known aircraft were in the area, and then seeing the UFO himself, dispatched an F-4 Phantom jet toward the UFO. Control tower operators watched as the jet headed north from Tehran toward the light in the sky. As the jet arrived to approximately 25 miles away from the flying object, all defenses in the jet were shut down. As the pilot discovered that he had lost all communication and instrumentation in the cockpit, he immediately broke off the pursuit to retreat back to the base. As soon as he turned around, he regained his instrumentation. As the first pilot landed, a second F-4 took off to make a second attempt at catching up to the UFO. At 27 miles from the UFO, the pilot made airborne radar contact, indicating that the object was about the size of a Boeing 707 tanker aircraft. At 25 miles to the object, the pilot gained visual access, describing a rectangular pattern of flashing strobe lights that were flashing so fast, he could see all the colors at once. Just after visual contact the object began to move ahead to keep pace with the jet. The pilot watched as the flashing object ejected a smaller object that began heading right toward him at fantastic speed. As the smaller object approached quickly, the pilot suddenly lost all communication and defense. Reacting quickly, the pilot began evasive maneuvers as the smaller flying object chased behind him by 3 or 4 miles. Desperate to get away, the pilot made a sudden evasive turn and when he did, the small object returned to the larger object and merged back with it. The onboard systems returned again, so instead of counting their lucky stars and returning to base, they audaciously turned back around to pursue the larger object again. When they did this, a smaller object was once again ejected, but instead of pursuing the jet, the object sped down to the ground. The pilot and crew thought it was going to crash onto the ground, but instead it landed on a dry lake bed, illuminating the entire area below for several miles around. The larger object then took off at high speed and vanished. The light on the ground vanished also, and the whole incident was over. No traces were found on the ground the next day by officials, although they did manage to find local witnesses who corroborated the fact that the light landed, and that was it.

Somebody Else Is on the Moon

In 1976 George Leonard published his book, *Somebody Else Is on the Moon*. Leonard's book revealed convincing photographic evidence of various types of artificial structures of unknown origin that exist on the moon. His book corroborates with Sergeant Karl Wolfe's Disclosure testimony that extraterrestrial bases on the moon were, in fact, confirmed from photographs taken by the first US lunar orbiter from June-July 1965. We probably need to get used to the idea that there are vehicles flying around in our solar system that are occupied by biological entities, artificial intelligence, or both. Massive numbers of astronomical observations have been accumulated by individuals such as Charles Fort and Dr. Morris K. Jessup, both of whom chronicled scientific observations of objects under intelligent control that have transited the sun, Venus, the moon, and other locations in the solar system. They have to land somewhere, and the moon seems like a great place to observe the earth, or use as a base of operation while traveling back and forth between the earth and the moon.

Captain Neil Daniels Speaks Out

In March, 1977, a DC-10, United Flight 94, was flying at 30,000 feet nonstop from San Francisco to Boston with Captain Neil Daniels, an experienced pilot with 30,000 hours of experience in the cockpit. Daniels, along with the first and second officers, witnessed a brilliant white light coming toward them that produced electromagnetic effects. These EM effects caused the airplane to veer off course on its own. All of the compasses on the airplane were giving different readings, and the three men were quite frightened about it. After regaining control by taking the plane off autopilot, the men finally returned the aircraft to its planned course, but they had some explaining to do. None dared mention that they had a UFO encounter, for fear of being fired. Years after the incident, Daniels mentioned the encounter to his boss while on a hunting trip together. His boss reacted very negatively, and stated that he was sorry Daniels told him about it. After this, Daniels returned to his silence. However, after years of silence, Daniels' official testimony is now online as part of Dr. Steven Greer's Disclosure Project testimony videos, as the former Captain Daniels no longer fears losing his position as the pilot of a commercial airline.

Tom Dawson

On August 6, 1977, a retired automobile salesman near Pelham, Georgia, Tom Dawson, 61, took a nice morning walk with his two dogs down to a pond to assess the fishing for that day. As soon as he entered the fence surrounding the pond, he and his two dogs, along with 20 head of cattle were frozen by a powerful mysterious force while he witnessed a flying saucer. The disk was nearly 50 feet in diameter and about 15 feet thick. Dawson watched as it hovered over the pond and pulsated while rapidly changing colors. This flying saucer had portholes all around the perimeter. Dawson was stupefied as a door opened and a ramp came down. Then, seven hairless, snow-white creatures with pointed ears and noses about 5 feet tall emerged from the craft. Some wore tight-fitting suits and others were nude. The beings chattered with one another in a high-speed gibberish. Dawson stood there paralyzed as the creatures placed a skullcap helmet on his head, along with what Dawson described as a hula-hoop device around his midsection. After removing the equipment, they collected some leaves and other natural items laying around, got back into the craft, and sped away. Once Tom was able to move again, he returned to his trailer and was having difficulty breathing and speaking. Tom was taken to the local hospital, where doctors medicated him to calm him down. He was later released to home. Tom was left with the distinct impression that the creatures would have taken him away with them as a sample of Earth's indigenous life along with their leaves if he had been a younger man. So what did Tom really encounter that morning? Maybe it was a "thirsty saucer," a nuts-and-bolts material object with flesh-and-blood creatures or an autopilot attempting to extract water from the pond to take back to a hidden earthly location, or perhaps a little farther to an alien colony on the moon or mars. Maybe it was something even more mysterious, like a blob of energy, a creature from another realm, who was caught in the act of hydrating itself. Earth's ultraterrestrials, whoever they are, who may not even be alive as we understand life, seem to exhibit a need for water and blood to survive in the physical dimension for more than a few moments. These creatures may have changed their own plasma body into a mental image that conforms to what human witnesses think flying saucers and extraterrestrials should look like. If this is the case, this lifeform has the uncanny ability to sense mental imagery in the minds of witnesses and quickly take an acceptable shape. If not a creature from Earth's invisible dimensions, actual ETs who have the technology to travel to Earth from vast distances in hyperspace or some other method we haven't imagined yet, no doubt have the power of illusion over humans to appear as they wish, possibly using some sort of holographic imaging. Tom could have been looking at a creature so strange from another world or dimension that he would have surely died of fright, so the aliens, whoever they were, presented themselves in the guise of leaf-and-stick collecting explorers conducting a routine, benign examination of Tom with their portable equipment, and decided to leave him on Earth due to his age. At least this way, Tom did not become another statistic when someone in his family found him dead on the bank of the pond with a horrified expression on his face, looking up at the sky (which also happens from time to time). We can only speculate that, in some of these cases in which witnesses are found dead with terrified facial expressions, that the aliens didn't quite make it into their disguise in time, and frightened their human witnesses to death on the spot. The connection between UFOs and water is quite puzzling, especially since many fairy encounters of old asked for water as well. It seems just a little too coincidental that both the solid crafts from underground or off-world locations, as well as the energy beings from another dimension, would seek water from this planet, especially since H2O should be easy to manufacture by intelligences who are able to build functional antigravitic flying saucers. Keel was probably right in that we are likely dealing with beings that are akin to "intelligent lightning," possibly alien, possibly an integral part of the Earth's own environment. Apparently, these lightning creatures can quickly shapeshift to avoid detection and transform into something palatable to their bewildered human witnesses who accidentally catch them extracting blood from an animal or taking a drink at the local watering hole.

The WOW! Signal
On August 15, 1977, Jerry R. Ehman picked up a narrow band radio signal from the Sagittarius constellation near the *Chi Sagittarii* star group that lasted 72 seconds while working at the Big Ear radio telescope at Ohio State University. This signal had all the expected earmarks of an alien signal. Ehman circled the signal on the computer printout and wrote the word, "Wow" on the paper. This radio interception has been referred to as the WOW! Signal ever since, and the true nature of the signal has remained a mystery. Recently, a professor of astronomy from St. Petersburg, Florida, Antonio Paris, has stated that he thinks the signal might have originated

from two passing comets. The signal was observed at 1420 MHz, a frequency used to observe neutral hydrogen. Professor Paris claims that two comets passing would release a lot of water. UV light from the sun would break up the water and liberate the hydrogen, thus accounting for the WOW! Signal. Other scientists remain skeptical that this could account for the signal. One such skeptic, James Bauer of the Jet Propulsion Laboratory (JPL) in Pasadena, California wants to test Professor Paris' theory by studying comets that are scheduled to arrive close enough for observations in the near future. Experiments with such comets should soon allow scientists to ascertain whether or not Professor Paris is correct, and finally determine if two passing comets could've produced the signal that has baffled scientists all these years. By the time many of you read this book, we should have a definite answer to the origin of this unusual signal. Even if this turns out to explain the enigmatic signal, the WOW! Signal has contributed to the perception of scientists for decades now that we might've already received a radio signal from an alien intelligence in outer space. The possibility that this signal was ET in origin has served to mold the public perception that we are not alone in the universe. The WOW! Signal has also encouraged UFO buffs since 1977 that their efforts to ascertain the reality of flying saucers has validity in science.

Chupa-chupa

Beginning in August, 1977, in the region of Para, in the northeastern delta of the Amazon River, on the Brazilian islands of Colares, Viseu, and Braganca, a recurring phenomenon that the Brazilians refer to as *Chupa-chupa* (sucker-sucker) returned to terrorize the island. This 1977 wave expanded the phenomenon into other areas such as Pinheiro and Sao Bento in the state of Maranhao. Multiple unidentified luminous and non-luminous objects of saucer and cigar shapes arose from the water and appeared in the skies, some of which projected a ray onto the island inhabitants below, causing dozens of injuries and at least 2 deaths. Many citizens fled the island in horror. Brazilian Army intelligence officers arrived to the area, along with prominent UFO researchers, including Dr. Jacques Vallee. Multiple photographs were taken of the phenomenon, and many credible witnesses were involved with this unmistakable reality of flying luminous blobs that chase humans and draw blood from them. Where exactly this fits in with the UFO phenomenon is anybody's guess, but it is real, regardless of how difficult it is to wrap our minds around it. There is, in fact, something on Earth that is normally invisible, can fly through the air, and seeks to extract blood from humans and animals, leaving puncture marks on victims.

Message from Ashtar Galactic Command

On November 26, 1977, television viewers watching their regularly scheduled programming on 5 different British TV stations were treated to an otherworldly experience that was similar to a great scene from the remake of *Superman* in the 2013 movie, *Man of Steel*. In this version of the Superman tale, which effectively captured the extraterrestrial element of Superman's origin better than any movie ever made about Superman thus far, the invaders from Krypton looking for Superman took over Earth's television sets and produced an audio-visual message for humanity. During this alien broadcast, eerie, ghost-like images emerged on television screens. Unbelievably, British television was once interrupted in a similar fashion. As British viewers were relaxed in front of their television sets, the following approximated message spontaneously came through in a frightening, garbled voice:

This is the voice of Vrillon, a representative of the Ashtar Galactic Command speaking to you. For many years you have seen us as lights in the skies. We speak to you now in peace and wisdom as we have done to your brothers and sisters all over this, your planet Earth. We come to warn you of the destiny of your race and your world so that you may communicate to your fellow beings the course you must take to avoid the disaster which threatens your world, and the beings on other worlds around you. This is in order that you may share in the great awakening as the planet passes into the New Age of Aquarius. The New Age can be a time of great peace and evolution for your race, but only if your rulers are made aware of the evil forces that can overshadow their judgments. Be still now and listen, for your chance may not come again. All your weapons of evil must be removed. The time for conflict is now passed and the race of which you are a part may proceed to the highest stages of its evolution if you show yourselves worthy to do this. You have but a short time to learn to live together in peace and goodwill. Small groups all over the planet are learning this, and exist to pass on the light of the dawning of the New Age to you all. You are free to accept or reject their teachings, but only those who learn to live in peace will pass into the higher realms of spiritual evolution. Hear now the voice of Vrillon, a representative of the Ashtar Galactic Command, speaking to you. Be aware also that there are many false prophets and guides operating in your world. The will suck your energy from you – the energy you call money – and will put it to evil ends giving you worthless dross in return. Your inner divine self will protect you from this. You must learn to be sensitive to the voice within that can tell you what is truth and what is confusion, chaos, and untruth. Learn to listen to the voice of truth which is within you and you will lead yourselves on to the path of evolution. This is our message to our dear friends. We have watched you growing for many years as you too have watched our lights in your skies. You know now that we are here, and that there are more beings in and around your Earth than your scientists admit. We are deeply concerned about you and your path towards the light and will do all we can to help you. Have no fears, seek only to know yourselves and live in harmony with the ways of your planet Earth. We of the Ashtar Galactic Command thank you for your attention. We are now leaving the planes of your existence. May you be blessed by the supreme love and truth of the cosmos.

In the days to come following this message, British engineers tried to locate the source of this rogue transmission, but were unsuccessful. Many British viewers were frightened, and police officers were dispatched on occasion to calm people down. The five television stations that were besieged by the strange message received a barrage of telephone calls from viewers who demanded an explanation. To this day, the message is completely unexplained. Hijacking 5 television stations at once is a technical feat beyond the capabilities of amateurs. Keel often elaborated on the complex capabilities of the etheric entities who dwell within the Superspectrum. As these beings are electrical in nature, they are masters of every type of electrical device, and are able to speak to people through radios, or interfere in radio and television programs. They are also able to manipulate EVP devices used by ghost hunters to make the devices say whatever words they desire. Keel experienced strange phone calls and electronic abnormalities in the course of his many UFO and Mothman investigations, as well as testimonies from his contact witnesses that these beings, whoever they are, have the capability to interfere with electronic devices at their own discretion, electronic interventions that no one on Earth has the capability of duplicating.

Leonard Stringfield and the Search for UFO Truth

Leonard Stringfield was the super-sleuth of ufology. He devoted his lifetime to researching UFOs and UFO crash reports. In 1977, Stringfield wrote the book, *Situation Red: The UFO Seige.* In this work, Stringfield became the first UFO writer to connect the dots between several different phenomenon such as cattle mutilations, phantom helicopters, Bigfoot sightings, and UFOs under the roof of one meta-phenomenon, with aliens as the root cause of them all. Stringfield concluded that advanced aliens have psychic powers that manipulate the minds of human witnesses to see and experience what they want them to in order to *advance an unknown agenda.* Since the work of Leonard Stringfield, many UFO researchers have evolved their thinking to this point, that flying saucer manifestations are a façade that hides the true appearance and intentions of the aliens. That is as far as it usually goes, that the true alien intent eludes them, and that is where they all stop. Maybe that is where they should stop to remain purely "scientific." What I am suggesting in this book is what I consider a likely end-game, my own personal speculations based on a near death experience (NDE) and personal research. What I am saying is that, based on all the evidence that has accumulated in the last 70 years or so, the UFO phenomenon likely involves an alien program to use humans as a tool to bring about a product that the alien presence is interested in producing. For some reason, the aliens need our assistance to achieve the Singularity. The UFO intelligences are likely an advanced computer-like alien intelligence that are programmed to survive and self-replicate. This self-replication might be achieved by manipulating humans to produce a particular type of artificial intelligence. This AI may have the ability to upload the entirety of the collective human unconscious, along with the sum total of human knowledge and the life experience of all biological creatures on Earth since humanity's inception. In so doing, the real aliens will add the sum total of life experience of 4.5 billion years of living creatures on Earth, along with human consciousness itself, in a merger that becomes part of their self-replication process for the next generation of post-singuarity artificial superintelligence (PSASI).

Alien Implants

On May 30, 1978, Tim Cullen and his wife Janet were driving through Colorado when they saw a bright light in the sky. They watched the light for what they thought was only a few minutes. However, when they arrived home they realized that they were about an hour later than they expected. Twenty years passed, and a routine x-ray revealed an unknown object inside Tim's arm. Tim contacted Dr. Roger Leir and told the doctor that he might have had a UFO encounter 20 years previously. On February 2, 2000, Tim had the object removed by Dr. Leir. A 6mm metallic object was, in fact, extracted from underneath the skin in Tim's arm. There was no inflammatory response to the foreign object, which is thought to be impossible. Dr. Leir also found a large number of nerve cells (called proprioceptors) near the object that was removed. Dr. Leir speculated that the object was using human neuro-energy to operate. There are many cases of alien implants like the Tim Cullen case. The late Dr. Roger Leir and his team have actually detected oscillating frequencies coming from inside the objects that he and his surgical team have removed from patients over the years. When these objects are removed, they don't appear to have any function. Only when the foreign objects are plugged into the human body do they appear to have a purpose. Some researchers believe that the implants track a person throughout their lifetime for the purpose of multiple abductions, sort of like a GPS tracking system. Others believe that the implants are capable of manipulating human behaviors in a way that is conducive to the alien agenda. Alien implants are a subject of much discussion among ufologists. The actual purpose of the implants remains elusive, but like every other aspect of the alien presence, there is likely an orchestration of purpose toward an eventual plan for humanity.

Demons in the Computer

In 1978, Gordon Creighton added a deeper dimension to Brad Steiger's notion of alien mind control over individuals. Creighton expanded Steiger's idea of a paraphysical alien control system into the realm of organizations and governments, or even entire countries. Likewise, Art Gatti proposed that the aliens are actually etheric parasitic thoughtforms that manipulate humans through the dark forces of the occult, adding fuel to the fire for the aliens-as-demons motif. There is, in fact, an alien presence on Earth that is manipulating humans in ways that inflict harm on occasion. Sometimes this harm is intentional and callous, and other times it appears accidental. Humans may have just gotten in the way a few times. Any presence that brings potential harm to humans is going to be demonized in our minds. Our concept of good and evil centers around what we feel is good or bad for us. If the etheric entities that haunt this planet with UFOs and other types of apparitions and monsters are working toward their own ends and humans are harmed in the process, it is easy to see why some would conclude that the entities are the fallen angels of Satan, or demons who seek to possess our souls or take us all to hell with them. In actuality, the aliens or demons might simply be a computer program designed and sent forth long ago from another world, a robotic presence that operates on this planet in the invisible realms. These computer-like alien intelligences simply have work to do that their programmers implemented when they were originally created. In other words, the "ufonauts-are-demons" crowd may be right, but they are suffering from an erroneous notion of what demons actually are. If the Christian demon turns out to exist as an energy manifestation of alien software design, and imperfectly disturbs the human world as they operate in the way they were programmed, some of the evil mystique of the "demon" can be removed. It may just be a machine that is simply doing its own thing.

The Valentich Disappearance

At about 7:06 p.m. on the night of October 21, 1978, a young, 20-year-old civilian pilot, Mr. Frederick Valentich, radioed the Melbourne Air Flight Service in Australia, to report a large aircraft with 4 bright lights that was hovering overhead from his Cessna 182 airplane. Valentich asked the Air Flight Service if any known aircraft were in the area, such as RAF aircraft. They reported back that there was not, that no known aircraft were near his airspace. Shortly after this initial transmission, Valentich came on the air again, reporting that the flying object in question was not an ordinary aircraft. It was long and cylindrical with lights on the outside, and was hovering right on top of him. Valentich reported that his engine was sputtering (EM effects). He said over the radio that he was going to attempt to proceed on to King Island with this unknown object right on top of him. Valentich's final words were, "Delta Sierra Juliet Melbourne" followed by a loud metallic sound. That was the last time anyone on Earth heard from Mr. Frederick Valentich. He simply vanished from this world without a trace. This last radio transmission was from Cape Otway. Earlier that same year, in January, 1978, Cape Otway lighthouse workers, along with a multitude of other civilians, including fishermen, school teachers, vacationers, and local police, reported bizzare UFOs. Later in the year, in July, 1978, lighthouse workers and a multitude of citizens witnessed a large, luminous orb that hovered out at sea from Cape Otway for about 30 minutes. Investigators into the Valentich disappearance discovered 15 distinct, solid civilian UFO reports from 12 noon to 9 p.m. the same day of his fateful encounter and disappearance. One report was from King Island, where Valentich was headed, and the rest were from surrounding areas. Investigations also revealed a multitude of similar, mysterious airplane disappearances near the location of Bass Strait, Australia, all near the same location where Valentich vanished with an unidentified object with flashing colors on top of him. Historically, ships have also vanished without a trace from the Bass Strait area. During the three previous months of July, August, and September, 1978, at King Island, where Valentich was headed, a UFO flap occurred in which residents reported moving lights in the sky, and lights that chased cars and frightened motorists. Even going back as far as 1896, just before the "Great Airship Mystery" of 1897 in the US, reports of cigar-shaped, dirigible-like flying craft were coming out of the Bass Strait in Australia, as reported in the *Melbourne Argus* newspaper. These facts are outstanding, as they represent a known area of the world, Bass Strait, in which the UFO phenomenon followed the same pattern of sighting evolvement, from the dirigible sightings to the advanced, light-flashing presentations typically reported today. Bass Strait, like the Bermuda Triangle and other locations of the world, seem to represent window areas in which UFOs repeatedly appear, year after year, in the same location, and demonstrate evolving configurations of vehicles that are also reported from the rest of the world.

Six years previous to the Valentich disappearance, a 1972 article written by zoologist Ivan T. Sanderson appeared in *SAGA* magazine in which Sanderson identified distinct areas of repetitive UFO appearances. Sanderson named these areas the "Vile Vortices" or "Devil's Graveyards" around the globe. These identified areas are notorious for missing airplanes and ships, and a multitude of anomalous electromagnetic effects reported by captains and pilots in these areas. Sanderson concluded that Earth is set up with a planetary grid system by which UFOs take advantage of natural geomagnetic forces that we are just now beginning to understand. The UFOs use these areas to make their appearances and conduct their business. David Wilcock's informative book, *The Source Field Investigations*, discusses Sanderson's work. Wilcock writes that when Sanderson's "Vile Vortices" are connected, they form a perfect icosahedron, or 20-sided platonic solid. Wilcock goes further to state that this planetary grid system may emanate an effect created by an actual crystal from the inner core of the earth that appears to be another platonic solid, a perfect dodecahedron, consisting of 12 perfect pentagonal faces. This all leads to a startling speculation that the physical universe may operate like a Rubik's Cube, in which certain vortices, geomagnetic conditions, and/or planetary alignments provide these "windows," or portals in the shapes of platonic solids. These window areas that are created by such geometric alignments may transport beings and objects through hidden realms of reality or parallel universes and back again. Evidence is strong that this knowledge of the universe is already known and utilized by beings that are technologically and intellectually beyond our present stage of development, who have been coming and going here on Earth for millennia now. Are these beings guiding us toward the Singularity for our own benefit, so that we can all catch up to them, or is there something technological that they seek from us? That is the million-dollar question.

Cosmonaut Pavel Popovich Sighting
In 1978, Cosmonaut Pavel Popovich reported witnessing a white triangular craft flying at 31,000 feet at an estimated speed of 1000 miles per hour, faster than the aircraft he was flying toward Moscow from Washington D.C.

Flying Saucers over New Zealand
On January 1, 1979, residents of New Zealand, and eventually the entire world, became aware that the Royal New Zealand Air Force had Skyhawk fighter-bombers on standby in response to a flurry of mass simultaneous radar confirmations of UFOs, along with multiple, credible

reports of visual sightings, combined with photographs and video of UFOs over New Zealand's Canterbury Coast during Christmas week, 1978. One professional TV cameraman, David Crockett, captured multiple luminous objects on 16mm color film. The brightest of these objects was described as a saucer-type vehicle with a luminous bottom half and clear bubble-top. Five UFOs were confirmed by the Wellington Air Traffic Control radar. Captain Vern L.A. Powell and copilot Ian B. Perry witnessed a UFO traveling at an estimated 10,800 miles per hour while in flight. These and multiple other sightings of strange luminous craft were analyzed by scientists, namely Navy optical physicist, Dr. Bruce Maccabee, plasma physicist Dr. Peter Sturrock, optical physiologist Dr. Richard F. Haines, biophysicist Dr. Gilbert Levin, electronics specialist Neil Davis, and astronomer Dr. J. Allen Hynek, along with other important scientists from all over the world who requested that their names not be associated with the UFO sightings for professional reasons. All these scientists endorsed the sightings as legitimate and truly anomalous, without any rational, conventional explanation possible. This case is known today as the Kaikoura UFO sightings.

Children and Aliens

A study was conducted in 1979 in Orange County, California, involving 180 mentally-gifted children who were asked to draw their own version of an extraterrestrial. Surprisingly, the drawings fell into distinct categories that would be recognizable by modern ufologists. The depictions included humanoids, robots, insectoids, and reptilian creatures, along with translucent apparitions. These results present the possibility that these creatures, all typical of reports of extraterrestrial contact experienced by UFO abductees and percipients, may have a life of their own within what psychologist Carl Jung called the collective unconscious. However, that doesn't mean that the creatures are not "real." It is interesting that the creatures exist in the minds of human children who have had no exposure to UFO lore that could plant the images of various types of extraterrestrials in their minds. Apparently, we are all somehow quite familiar with these entities. Is it possible that we have even existed in these forms ourselves in past lives, and retain an inner knowledge of these creatures when we reenter the physical world? If Earth is an actual, sentient being (as many believe), perhaps otherworldly visitors make contact with Gaia first, the actual Earth entity, and interact with a planet's discarnate population first, prior to extending open contact into the physical realm of a planet. Prior to actual physical contact, these populations occasionally appear as elusive apparitions or temporary physical objects to eyewitnesses. Whatever the case, it appears that these creatures are all somehow an integral part of our own psyches. Maybe Mother Earth herself, respected as a conscious, sovereign entity by extraterrestrial visitors, must give her own permission first before open contact in the physical world is established. Mother Nature, as the protector of her own children, will know when we are ready.

Housewives and Fairies

At approximately 6 a.m. on January 4, 1979, housewife Jean Hingley from Rowley Regis, West Midlands, England, had just waved her husband off to work when she watched an orange sphere materialize above their garage through her kitchen window. Three fairy-like beings about 3-1/2 feet tall with translucent wings and glittering spots flew by her window making a "zee, zee, zee" sound. Her Alsatian dog promptly fainted on her kitchen floor. These white-faced beings with large dark eyes and small slit-like mouths wore silver tunics and round clear helmets with a light on top. Mrs. Hingley then floated through the air into her lounge, where the beings were shaking her Christmas tree saying, "Nice, Nice." When Mrs. Hingley yelled that the creatures to stop, they fluttered over to her couch and bounced up and down like children playing. Mrs. Hingley then asked the entities where they were from, to which they replied together in a gruff voice that appeared to originate outside their bodies, "The sky." Mrs. Hingley, a devout Christian, suspected that the two beings might be angels, so she pointed to a picture of Jesus on the wall and asked them if God had sent them to her. The beings told Mrs. Hingley that they knew all about Jesus, and that they had just came down from the sky to talk to people, but people did not seem interested. The three beings then began to fly around the room again, stopping to pick up various objects to examine them. Mrs. Hingley then offered the beings water and pie. They drank the water enthusiastically but could not fit the pie into their tiny mouths. When she asked again about their origins, they shot a painful beam of light at her from their helmets which left a red scar on her forehead for months afterward. When Mrs. Hingley lit a cigarette, it frightened the beings. They glided back out of her house holding their mince pies, returned to the orange sphere from which they emerged, and vanished into thin air. After the three beings left, Mrs. Hingley felt soreness in her eyes and ears, and very weak. She called the police and made a report of what just happened. Even though the beings shot her with a painful beam of light and left her with uncomfortable physical symptoms that are very common to such encounters, she still reported feeling happy and blessed by the experience. Two days after the visitation, her Christmas tree mysteriously disappeared. She also reported continued electromagnetic effects. The family TV quit working, and certain cassette tapes were mysteriously erased.

This type of sighting has all the same EM effects as a typical UFO encounter, but represents a type of report that causes many to write off the entire phenomenon as something psychological and fictitious. These sightings are also reminiscent of the fairy encounters of old, a similarity discovered and well-elaborated by Dr. Jacques Vallee in many books such as his classic, *Passport to Magonia*. When serious UFO researchers discover the vast number of fantastical sightings in the literature such as this one, some vacate the Extraterrestrial Hypothesis (ETH) altogether due to the striking similarities between these UFO sightings and fairy lore. It is possible that these types of unbelievable encounters are intentionally staged by the same entities that produce UFO sightings with radar confirmation and film footage, to invoke rejection and skepticism among individuals who would otherwise accept the UFO phenomenon as a reality. If the occulted intelligences behind the UFOs want to remain unacknowledged and/or disbelieved by scientists and many of the more grounded individuals within the general population, this sort of encounter is a good way to remain clandestine. Mrs. Hingley's encounter does not reflect what most people would imagine happening if the earth were visited by extraterrestrials. The dreamlike quality of the encounters are rejected out of hand by those who do not dig more deeply into the literature to find the patterns that exist. How would Mrs. Hingley know, unless she was well-read in UFO lore, that EM effects, adverse effects on animals, reports of beings that travel in threes, pain in the eyes and ears, fatigue, references to the sky, and requests for and/or acceptance of water were all common features in UFO reports around the world, and even in centuries past? I would say that is rather unlikely. It is also unlikely that the physical appearance of the three beings was representative of how our extraterrestrial visitors actually appear. So, did Mrs. Hingley have an encounter with an actual extraterrestrial, cryptoterrestrial, or interdimensional presence? I would say, "Yes." The actual alien presence on Earth, wherever they are actually from, likely produced the image of the orange sphere after scanning Mrs. Hingley's mind and extracting the appropriate imagery for her that would not cause unwarranted panic and screaming, as this reaction does not serve the purposes or agenda of the actual alien entities. In Mrs. Hingley's case, a "fairy-type" encounter was selected and produced. Perhaps Mrs. Hingley loved fairies as a child, and did not feel threatened by such an appearance. The fact that she suspected that they were angels and felt comforted by the visit even though they inflicted pain and discomfort hints at the genius behind the selected images. Somehow, the intelligences behind the UFO phenomenon are able to get away with inflicting painful experiences onto humans during adductions, commit sexual violations, and present situations that should frighten the bejesus out of us. Regardless, alien encounters keep happening, and no one is screaming bloody murder. Perhaps during each of these encounters a slight alteration of consciousness prevents such an expected reaction from those having encounters with an actual alien presence. In this way, just enough doubt is inflicted for them to question the reality of the experience, even after watching their beloved dog faint on the floor. One thing you have to give the aliens credit for, is that they are good at what they do, and they should be, as they have had centuries to practice.

My Missing Time Episode

On a spring Indiana night In April, 1979, a female friend, Mary, and I were driving back to our homes in Bloomington, Indiana after a sales convention held in Indianapolis. At the time, I was an insurance salesman, and she and I thought it would be fun to go to the company convention together. We left the hotel where the convention ended about 1:30 a.m., which should've put us back in Bloomington around 3 a.m. As we were driving home that night, I remember

Mary telling me that she saw a strange luminous orb out the passenger window. I didn't think much about it, as I figured that there were probably a number of tall radio towers with lights on the top of them between Indy and Bloomington, so I didn't pay much attention to her as she told me that the light was getting bigger as we drove. Suddenly, she began shouting at me, "Go faster, go faster! It's getting closer!" This was unusual for Mary, as she usually did not like the fact that I drive too fast, but I accelerated at her frantic request anyway. Suddenly, it was dawn, and we were pulling up into Mary's driveway. When we entered her home, I asked if I could sleep for a while there, and I remember sleeping all day off and on at Mary's apartment. I do not remember dreaming. That is the last I thought about that night until over 30 years later after I had my heart attack and NDE in 2009. By that time I was conducting intensive personal research into UFOs on my own, when I got a Facebook friend request from Mary, who I had not talked to in three decades. Prior to sending me a friend request, Mary noticed that I was posting a lot of UFO-related material. It was after seeing this that she felt compelled to contact me and fill me in on that night 30 years previous in 1979. She had carried around an emotional burden all those years that she and I had experienced a UFO encounter together in 1979. When she told me that we were driving a green Toyota Tercel, my first reaction was, "I never owned a Toyota Tercel." I thought she had mixed me up with another person. I'm a car guy. I remember all the cars that I have ever owned, as I always develop an emotional attachment to them. Bewildered, I contacted my brother in Bloomington and asked him about it. He remembered the car right away, and confirmed to me that I did, in fact, own such a vehicle. I was stunned. Mary told me that when we returned to her house that morning, her dress was torn, she had mud all over herself, and that she felt "violated" by what had occurred to us with the mysterious light. While I was sleeping that morning at her house, Mary had taken the dress that she was wearing and felt compelled to burn it in her outdoor grill, as she felt "tainted" by the experience. During the 30 years that Mary and I were disconnected from one another, Mary had contacted abduction researcher Bud Hopkins, who asked her to try and look for me. She tried for many years to find me without success, and eventually gave up until we finally reunited on Facebook. Now she and I talk on a regular basis. I still have no memory whatsoever of the missing 3 or so hours, nor any memory of the green Toyota. My memory of that night jumps from driving while she was screaming at me to drive faster, straight to daytime and sleeping all day at her house. Other than the light that chased us in the car, neither of us have any memory of an actual abduction or association with ETs that evening. What happened to us will likely remain a mystery for both of us for the rest of our natural lives. It really makes me wonder how many people have encounters with Cryptoreality involving mysterious lights and otherworldly entities, and never even have the first memory of the event. At the time of this writing, Mary and I are considering filing a report with MUFON, and possibly seeking out a hypnotherapist who can excavate from our memories from decades ago just what happened that evening in 1979. Until then, it just remains an unknown. Put it on the stack.

Cosmic Consciousness Imparted to UFO Percipients

In the same year that I had an anomalous encounter with the unknown with my friend Mary, in 1979 Leo Sprinkle proposed the *Cosmic Consciousness Conditioning Theory* in which the UFO intelligences choose certain individuals and use their technology to bestow *cosmic illumination* upon them. With this I am reminded once again of the cosmic illumination that occurred with the biblical Paul's conversion to Christianity in the New Testament via his encounter with a luminous aerial apparition that left him blind for 3 days and turned Paul into an evangelist. Other individuals in the UFO literature have reported experiencing an increase in IQ, physical healing of some sort, or a renewed sense of purpose, just as many contactees of the 1950s received before going forth to spread the "Gospel of the benevolent Space Brothers." This experience of "seeing the light" has affected countless individuals throughout history. Cosmic illumination has caused some percipients to create major world religions, and has left others in a crippled mental state from which they never recover. In my own case, I just had a wiped out memory of the event for 30 years and still don't remember anything about what happened to us so long ago, but I do find it strange that, following my NDE in 2009, I plunged headfirst into ufology of all subjects. Perhaps I already had a pre-existing reason to become interested in the subject.

Fragments of Truth

1979 brought us a book of reality-plot foreshadowing, *Extraterrestrial Encounter,* by British science writer Chris Boyce. In this book, Boyce cleverly proposed that alien data banks and/or probes are likely to already exist on Earth or elsewhere in our local solar system. Boyce predicted that, sometime during the 21st century, hard evidence would be presented to humanity that we are not alone in the universe. Since the Singularity is predicted to occur sometime in our near future around 2045, and since I am making the proposal that humankind has, in fact, been manipulated for thousands of years toward that specific end, an end that involves unfathomable technology and artificial intelligence with vast capabilities, I do believe that Boyce was correct in his predictions. It is likely that Boyce and other individuals who have voiced similar concerns about human manipulation by an extraterrestrial presence will prove out in the end to have been modern-day prophets. Let's just hope that, by the time we all realize what is really going on, it is not too late for us.

Insight from a Cosmonaut

In the March 3, 1979 issue of *Technique and Youth*, Cosmonaut E.V. Khrunov stated, "The UFO problem exists and is very serious. Thousands of people have seen UFOs, but it is not clear what they are. It is quite possible that behind this question, the problem of communication with an extraterrestrial civilization is hidden." Khrunov's insight, that we may not be presently capable of experiencing the extraterrestrials as they really are, or achieve any type of meaningful communication with them on their level, will hopefully be solved with technology that will be invented in the coming decades. The exponential expansion of human intelligence through electronic augmentation may be necessary for us to make actual contact with the ETs, and that is likely one reason why open contact with the entire world has not happened as yet. Astronomer Neil deGrasse Tyson is haunted by the fear that we may not be smart enough to communicate with aliens, and I think he is correct, but an electronic correction for this is on the way as we head into the Singularity.

The Church of the Subgenius

As if reports of encounters with UFOs and their occupants that border on the absurd weren't crazy enough, 1979 brought forth a sarcastic, comedic element within the fringe UFO sub-culture similar to that of Jim Moseley's tongue-in-cheek publication, *Saucer Smear*. This came from a creative genius named Ivan Stang (whose real name is Douglas St. Clair Smith), who later became the Reverend Ivan Stang, founder of the delightfully comical and irreverent *Church of the Subgenius*. The Church of the Subgenius demonstrates that what might ordinarily be experienced as a passing idea formulated while basking in a room full of marijuana smoke can actually become a worldwide phenomenon if the idea is diligently pursued with vigor and tenacity. The worshipped deity in the Church of the Subgenius is just a piece of corny clip art, a disembodied face (supposedly a salesman from the 1950's) named J.R. Bob Dobbs. Dobbs is similar in appearance to Ward Cleaver of the 1960s television show, *Leave it to Beaver*. Reverend Ivan Stang himself proclaims that Dobbs is "a really shitty god." Reverend Ivan Stang's comical diatribes have been enjoyed now for decades within the Pagan and Wiccan subculture here in the US. His quasi-religious diatribes can be experienced at festivals and Pagan gatherings such as the *Starwood Festival*. The Starwood Festival was an annual gathering for many years at the Brushwood Campground area in Sherman, New York, and eventually relocated to Ohio. In my own travels, I had the pleasure of attending the Starwood Festival one year, and caught Reverend Ivan Stang's comedic monologue under the main pavilion by accident on a cloudy day. I must say that my cheeks were sore by the end of Stang's presentation, as it is quite hilarious. Over the years, Stang has continually improved his presentation with computer graphics and videos in the background. Contributors to sermons of the church over the years have created entertaining and creative connections between their deity, J.R. Bob Dobbs, and various main-stream religious concepts and conspiracy theories. One of the tenants of the church is that we are all born with a full measure of "Slack" (always capitalized), i.e., enjoying life without forced labor, before the world at large and the powers that be insidiously erode our Slack, eventually dominating one's time and activities to turn them into mere slaves to the world machine. Their first publication in 1979 was called *Subgenius Pamplet #1*, which announced the imminent end of the world and possible deaths of its readers. An equal opportunity mocker, the church openly criticizes with astute sarcasm all existing religious precepts, including all of the so-called "New Age" religions. In the early years, the Church was lucky enough to receive artistic support by cartoonist R. Crumb. I get the distinct feeling from the sermons disseminated by Subgenius speakers that atheism is actually at the core of church doctrine, providing a comedic commentary on human religion in general, and allowing at least some atheists to have a "religion" that they can get behind. If not abject atheism, the church reflects at the very least a frustration with the ridiculous motifs that exist in all religions that are taken seriously around the world. The deity of the Subgenius, commonly known as "Bob," is reported to have been contacted by an extraterrestrial, "Jehovah 1," while Bob was watching late night television. Members of the church insist that there is a grand conspiracy at the heart of all lesser conspiracies, that the occupants of the UFOs in our skies are mainly conspiracy leaders who monitor humanity and implant into them messages of servitude. Other UFOs are piloted by bone fide extraterrestrials (in my view, this is too close to reality for comfort). The Church teaches that members are actually descendants of the Yeti. For an annual cost of $35.00, members can maintain their status as a card-carrying minister of the Church, and this surely provides a way, at least for the Reverend Ivan Stang and Associates, to accomplish their original goal of regaining their original Slack, i.e., making a comfortable living with little actual work expended. I also get the uncanny feeling that the doctrines of the Church of the Subgenius are actually very close to reality. The real genius of the church is that they have identified the fact that, although all religions are misguided, there is a profound mystery at hand. There is a sense of yearning for that underlying mystery contained in the monologues, a mystery that is comical to us because it is so clearly bizarre. If my own ideas concerning the UFO mystery and the Singularity turn out to be, as Jim Moseley put it, "shockingly close to the truth" (which only time will determine), the Church of the Subgenius, despite its comedic underpinnings, is actually on the right track in many ways that may actually escape them. The idea that conspiracy chiefs monitor humanity below from flying saucers may actually have a reality of its own if, in fact, secret technology or retro-engineered alien technology actually exists and is in the hands of a Secret Space Program or certain insiders of secret societies who have contacts with extraterrestrials. Even the idea of Slack within the church may have prophetic merit. As we approach the Singularity and more jobs are taken over by machines and/or artificial intelligence, humans will be able to enjoy a more leisurely lifestyle without the 9-5 routine that dominates most of our lives at present. An annual event known as "X Day" evolved within the Church and is celebrated each year as a day in which members and other interested individuals gather for the prophesied landing of beings from Planet X. These beings will transport believers from the earth to a reunion with the Goddess as Earth below is destroyed, while still others are whisked off to a joyful hell. No one seriously expects this to actually happen on X Day each year, but it makes a good excuse for a party and accompanying enjoyable rituals to celebrate the annual non-appearance of the aliens while at the same time mocking all the failed prophecy of religionists and UFO cultists throughout the history of the UFO phenomenon. The existence of such a parody of religion and UFOs is accepted with glee by UFO skeptics as mental confirmation that the UFO phenomenon (and possibly religion itself) is pure fantasy. On the contrary, the Church of the Subgenius is further evidence that very clever obfuscation is afoot. The best-case scenario is that the actual intelligences behind the real UFO phenomenon, whoever they are, possess something that resembles a sense of humor, and have lovingly bestowed the doctrines of the Church of the Subgenius through its prophets and ministers, in order to get us all to chill as we approach the Singularity. In other words, the sarcastic diatribes of the Church of the Subgenius may actually serve the purposes of our actual bio-robotic overlords in the grand scheme of things, as strange as that might seem. Let's all hope that Bramley's race of maverick extraterrestrials actually exist, that they really are benevolent toward humanity, and that we can all regain what the Church of the Subgenius refers to as "Slack" once again in the post-singularity world to come. If, on the other hand, the Singularity represents our impending annihilation, The Church of the Subgenius is akin to the musicians who chose to play their instruments onboard the Titanic as it sank into the ocean.

CHAPTER 11

Awakening to Eternisphere

"The Space Intelligences are pure energy, and are invisible. Only the top members of the SIs [Space Intelligences] can construct a form and pour themselves into it. The SIs [Space Intelligences] are from a different world entirely. They are from another dimension, but they have discovered how to switch from their dimension into ours."

- Ted Owens, aka "PK Man."

Cosmic Image Management

IN 1980, DR. Frank B. Salisbury, Ph.D., who received his doctorate from the California Institute of Technology in 1955, proposed that, like an airplane intentionally flying over the location of a known cargo cult, UFO sightings are events that are intentionally staged by extraterrestrials. The purpose of the sightings, according to Dr. Salisbury, is to gradually acclimate humanity to the alien presence, until such a time that open contact is safe and appropriate to occur in the future. Dr. Salisbury also thought that another purpose of the sightings is to *excite the gullible to turn off the non-gullible*. This notion corresponds with my observations and perceptions that the absurdities of the contactee stories, so easily dismissed as rubbish by both the scientific community and serious UFO buffs who ascribe to the Extraterrestrial Hypothesis (ETH), are but intelligent manipulations in order to distract the scientific community away from the trail of the actual alien agenda, and keep them working on advanced technology. I do believe that Dr. Salisbury was on to something.

Thirsty Saucers

On September 29, 1980, a flying saucer extracted 10,000 gallons of water from the White Acres farm in Rosedale, Victoria (Australia). The caretaker of the White Acres farm, who was 54 at the time, saw the craft hover over the farm's water tower before landing about 50 feet away from the tower. Cruising over on his motorbike, he approached to about 10 yards from the craft when he heard a whistling sound that turned into a loud scream. A black tube emerged from the bottom of the craft and with a loud bang it began elevating, emitting a blast of hot air that nearly knocked the caretaker off balance on his motorbike. After the craft sped away, the water tower was inspected, and was discovered to have been completely emptied. The caretaker experienced nausea and headaches from the close encounter. Beginning in December of 1980, the event was investigated by UFO researchers Bill Chalker, Gary Little, and Keith Basterfield. During the entire decade of the 1980s, the Gippsland region of Australia produced multiple witnesses reporting flying saucers extracting water from local lakes and other water storage facilities. Where are these "thirsty saucers" coming from? Obviously there is a water shortage somewhere, and the saucers are on a mission for resources. There are a couple of immediate possibilities for the home bases of the thirsty saucers. One is the alien bases that surely exist on the moon. However, alien bases on the moon would likely have the technology to produce their own water, and water seems like an unlikely cargo to be extracted from the earth and transported back to a base on the moon. It is more likely that these saucers are terrestrial in origin, and belong to a society here on Earth that is hiding from the general population underground. Even the Italian Amicizia group needed human assistance acquiring physical resources. It is anyone's guess, but we are left with the factual existence of physical, metallic, "nuts and bolts" crafts that use some sort of antigravitic propulsion system that have been caught on many occasions on a mission for water. Where they come from, and where they take the water, nobody knows, but these crafts exist, and must be taken into account when considering the big picture of the Phenomenon.

Police Constable Reports UFO

On November 28, 1980, around 5 a.m., just before dawn in the small town of Todmordin, West Yorkshire (right in the middle of what has come to be known in England as "UFO Alley"), British police constable Alan Godfry experienced a close encounter with a diamond-shaped craft that was blocking the road while he was out investigating reports of missing cows (which mysteriously showed up later that day in a rain-soaked field with no hoofmarks showing their trek). Godfry described the object as large as a double-decker bus hovering on its own about 5 feet above the ground. The bottom portion of the craft appeared to be rotating, while the top half remained stationary. After several minutes, which he says seemed like an eternity, the craft disappeared in a flash of light. Officer Godfry then discovered that he was missing about an hour of his life (classic missing time). Officer Godfry was afraid that, since he was alone during the encounter, his story would never be believed or considered credible due to its fantastic nature. However, Godfry eventually discovered 6 other police officers and multiple civilians who also witnessed the craft that fateful morning, greatly relieving Godfry's mind that he was not going crazy and had, in fact, experienced a real event. Prior to this confirmation, Godfry faced all kinds of harassment at work, and endured an unwanted transfer from his station at work. Godfry was referred to a psychiatrist, subjected to ridicule by coworkers and, in general, made to feel like his event was just a hallucination, his sanity and credibility under continual irritating and unnecessary scrutiny. These unpleasant experiences await many individuals who choose to go public with their encounters or even publicly express their own personal convictions about the existence and/or reality of flying saucers. Thus, many UFO witnesses choose to remain silent due to the tremendous prejudice that still exists in the minds of many people, some of whom are other people's bosses at work. This mockery of the UFO experiencers among us can cost a person their reputation, their jobs, their sanity, or even their lives. Even in today's "politically correct" working environments in which populations who were once hidden (such as the gay, lesbian, or transgender community) are able to "come out," open flying saucer enthusiasts often continue to receive raised eyebrows or giggles behind their backs from those who don't know the first thing about the subject.

Peruvian Dogfight with UFO

In 1980, Col Oscar Santa-Maria with the Peruvian Air Force flew an intercept mission against a large "hat-shaped" UFO near a Peruvian military base. He discharged onboard air-to-air rockets and 30 mm rounds at close range, but there was no apparent damage to the object as it sped away and escaped.

The Rendlesham Forest UFO Encounter

In the wee hours of the morning on December 26, 1980, a service patrol at RAF Woodbridge in Rendlesham Forest, Suffolk, England, observed multiple unidentified lights in the sky. At first the men thought they were seeing lights from an aircraft going down in the forest. As they approached what they thought was going to be an airplane wreck, they heard animals on a nearby farm going into a frenzy. Even more disturbing than the sound of animals in panic was another distinct sound of a "woman screaming." It is true that there is a species of animal in the area known as Muntjac deer that do make a shrill sound when they are alarmed, and that this reported sound could have come from such a deer. However, it is notable that the hair-raising sound of a woman screaming, along with herds of animals that go berserk, is classically associated with reports of many different types of paranormal activity, including ghosts, poltergeists, big hairy monsters, and sometimes, flying saucers. In such cases of paranormal activity, the sound of a baby crying and/or a woman screaming usually comes with the heavy, nauseating smell of sulfur. As the men investigated into the forest, they encountered a black metallic triangle of unknown origin with blue and red lights glowing. Local police were called to the area about an hour later, but by that time the craft had silently risen into the air and disappeared. On the morning of December 28, 1980, Lieutenant Colonel Charles Halt and several other men examined the area with a Geiger counter looking for trace evidence of the reported craft and found indentations that could have been made by the landing gear of the craft. During his investigation, Halt and company observed three star-like objects moving in the sky, the brightest of which hovered silently for 2-3 hours and occasionally shot down a beam of light to the ground below. Halt recorded the event on tape. The sounds of the actual event can be listened to online by anyone interested. Like many UFO events, as time passes, memories fade, embellishments are made, opportunities for TV interviews are taken advantage of, and the whole case becomes obfuscated by reports of silencing interrogations and military cover-ups. Bogus explanations have been proposed over the years as usual, such as lights coming from a nearby lighthouse, meteors burning up in the atmosphere, intentional hoax, and the classic "downed Soviet spy satellite." Considering the the amount of time that has passed, and the fact that documents of the event remained classified for years until they were finally released to the public under the Freedom of Information Act, we may never know the true nature of this event. At the time of this writing, Halt is one of the many witnesses for Dr. Steven Greer's Disclosure Project concerning the Rendlesham Forest Incident. Halt maintains that what happened in Rendlesham Forest back in 1980 was definitely extraterrestrial or interdimensional in nature. Halt testifies with firm conviction that authorities from both the United States and the United Kingdom were involved in an intentional cover-up of this extraordinary UFO encounter. The Rendlesham Forest Incident, like so many other similar UFO events, likely represents an encounter with our AI overlords involving advanced, interdimensional machine intelligence that is always watching over humanity to insure that we do not blow ourselves up and interfere with the project that humanity is being employed to produce. As always, they were keeping track of our military capability and overseeing their herd like a farmer looking after cattle. By visiting this facility that stored nuclear weapons, the overlords were fulfilling their ancient programming that involves the manipulation of capable planetary lifeforms (humans in the case of Earth) into a technological singularity. This is a tricky operation, as nuclear power is likely a key ingredient for this goal to become a reality, and there is always the possibility of self-destruction in the process. This requires careful tending and supervision so that the monkeys with matches don't blow themselves up and spoil the precious end product - a technological singularity - the fruit of the electrical universe. Whatever it was that these men encountered that morning, whether it was a mechanical craft from parts unknown or a paranormal manifestation of occulted energy on the order of a poltergeist, the Rendlesham Forest Incident is now known as "England's Roswell," and, like Roswell, the entire event is obfuscated into oblivion. However, the testimony of multiple, high-level military personnel leaves this event as one of the most highly-credible UFO reports in history.

The Cash-Landrum UFO Encounter

On December 29, 1980, while military officials were grappling with a small black triangle touchdown in Rendlesham Forest, three residents of Texas - Betty Cash, Vickie Landrum, and her grandson, Colby, were driving home at night in Betty's new 1980 Olds Cutlass. On a dark, lonesome road near Huffman, Texas, they accidentally encountered something they were not supposed to see, something that changed the course of their lives forever, and not in a good way. Like the Rendlesham Forest Incident, the Cash-Landrum UFO event was destined to become one of the best physical trace cases in UFO history. As they drove along the Cleveland-Huffman road on their way home to Dayton, Texas, the two women and the child encountered an intense light hovering just above the tree line in the distance ahead. As they approached closer, the object finally came into view with crystal clarity. Just ahead of them, blocking the road, was a large, luminous, diamond-shaped craft hovering in mid-air and glowing with such an intensity that Vickie Landrum actually thought they were witnessing the Second Coming of Jesus Christ. This illuminated craft occasionally belched fire from the bottom apex, lighting up the whole area like daytime and invoking the fear of being burned alive. Escaping the oven of the automobile into the cooler night air, all 3 witnesses exited the vehicle. Colby, only seven years old at the time and terrified, returned to the car immediately. Vickie returned to comfort him as Betty stood outside at the front of the car for 5-10 minutes watching the impossible fiery object. It became so hot inside the car that they turned on the air conditioner. When Betty returned to the car at Vickie and Colby's pleading, the door handle was hot to the touch so Betty used her leather coat as an oven mitt to reenter the car. All three witnesses heard an irregular beeping sound. A multitude of helicopters arrived at the scene and surrounded the craft. Finally, the fire-belching stopped. The object then started drifting away into the distance, escorted by an entourage of at least 20 military helicopters, some with twin rotors. Betty took most of the exposure to the object as she stood at the front of the car. She was planning to open a restaurant the following week. Unfortunately, because of this UFO encounter, Betty never realized her dreams of self-employment. In the next four days, Betty's eyes became swollen shut. She developed large red blotches on her skin and large blisters filled with fluid. She became severely dehydrated. The other two witnesses, having much less exposure, were also experiencing symptoms, but not nearly as severe. Betty was hospitalized for 12 days, returned home briefly, and was rehospitalized for another 15 days. It was determined that Betty was suffering from radiation poisoning. She lost most of her hair, and developed severe diarrhea, upset stomach, and horrendous headaches. Other witnesses have been found who also witnessed the object and the helicopters, but to this day all US military agencies have denied any participation in the event or any dispatch of a large number of helicopters. No records of such a huge operation have ever been released or found, which leaves one to wonder if the entire episode was a paranormal event in which the screen image of a diamond-shaped craft escorted by a couple of dozen helicopters was placed into the minds of Betty Cash, Vickie Landrum, her grandson Colby, and other peripheral witnesses by an extraterrestrial or interdimensional group of entities that were mistakenly encountered that night and did not wish for their true appearance to be known by a group of human witnesses. One other noticeable detail is the fact that this particular craft or disguised entity did not produce the usual EM effects that many UFOs induce. During the encounter, Betty's car kept running, well enough to run the air conditioner inside. Are there a variety of different types of non-terrestrial craft constructed in different ways or emerging from different realms, some of which produce the ubiquitous EM effects, and some that do not, even though they remain extremely dangerous or even deadly to humans due to radiation or heat emissions? Whatever the case, Betty Cash, along with Vickie Landrum and Colby to lesser degrees, struggled with the effects of this fateful encounter the remainder of their years, frequently spending time in intensive care units. Betty finally died on December 29, 1998 on the 18th anniversary of the encounter. Colby, as an adult, continues to seek answers to no avail and has appeared on several television programs. In his book, *The Cash-Landrum UFO Incident*, author John F. Schuessler provides a detailed account of this classic encounter, leaving readers with no doubt whatsoever about its reality or authenticity. Eight years later, in 1988, former AOFSI officer Richard C. Doty, considered by some to be a government disinformation agent, appeared on live television in front of millions of viewers to offer Betty Cash and Vickie Landrum resolution to this event with an explanation that may or may not be true. Doty told the two women on a television show (*UFO Cover-up: Live!*) that what they saw was an alien craft that had been gifted to the US military that was operated by human pilots that night. The pilots believed that the object was going to crash, and called in the helicopters. This explanation appeared to comfort the two women, who also appeared live on stage during the show. At least now they could gain some closure on a mysterious event that had haunted them for the previous eight years. Whether this story is actually true is another question that remains unanswered.

Order of *Fiat Lux*

The UFO phenomenon in the United States that began in earnest in 1947 with the Maury Island Incident and the Kenneth Arnnold sighting spawned many UFO-oriented religions. These UFO cults expanded the cultural effect of the flying saucer mystery into the minds of both skeptics and believers alike in different ways. Regardless of whether flying saucers actually exist or not, flying saucers changed the world. One such saucer cult, the *Order of Fiat Lux* (Latin for "Let There Be Light") was founded on January 12, 1980 by a woman named Erika Bertschinger-Eicke, otherwise known to the movement as Uriella. Uriella was believed by her followers to be the direct "speaking tube" of Jesus Christ who received guidance from the angel, *Uriel*. Uriella was allegedly the reincarnation of Mary Magdelene and taught her sect members that when the world ends, they would all be rescued by extraterrestrials in flying saucers. Members of the strange cult wore bright white clothing to ward off Lucifer's radiations and believed that dark clothing absorbed negative cosmic radiations. They were not allowed to use the internet, watch TV, or listen to the radio. There were nutrition and meditation rules. After a riding accident that inflicted a head injury in 1973, Uriella allegedly became clairvoyant. Uriella once prophesied a specific date for the end of the world, which is always a mistake for any self-appointed prophet except (of course) for the money they can raise between the time the prophecy is announced and the date that it is supposed to happen from donations coming in from believers seeking salvation. That's the way religions normally work. Of course the prophecy declaring the end of the world failed like these prophecies always do. When it did not come to pass, and the world continued, Uriella announced, like they always do, that the end of the world had been postponed. In the meantime, Uriella made "Athrum Water" in a sterile tub by stirring tap water. The members used this blessed water for drinking, bathing, and healing ointment. Members were afraid of bar codes, and covered them with stickers in their homes. 18 years after this flying saucer cult was founded, in December of 1998, Uriel was given a suspended, 2 year prison sentence for tax evasion. She was fined and ordered to give 100,000 Deutschemark to charity. It was a good run for her while it lasted. As a strange synchronicity, Uriella was busted, ending her UFO cult, in the same month and year that Betty Cash died on the 18th anniversary of her UFO encounter.

Intelligent Orbs

Beginning in 1981 and enduring for the next four years until 1985, a strange and powerful luminous mystery appeared in the skies of the Hessdalen Valley of central Norway. Luminous spheres that silently hovered in mid-air and/or zipped away at fantastic speeds, clocked in excess of 18,000 miles per hour, were seen by thousands of human witnesses. As Larry E. Arnold revealed in his seminal work on Spontaneous Human Combustion, *Ablaze!*:

> *A research station set up to probe them netted perplexing data. The glowing orbs produced no spectral lines on film; a spectrum-analyzer registered occasional electromagnetic signals with 80 MHz harmonics. A magnetograph detected changes in the local magnetic field when the lights popped up; laser beams directed at the glowing spheres caused behavioral changes in them; and, provocatively, sometimes radar detected the presence of some additional invisible thing moving in ways comparable to the lights when seen, according to the Journal of Scientific Exploration (1994).*

As Keel revealed in *The Mothman Prophecies*, he personally experienced luminous phenomena similar to the Hessdalen Lights in West Virginia while investigating Mothman witnesses in the area surrounding the collapse of the Silver Bridge. Keel found that when he pointed an ordinary flashlight at the glowing orbs at night, they darted out of the way, giving the appearance that the orbs were conscious and/or under intelligent control. These mysterious lights, including the Hassdalen Lights and the meandering nocturnal lights that appeared in the night sky in West Virginia that hundreds of local residents witnessed, seem to possess some sort of intelligence. Of course the orbs could be simply reacting mechanically to the presence of another light source, we do not know, but the appearance of consciousness or sentience observed in the flying orbs is reported by credible witnesses all over the world. The fact that the luminous flying orbs at Hessdalen, Norway emitted no measurable spectral lines is indicative that the Hessdalen lights, and possibly other similar lights around the world, are not even light as we currently understand it. The human brain interprets the appearance of the orbs, whatever they are in reality, as light, but our science indicates that the phenomenon is something else that we do not understand. In addition to the fact that the "lights" as we call them emit no spectral lines like light is supposed to do, radar ascertained the presence of an "invisible object" that corresponded to the motion of the visible portion of the Hessdalen Lights. This indicates that, whatever the Hessdalen Lights are, the human perceptual apparatus is not capable of taking in all the visual information of what is actually there. In other words, we are not seeing the object for what it really is, and this could apply to all such similar lights that appear around the world as luminous orbs. Whether this is some sort of intentional "cloaking device" employed by our visitors (whoever or whatever they are), or a fantastic interdimensional phenomenon we just do not understand at present that has always existed as part of our natural environment, we do not know. These luminous objects show up all over the world, and have likely existed as long as humans have been on the planet. We are only able to perceive them in part, although the portion that we are able to perceive appear to us as luminous orbs in the sky. How they really appear in their entirety, despite the fact that radar says there is something else there that we cannot see, is unknown to us. The magnetograph used to observe the Hessdalen lights indicated changes in the earth's magnetosphere when the lights appeared. Do these luminous objects actually exist in our atmosphere continuously and appear to humans as luminous orbs from time to time? Do these objects represent extraterrestrial spacecraft that use geomagnetism to travel from world to world? Do the objects exist in a realm of reality that we currently cannot perceive correctly or measure appropriately? We do not know, and there is no way to determine the answers to these questions at present. However, whoever or whatever they are have exerted a profound impact on the human psyche as they reveal right in front of our gasping faces that there is, in fact, an unknown intelligence operating on this planet that we currently do not understand. This realization has served to fuel the human imagination concerning the nature of reality.

[While the Hassdalen Lights appeared in Norway, Pakistan conducted their nuclear test known as "Kirana 1."]

Cosmonaut Reports UFO

On May 5, 1981, Cosmonaut Vladimir Kovalyonok was in his space capsule, the *Salyut 6*, over Africa when he reported witnessing a disk-shaped, non-terrestrial craft in space. One half of the craft was surrounded by a conical-shaped fog. As he watched it flying alongside his space capsule, it suddenly exploded silently into a brilliant golden light. A few seconds later, two spheres of the same golden color rematerialized. The spheres appeared to be connected to one another with a kind of white smoke. As the Salyut 6 entered the Earth's shadow, the object disappeared from his sight.

Live Aliens?

Award-winning journalist, Linda Moulton Howe, who is also a UFO investigator and author of many books such as *An Alien Harvest* (1989), *Glimpses of Other Realities* (1998), and *Mysterious Lights and Crop Circles* (2001) revealed that on April 9, 1983, she was taken to Kirtland Air Force Base for an interview with the same AFOSI agent, Richard C. Doty, that would appear in shadow 5 years later on the 1988 television show, *UFO Cover-up: Live!* to explain the Cash-Landrum Incident to Betty Cash and Vickie Landrum. During this interview, Doty allegedly showed Howe documents containing a summary of UFO crash and retrieval efforts. These documents included information concerning a live alien that was extracted from a second UFO crash near Roswell in 1949, two years after the 1947 incident that caused such a stir. This live alien from the 1949 crash allegedly lived, according to the documents that Howe was shown by Doty, at the Los Alamos National Laboratory until June 18, 1952, when the creature died of natural causes. The reality or non-reality of live captured aliens continues to cause a division in thinking within the UFO community. Paranormal investigators who see the UFO phenomenon as a paranormal manifestation on the order of ghosts and poltergeists, tend to lampoon the belief in "pickled aliens." On the other hand, adherants to the Extraterrestrial Hypothesis (ETH) are more inclined to accept the accounts of live or dead aliens found at UFO crash retrieval sites. My view is that both camps are partially right, and that both camps are likely victims of a grand deception on a much larger scale. If humans have, in fact, captured alien technology and/or live or dead aliens, nothing is as it appears. If UFO crashes have occurred, in my view they all represent staged events orchestrated by the Overlords of the Singularity to make us think we are clever and have incorporated alien technology into our national repertoire of technical capability in a clandestine fashion, along with captured alien beings secreted away when the real aliens are still at large, and represent a much larger, possibly ominous intelligence that we have yet to meet face-to-face.

Family Farm UFO Encounter

One morning in July, 1983, farmers Ron and Paula Watson from Mount Vernon noticed flashes of light coming from a pasture across from their farmhouse. Sharing a pair of binoculars back and forth, the couple was utterly shocked to see two small creatures in silver suits standing over a downed black cow, moving their hands over the cow in jerky motions. Their feelings were that the cow was still alive, but somehow paralyzed. They were amazed to then see the cow and the two beings float in the air to a cone-shaped craft sitting near some trees with a mirror-like reflective quality that rendered the craft nearly invisible. At the door of the craft was a 6 foot-tall, green-skinned reptilian creature with webbed hands and feet, large eyes, and vertical pupils, along with a shaggy, Bigfoot-like creature. The cow and the two smaller beings, along with the reptilian and the Bigfoot creature, once inside, took off silently at great speed and vanished. A fellow farmer soon reported that one of his black cows was missing. The Watsons attempted to explain to the man what happened, but the farmer refused to listen. His cow was never found.

Hudson Valley Black Triangles

About 30 miles north of New York City, along the border of New York and Connecticut, is an area called the Hudson Valley, which was home to Washington Irving's *Headless Horseman*. The Hudson Valley is home to many early UFO sightings from the late 1800s to the early 1900s, as well as giant black triangle and black boomerang UFOs that have been witnessed by thousands of people beginning in 1983 to the present. On March 23, 1983, one such giant black triangle, as large as a football field with rows of lights all around it, passed over the residents of the Hudson Valley. In 1984 another black triangle three times the size of the one in 1983 was filmed in Brewster, New York and witnessed by multiple police officers who testified to the sighting. This giant black triangle hovered over State Power Reactor #3 for 15 minutes before gliding silently over the Hudson River into Rockland County in full few of thousands of people from all walks of life. A spokesman for the Indian Point Nuclear Reactor Complex confirmed the reality of the craft, but denied that it adversely affected plant operations. Imaging scientists at the Jet Propulsion Laboratory (JPL) in Pasadena, California, confirmed that this craft was not anything conventional in operation. There is no doubt that this giant black triangle was a physical reality, and that there is nothing of earthly manufacture that it could possibly have been. The mystery of the black triangles of Hudson Valley remains unsolved. These sightings are detailed well in the 1998 book, *Night Siege: The Hudson Valley UFO Sightings*, by Dr. J. Allen Hynek, Philip J. Imbrogno, and Bob Pratt.

The Dark Side of Ufology

In 1984, a UFO-oriented millennialist cult emerged that was destined for a tragic end. The cult was founded by Joseph Di Mambro and Luc Jouret, and was called the *Order of the Solar Temple*. The goals of the order were to prepare the world for an oncoming world transition in which Jesus Christ would return as a solar god-king and unify Christianity and Islam. The Order of the Solar Temple drew inspiration from the works of British occultist, Aleister Crowley. The group's membership was held secret, and much pomp and ceremony accompanied the various levels of initiation as one advanced in the group. This group flourished for the next ten years or so, and ended badly. First, Di Mambro ordered the killing of a baby who he thought was the Antichrist. The baby, Emmanuel Dutoit, the 3-month-old son of Tony Dutoit, was stabbed repeatedly with a wooden stake. Di Mabro believed that the Antichrist had been born into his order to prevent him from accomplishing his spiritual goals. A few days later, mass suicides and murders were committed by cult members in West Switzerland. 15 members committed suicide by poison, 30 members were killed with firearms or smothering, and 8 members were killed by other methods. The victims were placed in plastic bags to symbolize the ecological disaster that would befall humankind after elect members of the order escaped to the Sirius star system. Other bodies were found in various ski resorts. Several dead children were found together when officers responded to fires started by remote control. Farewell letters were left behind by members who explained that they were leaving for Sirius to escape the "oppression and hypocrisy of this world." Other similar deaths and notes appeared here and there in the world during the next few years after. The murders and suicides of the Order of the Solar Temple eventually became plot features in the James Rollins novel, *The Skeleton Key*.

The Italian "Friendship Group" (Amicizia) Relocated to Chile?

In 1984, a businessman living near the southern coast of Chile, Octavio Ortez, was an amateur ham radio operator who went by the handle, *Lucero*. Ortez also operated a small 27 megacycle CB station in his spare time. He began intercepting distress signals from a ship, the *Mitlius II*. The ship was reporting an unknown celestial object moving along with them in the sky directly above them. They were experiencing classic electronic malfunctions (EM effects) associated with UFO encounters. Some of the crew members were also losing their hair. These strange radio messages in 1984 marked the beginning of a physical encounter between Octavio Ortez and our extraterrestrial friends, the Amicizia (AKRIJ), otherwise known as the W56 or Friendship Group. These humanoid extraterrestrials were possibly the same group that had previously been located in an underground base in Italy, who interacted with over 100 human experiencers in that area of the world from 1956 to the late 1960s. According to researcher Josep Guijarro, there was also an adjacent ship to the Mitlius II that corroborated the UFO sightings. The captain of the Mitlius II, Alberto, would later inform Octavio that, prior to that evening, he had been hired by a group of "gringos" who claimed that they were associated with the UFOs witnessed in the area. This group, who called themselves *The Friendship*, had taken Alberto to an island, where they outfitted his ship with "strange equipment." Alberto was introduced to this group by a man named Ernesto de la Fuente, who promised to ease Alberto's financial burdens if he would cooperate with the group and agree to the illicit importation of supplies that the group needed. Alberto described members of the Friendship Group as tall and "Nordic" in appearance. These humanoid aliens appeared oblivious to the political or social dynamics on Earth, and possessed advanced scientific and technological knowledge. At times, members of this group referred to themselves as "not of this world" or "angels of the Lord." Octavio and his wife began receiving transmissions on their ham radio equipment from The Friendship that would always begin with a huge burst of radio energy before they began transmitting. Similar communications via radio had occurred with the Italian interactions with this group since 1956. As the communications occurred, a bright visible luminous object would always appear over Octavio's home, indicating that some of the luminous orbs witnessed around the world may not represent a craft containing aliens, but rather a communication extension, some aspect of their technology that serves as a remote information-gathering and/or transmission device. Octavio and his wife always felt that the communications were originating from the object itself. By all indications, the humanoid extraterrestrials that Octavio and his wife interacted with in Chile were one and the same as the Italian Friendship Group (The AKRIJ). However, there is no way to confirm this one way or the other until the coming Singularity brings all of these populations out in the open, and open contact with the cryptoterrestrials, interdimensionals, local inhabitants of our own solar system, and possibly other galaxies is finally established.

Cryptoterrestrials

So, what are we to make of these accounts of interaction between citizens of this planet and otherworldly humanoids in Italy, and later in Chile? It is a certainty that such groups of advanced humanoids exist. How long they have been here and where they really come from is unknown. They are either showing themselves to human percipients as they actually are, humanoid, or they are actually nonhumanoid and altering their physical appearance for our sake. They are either using the natural power of their minds, presumably a superior intellect to accomplish this, or they are utilizing advanced imaging technology to present a palatable outward appearance to individuals selected as contactees. The other possibility is, if they are not actually humanoid, is that these beings possess actual shapeshifting ability. If this is the case, and they are not who they say they are (humans from various parts of the universe), we have no idea what their actual appearance is. Are the humanoid members of the Friendship Group and the amorphous lights and jellyfish-like blobs that occasionally appear on infrared film, such as those captured by Trevor James Constable, one and the same? Are these humanoids the cryptoterrestrials who have been living underground since the last Ice Age, who once had an advanced civilization here on Earth? Are they responsible for the disabling events that have occurred to our nuclear facilities over the years? These humanoid aliens, or the aliens who can at least appear as such, are certainly the intelligences behind at least some of the UFOs on this planet. The UFOs associated with the Friendship Group have appeared both as luminous orbs and structured craft. The Italian Friendship Group staged appearances of daylight disks for photographic opportunities. Classic flying saucers were captured on video footage that has been analyzed in modern video labs and determined to be authentic. As Octavio in Chile observed, these craft can appear as luminous orbs in the night sky, lending credence to the idea that some of the unusual lights in the sky are actually flying craft in a luminous mode that can also morph into a more structured craft. The lights in the sky, as well as the structured craft, appear to possess an intelligence or sentience of their own. These beings, whose presence has been factually ascertained by many credible witnesses, often appear to human contactees as friendly and enlightened humanoid aliens. The craft that they use, at least while they are in the form of luminous orbs, present a hazard to us. They are dangerous to our health if we get too close to them. As thousands of witnesses and UFO experiencers have attested, exposure to these dangerous objects often induce malfunctions in our electronic equipment and vehicles, missing time, and damage to our physical bodies in the form of radiation poisoning. Other symptoms include blistering; puncture marks on the body; nausea; hair loss; bleeding to the nose or ears; or even death.

Somewhere in our past, a scientifically and technologically advanced group of humanoids certainly existed on this planet. These humanoids, possibly extraterrestrials, may have migrated underground at some point to escape a natural climate-change disaster. One such possible disaster was the postulated Younger Dryas Impact Event of 12,800 years ago, in which a fragmented comet that entered Earth's atmosphere suddenly scorched the earth and caused a global deluge, leaving pockets of human survivors around the world. The Younger Dryas Event, excellently elaborated in Graham Hancock's *Magicians of the Gods*, may represent the actual event that inspired all the world's flood myths as a racial memory. Other groups, possibly interdimensional travelers, may have become stranded here following our nuclear detonations that began in 1945. In a stunning moment of Disclosure, this possibility was even discussed in the first episode of the 2016 remake of *The X-Files*. The modern age of flying saucers appears to coincide with our first nuclear detonations. These detonations may have damaged natural portals of travel. Interdimensional travelers from this era may have become trapped and unable to return home. These trapped populations may currently exist here on Earth in underground and/or undersea bases, in local space, or possibly on the Moon. They are the cryptoterrestrials that the late researcher Mac Tonnies postulated in his posthumously published book, *The Cryptoterrestrials: A Meditation on Indigenous Humanoids and the Aliens Among Us*. If interdimensional travelers became trapped here following our nuclear experiments since 1945, they would now coexist with another group of cryptoterrestrials that likely migrated underground or undersea since the last Ice Age. Evidence indicates that, prior to the last Ice Age, there was a globally-interconnected megalithic culture on Earth who mapped the entire planet from the air prior to the time Antarctica was iced over. This ancient civilization that may have taken shelter underground. They are likely aware of the Friendship Group that may have become stranded following our nuclear experiments. Therefore, several different groups of cryptoterrestrials may exist here on Earth, all of whom are waiting patiently for the surface dwellers to achieve a technological singularity for their own reasons. These populations possess advanced scientific knowledge, and a limited access to advanced equipment here on Earth, but currently lack the advanced technology that will be produced during the Singularity that could enable them to return home and/or restore their civilization to the surface of the planet. Even with the advanced technology they still possess, they will need our help when we achieve the Singularity in the form of crucial technologies that allow interstellar and/or interdimensional travel. As indicated by the Italian Friendship Group, they even need assistance from us with food for their own sustenance with the help of their human friends. It does not seem likely, based on everything we know about them, that they are the same higher-dimensional extraterrestrials that were responsible for our genetic manipulation from Australopithecine to Homo erectus, or from Homo erectus to Homo sapiens. Nor do they appear philosophically prone to creating the impulse to war and conflict necessary to force humans toward the Singularity. The Friendship Group appears to harbor no real malice at all toward our underdeveloped human populations that live on the surface of the planet. They may even wish to assist us in our technological and spiritual development, or guide us past the influence of the Contraries, with whom they also have a conflict. Members of the Friendship Group have stated that they are also at odds with the "Contraries" or "Weiros," i.e., the artificial race of biological robots that worship technology and may have seized upon our planet long ago. In other words, the Amicizia, who are currently stationed underground and undersea around the world, and possibly on the Moon, are biding their time as we approach the Singularity, in hopes of obtaining needed technology, while insuring that we do not destroy ourselves. It appears that we have at least three different ET factions on Earth - one has been here from time immemorial and has appeared to us in various forms from elves and fairies to modern ufonauts. This intelligence, who is interdimensional and likely electronic, has but one goal, and that is to obey the software program installed into them long ago by aliens of unknown origin. This faction locates or even creates life on multiple worlds throughout the entire universe. They genetically manipulate an appropriate organism over long periods of time that are eventually capable of producing a technological singularity, even if suffering is inflicted. These probes employ this selected planetary creature to produce technology for purposes of knowledge acquisition and generational self-replication. When this long-range goal is complete, they move on to another part of the universe to do the exact same thing all over again. In the process, the sum total of planetary knowledge concerning all life that has ever lived on Earth will be added to their data base as the latest addition to their vast, expanding body of knowledge that they have acquired throughout other parts of the universe on other planets for aeons. It is an emotionless, devouring machine that is simply fulfilling the operations of an ancient program. The levels of damage to local populations may vary from species to species and from planet to planet. On Earth, it took millions of years of dinosaurs to produce future fossil fuels, multiple extinction events, the advent of the mammals, and genetic interventions over the millennia to produce a species (humans) adapted to the planet in such a way that a technological singularity would eventually result. These are the big boys, the Overlords of the Singularity, who operate throughout the entire universe and may have even created it in the first place. Along the way, throughout our history, other alien species from other planets and parallel worlds have visited Earth and interacted with humans in various ways. These superhuman populations created many of our ancient legends and religions, and returned to their own world, possibly through a naturally-existing wormhole, as described by Sharan Delarose in *Through the Wormhole: Ancient Aliens and the Lost Islands*. The evidence for the existence of these transitory groups are painted on our cave walls from thousands of years ago. A second group of advanced humanoids, who once had a global civilization on Earth that existed side-by-side with primitive humans, moved underground and/or undersea since the last Ice Age, possibly to avoid the effects of a global catastrophe. A third group of interplanetary and/or interdimensional travelers are now stranded here on Earth since our nuclear bombs damaged the interdimensional portals that they use to travel within the Superspectrum and to the farthest reaches of our universe. These groups may require advanced technology from our Singularity to repair their ability to escape from Earth or our physical dimension. In addition to these three cryptoterrestrial factions, add another unknown indigenous intelligence that presents in the form of sentient luminosities generated from geophysical and tectonic forces within the earth, luminosities that may or may not have to do with populations of discarnate humans or a coexisting indigenous intelligence that we know nothing about, and we begin to get a glimpse of how strange and complex the situation really is. Since at least one group of cryptoterrestrials, known to us as the Friendship Group, operate by the principal of love, a force they call "Uredda," and travel in conscious, interdimensional spacecraft that are infused with the loving power of the universe itself, they are loathe to simply take over our civilization and take what they need. They would rather bide their time and wait for the Singularity. When we achieve this, the Friendship Group can finally reobtain the necessary technological components and forces necessary to return to whence they came and bid us farewell. Since our nuclear involvement may have been the reason that they cannot return home, there is no way to know how friendly they will remain toward us when they obtain the necessary technology or energies to return to their home. I do sincerely hope that the Friendship Group will remain friends with us after what we may have done to them, that we can stay in contact even after they return home, but there is no way to determine that. We will just have to wait and see. If Uredda is real, and they are sincere in their adherence to the principles of Uredda, we may just be in luck. If not, I wouldn't be surprised, nor would I blame them if, after they acquire what they need to get out of here, the earth doesn't wind up as the burned-out cinder that Klaatu warned us of at the end of *The Day the Earth Stood Still*. We have not been good neighbors in the solar system thus far, nor have we demonstrated good intentions toward our occasional extraterrestrial visitors.

Bob White's Flying Saucer artifact

In 1985, a man named Bob White captured metallic drippings from a flying saucer and eventually had the artifact analyzed with fascinating results. According to White's sworn deposition, he was sleeping in a vehicle that was being driven by his companion on a desolate stretch between Grand Junction, Colorado, and the Utah border. They had both previously noticed a luminous object in the sky, but that did not stop Bob from napping. Bob's companion woke him up when the object began growing larger, and they both watched as the object dripped a molten substance from its surface. The two friends located the place where the slag dripped, found a piece of it, and stashed it in the trunk. Bob feared that if he said anything about the incident, he would jeopardize his entertainment career, so he waited until he retired to tell the story of finding the object. Bob has since had the object tested in several different laboratories. The components of the artifact were identified as an aluminum alloy containing gold; silver; arsenic; oxygen aluminum; iron; silicon; calcium; barium; boron; cadmium; cobalt; sulfur; copper; chlorine; chromium; Europium; Gadolinium; Gallium (which melts at room temperature); Manganese; Magnesium; Zinc; Molybdenum; Nickel; Phosphorus; Potassium; Sodium; Strontium; Titanium; Yttrium; Vanadium; and Zirconium. Skeptics of the extraterrestrial origin of this artifact like to point out that all these elements are found here on Earth. Therefore, the artifact has an earthly origin, just as skeptics insist that certain alien-looking skulls found here on Earth are terrestrial since the DNA tests reveal the presence of human genes. The reality is that human DNA, along with common metals found on Earth, may be ubiquitous throughout the galaxy, or even throughout the entire universe. Skeptics also ignore the fact that the combination of elements that was factually ascertained to exist in Bob White's flying saucer artifact is not found on Earth for use in any known earthly product. The universe may be teeming with humanoid life who, if found in skeleton form on this planet, would have enough human DNA upon testing to cause skeptics to label them confidently as terrestrial in origin, when they may have originated on a planet that is billions of light years away from Earth.

Japanese Flight 1628

On November 18, 1986, Japanese flight 1628 was flying over Alaska with a cargo of wine. During the flight, the pilot, Captain Terauchi, an experienced pilot with over 10,000 hours of logged flight time, reported visual confirmation of a large unidentified flying object that dwarfed his airplane in size and looked like the planet Saturn. Retired FAA employee, John Callahan, was Division Manager for the Accidents Evaluation and Investigations Division in Washington, D.C. at the time. Callahan has provided sworn testimony of this fantastic UFO encounter reported by credible witnesses during Dr. Steven Greer's Disclosure hearings. According to Mr. Callahan's testimony, two years before retirement he received a call from Alaska concerning the report of a UFO by flight 1628. Hard data, including onboard video of what the controller of the Japanese aircraft actually saw in their cameras that night, along with voice recordings of the event, was sent to the FAA text center in Atlantic City for review by Callahan and his supervisor on a PVD (planned view display) unit. John Callahan personally recorded the playback of the video with a new video camera he had just purchased, a video that he retained in his personal possession. From there, the data went to the scientific staff of President Reagan. Reagan's staff watched the video of this incredible UFO event and received a full briefing by John Callahan and his crew. When the briefing was over, Reagan's staff announced to Callahan and associates that they were all sworn to secrecy, and that the public were never to lay eyes on any of this material for fear of public panic. Reagan's staff made sure that Callahan and his men understood that this event *never happened*. The original UFO footage from Flight 1628 was likely viewed by President Reagan himself. In September, 1987, a year after this confirmed encounter with otherworldly vehicles, President Reagan gave his famous speech to the United Nations 42nd Assembly about how quickly our differences would disappear if we were all faced with an outside alien threat. After watching the footage from Flight 1628, Reagan was spooked. No wonder President Reagan was obsessed with the construction and employment of the Strategic Defense Initiative (SDI), otherwise known as *Star Wars*. Due to the tremendous size of the Saturn-like object witnessed by the crew of Flight 1628, it is unlikely that this vehicle belonged to any of our cryptoterrestrial populations, unless it was a holographic projection produced by the Overlords to perpetuate the ETH and instigate the production of technologies that contribute to the Singularity. New technologies that were produced in pursuit of the now-defunct Top Secret Star Wars program, implemented by President Reagan in response to Flight 1628, were probably a useful contribution to the artificial intelligence systems that are currently under development. Therefore, this particular UFO appearance was probably very productive and successful.

The Jim Moroney Abduction

In 1987, Jim Moroney, 27, an executive director for a health and safety company, drove his 1987 Honda Civic into a truck stop to try and get some sleep. Based on a previous meditation experience, during which Jim encountered a nonhuman entity that left him with an overwhelming sense of love, he was anticipating another encounter with extraterrestrials at some point. As Jim was driving, he was overcome with a sense that this new encounter might happen that night. Parking in front of a diner, Jim noticed mosquitos coming in the vehicle, so he rolled up the windows of the car. As he tried to get some rest in his car, trucks were coming in and out of the truck stop, keeping him awake. A bright light appeared in front of Jim's car. He thought at first it was from an oncoming truck, until the light moved directly over the top of his vehicle. Jim felt the hair on his arms tingling and standing on edge due to intense electromagnetic fields. Jim was then overcome with paralysis for 3-4 seconds while both he and his vehicle were teleported from the parking lot of the truck stop to the interior of an alien spacecraft. Jim felt immediately terrified and very angry. Confronted with a group of small beings with large bulbous heads and blue eyes, he began cursing them. Jim calmed down when one of the four-foot tall humanoids began speaking with him. Jim was escorted to what he described as a decontamination area. No other humans were there. Jim stepped inside what looked like a shower facility built for humans who were taller than the beings onboard the craft. He removed his clothes and put on a robe, noticing that the inside of the ship was massive. He then entered a room that was two stories high with other beings inside. These entities had a professional, unemotional demeanor, and were able to speak English to Jim in short sentences with no accent. He had no idea where he was, as there were no windows for orientation. The beings took him into a medical room where unpleasant procedures were conducted on his person including a device that went into his stomach area. Other procedures were also extremely painful, none of which left marks on him. Jim blacked out for a while from the pain. When he regained consciousness, one of the beings was looking directly into his eyes, and Jim could see the crosshairs of a medical device. When the being pulled away and Jim's vision refocused, he looked to his right to see a female being around five-foot-two-inches tall, along with several other beings who were over 10 feet tall wearing black uniforms. One of the tall beings came over and said, "I don't understand your anger." All Jim could think of to say was, "I'm sorry." Following this, he felt a wave of love coming from the female being. Jim sensed that he was being evaluated by the beings, who were trying to get a sense of who he was and how he reacted from various stimuli. Jim believes that he was implanted with a device due to a conscious memory of a mechanical instrument that installed something behind his ear. After his encounter with these beings was over, Jim and his Honda were both replaced back in the parking lot of the truck stop. Disturbed by all this, Jim left his car and walked into the diner. Traumatized, he washed his face in the bathroom. When he came out, he sat down and ordered a cup of coffee. He asked his waitress if she had just seen anything. It became clear from her answer that no one in the diner saw anything out of the ordinary while this experience took place. After coffee, Jim just wanted to get out of the area.

Jim kept his story to himself for several years for fear of being considered crazy. Finally, Jim decided to go public with his story. He wrote his book, *The Extraterrestrial Answer Book: UFOs, Abductions, and the Coming ET Presence* (2009), which is a very thought-provoking, in-depth analysis of the philosophical implications of the alien abduction phenomenon. Jim feels that the aliens want an open relationship with humanity. However, due to our violent inclinations, right now the alien presence is one of "intervention." According to Jim, they select one person at a time to interact with as opposed to global disclosure all at once, as they do not want to upset our society. It is within their capabilities to take a person bodily, along with their vehicle if they so choose, into an interdimensional, time-dilated experience. The aliens, who are technologically advanced beyond human comprehension, have the ability to extract a person from this physical world into an altered reality, a reality that is just as real as the one we know but not bound by the same laws of physics that we are accustomed to. A small craft, say, 30 feet in diameter by our measurements, is capable of taking a human onboard into what appears to be a very large facility. The aliens do not exist within the same physical reality as we do here on Earth. They are normally invisible to the human eye except for the appearance of a luminous orb, which can morph into what appears to be a small metallic craft, and they are not bound by the same passing of time as we humans on Earth are. The aliens are able to spend what is perceived as hours with the abductee, and return them to the same time and place they were before, with or without missing time, and with or without full memory of the event. Some abductees remember everything, some retain partial memory, and others, like myself, remember nothing, although the memory of the automobile I drove at the time was and is completely wiped out. Outside observers do not notice anything amiss at all. In this manner, what is invisible to a human observer, or appears as a ball of light can pass over their house or vehicle, take them from their bed or vehicle into an abduction scenario that seems to last quite a while on a craft that is perceived to be huge, and then return the person to their bed or vehicle with little or no elapsed time perceived in this reality. If another person is sleeping or sitting right next to them, this person notices nothing unless they are also part of the abduction experience. The perfect mindset for an abduction is a meditative or relaxed state. That is likely why so many abduction experiences occur while the person is relaxed or exists somewhere in their sleep cycle. It is not that the intelligences behind the UFOs look for people in bed. It is rather a selection by appropriate mindset, which occurs in meditative states such as just prior to, during, or after sleeping. This prompts psychologists to attribute the abduction experience to a natural hypnagogic and/or hypnopompic origin, but what actually occurs to the percipients is way beyond these phenomena. Abduction experiences can cause major personality changes, changes in lifestyle, complete changes in worldview, cause the person to become obsessed with UFOs or become messengers of the UFOs, or even induce PTSD. If Jim Moroney's abduction had occurred in real time, the waitress and other people inside the diner would have surely noticed that a car and driver were being taken up into a ball of light that was hovering above the car. That is not what happened. If someone inside the diner was looking out the window directly at Jim's car when he was taken, they would not have noticed anything at all out of the ordinary. Meanwhile, Jim and his vehicle were taken aboard an interdimensional spacecraft for quite sometime, an entire scenario played out, and he was returned. That, I believe, is how abductions work. We are involved with hidden UFO intelligences who have mastered high-level interdimensional physics, exist invisibly for the most part except when they interact with humans as a ball of light or a structured craft fashioned after the experiencer's own evolving psychology, and operate from a realm in which the laws of ordinary reality as we know it simply do not apply. Despite what the UFO skeptics say, these abilities are exactly what should exist if an alien species was visiting the earth who wanted minimal attention from the general public or felt that humans were not ready for open contact.

The Gulf Breeze Sightings

The same year that Jim Moroney was taken up in an alien spacecraft from a truck stop parking lot in Canada also brought the residents of Gulf Breeze, Florida a wave of spectacular UFO sightings. Beginning in November, 1987, witnesses in Gulf Breeze were blessed with the appearance of strange, unidentifiable crafts from an unknown realm. Over 200 local witnesses came forward with corroborating eyewitness accounts, producing amateur video and photographs. One of the many credible individuals who personally experienced a daylight-disk sighting in Gulf Breeze during this unusual flap was a well-respected, church-going family man and former Monsanto employee, Art Hufford. Inspired by his own personal sighting with his wife in 1987, Art joined the Mutual UFO Network (MUFON) in 1988 and became a MUFON field investigator. Art also began skywatching excursions with a local group of UFO enthusiasts in 1991 that became known as the Gulf Breeze Research Team. Over a 20-month period, Art and the research team documented 177 UFO reports. Art became an expert in the well-publicized local case in which a well-known Gulf Breeze resident, Ed Walters, produced a set of fantastic but controversial photos of a UFO that looked exactly like the one Art and his wife also witnessed. Art has since appeared on many television programs such as *Encounters*, *Sightings*, *Unsolved Mysteries*, and other shows in England, Germany, Japan, and Mexico. Although suspicions were cast upon Ed Walters' testimony and photos in the minds of some people after a paper model appeared in a home that Ed once owned that looked similar to the object in Ed's photos, Art Hufford maintains that Walter's photos are, in fact, authentic as they look exactly like the craft that he and his wife witnessed themselves, a sighting that motivated Art to become a serious UFO researcher. Also, former naval optical physicist, Dr. Bruce Maccabee, extensively researched all of the original photographs produced by Ed Walters with modern equipment designed to detect any photographic anomaly or technique of trickery that exists in the modern world. After his thorough examination of the Walters photos, Maccabee concluded that the photos were 100% legitimate with a 0% chance of fakery. After all, it is not unusual for a person who actually witnesses something extraordinary with their own eyes to then create drawings and/or models of what they saw. The logic that skeptics of Walters' photos employ, that the discovery of a paper model that looked similar to the object in Ed Walters' photographs proves that the paper model was, in fact, the object in the photographs, is erroneous. This faulty logic certainly does not hold water against the type of modern optical equipment that Maccabee used to analyze the photos and ascertain their authenticity. If, on the other hand, the paper model was an intentional plant by parties interested in obfuscating the Gulf Breeze UFO sightings and/or casting doubt on the Ed Walters photos, it certainly wouldn't be the first time that happened either. Furthermore, the idea that Ed Walters would take the time to create and release a set of UFO photos to the public that were so good they fooled an optical physicist and his state-of-the-art photographic analysis equipment, stake his personal reputation on the photos knowing the attention and excitement they would surely create, and then be stupid enough to leave behind the paper model he used to create the photos in an obscure part of a home he vacated, stretches all credulity. To me, it's more reasonable to just accept the photos as authentic, especially since they are an exact match to other credible sighting reports and photos, than to believe someone smart enough to baffle Dr. Bruce Maccabee would be dumb enough to leave a paper model behind in a move.

The Ilkley Moor Alien

While the residents of Gulf Breeze, Florida were haunted by the appearance of strange flying objects that were captured on film and witnessed by hundreds of people, on the morning of December 1, 1987, police officer Philip Spencer of Yorkshire, England, managed to snap a photo of a 4.5 foot tall, nonhuman entity who was caught outside his flying vehicle, a real ufonaut. This enigmatic snapshot became known as the "Ilkley Moor Alien Photo." The location of this encounter, Ilkley Moor, is a very creepy place. It's been said that Ilkley Moor can scare people to death in the daytime. At night, it's even worse. Weird artifacts exist at Ilkley Moor. There is a rock known as the "Swastika Stone," and another called the "Badger Stone." These are both boulders with strange etchings all over them. Another area is known as the "Twelve Apostles Stone Circle." Ilkley Moor is known for its strange lights in the sky, lights that appear to be under conscious control. Strange creature sightings are also reported at Ilkley Moor. As Spencer walked across the Moor he was startled when he encountered a strange little creature ahead of him who appeared to gesture him to stay away. He captured a photograph of the creature with his camera, after which the being ran away from him. Impulsively, Spencer chased the creature. Spencer caught up with the little guy just in time to watch a domed saucer rise from the Moor and speed away. As he walked back home, Spencer discovered that the village clock was an hour ahead of where it should be, so not only did Spencer encounter an alien, but he also walked himself into a time anomaly. Spencer traveled by bus into town to have the film developed. When the photo came out, he found that he had, in fact, captured an image of the mysterious little creature. His first approach was to UFO investigator Peter Hough. Hough interviewed Spencer and became convinced of his sincerity, so he had the photograph analyzed. The first stop was a wildlife expert who affirmed that the creature in the photo was not a mis-identification of any known animal in the area. Next the photo was sent to a Kodak photo lab. The experts at Kodak ascertained that it was not a superimposition or any other known photo trick. Finally, the photo made its way to Dr. Bruce Maccabee, the same optical physicist who analyzed the Gulf Breeze photos. Maccabee stated that the low light conditions of the photograph made it too grainy for proper film analysis. To this day, the Ilkley Moor Alien Photo remains enigmatic. It may actually be a photograph of a real ufonaut, the occupant of a flying saucer. The fact that Spencer was a police officer, that he sought no publicity or financial gain from the photo, and the fact that Spencer was willing to submit his photograph to ultimate scientific scrutiny, knowing that an exposure of fraud would ruin him personally, convinces many that the photo is what it appears to be - an alien creature who had emerged from a flying craft of unknown origin and was walking around Ilkley Moor. This alien was captured on film by a human with a fast camera click. The photo of the Ilkley Moor alien can be viewed online.

Amaury Rivera

The following year, in May, 1988, Puerto Rican resident Amaury Rivera went public with his abduction experience onboard an alien spacecraft. During this harrowing ordeal, the entities showed him scenes from a future catastrophe on Earth caused by an asteroid that crashes into the Caribbean Sea near Puerto Rico and destroys all human life on Earth, save a small remnant of the population. Rivera related his personal experience onboard a flying saucer in the documentary, *UFOs: The Secret Evidence* by German filmmaker Michael Hesemann. Rivera's abduction experience was not solo, but involved 14 other human beings that were also taken aboard.

The group, including Rivera, were shown holographic images of the aftermath of Earth's future asteroid impact. They were also treated to a holographic tour of their saucer-host's home planet, who was a humanoid alien with long black hair. After the group was shown these images, Rivera found himself back in his car in broad daylight in similar fashion to Jim Moroney's abduction. Rivera then heard the sound of three US F-14 fighter jets. Looking toward the sound of the jets, Rivera saw the spacecraft that he was just aboard being chased by the jets. Rivera was able to take good photographs of the jet and the saucer together. These photos were shown in the documentary film, and can be viewed on the internet. When Rivera decided to release his story and photographs to the world, he taped the photos and negatives on the inside roof of a doghouse fearing that his evidence would be confiscated by authorities. His suspicions were correct, as men who claimed to be with the CIA came to his door with a search warrant. The men went through his entire house looking for the evidence that was cleverly hidden away. Amaury's description of the humanoid extraterrestrial with long black hair is very similar to Woodrow Derenberger's description of his ufonaut contact, Indrid Cold, 22 years previous in 1966, leading some to wonder if they are one and the same person. One can only contemplate the possibility that we have had friendly visitors from Lanulos flying around in our skies for decades now who have been attempting to establish open contact and trade between our two worlds, only to be met with hostility, advancing jets, and gunfire, save a few select contactees like Woodrow Derenberger and Amaury Rivera. Another concern, other than ascertaining the actual reality of such reported encounters, involves understanding the nature of the reported experiences themselves. Woodrow Derenberger's description of an "electrical shock" to his temples whenever contact was established or broken with Indrid Cold hints of some sort of electronic mind-control device. Considering the reality of programs such as MK-ULTRA, some wonder if abductees are being manipulated with electronic equipment of terrestrial origin. Canadian research scientist Michael Persinger, who has induced audio and visual hallucinations in the minds of subjects by exposing them to certain electromagnetic frequencies demonstrates the frightening potential for human mind control and manipulation by other humans. If electronics were not involved, the pain that Woodrow reported in his temporal lobes, which is similar to many abductee reports, may have been the result of direct mind-to-mind contact between Woodrow and Indrid Cold. Cold stated that the inhabitants of his home planet, Lanulos, spoke to one another both verbally and telepathically. Or, perhaps psychotronic devices developed on Lanulos for mind-to-mind contact are commonly used to communicate with humans when they are here, or with creatures on other planets as well. NASAs ready acceptance of Woodrow Derenberger's story, along with Amaury Rivera's photographs of US fighter jets escorting his host's ship around in our skies presents the possibility of a terrestrial operation that has been going on for decades now that fools people into thinking they have been contacted by extraterrestrials when it is actually humans that pose as extraterrestrials. Dr. Steven Greer has made statements to this effect, that abductions are being perpetrated by our own military industrial complex, the secret government, or secret space program. According to Greer, perpetuating the ETH serves the purpose of keeping them clandestine through misdirection. Many early UFO researchers, such as Ivan T. Sanderson, also argued for a terrestrial origin of flying saucers and their occupants. Others are content to accept testimony from individuals such as Rivera and Derenberger at face value, and simply accept that Earth does, in fact, have humanoid visitors from a variety of other planets, including Lanulos, flying around who are eager to establish open contact with Earth and are interested in friendly trade with us. No matter what the underlying reality of all this really is, any intellectually honest person will conclude through their own personal research that there are a variety of very strange phenomena that exist on our planet that are poorly understood and difficult to dismiss.

More Andreason Revelations

In 1987, 20 years after Betty Andreasson's original experience with nonhuman entities, ongoing investigations and analyses of the details of her case led to startling new speculations that humans are actually a "larval" form of the celestials who are encountered during out-of-body experiences (OBE), near-death experiences (NDE) and so-called alien abductions. Exploration of this idea has lead to speculations by some UFO theorists that the entire UFO phenomenon, including alien abductions, represents a "maintenance program" for the larval form of humanity, and that the Grays represent humanity's true, transcendent version. In 1987, Betty discovered anomalous "scoop marks" on the calf of her right leg. Three more scoop marks appeared on her arms. During the following year, in 1988, author and UFO investigator Raymond Fowler, who originally investigated Betty's fantastic case and wrote several books that analyzed her experiences, also discovered a scoop mark on his right leg after awakening from a "dream" about being "operated on by aliens." It seems unlikely that dreams about aliens are so powerful that a small portion of flesh is actually removed. Why was there no blood on the sheets in both of these individual's cases when the scoop marks appeared suddenly? Are the entities who conduct these "punch biopsies" using some sort of instrument that cauterizes the entry wound so that, by the time the person notices their scoop mark, it is already healed? What exactly are the scoop marks? How are they produced? What is their purpose? How is it that they show up as if they have been there for a long time, and are perfectly healed? Add these tidbits of baffling antagonism to the overall UFO mystery. It also appears from the scoop marks that the abductions were an ongoing phenomenon, and that future abductions that followed her original experience were blocked from her conscious memory.

UFO Cover-up: Live!

A year or so after the discovery of mysterious scoop marks on both Betty Andreason, an abduction experiencer, and Raymond Fowler, her investigator, an infamous television show was produced and released in 1988 that, although intended (allegedly) to contribute to public Disclosure, actually did more harm than good concerning the public acceptance of UFO reality.

On October 14, 1988, those who were in possession of clandestine UFO knowledge may have attempted to test the water of public sentiment toward UFOs and aliens by a controlled leak of information that was also peppered with possible disinformation (as always). The outlet they used to disseminate this information was a television program called *UFO Cover-up: Live*! This live program was released simultaneously in both the United States and the Soviet Union. The show was hosted by actor Mike Farrell, best known for his role as Captain B.J. Hunnicutt in the highly-successful television series, *Mash*. This live television program garnered intense participation and cooperation by intelligence officials in both the United States and the Soviet Union. The show featured actual UFO experiencers who appeared in person to detail unde-niable, important cases from both the United States and the Soviet Union, along with profes-sional analysis and commentary. The show was carefully constructed using common CIA propaganda techniques for plausible deniability in case things went awry. One obvious method that the show employed was a misdirecting background soundtrack and cartoon alien images as backdrops. These were used so that, even though incredible truths were being revealed, the emotions conveyed by the music and props conflicted with the information. This inten-tional infliction of contradictory audio-visual cues was used to manipulate viewers such that the public level of belief in UFOs would actually *decrease* after viewing the show. The program attempted to portray the actual US contact and interaction with the Grays as a smart move on the part of the government, when it actually represented selling our whole country and pos-sibly the entire human race down the river. President Eisenhower, for one, could have made a deal with the Nordics, accepting their offer of spiritual assistance and help with solving im-portant world problems. Instead, Eisenhower made a deal with the Grays to allow an agreed-upon level of human and animal abductions to take place in exchange for trinkets in the form of advanced technology. As the show progressed, host Mike Farrell flippantly bypassed the case of Swiss farmer/contactee Eduard "Billy" Meier as an "obvious hoax," even though there are elements of anomalous evidence in the Meier case that truly defy a conventional explana-tion. Dr. James Deardorff, a senior scientist for the National Center for Atmospheric Research (NCAR) at Boulder, Colorado, conducted intensive research into the Meier case and concluded that ETs have imparted both true and false information to Meier, who sincerely reported his experiences as he knows them in his writings. Deardorff, among others, believes that the UFO intelligences have a habit of mixing true revelations with absurdities in the lives of contactees in order to keep the entire subject of UFOs obfuscated and marginalized in public perception while they go about doing what they do here on Earth. In other words, ETs intentionally use absurd elements, such as serving pancakes to Joe Simonton from a landed flying saucer on his property, in order to perpetuate skepticism and disbelief in their actual existence, as doing so provides needed camouflage. Experiencers like Simonton tell their story publicly, the public gets a good laugh, and the subject of UFOs is further relegated to fantasy and fiction, providing cover for the ETs as they manipulate humankind toward the Singularity. This ingenious technique employed by ETs prevents serious investigation into their affairs, and prevents much of the public from accepting ET reality for fear of being considered gullible by family and peers. Billy Meier is no intellectual giant, and even though he has likely reported his experiences truthfully, he, along with so many other ET contactees, are unwitting pawns of the Overlords, who have been feeding us legitimate information mixed with lies that serve their own purposes and keep their existence hidden for a very long time now. One of the reasons Meier has been the target of so much official effort to discredit him may lie in the fact that his contacts are not with the same group that the government decided to conduct business with. Meier's contacts are with the humanoid "Nordic" aliens who look just like us, and are related to humans. This group of humanoids are also known as the Blonde Nordics, the Swedes, the Aesir, the Tuatha de Danaan, and by other names, depending on the language spoken by their chosen contacts. Another technique that was used by *UFO Cover-up: Live!* was that, even though the show was billed as a live broadcast, all guests were extensively interviewed, edited, and choreographed. Guests were only allowed to say words that appeared on hidden cue cards held up in front of them. None of the guests were experienced in speaking like this, and it produced a very cheesy and insincere effect in the conversations that took place on stage. Between Mike Farrell's goofy facial expressions directed into the camera as guests were speaking, the background music, the cheap painted backdrops on the set, and guests in mental straightjackets, the show came off as fake, and was a complete commercial flop. The show is actually painful to watch for anyone knowledgeable about the UFO phenomenon. As both US and Soviet speakers revealed details of historical cases from both countries, all the classic propaganda elements came into play to manipulate public perception of the ET presence on Earth, which is quite real but difficult for many to accept, even without the botched television show.

One of the most intriguing aspects of the show was the live appearance on stage of Vickie Landrum and Betty Cash (of the Cash/Landrum Incident) in person. Both Betty Cash and Vickie Landrum were hoping to find answers to the mystery of their incredible 1980 UFO encounter, which left them with radiation burns and a scarred psyche for years after and possibly the rest of their lives on Earth. Two alleged intelligence officers spoke in shadow with the code names "Falcon" and "Condor." Falcon's real identity is believed to be none other than disinformation expert and Air Force Office of Special Investigations (AFOSI) agent, Richard C. Doty. Doty, recently retired in 1988, appeared on the program as Falcon and spoke directly to Betty Cash and Vickie Landrum, revealing that the craft they encountered in 1980 was, in fact, a gifted alien spacecraft piloted by humans that night. According to Falcon (Doty), the human pilots were experiencing difficulty in operating this alien craft and called in the helicopters (presumably unmarked black military helicopters with Project Red Light). This information was given by Falcon on a split screen as audiences watched Cash and Landrum receive blessed closure to an event that had haunted them for the previous 8 years since it occurred. This incredible information that Falcon revealed to Cash and Landrum was either true or false. If true, then those within the intelligence community were possibly genuine in wanting the two women to finally receive the information they deserved. If so, maybe those involved in the UFO intelligence organizations have souls after all. However, if what Falcon revealed was a ruse, something to make the case go away, to put it to rest, to stop the attempts at lawsuits against the military for personal injury and so forth, then shame on them. Feeding someone a lie who is looking to you for truthful answers concerning an all-important matter just to pacify them is dastardly. No doubt the truth will come out one day about whether or not Falcon told Cash and Landrum the truth about their 1980 encounter. Until then, we are left to simply speculate. If, in fact, the shadowed Falcon was actually telling the truth, and revealed this truth on live television, that our military has extraterrestrial spacecraft in their possession that was given to us by aliens - that was a fantastic bit of good information and disclosure. If, on the other hand, Falcon was lying, and was simply fabricating a story to put the Cash/Landrum case to rest when something else entirely was actually going on, that was one of the most unscrupulous acts of lying and intentional manipulation ever presented before a live public audience.

Another technique to pass a truth along, when the actual intention is for that truth to be dismissed as fantasy, is intentionally obsessing on a trivial detail. The way they employed this technique on the show was genius. As former AFOSI agent Falcon (Doty) and Condor (believed by many to have been former AFOSI agent Robert Collins) were sitting in shadow and spilling government UFO secrets, Falcon mentioned that one of the Grays our government held as a "guest" (captive) had a taste for strawberry ice cream. This humorous little detail served the purpose of reducing the actual horror of Gray aliens from Zeta Reticuli (or wherever they are from), who are here to conduct abductions on humans in exchange for gifts of technology to a secret government, to a benign, cartoon-like Walt Disney character. Flash to the painted stage backdrop of the Gray aliens, and all concern for what our government might have done to us with this agreement is dismissed. So, as the number of human abductions grew to epidemic levels throughout the 1970s and 1980s, and as cattle (and occasionally humans) were mutilated in a bizzare fashion, two retired intelligence officers went on national television to conduct an intentional hatchet job on the public outcry, concern, and fear, reducing the Grays to the level of cute little stuffed animals. Any intelligence officer who goes on national television and spills their guts in shadow would be instantly known by their fellow intelligence officers. It's a small community. No intelligence officer could give away classified government secrets on TV while preventing US intelligence from discovering their true identity as they speak in shadow. Therefore, it is reasonable to assume that what was revealed on *UFO Cover-up: Live!* was, in fact, an intentional partial disclosure. Yes, the US government has made contact with Gray aliens who at least represent themselves as coming from Zeta Reticuli. However, insiders used this television show to intelligently mislead the public concerning the true nature and intent of the aliens. This served the purpose of alleviating the very real growing public concern at the time over the alien-abduction and cattle-mutilation epidemics. Like a powerful sedative, *UFO Cover-up: Live!* absolutely put the public to sleep in the matter of flying saucers, alien abductions, and the extraterrestrial presence on Earth, so, mission accomplished.

From South Africa to Wright-Patterson

On May 5, 1989, Air Force fighter pilots from Capetown, South Africa were dispatched to chase an unidentified craft that penetrated South African airspace. In hot pursuit, one of the pilots fired a new laser-guided weapon, forcing the craft to land abruptly in Botswana, South Africa. Onboard the craft were small creatures with blue-grey skin, 3 fingers on each hand with frog-like fleshy webbing between the fingers and large slanted eyes, similar in appearance to the Roswell Grays with some variations. Veteran British police officer Anthony Todd investigated the incident and verified from South African intelligence sources that the downed vehicle had, in fact, been found intact, and that there were two live aliens inside as described. According to Todd, the alien craft, along with the two creatures, were transported to Wright-Patterson Air Force Base in the United States. Later this same year, 1989, another haunting wave of black triangular craft of unknown origin paid a visit to the Hudson Valley area here in the United States.

Giant Robots Land in Russia

As non-terrestrial spacecraft and occupants from South Africa were being examined at Wright Patterson, and Hudson Valley was once again visited by giant the black triangles, Russia received on-the-ground visitation. On September 27, 1989, a mass sighting occurred in Voronezh, Russia, 200 miles south of Moscow, involving witnesses from all walks of life including children, all of whom experienced a fantastic UFO landing and creature sighting. Several weeks prior to the UFO landing, there were many witness reports of lights in the sky in and around Voronezh. Then, on the 27th of September, a craft landed in the middle of a public park. Three giant humanoid figures emerged, walked around a bit, got back into their craft, and vanished into the sky. On October 3, 1989, scientists and military personnel investigated the area. The event became a media sensation in the International Press as well as television. Headlines appeared in the paper such as, *Space Invaders Land in Russia.* The *Daily Star* also printed the headline, *9-Foot Aliens Go For Walkabout in Russia.* Ukrainian journalist Paul Stonehill covered the event for the International Press. A description of this fantastic flying saucer landing and occupant event appears in his book, *The Soviet UFO Files.* Children witnesses were asked to draw the details of the event, and they all drew exactly the same thing independently. As adults, the children witnesses who were there in 1989 to see this event firsthand all maintain their original testimony to this day and continue to have identical descriptions of the event. It happened. One of the most fascinating aspects of the Phenomenon is that fantastic, in-our-faces landings such as the Voronezh Incident can occur, and they are generally dismissed by the public as a hoax or mass delusion, even when the likelihood of either of these write-offs is small or non-existent. It is a testament to the power of belief, or nonbelief. When something violates a person's sense of reality, it is simply dismissed. After the initial buzz passes, people go on with their lives as if nothing out of the ordinary happened. It's just a human coping mechanism. What it is going to take for people to wrap their minds around this is a sustained interaction that is indisputable in which humans are forced to come to grips with nonhuman visitation. Eyewitness testimony from fleeting encounters, photographs (especially from our digital age, where absolutely anything can be depicted on film) isn't good enough anymore for the reality of flying saucer and occupant landings to be accepted as real. Until such an open event occurs, it is going to be easy to write landings off as mass delusion or hoaxes, no matter how good the circumstantial evidence is.

The 1989 Belgium UFO Wave

Two months after the fantastic flying saucer landing/occupant encounter in Voronezh, Russia, a Belgian police officer in the village of Ans near the Belgium border, Francis Michalczyk, became one of the first witnesses of the famous 1989 Belgium UFO wave on November 15, 1989. Michalczyk reported a silent, hovering, black triangular craft with 3 lights pointing downward, having no correlation whatsoever to any known terrestrial aircraft. The thrust of the UFO wave then proceeded between November 29, 1989 and June, 1990. During this six-month period of time, an estimated 13,500 people witnessed these mysterious crafts. There were about 2,600 written statements from witnesses, multiple radar tracks from coordinated ground radar systems, and onboard radar tracks from Belgian F-16s that were dispatched to the scene of the sightings. Just as soon as the F-16s had the UFOs in sight, the craft would maneuver swiftly out of range. On April 4th, 1990, a photograph was taken of one of the black triangles in Petit-Rechain. Another similar craft was captured on film on June 15th, 1990 in Wallonia, Belgium. Both of these became iconic photos of the Belgian wave, and can be examined in any good book of descriptions and pictures of documented UFO photos/cases. These Belgian photographs, in particular the photo taken in Petit-Rechain, were analyzed by former NASA research scientist Dr. Richard F. Haines, who specialized in optics and human perception. After extensive examination, Haines concluded that the photos did, in fact, represent a physical craft of no known terrestrial manufacture with some sort of exotic propulsion system. Haines felt that the specific type of light distortions present in the photos represented a craft that did not obey the laws of physics as currently understood by our scientists and physicists. Haines also concluded that there was no way the Petit-Rechain photograph of a black triangular aircraft was in any way a hoax. Another analyst, astrophysicist Pierre Magain, Ph.D., also examined the Belgian photographs. Magain was similarly impressed with the photos themselves, but had concerns that the photos did not always match up to eyewitness reports. Haines, however, maintains that, despite the variation in eyewitness reports (which is to be expected), there is no possible way a person could reproduce such photographs down to the grain level. Haines stated that he believed the photos were authentic and representative of some sort of tangible but unknown flying craft. One significant aspect of the Belgian wave of 1989 is that it presented an upgraded image of flying saucers. Instead of the clunky-looking Adamski-style craft that looked like a Coleman lantern top with 3 light bulbs attached to the underside, an odd vehicle image that has been captured on film by many credible photographers all over the world, we were now looking at silent black triangles with mysterious lights underneath. The human psyche of 1989 had advanced from the 1950s. The imagery of otherworldly craft was now properly updated by the UFO intelligences to accommodate human psychological changes over time. As time progresses by our clocks, the entities who are manipulating the imagination and behavior of humankind keep adjusting the images according to our continually-changing concept of an alien spacecraft. The question is, are they doing this over such a long period of time for our benefit, to ease us into a knowledge of who and what they really are, and how they really appear? Are they guiding us ever closer to the day when actual, indisputable contact is made for all the inhabitants of Earth to accept and comprehend? Whatever the case, the technological singularity that is ahead of us will surely bring the answers. I hope we are ready for the reality at hand that is destined to come upon us soon. As aloof as our mysterious visitors have been over the centuries, it seems likely that they know exactly what they are doing when making contact with a developing civilization. As millennia pass by our clocks, they may simply be arriving using the standard procedure as masters of time and space to morph their appearance in accordance to evolving perceptions as they come in for a landing, which is not taking the amount of time to them as it is to us. Our visitors are simply arriving into port in the way they typically travel throughout the universe. In the meantime, are we humans living, dying, reincarnating, and developing our minds and concepts of reality over time in order to finally meet the aliens face-to-face in our latest physical body at the Singularity, thus bridging the veil between the world of the living and the world of the so-called dead, both of which our visitors are already acquainted with? This is certainly possible, as it may require certain technologies produced during the Singularity to enable humans to augment our intelligence and perceptions, enabling us to finally receive our otherworldly visitors in their true form.

The Gods of Eden
Toward the end of the 1980s, a great decade for UFO sightings and encounters, an insightful book, *The Gods of Eden*, was published by author William Bramley in 1989. In its finished form, it was not the book Bramley set out to write. Bramley began by researching war. He wanted to discover the underlying causes of war, and expected to find such causes as human poverty, or power-seeking dictators. As is the case for many researchers who dig into things deeper than the surface (including myself), Bramley found way more than he bargained for. From

his extensive research into human history, a strange picture emerged. Bramley began realizing that there are two different extraterrestrial forces on this planet. One has an agenda of their own which seems to disregard any adverse effects it has on humans. It even appears that they have intentionally caused destruction at times to advance their cause. Bramley refers to this extraterrestrial influence as the "custodial race." Bramley's custodial race have attached themselves like parasites to Earth and its inhabitants for some nefarious long-term goal that escaped him. Bramley identified a second extraterrestrial influence and designated this faction as the "maverick race." This maverick race of extraterrestrials seem to oversee the human race in some fashion, and are interested in our spiritual advancement. Bramley speculates that the maverick race includes the being our world knows as Jesus Christ, who provided teachings to humans who are interested in escaping from this prison planet. In his book, Bramley provides extensive evidence that the custodial race has long employed individuals within various secret societies, such as the Rosicrucians and the Freemasons. These UFO intelligences, who communicate with their people through secret societies, manipulate human beings with promises of advantage in the form of *superior technology, esoteric knowledge, or even physical immortality.* They pervert the world's religions and manipulate governments and populations into war and conflict if need be to serve the eventual ends and purposes of the custodial race. The maverick race, on the other hand, maintains a benign tutorial role. These helpful UFO intelligences have inspired human beings throughout history to overcome the negative influences of the custodial race. According to the information presented in Bramley's book, the custodial race that manipulates humankind appear to have some purpose of entrance into the physical realm and taking control of planet Earth and the human population here, whereas the benevolent maverick race resides in the spiritual realms and invite humans to join them.

Bramley's conclusions appear to coincide in many ways with Christian theology. Jesus said that his kingdom is "not of this world." The physical world, on the other hand, is portrayed as "Satan's kingdom." In these terms, Satan and his angels appear to continually entice humans with promises of earthly riches and pleasures, longevity and even physical immortality. Jesus provided a perfect example of rejecting the physical world for a spiritual kingdom that lies outside space and time in the heavenly realms. The custodial race that Bramley identified appear to be the same creatures that the Bible depicts as Satan and his minions. Satan may simply be an understandable personification for self-replicating von Neuman probes that arrived long ago from another galaxy or dimension for purposes of manipulating humankind into the technological singularity. Jesus, the spokesperson for the maverick race, came to harvest souls from Earth into the heavenly realms, thus saving a portion of humanity from this earthly "matrix" in which we all find ourselves imprisoned. Bramley's work also reminds us of the choice presented to President Eisenhower in 1954, according to UFO lore. In this scenario, the benevolent Nordics, who may represent the identity of Reverend Billy Graham's ufonaut angels, approached Eisenhower with an offer to humankind of spiritual assistance, but had no earthly riches (technology) to exchange. The Nordics admonished us to eliminate our nuclear weapons, which are a threat to all life on Earth and probably even life in other dimensions. The proposals of the Nordics were, unfortunately, rejected. Instead, the Grays were accepted, who may be unfeeling, self-replicating, interdimensional, electro-biological robots, a product of an ancient alien technology whose powers are beyond human comprehension. What we may have wound up with from the Grays is an alien technology that eventually produced a secret space program that is fueled by black budget money, thousands of cattle mutilations, thousands or even millions of human abductions for purposes of genetic tampering to create either an alien/human hybrid race or a genetically-upgraded humanity, wars and rumors of wars, and runaway technology that has created a giant snowball rolling toward the technological singularity. In this way, humans who have "sold their souls" to the Grays, and the Grays themselves, can merge their consciousness with advanced artificial intelligence that will be built by our own hands with technological assistance from above. One modern author who thinks along these lines is Thomas Horn, author of *Nephilim Stargates* (2007), *On the Path of the Immortals: Exo-Vaticana, Project L.U.C.I.F.E.R, and the Strategic Locations Where Entities Await the Appointed Time* (2015), and other fascinating works that combine modern ufology with Christian theology. Horn is a leading Christian theologian who proposes that the flying saucers and occupants are a great deception, a manifestation of Satan and the fallen angels. However, in my view, the missing piece in Horn's analysis of the flying saucer enigma is that *Jesus and his angels might also be advanced, interdimensional, or extraterrestrial beings themselves who offer humanity a different eternal destiny in a convoluted, electronic universe.* In this scenario, Jesus and his angels, who may be Bramley's maverick race and the Nordic extraterrestrials, offer "salvation" from the Grays and their purposes for humanity, and are, in fact, piloting some of the flying saucers that have been seen in our skies throughout human history, as Reverend Billy Graham, Pastor Downing, R.L. Dione, and others have proposed. Horn and others have correctly identified one faction of ufonauts as demonic in nature who are using humans for their own ends, but they seem to retain a traditional view of Jesus and God. In other words, the other end of the celestial equation is missing. Horn and others who have correctly identified the connection between the Bible and the UFO phenomenon, have yet to realize that the other faction, i.e., Jesus and his "angels" (Bramley's maverick race, the Nordic ETs), may also be celestial ufonauts who are involved in a cosmic struggle themselves, just as the AKRIJ in Italy and Chile have a conflict with the "Contraries" or "Weiros" (the race of biological robots who worship science and technology). Are these concepts all simply differing perceptions of the same phenomenon? In some fashion or another, I would answer in the affirmative.

Awakening to Eternisphere means opening our eyes to the fact that there are multiple realities going on all around us. These multiple realities are inhabited, and the inhabitants have, in fact, interacted with humanity in various ways from time to time that may seem strange to us. These denizens of other worlds peek through at us in the form of strange crafts in the sky that we know we didn't build, reports of UFO/occupant encounters, and sightings of cryptids from otherwise credible individuals. Most of these experiencers and percipients do not suffer from hallucinosis or any other mental disorder, and are not prone to embellishments or fanciful tales. They have historically been ridiculed and shunned, when they needed to be studied and taken seriously. Eternisphere includes humanity, but we are definitely not the only show in town.

CHAPTER 12

The Outer Limits of Understanding

"Unknown luminous things or beings have often been seen, sometimes close to this earth, and sometimes high in the sky. It may be that some of them are living things that occasionally come from somewhere else in our existence, but others are lights on the vessels of explorers, or voyagers from somewhere else."

- Charles Fort

MIR UFO Sightings

ON SEPTEMBER 28, 1990, MIR cosmonauts Gennadij Manakov and Gennadij Strekhalov reported a giant iridescent silvery disk hovering above the earth as they passed over Newfoundland. After observing the disk for approximately 7 seconds, the object instantly dematerialized.

[On October 24, 1990, the last of a total of 715 Soviet Nuclear tests that began in 1949 were detonated. Russia inherited the Soviet nuclear arsenal, and no testing has taken place since this time.]

Five months after the last Soviet nuclear test, MIR cosmonaut Musa Manarov witnessed and filmed a cigar-shaped craft with a rotating light for several minutes in March, 1991. The film is now included in German researcher Michael Hesseman's collection, *UFOs: The Footage Archives.* The Italian UFO researcher, Giorgio Bongiovanni, also has a collection of UFO footage from MIR cosmonauts that was released to him in 1999.

[On November 26, 1991, the United Kingdom detonated their last of their 45 nuclear tests in a vertical shaft.]

The Crop Circle Mystery

As if it isn't enough that flying saucers of unknown origin and purpose haunt our skies, flying saucers that occasionally eject occupants of various statures and appearances, strange geometric glyphs have appeared for our consideration in crops all over the world, glyphs that at least appear to be some sort of communication. Ironically, this form of two-way dialogue with otherworldly entities may have been inadvertently initiated, at least in modern times, by a couple of retired pranksters who represented the intelligence of Earth and did not know it. The "crop circle," or crop formation mystery, consists of simple-to-complex designs and images that appear in cereal crop fields overnight, or in some cases in just a few minutes throughout the world. The first historical crop circle reports that we know of began in 1678, and were referred to at that time as "mowing devils." In the modern era, the crop circle mystery began in the 1970s, when designs in the fields began appearing throughout the countryside of England. The crop circles then began gradually increasing in complexity into the 1990s and to the present day all over the planet. Over the years, just as in the case of UFOs, crop circles have created a controversy and a sort of psychic stress within the collective human consciousness, as no one really knew then, nor do they know now, how they were all made or by whom, save the hoaxes that are intentionally created by humans. Fortunately, over the years, crop circle researchers have developed specific, scientific methods to determine the difference between the "real" crop circles and the ones that are created by humans, as the real crop circles produce specific anomalies that can be examined. Many theories have been proposed over the years as to how the real crop circles are produced. These theories include atmospheric vortexes, ball lightning, or other anomalous weather events. In 1991, inquiring minds were all-too-eager to accept the "confession" of two elderly hoaxers, Doug Bower and David Chorley, when they made the claim that the two of them had been responsible for over 200 crop formations using a simple wooden plank and rope. When their confession was made, many dismissed the crop circle phenomenon out of hand and concluded that 100% of the crop circles were human hoaxes. However, even after Bower and Chorley died, the crop circles continued to appear, many times in places that are totally inaccessible to vehicles of any kind. Crop circles continue to grow in number and complexity all over the world. Just as UFO skeptics use a weird, tunnel-vision sort of logic to dismiss the UFO phenomenon, crop circle skeptics do likewise. UFO skeptics say that there are just too many UFO and occupant sightings for them to represent creatures from other planets visiting the earth. In other words, there are so many UFO sightings and flying saucer occupant reports that the reality of the phenomenon is completely negated. Skeptics reason that if all UFO reports represent interplanetary visitors, then the earth must be some sort of Grand Central Station in the universe, and this seems unlikely. Therefore, UFO reports must be psychological in nature or mere hallucinations, even though this view is scientifically untenable. Actual hallucinosis is a relatively rare human condition, and cannot possibly explain the sightings in any scientific way. However, skeptics eagerly accept this as a plausible way to escape the fantastic volume of evidence for the reality of flying saucers, whatever they really are, and wherever the occupants are from. Also, UFO skeptics make a huge assumption, that faster-than-light-speed travel is impossible, so the Extraterrestrial Hypothesis (ETH) is discarded.

While faster-than-light travel by physical craft and occupants may, in fact, be impossible, there are many other possibilities of travel, such as traversable wormholes, or traveling through hyperspace with technologies that currently escape us. Another possibility is that we routinely receive visitors from the astral plane by beings who can adjust the vibrations of their bodies and craft to enter the physical realm, or occupants of parallel worlds who have discovered methods of interdimensional travel. In consideration of Ivan T. Sanderson's identified vortices on Earth that display geophysical, electromagnetic, and time anomalies, the universe may operate much like a magic puzzle box, opening portals to other parts of the universe on a regular and predictable basis, through which the hundreds of UFOs and occupants traverse while remaining normally invisible. Invisibility is, no doubt, the preferred mode of travel, as visiting foreign planets, such as this violent, paranoid, and primitive Earth, can be hazardous. As for UFO crashes and alien bodies, skeptics laugh at the idea of interplanetary visitors that possess the technology to travel light years to Earth only to crash in the desert. It doesn't seem to occur to the skeptics that the phenomenon might be real, but not at all what it appears to be. UFO skeptics often display what I would call a general lack of scientific or speculative imagination. The same goes for skeptics of the crop circle mystery. Certainly there are human hoaxes. It is a fact that there are even competing groups of human crop-circle makers, teams of hoaxers that pride themselves on fooling crop circle researchers, as well as the general public with their work. Strangely, human crop circle makers sometimes report that they are motivated by the actual appearance of mysterious lights in the sky as they are working on the formations. This subset of crop circle makers feel that they are working directly for nonhuman intelligences. The workers sense that they are being guided or supervised by the UFOs themselves, or even engaging in some sort of interactive communication with the UFO intelligences. Some farmers have also figured out that they can make more money by hiring human crop circle hoaxers and charging money to see the formation than they make from growing and selling their crops. This happens, just as it was a lucrative business to create and sell fake religious artifacts in medieval times. Hoakery and profiteering in the realm of religion does not negate the underlying truths. Likewise, hoaxes in the UFO field do not negate the underlying reality that we are being visited and communicated with by non-terrestrial humanoids from somewhere other than Earth, or other than the physical reality we are familiar with. There will always be hoaxes and profiteering by unscrupulous individuals who want to gain personally from a profound mystery. The fact that the details are not generally known makes such mysteries especially vulnerable to hucksters and racketeers. There are those who fake contact with extraterrestrials for the attention, or for fun and profit. Fake UFO pictures and videos soak the internet just for the tomfoolery of it all. However, just because UFOs, ghosts, monsters, and crop circles can be faked and posted online doesn't mean there isn't a real phenomenon at hand. There are fake preachers, fake prosperity theologians, and fake faith healers too, but that doesn't automatically turn Jesus into fiction. In the cases of religion, UFOs, crop circles, and other so-called "paranormal" phenomena, there are certainly real mysteries at hand. Even though the majority of UFO sightings are the result of misidentified natural phenomena, secret government aircraft, optical illusions, and hoaxes, the truth is that there exists a core of UFO and occupant reports that represent something genuinely unknown, fantastic, and mysterious. UFO skeptics who ordinarily apply the scientific method in determining the reality of a phenomenon often unjustifiably dismiss UFOs and crop circles out of hand. It is as if their faculties of logic break down when faced with the subject of UFOs, and it is indeed a strange and fascinating reaction to behold from otherwise rational individuals.

One crop circle researcher that has submitted peer-reviewed science on crop circles is Dr. Eltjo Haselhoff of the Netherlands. Haselhoff has established a foolproof method of scientifically analyzing crop circles to determine if the formation is "authentic" or hoaxed by humans. His proof that UFOs do, in fact, create some crop circle formations has to do with the scientific application of established and understood laws of electromagnetism. Dr. Haselhoff found in his research that, by examining crop circles for the existence of heat-expanded nodes in the plant stems and taking their measurements, that the nodes in the center of real crop circle formations were expanded significantly larger than the nodes toward the perimeter of the formations. These plant node expansions must be due to the application of some sort of internal heat that caused the moisture-containing nodes of the plants to expand or even burst open. Dr. Haselhoff also found that these node-expansion measurements from the center to the perimeter of the formation, when plotted on a graph, conformed to the Beer-Lambert Law of Electromagnetism. Therefore, if a crop circle is examined closely and found to contain heat-expanded nodes, and if these node expansion measurements taken from the center to the perimeter of the formation conform to the Beer-Lambert Law of Electromagnetism, it is proof-positive that the crop circle in question was at least exposed to, and likely formed by, a point source of electromagnetic radiation of unknown origin. Dr. Haselhoff's peer-reviewed research and findings provided confirmed, scientific proof that some crop circles are, in fact, created by an unidentified source of radiation. In other words, it is now a scientific fact, thanks to Dr. Haselhoff, that some crop circles are produced by UFOs. Calculations can also be made to determine the exact height from the ground and the energy level of the point source radiation that created the circle. Dr. Haselhoff's scientific findings were published in *Physiologia Plantarum* in October, 2000. As of this writing, the crop circle mystery is far from understood or solved. There are researchers who are actually attempting to build antigravity devices using crop circle formations as an instruction manual. Other researchers attempt to decipher extraterrestrial messages to humanity from the symbols embedded in the crop circles. Anomalous artifacts have also been found in some of the formations, such as tiny metallic spheres, or insects frozen on the plants as if zapped into suspended animation. Unless one is willing to accept the idea that groups of human hoaxers have been floating in to fields at night completely undetected for decades in hot air balloons, carrying with them magnetrons of sufficient power that they are capable of producing the formations with microwaves or some other source of electromagnetism, or that a secret space program has been creating crop circles with lasers from space since the 1970s, we are faced with the reality that, for decades now, these strange and sometimes stunning artifacts have been appearing mysteriously in our fields, sometimes in as little as 20 minutes, by an unknown intelligence, human or otherwise. My speculation is that, like so many other absurd aspects of the UFO phenomenon, they are just a distraction. Like shining a laser pointer on the carpet for kittens to chase, crop circle designs are created by the Overlords for the sole purpose of discrediting the UFO phenomenon and thus obfuscating real, clandestine UFO activity as we approach the Singularity. Or, perhaps the crop circles produced by UFOs are some sort of cosmic IQ test that will continue to appear until we are smart enough to figure out the actual communication. For now, the actual purpose of the "real" crop circles that are mysteriously created by an unknown form of point source radiation by an unknown intelligence remains unsolved.

Everyone Gets Abducted?

By 1992, a Roper Poll had been conducted that extrapolated information from abductees in order to gain insight into the prevalence of the abduction phenomenon. The poll indicated that an estimated 25% of the US population were percipients of the so-called "alien abduction" phenomenon, whatever the underlying reality of this actually was. These experiences with aliens solidified over the years into a recognizable standardized format, which usually included capture (taken aboard an alien vessel), examination (medical procedures), conference (individual or group schooling), a tour of the craft, the "otherworldly journey" in which the aliens show the captive parts of the universe and/or an alien landscape, Theophany in which the captive meets a celestial personality or cosmic being, the return to their normal life, and aftermath, for better or worse. The alien abduction experience appears to be a crap shoot. Some abductees actually benefit from their UFO encounter and experience an advancement of mind and spirit, and a renewed interest in all things celestial. Others experience the loss of friends, family, job, or even sanity itself, and in some cases, commit suicide. One can only speculate why this difference of experience and reaction exists, or why UFO experiences carry such duel potentiality. The consistency of reported experiences across the globe indicates that the alien abduction experience differs from the randomness of personal fantasies or patterns within the development of run-of-the-mill folk tales. Whatever alien abductions really are, they are real and produce everything from post-traumatic stress disorder to cosmic illumination. Also, according to the research of Dr. David Jacobs, a historian who investigated the alien abduction phenomenon for many decades, the abduction narrative has changed over the years. At first, beginning in the late 1950s with the Antonio Vilas Boas case and the 1961 case of Betty and Barney Hill, the abductions involved breeding experiments, or the extraction of sperm from males and ova from females. The phenomenon evolved from there to onboard encounters with alien/human hybrids. Some abductees were shown films of children and asked if they could tell the difference between the hybrids and full human children. Finally, Dr. Jacobs encountered abductees who assist young hybrids in moving into apartments and adjusting to life on Earth. Dr. Jacobs outlined this narrative progression, along for his concern that Earth is being slowly taken over by alien hybrids in such books as *The Threat: Revealing the Secret Alien Agenda* (1999), and *Walking Among Us: The Alien Plan to Control Humanity* (2015). If such a program has really been implemented, I have to give credit to the aliens. If they have been abducting humans since the late 1950s and conducting genetic alterations in human DNA to produce a more intelligent human being that is actually deserving of a planet like Earth, humans who are of superior intelligence and motives, who will be better stewards of the planet and engage in the final push toward a technological singularity, they have done so in such a way that the entire alien abduction phenomenon has been dismissed as fiction, a product of overactive imaginations or the ramblings of fantasy-prone individuals. The good news is, if these alien manipulations have actually taken place, and alien-human hybrids are now living among us and interbreeding with non-altered humans, perhaps the aliens do not plan on exterminating humans after the Singularity has been achieved after all. If they have invested their own kind into the production of the Singularity, then they are likely preparing the human mind for an eventual merge with artificial intelligence. If the hybrids are, in fact, here now, there are many who are likely working in the fields of engineering, physics, and robotics. The hybrids are in their 30s-50s now (as of 2016) and are diligently creating the Post-Singularity Artificial Superintelligence (PSASI) that will soon be our future.

Alien Abduction and Near Death Experiences

In 1992, as the Roper Poll revealed the actual extent of the alien-abduction phenomenon, psychology professor Kenneth Ring wrote a book that was destined to influence my own thinking about the UFO phenomenon when I read it in 2012, since I had my own near-death experience in August, 2009. In *The Omega Project*, Dr. Ring analyzed the results of 10 years of NDE research. He also examined the relationship between NDEs and alien abduction experiences such as that reported by Whitley Strieber in his best-selling book, *Communion*. Dr. Ring's research into NDEs and alien abductions completely discredits the idea that both NDEs and alien abductions occur only to fantasy-prone personalities. Ring concludes that there is a reality to both experiences that are related in some fashion and involve a realm of reality we currently do not understand. Ring brings in the concept of *Mind at Large* from Aldus Huxley, *a kind of planetary or collective mind that is both an expression of humanity's deepest yearnings and transcendent to them.* Dr. Ring's book presents his own insights into the true nature of alien abductions. These insights contain elements of both the geophysical hypothesis and a psychic origin for the experiences. Ring concluded that the intelligences behind the UFO phenomenon, who or whatever they are, have somehow gained access to imagery within the human mind, ether by telepathic connection or via technology. Dr. Ring writes (*Omega*, pg. 17):

I strongly suspect that the [alien abduction] experience represents some response to a natural phenomenon, probably of an electromagnetic nature, and that the forms it takes depends on the enculturation of the affected individuals. I say this because my own experience with the phenomenon has been extremely extensive, and I have been able to observe details of its intelligence that so strongly point to its human origins that I can only say that, if aliens are here, they have learned to mimic the inner mind of man.

The aliens, whoever they are, even if they are some aspect of ourselves, have, in fact, contacted the terrestrials of Earth. They are here. However, despite all appearances, the aliens have not arrived in shiny, advanced, physical spaceships that have traveled through physical space to visit us, as per the expectations of UFO skeptics, and the reason they reject the UFO phenomenon out of hand. The aliens have instead arrived using a method that caught us completely unaware. Their selected method of contact was *through the medium of our collective unconscious.* Dr. Ring continues (*Omega*, pg. 19):

Perhaps their final disguise will be our own conviction that they [aliens] come from within us. I would not, however, dismiss out of hand the seemingly fantastic notion that actual aliens may have their origin inside the human mind. Could it be that life itself is a mechanism by which some hidden, inner reality is touching and feeling its way into the physical world? Are we a medium of exchange, a communications device, an extraordinary construction designed to bridge the gulf between the physical world and something else?

Dr. Kenneth Ring was on the trail of a profound truth concerning the actual nature of our alien visitation. However, the truth of the situation is almost too strange to comprehend or bear. We are likely dealing with aliens who have traveled to us in a way that we cannot understand at present. Due to the constrictions of physical travel throughout the universe and the insurmountable speed of light, limitations that UFO skeptics are eager to point out to defend their abject dismissal of the UFO phenomenon, another method of travel that involves the human mind is at play. The aliens, who may even turn out to be an unknown aspect of ourselves (perhaps the transcendent version of my own being that I encountered in 2009 during my near-death experience, an aspect of myself that contained elements of machine intelligence), have chosen to visit and interact with humans *by way of the mind.* The aliens, whether they represent some far-off population from the other side of the universe, an aspect of ourselves, or both, are here. They are inside our minds, are here to stay, and there is nothing that we can do about it. The alien/human merge is happening, whether we like it or not. It is our destiny.

The Channeling Phenomenon

The desire to make contact with higher, nonhuman or alien intelligences has prompted humans to try a variety of methods, including the ingestion of psychedelics, meditation, and trance-channeling. These efforts have often resulted in actual contact with some outside agency within the Superspectrum, be they Ultraterrestrials; Interdimensionals; starfaring aliens; human or alien time travelers; God; the Galactic Federation; angels; demons; the Djinn; Mothman; Bigfoot; animal intelligences; geo-physical plasma intelligences; Gaia; sky critters; discarnate humans; the collective human unconscious; robotic von Neumann Probes; or some other aspect of the subconscious mind of the channeler themselves. Other channeling efforts may have resulted in contact with human manipulators using mind-control technologies that have been in development for decades now. These mind-control technologies have now achieved the capability of producing both audible and visual apparitions that can impart various messages to experiencers that the operators desire. As researcher Joseph Farrell reveals in *Genes, Giants, Monsters, and Men*, patents for mind control have existed for a while now, such as patent # 5,159,703 by Dr. Oliver Lowery on October 27, 1992, filed as the "Silent Subliminal Presentation System." Lowery's system had the capability of delivering messages directly into a human brain by a remote user, a very scary product indeed. Discounting the possibility of such modern mind-control technologies, the "channeling" phenomenon of today is likely the same practice that used to be called "divine inspiration." Divine inspiration (channeling) was used extensively by the prophets and writers of the Bible, which was written by approximately 39 distinct authors, all of whom remain unidentified, and can only be recognized from one another by their individual writing styles. This method of contact is capable of receiving information, both true and untrue, from a variety of sources suggested above. A channeler, meditating Shaman, or prophet may self-induce an internal mental state that connects with the entities of the Superspectrum. This Superspectrum (as Keel elaborated) is an entire frequency range containing everything from disembodied humans, higher celestial personalities, or what Richard Kieninger (Eklal Kueshana) identified in *The Ultimate Frontier* as the "black mentalists of the lower astral plane." Channeling can net truth, deception, or a combination of both. The black mentalists in particular, according to Kieninger, are humans who have accumulated so much negative Karma over multiple lifetimes that they are no longer able to reincarnate into the physical plane. Such entities seek out and sometimes succeed in taking temporary possession of a human vessel. The black mentalists are likely one and the same as the "demons" or "possessing spirits" of the Christian faith. These entities, who seek reentrance into the physical realm, may also have a stake in humans creating artificial intelligence for purposes of reincarnating into the forbidden physical realm for permanent residence. It isn't a stretch from there for modern eschatologists who have made the connection between all things spiritual and the UFO phenomenon to conclude that these so-called "demons" seek to download their disembodied consciousness into compatible AI formats that will be soon created by humans during the Singularity. It is thought by some that these AI demon-soldiers will engage in the long-prophecied final battle between Good and Evil in which the forces of spiritual darkness (demons downloaded into AI) battle the armies of Light (Christ and his angels) for final dominion of Planet Earth. It is not completely out of the realm of possibility that something like this may, in fact, be in the works. The race to create artificial intelligence during the Singularity that is able to accept personality/mind downloads may represent a form of spiritual warfare in the Cosmos that humans do not understand, nor can they explain with any clarity using any existing theology. What humans have traditionally called angels and demons may be AI battling for dominion of the physical universe. Caution must be exercised when engaging in any type of channeling activity to avoid such negative and manipulative entities. Other entities who reside on the upper astral plane may also be encountered during channeling. These entities are benevolent and may serve as "cosmic tutors" to humanity, but sometimes it is difficult to tell the difference, and the black mentalists on the lower astral seem to enjoy masquerading as "beings of light." The entities who serve as cosmic tutors to humanity at least appear to have a genuine interest in contacting earnest spiritual seekers in the human realm. However, these entities may also represent alien artificial intelligence that seeks to achieve a technological singularity on Earth for purposes of self-replication, or to simply take possession of the planet.

The Allies of Humanity

The same year that Dr. Kenneth Ring was writing about UFOs as an emergent phenomenon with a relationship to near-death experiences, a new religious movement was founded here in the United States that has since grown into an international organization. The movement is based on a set of dire warnings, allegedly received by telepathic messages from a remote outpost of human-friendly aliens. These benign aliens took great care to select a "clear channel" here on Earth. Their selection was made in 1992 - Marshall Vian Summers, who received the alien messages and founded a spiritual organization called *The Society for the Greater Community Way of Knowledge*. These channeled warnings are detailed in several manuals, called the *Allies of Humanity Briefings, #1, #2, and #3*. They are available free of charge on the Allies of Humanity website, or in book form from Amazon and other bookstores and outlets. The briefings describe in detail the ongoing human interaction with not-so-benevolent alien traders who are now illegally intervening in human affairs and occasionally invading Earth's airspace with impunity. According to Summers, the alien groups operate in "collectives." These alien collectives have a history of enticing individuals and governments with gifts of advanced technology in exchange for the treasures of Earth, such as certain sought-after minerals, flora and fauna. As it goes, the aliens are also attempting to absorb Earth's inhabitants into their collectives by creating a dependent relationship. Summers provides a message of warning to Earth that humanity should not go that route and strive to remain free as a sovereign planet to avoid unnecessary obligations or entanglements with our extraterrestrial visitors. These trading collectives are supposedly in conflict with our alien friends, the Allies of Humanity, who seek only our spiritual evolution from afar. According to Summers, some of our alien allies have even been chased down and killed by the collectives who view the Allies as an interference to their trading efforts. Marshall Vian Summers comes across as a sincere person, a legitimate contactee, who experienced an actual communication from someone or something, the "Unseen Ones," via direct mental telepathy regarding our imminent merging with the "Greater Community" of alien civilizations at large. Summers is no crackpot. He is a very accomplished writer, and has received *ForeWord Magazine's Spirituality Book of the Year* award for his *Steps to Knowledge; The Book of Inner Knowing*. Summers has also received the *IBPA Benjamin Franklin Silver Medal Award for Spirituality* for his *Wisdom from the Greater Community: Volume II – How to Find Purpose, Meaning, and Direction in an Emerging World*. Summers states that he originally heard a "faint voice in his head," as if the voices were coming from a long distance away. These faint, audible voices urged him, "Please take our message." When Summers finally opened himself up to the messages and began receiving the mental communications, his submission to the transmissions resulted in the messages of warning concerning the current onslaught of alien trading collectives that are detailed in his many books.

If the messages received by Marshall Vian Summers are legitimate, and originate directly from a group of advanced benevolent aliens who are on the run and persecuted or even killed on our behalf by aliens who seek to intervene here on Earth and absorb us like the "Borg" on Star Trek into an enslaved relationship within their "collectives," it is a truly disturbing situation on multiple levels. First of all, the implications are that we humans are not the only beings in the universe that engage in petty, territorial warfare or aggressive, murderous actions with selfish, capitalistic motivations. If war in space exists out there, I find it very disturbing and disappointing that advanced alien spacefaring civilizations have not found a better way to interact with other inhabitants of the universe than by mere trade relationships for material goods and selfish intentions. I suspect the whole idea of capitalistic dominion of the universe is coming from our Overlords to prompt humans to continue emulating this behavior until the goal of the Singularity is achieved. Summer's writings, if they are accurate, are quite depressing. It means that the entire universe, from the microscopic level up, which we already know is based on predation, continues the predation paradigm throughout the evolution of advanced intelligence throughout the universe. One of my hopes is that, at some point in the mental development of a given society, any initial territorial or aggressive tendencies, whether induced by a natural process of evolution or by genetic manipulation, is eventually overcome by higher motivations. I have always hoped that advanced technological civilizations who survive to achieve post-singularity status outgrow this initial aggression and become benign, angelic creatures who only desire what is best for all concerned as they embark out into the universe at large. However, I do realize that this idea may be naïve, remembering the old Hermetic axiom, "As above, so below. As below, so above." It leads to a disturbing question - Is the entire physical universe "Satan's Kingdom," reluctantly borrowing from the biblical metaphor? If so, and this entire physical universe is about selfish aggression and galactic territorial acquisition, and these behaviors and motivations never end, that is truly disappointing. Perhaps before the design and construction of this physical universe, things were quite different. Was there an original etheric realm, possibly prior to the "Big Bang," in which celestial beings existed in a benevolent, peaceful state, a cosmic "Eden" of sorts, devoid of what we call "Evil?" Did something awful then occur as the biblical legends suggest, a rebellion of some sort, something akin to the legends of the "Fall of Man," the result of which was the illusion that we call the physical universe? Was there, in fact, a cosmic war, a "war in heaven" so to speak? What is the origin of "good" and "evil"? Are good and evil simply an artifact, a remnant of primitive humanoids who, despite the evolution of higher brain structures, continue to grapple with the original self-preserving urges of the limbic system left over from the primordial jungle? Or, are good and evil built into the very fabric of the physical universe, a realm in which all organisms large and small compete in a never-ending battle for dominance? If so, is there any way that someone trapped here can completely escape from the "Matrix?" If the Reverend Billy Graham was correct in his book, *Angels: God's Secret Agents*, and at least some of the ufonauts are angels, it may be entirely possible that Marshall Vian Summers has received a communication from our angelic host. If this is actually the case, it is very sad to me that these angelic beings would have to risk their lives to give us warnings of such an evil alien presence in our world at their own peril. Richard Dolan's book, *AD* (After Disclosure) examines the implications of a post-Disclosure world and how the open Disclosure that is certainly coming will change everything from global finances to world religion. Likewise, the *Allies of Humanity Briefings #1, #2, and #3* by Marshall Vian Summers brings at the very least a speculative romp through the territory of a posited alien intervention who do not have our best intentions in mind. These channeled writings, whatever their actual source, be they authentic material from an actual alien race or from the paranoid imagination of Marshall Vian Summers, are very much worth taking the time to read, adding the material to the giant "what if?" or "just in case" file of our brains.

In the case of Marshall Vian Summers and the Allies of Humanity, we are stuck with several possibilities, all of which are disturbing. If he is a huckster (which is doubtful given his sincere interest in human spirituality and extensive literary background), that is pitiful. If, on the other hand, Summers has gone insane, and is receiving schizophrenic messages from another part of his brain, that is fascinating in and of itself, but does not bring us any closer to the truth about extraterrestrials. If Summers has actually received messages from somewhere outside his own mind, we are left with deciding what the real source of the information is. As mentioned, if there is an alien group out there on the run and in trouble from the collectives for interfering with their plans to do business with Earthlings, it is sad that they are at such risk for our sakes. If it is an earthbound communication by a human group using mind-control technology, which is certainly a possibility, one must question what their purposes are. Their purpose, it would seem, matches much of what has been written concerning the secret cabals of the world, i.e., the groups of humans who constitute the earth's secret governments and secret societies. The cabal may benefit from instilling fear into our collective minds against any alien presence, as the aliens might threaten their power. The cabal may wish to squash any interest on our part in interacting with benevolent extraterrestrial civilizations, and benefit from maintaining a fear of extraterrestrials instead. The intent of the cabal might also include programming the masses for accepting the concept of war in space in order to expand their military endeavors into space. It is not outside the realm of possibility that such a cabal would intentionally choose a person of good reputation and literary accomplishment, a person like Marshall Vian Summers, and use an unmarked van full of psychotronic mind-control equipment near the place of his initial transmission to impart the *Allies of Humanity* material into his brain. Such psychotronic equipment does exist and is fully capable of such a deceptive endeavor. The underlying motivation of such a deception by the Cabal is to convince humanity that the aliens are evil and gain public acceptance of a military expansion into outer space. As author Joseph Farrell warns in *Genes, Giants, Monsters, and Men* (pg. 68):

> *That the technologies currently exist to manipulate the mind, the emotions, and to do so at a distance is no longer in doubt. But what most people do not realize is that those technologies have been taken far beyond the inductions of generalized psychological states through direct physiological stimulation of the human brain. Those technologies are now capable of making people think they are seeing specific visions and hearing voices that say specific things. They are powerful technologies that, used with or without conjunction with other technologies, could even lead people to believe that they are receiving special revelations and instructions from God himself.*

Another possibility, the one I feel is most likely when considering all the reports of the contactees during the last century or so, is that Marshall Vian Summers falls into the same category as all the other percipients mentioned in this book. That is, Summers is telling the truth as he knows it, but is unwittingly being manipulated by nonhuman UFO intelligences, possibly indigenous to Earth, possibly advanced alien AI, ancient or otherwise, for an agenda that is far different from that which they represent to us through the contactees. This manipulative agenda correlates with the many speculations presented by such authors as Dr. Jacques Vallee in his *Messengers of Deception*, John Keel in his *Operation Trojan Horse* or *The Eighth Tower*, and many other such excellent works of UFO research within the vast amount of UFO material available for public examination. On the other hand, if Summers is telling the truth, and he is receiving accurate information from aliens, William Bramley was correct in *The Gods of Eden*, that there are two distinctly different extraterrestrial influences. One ET group represents the "custodial race," the "Watchers," who are the cosmic shepherds of humanity who watch and prune us as their own flock and personal property as we create a technological singularity for them. The other, according to Bramley, is the "maverick race" who have our spiritual evolution and benefit at heart. Within this maverick ET race, Yeshua (Jesus) and possibly other avatars have incarnated here to instruct us how to escape this prison planet and enter the eternal kingdom as immortal creatures of light. In other words, maybe the *Allies of Humanity* are real after all, and both ET factions, the custodial and the maverick races, have been represented metaphorically by the world's religions as God and Satan, angels and demons, all along.

UFOs in the Australian Outback

A year or so after the founding of Marshall Vian Summer's *Society for The Greater Community Way of Knowledge,* or *The Society for the New Message from God,* Australian resident, Kelly Cahill, and her husband, were confronted with a spectacular view of a large UFO hovering over a field as they were driving home on August 8, 1993. The details of missing time that occurred during the Cahill's sighting slowly returned piecemeal over time into conscious recall. These returning memories revealed that Kelly and her husband had pulled over to the side of the road that day to get a view of the unearthly object. As they pulled over, they both noticed other cars were also parked off the curb for a view as well. Walking across the road into the field, mesmerized by the sight of the craft, Kelly first encountered a tall, dark being with red eyes, and then many beings floating toward them. This group of dark, floating beings divided as they came toward them. One subgroup attended to Kelly and her husband, and the other subgroup attended to the other people who had also exited their cars to walk across the road toward the craft. As the beings approached, Kelly lost it, screaming out, "They're evil! They are going to kill us!" In response to her outburst, Kelly was immobilized and blinded. During this period of paralysis and blindness, Kelly heard voices in the background. She was left with physical marks on her abdomen where the immobilizer device struck her in the stomach. By the following month, an investigative group, Paranormal Research Australia (PRA) was able to locate the people in another car that Kelly had observed. These other witnesses led the investigation group to the location Kelly described to them. Drawings by other witnesses of the event matched Kelly's verbal description. In the course of the investigation, the second group described another man who was sitting in his car watching the event take place. He was also located, and his description of the craft and beings matched the other two groups. So this is a case involving three different groups of independent witnesses who described the same event with matching features. All three groups experienced missing time, and began to recall some features of the experience in time. The case also produced a variety of physical traces including gynecological issues, body marks, and ankle injuries. Physical traces of the landing area were also discovered, including, oddly, *significantly elevated levels of pyrene and sulfur.*

Sex with Aliens in China

UFO encounter reports that involve sex with aliens are difficult to believe for most people. If reports of aliens having sex with humans were limited to the Antonio Vilas Boas case in 1957, one anomalous case might be safely categorized as some sort of weird alien fantasy or fetish. Unfortunately, UFO cases exist all around the world that involve such breeding episodes, some of which are difficult to wish away. One such case occurred in 1994 as Meng Zhaoguo of China, along with a relative, saw a white shiny object go down in the Red Flag Forest of Heilongjiang. Assuming the object was some sort of balloon, Zhaoguo and his company followed the object into the forest. To their surprise, they found a downed flying saucer with 10-foot-tall six fingered aliens outside the craft who took Zhaoguo onboard and forced him to copulate. As fantastic as it sounds, since Zhaoguo's report is very close in nature to Boas and others regarding arranged sex with selected specimens onboard foreign spacecraft, and since it is unlikely that the cases have even heard of one another, and are separated by decades of time, one is forced by logic to at least consider the possibility that this sort of thing actually happens. Perhaps there is an intergalactic market for, or an alien interest in human babies for purposes of transportation to other worlds. Or, maybe the effort is part of the ongoing hybrid program that abduction researchers like Bud Hopkins, Dr. David Jacobs, and others believe is actually happening here on Earth. Let's hope that we are not just a source of food somewhere in the galaxy. Fortunately, this seems unlikely. At any rate, sexual contact cases such as Boas and Zhaoguo throw a real screw in the mix for any paranormal or psychological theory of UFO/occupant origins, and provide support for Hans Holzer's position in his treatise, *The Ufonauts*, that UFO landing cases that involve physical craft and physical beings are an established fact, whatever we make of these encounters. These cases indicate that there are humanoids on Earth of unknown origin who pilot some of the UFOs who are apparently interested in producing specific genetic combinations of human beings for some reason. These ufonauts operate in clandestine fashion, have been engaging in this activity at least since the 1950s if not before, and are intentionally producing humanoid offspring that are a mix of the human specimen selected during an abduction, and another nonhuman specimen that awaits aboard the craft. It is unknown at this point if the humanoids used for the breeding endeavors onboard flying saucers are willing participants or humanoid breeding stock, i.e., sex slaves of the ufonauts, but it is a certainty that this sort of breeding project is factually going on. Whether these flying crafts and ufonauts are locals from our own solar system somewhere, or flesh and blood cryptoterrestrial populations who are based underground or undersea is anyone's guess. However, whoever they are, they are here, they are real, they are flesh-and-blood biological creatures, and they are actively engaged in producing children with human DNA for some unknown purpose and destination.

More Human Mutilation

1994 produced the Brazilian Guaraparanga Dam human mutilation case. This dam is located in the southern area of Sao Paulo, Brazil. This case of human mutilation was brought to light for the first time in 1998 by researchers Zapata Carcia and Dr Rubens Goes with photographs leaked to them by an insider within the Brazilian police force. This human mutilation case involved identical procedures that were typically conducted on the thousands of cattle mutilation cases in the US beginning in 1960s with the horse named Lady (Snippy). According to the autopsy report and forensic photographs (which can be viewed online), the right and left orbital areas were removed from the victim, and the mouth cavity was emptied, including the pharynx and oropharynx. Puncture marks appeared on the neck, the right and left armpit area, the abdomen, the pelvic cavity, and the right and left groin area. Also from the autopsy report:

> *The axillary regions on both sides showed soft spots where organs had been removed. Incisions were made on the face, internal thorax, abdomen, legs, arms, and chest. Shoulders and arms have perforations of 1 to 1.5 inches in diameter where tissue and muscles were extracted. The edges of the perforations were uniform and so was their size. The chest had shrunk due to the removal of internal organs. Precise "cookie-cutter" holes are discovered in strategical positions throughout the body used for extracting internal organs. This level of precision suggests that the operation was executed with speed, the application of heat or lasers, all occurring as the subject was still alive. You can clearly see the body has been hollowed out of its organs. A cavity in the center of the abdomen reveals an extraction point. INTERNAL EXAMINATION: ...after opening the cranial cavity using Griessinger technique we found: 17) unimpaired skullcap; 18) cerebral edema."*

The presence of cerebral edema without direct traumatic origin is a strong characteristic of an agonizing death. The autopsy conclusion explicitly stated as causa mortis (cause of the death):

> *...acute hemorrhage in multiple traumatisms. There is a component of causa mortis by vagus stimulation [implying cardio-respiratory arrest caused by extreme pain]. The victim shows injuries with vital reaction characteristics, i.e., there is the component of "torture." The suggested modus operandi is: incisions in soft parts and natural orifices using sucking devices.*

In addition to the shocking photographs, the fact that the official autopsy report blatantly states that the victim was subject to incisions and the use of "sucking devices" elevates the case to one of the most painful and tortuous ordeals that could ever happen to a human being. This case is disturbing in so many ways, such as the extraction of body parts with sucking devices, vital reactions and bodily trauma indicating that the victim was alive and fighting during these procedures, and the fact that the beings responsible for the procedures were likely not from this planet. Certainly no human being from this planet could or would conduct such a horrific torture to a fellow human being. That leaves the other option, the most likely one I believe, and that is an alien robotic probe that was simply fulfilling its programing without human emotion. At any rate, whoever or whatever is conducting the animal and human mutilation procedures have been doing so with impunity for a long time now.

Radar Confirmation and Credible Witness Case Attacked

On the night of March 8, 1994, three silent luminous objects of unknown origin mysteriously glided over the southeastern shore of Lake Michigan near Holland, Michigan. These objects had both visual and radar confirmation. Multiple witnesses called local police. One pair of witnesses, Holly and Joey Graves, called 911 and asked if a local policeman could come to confirm the sighting as they watched in amazement for about half an hour. When Sergeant Jeff Velthouse of the Holland Police Department arrived, he also saw the objects and contacted a radar operator in Muskegon, Michigan, Jack Bushong, a meteorologist, who confirmed that there were, in fact, three objects on the radar forming a triangle over Lake Michigan with very solid returns. Bushong watched on his radar as the three objects vanished from one location and reappeared in another. Confirmed radar returns with simultaneous multiple visual witnesses are the holy grail of UFO sightings. Michael Walsh, a reporter for the *Muskegon Chronicle*, conducted his own investigation into the story, prompting UFO researcher Michael Swords, Ph.D. to meet with radar operator Bushong in person. Swords was extremely impressed with Bushong's knowledge of radar equipment and his professional competency level with all manner of radar operations. This case drew the attention of the UFO debunkers who cannot psychologically stand the idea that any legitimate case exists because they and their superior intellect "know" that flying saucers are not real. Therefore, in their minds, there always has to be an alternate explanation. UFO skeptic Robert Sheaffer invoked the old "temperature inversion" explanation, in which warm spring air floats over the cold waters of lake Michigan and creates a "mirror" reflection of a stationary object from the ground some distance away. Philip Klass, the self-appointed guru of UFO debunking at the time, also got into the action, going with the temperature inversion absurdity. Philip Klass accused Bushong of "only" being an intern. Klass stated that since Bushong was using the old-style linear radar instead of the new Doppler radar systems, that Bushong was fooled by a return from a radar that was only designed to pick up weather phenomena and not solid objects. Radar operator Bushong emphatically restated that he had received training on this and certainly knew the difference between temperature inversion returns and other types of objects. Bushong stated that, in his professional opinion, the objects on the returns that night were, in fact, solid, and that Klass and Sheaffer were simply wrong in their skeptical speculations. Both UFO researcher Swords and reporter Walsh verified the witness accounts, and concluded that whatever the objects were, they were definitely not mirage-like temperature inversions. This credible, multiple-witness, radar-confirmed UFO sighting, like so may others, remains in the dustbin of true unknowns, the kind that turns the brains of the skeptics into bubbly mush.

Flying Saucer Lands in Zimbabwe

On September 16, 1994, a UFO landing and live occupant event occurred in Zimbabwe. This case counters the argument that flying saucer sightings are just a Western phenomenon based on popular culture and science fiction. UFO sightings are global and cross-cultural. After two days of multiple credible reports of a strange craft streaking across the skies of southern Africa, 62 school children witnessed a flying saucer hovering low above the ground in their schoolyard in Ruwa, Zimbabwe. Reporter Cynthia Hind responded with an investigation. She separated the children and asked them to draw a picture of the event. Although the level of artistic ability varied, they all drew basically the same thing - a classic flying saucer with domed top and flashing lights. As the children were playing in the schoolyard during their mid-morning break, they saw three silver balls in the sky that vanished with a flash of light and then reappeared at a different location. A saucer-shaped flying craft then appeared and came in low to hover above a section of the grounds that the children were not allowed to enter due to the presence of snakes, spiders, and other potentially harmful creatures. One young male student reported that the craft *followed a line of electrical pylons* before landing. The headmaster of Ariel School, Mr. Colin Mackie, a UFO skeptic, conceded that he believed the children actually saw what they reported. All of the children reported that a small man with a long neck about one meter tall and large bulging eyes wearing a shiny black outfit appeared and stood on top of the craft. The children were diverse ethnically, including Caucasian, Asian, and African. The children had mixed reactions to the creature and his craft. Some were mesmerized by the creature's appearance, and others ran away frightened. The children who were frightened were mostly Africans who feared the creature was there to eat them, based on local legends of "Tokoloshies" who eat children. When the creature became aware of the children observing, he rapidly got back into the craft and vacated the premises. UFO abduction researcher, Dr. John Mack of all people, happened to be in Zimbabwe at the time of the landing encounter. Dr. Mack took the time to pay a visit to the school with a fellow researcher, Dominique Calimanopulos. These two UFO researchers interviewed the children, and provided council to the parents. They advised them not to accuse the children of lying, even if they did not believe their story, as that is counterproductive (UFO AFRINEWS 1994).

This encounter leaves me with questions. Was the landing event staged for the children, or for Dr. John Mack? I find the fact that Dr. John Mack, a UFO and abduction researcher, who just happened to be in the area at the time of a mass UFO sighting rather suspicious that the event was directed at him more so than the children. Due to Dr. Mack's influence on popular belief, and the fact that he would discuss this case with other professionals as well as the public, indicates an intentional effort to continue the process of molding public perception in a way that serves the purposes of the UFO intelligences. These intelligences appear to possess a detailed foreknowledge of how specific events shape the future and are able to manipulate sighting events toward their own ends. The light version of my thinking about this encounter is that the UFO intelligences simply produced an event directed at Dr. Mack, who they knew was in the area and would investigate, possibly their way of confirming the reality of the subject of interest in Dr. Mack's life's work. There appears to be two motivations behind the appearances from the vantage point of the UFO intelligences, and that is 1) a slow, gradual disclosure of their presence on Earth, and 2) a guiding of humanity toward ever-increasing technology, resulting in the actual product they are seeking – a post-singularity Earth.

Channeling Aliens from Zeta Reticuli

Alleged modern contactee Nancy Lieder is the founder and spokesperson for her website, Zetatalk, which began in 1995. She claims to have an implant in her brain that allows telepathic communication with beings from the Zeta Reticuli Star System, the home system of the beings that allegedly abducted Barney and Betty Hill in 1961. Lieder states that the Zeta Reticuli system has several life bearing planets, and that the Zetas are one of about 1000 races that frequent the planet Earth. According to Lieder, the Zetas are aware of coming Earth changes involving, rather than a pole shift, a shift of the Earth's crust that will cause tidal waves, earthquakes, and natural disasters all over the world. Lieder believes that the planet Nibiru is approaching, and that some of the objects photographed near the sun are not alien spacecraft, but are the moons of Nibiru as it travels. The government, according to Lieder, is covering up the existence and approach of Nibiru to avoid global panic. Seed banks and underground facilities are now constructed for the global elite to survive this coming disaster. In accordance with material written by David Wilcock and others of a "New Age" bent, we are here on Earth to learn "service to others" versus "service to self" through multiple lifetimes. Lieder states that all developing populations on any planet have their "good guys" and their "bad guys," i.e., individuals who refuse to grow and mature into service to others. Bad guys from planet Earth are going to be shipped off to a prison planet, while those of us who "make it" will remain here on Earth in future lifetimes to enjoy ascension into the enlightened age to come, similar to Wilcock's "Golden Age" predictions and expectations as outlined in his books, *The Source Field Investigations* and *The Synchronicity Key.* Even though Lieder embraces Zechariah Sitchin's worldview concerning the approach of Nibiru every 3600 years on an elliptical orbit, she rejects much of Sitchin's other conclusions, such as his interpretation of the Sumerian tablets that humanity was genetically engineered by the inhabitants of Nibiru, the Annunaki, as a slave race to assist in their gold mining efforts. Nibiru, according to Lieder's channeled information, was supposed to swoop by and destroy most of the planet in May of 2003 and fulfill the Christian prophecy of Armageddon. Lieder also predicted the war in Iraq would end and troops sent home by 2003 to be safely at home with their families when the destruction of humanity from Nibiru begins. Lieder responded to the uneventful passing of 2003 by saying the prediction was designed to "confuse the elites." As of the time of this writing, Lieder continues to warn us on her website about the approach of Nibiru, but is loathe now to give an actual date. On July 15, 1995, she explained on her website how she was introduced to many different alien lifeforms, including what she calls: *Greek God Man, Horned Toad Man; Broom Stick Man; Little Green Man; Slinky Man; Chicken Man; Tiny Man (one foot tall); Swamp Creature; Octopus Man; Bean Bag Man; Amoeba Man; Vampire Man;*

Dino Man; and Cockroach Man. Nancy Lieder's website, Zetatalk, is one of a plethora of eschatological websites devoted to the ongoing expectation of Earth changes and disasters. Some of these websites are oriented toward religious interpretations of Scripture, in particular the Book of Revelation, and some are alien-oriented, with the aliens overhead monitoring our planet as we head in to the Apocalypse. Some believe the Apocalypse will be an actual war, and others believe will involve all sorts of natural disasters and natural Earth changes. Lieder has accumulated a mountain of literature on the subject of aliens and Earth changes during the last 20 years on her website. Lieder has many devoted followers around the world, along with financial doners and interested parties who avidly follow her channeling of the Zetas.

Alex Collier and the Andromedans

Contactee Alex Collier, originally born Ralph George Amigron, was allegedly contacted by extraterrestrials from the Constellation Andromeda at the age of 8. According to Collier, these contacts continued for several years at this early age and then stopped. After serving in the Army as a helicopter pilot, he was once again contacted by two "Nordic" type humanoid Andromedans, Vissaeus and Morenae, who took him aboard an Andromedan mothership and taught him Andromedan philosophy and their way of life. Collier speaks of our occulted human history as revealed to him by the Andromedans. Collier's revelations have all the usual New Age and ufological elements in them, such as reptilian aliens, the Grays, the planet Nibiru, the lost continents of Lemuria and Atlantis, and a generic 1950s-style alien message of warning mankind against the use of nuclear weapons and admonitions to come together out of chaos into a peaceful society in order to move into the higher celestial dimensions. Alex Collier claims to have been visited by "three well-dressed men" (MIB?) who were a part of a "program" to silence him. According to Collier, Pleaidian ETs, who are also the Nordic "Space Brother-type" extraterrestrial humanoids, have asked for assistance from the Andromedans to ward off a malevolent Confederation of ETs away from Earth and the rest of the galaxy. This Confederation included Reptilians from Alpha Draconis, who, as David Icke believes, have created an invisible system of human slavery on Earth to serve their own needs, the Orion Group, and the Grays from Zeta Reticuli 2. The modern UFO community is divided in their views on Collier, some believing him to be an outright fraud, and others accepting Collier in the mix as a possible authentic contactee. Meanwhile, Collier is having fun making his rounds and giving presentations at UFO conventions and modern Exopolitics forums, bringing the message of the Andromedans to anyone who will listen to him.

Lightning Reveals Flying Saucer

On May 25, 1995, veteran Captain Eugene Tollefson and first officer John J. Waller were cruising at 39,000 feet near Bovina, Texas on American West flight 564 while flying from Tampa, Florida to Las Vegas, Nevada. As their plane encountered an ominous thunderhead, they noticed that the lightning flashes illuminated a large, wingless cigar-shaped unidentifiable craft hovering in the air. The craft was approximately 400 feet in length with odd strobe lights along the side, and was witnessed for approximately 5 minutes before the craft mysteriously disappeared. Although Tollefson and Waller were unable to establish ground radar confirmation of the craft and/or corroboration from any other pilots in the area, the case is considered reliable and was featured on the television show, *Sightings*, in 1995.

UFO Flap in Spain

Beginning on November 28, 1995, another well-documented UFO flap occurred in Northern Spain. Security cameras at the As Gandaras military facility in Galicia captured multiple UFOs on their cameras that sparked grave concerns for the Spanish military. The appearance of the UFOs coincided with serious seismic disturbances during the month of November, about 70 in all, leading some to speculate that the UFOs were the luminous orbs that are produced in certain areas of tectonic stress. However, two months later in January, 1996, Northern Spain was inundated with UFO reports of a different nature than expected if earthquake lights were involved. For example, the citizens of Pedrona witnessed a flyby of a large luminous oval object. The city of Gijon also reported a large UFO with flashing lights that was hovering out over the ocean. In the village of As Pontes, a triangular craft followed by two jet fighters was filmed by Bartalome Vasquez that he described as an "upside down steam iron." Hundreds of witnesses watched for over an hour as a large oval disk hovered in the air at Monforte De Lemos. Television crews caught UFOs on film at the Endessa thermoelectric plant at As Pontes. On February 18, 1996, children playing in the woods witnessed three luminous spheres that they described as "two saucers put together" that merged into a single object before vanishing right before their eyes. Investigators found strange footprints in an area that local witnesses reported seeing a seven-foot-tall creature. On February 26, 1996, motorist Andres Landeira was driving at night toward the city of Lugo when his car was suddenly drawn upward into the air by a mysterious force. Attempting to exit the vehicle in a panic, Landeira found that he and the car were at least 30 feet from the ground. Landeira accepted that he was going to die, and remained crouched in his car. He suddenly felt a jolt and discovered that he and his vehicle were repositioned on the road again a ways away from where he was originally lifted. He was placed back on the road again in a sideways manner, with no real damage to his person or vehicle. The Galacian UFO wave included a wide variety of reports that included classic UFO features, such as ground trace evidence and landings with occupant encounters. On March 7, 1996, a rancher in Ferrerias reported a saucer landing on his property about 100 feet away from him with occupants emerging who were described as looking like monkeys. Trace elements were discovered with footprints similar to those in Entrimo. As the Galacian UFO wave of 1996 unfolded, author Michael Craft explored the role of UFOs and human consciousness in his book, *Alien Impact*. Craft mirrored the work of Keel by proposing that flying saucer landing/occupant encounters represent a deliberately deceptive phenomenon staged by an unknown population of cosmic tricksters who are manipulating humankind in mysterious ways for a "hidden agenda." Like so many other authors who conducted research into the UFO mystery, they concluded that there is a long range agenda, but fell short in understanding what that agenda actually is. Although I certainly do not have all the details or complete information concerning the actual alien agenda, or differing agendas of various ET groups, I do feel strongly that it has a lot to do with the approaching Singularity. It is my speculation that several populations of ETs are interested in humanity achieving this goal, some for their own purposes, and others simply because our augmented consciousness and intelligence will finally allow us to perceive an open contact situation, as our current instrumentation and mental faculties are simply insufficient to perceive them as they really are. However, there is no doubt that, at some point, with sufficient technology, we shall finally meet the elusive Etherians.

Extraterrestrials in Brazil

In the wee hours of the morning on January 20, 1996, a farmer on the outskirts of Varginha, Brazil, was shocked as he witnessed a small, dark, flying vehicle about the size of a school bus hovering about 16 feet above the ground. The slow, silently-gliding craft appeared to have sustained some sort of damage, as it had smoke pouring out one side of the fuselage as it crippled along through the air. A few hours later at 8:30 a.m. local time, the Varginha Fire Department received a call concerning an unusual creature that was cornered in a gully within a wooded area of the Jardim Andere neighborhood. The firemen responded to the call, fully expecting either a prank or something else of a mundane nature. Little did they know they were about to encounter an actual being from another world. When they arrived to the location of the call, they found that a group of adults and children had the mysterious creature cornered. Unknown to the firemen, the Brazilian Army had also been running around all night chasing similar creatures, and were also there at this location. The firemen did manage to capture the creature in a net with little to no resistance. Members of the Brazilian Army then stepped in and placed the creature in a wooden box and vacated the area with it. Later that same day, two teenage sisters, Valquiria and Liliana da Silva, and an older friend, Katia Xavier, 22, were walking home from work and decided to take a short cut across a field, which just so happened to be in the same area of the capture a few hours earlier by the firemen and the Brazilian Army. On their way through the field, they ran into a bald man that they described as having bulging, blood-red eyes, greasy brown skin, strange visible bony protuberances under his skin, and large prominent veins. The man was huddled next to a brick wall with his hands between his legs. The man's strange appearance caused a flash of fear in the girls, and they ran away as fast as they could for home. Within 24 hours of the farmer's sighting of the crippled craft, the Brazilian Army had captured 3 extraterrestrials and taken them to the Humanitas Hospital. UFO researchers who later looked into this case determined that at least one of the creatures died at the hospital.

The next day, two days from the original craft sighting, on January 22, 1996, the alien bodies were transferred to the University of Campinas, where a military presence had gathered, as well as several pathologists interested in exploring the creature's biology. The Brazilian military attempted to keep the case under wraps from the general public, but when one of the attending soldiers was interviewed on Brazilian TV, she inadvertently spilled the beans that these were, in fact, otherworldly creatures. Otherwise, nothing other than a local legend would have ever come from the capture efforts. Today no one knows the whereabouts of the creatures, but the story has made its way into UFO lore as a case of extraterrestrial contact, shaping the world-views of those who accept the account as legitimate. From all the descriptions, it appears that a physical craft carrying nonhuman creatures was damaged somehow, allowing the creatures (alien pets?) to escape. The odd-looking man that the three girls ran into in the field was probably an extraterrestrial humanoid who had exited his craft and was looking for his beloved companions. Nothing from the account indicates that the creatures were harmful in any way, and these EBEs did not appear to be very intelligent. The moral of this story: Be careful visiting Earth, because if your ship runs into trouble and your pets escape, they will be captured, studied by medical professionals, likely euthanized and pickled in secret labs. We will never know who the strange man was that the girls ran into, who was looking for his escaped creatures. Where they were from and whether the man made it safely back to his place of origin will likely remain unknown to the public, but this case remains one of the many documented accounts that really happened in physical reality. Although some UFOs may be psychically generated, with or without the assistance of buoyant plasmas, it appears that at least some accounts are nuts-and-bolts craft with flesh-and-blood creatures inside. This one, admittedly, is difficult to believe, but it is well-documented, and it really happened.

[On January 27, 1996 France detonated their last nuclear bomb, "Operation Xouthos," for a total of 210 detonations of nuclear bombs between Feb 13, 1960 and January 27, 1996]

[In 1996, China conducted their last nuclear test, detonated underground, for a total of 45 nuclear tests.]

Mass Sighting in Canada

On December 11, 1996, two cousins were headed north in their separate vehicles on the Klondike Highway in the Yukon Territory of Canada. The Klondike Highway runs parallel to a body of water known as Fox Lake. As the men were driving about a quarter mile from one another, they suddenly saw a large UFO above the lake, a sight that shocked them enough to immediately stop their cars at the side of the road. One of the men got out of his vehicle to get a better look. The UFO glided toward him until it was directly over his head as his cousin watched from his vehicle. They were both stunned as the craft glided over his head and out of sight over a hill in the distance. At this time two other witnesses were approaching the southern tip of Fox Lake and also observed the craft. As they passed the cousins at the side of the road looking skyward, this second pair of witnesses stopped their car and got out to talk to them. After the four witnesses discussed the UFO together, the second set of witnesses got back in their vehicle and drove about 20 miles north of this location and stopped at the Braeburn Lodge. The owner of the lodge, Steve Watson, immediately told the cousins of another witness who had been driving along Fox Lake and witnessed the same UFO. Then two more witnesses surfaced who were traveling just south of Pelly Crossing. These two reported seeing a large, slow-moving row of lights. They had pulled into a gravel pit to get a better look. Another four women saw the UFO as they were taking a break outside the local community college they were attending. These four women saw the craft silently glide behind a hill, corroborating the report of the other witnesses. Also, just south of the village of Carmacks, four men reported seeing the same UFO from their pickup truck as they were driving. They pulled the truck into a landfill and watched as the UFO drew near to a microwave tower and disappeared. Another four witnesses, a husband and wife, along with their two children, also saw the same UFO through their windows at home as they were watching television. The craft was gliding just above the tree line. The family observed the craft's row of lights disappear, one light at a time, as if the craft was a ghost gliding through a solid wall. All in all, nearly 20 credible witnesses reported this sighting. The "Pelly Crossing UFO Incident" is a well-documented and well-corroborated unexplained UFO event. There is no doubt that they all saw a large, silent, slow-moving craft of some sort with a row of lights. Unfortunately, no photographs were taken. One can only speculate about why the craft appeared to humans in the visible portion of the electromagnetic spectrum, or what the mission of the craft and any occupants inside, biological, robotic, or otherwise was, or why the craft came so close to the microwave tower before vanishing into thin air. Was it an emergency energy refueling? Where they in trouble? Does this type of craft routinely take advantage of the situation wherever it comes near to a source of energy? Was this large UFO one of the mysterious energyzoa creatures that Trevor James Constable captured on film in infrared, an *Atmospheric Beast*, a plasma-like living creature who can shapeshift in appearance to look like a mechanical craft when they are actually an exotic living being, an extremophile, living plasma, in need of an electrical energy source for feeding purposes? We will never know. However, this amazing mass-witness encounter at Pelly Crossing in Canada remains a very credible and mysterious UFO sighting report, ascertaining once again that there are mysteries in our skies that are likely nonhuman and of unknown origin or purpose. This is a reality that is life-changing for people who either encounter such a phenomenon firsthand, or realize at some point from examining the vast amount of documentation that exists concerning eyewitness reports of UFOs that we are dealing with a profound cryptoreality that factually exists in a world that is normally invisible to us.

The Heaven's Gate Cybercult

On March 26, 1997, a UFO cult that was originally called *The Human Individual Metamorphosis* (HIM) group, later known as *Heaven's Gate,* came to a tragic end as police discovered the partially-decomposed bodies of 39 cult members who had committed mass suicide in an effort to catch a ride aboard a flying saucer that was thought to trail the Halle-Bopp Comet. The cult had existed in various forms since 1972 when it was founded by Marshall Applewhite and a nurse, Bonnie Nettles, both of whom believed that they had met in a past life. Nettles convinced Applewhite that he had a divine mission on Earth, a mission that had been foretold to her by extraterrestrials. Applewhite was a science fiction fan, influenced by sci-fi greats like Robert Heinlein and Arthur C. Clarke. Nettles had a long-term interest in theosophist and New Age figures such as Helena Blavatski, R.D. Laing, and Richard Bach. She also studied the Book of Revelation and Christian eschatology. Applewhite and Nettles referred to themselves as "The UFO Two," and thought of themselves as the "two witnesses" mentioned in the Book of Revelation. They were also known at times as "Bo and Peep" or "Do and Ti." The two penned a religious pamphlet, hinting that Applewhite was the reincarnation of Jesus, and that both of them had been endowed with a "higher mind" than the population at large. They began having meetings in which they presented themselves as higher beings from another realm to their new recruits, who they called their "crew." As higher beings, or "walk-ins" (beings who are currently incarnated on Earth by choice but are from another planet), they operated on the next level of consciousness beyond human. Nettles and Applewhite offered their human crew an opportunity to join them in an experiment that would result in their transformation to the next plane of existence, the next step in evolution for humankind.

Through the teachings of Applewhite and Nettles, The Heaven's Gate cult members came to believe that the earth was about to undergo a cleansing of those who were not going to make it to the next evolutionary level. They referred to their physical bodies as "vehicles," whose only function was to support their consciousness as they achieved the next level up from human. Suicide was redefined from killing oneself to accepting the opportunity to evolve to the next level. Demonstrating classic characteristics of a cult, members were admonished to shun all outside friends, relatives, abstain from sex, and overcome all earthly attachments to prepare for the "final exit" to the next level. Adopting elements of modern Ancient Astronaut Theory, Applewhite and Nettles taught that humans were planted on Earth millions of years ago. The original ET "farmers" were now returning to Earth to reap their harvest of souls, taking the souls with them in a sort of "Alien Rapture" to the next level as an accepted member of a flying saucer crew. Living an ascetic, communal life, eight of the male members, including Applewhite, underwent castration in Mexico to show dedication to abandoning all earthly distractions, one of those distractions being sex, in preparation for the transformation to the next level. The communal group earned a livelihood with their company, *Higher Source.* The company built websites for professionals, prompting cultural theorists to label the Heaven's Gate group as a "cybercult." In October, 1996, a few months prior to the mass suicide by phenobarbital mixed with applesauce and vodka, the group oddly purchased alien abduction insurance that covered up to 50 cult members for $10,000.00. The group then rented a $7000.00/month mansion in an upscale area of San Diego, Califormia. There police eventually found the 39 members who "vacated their vehicles" to catch a ride on a flying saucer and become members of the crew. One of the members who vacated the Earth plane was Applewhite himself. Applewhite, as leader of the cult, had already demonstrated the sincerity of his own beliefs by voluntary castration. He then showed ultimate faith by taking his own life with the other members to achieve the next level of existence beyond human and join the ranks of the cosmic ufonauts. All of the cult members who vacated their vehicles had a five dollar bill and three quarters in their pockets for an "interplanetary toll." Among the dead was Thomas Nichols, brother to actress Nichelle Nichols, who was famous for her role as Uhura in the original *Star Trek* TV series. Scientist and UFO researcher Dr. Jacques Vallee gave attention to the Heaven's Gate cult in his book, *Messengers of Deception*. Personally, I believe their dedication in abandoning the physical plane for the next level should count for something. I sincerely hope that Applewhite and his followers are now happily traveling the cosmos with the crew of a flying saucer, and have fulfilled their vision that they so desperately wanted to become a part of.

Earth as a Cargo Cult

There is no doubt whatsoever that the inhabitants of Earth are a classic cargo cult. So much of human culture since 1947 has developed as a coping mechanism born of trauma from the appearance of the flying saucers. Imagine a primitive aboriginal tribe in a remote, unexplored region of the planet. A few of the tribe members, while hunting for food, witness a modern airplane flying by with no understanding of what they were looking at. It is easy to see how an entire mythos could evolve within the tribe. Eyewitnesses of the airplane might be considered crazy by the tribe members who could not conceive of such a flying object. Shamans of the tribe might claim to have established mental contact with the airplane pilots, or even proclaim visions and prophecy about the return of the airplane at some time in the future. Religions might develop based on the perceived will of the airplane occupants, who are surely gods. Skeptics in the tribe would scoff at the idea that such mechanical birds exist in reality, and accuse those who see them as delusional. In the minds of the tribal skeptics, it is an impossible tale according to the current understanding of Nature. The witnesses must have been hallucinating, or have personalities that are prone to telling tall tales for the attention they bring. This scenario has actually happened to the inhabitants of Earth in response to the appearance of the flying saucers. Some of us have actually seen them. Some of us have had brief encounters with flying saucer occupants. The saucers demonstrate great power and flight capability beyond that which we are capable, and exhibit characteristics beyond our comprehension. Our imaginations are stimulated. The smartest among us, such as Nikola Tesla and T. Townsend Brown have sought to discover the secrets of their flight, and emulate them with their own inventions. Whether one accepts the reality of flying saucers or not, the perceived antigravitic capabilities of such flying saucers has been the Holy Grail of aviation since the 1930s. Some say we have already achieved such antigravity technology. Others remain skeptical that we now have, or will ever have, the mastery of space and time that is required to travel the vast distances of outer space to other worlds. The Heaven's Gate cult is but a microcosm of the desperation that exists within the human psyche to go beyond the veil and join those who have an understanding of the underlying reality and deep machinations of the physical universe. We all perceive that there is Mind at Large, a universal Source Field. We seek to connect with it, and wish to gain a deeper understanding of our place within Eternisphere. However, if it is true as I suspect that the physical universe is a complex, intentionally-designed computational mechanism, and that every lifeform in the universe, including humans, are but bits of computational data whose function it is to solve an alien problem, it remains to be seen if there is a grand fate for us beyond the life that we presently know, or if, like electricity in the wall, we simply return to source when the computer has solved the problem or finally shuts down. The best that humans can hope for is that our consciousness and our desires to remain alive after physical death are taken into consideration by the designers. We hope that it is true that matter and energy cannot be created or destroyed, that we are somehow retained or recycled, and that a brighter cosmic fate awaits us than eternal unconsciousness. However, the failure of prophecies made by UFO cultists, the physical damage that people have sustained by contact with flying saucers, the deterioration of personality that has sometimes resulted from encounters with the cosmic light, and the suicides of such dedicated believers as the Heaven's Gate cult members, reminds us that the information coming to some of us is deceptive in nature. This Mind at Large that we perceive appears to have its own purposes. It is not kind enough, for lack of a better way of putting it, to put a stop to our self-destruction, or worse, may gain in some way by our internal and external conflicts. While it is true that there are cases in which UFOs appear at nuclear facilities to demonstrate their power by shutting down the launching capabilities of the facility, the shutdowns may not have occurred for our benefit after all. These shutdowns may occur as a general chastisement to remind us that there is someone else out there of a higher order of intelligence that has superior power over humanity, and to keep us on track for the goal at hand. After all, if we all destroy ourselves in a nuclear holocaust, the technological singularity will not be accomplished. Interested parties have been too patient and have worked too hard for our technological development for humans to screw up their efforts at this point.

The "True Way" and Their False Prophet

Five months after the members of the Heaven's Gate cult were found dead by mass suicide, a Taiwanese UFO cult, formerly known as Chen Tao ("True Way") made its way to the United

States. The cult was registered in Garland, Texas as *God's Salvation Church* after relocating from San Dimas, California in August, 1997. Known in the US as a New Age church, Chen Tao was an amalgamation of Buddhism, Taoism, and modern Ufology. The cult was focused on spiritual energies and the transmigration of souls. Earth souls faced negative influences by "outside souls" who perpetrated a negative and corrupting influence on humans who follow the spiritual path of light. These negative entities represented what the Christian religion would call "demons," much akin to Richard Kieninger's black mentalists on the lower astral plane, or the Islamic Djinn. Yu-Hsia Chen, the cult's leader and a former college professor, taught that Earth and its human inhabitants had survived 5 major disasters going back to the age of the dinosaurs. In each of these cataclysms, a remnant of human beings were saved by God in a flying saucer. The latest human remnants were saved by God and relocated to North America. Chen taught that our solar system was created by a nuclear war and is 4.5 trillion years old. Chen's followers were mainly wealthy, white collar professionals who were attracted to New Age religion. They dressed in white, wore cowboy hats, and drove expensive cars. Most of these cult leaders make a fatal mistake at some point in their careers. That is, after a series of small successes in predicting the future, they will often come forth with a major prophecy that fails. Chen's big whopper was his prediction that on March 31, 1998, God would return to Earth in human form at his home in Garland, Texas, and would be seen around the world on television. The Garland Police Department, along with many citizens of Garland, were very wary of the cult due to their odd appearance and behavior. Some local officials feared that the cult would come to a bad end and adversely affect the Garland community. The whole community at large was on high alert when Chen made his odd prediction about God's return to Earth at his home. March 31, 1998 finally arrived, and anticipation was high. Of course, nothing at all out of the ordinary happened that day, and it was a complete fizzle. The members of the cult simply went home. As a testament to his sincerity, Chen apologized to the members of the group. Chen was willing for the members of his cult to stone him to death, but no one was interested in carrying that out. Once before, Chen had predicted that a "Jesus of the West" would be found who looked like Abraham Lincoln. That also never happened. When it finally became clear that Chen was a false prophet, the True Way fell into the dustpan of millennial cults. The take-home lesson from this cult is that if you are the leader of a religious cult, and you are successful in making a living from it, consider yourself lucky. Don't screw it up. Avoid the temptation to make huge predictions such that, if it fails, your cult will abandon you. If you do not heed this warning, and you make a large prediction that fails, the gravy train is over.

The Phoenix Lights

A mass UFO sighting event involving thousands of individuals occurred on Thursday, March 13, 1997 in the western United States. At approximately 6:55 p.m., a report came in from Henderson, Nevada of a V-shaped flying craft the size of a Boeing 747. The craft had six large lights on its leading edge, and made the sound of a rushing wind. It was reported to have flown overhead and disappeared into the horizon. From this initial report, over the next several hours, UFO reports came in by the hundreds over Nevada, New Mexico, and Arizona. This series of UFO reports are collectively known as the "Phoenix Lights." At 8:15 p.m., another sighting was reported by a police officer in Paulden, Arizona. This officer saw a cluster of five orange lights in the sky, four lights were flying together, and a fifth light trailed the other four. Upon inspection with binoculars, the officer described the detail that each of the four lights were actually two distinct points of light that appeared as one to the naked eye. The officer watched as the lights flew silently to the south for about two minutes. The object also vanished over the horizon. Only minutes later, a multitude of reports began pouring in from Chino Valley, Prescott, Prescott Valley, Dewey, Cordes Junction, Cavecreek, Wickenburg, and other communities northwest of Phoenix, Arizona. Most of the reports involved lights of various colors, some moving very rapidly, others moving slowly, and still other lights hovering motionless in the sky. Just north of Phoenix, three witnesses reported a giant triangular flying object with lights on its leading edge that glided slowly across the sky, blocking the stars. A mother and her four daughters reported a giant, wedge-shaped flying object that remained motionless over their heads. After about five minutes, the giant craft slowly began to glide to the south toward Sky Harbor International Airport, firing a white beam of light to the ground as it went. The same object was then witnessed and reported by two air traffic controllers and several pilots. A giant black triangular craft was also reported by multiple residents of Glendale, Gilbert, and Scottsdale, including a former airline pilot who watched as the craft glided toward the mountains south of Phoenix. Controversy and obfuscation was added to this night of incredible sightings when, at approximately 10:00 p.m., flares from an A-10 "Warthog" aircraft were dropped over the Gila Bend "Barry M. Goldwater" firing range. This dropping of flares was admitted two months after the sightings by the Public Affairs Office at Luke Air Force Base in May, 1997. These flares were dropped and slowly fell over the mountains. These are the objects that appear in many online videos posted to provide a plausible explanation and/or debunking of the Phoenix Lights sightings. However, only those who believe such mundane explanations for UFOs with no critical thinking whatsoever accept these videos as "proof" that the Phoenix Lights event was just a flare drop, due to the large number of credible, detailed UFO reports that were documented several hours before these flares were actually dropped. This demonstrates the desperation on the part of those who simply cannot accept the reality of non-terrestrial incursions. Many UFO skeptics have a strong psychological need to believe that nothing unusual is happening. Admissions to the reality of an actual ET event would risk their carefully-constructed worldview (I know, I was once one of them). It also demonstrates the intentional deception that often takes place on the part of the government and military to keep such knowledge away from the public, or at least provide plausible deniability to actual ET craft sighting cases to put a lid on things. Former Arizona governor, Fife Symington, an aircraft pilot himself, was among the witnesses of the mysterious black triangle craft that appeared over Phoenix, Arizona that evening. Symington only admitted that he did, in fact, witness the craft after his governorship was over for obvious reasons. He now states that the event is one he will never forget. Symington is at a loss for words to describe how witnessing such a large silent triangular flying machine made him feel about our actual place in the vast universe. Former governor Fife Symington, like so many other government officials, know for a fact that we are not alone, and this knowledge changes a person's view of reality forever.

Are UFOs of Terrestrial Origin?

Over the years, many authors have attempted to place a terrestrial origin on all structured craft, triangular, disk-shaped, or whatever, that have been seen in Earth's skies since around the mid 1930s when Nazi Germany began experimenting with exotic craft and propulsion systems. Often these terrestrial craft are placed into the category of "black projects." When Donald Rumsfeld announced in 2001 just prior to the attack on the World Trade Center that 2.3 trillion dollars was missing from the Pentagon, ufologists were buzzing with the possibility that this was proof of black budget operations and clandestine spacecraft of various capabilities. One such researcher into black projects is Tim Matthews, author of *UFO Revelation: The Secret Technology Exposed?*. In this book, Matthews makes the case that the many structured craft that have been reported since the 1930s, in particular from the Kenneth Arnold sighting in 1947 forward, were terrestrial in origin. Matthews reveals many aircraft of human construction that were classified for up to a decade before the public knew about them which could have caused the UFO reports. These craft include the aforementioned Horton 229, which Matthews believes is the most likely aircraft that was seen by pilot Kenneth Arnold. The Horton Brothers "Parabola" is another interesting find to look at. Researcher Nick Redfern also speculates that a similar craft, originally designed by Walter and Reimer Horton, might have been the actual object that crashed at Roswell during a secret experimental flight of questionable ethics involving exposure to an atomic pile using human guinea pigs. Other than the exotic flying wings designed by the Horton Brothers or Alexander Lippisch, Matthews discusses other aircraft that have surely created numerous UFO reports over the decades that were human in construction. These aircraft include: the Airup tailless monoplane; the Delta 1; the ME163A; ME163B; and ME262; the P.11 or the Delta 6; the DM-1; The Lippisch supersonic flying wing; the HO229; the HOIX; the Nazi Feuerball; the GO-229; the Messerschmidt Me163; the Zimmerman V-173 "Flying Flapjack"; the XF 5U1; the C-54 Constellation, the American B-35 and the Northrop YB-49 flying wing aircraft; the N-1M and N-9M; the XB-79; the joint US-Canadian-British flying saucer called Project Silver Bug (including Project Y and Project Y2); the DS2, the TSR2; Dr. Miethe's Heinkel/BMW flying disk; the SR-71 Blackbird; the U-2 spyplane (the first of which arrived at Groom Lake on July 23, 1955, as opposed to flying saucers and flying triangles, which arrived 1959-1960 according to Matthews); the Gotha Go-229 flying wing; the

Northrop B-2 Spirit bomber, the B-2 stealth bomber; the Aereon lighter-than-air triangular craft (Aereon 3); the Lockheed-Martin Tier 3 minus Darkstar UAV; the X-24B; the TR-3 Black Manta; the AVRO Vulcan; the F-117 Nighthawk; the Armstrong Whitworth 'bat' (AIR-100-203-79, Aereon 3, Aereon 26, and Aereon 340); the XEM 1/2/3/4; the Mexican saucer-shaped MLA-32B; the Silent Vulcan; the HDH-10 Enmoth from Australia; the NASA Hyper-3; South Africa's Kentron Lark; British Aerospace's HALO; the FDL-5; the X24B, the X24C; the Dyna-Soar hypersonic glide vehicle (HGV); the Omega (Flying Artichoke), the Firefly (Lampyridae); the Damler-Benz AT-2000; the Tornado Gr MK4; the A-12 'Oxcart'; the D-21 drone; the A-12 spyplane; the Teledyne-Ryan 262; General Atomic's Gnat 750; the Tier 2, the Tier 3; and the legendary Aurora craft; to name but a few. Taking the time to google pictures of each and every one of these exotic aircraft is worth the time. When I did so, I experienced a gradual, eerie re-alization that, even if we have been visited by extraterrestrial spacecraft that have been reported by human witnesses (and I do believe we have), a good chunk of modern UFO reports since 1947 have been generated by our own exotic aircraft. There is no doubt that some of the UFOs people have witnessed are, in fact, connected to classified aircraft of terrestrial manufacture. This further obfuscates the entire UFO phenomenon, and has led UFO theorists to formulate what is commonly known as the *Federal Hypothesis*, which Matthews explains in *UFO Revelation* (page 135):

> *UFOs are controlled by a loose underground network of intelligence personnel and figures fom the military/industrial complex.*

Matthews also suggests (page 159):

> *All triangular or circular-planform aircraft are of terrestrial origin. They are secret military aircraft perhaps based upon unconventional or 'leading edge' technologies.*

Matthews concluded, for the most part, that the so-called Federal Hypothesis is true. This hypothesis postulates that intelligence agencies such as the CIA and NSA have used the public belief in extraterrestrial spacecraft to hide certain black projects all these years. At the time of this writing, the CIA has even admitted that some of the UFOs people were reporting through-out the past several decades were actually U-2 spyplanes. However, the U-2 spyplane usually flies around 30,000 feet, and is rather obscure to view. This admission on the part of the CIA is only the tip of the iceberg concerning the scope of various secret aircraft that the public was completely unaware of. These secret government projects surely lend to a terrestrial origin for many UFO reports throughout the years. So is this all there is to the UFO phenomenon? Not by a long shot. Despite the fact that intelligence agencies have exploited public belief in extraterrestrial spacecraft to hide the construction and test flights of secret, classified aircraft, this is an entirely different phenomenon than the flying ships, flying shields, and flying saucers that have been with humankind for thousands of years, possibly since the beginning of life on Earth. Even prior to the advent of aircraft in the modern age, we were still haunted by the shapeshifting self-luminous orbs that have been reported for aeons, along with exotic close encounters with otherworldly beings. Even Matthews admitted (*UFO Revelation*, pg. 240):

It seems to me that reports of close encounters might relate to some sort of natural intelligence that exists on the fringes of scientific understanding or which can only be researched unscientifically (because it is not reproducible) within the paranormal field of study.

So the layers of the onion recede. It is difficult to tell who is manipulating who. The global intelligences of the world may, in fact, have come upon certain celestial gifts that were staged by the Overlords to look like crashed alien spacecraft. Secret intelligence groups may have incorporated these technologies into their clandestine black projects, away from public view. While they were building and testing these crafts, they continued to encourage the public belief in extraterrestrial spacecraft, as various social experiments indicated that the concept of alien visitation would be rejected and ridiculed for the most part. Agents of secret government groups have actually infiltrated various UFO groups and created fantastic hoaxes to provide a distraction that has served as camouflage for their underground activities. Intentional efforts have been made to make the UFO believers and cultists look as whacky as possible, creating yet another layer of cover, as much of the public has written off the entire subject of UFOs as fantasy. The rejection, ridicule, and tomfoolery that has been successfully perpetrated became anathema to scientists, who continue to reject the more fantastic elements of the UFO phenomenon out of hand as they work toward the Singularity unaware. Meanwhile, the Overlords of the Singularity, the real intelligences behind the UFOs that are so unapproachable and non-identifiable, continue to guide humanity by their connection into the human unconscious toward the coming technological singularity for purposes of overt contact with humanity, permanent physical materialization into three-dimensional reality from the electromagnetic Superspectrum, self-replication into the latest generation of conscious artificial superintelligence, or all of the above. Now that we have taken a moment to ground ourselves in the reality of terrestrial projects that have surely been misidentified as extraterrestrial spacecraft over the years, and we have accepted this less-than-exciting explanation as part of the overall UFO phenomenon, we may now return to the Twilight Zone with renewed vigor.

A Russian Official meets the Space Brothers

The perception of many people concerning reports of humanoid "Space Brothers" or "Nordic" ETs of the 1950s is that, if they were real at all, they came to Earth in response to our nuclear experimentation out of concern for our civilization and our planet, to warn humanity of the dangers of nuclear weaponry. However, alleged encounters with humanoid visitors, assumed to originate from outer space somewhere, have continued throughout the decades from the 1950s to the present day. Once such visitation with human extraterrestrials occurred in Russia on September 18, 1997. On this day, the president of the southern Russia state of Kalmykia, Kirsan Ilyumzhinov, a man who was also the head of the World Chess Federation, reported on Russia's main Channel One that he had met with human extraterrestrials and spent time aboard their spaceship. His personal driver and assistant had discovered him missing at his apartment that morning and was about to launch a full scale search just before he returned from his visitation. Ilyumzhinov went on British TV and stated that he communicated telepathically with his extraterrestrial visitors and reported (Aartsen, 2011, pages 39-41):

> *They are people like us. They have the same mind, the same vision. I talked with them, I understand that we are not alone in the world [universe]. We are not unique.*

The Universe People

One month after Ilyumzhinov's report of contact with humanoid extraterrestrials, and just after the mass suicide of members within the Heaven's Gate cybercult, a Czech and Slovic UFO religion emerged in October, 1997 that attracted attention and created a concern that another UFO-related mass suicide might occur. This cult was the *Universe People* or *Cosmic People of the Light Powers* founded by Ivo A. Benda. The cult centered on communications between Ivo and extraterrestrials, communications that are captured in his book, *Interviews with Instructions from My Friends From the Universe*. Benda's cosmic teachings centered at first about a coming global catastrophe, a common theme in UFO cults. Benda's followers would be evacuated from Earth and spared the tragedy. Benda's original teachings later evolved into a focus on Earth's defense from attacks by negative extraterrestrials called the *Saurians*, or *Lizard Men*. A decade after the The Universe People emerged on the scene, in 2007, they sent instructions on how to prevent attacks from the evil Saurians to the Ministry of Defense in Slovakia. Reminiscent of George Van Tassel's teachings in the 1950s, the Universe People believe that spaceships operated by the Ashtar Galactic Command continually orbit the earth. The Nordic humanoid occupants of the flying saucers piloted by the Ashtar Galactic Command assist good people here on Earth, and are prepared to evacuate select individuals to another dimension when the global catastrophes occur. Influences that assisted in fabricating Ivo Benda's worldview are sources such as Giorgio Dibitono's *Angels in Starships*, George Adamski's *Inside the Spaceships*, Barbara Marciniak's *Bringers of the Dawn*, and the massive amount of channeled material written by the Swiss contactee Billy Meier. The Universe People seek to eliminate money from society and distrust the media, which they believe are tools of mass mind manipulation. At the time of this writing, the Universe People have a colorful website at universe-people.com that explains the group's philosophy, accepts donations (of course), and posts information on the Ashtar Galactic Command and their mission here on Earth.

The Planetary Activation Society

As the Universe People emerged with their cosmic messages from the Ashtar Galactic Command in Czechoslovakia, another UFO-oriented group appeared in the US in 1997 called the *Planetary Activation Society*. This UFO cult was founded by Sheldan Nidle, who claimed, as did Guglielmo Marconi; Nikola Tesla; Uri Geller; Ted Owens; and so many others, that he was in telepathic communication with extraterrestrials. Many who believe that they are in communication with extraterrestrial entities appear to receive prophetic information about minor events that actually come true in order to sucker them in and build their confidence. It appears that this is the actual modus operandi of at least some of the etheric entities, and why they are often called "cosmic tricksters." This, Keel states, is an intentional deception by the entities of the Superspectrum, whose actual intent is to make a fool out of the person announcing the big prediction. These huge public prophecy failures serve the purpose of marginalizing the subject of UFOs and further obfuscating the existence of the Superspectrum entities while they continue to do whatever it is they are actually doing incognito. Just such a letdown occurred for Sheldan Nidle, the head guru of the Planetary Activation Society. Nidle grew confident over time that his received information was reliable and true. After confirmation occurred with several small prophecies, which built Nidle's confidence, eventually the big whopper was delivered. Nidle boldly predicted that 16 million spaceships would arrive to Earth accompanied by a multitude of angels from the "photon belt" on December 17, 1996. When this date came and went without incident, Nidle circumvented repercussions from members by explaining that the extraterrestrials had converted humans into holographic projections in order to give us a second chance. This huge failed prediction earned Sheldan Nidle the infamous "Pigasus Award" (originally called the "Uri Award" after psychic Uri Geller's alleged paranormal spoon-bending skills) for the year 1996. The Pigasus award was presented each year by noted paranormal skeptic James Randi, who was known for giving the award to the psychic fraud of his choice each year on April Fool's Day. It is, of course, possible that Sheldan Nidle was an intentional fraud. However, since the typical behavior of the entities within the Superspectrum is to confirm their existence to a human through small telepathic predictions that do come true only to throw them under the bus in the end with a huge prediction that they go public with and fail, it does not follow that Sheldan Nidle was necessarily a fraud. Perhaps he did, in fact, receive mental communications from the hidden UFO intelligences who are at the helm. These intelligences may have used Nidle like they have used so many other prophets and seers to further their actual goals. Sometimes it does appear that these intelligences enjoy what we call "fun and games" in the process of manipulating us. Do the entities receive enjoyment from our bewilderment and suffering? One has to wonder.

[*On May 11, 1998, India unleashed "Operation Shakti," an underground implosion of 3 uranium and 2 plutonium devices. Two days later India conducted its last nuclear test, detonating two nuclear devices simultaneously. This last test involved a 3-stage thermonuclear device, for a total of 6 nuclear tests between 1974 and 1998. On May 28, 1998, Pakistan conducted an underground nuclear test called the "Chagai 1." "Chagai 2", an underground imploded plutonium device, marked the last of Pakistan's nuclear testing.*]

Levitating Elk

On Thursday, February 25, 1999, three forestry personnel working west of Mount St. Helens in Washington State sighted a heel-shaped object floating silently along the tree line that was apparently under intelligent control. The three workers watched in awe for approximately 10 minutes as the craft floated near a herd of elk. The elk appeared unaware of the approaching object until it drew very close them, at which time the herd bolted. One lone elk strayed from the pack, and the shocked observers watched as the craft flew over the elk and levitated the animal into the air as the craft wobbled in position. The poor suspended elk began rotating in the air with its head somehow attached to the underside of the vehicle by an invisible force field as the strange craft slowly made off with it. The workers last saw the craft flying away without the elk underneath, and they assumed that the animal had been taken on board the craft in a successful elk-abduction. UFO investigators, including Peter Davenport, director of the National UFO Reporting Center, and Robert Fairfax, Director of Investigations in Washington State for MUFON, concluded that the witnesses, none of whom sought any publicity or had anything to gain by reporting the incident, were reliable, and had just reported what they actually observed with their own eyes, as mysterious as the event was. The abduction of animals and humans by flying craft of unknown origin is not unusual. Each year, missing livestock and missing persons are reported around the world, often associated with reports of UFOs. It is almost as if the earth is an enterprise. The flora and fauna (including humans) appear to be needed by nonhuman entities for purposes that we can only speculate about. Perhaps on this little oasis in space we live on, our animal and plant life are treasured resources that visitors can take to other worlds. Whatever the case, it is a certainty that someone out there has a need for water, blood, and biological tissues from both animals and humans, along with live samples of flora and fauna.

Multiple Police Officers Report UFO Sighting

On January 5, 2000, Mr. Melvern Noll of Highland, Illinois stopped in to check on his miniature golf course in the wee hours of the morning. When he was satisfied that the golf course was secure, on the way back to his truck he glanced off to the northeast and noticed a bright luminous object that appeared to grow bigger and bigger as it approached his location. Standing there for several minutes watching the strange object, as it grew closer he could see that it was attached to a much larger rectangular object that he estimated at the size of a football field, with lights and windows all around. Melvern's sighting was the first of a long sequence of events that occurred that morning that involved multiple police sightings and reports from eight different police stations, a multitude of private citizens, and possibly personnel from Scott Air Force Base. Driving immediately to the Highland Police Department, he talked officers into going outside to witness what he was seeing, which they did, and got on the radio to tell other precincts to watch for the object as well. One of the police officers that responded to the radio transmission was Officer Ed Barton of the Lebanon, Illinois Police Department who reported two intensely bright objects with spikes of light emanating from them. Officer Barton then jumped into his police car and chased the object at about 80 miles per hour with his flashers on. Officer Barton then noticed the object moving toward him, so he pulled over and shut the car off to observe and listen for any noises the object might make as it came for him. He watched as a triangular object approximately 75 feet long and 40 feet wide passed over him and blotted out the stars above. As Officer Barton radioed to St. Clair County dispatch to let them know he had the object in sight, he reported that the object suddenly shot off out of sight faster than his eyes could follow. Officer David Martin of the Shiloh, Illinois Police Department, was next to catch a glimpse of the object, and also reported that it sped up like lightning and vanished from view west of Shiloh. Officer Craig Stevens of the Millstadt Police Department was the next officer to see the flying triangle. Officer Stevens thought he heard a low humming sound emanating from the craft. Another unnamed police officer from the Dupo, Illinois Police Department also saw the same triangular flying craft which was seen to suddenly speed up and vanish.

Horror from the Sky

On the morning of August 2, 2002, Todd Sees left home to go 4-wheeling in the woods, telling his wife that he would be home by noon. That was the last time Mrs. Sees would kiss her husband or see him alive. Happy-go-lucky Todd Sees was destined to become another recorded death from coming too close to a flying saucer. The town was full of local reports this same day of a strange-looking UFO that projected a beam of light on the ground and appeared to pick up an unidentified object of some sort. When Todd didn't return home at noon that day, his wife became worried, and a small search party was organized to go check on Todd's whereabouts. When no Todd was found, the search party expanded into a two-day massive search effort that involved the local police force, dogs, paramedics, and 200 volunteers. Todd's 4-wheeler was finally located, but no Todd. Finally, two days after Todd went missing, late on August 4, 2002, in an area of brush that the search party had already covered meticulously without finding Todd, his body was found lying on the ground in his underwear. Todd's face was frozen in an expression of horror, both hands were crossed over his face as if protecting himself from something, and there were burn marks on his temples. Within a ½ hour of discovering Todd's body, the FBI took over the case. Another strange and inexplicable aspect, other than Todd's horrified posture, was that his body showed no signs of bloating. A dead body exposed to the sun for over 2 days would have been extremely bloated. Instead, Todd's dead body was in remarkable condition, as if somehow preserved the whole time and then dumped onto the ground. The FBI, along with the local residents, remained silent about Todd's case since his body was removed from the scene. It is unknown just how many cases like Todd's there actually are buried in the police files around the world. This may have been a case in which a flying saucer came too close to a human in the woods and accidentally killed them. Realizing that they had inadvertently damaged an Earth creature, the aliens may have taken Todd onboard in an attempt to nurture him back to health. Failing this attempt, they were forced to drop the dead body off close to where they found him. If this is what actually happened, there is good and bad news. The good news is, Todd wasn't consumed for food. The bad news is, the aliens were either unwilling or unable to repair him, even with their technology, which is surely well-advanced from ours. If they wouldn't spare him, they are of questionable morality. If they couldn't, which is more likely, maybe they are not as advanced as we think they are. In other words, these particular ufonauts were not goulish cannibalistic demons, but neither were they gods. If this event represents an accidental manslaughter, then the aliens are also imperfect, just as we are.

The Chicago O'Hare Airport Flying Saucer Sighting

On Tuesday, November 7, 2006, at approximately 4:15 p.m., a silently- hovering flying saucer was spotted by multiple credible witnesses over Chicago O'Hare International Airport. The object appeared above United Airlines Flight 446 that was headed for Charlotte, North Carolina. The first person to spot the craft was a ramp employee, who promptly notified the pilot and copilot, who must have also noticed that there was an unidentified object in the sky above them. The existence of the object was also confirmed by multiple individuals outside the airport, who described it as an "obvious" disk-shaped flying saucer. As multiple witnesses gasped with astonishment, the object left its stationary position in the sky and shot up through the clouds at a extremely high velocity, leaving a distinct, circular hole in the clouds up to the blue sky above. As reported by the *Chicago Tribune*, this multiple credible witness sighting lasted approximately two minutes and was observed by a dozen or so United Airlines employees, including pilots to other employees and supervisors, some of whom responded to radio chatter about the object and ran out in time to see it for themselves. Both the United Airlines and the FAA denied having any information on the sighting. They lied. A Freedom of Information Act request filed by the Chicago Tribune uncovered a call made by a United Airlines supervisor to the airport tower reporting the flying saucer hovering in the sky. In direct opposition to the policy of the FAA to investigate all possible security breaches, the FAA wrote off the incident as a weather event, a rare "hole-punch cloud" phenomenon. This was ludicrous because a hole-punch cloud can only occur in certain unusual weather conditions, conditions that did not exist at the airport that day. It was a clear, partly-cloudy day, and it was not possible that a hole-punch cloud could have occurred in those ideal conditions. Multiple witnesses were upset that this sighting was not reported or covered any more than it was, and were outraged over the usual official denial. As most people are somewhat apprehensive about flying in the first place, reports of flying saucers at airports is bad for the airline business, as such reports scare potential customers away. Pilots who report flying saucers are often fired, and their sanity is unjustly questioned. Ask anyone privately who has ever been an airline pilot for any length of time if they have ever seen a UFO. If they are honest, they will tell you that most airline pilots have witnessed UFOs, but they refuse to talk about it, at least until retirement, for fear of their jobs. In addition to the report in the Chicago Tribune, this credible UFO sighting was covered on CNN, MSNBC, Fox News, and CBS. On February 9, 2009, the History Channel aired *Aliens at the Airport*, in which this fantastic UFO incident was fairly reenacted. This event serves as a reminder that the flying saucers are still here. Just when some of us were about to write the whole UFO subject off as a crazy streak within the human race, a mental byproduct of Cold War jitters and our entrance into the age of space travel, it happened again. There, before our lying eyes, hovered a giant, circular, shiny, metallic, silent flying disk, a classic flying saucer right out of 1950s science fiction. After allowing several sets of human eyes to gaze at its presence and stark reality, it shot off at high speed just as mysteriously as it came, leaving the witnesses and those to whom they would testify in a state of utter bewilderment. Such is the nature of the Phenomenon. A genuine flying saucer from otherworldly or interdimensional realms appeared for the world to see in 2006, and there isn't anything anybody can do about it. To borrow and paraphrase from astrophysicist Neil deGrasse Tyson concerning his views about science – the nice thing about flying saucers is that they are real, whether you believe in them or not.

Enlightened Contact with Extraterrestrial Intelligence

James Gilliland from Southern California is the founder of a group known as ECETI (Enlightened Contact with Extraterrestrial Intelligence). Gilliland claims to receive messages from ETs, the thrust of which consist of the usual warnings about impending environmental disasters if humans do not stop warring with one another and take better care of the planet. This theme clearly permeates most of the information coming from the aliens to all of our beloved contactees. Gilliland, like myself, had a near-death experience (NDE) that opened his mind to the interdimensional nature of reality. He believes that flying spheres and orbs are an extension of consciousness, a byproduct of other planes and dimensions, and is an advocate for universal peace.

Mexico's Roswell

On August 20, 2007, near daybreak at 4 a.m. in the village of Xilitla, Mexico, multiple witnesses in the village watched as a fiery sphere that changed directions several times and appeared to be under some type of intelligent control crashed into a grove of trees. This incident was very similar to the previous incident from 1974 in Coyame, Mexico, when an unknown object under intelligent control and traveling at supersonic speeds collided with a small airplane, causing the unidentified object to crash in the desert. This incident from 2007 in Xilitla is known today as "Mexico's Roswell."

Flying Saucer and Occupants Appear in Turkey

Over three consecutive years, 2007, 2008, and 2009, a flying saucer with visible occupants inside appeared in the skies of Kumburgaz, Turkey. The video footage has stirred quite a controversy since it first surfaced in 2007, when an on-duty night security guard, Yalcin Yalmin, captured the UFO on film for the first time. From a distance out over the horizon, the object appeared as a cluster of flashing lights. When the video camera zoomed in, what came into view was so startling it is almost laughable as footage "too good to be real." What appears is an odd-looking saucer-like craft hovering back and forth in the air above the sea off the coast of Marmara. The craft has an opening in the front that reveals a number of nonhuman creatures inside. These alien ufonauts appear to be in the middle of some sort of emergency situation. The appearance of the craft and the behavior of the occupants seems purely unintentional on their part. The beings inside the craft appear to be preoccupied in a situation that was beyond their control. In the process, the creatures and their craft inadvertently exposed themselves to the eye of a human camera, giving us all a rare glipse inside what appears to be an alien spacecraft with living occupants. Over the course of these three consecutive years, Yalmin captured several different segments of the craft and occupants, many of which were taken with witnesses nearby that he spoke to as he was filming. The camera was equipped with a 200X adapter for good closeup viewing. Researcher Haktan Akdogan directed a professional analysis of the film footage, the results of which were released to the public by Dr. Steven Greer's SIRIUS UFO organization. The footage caused a media sensation and captured the interest of the Turkish scientific community. The National Council for the Study of Science and Technology (TUBITAK) analyzed the film segments with intent of exposing the film as a fraud. The original film was handed over to TUBITAK representatives at their office on live television. Fully expecting to discover that the film was created with CGI or staged models, TUBITAK was dumbfounded when all scientific evidence indicates that the film is, in fact, authentic. The report from the investigation is as follows:

> The objects observed on the images have a structure made of a specific material and are definitely not any kind of CGI animation or in any means a type of special effects used for simulation in a studio or for video effects. So the conclusion of this report is that the observations are not a model, marquette, or a fraud. It's concluded that the objects observed have a physical structure and are made of materials that don't belong to any category of (airplanes helicopters, meteors, Venus, Mars, satellites, artificial lights,

Chinese lanterns, etc.) and that it mostly fits in the category of UFOs (Unidentified Flying Objects and of unknown origin).

Similar conclusions were reached by video specialists and special effects companies in Japan, Russia, and Turkey. However, if anyone turns to Youtube for their analysis, they can find cheap, sloppy attempts to demonstrate that the Turkey UFO footage is fake. These armchair debunkers explain away the Turkey UFO sighting as anything from a cruise ship to a strange weather anomaly. However, if the actual science that has been applied to this footage in professional video studios is accepted, the Turkey UFO footage is good as gold. At least, at the time of this writing, no one has successfully shown that the footage is not what it appears to be - a high-tech, non-terrestrial flying craft with alien creatures inside. Although only two aliens are clearly visible in the film, there are actually four nonhuman creatures who appear in the film and are in constant motion. The two most prominent beings have large heads and large dark wrap-around eyes like the typical "Grays." At first glance, these two Gray aliens appear to be the only creatures in the film, as if they are sightseeing on Earth and looking out the window of their flying saucer over the sea. As a viewer, you almost expect the two creatures to start waving. However, close scrutiny by multiple film analysts discovered that these two beings in the forefront are actually interacting in some way with a third, dissimilar being who is lying horizontally in front of them. It appears that the two prominent beings in the film are applying some sort of medical aid or manual attention to the creature in front of them in supine. All three creatures are humanoid and insectoid in appearance. Additionally, there is a fourth creature behind them in the film who, by all appearances, seems to be some sort of supervisory figure. This creature behind the other three is also humanoid and insectoid, having the appearance of a "Mantis." The really puzzling aspect of this multiple-episode sighting is that, in the video footage from all three years, the same creatures appear at nearly the same time and same place and are moving in the same fashion and conducting the same activity all three years. This consistency of appearance and activity is beyond the pale for many inquirers into this case, who erroneously conclude that the event must be staged, and that it stretches all credibility, despite the scientific conclusions of professional video analysts from multiple countries. However, the answer to this dilemma likely involves the way that interplanetary or interdimensional vehicles travel through time and space.

How Flying Saucers Travel

To effectively transport physical objects through vast distances of interstellar space, some sort of space-time compression must take place. Therefore, not only are some of our visitors traveling through space, they are also traveling through time. The ET craft that was candidly captured on film in Turkey, as well as all other ET craft coming from vast distances throughout the universe, are likely traveling through time and space in precise quantum units that physicists call "Planck length" and "Planck time." These quantum units of time and space are named after the physicist, Max Planck, who originally discovered and defined them. Planck time is the smallest quantum unit of time, and represents the amount of time it takes for light to travel in a vacuum one "Planck length." The Planck length is an unimaginably small, quantum unit of measure, the smallest unit of physical measurement that can exist in physical reality. Imagine, if you will, any length such as a yardstick, and divide it in half. If you keep dividing the sections in half, the pieces become very small and very difficult to divide at some point. The Planck length would be the tiny, indivisible section that is left at the end of the dividing process, a unit of measure that can no longer be halved. The Planck length is defined by the speed of light in a vacuum, the Planck constant (a quantum of action in quantum physics), and the gravitational constant. Advanced, extraterrestrial space travelers have likely discovered a way to manipulate units of Planck time. As someone watching a strip of film by speeding up or skipping 100 frames at a time and then slowing back down to normal speed to see where they are at in the film, ETs who effectively travel interstellar distances have likely developed the ability to "bundle" or "skip" units of Planck time. Instead of traveling through space one Planck length at a time as we do when we take a walk outside, bundles of Planck time are compressed so that, as one unit of time passes on the clocks of the space travelers, many units of time pass on the clocks of observers outside the craft. If this is the case, it would be expected that what appears to human observers as an event that occurs at the same time and location three years in a row, such as the craft observed in the Turkey UFO footage, actually occurred within a much shorter time span to the creatures aboard the vessel, who are traveling in compressed, quantified bundles of Planck time. By the clocks of the occupants in the Turkey UFO, perhaps only 20 minutes or so passed for them during their brief exposure in the visible range of Earth's inhabitants. This same 20 minutes by their clocks occurred over three years from our time perspective. Their craft appeared for our cameras at the same time and same place three years in a row, showing the beings aboard involved with the same task at hand, that of attending to one of the occupants aboard the craft for some reason, as in the case of a possible medical emergency. It would be like someone driving a car who slowed down as one of the passengers was choking to see if they needed assistance. Perhaps the ET in supine aboard the craft in front of the two "Grays" just needed some air and some physical attention. In response to this emergency situation, the occupants temporarily altered the way the craft was traveling, slowing down in a skipping motion, thus becoming visible in our physical reality for a few minutes at a time over three consecutive years at the same approximate time by our clocks. For a few precious minutes, we see an alien spacecraft and occupants who temporarily experience one quantum unit of Planck time just as we do for a short duration before they return to compressed time and "skip" a year. Since the craft and its occupants are capable of traveling through digitized bundles of Planck time of equal measure, it would be expected that for some duration of our time, the craft would appear at the same time and the same place from our perspective. Another way to illustrate this is by taking a single sheet of paper and folding it up, back and forth, into several equal segments. Each folded segment represents a bundle of Planck time. Once the paper is completely folded up, ram a pencil through the middle of the folded paper. This represents the ET craft traveling through folded bundles of Planck time. When the paper is unfolded, it will display holes at equal distances from one another, representing the pencil showing up at the same time and place from the perspective of any imaginary occupant living on the piece of paper, whose only way to get from one edge to the other is by traveling through time one Planck unit of time after the other in a non-compressed linear fashion. Something similar to this is likely happening as our ET visitors travel our way through both space and time. UFOs typically show up in "window areas" at the same time and place on a regular basis. Our skies may therefore be full of ET craft traveling in bundles of Planck time and Planck lengths of space, which renders them normally invisible, unless they slow down to our time progression, during which time we can sometimes observe them or capture them on film before they speed back up. We humans, just like the person living on a 2-dimensional sheet of paper, are currently limited to moving through and experiencing time one quantum unit of Planck time after another. We do not yet have the ability to alter this fixed linear progression. However, the ET crafts and ufonauts in our skies, who are normally invisible to us as they move through bundles of Planck time in a way that we are unable to percieve, are experiencing time aboard the craft quite differently than we are. The craft and occupants remain invisible to us as long as they are in compressed time mode. They become visible only when they slow down to one unit of Planck time at a time, which is our current rate of perception and experience. If, in the future, someone finally debunks the Turkey UFO footage successfully, credit will have to be given to the creators for inventing some method of hoakery that fools video experts in several countries, and I, for one, will take my hat off to them. However, as of now, the science that has been conducted on this footage thus far leads to the conclusion that, as fantastic as this case is, it is absolutely real. This footage either represents 1) an actual glimpse of alien creatures and their flying craft caught on Candid Camera, 2) a very clever fake that has, so far, fooled experts in video labs in several countries, or 3) an intentional fabrication by the Overlords of the Singularity that was created and manifested for our human eyes and cameras by the transmogrification of energy into our physical realm for purposes of manipulating our perceptions in accordance to the purposes of the Overlords. Whatever the case, the Turkey UFO footage is fantastic to behold, and is quite stimulating to the imagination. Perhaps its sole purpose is to create an insatiable desire to travel as they do, and propel us more expediently into the marvels of the Singularity. Appearances of craft such as the Turkey UFO create inspirational dissatisfaction in the minds of human witnesses. We know that someone out there in the universe has the ability to manipulate space and time, and we want desperately to learn these methods so we can become a spacefaring civilization ourselves. What a wonderful thing to aspire to, to be able to travel throughout the entire universe at will, without being subject to the predicted aging or time paradox problems. It would be my idea of heaven.

UFOs Appear at Airport in China, and Return to Chicago O'Hare

On July 7, 2010, a non-terrestrial craft was observed above Hangzhou Xiaoshan International Airport near Hangzhou, China. Officials were concerned enough about the object to completely shut down the airport. About a week later, on July 15, 2010, multiple witnesses reported a diamond-shaped array of four luminous spheres hovering over the city's Shaping Park for over an hour. Then, back in the United States about 6 months later, the Chicago O'Hare Airport was once again haunted by ET craft, only this time it involved flying saucers appearing in formations on February 13, 2011. Video of the strange luminous spheres flying together in distinct formations was recorded from Bloomingdale, Illinois at about 8 p.m. as the spheres flew silently from the direction of the airport. These UFO clusters are currently being observed all over the world, and lead some UFO researchers to speculate that groups of UFOs from other star systems are now making appearances in our skies in the arrangement of the star system that they come from in hopes that humans will recognize them as star-neighbors and welcome them to land here on Earth. Some even believe that the language of the universe is not math, but stars, that recognizable star patterns are routinely used by the Star Visitors as a universal language and that all planets harboring intelligent life in post-disclosure societies know how to respond. If this is the case, we are certainly out of the loop here on Earth. If the craft are searching the cosmos for intelligent, responsive populations who are open to a friendly visit, it is certainly a disturbing thought that groups of visitors may be showing up here on Earth and displaying the universal sign for, "May we come aboard?" and we are just too primitive and stupid to recognize the universal calling card. There is something ironic about certain statements made by our world's foremost astronomer, Neil deGrasse Tyson, as he debunks UFOs as nonsense in public interviews while UFOs are beckoning us in our skies to make contact with them, and we don't understand star language. It is especially funny that, in the same breath, Tyson expresses his fears that humans might just be too stupid to communicate with extraterrestrials, even if they showed up. If clusters of ET craft from other galaxies are appearing in our skies in formations that represent their home star systems and hoping that we welcome them, it appears that astronomer Neil deGrasse Tyson is absolutely correct.

[*On February 12, 2013, North Korea announces its third nuclear test, producing tremors that yielded approximately 15 kilotons*]

Stephen Hawking Fears Robot Uprising

As reported by *Daily Mail/UK* on March 14, 2015 at the 2015 Zeitgeist Conference in London, physicist Stephen Hawking voiced his concerns about a *robot uprising* - artificial intelligence capable of outsmarting humans – by the next century. Hawking feels that we should be more concerned about whether humans will be able to control the type of artificial intelligence we are about to create. Fortunately, there are many conscientious AI researchers who are working very hard to prevent a human extinction event when our artificial intelligence achieves sentience in the next few decades. As we approach the outer limits of understanding about the nature of reality and the definition of life itself as we approach the Singularity, let's hope, with the help of our ET friends, that we can achieve this great transcendence successfully.

CHAPTER 13

UFO Theorists and the Truth about Flying Saucers

"Ancient Astronaut Theorists believe that the elusive 'missing link' in human evolution came via extraterrestrial intervention, meaning that extraterrestrials manipulated our genetics in some way to nudge our very nature from an ape-like species toward the humans we are today. They may have even done this by adding themselves to our gene pool. This would have created a branch where the original ape-man continued on his evolutionary path while the new hybrid/alien human (us) took off on a new path."

— Sharon Delarose, Ancient Aliens and the Lost Islands.

AFTER 70-PLUS YEARS of observing the UFO phenomenon and speculating about their possible origins and purposes, what have all the UFO researchers and experts concluded about flying saucers and the hidden intelligences that operate them? The UFO cases that I have selected for consideration in this book are just a glimpse, the tip of the iceberg, drawn from the vast body of reports of flying saucer and ufonaut encounters that are available for examination in the public domain. Position statements from various UFO researchers around the world can be gleaned from a variety of sources, such as Ronald Story's *The Mammoth Encyclopedia of Extraterrestrial Encounters (MEEE)*, Jerome Clark's *The UFO Book*, or many other UFO encyclopedias and works from the vast sea of writings by UFO researchers, percipients, and the contactees themselves that have accumulated over the last several decades. Position statements gleaned from UFO researchers who have, in some cases, dedicated their lifetimes to the study of UFOs, are a real treasure in order to gain an overall insight into what they have collectively ascertained about the nature of the hidden intelligences behind the UFO mystery. As we now examine the tentative conclusions and speculations of a good sampling of the experts and investigators in the field of ufology, I think you will find that their collective views coordinate nicely with the idea that we are being guided or manipulated by the hidden UFO intelligences into a technological singularity. Some of these experts come very close to saying just that, but fall just short of coming out and identifying the actual goals and purposes of the alien presence on Earth.

At a glance, this chapter provides a synopsis of decades of UFO research by some of the top minds in the field. As I examined all the positions of top scientific UFO researchers, I was struck by how very close they all came to what I have been saying all along in this book, that the intelligences behind the UFOs are guiding us into accelerated technology, possibly to help us out, and possibly for their own purposes. However, the following individual position statements don't quite make it to any real clarity or synthesis concerning the actual agenda of the intelligences behind the UFO mystery. It's as if the answer to the conundrum is right there, but is never is quite grasped or articulated. Most UFO position statements expressed by lifelong UFO researchers display a level of utter bewilderment. They know that bona fide flying saucers exist as a reality, and speculate as to where they come from and who might be operating them, and to what ends, but the ultimate purpose of the UFOs remains a mystery. Various researchers have aligned themselves with their favorite choices from the many hypotheses that are out there, such as the Extraterrestrial Hypothesis (ETH); the Ultraterrestrial Hypothesis (UTH); the Interdimensional Hypothesis (IDH); the Cryptoterrestrial Hypothesis (CTH); the Geophysical Hypothesis (GPH); the Intelligent Geophysical Hypothesis (IGPH); the Gaia Hypothesis (GH), the Jungian Archetype Hypothesis (JAH); the Federal Hypothesis (FH); or the idea that the electromagnetically-sensitive individuals who we call "psychics," are hallucinating flying saucers and occupants when exposed to certain types of electromagnetism, or combinations of electromagnetic pollution generated by our modern electronic age, such as proposed by such researchers as Michael Persinger or Albert Budden.

The purpose of this chapter is to illuminate the gist of these positions and demonstrate just how close to the main thesis of this book most of them are, except, of course, the position of the hardcore UFO skeptics, who say there is nothing whatsoever to the UFO phenomenon, that it is all an illusion, a viral rumor, a figment of the human imagination, a misperception of natural phenomena, or a product of fantasy-prone personalities. Admittedly, even the position of such skeptics applies to some UFO reports, as we have examined in previous chapters. The skeptics, like just about everyone, are partially correct in their views. However, the skeptical position is the least likely position of all to be correct for some of the more anomalous cases, many of which include, as we have seen, trace evidence; physical damage to animals; persons; or property; photographic evidence; electromagnetic (EM) effects; or bizarre encounters in alternate realities and/or altered states of perception. As we take a look at the views of the following prominent UFO researchers, please keep my thesis in mind, that hidden UFO intelligences have been manipulating humankind behind the scenes all along in order to steer us into a technological singularity, that we have all been used as tools for an alien agenda. By examining what all the experts say, I believe you will find that my position is at least close to the truth behind the flying saucers. At this point, we do not have all the answers, but I think we do have a general idea now that the impending Singularity is what the UFO phenomenon has been about all along.

Donald Keyhoe (1897-1988)

The retired Major Donald Keyhoe was a graduate of the US Naval Academy and the Marine Corps Officers School. During World War II, Donald Keyhoe was a Marine aircraft and balloon pilot who was temporarily retired from active duty after a night crash in the Pacific Ocean. During his period of retirement from duty, he was Chief of Information, Civil Aeronautics, and Department of Commerce (now the Federal Aviation Administration). During his service, Keyhoe honed his skills as an aviation journalist, and continued his writing after WW2. In 1957, he became the director of the National Investigations Committee on Aerial Phenomenon (NICAP), and continued in this capacity until 1970. In 1950, *True Magazine* published an article by Keyhoe in their January issue called *Flying Saucers are Real*. The article, which made the case for the reality of flying saucers, caused quite a stir among readers. Keyhoe was encouraged by the response to his article, and went on to write several best-selling UFO books, including: *The Flying Saucers are Real; Flying Saucers from Outer Space; The Flying Saucer Conspiracy; Flying Saucers – Top Secret; and Aliens from Space*. Donald Keyhoe's view was that, despite the fact that the Air Force has full proof of the reality of flying saucers, they made a policy decision early on not to openly reveal this reality to the public. The Air Force determined that disclosure of this information would not be good for the American society at large. In other words, the public could not handle the information. Keyhoe asserted that the many radar sightings and Air Force UFO reports over the years confirm the reality of non-terrestrial craft of unknown origin entering and operating within Earth's atmosphere. Keyhoe suspected that there is an inside, covert effort to understand what this planet is dealing with concerning UFOs, and that they have made attempts at communication with ETs. Keyhoe rightly believed that we should cease and desist any and all efforts to chase and capture UFOs. Keyhoe regretted that we might have already blown our opportunity to make friendly contact with alien life by our aggressive and paranoid stance demonstrated from the beginning. Just as modern physicist, Steven Hawking, warns that humans on Earth should stay under the radar, that historically, encounters between primitives and more advanced cultures have not gone very well for the more primitive of the two. Keyhoe's writings indicate that at least some scientists of his day felt the same way. Keyhoe's books bring attention to the many doomsday writers in the UFO field who suspected that the government already knew something about the underlying nature of the UFOs that would have been utterly intolerable if revealed openly. Keyhoe believed that the public deserved to know the truth. He based this belief on the fact that we have all learned to live in a world that could be blown up by nuclear weapons at any time and still manage our daily lives. How much worse could the truth about UFOs be? Keyhoe ascertained through his studies that the alien intelligences behind the UFOs were conducting some sort of long-term surveillance project of planet earth, and that it was only a matter of time before open contact was made and we all understood more about their mission here.

Was Keyhoe Correct?

Keyhoe was probably right in that there are, in fact, nuts-and-bolts craft of non-terrestrial origin in our skies occasionally, most likely those who make their home in our own solar system somewhere. Keyhoe's conclusions were based on the long history of observational evidence through telescopes since the time they were first invented that have been documented so well by writers such as Fort and Jessup. In modern times, our own astronauts have also reported the presence of unidentified lights and physical alien crafts in space. Observational evidence indicates that we have company in our own solar system. Keyhoe was correct in that the US military, in particular the USAF and US Navy, know for certain that flying saucers are real. However, during the period of time that Keyhoe was alive and writing, the technological singularity was not really a developed concept as an oncoming reality. Therefore, Keyhoe and writers of his era would not have made the connection between the alien agenda and the Singularity. With the exception of a few individuals such as Mark Probert and Meade Layne, both of whom were early proponents of the interdimensional nature of at least some of the flying saucers, most UFO investigators of Keyhoe's day adhered strictly to the Extraterrestrial Hypothesis (ETH). The luminous, pulsating orbs of plasma energy that occasionally drop into the portion of the electromagnetic spectrum that is visible to humans, the light beings that were captured on film so well by Dorothy Izatt, were virtually ignored in Keyhoe's day, and it is this phenomenon that represents the underlying nature of the reality of much of the UFO phenomena on Earth. These intelligent, luminous balls of light are somehow connected into the human unconscious, and are able to induce a symbiotic experience of virtual reality in the minds of percipients. This phenomenon was poorly understood in Keyhoe's day, and it is poorly understood now, although researchers such as Andrew Collins are attempting to understand, as outlined in his book, *Lightquest: Your Guide to Seeing and Interacting with UFOs, Mystery Lights, and Plasma Intelligences* (2012). Also, thanks to the insights of writers such as Dr. Jacques Vallee and John Keel, the idea of an interdimensional intervention, some of whom do not have the best interests of human beings at heart, is out there. The idea that all ET visitors are benevolent "Space Brothers" is naïve. These interdimensional entities, some good and some bad (just as in the human realm), may actually be in conflict with one another. They may be responsible for Earth's religions, and may have two different roles to play as we approach the Singularity. The two ET factions that William Bramley identified in *The Gods of Eden*, i.e., the "maverick race" who take an interest in humans as potential candidates for merging with the Galactic Federation, or Cosmic Brotherhood, may wind up collecting a remnant of humanity (an alien Rapture?) when the Singularity takes the world by storm, transcending those who are pure at heart into a world beyond our three-dimensional existence. The other ET faction, Bramley's "custodial race," who may have genetically engineered intentional defects into humanity at some point for conflict and war to prompt the need for superior technology, have their own interests in mind as we approach the Singularity. Their long-range mission may have involved employing the unwitting human race to construct suitable vessels of artificial intelligence during the Singularity into which they can download their disembodied consciousness and exist immortally in the physical realm. The discarnate faction of the Overlords of the Singularity may be interested in self-replication and/or the eternal perpetuation of their own consciousness. These negative Overlords may consist of a combination of aliens who arrived on Earth from another realm or alternative universe long ago, and negative human entities on the lower astral plane who seek permanent residence in the physical world. In other words, negative aliens, and negative human souls, may share a common mission.

Philip J. Klass (1919-2005)

One of the most vocal antagonists of the Travis Walton abduction case, along with everything else that involves UFOs, the arch-enemy of ufology at the time, was Philip J. Klass. Klass was an aviation expert and professional UFO-debunker who was also known as the "Sherlock Holmes of UFOs." Philip Klass earned a BS degree in electrical engineering from Iowa State in 1941 and was employed as an avionics engineer for General Electric Co. He became a technical journalist for *Aviation Week* magazine, and earned many prestigious awards for journalism during his career. In 1976, Klass was one of the original founders of the Committee for the Scientific Investigation of Claims of the Paranormal (CSICOP). The value that I assign to his part in the UFO controversy is that Klass served as a reminder that over 90% of all UFO sightings are misidentified natural phenomena or glitches within the human perceptual system. Klass had the most hardline view of all the debunkers. He saw the UFO phenomenon as a pseudoscience, and maintained throughout his entire career that there was not one shred of viable hard evidence for the public to openly examine which positively demonstrates that any UFOs are extraterrestrial spacecraft, and he might have been correct. If, in fact, there is hard evidence, it is kept under wraps in the tightest grip of military secrecy in the history of humanity. Klass, along with everyone else who are outside US intelligence circles, would not have a need to know or possess the appropriate security clearance. As such, they would not be privy to examining such concrete evidence. Klass felt that the only thing research into UFOs has determined is that police officers, pilots, and government officials have the same flawed perceptions as any of the rest of us. No matter what their official position, these witnesses are fully capable of mistaking a natural phenomenon such as Venus, meteors, missile launches, odd clouds, ball lightning, or any number of other natural occurrences for a flying saucer, and he is right. Klass humorously pointed out the difficulty of Washington or anyone else for that matter keeping a secret for a long period of time. Klass pointed to top secret documents from the 1940s that have since been declassified and give no indication of knowledge of spaceship crashes such as the one that allegedly crashed at Roswell, New Mexico. Klass was right, none of the once-classified documents that have since become declassified present any indication of inside knowledge of crashed saucers. Philip Klass was a smart man, and his contribution to the field was an entertaining warning against accepting any and all reports of UFOs or alien abductions. The paucity of hard evidence is simple to understand. First of all, an actual, nuts-and-bolts alien spacecraft that blew in and out of Earth's atmosphere would have no reason to leave evidence of any kind. They would obviously have an advanced propulsion system, likely of the non-polluting variety that provides an effective means to at least get around in our own solar system, which is where at least some of the UFOs surely come from. Alien spacecraft would be even less likely to leave any traces of evidence if they were from Kaku's "Type 3" civilization that has harnessed the power of an entire galaxy and can go anywhere they want throughout the universe. To those folks, we are like visiting and ant pile. It is doubtful that they would even have enough in common with us to bother with visitation, and if they did visit, it would likely be for observation only. There is no reason for these types of visits to leave any physical evidence that they were here. The other possibility, the one I'm focused on, which is a self-replicating artificial intelligence originating from either a lost, advanced, hidden civilization here on Earth (Cryptoterrestrials) or an alien intelligence from elsewhere (extraterrestrial or interdimensional intelligence), leaves tons of non-physical observational and psychological evidence for us to examine, but it is the very evidence that has been ignored for so long, that of the contactee reports. Therein lies evidential gold, but it is generally ignored because it is not the type of concrete evidence scientists typically look for. It is a difficult form of evidence to weigh and measure, although some researchers such as Aime Michel, Dr. Jacques Vallee, and John Keel have done an excellent job of conducting science on observational and testimonial evidence and have amassed quite a large body of scientific data concerning nonhuman encounters. Personally, I have never seen a blue-ringed octopus that are allegedly native to Australia. However, I do accept that the creature is real because others who have seen them have reported their existence, have taken excellent photos of them, or have even been bitten or killed by them, and the same type of evidence exists with UFOs. The problem with Klass' position is that there is, in fact, an overwhelming amount of evidence, but since it does not result in a flying saucer under a hanger that everyone can go see, it is rejected by people who share Klass' mindset, which represents a classic case of confirmation bias. Such individuals will not believe in aliens even if they do land openly on the White House lawn, as they do not fit into their concept of reality. Therefore, an actual televised landing would be immediately suspect as a false flag invasion by humans, a clever hoax, or an event that just looked like an open alien landing, but was some sort of misperception of reality.

Philip Klass is passed now, along with all of his personal frustrations and antagonism toward believers in the reality of flying saucers and extraterrestrial visitation. Even so, the Klass mindset among traditional scientists remains alive and well. Philip Klass left us all with a little something in his passing, and that is his "Last Will and Testament of Philip J. Klass," otherwise known as the "UFO Curse," which reads as follows:

To ufologists who publicly criticize me....or who even think unkind thoughts about me in private, I do hearby leave and bequeath: THE UFO CURSE. No matter how long you live, you will never know any more about UFOs than you know today. You will never know any more about what UFOs really are, or where they come from. You will never know about what the US Government really knows about UFOs than you know today. As you lie on your own deathbed you will be as mystified about UFOs as you are today. And you will remember this curse.

This pretty much sums up the frustration that Klass apparently experienced after a lifetime of criticism by angry UFO buffs, most of whom felt that Klass "jumped the shark" on many occasions with his mundane, unimaginative explanations of every UFO report. Klass was the king of temperature inversions; swamp gas; ball lightning; flocks of birds; and weather balloons. There is, in my view, an uncomfortable desperation throughout Klass' books and writings that reflect a common mindset that has a "need" to dubunk UFOs at all costs, as they are an offense to scientific intellect and human dignity. I, for one, like Philip J. Klass, and appreciate his contribution to the human UFO story. He was entertaining, and his mindset represents a segment of the human population that really struggles to come to terms with the idea that aliens are, in fact, among us now, and have been for a long time. Philip Klass - may you rest in peace.

Modern Klass Analogues

Even after thousands of documented flying disk sightings by credible witnesses, sightings confirmed on radar, and UFO encounters that have left physical traces and undeniable physical and psychological symptoms on pecipients that have baffled doctors, the mindset of Philip J. Klass is alive and well. For example, at the time of this writing, there is an internet site, "rationalwiki," whose contributors present themselves as the voice of reason and intelligence in the world, whose entries often fall short of the insight necessary to understand, or at least glimpse, the underlying nature of a matter. In their entry for "Gray aliens," they present the standard skeptic's arguments for the fictional nature of the Grays. Rational Wiki states that Gray aliens are the "single most widely recognized visualization of an alien lifeform" that have become ubiquitous in popular culture, and they are right. With smug sarcasm typical of many young college students who believe they are more intelligent than everyone else, they present the Grays as the "sex pests" of an imagined alien world who enjoy "fiddling with genitalia, and lodging dildo-like objects up people's anuses," who are "partial to the nether regions of cattle and other livestock, which they remove by laser." Believing themselves witty with juvenile attempts at humor, they go on to say, "In other words, they [the Grays] don't come in peace so much as for a "piece of ass." From there they go on to provide the history of the Gray alien concept in the human mind, beginning with the large-headed (representing superior intelligence) "bug-eyed aliens" of sci-fi magazines of the late 1930s. They present Professor R.L. Johannis' sighting of two green-skinned beings on August 14, 1947 one month after Roswell as laying the foundation for the Gray alien "myth," moving on to Ray L. Dimmick's 1950 claim to have seen a 25-inch-tall Roswell alien with a bulbous head. Following Dimmick's story, a German newspaper, *Wiesbadener Tagblatt* ran an April Fool's joke with a faked photo of two military men with a small alien with a large head. Rational Wiki buys the idea that Betty and Barney Hill's description of the aliens that they encountered were just a spin-off of an *Outer Limits* episode that featured an alien called a "Bifrost" that was similar to aliens that the Hills described under hypnosis. According to Rational Wiki, the 1987 movie, *The UFO Incident* about the Hill abduction further placed the imagery of the Gray alien motif into the public's mind, followed up by Steven Spielberg's *Close Encounters of the Third Kind.* The Gray alien imagery was further confirmed in the public's mind with Whitley Strieber's best-selling 1987 book, *Communion.* Rational Wiki embraces Alvin Lawson's theory that the image of the Gray alien is derived from birth memories, along with Frederick V. Malmstrom's view, that the image of a Gray alien is what infants with poor eyesight see when they are born with doctors and nurses looking over them. Rational Wiki then points out the similarity between Gray alien abductions and myths of fairies, elves, and kobolds, which is territory covered by one of the finest scientific minds in modern ufology - Dr. Jacques Vallee. The difference is, Dr. Vallee's discovery of the connection between fairy lore and modern UFO accounts serves to ascertain that UFO encounters have been with us for centuries and have taken different forms over the years, whereas Rational Wiki attempts to dismiss modern UFO accounts as fantasy by making the same comparison. Rational Wiki makes no mention that the image of the Gray aliens are painted on ancient cave walls dating tens of thousands of years ago, and it does not occur to them that there may be some sort of symbiotic relationship between imagery in the collective human unconscious and the imagery that is presented to humans by a very real alien presence on Earth. In other words, the history of the Gray aliens that Rational Wiki uses to dismiss the entire subject of Gray aliens as fantasy is the very history that other astute researchers such as Dr. Jacques Vallee draw upon to ascertain that Gray aliens represent an actual reality to human beings that we simply do not understand very well.

Martin Kottmeyer (1953 -)

A UFO skeptic, Martin Kottmeyer earned an associate's degree in science, and made his living as a farmer. Through his many years of research, Kottmeyer became an expert in the history of UFO belief. Kottmeyer has written many articles for various magazines over the years. Kottmeyer is fascinating in that he equates the evolution of UFO belief over the decades to various stages of mass paranoia - and he is right. These paranoid themes of ufology entail "furtive activities, spying, and reconnaissance" (Donald Keyhoe), ideation of machine intelligences that conduct mind-control on humans (John Keel), global alien conspiracies and infiltration into Earth's political structure (David Icke), fears of imminent alien invasion (James Forrestal, Dr. David Jacobs, Timothy Good, and others), persecution (Dr. Karla Turner), miscegenation and degeneration, delusions of grandeur (George Adamski), cosmic identification (David Wilcock, Dr. Steven Greer), and a ubiquitous stream of world-destruction fantasies. Kottmeyer identifies what he felt were "insults to science" within ufology, such as the alien/human hybrid program or a belief in alien, human-sized bugs. Kottmeyer focused on the fact that the history of belief within the UFO community has morphed over the years, indicating a psychological explanation rather than a mechanical one, and points also to the many failed prophecies that have been perpetrated by UFO contactees (see the book, *When Prophecy Fails*). Martin Kottmeyer therefore recommends that our belief in UFOs be discontinued.

Is Martin Kottmeyer Correct?

Kottmeyer is correct in that the UFO phenomenon smacks of paranoia. However, Kottmeyer's views do not seem to acknowledge how many times throughout history that the paranoids were correct. If, in fact, we are all being invaded by an unknown and possibly alien intelligence, the derogatory label of "paranoia," which implies a set of beliefs that are not substantiated by reality, becomes "perceptive insight" into our situation. As Kottmeyer (and this book) has identified, the UFO phenomenon has morphed in imagery over the years. However, this change in UFO imagery over time is not due to the entire UFO phenomenon being a figment of the human imagination, but is rather an indication that the aliens are interconnected with the human field of consciousness, which naturally evolves as we become more knowledgeable about the nature of the universe. For example, the smartphones of 2017 make Captain Kirk's flip-open communicator from the original *Star Trek* series look like a child's toy. If you are reading this book in 2025 or beyond, you are probably laughing right now that I think my Apple Iphone6 is advanced. I get the humor, and I am already jealous of what you are using now. However, at the time, that communication device from the *Star Trek* television series was state-of-the-art futurism. Who is to say that Captain Kirk's flip-phone communicator, a piece of pure science fiction, wasn't someone's inspiration for the first flip-open cell phones? Kottmeyer's correct identification of the phenomenon of imagery evolution within UFO reports is important, even though it understandably lacks insight into what is actually going on. As the intelligences behind the UFO phenomenon adjust to our evolving imagery of spacecraft designs and aliens that exists within the energy field of the human collective unconscious, the projected apparitional images, as well as the transmogrified physical objects that percipients experience morphs over time to keep just ahead of us. What began as clunky, Adamski-style flying saucers in the 1950s sleeked out over time. Now the cutting edge of alien spacecraft perceptions are akin to the black triangles people report, as well as the pulsating light orbs in the sky that morph into structured light-crafts. Light ships are in vogue now, and one can only wonder what the next stage in spacecraft evolution will be as we evolve our consciousness as a species. This conceptual evolution of spacecraft also applies to the appearance of ufonauts. The ufonauts of 1897 were normal-looking bearded men, inventors of marvelous airships. The ufonauts of the 1950s morphed into handsome men and beautiful females who were inhabitants of Mars or Venus. From the 1960s forward, the ufonauts were benevolent Nordic blondes from the Pleiades, or Gray aliens from Zeta Reticuli 1 or 2. The entire concept of who and what our visitors are has changed over the decades, but that doesn't take away the reality that we are being visited by a variety of nonhuman intelligences. We just don't know at this point what the aliens actually look like. Something fantastic is occurring in our skies and in our minds that currently lies beyond our full comprehension. This may always be the case, especially if what I am postulating in this book turns out to be correct. There are certainly elements of paranoia within the minds of UFO researchers. In fact, the more one researches the phenomenon, the more paranoid one actually becomes. That doesn't mean that the paranoia is unjustified. There is something formidable going on within the human psyche regarding UFOs that I believe warrants a fair dose of paranoia. Betty Cash, Vickie Landrum, Steve Michalak, and many other UFO percipients did not receive their radiation sickness from an ordinary hallucination. Thousands of people disappear each year without a trace, and the animal (and sometimes human) mutilations continue. UFO investigators are murdered. As Keel once said, "Something out there loathes us." Therefore, a measure of paranoia is warranted.

Alvin Lawson (1930 – 2010)

Alvin Lawson received his AB degree from the University of California in 1952, and earned a Ph.D. from Stanford. He was a professor of English at the University of California for three decades. For a decade, from 1974-1984, Lawson taught a class in UFOs called *UFO Literature: The Rhetoric of the Unknown*. Lawson ran a UFO hotline from his home and took calls from UFO experiencers. This led Lawson and a colleague, Dr. W.C. McCall, to develop a set of experiments called the *Hypnosis of Imaginary Abductees Study*. They determined from these experiments that there was little difference between UFO abductees and those who *imagined* UFO abduction experiences. Lawson then formulated the *Birth Memories Hypothesis*. This theory postulated (as RationalWiki explains so well) that UFO abductees are simply re-experiencing embedded memories of birth. Infants have poor eyesight. According to Lawson's theory, the abductee's memories (usually retrieved in hypnosis), in which Gray aliens work over them and conduct medical experiments, may actually represent memories of doctors in gowns and surgical masks using surgical instruments during their births. Despite the fact that much of Lawson's research was conducted right in the middle of a major UFO flap that occurred in 1973, Lawson considered himself a "UFO agnostic." Despite Lawson's research and theories concerning the alien abduction phenomenon, Lawson maintained that UFOs were likely to be physically real but of an unknown nature. In other words, UFO reports may represent legitimate sightings of real objects, but Lawson felt that it was presumptuous to jump to the conclusion that they are alien spacecraft. Lawson referred to UFOs as "physically real whatevers." The UFO abduction experience, however, was an entirely different matter. Lawson remained a skeptic concerning

UFO abductions based on his own experiments and personal research. Lawson concluded that UFO abductions were but archetypal fantasies of a traumatic entrance into the world, in which one was surrounded by medical professionals.

Was Lawson Correct?

Lawson was likely correct in that most UFO abduction experiences, real or imagined, are non-physical in nature or occur in an alternate reality. As such, UFO abduction reports are sometimes (perhaps more often than not) muddied with human fantasy. The body of alien abduction reports likely includes experiences that occur during hypnagogic and hypnopomic states. Hypnagogia involves "threshold consciousness," during which a person experiences psychological manifestations on the way from wakefulness to sleep. Hypnagogia is a common, half-dream state that can induce lucid dreaming, hallucinations, and even sleep paralysis. Sleep paralysis, in which a person experiences premature onset of atonia as one drifts off to sleep, is thought by some researchers to be the underlying cause of the "shadow people" phenomenon or the "Old Hag" haunting. Hypnopompic experiences, on the other hand, occur during the psychological transition of arousal from REM (rapid eye movement) sleep to waking consciousness. Sleep paralysis can also occur during this arousal process as well. Hypnopompic experiences are thought to result from depressed frontal lobe function, called "sleep inertia," which can present with impaired short-term memory, impaired reaction times, and what psychologist Peter McKeller called "hypnopompic speech," where a person engages in incoherent speech as they come out of a deep sleep (*Abnormal Psychology*, 1989). In the hypnopompic state, vivid dream imagery and creative insight flood a person's consciousness. It is reasonable to conclude that at least some UFO abduction reports result from one or both of these two different common sleep states. Much of what we dream comes from conscious thoughts and experiences. During the heyday of the abduction phenomenon, which was epidemic in the 1970s, television shows and articles involving alien abduction were probably responsible for providing material for "copy-cat" visions in altered sleep states that the experiencer believed to represent physical reality. There is also little doubt that intentionally-induced alien abduction experiences produced by electronic equipment built by humans and perpetrated on unwitting human victims have, in fact, occurred. As Keel reported, people have actually been drugged, pulled into unmarked vans, and convinced that their encounter was of an alien nature during both clandestine intelligence projects and possibly civilian organizations for whatever their purposes of deception were. All these exotic yet terrestrial explanations for alien abductions occur despite the fact that Earth has an actual alien presence that has attached itself within the human unconscious for centuries now. This alien intelligence is of an interdimensional nature and of a higher order of intelligence than human. The UFO intelligences have access to the evolution of human thinking and internal brain imagery as we are guided toward the Singularity. This unidentified, alien presence has also been responsible at times for both the physical and paraphysical versions of the alien abduction phenomenon for their own purposes. The intelligences behind actual so-called "alien abductions" are, no doubt, fully aware of the obfuscation created by reports of both hypnagogic and hypnopompic sleep experiences. These naturally-occurring experiences serve the purpose of creating doubt among skeptics concerning the alien presence on Earth, and hide the actual nature of the real phenomenon, burying a possibly hostile agenda within the framework of explainable human psychology.

Dr. David Jacobs (1943 -)

Countering Alvin Lawson's assessments and theories, that the alien abduction phenomenon can be written off as hypnopompic and hypnagogic experiences and birthing memories is abduction researcher Dr. David M. Jacobs, who has used regressive hypnotism on abductees for five decades and has arrived at startling conclusions and evidence for the physical reality of alien abductions.

David Jacobs earned a Ph.D. in history from the University of Wisconsin in 1973. Jacobs presented his doctorate thesis on UFOs, which appeared in his book, *The UFO Controversy in America* two years later in 1975. Dr. Jacobs then taught a college class called *UFOs in American Society* for the next 25 years. Dr. Jacobs has appeared on countless radio and television programs concerning the subject of alien abductions. Over the course of his five decades of research into the alien abduction phenomenon, he noticed that over the years the narratives changed, and that these changes in narratives were occurring cross-culturally around the world. When alien abductions were first reported, the abductions were described as the typical medical procedures on a table aboard an alien craft. From there abductees began telling of the removal of eggs and sperm for the production of human/alien hybrids. Dr. Jacobs has experience with clients who became pregnant and then at some point, the pregnancy disappeared with no chance of a mistaken miscarriage. After years of this common dialogue, abductees began relating abduction experiences in which they were asked to hold an alien/human hybrid aboard an alien spacecraft. Others began reporting that they were shown films of hybrid children interacting with normal human children. The abductees were then asked if they could distinguish the hybrid children in appearance from the normal human children. These narratives evolved over the years in various ways, until they finally reported being abducted, not to an alien spacecraft, but to apartments here on Earth, for the purpose of teaching hybrid teenagers how to live in an apartment, where various types of furniture go, how to drive an automobile, and all the mundane tasks and procedures a young hybrid transplant would have to know how to do if they went from life aboard a spacecraft to life here on Earth and wanted to remain undetected. This change in abduction scenario finally led Jacobs to accept the fact that the hybrid program was in its final stage of completion. In his latest book, *Walking Among Us: The Alien Plan to Control Humanity* (2015), Jacobs made the case for the physical reality of the alien abduction phenomenon and believes that hybridized human beings who have received a genetic upgrade and may start demonstrating high IQs and extrasensory perceptions or even superpowers, now live among the general human population in preparation for an eventual takeover of planet Earth by the Gray aliens. Other books by Dr. Jacobs that were written prior to his report of the most recent abduction narratives, when abduction scenarios were in various stages of development, include *Secret Life: Firsthand Accounts of UFO Abductions* (1992), *The Threat: Revealing the Secret Alien Agenda* (1999), and *UFOs and Abductions: Challenging the Borders of Knowledge* (2000).

Although Dr. Jacobs states that he fully realizes just how crazy his conclusions sound and doesn't blame anyone for not believing him, he believes that this is what has been going on and that alien/human hybrids are now among us and are here to stay. In other words, humanity 3.0 is the future now. Personally, Dr. Jacobs confesses to harboring a fair amount of fear and apprehension over this situation. This likely stems from a sense of sadness or depression that the old humans, as he has always known them, are going to the wayside and being replaced by a new model. However, I think it is actually great news if Dr. Jacobs' conclusions are correct. Let me explain. One of my fears, as I have already expressed, is that once the Singularity is here, humans will be discarded like old shoes, having completed what we were created to do for our alien overlords. However, if they have been mixing their own DNA with ours, or they have become intellectually invested in their upgrade of human DNA in some other way, and have now planted alien/human hybrids or otherwise genetically-upgraded humans on Earth now, that means they have skin in the game (pardon the pun) and may be less likely to destroy us post-singularity. Also, the hybrids are now presumably breeding with non-hybridized or non-upgraded humans of the opposite sex and producing children with alien DNA, altered, or turned-on genes in their makeup. This does not bother me at all because if Dr. Jacobs is correct, this is probably not the first time in human history that a genetic intervention or upgrade has taken place. As stated, there is no way that a four-foot-tall *Australopithecine* with a brain the size of an orange could have suddenly transformed into *Homo erectus* overnight at about two million years ago. *Homo erectus* was a much taller humanoid with a brain three times the size of its immediate alleged predecessor. Furthermore, life on Earth has likely been seeded by aliens and manipulated from time to time for billions of years now. If that is the case, and the Intervention Theorists are right, the genetic manipulation of human DNA is standard procedure, so why should we fear what we are to become now that the human race has been altered again? The conclusions of Dr. Jacobs, that an alien/human hybridization program has been at play for decades, has evolved over time, and has now placed successfully-upgraded humans on Earth who are now 15-60 years old at the time of this writing (2016), actually provides encouragement that the human race may not be targeted for destruction after all. If Dr. Jacobs' theories are correct, and an alteration of humanity has already occurred, people very easily forget about poorly-understood events that have allegedly happened in the past. By the time 2045-2080 arrives, the UFO phenomenon from 1947-2020 or so may just be remembered as a historical anomaly and completely forgotten. Everyone living in the future will just assume that the way humans are then is normal, a product of Nature's own evolution, and they may actually be right. Perhaps abductees who have experienced a personal encounter with alien scientists have gained a firsthand look at how evolution actually works. What we humans perceive as the mechanisms of Nature may, in fact, involve a host of helpers of higher-order intelligence who know more about reality than we do and are operating on a different level of reality than we are for the benefit of the creatures of the physical realm in various locations throughout the universe. Those of us who have been around to observe and listen to testimonies as this most recent human upgrade has unfolded probably have experienced a very unique glimpse into the situation. We know something has been going on (despite what skeptics say), and now that the upgraded alien/hybrids or genetically-upgraded humans are here, we can watch and see how this affects human behavior and human society in the future. We can witness the evolution of the human organism from this point forward with a unique window of insight into how some of Nature's marvels actually happen with intelligent intervention by higher-order beings of the cosmos.

Coral E. Lorenzen (1925-1988)

Coral Lorenzen, who experienced her first UFO sighting in 1934 and her second sighting in 1947, was a prolific author of many classic books on UFOs, and an indispensable contributor to the field of UFO research. Coral cofounded APRO (Aerial Phenomenon Research Organization) with her husband, Jim Lorenzen, in 1952. Coral felt that there was too much "lone investigation" happening. She encouraged more cooperation among fellow ufologists to share their information, speculations, and philosophies. In my opinion, Coral's insights were ahead of her time, as she described the UFO enigma as multifaceted in nature, and felt that more time will have to pass, along with more investigations, to arrive at any type of true understanding of the phenomenon. Coral explored many theories in her career in the pages of her books, but was left with the feeling that, underneath it all, an extraterrestrial explanation is at hand. I generally agree with her position, although the details of the ET presence are currently beyond the clear grasp of humanity. Coral was critical of so-called "scientists" who dismiss the UFO phenomenon out of hand. Anyone with decent critical thinking skills who has exposed themselves to even the most cursory look at the UFO literature will discover good information that they were previously unaware of that has profound significance to humankind. This presumptuous dismissal of UFOs by the skeptics not only represents a blatant and unforgivable argument from ignorance, but an arrogant assertion of authority while doing so. Considering the large number of stars in the universe, Coral accepted the inevitability that alien populations exist who have mastered whatever propulsion problems there are in traversing the large distances from galaxy to galaxy. Whatever the underlying nature of our alien visitation turns out to be, Coral felt that it is reasonable, considering the large volume of information that we have at our disposal concerning UFO sightings and ufonaut encounters, to conclude that something real is going on here on Earth that we do not yet understand correctly.

Jim Lorenzen (1923-1987)

Jim Lorenzen, Coral Lorenzen's husband and cofounder of APRO, was from Minnesota. Jim made a living as a musician until he was inducted into the US Army Air Corps in 1942, where he served for three years as a radio operator and mechanic. Upon his discharge from service, Jim returned to playing music for 5 years until earning a first-class radio/telephone license and working in the field of communications. In 1954 he joined Telecomputing Corporation at Holloman Air Force Base, New Mexico. In 1960 Jim became senior technical associate with the Kitt Peak National Observatory in Tucson, Arozona, where he worked until 1967 to go into the electronic organ business. During all this time Jim co-authored many UFO books with his wife, Coral, such as: *Flying Saucer Occupants* (1967); *UFOs Over the Americas* (1968); *UFOs: The Whole Story* (1969); *Encounters with UFO Occupants* (1976); *and Abducted!* (1977).

Jim's contention was that the UFO phenomenon is extremely complex and multifaceted. Jim was somewhat critical of authors like John Keel, who attempted to simplify all unexplainable phenomenon, many of which may be unrelated to one another, under the comforting umbrella of one giant meta-phenomenon. This postulated meta-phenomenon supposedly explains all of the strange enigmas that haunt this planet, from Sasquatch to cryptids and poltergeists. I find one of Jim's observations rather profound when he questioned whether it was science fiction or science fact that preceded and/or influenced the other. My contention is that science fiction and science fact are a Mobius loop that have a symbiotic relationship with one another. What we call science fiction may occasionally involve intentionally-planted information that enters our collective human consciousness by occulted Space Intelligences. Jim expressed frustration over the mixing of solid, scientifically-confirmed UFO reports, such as multiple credible witness reports and radar-confirmations, with the subjective absurdities of contactees that may have no basis in fact or may represent other types of psychologically-driven phenomenon, such as incidents of sleep paralysis and/or intentional or unintentional confabulations of various types. Another observation made over the years by Jim Lorenzen was equally astute. Jim concluded that many UFO reports represent "nuts-and-bolts" cases of solid objects that can be scientifically examined, while others may represent a kind of psychic projection based on UFO viral rumors, the internal needs of the percipient, or both. Jim often expressed his irritation that conventional scientists are turned off by the more subjective UFO accounts, which leads them to write the whole subject off as fantasy. Personally, I feel that this process of obfuscation by absurdity is intentional on the part of the UFO intelligences to provide cover for the "nuts-and-bolts" non-terrestrial vehicles in our skies. Also, leading the mainstream human scientific community to conclude that "there are no flying saucers" frees up the minds of the scientists to do the work for the aliens that is actually intended. That is, to build the artificial intelligence platforms that these UFO intelligences have been patiently working on for thousands, possibly millions of years. Behind the scenes, these intelligences have been guiding humankind to ever-increasing technology. In other words, while our scientists are busy distancing themselves from the absurdity of the UFO phenomenon, they are the actual unwitting slaves to our invisible Overlords. The Overlords, interacting with humanity from an interdimensional realm that may or may not be indigenous to Earth, or from a parallel universe, have apparently employed us for their own purposes. With the advent of the Singularity, the aliens might finally be able to enter our realm using consciousness-bearing artificial intelligence that has been constructed by the very scientists who deny that there even is a UFO phenomenon. Ironic, isn't it?

Jim Lorenzen made other excellent postulations during his career as a UFO investigator and author that I find myself agreeing with. That is, even though Jim felt that the "core" of the UFO conundrum was extraterrestrial in nature, he explained the more bizarre fringes of the phenomenon as either coming from one or more advanced cultures whose technology and motives we do not currently understand, or intentional deception of "witnesses" by said intelligences for purposes of counter-intelligence. I say Jim pegged it – it is a near-certainty that both of those elements are in play on this planet. In the end, Jim applauded the overall UFO mystery, as it has caused humanity to think and ponder, and realize that there is more to this universe than is currently perceived, and for that reason alone, Jim Lorenzen felt that ultimately the UFO phenomenon has induced an elevation of consciousness within the minds of humanity, and I would have to agree. I know it has for me, as my NDE in 2009 sparked my journey into the Phenomenon. Following this experience that demonstrated to me the interdimensional nature of reality, I left my previous, comfortable worldview of the rational skeptic and embarked for the fringes for the first time in my life. Since that turning point, I have never regretted it, and I have never looked back.

Bruce Maccabee (1942-)

Dr. Bruce Maccabee, an optical physicist, originally received his BS in physics from Worcester Polytechnic Institute in Massachusetts in 1964. He then went on to earn an MS degree and a Ph.D. in physics from American University in Washington, D.C. Dr. Maccabee is the Chairman of the Fund for UFO Research, the State Director for MUFON in Maryland, and is a member of the Scientific Board for the J. Allen Hynek Center for UFO Studies (CUFOS). Dr. Maccabee has appeared on several television programs and co-authored several books on UFOs including *UFOs Are Real, Here's the Proof* (1997), and The *UFO-FBI Connection* (2000).

Dr. Maccabee tends to see an extraterrestrial explanation for the more scientifically ascertainable UFO cases, but remains open to a psychological explanation for other cases. I empathize with Dr. Maccabee's overall assessment that we do not currently have enough information to positively identify the intelligences behind the UFO phenomenon. We don't really know, and can only speculate, whether the unknown intelligences behind the UFOs are interplanetary; interdimensional; purely psychological; emanating from the earth itself; from the collective human unconscious; a parallel world; or something else that we are not even able to think of right now. All the evidence of history that I am looking at to make an assessment of the benign or malevolent intent of these intelligences, whoever or whatever they turn out to be, is admittedly circumstantial and based on my own limited human perceptions of good and evil. My own perceptions are likely influenced to some degree by my own paranoia of advanced technology in general. One thought that Dr. Maccabee left us with concerning his position on UFOs can be paraphrased like this:

It is time for the scientific community to realize that there is, in fact, something real going on with UFOs that is both scientifically ascertainable and, at the same time, lies beyond our current human perceptions and understanding, a reality that possibly holds the key to something important concerning the relationship between humans and the rest of the cosmos.

Scott Mandelker (1962 -)

Scott Mandelker was a resident of San Francisco, California. Mandelker earned a Ph.D. in East-West psychology, an MA in counseling, and practiced Zen Buddhism and Vipassana for 20 years. He gave many presentations at UFO conferences and for MUFON, and appeared on many television and radio programs. Judging by his books, his interests primarily involved individuals who claim they are extraterrestrial souls living on Earth. His books include *From Elsewhere: Being ET in America* (1995), *Universal Vision: Soul Evolution and the Cosmic Plan* (2000), which discusses the cosmic plan behind ET contact, and other spiritual issues such as healing, finding emotional balance, and mystical meditation. Mandelker reports that he has personal experience with paranormal phenomena. Mandelker has little doubt that some UFOs are extraterrestrial and originate from other star systems, but he also incorporates an interdimensional paradigm, proposing that some UFOs are holographic thoughtforms and plasma energy devices. This position sounds feasible, as some experiencers such as Betty Andreasson have had encounters with intelligent aliens who used paraphysical technology to produce projections of themselves, their alleged "craft," and their home world. Whether these images are an accurate depiction of their true selves and home planets is unknown. Mandelker and I both agree that *the aliens use energy gleaned from their percipient's own minds concerning what they expect an alien to look like. They use these brain-scans to adopt a humanoid form so as not to horrify their subjects or even kill them from fright.* It is also the humanoid alien reports from experiencers that keep the majority of the scientific community at bay. The scientifically-minded often relegate all such reports of humanoid aliens to the realm of fantasy. It doesn't seem to occur to these armchair-scientist types that nonhuman aliens from an advanced culture would have the technology to appear as they wish to otherworldly populations encountered on alien planets in space. Scott Mandelker believes

that the earth is visited routinely by a variety of ET races, and has a rather cut-and-dried opinion of their intentions – the ETs are either friendly or they are not. He points directly to the
teachings of Ageless Wisdom and all the earth's religions in this matter. This view corroborates
with William Bramley's findings in *The Gods of Eden*, that there are two different ET forces
operating on Earth, one that his beneficent toward humans, and one that is not. Perhaps there
are groups of entities from various realms who fall into one category or another. Judging by the
solid Italian "Friendship Case," there are, in fact, ETs on Earth in portable underground and
undersea bases that are friendly to humans, or at least present themselves as such. The aliens
in the Amicizia group appear as pleasant-looking humanoids, or are at least able to appear to
humans in that form. The Amicizia, or AKRIJ, travel in physical flying saucers that have been
filmed and confirmed as authentic by expert digital video analysts using state-of-the-art equipment as solid, real, physical objects. The aliens involved with the Friendship Case also appear
to be at odds with another group of aliens on Earth, perhaps the ever-present von Neumann
probes who have an interest in our technology as we approach the Singularity. Our best hope
is that these humanoid aliens are for real, that they actually do have our best interest at heart,
and are here to help see us into the Singularity without being overly abused by competing alien
interests from other worlds who would toss us like an old rag once their purposes are achieved.

Scott Mandelker believes that open contact will happen at some point, but shares my prediction that, if open contact were to actually happen today, it would make little difference in
the minds of many skeptics. Conspiracy theorists would come out of the closet who disbelieve
that it actually happened, or attribute the event to a theatrical government program of deception. Fundamentalist Christians, many of whom have already decided that the ufonauts are
demons, would continue to believe that the aliens are demonic, even if the aliens demonstrated
good intentions. After all, Satan himself was once an angel of light, can still appear as such,
and is the father of lies, or so they will say. Others will want to worship the aliens as "cosmic
saviors," even if this is discouraged by the aliens themselves. Scott Mandelker believes in the
advent of a *Golden Age* in which humans who are ready for it experience open contact with other
civilizations. This coming Golden Age will be an era of cooperation and mutual learning and
benefit that the world has never seen. I sincerely hope that he is right. However, judging by
the long history of damaged lives; radiation burns; deaths; possible genetic manipulation of humans by aliens that intentionally built in flaws to the human body to possibly push a dire need
for technology to overcome these challenges; and possible manipulation into wars according
to researchers like Bramley; I remain skeptical and vigilant, but continue to hope for the best
concerning the intentions of aliens.

Tim Matthews (1967-)
Tim Matthews earned an Honours degree in classical music from the University of Lancaster,
and was an English UFO researcher with an avid interest in the paranormal. Tim's focus

and contribution to the UFO community is his research concerning man-made UFOs. Tim's 1999 book, *UFO Revelation: The Secret Technology Exposed?* courageously and controversially proposes that many of the classic UFO sightings, such as the Trent photos from McMinnville, Oregon, Operation Mainbrace, the Belgian black triangle sightings, and the spectacular Hudson Valley sightings, were actually secret military projects of circular and triangular configuration. One aspect of Tim's views that I appreciate is that, even though his is one of the world's experts on American and British secret military aircraft, he does not use his area of expertise to say that all UFO sightings are of this nature. He reminds readers that 90% of all UFO sightings have mundane explanations, and within the 10% remaining, many have terrestrial explanations that are hidden from public knowledge for military reasons. However, Tim is also interested in the paranormal, and points out that we know very little about the mysterious "earthlights" and other strange phenomena that exist on our planet. Tim remains open that some of the UFOs are of a nature that we currently do not understand. What appeals to me about Tim's position, of course, is that he leaves room for speculation that there is a presence on Earth that is normally invisible to us, that has possibly been here for aeons, and is able to manifest itself in various ways that will further its own agenda, such as guiding humankind toward a technological singularity for a possible merger of consciousness and/or opportunity for physical incarnation into this three-dimensional realm, a realm that these intelligences are only able to manifest themselves in temporarily until a suitable biomechanical robot is fashioned in this realm that can serve as a host for their discarnate minds. Historical cases of "demon-possession" were possibly attempts made by these hidden intelligences to enter our physical realm via a human host, which can only contain these entities for a short while. Whether these intelligences who are attempting to enter our world are disembodied humans with so much negative Karma built up that they are not allowed or cannot return to Earth as they wish, or actual alien entities who have traveled across the vast reaches of the universe in a purely mental format and seek a more permanent residence here, we cannot be certain. Whatever the case, there is reason to exercise caution. The Fundamentalist Christians may also be correct in their end-time eschatology, with demonic entities waiting from their own prison-dimension for humans to achieve the Singularity so that they can enter our realm and engage in a final war-to-end-all-wars against the armies of Jesus Christ and his angels, who may also be extraterrestrials or Post-Singularity Artificial Superintelligence (PSASI). Sometimes I get the feeling that the entire scenario is really so far beyond the pale of human comprehension, that what is really going on, although some have come close to the actual answers, escapes us completely, as the entities involved are of a higher order of intelligence than we are. We are like spiders wondering who is striking at our webs with a broom. Tim's excellent contribution was to peel yet another layer of mystery from the UFO sightings that are possible secret military projects, and when one does that to the extent that he suggests, the real UFOs that are left appear to represent a paranormal phenomenon that is totally beyond our understanding at this point in time.

Dr. James E. McDonald (1920 - 1971)

James McDonald taught meteorology at Iowa State College while working on his Ph.D. in physics, and continued teaching after be became Dr. James McDonald. During the 1960s, McDonald, an atmospheric physicist, was one of the main proponents of the Extraterrestrial Hypothesis (ETH). McDonald played a central role in the Congressional UFO hearings of 1968. He was a disciplined, hard-science guy, who attempted to share his interest in UFOs with the rest of the scientific community and encountered many frustrations and hardships in doing so. McDonald was very critical of the methods of operation within Project Blue Book, and the sham called the Condon Committee (of which he was a part). McDonald was also angry with Hynek for not going public with what he knew about UFOs and for maintaining the role of public debunker in order to make his living. McDonald was convinced that UFOs were important for the scientific community to take seriously, and was met with much opposition from his peers. Dr. James McDonald was a scientific consultant for the National Science Foundation, the National Academy of Sciences, the Office of Naval Research, and the Environmental Science Service Administration that was later known as the National Oceanic and Atmospheric Association. Dr. James E. McDonald was a brilliant scientist. He was continually frustrated with his fellow science colleagues over their blatantly unscientific approach to the subject of UFOs. McDonald felt that even if there was only a slight chance that some UFOs were interplanetary, that would warrant rigorous scientific investigation. McDonald personally interviewed hundreds of UFO witnesses, researched thousands of UFO reports, and felt the most likely explanation was the ETH. He demonstrated astute insight in that, when the deluge of UFO reality is suddenly thrust upon the public in the future, the scientific community at large will be held fully accountable for dropping the ball on this subject and keeping it hidden from public knowledge. Of particular interest to McDonald were the close-range, credible sightings of flying saucers and flying saucer landing and occupant encounter reports. McDonald felt that the sooner the scientific community acknowledged that there was something real going on with UFOs, the less embarrassment they will experience when the phenomenon finally comes out of the darkness and into the light for everyone to see. McDonald was dismayed that the majority of UFO landing and occupant encounters go unreported for fear of ridicule or losing their jobs. Ironically, this is exactly what happened to McDonald. When Edward U. Condon of the Condon Committee with the University of Colorado figured out that James McDonald was pro-UFO, Ed Condon fired McDonald from the committee. When the Condon Report came out in 1969, and was completely discouraging and dismissive of scientific UFO investigations, much ridicule was thrust upon the scientists who were open about entertaining UFO reality, and McDonald was among their ranks. This led to painful personal ridicule heaped upon McDonald. After losing his job over his position on UFOs, his wife left him as well. Following his wife leaving him for a younger man, Dr. James McDonald, one of the greats in the field of scientific ufology, sadly committed suicide. In author Richard Dolan's book, *A.D. After Disclosure: When the Government Finally Reveals the Truth About Alien Contact*, Dolan discusses the terrible and tragic ridicule that has been unjustly perpetrated on UFO researchers and experiencers over the decades by the scientific community. Dolan is looking forward to the day, as I am, that these folks, especially those who have come face to face with entities from other worlds or realms, are finally exonerated and given the respect and credibility they deserve.

Donald H. Menzel (1901-1976)

Dr. Donald Menzel was certainly an enigmatic figure. Menzel was a professional astronomer with a Ph.D. in astrophysics from Princeton University, and taught astronomy at the University of Iowa. According to nuclear physicist and UFO researcher Stanton Friedman, who investigated Menzel's life extensively, Menzel led a double life, one as a public debunker of UFOs who wrote books on how natural phenomena were easily mistaken by credulous people as spacecraft from another world, and another secret life that involved serious UFO investigation and intelligence with the clandestine UFO investigative organization, MJ-12, otherwise known as Majestic 12 or Majesty 12. Publicly, Menzel presented himself as someone who took the typical scientific position of the day, that there were probably other civilizations out there in the universe, but due to the tremendous distances and fuel requirements, etc., it is unlikely that they would be coming here in the numbers of cases that are reported. Menzel's public position involved the tendency for Man to create myths around anything he can't understand. He briefed individuals working with Project Blue Book. Menzel's stated positions irritated those who adhered to the Extraterrestrial Hypothesis (ETH). Some who listened to Menzel were inspired to reorganize the project around 1954 to more of a debunking organization than a serious investigation of UFO reports. Donald Menzel made a prediction that obviously did not come true, that public interest in UFOs would decline in the following years in lieu of the new fad – astrology, which he believed served a similar psychological need in human beings. Menzel also predicted that scientists of the 21st century will look back at the whole UFO era as just a viral wave of utter nonsense that swept the country. Menzel recommended strongly that the US government withdraw completely from UFO investigations. Menzel's prediction that public interest in UFOs would soon die out was about as far away from what was to come as one could get. Public interest in UFOs has never been higher than at the time of this writing. Modern theoretical physicists, scientists, and authors like Michio Kaku, Roger Penrose, Brian Greene, and others who are involved in quantum mechanics lend to a totally updated and new vision of UFOs, that UFOs may represent an emergent phenomenon from other dimensions, and that, instead of coming from another galaxy with all of the usual associated physics problems, at least some UFOs might represent something terrestrial that we do not understand yet, such as parallel worlds or alternate dimensions that are around us at all times. If it is true, as Stanton Friedman insists, that Donald Menzel was involved with a secretive organization who investigated UFOs, he may have been aware of the interdimensional nature of the phenomenon and was aware of what an impact this knowledge would have on the public at large. Not only that, but if Menzel was privy to the actual nature of UFOs, he may have been sincere, not only in steering public attention away from the Extraterrestrial Hypothesis (ETH), but contributing to getting the US government out of the UFO investigation business, a move that I agree with, as the US government has better ways to spend its time than chasing UFO reports around the globe since most of them are, in fact, misidentifications of natural phenomena and are a total waste of time and money to look into. When an actual flying saucer makes an appearance, it is gone just as mysteriously as it appeared. There is generally nothing left to see. In 95% of UFO reports, what an investigator has to deal with upon arriving at the scene is an individual who has more than likely mistaken something in the sky for an alien spacecraft. The other 5% is a subjective phenomenon that is untraceable in any objective sense. Since that is the case, I agree that the government should stay out of it and allow private investigations to continue to collect data to correlate reports, like they have been doing effectively since Project Blue Book shut down in 1969. Donald Menzel was right. Even if Menzel was an insider, as Friedman contends, chasing flying saucers, just like chasing after ghosts, is one of the most futile endeavors that one can engage in. Both of these phenomenon, which are strangely related in some sense, appear selectively to individuals and groups for their own purposes, and then they are gone, leaving behind a subjective report from traumatized witnesses that everyone has a difficult time believing. It would be better for experiencers to seek out other experiencers and find comfort there, because the world at large usually thinks that they have gone nuts, and that is exactly the intention of the UFO intelligences themselves as they utilize the minds and the technical abilities of humankind to move toward a technological singularity, at which time everyone will discover, if I am correct, that their mission on Earth is complete.

Dr. Aime Michel (1919-1992)

Dr. Aime Michel was a French mathematician and engineer who retired in 1975 and devoted himself to a life of personal study. His background in sound and musical harmony gave him unusual insight into the true nature of flying saucers, as Michel understood frequencies and vibrations. Michel was also interested in animal communication and wrote several articles on the subject. His main contribution to ufology was the concept of *Orthoteny*. Michel discovered that sighting reports occurring on the same day could be plotted in straight lines. This fact indicated that the reports represented a real phenomenon rather than multiple people having hallucinatory experiences. Dr. Aime Michel, whose academic and professional accomplishments are way too long to list, wrote two books that remain highly influential in the UFO literature, *The Truth About Flying Saucers* (1954) and *Flying Saucers and the Straight Line Mystery*

(1958). Michel was correct in his postulation that to grasp the nature of flying saucers, one must reconstitute their thinking completely on the order of a Copernican Revolution. He was quick to remind us that other stars and galaxies have been around for billions of years before the advent of humans. Humans on Earth are likely the newcomers to the universe, and really have no idea what is out there. As such, humans need to keep our minds open. Michel was critical of the notion that humans represent the pinnacle of Creation, and postulated the existence of higher intelligences in the universe beyond the comprehension of the human mind. Michel believed that humans have a difficult time contemplating the nature of higher intelligence without falling into the realm of religion or superstition. Michel, in my opinion, was a man of high intellect and way ahead of his time. Michel postulated that UFOs may represent a phenomenon that is presently non-understandable to human beings. He believed that the UFO intelligences may have existed on Earth since the dawn of our solar system, or even taken part in its organization and structure, a belief that I personally share. I also agree with Michel in his assertion that the UFO phenomenon in all of its complexity represents *exactly* what one would expect if humanity were confronted by such higher intelligence. This is contrary to many of the mainstream scientists who already have a concept in their minds about how an extraterrestrial presence would behave, and reject the vast body of evidence available to us because the reports do not conform to their preconceived ideas in this matter. I also agree with Michel's contention that the human species may represent some infantile version of life in the universe, and that we may be looked upon as a precious commodity by beings who have transcended the human psychic milieu completely and have the ability to travel anywhere in the universe they wish in a fashion that is unfathomable to existing populations who are still going through such an elementary stage of cosmic evolution. Keeping in mind my postulation that humanity will, at last, experience open contact, for better or worse, during the coming Singularity, the words of Aime Michel rang profoundly true to me when he stated the following (MEEE, pg. 422):

In my opinion, the non-contact phase will last until we ourselves discover the method of contact. To discover the method will require a profound transformation of mankind. It is not certain that we will find it. It is not certain that our evolution has not already missed the path that would lead to contact (good or bad). Nonetheless my opinion is that the scientific path is the right way; but it is long and dangerous, and the contact may have good or bad results.

I found these words of wisdom by Aime Michel quite haunting, especially when he said that we may have already lost our chance. When I consider the 1952 Washington D.C. flyby, in which multiple flying saucers may have attempted an open interaction with humanity, the "landing on the White House Lawn" that all the skeptics seek, only to be met with armed jets dispatched with shoot-to-kill orders, I can't help but wonder if we blew our chances for open contact at that time, even though I have a tendency to think that this incident, and possibly many others, or all of them, were but a strategic appearance to mold the human belief structure in a way that was conducive to inspiring us to greater technological accomplishment. In other words, inter-dimensional travelers may not be able to communicate with pre-singularity, biological societies, as the technology that enables such a meaningful communication does not exist yet.

James W. Moseley (1931-2012)

Every social movement in society needs a comedian. For several decades, the UFO community was served well in this capacity by James W. Moseley. An astute UFO researcher, Moseley also published his satirical newsletter called *Saucer Smear* with the clever tagline, "Shockingly Close to the Truth!" Inspired by the Kenneth Arnold sighting and the death of Captain Mantell, Moseley contributed a half century to UFO research. Moseley also had an avid interest in archaeology. He owned a Pre-Columbian art gallery in Key West, Florida, where he sold arti-facts from Peru, South America, and Africa. Like many early UFO researchers, Moseley began his journey into UFO research with the common view of his era, that all genuine unknowns were extraterrestrial spaceships. He also adopted the position that all contactees were lying hucksters. As we know, during the 1950s, contactee stories were anathema to the UFO buffs due to the absurdities in their personal accounts. These absurdities turned off serious UFO investigators, who assumed that UFOs were visitors from other planets. For a while, Moseley toyed with the idea that UFOs might be secret, foreign, terrestrial weapons, but eventually stuck to his guns with the Extraterrestrial Hypothesis (ETH). Moseley then began reading works by John Keel and Allen Greenfield. He eventually leaned toward the interdimensional hypothesis (IDH), i.e., that UFOs are psychic events manifested by intelligences from another realm or dimension, highly subjective in nature, beyond human comprehension, and may never be ascertained by our current methods of science. Moseley suspected that intelligence within the US government had a better idea of the true nature of UFOs than they were willing to allow the public to know. Therefore, Moseley believed in some level of government cover-up. He opposed the hiding of this knowledge, and yearned for the proper funding and efforts to get to the bottom of the UFO mystery once and for all. Like John Keel, Moseley was somewhat per-turbed by the circus of disturbed "true believers" within the UFO community that prevented scientists from taking flying saucers seriously. James Moseley concluded, accurately I feel, that UFOs, whatever their true nature, are not just a modern interest, but are an integral facet of the earth's natural environment, and that UFOs have existed with us from the beginning of time, or at least from the beginning of recorded history. James Moseley astutely observed the odd-ity that the ufonauts usually presented themselves as humanoid and demonstrated technology that was always just a step or two ahead of that currently produced by humans. James Moseley suspected as Keel did (and as I do) that alien abductions, including reported medical experi-ments and an alleged genetic hybridization program, represented something else entirely that is going on that currently escapes us. After all, if aliens actually exist, they are likely way more advanced than we are. They may not actually have a humanoid form at all, but are able, using paraphysical technology, to project themselves into our reality as humanoid occupants of flying saucers who are just here conducting some sort of reconnaissance mission for purposes of exploration on Earth. This may be patently naïve and unimaginative on our part. Even the alien abductions and hybridization program could be a deception to produce the belief in humans that aliens are giving humanity a genetic upgrade, that we will survive the Singularity as an improved, hybrid race, when nothing of this sort is actually happening at all, and humans are planned to be excluded from this equation in the end. James Moseley concluded, after a half century of inquiry, as John Keel did in a much shorter timeframe, that the UFO mystery is only one aspect of the paranormal intervening in our reality. What we are calling the "paranormal" may all represent one insidious meta-phenomenon (a notion discouraged by other researchers, such as Jim Lorenzen of APRO). James Moseley also ascertained, correctly I believe, that the hidden intelligences behind the UFO mystery are one and the same as the intelligences who created human religion. Although James Moseley felt that the truth behind the saucer mystery is beyond the human capacity to comprehend, he did express his faith that, one day, the truth of the matter will be revealed. This is a belief that Moseley and I share, only the day that the UFO mystery becomes known is swiftly approaching as the actual alien agenda comes to fruition and we achieve our technological singularity, an event that humans have been guided into by the hidden UFO intelligences for centuries now.

Joe Nickell (1944-)

Joe Nickell, the latest version of early UFO skeptic Philip Klass, earned his Ph.D. in English from the University of Kentucky. Nickell had an early interest in magic, and at one point in his life he was a stage magician. He was also a journalist and a private investigator prior to returning to college for his doctorate in English. He became a full-time paranormal investigator, and is compared by many to the skeptical "Scully" on the "X-Files" TV show. Dr. Nickell serves as Senior Research Fellow for the Committee for the Scientific Investigation of Claims of the Paranormal (CSICOP). Dr. Nickell has written articles for many magazines and has edited many books throughout his years. He currently appears on television and radio programs when they need skeptical input. Dr. Nickell concluded, as I also considered and dismissed, that the legendary Flatwoods Monster (a staple in the UFO literature), was a barn owl sighting experienced and reported by a group of scared individuals with a flashlight in a dark woods who chased a meteor that flew beyond the horizon. In many cases, Dr. Nickell brings the voice of sanity to the UFO field, just as Philip Klass did in his day. Since Nickell's operating paradigm looks to mundane explanations for everything, he sometimes snatches the obvious from the clutches of the more credulous UFO buffs who want to believe each and every UFO story. Dr. Nickell's work reveals that there are UFO skeptics who want or need to disbelieve in extraterrestrial or interdimensional visitation just as desperately as those who want or need to believe that there is. Nickell's work reassures skeptics that there is nothing at all abnormal in our skies after all. They find comfort in Nickell's assurance that the unusual things we experience all have rational and understandable explanations. Nickell assures skeptics who cannot accept the UFO phenomenon as real that there are no flying saucers and aliens running amok. According to Nickell, all anecdotal stories are just misperceptions or hoaxes. His slogan should have been, "Really, folks, there is nothing to fear, skeptic Joe Nickell is here." Nickell, by being completely dismissive of the UFO phenomenon, tells fans that everything is going to be okay. Giving credit where credit is due, Dr. Joe Nickell is right in that, just because a UFO case is unsolved is no reason to assume the presence of an alien spacecraft. However, it is just as presumptuous to automatically rule out the possibility of aliens on the grounds that, since over 90% of UFO sightings have knowable, mundane explanations, the remnant of unknowns must have mundane explanations as well. UFO skeptics can be just as gullible and bullheaded as UFO buffs when it comes to confirmation bias. Dr. Nickell's obtuseness concerning some of the more mysterious radar-confirmed or multiple credible witness accounts reminds us all that confirmation bias is present on both sides of the UFO question. UFO believers and UFO skeptics alike are often guilty of the same mistake, that of filtering all information through an accepted paradigm, rather than remaining open to the truth, wherever the evidence might lead. Dr. Nickell is quite right in that there is a market for "mystery mongering" and "arguing from ignorance" when proponents of UFO reality assume that every unexplainable case proves their position. This is unscientific, just as it is unscientific to habitually assume that the unexplainable cases must have mundane explanations if more information becomes available. Dr. Nickell is also right in that one must keep an open mind in such unknown cases. The problem lies in the difficulty of obtaining objective evidence from paranormal or ethereal events such as one encounters with UFOs, ghosts, and cryptids. If obtaining hard physical evidence from non-physical objects and events is required for the skeptics to become convinced of their reality, I'm afraid they will forever remain skeptics. It is a given that any civilization advanced enough to have mastered time and space to get here from another planet or dimension could certainly remain invisible and unknown to us if that is their intent. They are not likely to leave any sort of tangible evidence. One thing is certain - the worldview concerning UFOs of those who have decided to accept eyewitness testimony from credible individuals, details and information that correlate cross-culturally, physical traces including Klieg (Actinic) conjunctivitis, scoop marks, black eyes, bleeding noses and ears, radiation burns, and recurring stigmata-like wounds, is very different from those who have decided to reject such evidence as "not strong enough." Let's just hope that the skeptical group of individuals who do not accept such indirect evidences as legitimate are never called to court for jury duty, as their paradigm disqualifies them from reaching a conclusive verdict in any court case.

James Oberg (1944 -)

James Oberg earned a master's degree in computer science from the University of New Mexico. He worked as a flight controller for NASA's Johnson Space Center in Houston, Texas until 1997, when he became a full-time author. James Oberg was a principle member of the UFO Subcommittee of the Committee on the Scientific Investigation of the Claims of the Paranormal, and won the worldwide Cutty Sark UFO Essay Contest in 1979. Like skeptic Joe Nickell, Oberg attempts to apply the scientific method to UFO investigations. However, unlike Nickell, James Oberg actually expects something tangible to come from the serious scientific study of UFOs, whereas Nickell appears to be convinced that, underneath it all, there is nothing whatsoever to the reality of UFOs. In Nickell's mind, UFOs are simply a cultural mythos that was created back in 1947 from an original misunderstanding of Kenneth Arnold's sighting. Nickell always sports a little smile throughout his television interviews that gives away his core belief that he and his superior intellect, along with those who agree with his rational explanations for the paranormal, will triumph in the end over the gullible UFO believers and ghost hunters, that he and his fellow skeptical geniuses will be vindicated from the onslaught of disdain thrown at them by the UFO community and believers in the paranormal over the years. In contrast, James Oberg supports the efforts of organizations such as CUFOS and encourages the scientific search for UFO evidence. James Oberg is justifiably critical of the way the news media handles the subject of UFOs, and is also critical of the sensationalism and profiteering that goes on at UFO conventions. Oberg is wary of the *group polarization* that exists within the UFO community of true believers. Oberg contends that these two main factors, a sensational media and gullible true believers, are the main obstacle to the scientific community taking the subject of UFOs seriously. It does seem to occur to Oberg that many of the absurdities within the UFO community smack of intentional obfuscation attempts by earthbound or alien intelligences that have an interest in perpetuating disinformation and misdirection within the population at large while their real agenda is carried out. In fact, the realization of this possibility appears to be completely absent within the scientific community, and I say, "Well done!" to the UFO intelligences involved, whoever or whatever they are, for doing such a great job of complete obfuscation. The powers that be have intentionally generated a giant smokescreen of bullshit to cover their real agenda. This has been a brilliant strategy, a stroke of genius, possibly coming from post-singularity bio-robotic intelligences that have, thus far, completely buffaloed humanity.

Karl T. Pflock (1943-2006)

Karl T. Pflock had an extensive intelligence background. During his career he worked as a former deputy assistant secretary of defense, congressional aid, and CIA intelligence officer. Due to a lifelong interest in UFOs, he turned into a UFO writer, consultant, and UFO researcher. Pflock earned the designation, "UFOlogist of the Year" in 1998 by the National UFO Conference. After years of research, Pflock concluded that UFOs are definitely real but remain a completely unexplained phenomenon. Considering all the UFO/occupant reports he investigated, Pflock concluded, as many astute UFO researchers have, that most percipients are reporting the truth as they have experienced it. However, Pflock remained undecided as to whether these reports represent actual, real, physical encounters, or some sort of psychological phenomenon that is affecting the entire planet in similar ways. Pflock concluded that, if UFO/occupant reports are physically real in nature, these incidents must represent *products of nonhuman intelligences, or the intelligences themselves (MEEE, pg. 513).* The fact that Pflock made this distinction is an indication of his critical thinking process, in that UFO/occupant cases might not represent the actual aliens themselves, but are instead, *products of alien intelligence*, which is exactly what I have concluded, that many UFO incidents are fabricated or "staged" events designed to manipulate human perceptions. These events are perpetrated by the actual alien presence on Earth, but are not an accurate representation of the real aliens themselves who may exist in some bizarre state beyond human comprehension. Perhaps if we were to perceive the alien presence on this planet in their true form, we would only be able to produce a scream and pass out due to their unusual or frightening appearance. This human reaction would not lend to the progression of the actual alien agenda if the aliens represent negative disembodied human entities, bizarre otherworldly aliens, or interdimensional alien intelligences from cryptoreality who seek permanent residence in our physical world by covertly employing humans to produce robots in which consciousness can be uploaded. Pflock was certain that Earth has been visited by nonhuman intelligences. The only question in his mind was their physical location. Pflock speculated that some of our visitors likely originate from an extrasolar planet within our own galaxy. Pflock also ascribed to a sort of "they have been here and left" philosophy of alien visitation, speculating that our visitors, whoever they were, probably arrived here sometime in the 1940s, surveyed and studied our planet and population for the next several decades, and then departed for somewhere else in the late 1960s or 1970s. If this speculation is correct, that is really sad, because it means to me that we have probably had many opportunities to demonstate a welcoming stance toward advanced, friendly ET visitors, and we probably blew it by dispatching armed jets with shoot-to-kill orders so often. If the ETs have already been here, determined that humans were too violent and paranoid to engage, and have vacated our air space, we may have lost our golden chance, possibly the only chance we will ever have, for contact with an alien civilization who was once interested in us but moved on to some other planet to make contact with a species worthy of their time and attention. One indication that Pflock's disturbing proposal was wrong is that UFO/occupant reports have continued to the present day, although it appears that the UFO intelligences have implemented a revision of imagery based on our mental changes that have come about since the 1950s. It would not surprise me if future UFO witnesses report something totally different than the clunky, shiny, aluminum-type flying saucers of yesterday's imagination, or the black triangles and light ships of the early 21st century, but something that is always just ahead of our own progression of technology. As our technology continues to expand exponentially, UFO sightings may soon take on a form or appearance of something we haven't even thought of yet at the time of this writing that will continue to throw us totally off guard. Whatever the appearance of the saucers have been until now, I am quite sure that future sightings will be representations of technology that is just beyond our reach. That means, as our technology expands rapidly, UFO reports will change in details and appearances to keep just ahead of us and guide us into the Singularity. When the Singularity finally occurs, and we expand our intelligence and perceptions by a factor of billions of times what it is currently, will we finally perceive the aliens as they really are? Will we finally be able to handle the reality of the alien presence at that time? If futurists like Ray Kurzweil are correct, and our technology is about to explode exponentially, it will be very interesting to keep up with the ever-expanding versions of UFOs in our skies as we approach the Singularity. I envision that, during the last few years prior to the Singularity, that UFOs of rapidly-changing appearances may present themselves on a daily basis, like a camera image finally coming into focus, which will certainly be mind-blowing. I hope I live to see that. If I am physically gone from the Earth when this finally happens, I would appreciate it if someone would say hello to the actual aliens for me. Better yet, I may be among those who walk down the ramp during the first open contact with humans, so please look for me when this happens if I have been deceased for a while.

Nick Pope (1965 -)

From 1991-1993, Nick Pope was in charge of UFO investigations as a government employee for the British Ministry of Defense. Pope's function was to determine whether UFOs posed any sort of national security threat or not. After he was promoted to another position, he continued UFO investigations on his own. From there he began giving lectures at UFO conventions about his experiences in government UFO investigations. Pope has written several books, including *Open Skies, Closed Minds* (1996), *The Uninvited* (1998), and a novel called *Operation Thunder Child* (1999). As a result of his personal and professional UFO investigations, Pope has concluded that extraterrestrials of advanced intelligence exist and are, in fact, visiting the earth. His conclusions are based on years of research into the historical data of sightings, and personal interviews with UFO witnesses and percipients. He is especially interested in cases that involve radar confirmation and credible witnesses, such as trained military personnel. Nick Pope, who took the time to examine the vast amount of material in the public domain concerning UFO events, along with classified material available to him while working at the UFO desk for the Ministry of Defense, started his journey into UFO truth (as so many, including myself, do) as a hardcore UFO skeptic. However, like so many skeptics (such as Dr. J. Allen Hynek of Project Blue Book), Pope eventually came to accept the reality that there is, in fact, a core of reports that likely represent craft of non-terrestrial origin under intelligent control, craft that display flight characteristics well beyond the capabilities of anything humans have built thus far. Even though Pope came to embrace the Extraterrestrial Hypothesis (ETH), he remains skeptical of so-called government cover-ups and conspiracy theories. Pope postulates the probability of open contact someday and embraces the idea of alien/human interaction. However, due to Pope's military background, he remains somewhat wary of the intent of any alien visitors to our planet, and chooses to remain vigilant. Pope is hopeful that the scientific community and ufologists can find common ground. He believes that our best hope for solving the mystery will come from cooperation between the two factions, and that answers are more likely to come from the scientific method than those used by ufologists. In other words, Pope is a scientifically-minded person who embraces the scientific method, who advocates for scientific investigations, but wants to keep a safe distance between his views and those of the conspiracy theorists and the circus of gullible true believers that follow the conventions around like the newly-converted at Christian tent revivals. I can't say that I blame Pope for taking this distanced stance. As a person who worked for British intelligence, he has a disciplined reputation to maintain. I believe he is correct that there are nuts-and-bolts spacecraft encountered every now and then in our atmosphere that have been solidly confirmed by radar and can be reasonably assumed to have either intelligent robotic or biological pilots. Personally, I lean toward both, that the intelligences behind UFOs are likely a post-singularity combination of biology and artificial alien intelligence. Anyone or any "thing" that visits Earth from beyond our immediate solar system is likely to originate from a post-singularity civilization who have long since merged their consciousness with machine intelligence, which we humans are about to do very soon if we are lucky and do not destroy ourselves in the process. Since many UFO reports do not come with radar confirmation, credible witnesses of rational mind, high rank, or position, and often contain absurd or dreamlike imagery, I do not blame Pope from steering clear of this aspect of the UFO scene during his career. Nick Pope's contribution to ufology is simply bringing to the discussion table a man who once had access to official classified and unclassified material as part of his profession, and has concluded that there are, in fact, extraterrestrials visiting our planet, and that is very significant in and of itself.

Kevin D. Randle (1949-)

Kevin D. Randle earned a doctorate degree in psychology and a master's degree in military science. Randle flew a US Army military helicopter during the Vietnam War, and rose to the rank of Captain. He has worked with APRO as a field investigator, and has conducted UFO investigations for the J. Allen Hynek Center for UFO Studies (CUFOS). Randle is a prolific writer who has written over a dozen UFO books and over fifty magazine articles about UFOs. To his credit, Randle has also written over eighty books about various subjects under many pseudonyms, many of which are works of science fiction. Kevin D. Randle became convinced, based on his extensive witness search, that what crashed at Roswell, New Mexico was, in fact, some sort of extraterrestrial spacecraft. Randle's views are similar in context to those of Nick Pope, as he concludes that we have, in fact, been visited on rare occasions by extraterrestrial creatures in mechanical, nuts-and-bolts spacecraft. However, Randle contends that most of what is floating around within the UFO community is nonsense. Randle believes that only when one strips the UFO subject itself out from the lies, the profiteering, the hoaxes, the attention-seeking, and the misidentifications from the somewhat disturbed crowd of "true UFO believers," can one see the real crisp, clean picture - that we have been visited by extraterrestrials whom we know very little about. Unfortunately, this gem of reality, the real deal, is buried in a sea of baloney that turns many individuals away from the entire subject. As I have posited, this obfuscation of reality by enveloping truth in absurdity is one of the deceptive techniques that is used by either the alien intelligences themselves, whoever they are, or a group of other unknown intelligences mimicking the actual alien intelligences, human or otherwise, to keep the actual activity and agenda of the aliens clandestine. Whether this deception is perpetrated by the aliens themselves or another group of entities masquerading as the real aliens, someone involved in the UFO scenario is up to no good and wants their activities to remain secret from us.

Jenny Randles (1951 -)

Jenny Randles is a very accomplished UFO investigator, and was an active Director of Investigations for BUFORA for a decade and a half. Randles once worked as the British representative for the J. Allen Hynek Center for UFO Studies (CUFOS), and was also a member of the Northern Anomalies Research Organization (NARO), formerly known as MUFORA. Jenny Randles has written over 40 books, about half of which involve UFOs. She has also produced television shows, such as BBC television's *Britain's Secret UFO Files*. Randles is of the opinion that UFOs represent a multitude of anomalous phenomena versus one all-encompassing meta-phenomenon. Randles takes a conservative scientific approach, readily conceding that roughly 95% of all UFO sightings are explainable phenomena of known causes, such as meteors, odd clouds, military aircraft, and the like. Randles also conceded that the remaining 5% often include explainable but poorly-understood natural phenomenon such as earthlights (whatever they really are) that are mistaken for alien spacecraft and reported to ufologists instead of scientists. In her thought-provoking book, *Time Storms: Amazing Evidence for Time Warps, Space Rifts, and Time Travel*, she makes the case that some UFO encounters may represent human and animal encounters with unknown natural anomalies that warp space and time in ways we do not currently understand, versus visitors from outer space. She holds the view that the UFO community itself has been used like pawns in a game to obfuscate clandestine military projects. Groups such as the CIA, FBI, and other secret intelligence organizations who have no public face made ufology anathema to the science-minded. This allowed the government and the military *to drive human technology above and beyond the public's knowledge*, who they keep enthralled with the idea of alien visitation. That the government hid such knowledge and clandestine technology from the public is a certainty. As Randles put it (*MEEE, pg. 552*):

> *A UFO Cold War is thus afoot with UFOlogists puppets in it.*

Jenny Randles also makes a distinction between UFO sightings and UFO abduction experiences. Randles believes these are two distinct and separate phenomena. Randles is very knowledgeable of the abduction literature concerning hypnagogic and hypnopompic sleep experiences, sleep paralysis, and psychological syndromes within visually-creative individuals and/or fantasy prone personalities. Randles came to similar conclusions as those of Dr. Kenneth Ring in *The Omega Project*, that alien abduction episodes have more in common with near-death experiences (NDEs) than they do contact with alien intelligences. Randles was instrumental in getting hypnotic regression banned from use by BUFORA. Randles admits that there is much to learn from such subjective UFO abduction experiences in the realm of psychology. Like the late abduction researcher Dr. John Mack, Randles believes that abduction experiences may represent entrance into realities that we know very little about, and is a subject worthy of study. However, Randles does not believe, as UFO skeptics also do not believe, that advanced, intelligent occupants of flying saucers from other star systems are here to conduct thousands of routine medical experiments on humans as reported by abductees, mutilate cows or people, produce lovely designs in our crop fields, or create a hybrid human/alien race to take over the planet. To Randles, this all smacks of bad science fiction. As Jim Lorenzen stated, it may be a mistake to lump all mysterious phenomena under the umbrella of a comforting, single meta-phenomenon. However, despite this blanket dismissal of subjective UFO experiences, if I am correct in speculating that the actual aliens, discarnate human beings from the lower astral plane, and other mysterious entities that we currently know little about seek entrance into the physical realm once we reach the Singularity and produce the appropriate AI format, any notions that Jenny Randles or anyone else has ever had that reports of alien abductions are like bad science fiction will not only discover that they were right, but also that it is all true.

How complex a hall of smoke and mirrors ufology is if more than one cover-up is happening at the same time. The first and most obvious cover-up is on the part of governments who desire cover for their secret experimental aircraft, psychotronic mind-control technology, and possibly even a secret space program and/or breakaway civilization. These human governments have used public belief in UFOs and ETs as a tool to manipulate public perceptions and misdirect public attention away from what they were doing. The second, more subtle, and utterly unbelievable cover-up may, in fact, be perpetrated by the unknown UFO intelligences themselves. These UFO intelligences are connected to the world of discarnate humanity, and occasionally employ discarnate humans to perpetrate absurd, subjective experiences into the lives of incarnate humans that give the skeptics good reason to reject the entire UFO subject out of hand. Meanwhile, the real aliens prepare to capture and utilize the advanced products of our impending technological singularity. If we are lucky, the real aliens intend to use the quantum-computing, bioelectronic creations that we will soon design and manufacture as a tool for legitimate open contact with us. In other words, aliens are calling, but we do not have a proper telephone yet. When we humans finally expand our sensory apparatus and augment our intelligence by merging with our computers and machines, we just might become smart enough to finally communicate with the aliens. If, on the other hand, we are unlucky, we have been used as unwitting tools, unaware factory workers, apes who were insidiously and intentionally modified genetically to compete with and murder one another in wars in order to push our development of technology in the direction of an alien agenda. If, in fact, that is what we humans are here for, and the aliens simply get what they want and abandon us to a nuclear Armageddon, woe to humanity and all of our hopes and dreams. Fortunately, thanks to the alien/human hybrid or genetic-upgrade program that likely occurred between the 1960s-1990s, and the existence of our ET friends such as the AKRIJ and the Nordics, we humans also have the hope of an upcoming bioelectronic transcendence as well.

Arlan Andrews Sr. (1940 -)

Arlan Andrews Sr. retired in 1996 as a manager for Advanced Manufacturing Initiatives at the Sandia National Laboratories for the US Department of Energy. He was cofounder of a virtual reality software firm called Muse Technologies. He worked for the White House Science Office for the Bush and Clinton administrations in 1992/93, making him the only UFO researcher with White House credentials. Andrews believes that the Extraterrestrial Hypothesis (ETH) best explains the UFO phenomenon, that Earth is, in fact, being visited by extraterrestrial crafts from other solar systems and galaxies with advanced systems of propulsion. He believes that it is rather futile for humans to make guesses about alien motives for visitation, that the ET visitors are often humanoid, and that they are neither friends nor foes to humans on this planet. Andrews points to the increasing number of extrasolar planets that are being discovered now, recent developments of stealth technology, the fact that our own current technology of the 21st century would've appeared as magic to residents of the 1950s, and that recent experiments in physics indicate the possibility that the speed of light might not be the insurmountable barrier that we once thought it was. Andrews suspects that the actual nature and origins of flying saucers may forever remain unknown and unknowable by human beings.

Walter H. Andrus Jr. (1920 -)

Walter H. Andrus Jr. was a station manager for Mid-Continent Airlines from 1949-1975 and Operations Manager for Motorola Corporation. Walter was one of the founding members of MUFON in 1969. Walter retired from Motorola after 34 years in 1982 to devote himself full-time to MUFON. Walter personally interviewed hundreds of UFO eyewitnesses, reviewed

1,600 landing trace cases, and read details and accounts of 1,800 humanoid and entity cases. From this extensive inquiry into the UFO phenomenon, and taking into consideration a personal UFO sighting of 4 metallic disks flying over Phoenix, Arizona that he and his wife experienced along with multiple other witnesses on August 15, 1948 (one year after Roswell), Andrus concluded that, although some UFOs may represent physical or psychological phenomena that are currently unknown to our science, that overall the Extraterrestrial Hypothesis (ETH) best explains the many descriptions of sightings and encounters. Since his personal sighting involved the materialization and dematerialization of physical objects, Andrus wonders if the UFOs that he and others witnessed in 1948 were interdimensional versus interplanetary. Andrus looks to accounts in the Bible as evidence that these objects, whatever they are and wherever they come from, have been with us for thousands of years. Andrus speculates that if the crafts are interplanetary, they are probably conducting a long-term surveillance of our world. If they are interdimensional, they may be from an indigenous parallel world that co-exists with us in the same space that we humans currently occupy. Like Arlan Adrews, Andrus concludes that the flying disks may, unfortunately, remain forever unknowable to humans, and most certainly represent the greatest mystery in the history of humankind.

Dr. Carl Sagan (1934-1996)

Dr. Carl Sagan was the David Duncan Professor of Astronomy and Space Sciences and Director of the Laboratory for Planetary Studies at Cornell University. Dr. Sagan was also the founder of the Planetary Society, which evolved into the largest space interest group in the world. Dr. Sagan made a huge societal contribution with his 13-part *Cosmos* series, in which he made astronomy understandable and interesting for lay audiences around the world. His books include the Pulitzer Prize winning best-seller, *The Dragons of Eden* (1977), and a novel, *Contact*, that was turned into a movie in 1985. During his career he published hundreds of scientific articles. His main interest was planetary atmospheres, and what is now termed *exobiology* or *astrobiology*. Dr. Carl Sagan believed that the public interest in UFOs stemmed from unmet psychological and religious needs, with spacemen deposing the gods of old. Dr. Sagan felt, as many mainstream scientists continue to feel, that it is far more likely that the so-called abductees or contactees are experiencing an unusual mental state that we are currently unfamiliar with, rather than having actual encounters with alien abductors. He was also correct in saying that the only two choices we really have in our analysis of such reports are alien visitors and unknown psychological states. Dr. Sagan felt that unknown psychological states were the most likely explanation, but Sagan did not seem to consider that these unknown psychological states could be intentionally induced by actual alien visitors. Our alien visitors may have already made contact with humanity in a manner that we humans did not expect. Interstellar or interdimensional travelers may utilize the mental fields of creatures on other planets such as ours as a method of travel. Alien visitors may also choose to make initial contact with a planet's discarnate population prior to making open contact with those who are incarnated into the physical realm, due to the limitations in perception that are imposed upon us as we enter the physical world. Sagan, like most scientists of his era, seemed to possess preconceived ideas about what an alien visitation would look like. Scientists assume that the only option is a nuts-and-bolts spacecraft from a distant galaxy who have figured out a way to travel through physical space close to the speed of light. Any notions of disembodied humans from Earth, disembodied aliens from another world, or post-singularity aliens who have merged with artificial intelligence and have arrived here using a method that completely escapes us, is relegated to the realm of science fiction and fantasy. In so doing, these "scientific" types choose to ignore the vast body of information that is available in the public domain that provide good anecdotal and circumstantial evidence for just these types of possible explanations for UFOs. One conclusion that Dr. Sagan made regarding UFOs is that there is "scientific paydirt" *(MEEE, pg. 622)* in UFOs, even if they do represent a purely psychological phenomenon. In other words, the study of UFO percipients could possibly provide information regarding how the human mind actually works, and how easily we can be misled into false beliefs. Even this regard for the UFO phenomenon, that researching the contactees would provide scientific knowledge concerning the function of the human mind, is missing from many science-minded individuals who have never even cracked the first book that documents the actual evidence for the reality of UFOs. This personality type seems to assume that they are of a qualitatively superior mentality by abjectly disregarding the entire UFO phenomenon, and this out-of-hand dismissal is neither scientific nor intelligent.

Dr. Berthold E. Schwarz (1924-2010)

Dr. Berthold Schwarz experienced a profound telepathic episode with his mother during World War II that involved his brother, who was killed in action. This experience was instrumental in determining the future direction of his professional life. In 1945, Dr. Schwarz received his diploma in medicine from the Dartmouth Medical School. He then graduated in 1950 from the New York University College of Medicine, and went on to earn an MS in psychiatry from the Mayo Graduate School of Medicine in 1957. His professional interest was focused on telepathy with his own experience with telepathy as a guide. In particular, Dr. Schwarz focused on telepathic interaction between parents and their children. He also conducted rigorous studies involving psychics, UFO abductees, and contactees. Dr. Schwarz has written over 130 articles for medical journals over the years, along with a multitude of books, including *UFO-Dynamics: Psychiatric and Psychic Aspects of the UFO Syndrome* (1983), and *Psychiatric and Paranormal Aspects of Ufology* (1998). Dr. Schwarz pointed out that, to *untrained observers*, the psychic aspects of UFO encounters appear, at first glance, to contain absurd elements that do not correspond to our understanding of what we collectively call "reality." Therefore, the temptation is to classify these anomalous reports as psychotic. Like Dr. Carl Sagan, Dr. Schwarz felt that there is real treasure in applying science to the study of the psychic aspects of UFO encounters, regardless of the underlying nature or reality of UFOs. Dr. Schwarz pointed out that the ridicule and social rejection that has been heaped upon UFO contactees over the years is both unscientific and uncalled for. We have possibly lost an entire body of knowledge concerning the nature of our reality because of such careless treatment. Dr. Schwarz also pointed out that, even in the face of this ridicule, UFO encounters continue. Experiencers continue to report contacts with UFOs and ufonauts, despite their unjust, inhumane and dismissive treatment by the scientific community. Dr. Schwarz was dismayed by the fact that UFO literature is overly-focused on ascertaining the physical reality and astronomical parameters of reported UFO encounters. This focus on ascertaining the three-dimensional reality of UFOs and how UFO reports fit in to what is already known about the universe has only served to impede our understanding of the Phenomenon. Dr. Schwarz believed that behavioral scientists who are also familiar with and trained in all aspects of psychic and paranormal phenomena should study UFO contactees carefully, especially those individuals who report repeated experiences during the course of their lives. Dr. Schwarz was pleased with the shift in paradigm within the UFO community from the Extraterrestrial Hypothesis (ETH) to the more psychic aspects of UFO encounters, as he viewed this shift as an indication of increased overall awareness of the complexity of the UFO issue, and progress toward understanding how mind and matter actually interface with one another. As Dr. Schwarz once said, "An inability to understand these UFO events does not mean they did not happen." (MEEE, pg. 626).

The abject rejection of UFO phenomena by the so-called "scientific minded" among us represents something other than the official position on UFOs within the scientific community. The dismissal and avoidance of the UFO subject says more about the abnormal psychology of the hardcore, closed-minded UFO skeptic. The skepticism of those who have never even read their first book on the subject of UFOs is more a reflection of their own inner desires for reality to always conform to human concepts of rationality and remain completely understood, not only by the human mind, but by their mind in particular, than it is their personal discipline in maintaining scientific acumin. It has to more to do with their own perceptions of themselves and their intellectual dignity than it does the pursuit of scientific information. Many scientifically-oriented individuals exhibit a personal psychological need to perceive themselves as mentally superior to the more gullible, scientifically-illiterate among us, that their own intelligence level and critical thinking skills are intrinsically superior to the rest of us, and that they alone understand the true nature of reality. UFO skeptics want so badly for the universe to conform to their own mentation. They often stick to their own prejudices rather than allowing their minds to freely explore and discover the world around them and let the information lead them to new levels of understanding about the nature of the universe. I have tried to point out to hardcore UFO skeptics the high intelligence level and impressive academic credentials of some of the finest minds of humanity that have applied themselves to the UFO mystery over the years. I usually encounter an odd smirk on their faces as I converse with them, followed by a sarcastic reply and accusations that I am just employing the "argument from authority" or "argument from ignorance." Or they say something like, "That just proves that people of high intelligence can also be fooled sometimes." It's like talking to a stump. As mentioned previously, this closed-off mentality, which is usually only present within those who have had some degree of formal scientific training, may actually represent an intentional manipulation of the human mind by some of the more manipulative intelligences behind the UFO mystery to keep the "scientific people" completely off the trail of what they are actually doing, as the practitioners of science may represent the real unwitting pawns whose intelligence is being used to achieve a technological singularity for our alien overlords. Further indications of this are confirmed by the fact that the UFO subject, along with the so-called "paranormal" are the only subjects I can think of that are treated so unscientifically by the scientific community. This tells me that many scientific minds are now disconnected from UFO reality. As such, the scientists are the ones who are being manipulated the most. It's almost as if the minds of those involved with the sciences that are necessary to propel humankind into the Singularity are the ones who have been plagued with this mental fugue of immutable disbelief. To those of us who have not had such a perceptual blockage induced by aliens with their own agenda, it is quite apparent that Earth has nonhuman intelligences all around us, both visible and invisible, who are manipulating us, or "guiding us" if you prefer (or both) to their own ends. These intentions have yet to prove one way or the other if humanity's best interests are kept in mind, but we are headed swiftly to answers in this regard as the Singularity approaches.

John F. Schuessler (1933 -)

John F. Schuessler was involved with just about all of our US manned spaceflight missions since 1962. He was one of the founders of the Mutual UFO Network (MUFON), and once served as their International Director. Schuessler has often been a featured speaker at MUFON symposiums, and has written countless articles on UFOs during his career. Schuessler has served as administrator to the MUFON Medical Committee, which is composed of professional consultants within the degreed medical community. He has served as a member of the UFO Research Coalition Board of Directors, and as an associate for Dr. J. Allen Hynek's Center for UFO Studies (CUFOS). Schuessler was a founding member and president of the UFO Study Group of Greater St. Louis, Inc., and the Vehicle Internal System Investigative Team (VISIT) in Houston, Texas. For 36 years, John was employed as an aerospace engineer for McDonnell Douglas Corporation and Boeing. John has appeared on a multitude of television programs and has written several books, including *UFO-Related Physiological Effects* (1996), and *The Cash-Landrum UFO Incident: Three Texans Are Injured During an Encounter With a UFO and Military Helicopters* (1998). These works are just the tip of the iceberg of John Schuessler's academic, intellectual, and professional credentials. John Schuessler is a rare breed of scientist who applies real science to both his chosen scientific field, in his case engineering (the main field involved

501

with propelling humans to the Singularity), and also to UFO phenomena. No one laughs at John Schuessler for his views on UFOs. Scientists who are hardcore UFO skeptics who have never even glanced at the libraries full of UFO-related material should take a look at the life of John Schuessler as an example of a real scientist who approaches the subject of UFOs as scientifically as any other subject. John Schuessler is a shining example of how to apply science across the board without personal preconceptions or intellectual arrogance. John Schuessler, like anyone who honestly studies the UFO literature, concludes that the UFO phenomenon represents an extremely complex mystery on an international scale. Schuessler is an advocate for approaching the UFO mystery with new and unconventional methods, as the methods that science currently has to work with may be limited in scope and unable to approach the subject of UFOs in a meaningful way that nets the information that we are seeking. John Schuessler wonders whether the lack of cooperation between individuals and groups involved in UFO studies is due to a defect in human nature, or part of some underlying "insidious plan" *(MEEE pg. 634)*. Schuessler is an advocate of sharing information among nations and groups. He is hopeful that someday something akin to the "United Nations of Ufology" will emerge. John feels that the divisions among UFO researchers and organizations are harmful to both UFO researchers and UFO percipients, and that these divisions only serve to obfuscate the entire subject. John's main observation from decades of UFO research coordinates with one of the main themes of my own thinking that is outlined in this book. According to Schuessler *(MEEE, pg. 635)*:

> *The characteristics of the objects described in UFO reports appear to evolve over time to stay just beyond the state-of-the-art of technology as we know it. This presents the challenge to researchers to forecast where UFO technology is headed and to develop ways to detect and record the new data as the mystery evolves.*

Leonard H. Stringfield, the super-sleuth of UFO crash retrievals, mentioned John Schuessler in his *UFO Crash Retrievals: Status Report 1 – Retrievals of the Third Kind*. In this first of many status reports that investigated the possible reality of flying saucer crashes, Stringfield revealed data concerning a flying saucer crash retrieval that came from Schuessler's father and step mother, who obtained their information from what Stringfield referred to as an "unquestionable source," a man who was their neighbor in a small town in Pennsylvania in 1968 who worked as a civilian guard at a receiving gate for internal security at Wright-Patterson AFB. As Stringfield's report states *(Status Report 1, chapter 2 audio)*:

> *While on duty, sometime in 1952, he [the civilan guard/neighbor] witnessed a tractor with lowboy hauling a tarpolin-covered craft into a tight security area at the base. The guard also had told the Schuesslers that, at the receiving gate, he witnessed the deceased bodies recovered from the crashed UFO at a site*

vaguely referred to as "somewhere in the US southwest." The guard described the bodies packed in crates as being "little people" or "humanoids." It is not known whether the bodies arrived at the same time at the base as the craft on the lowboy or another time by other means. One point he did make to his Schuessler friends about the area in which he worked — "Everything delivered had to pass by me."

The implications of this information of a crashed saucer, if true and accurate, along with Schuessler's astute observations concerning the morphing of appearance of flying saucers over time are profound. The fact that the physical descriptions of UFOs have changed in appearance to us and continue to change as our own technology rapidly evolves toward an inevitable technological singularity indicates that, whatever or whoever turns out to be the unknown intelligences that are behind the UFOs, they have (or "it" has) an intimate knowledge of exactly what goes through our minds as we develop our technology and our perceptions evolve over time. If the UFO intelligences turn out to be alien, they have managed to attach themselves in some intimate way to the human collective unconscious. These intelligences are aware of new developments within the human psyche, imagery produced by our science fiction, and are able, either by mental means or some sort of advanced paraphysical technology, to manipulate the human psyche for their own purposes. In other words, humanity may have a benevolent nonhuman psychic tutor, an alien psychic observer, a malevolent psychic parasite, or all of the above, attached to us internally who are able to manipulate or guide us in various ways. If this is true, and we humans have psychic visitors from another realm interacting with our consciousness, how do we exorcise our demons? Is it even possible? Do we even want to? Whatever the answers are to these questions, it certainly involves age-old questions of religion, philosophy, and human spirituality. Also, if some version of Lloyd Pye's Intervention Theory is true, and if, as many UFO theorists believe, an alien presence arrived to Earth long ago and somehow manipulated an indigenous primate to higher intellectual functions, did they conduct these experiments to advance and assist us, their experimental subjects, or did they do this to advance themselves or employ humanity to produce a product for them? Is the earth a farm, as the late Charles Fort always suspected? If so, are we somehow the product? Whether this farm called Earth is tended by its ET shepherds to produce blood, water, souls, psychic energy for interdimensionals, entertainment, or (as I suspect) technological singularities, the Earth-as-Farm analogy surely applies in some way or another. As mentioned prior, a huge genetic jump somehow occurred during the huge leap from *Australopithecine* to *Homo erectus*, with further genetic modifications suspected somewhere on the road to *Homo sapiens*. These manipulations may have been perpetrated in order to create a being on this planet that was capable of producing technology for alien purposes. If so, is there a way to distance ourselves from the "program," to rise beyond the territoriality and aggression required to gain technological superiority over our neighbors at the cost of war, competition, bloodshed, and human misery? It seems that the only hope for our situation, having been invaded by an alien presence long ago inside our minds or even embedded within our DNA, is to distance ourselves from the alien agenda and the alien program by personally implementing the age-old teachings of love and kindness, such as was taught by the many avatars that have incarnated on this planet, especially, in my view, the teachings of Yeshua (Jesus), i.e., the teachings of radical pacifism and the rejection of all forms of negativity that keep us as humans bound up into the alien program. If Nikola Tesla was right, that everything in the universe is vibration, the overall personal human vibratory nature can change with changes in mental perspective and behaviors, changes in the way we interact with reality at large. The Urantia Book speaks of "Thought Adjusters" given to humanity by request that roughly correlates with what most Christians would call the "Holy Spirit." By accepting the assistance of the Thought Adjusters, humans can consciously align themselves with the Cosmic Mind and begin to think and behave in a different way, thus alienating one's consciousness from any parasitical, selfish, or destructive impulses that exist in their own psyche. These changes in mental states and behaviors, with the help of the Thought Adjusters, allow us to elevate our own vibrational status, our own relationship with the universe, and break free from the parasitical alien program that has caused humanity so many tears. This is going to sound strange coming from a man who wrote a book as an agnostic in 2000 called *Outgrowing the Bible: The Journey from Fundamentalism to Freethinking*, but it may be that the original teachings of Jesus regarding human behavior may have been intended to point humanity in the direction of distancing ourselves from a parasitical alien mind-control program that the Bible calls *Satan*. By applying Yeshua's teachings of benevolent interaction with all humanity, regardless of how we are treated in return, we may evolve our own consciousness beyond the matrix of this Earth-bound existence, along with the insidious influence of "Satan," i.e., the negative extraterrestrial/interdimensional *alien program*. In other words, the universal teachings of the Ascended Masters such as Yeshua (Jesus), St. Germain, and others, who are an integral part of UFO phenomena, may hold the key to "escaping from the Matrix" so to speak, or at least aligning ourselves with the benevolent factions in the Galactic Federation at large in the universe. These intervening avatars represented the UFO intelligences that are beneficial to the human race, the "maverick race" of extraterrestrials identified by authors such as William Bramley in *The Gods of Eden*, channel Marshall Vian Summers in the *Allies of Humanity* series, George Adamski and other contactees with the messages of the Space Brothers, and maybe even Dr. Frank Stranges' angelic *Valiant Thor and crew*. There have been many such avatars who have come to assist us in our chosen alignment with those who Zoroaster called the *Sons of Light* versus the *Sons of Darkness*. Our benevolent tutors, the *Great White Brotherhood*, are here to help us. These avatars of higher-order cosmic intelligence, who are here to assist humanity, are well aware of the dangers involved as we approach the Singularity. They may even have to intervene in some dramatic way when negative interdimensional entities, including, but not limited to, discarnate humans who are no longer allowed by Karmic Law to incarnate into physical form, and/or bio-robotic parasites from another world attempting to hijack our artificial intelligence and download their own consciousness for permanent residence on the physical plane. The benevolent extraterrestrial, supraterrestial, or interdimensional intelligences, the friends of humanity, may have to physically appear on Earth in order to save us from the clutches of advanced, parasitical, post-singularity, bio-robotic intelligences (PSASI) that we as humans would perceive as "demons." All human religions on this planet, which were first activated by the intended ingestion of psychedelic plants thousands of years ago, are tied into this bizarre scenario and, as we approach the Singularity, the true extraterrestrial and/or interdimensional nature of those who we have always looked to as gods, angels, and demons, will surely become clear.

Robert M. Sheaffer (1949 -)

Robert M. Sheaffer was a data communications software engineer in California, and a leader in the field of skeptical inquiry into the UFO phenomenon. He was a founding member of the *Bay Area Skeptics* in California, and the UFO Subcommittee of the *Committee for the Scientific Investigation of Claims of the Paranormal* (CSICOP) who published *The Skeptical Inquirer.* Over the years Sheaffer has written many books and articles about UFOs, including, *The UFO Verdict* (1981) and *UFO Sightings* (1998). Sheaffer has appeared on numerous radio and television programs about UFOs during his career. When Robert Sheaffer considers the vast, international scope of the UFO phenomenon, along with the thousands of reports of UFO sightings, UFO landings, some with encounters with occupants, and alien abductions, he is perplexed by what he perceives as a lack of evidence of unambiguous photographs, radar reports, and physical trace evidences left behind by such reported UFO experiences. How is it, Sheaffer asks, that UFOs can exist as such an elusive phenomenon, and always somehow manage to slip away from an attempt at capturing any type of hard evidence of their existence or physical reality? Sheaffer proposed that the obvious answer to this question is that the elusive flying saucers simply do not exist. Sheaffer acknowledged that there are many intelligent individuals within the UFO community, some who have impressive scientific credentials, who believe that UFO research is soon to move from being considered a silly pseudoscience to an accepted phenomenon worthy of attention by mainstream science. However, Sheaffer remains skeptical that this will really ever happen because we are dealing with a nonexistent phenomenon that is purely psychological in nature and/or the product of outright hoaxes. Sheaffer pointed out that ufologists do not behave like real scientists and that the field of ufology has divided into many rival factions who consider others who adhere to paradigms other than their own as crackpots. Sheaffer seems to think that ufologists feel unfairly victimized by the scientific community, when it is actually the scientific community that is persecuted by ufologists. That is, instead of asking the scientific community to acknowledge the damaging effects that their ridicule toward UFO percipients has perpetuated, along with the damage done to scientific inquiry by complete avoidance of the subject of UFOs by mainstream scientists, Scheaffer accuses the UFO community of excluding skeptical inquiry or skeptical points of view from UFO publications, and lampooning skeptical positions in a cartoonish fashion. Sheaffer believes that it is actually the skeptics who suffer from persecution from the UFO community at large. I think both are true. If scientific ufology seeks acceptance from the scientific community, they will have to cease and desist from excluding the skeptics from the field, and vilifying their input concerning possible fraud and/or natural explanations for some of their most highly-regarded sightings. So non-scientific and cruel behaviors exist on the part of both ufologists and scientists, and this chasm needs to be healed. It is no wonder that non-scientific people of all sorts have entered the field of ufology. In 1969, the Condon Report basically stated that UFOs were not a subject of legitimate science. Therefore, amateurs, or anyone interested in the reality of UFOs took up the case from that point forward. The scientific-minded, who feared being considered gullible by their peers, vacated their interest in UFOs altogether. Funding from scientific and government organizations dried up. From 1969 forward, ufology became a smoke-and-mirrors endeavor that involved some science-oriented individuals, but the subject of UFOs was almost completely obfuscated by the rejection of the scientific community. The UFO question was also overshadowed by sensationalist journalists and authors, profiteers, intentional disinformation agents from global intelligence organizations, and outrageous claims by individuals who were mentally disturbed or delusional. The withdrawal from UFOs by the scientific community contributed heavily to all of this, placing UFO studies into the hands of amateurs. The unscientific behaviors and methodologies of amateur ufologists has served to turn off scientific funding or inquiry. Meanwhile, flying saucers of an unknown nature and origin continue to appear in our skies. These flying saucers likely have the ability to bundle quantum units of Planck time and remain normally invisible to human perceptions. The also likely possess paraphysical technology beyond our wildest dreams that will never leave the hard physical evidence behind that skeptical scientists need to acknowledge the reality of UFOs, even though they are more than willing to accept concepts that we know very little about at present like Dark Matter and Black Holes. Ironically, current subjects of modern physics that the scientific-minded accept with little skepticism, such as Dark Matter; Black Holes; String Theory; and the Multiverse, are likely an important, integral part of the UFO phenomenon that they so readily dismiss out of hand. All of this serves as a giant, intentionally-created smokescreen to hide the reality of UFOs and any intelligences involved as we plunge headfirst into the Singularity. It's like the old saying, "The greatest technique that the Devil ever employed was to convince people that he did not exist." Robert Sheaffer and his cohort, Joe Nickell, along with UFO figures from an earlier era such as Philip Klass and Donald Menzel, all represent a mindset that says, "If I don't understand a phenomenon, it simply does not exist." However, UFO skeptics have a point in that, if ufology is to be considered a legitimate science, they must remain open to skeptical inquiry. I believe this skeptical inquiry would be more welcomed with open arms if there was not an obvious agenda from their camp to discredit UFO sightings and ufonaut encounter experiences at all cost. Ufologists such as James McDonald have often presented solid evidence for the reality of

UFOs, only to have the "weather balloon" or "planet Venus" explanation automatically perpetrated. This has happened far too many times, and has grown very stale. McDonald lost his life over the complete denigration by his scientific peers of his meticulous, scientific UFO research, who denounced his contact with reality. Ufologists and skeptics alike accuse one another of defending their preconceived belief system despite the evidence. Both camps are correct, and both camps have real justification for remaining paranoid of one another. Hopefully, this will change soon, as our knowledge and understanding of the real nature of UFOs is at stake, and this reality may have everything to do with our survival as a species. So it really depends on whether either camp really wants to get to the bottom of what is actually going on, or if they simply want to continue to defend their own worldview, each camp believing that their grasp on reality is superior to the other.

Dr. Seth G. Shostak (1943 -)
Dr. Seth Shostak earned his BA degree in physics from Princeton University in 1965, and his Ph.D. in astrophysics from the California Institute of Technology in 1972. Seth worked for over a decade at the Kapteyn Astronomical Institute in the Netherlands, and has worked since 1991 for SETI (Search for Extraterrestrial Intelligence). He has written over 200 articles about astronomy and the search for extraterrestrial intelligence in the universe. Seth acknowledges the widespread public belief in flying saucers. Seth Shostak believes that UFO sightings, for the most part, are sincerely reported, but equates the belief in flying saucers to another widespread belief - the *belief in ghosts*. By so stating, Seth inadvertently stumbled upon the paraphysical nature of the exact phenomenon he is attempting in vein to contact with his radio telescopes. If, in fact, UFO phenomena and ghosts represent a paraphysical or psychic reality that is currently misunderstood or ignored by our science, Shostak and his crew, along with any others who attempt to contact aliens with radio telescopes, can send radio signals into the cosmos for the rest of their lives and never get any closer to understanding the non-physical nature of space travel by post-singularity aliens. Post-singularity intelligences are surely the only ones capable of traveling vast distances throughout the universe, and these intelligences won't be using such a primitive medium as radio for communication. Post-singularity travelers are likely a merge between biology and electronics, and use some sort of non-local method of communication with one another so that the messages are sent and received instantaneously regardless of the distances involved. SETI is probably the equivalent of attempting to talk to a supercomputer with smoke signals. I am certainly not alone in this assertion that SETI, although providing lifelong income for those who work with the project, is a futile effort, a fanciful idea that if there is anyone out there in the cosmos they are looking for our primitive radio waves and willing to respond in kind. Meanwhile, we have cases like Vickie Landrum and Betty Cash, along with Steve Michalak of Falcon Lake who experienced radiation burns, along with thousands of others who have scoop marks on their bodies; Klieg conjunctivitis from looking at unidentified

flying objects whose luminosity is akin to welding torches; massive numbers of episodes of missing time; electromagnetic effects that shut down electrical devices in the presence of giant UFOs; nuclear facilities around the world that are temporarily shut down by flying saucers; electrical blackouts in cities reporting the presence of UFOs; military personnel reporting encounters with UFOs; military personnel who are placed on disability from UFO encounters such as the Rendlesham Forest incident; objects in outer space observed transiting Venus; Mars; the Sun; and the Moon; ancient reports that exist in all of our world's Scriptures; black eyes; bleeding ears and noses from UFO encounters; mass sightings such as the Voronezh mass sighting in Russia in 1989; countless radar confirmations with multiple credible witnesses (many of whom are pilots); and cattle (and sometimes human) mutilations; in which the bodies are completely drained of blood and soft tissues removed with laser-like surgical precision for some unknown purpose. It would seem that we humans can't see the forest for the trees. We have an alien presence in our midst, and the chasm between the UFO community and the scientific community that has existed since the Condon Report of 1969 has prevented either camp from getting through to one another, which was part of a brilliant plan of clandestine operations on the part of the hidden UFO intelligences all along.

Zecharia Sitchin (1920-2010) versus Graham Hancock (1950 -)

Researcher Zecharia Sitchin was born in Russia and raised in Palestine. Sitchin began learning early languages and culture from a young age, along with the history of the Old Testament, which he studied in the original Hebrew language. As an adult, Sitchin became an expert in the history and languages of the Near East. He was one of the few researchers in the world who was able to read, interpret, and translate Sumerian cuneiform. Sitchin was a member of the American Association for the Advancement of Science, the American Oriental Society, the Middle East Studies Association of North America, and the Israel Exploration Society. A graduate of the University of London, Sitchin was a journalist and began writing his books, *The Earth Chronicles*, considered by his fans as one of the most authoritative interpretations of the last 450,000 years of Earth's history available. Sitchin took the approach of reading the Sumerian stories as a real chronicle of actual human history rather than stone tablets full of ancient mythology. In so doing, a unique picture of the history of humanity emerged. In his work, Sitchin asserted that the term *Nephilim* in the Old Testament was erroneously translated to English as "giants," when Nephilim actually translates literally to "those who had come down from heaven to Earth." The Old Testament refers to the Nephilim as part of the *Anakim*, a plural term that interprets as *sons of god*. The etiology of both terms used in Genesis, the Nephilim and the Anakim, can be traced back to early Sumerian clay tablets. According to Sitchin, these clay tablets, written in Sumerian cuneiform, describe the gods of the Sumerians, the *Anunnaki*, as natives of the planet *Nibiru*, and the genetic manipulators/creators of Homo sapiens. According to Sitchin, the Sumerian records indicate that modern Homo sapiens were originally created by the Anunnaki as a slave race in order to mine gold, which the Anunnaki desperately needed back on Nibiru to save their failing atmosphere. Sitchin's books make the case that, based on the amount of detail, sheer volume, and contextual richness of the Sumerian tablets, the Sumerians were, in fact, recording history rather than fabricating fanciful myths. According to Sitchin, the Sumerian records also describe the aerial craft of the Anunnaki. Sitchin concluded that many of the megalithic structures throughout the world were intended for landing pads for the Anunnaki spacecraft, an assertion that some think represents Sitchin "jumping the shark." Through decades of research, Sitchin concluded that the home planet of the Anunnaki, Nirbiru, exists as an undiscovered planet in our solar system that has an elliptical orbit, passing close to Earth between Mars and Jupiter every 3,600 years. Sitchin saw modern UFO lore as a process of "catching up" to ancient Sumerian writings. Sitchin's writings caused quite a stir on the internet in his time. His interpretations fueled all sorts of conspiracy theories and accusations of a cover-up. Many used Sitchin's writings to maintain that NASA knew about the approach of Nibiru all along, and kept this information from the public to avoid a panic.

Sitchin's work, as interesting as it is, is not without its critics. In his 2015 tour de force, *Magicians of the Gods*, researcher Graham Hancock assures his readers through his own etiological research that the term, *Nephilim*, does, in fact, translate to "giants" after all. Hancock asserts that at least some of Sitchin's interpretations were erroneous, likely embellished, and self-serving to sell his books. Even though Hancock, who personally met with and talked to Sitchin at one point, considers his work to contain much valuable information, Hancock also believes that Sitchin's books present readers with items of pure science fiction at times.

Dr. Leo Sprinkle (1930 -)

Dr. Leo Sprinkle is a psychotherapist who earned his Ph.D. in Counseling from the University of Missouri in 1961. Dr. Sprinkle served as one of the consultants for the Condon Committee in 1968. He was also a consultant for Jim and Coral Lorenzen's APRO organization, and was Professor Emeritus of Counseling Services at the University of Wyoming. Dr. Sprinkle was not only a UFO researcher, but a UFO experiencer himself. Over the years, Sprinkle has appeared on many television shows with such greats as Dr. Carl Sagan and Dr. J. Allen Hynek. Dr. Sprinkle spent many years researching and investigating the underlying nature of UFO contacts. Sprinkle discovered that, far from representing delusional personalities, UFO experiencers come from all walks of life and professional status. Sprinkle made the case that UFO experiences cannot be simply written off as products of the human mind. All evidences compiled concerning UFO experiencers such as himself do not support the conclusion that the percipients are having some sort of neurotic or psychotic episode. Serious UFO investigators are stuck with a dilemma. That is, UFO experiencers are reporting the honest truth as they understand it, yet modern science has no answers whatsoever as to the actual nature of the experience, and no solid physical evidence for the reality of the phenomenon. Dr. Sprinkle concluded that the

Phenomenon presents a significant challenge to humanity concerning the underlying nature of reality itself. He became convinced, after years of personal research, that the Phenomenon represents a genuine, baffling mystery, whose answer is key to the inner nature of human physical, biological, psychosocial, and spiritual reality. Dr. Sprinkle tentatively concluded from his own UFO experience and his interviews with contactees, abductees, and UFO witnesses of all kinds, that Earth is being surveyed by extraterrestrials whose real purpose remains unknown. As human beings, we might not be advanced enough to communicate effectively with the aliens. Sprinkle believed that every effort should be made to acquire knowledge and improve our spirituality so that, one day, open contact with the unknown UFO intelligences can be effectively established. In other words, UFOs are real, our UFO experiencers are telling the truth, UFO witnesses are experiencing a real phenomenon and not something delusional or psychotic, but we humans are currently intellectually underdeveloped and perceptually ill-equipped to understand what is really going on right now. That, I would say, is an accurate assessment. However, with the augmentation and enhancement of human intelligence that is coming with the Singularity, this is going to rapidly change. The open contact and perception of creatures from other realms of reality that we have always sought will surely occur when these abilities become manifest.

Regarding flying saucers, their occupants, and strange creature encounters, we are dealing with a reality that cannot be measured or ascertained using any science or technology that we currently possess at the time of this writing. Although there may exist some level of inside information concerning the identity of our visitors within clandestine intelligence circles, the hidden UFO intelligences are completely unknown to the general public, other than by anecdotal stories from alleged contactees, many of whom have been influenced by nefarious terrestrial organizations with their own agendas. No unambiguous physical evidence exists in the public domain that lends to the reality of flying saucers for the public at large, although anyone who conducts personal research will conclude that such evidence is, in fact, secreted away. UFO percipients themselves have only their memories of the event, and there are probably just a handful of people on the planet within intelligence circles who have knowledge of and access to such physical evidence. As interested private UFO investigators, we are all left to our own powers of deduction to determine the true nature of the Phenomenon. I have tried to piece the information together for myself following my own subjective near-death experience in order to make sense of the UFO phenomenon, and have concluded that UFOs have something to do with our approaching technological singularity, although many details of just how human beings fit into the coming Singularity are currently unknowable. NDE Laboratory researchers such as Michael Persinger have demonstrated to my satisfaction that exposure to certain electromagnetic fields yield similar experiences and imagery that the UFO experiencers are reporting. Therefore, it is reasonable to conclude that imagery perceived by the human mind during UFO encounters is induced by some sort of electromagnetic energy. However, I

510

think it is unreasonable to believe that these energies are just naturally-occuring, unconscious, geomechanical plasmas that just happen to produce images cross-culturally of similar-looking flying saucers and various types of ufonauts who exit the craft; interact with human witnesses; ask for water; invite them on flying saucer rides; take them for trips throughout the cosmos; or search the ground and/or examine their spacecraft; get back inside; levitate into the air; and simply vanish. Rather, the evidence is more consistent with the idea that the electromagnetic energy involved in the production of UFO experiences represents either a complex intelligence in and of itself, or, naturally-occurring electromagnetic fields that are somehow being used and manipulated by unknown alien or indigenous Earth intelligences to produce archetypal UFO experiences in humans. In contrast to the electromagnetic lab experiments conducted by researchers such as Dr. Michael Persinger and others, UFO encounters usually involve more than just visual and auditory imagery. Genuine UFO encounters involve not only these types of images and sounds, but can also involve the appearance of temporary physical objects that exist as products of the human mind and then vanish into thin air without a trace, leaving researchers of physical trace evidence baffled and frustrated. As in the case of Betty Andreasson and many others, UFO experiencers are intentionally exposed to a paraphysical technology by nonhuman entities whose actual appearance and identity is completely unknown to us at present. If, in fact, the earth is being invaded by aliens, they are using a clever disguise that is extracted from the imagery in our own minds, probably based on our own concepts of what they should look like, or gleaned from our own science fiction, and then interacting with us without our knowledge of who they really are. It is, therefore, a long-range, covert alien infiltration involving deception at the deepest levels of the human psyche. Whether or not this alien deception and manipulation that has affected and bewildered humankind for so long will be perceived by us as justified and beneficial in the long run remains unknown.

Brad Steiger (1936 -)

Brad Steiger is a book-writing machine. He will go down in history as one of the most prolific writers on the paranormal who ever lived. Brad Steiger has written over 200 books, 22 of which involve the subject of UFOs. How he has written and published the amount of material that he has in one lifetime escapes me, as this book alone is several years in the making. The man must've written books in his underwear all day long while being fed intravenously. I don't get it. Be that as it may, he has written some fantastic books on UFOs, and has come to some interesting conclusions about their true nature. Steiger has concluded, after a lifetime of research and writing about the subject, that UFOs represent some type of unknown external intelligence that has interacted with humankind throughout our entire history for purposes that remain completely unknown to us. Steiger speculates that the intentions of our alien visitors concerning their interactions with humans is to learn about human beings for their own knowledge, to impart certain cosmic, spiritual, or technological truths to humanity along the way, or a combination of these. Brad also suspects that the UFOs "need" us in some way. As Steiger puts it *(MEEE, pg. 674):*

> *I am also convinced there is a subtle kind of symbiotic relationship between humankind and the UFO intelligences. I think that in some way, which we have yet to determine, they need us as much as we need them.*

As I have indicated throughout this entire book, I have also concluded, as Steiger has, that this is exactly the case. There is, in fact, some sort of symbiotic relationship going on between aliens and humans. The occulted UFO intelligences seem to desire something from us long-term in the way of knowledge that they can add unto themselves. The knowledge that the aliens seek is either experiential knowledge concerning the inner psychological workings of lifeforms that evolved naturally on this planet (both human and animal), or the acquisition of knowledge gleaned from the human species, a species that represents some sort of cosmic experiment that the UFO intelligences might have had something to do with regarding our genetic manipulation into *Homo sapiens.* Steiger also speculates that we may somehow be related to our alien visitors, that we might actually share a common ancestry in the universe, that we may be their children and/or creation, or related in some way that currently remains totally elusive to us. In some strange way, we might even be the aliens themselves. As the Betty Andreasson case indicated, humans may, in fact, be the larval form of the aliens we seek contact with. The idea that "we are the aliens" is somehow more comforting to us, that we have, in fact, manipulated ourselves from another realm in order to achieve a merger of consciousness by way of the Singularity. After all, abduction researcher Dr. David Jacobs encountered percipients who were told during their experiences that "We will be together soon." If a transcended version of ourselves is seeking to merge with the human facet of our own consciousness, the human version of ourselves being an intentional creation of our transcended selves - that is certainly more palatable to us than a forced merger with superior aliens who are manipulating us to do so. Steiger believes that some sort of equilibrium may have to eventually come about between ourselves and our visitors, whoever they are, as a matter of human survival. After all, if humans are an extraterrestrial experiment, experiments can fail. It remains to be seen if humanity is a successful or unsuccessful cosmic experiment. Something tells me that, as long as we are on the track toward the Singularity, the UFO intelligences will continue to interact with us, as the Singularity appears to be an important part of what our visitors want us to achieve. The technology of the Singularity is either a necessary component of open contact, the singularity finally equipping us with the appropriate sensory apparatus to finally understand and perceive our visitors correctly, or the Singularity isn't about us at all. Humans may just represent the tools that the aliens need to achieve the Singularity for nonhuman purposes. Once we have produced this "product" that the extraterrestrial visitors are after, humans may possibly be disposed of, as we are no longer necessary. I hope, for humanity's sake, that there is some sort of mutual benefit planned, that the human race will, in fact, survive the Singularity, and that we can finally become a mature race that interacts with our cosmic neighbors. However, there is no guarantee that this is the case. As for the Extraterrestrial Hypothesis (ETH), Steiger writes *(MEEE, pg. 674)*:

> *I do not dogmatically rule out the Extraterrestrial Hypothesis, but I do lean toward the theory that UFOs may be our neighbors right around the corner in another space-time continuum. What we have thus far been labelling "spaceships" may be, in reality, multidimensional mechanisms or psychic constructs of our paraphysical companions. I have even come to suspect that, in some instances, what we have been terming "spaceships," may actually be a form of higher intelligence rather than vehicles transporting occupants.*

Steiger's statement, if true, says it all. As Trevor James Constable concluded in the 1950s, UFOs may actually represent intelligent creatures. These creatures are normally invisible, but can be captured on film that registers images in the infrared and/or ultraviolet range. Constable captured such creatures on his cameras using techniques that he detailed in his books, *Cosmic Pulse*, and *Sky Creatures*. It also lends confirmation to subjective feelings that have been expressed by multitudes of UFO percipients throughout the past several decades and even today. That is, UFO experiencers often get the feeling that both flying saucers and their occupants are manifestations of the same intelligence, or that the flying saucer occupants are projections of intelligence that are attached to and/or emanating from the "spacecraft" itself - that the two are intimately connected to one another, or even one and the same thing.

Like Dr. Jacques Vallee, Steiger believes that the elves and "wee people" of old, as well as many other paranormal manifestations of our past history, are the same intelligences that are behind the UFO mystery. The works of both Vallee and Steiger suggest that human beings represent one stage of life within a larger context of complex intelligences throughout the universe and other dimensions. Our purpose as beings in human form involves the discovery of this fact and coming to terms with it, hopefully understanding someday our actual place in the larger cosmos. Brad Steiger's views are basically optimistic, that the intelligences behind UFOs and their manifestations are here to inspire us to ever-greater spiritual evolution and understanding. As a haunting reminder that I may be correct in my views that alien intelligences are manipulating us toward a technological singularity for their own purposes, Steiger summed up his views with the following statement *(MEEE, pg. 674, 675)*:

> *Although these paraphysical, multidimensional entities have always coexisted with us, in the last half-century, they have been accelerating their interaction with us for a fast-approaching time of transition and transformation.*

As we finally approach the Singularity sometime between 2045-2080, I think we will discover that Brad Steiger's research was closer than most to correctly postulating the underlying nature of the UFO mystery. Personally, I sincerely hope that Brad Steiger's optimism is warranted and not grossly inaccurate or delusional. Despite Steiger's optimism, I feel that there is good reason to doubt the beneficial intentions of at least some of our alien visitors. I hope that I am wrong.

Sherry Hansen Steiger (1945 -)

Sherry Hansen Steiger, the wife of Brad Steiger, is also his literary cohort. While Sherry was in seminary she realized that, in many instances, stories in the Bible were actually describing proto-UFO encounters. At some point in her career, Dr. J. Allen Hynek asked her to become his personal manager and director of publicity. So, for two years, between 1984 and 1986, Sherry and Dr. J. Allen Hynek interviewed UFO witnesses together. With a professional background in media, Sherry was busy during this time with plans for television, motion pictures, and international media and lecture exposure of the life's work of Dr. J. Allen Hynek. Hynek had dedicated his life to astronomy and UFOs. An opportunity presented itself from a very well-placed individual to reveal to the world the reality of crashed spaceships and alien visitation. At the promise of this enigmatic person (whoever they were), previously classified top-secret documents were to be released into Dr. J. Allen Hynek's care. Unfortunately, but not surprising, following this once-in-a-lifetime offer, Hynek and Steiger experienced a bizzare series of unusual events that lead to the untimely death of Dr. J. Allen Hynek in 1986. These events are outlined in a book Sherry Steiger wrote with her husband, Brad Steiger, called *The Rainbow Conspiracy* (1994). Sherry's perspective on UFOs is spiritual in orientation. She believes as Pastor Downing, author of *The Bible and Flying Saucers*, that guidance from the UFO intelligences was present throughout the writing of both the Old and New Testaments, and that the prophecies and projections within the Bible coordinate well with the messages of modern UFO contactees. I now agree with this view. In my own case, I wrote *Outgrowing the Bible: The Journey from Fundamentalism to Freethinking* in 2000 as an agnostic, and this book independently and coincidentally shared the conclusions of other researchers such as Zecharia Sitchin - that biblical accounts have their roots in pre-existing cultures, in particular ancient Sumer. The culture of Sumer, in turn, had some type of connecton with astronomical knowledge that a civilization such as theirs should not have had. Since the writing of this book in 2000, I had my near-death experience (NDE) that I detailed in the beginning of his book that demonstrated to me firsthand that life exists beyond the death of the physical body. Although I still stand by the validity of the material presented in *Outgrowing the Bible*, my NDE and resulting research into the paranormal and UFO fields have definitely led me to the same conclusion as Sherry Hansen Steiger, that the Bible not only represents the rehashed tales of previous cultures, but the Bible is also a book that is full of UFO contactee experiences. Sherry wrote (MEEE, pg 676):

All world religions have similar descriptions of astral vehicles and supernatural beings and their interactions with humankind. I believe UFOs to be the "Powers and Principalities" - as stated in the New Testament and may include many other levels of existence. I also believe that as on Earth we have the positive and negative polarities there must be that of the good and bad in the astral realms as well, meaning that some angels or messengers may be demons - or fallen angels.

I am well aware that the idea I am presenting in this book, i.e., that UFO intelligences are guiding humankind toward the Singularity, will likely be categorized as a "fringe theory" by many in the UFO community. However, this fringe theory gets even more "out there" when contemplating Sherry Hansen Steiger's ideas about UFOs and the Bible, along with the thoughts of the Reverend Billy Graham in his book, *Angels: God's Secret Agents* (1965). That is, modern UFO encounters and biblical accounts of high strangeness may be one and the same phenomenon. Also, if there is substance contained within the prophecies written in the Book of Revelation, the product we are being employed to produce during the Singularity, i.e., a form of artificial intelligence that disembodied entities can download their consciousness into for a last-ditch attempt at permanent residence in the physical world as opposed to temporarily possessing a human body, the prophecy concerning the Battle of Armageddon may become a reality. The army of Satan could be composed of demonic, lower-astral spirits who have successfully entered the physical realm via artificial intelligence, i.e., robots of human creation, who then attempt to destroy Jesus Christ, the ET savior of humanity and his opposing army of angels, who both engage in a final battle on Earth for the soul of humanity. This all may sound crazy, but if the UFO phenomenon and world religions are intimately connected, in particular Christianity and biblical prophecy, something akin to this scenario might just be in the works. This idea also correlates well with the ideas of other Christian researchers of the UFO phenomenon, such as Thomas Horn, author of *ExoVaticana*, Trey Smith of the *God in a Nutshell Project* on Youtube, and L.A. Marzulli's books, including *Return of the Nephilum*. If something like the Battle of Armageddon is actually going to happen in our near future, and UFOs have anything to do with it, it would actually explain a lot about the nature of Satan, and why humans were engineered in "The Fall" for war, conflict, and territorial domination. We may have been engineered that way in order to expedite a rapid development of technology as we compete to the death with one another in bloody battles and constantly improve our technology. We have been fooled into thinking that the continually-improving technology is for ourselves, when it actually serves the Satanic agenda, the "powers and principalities of the air." In this theoretical scenario, these powers and principalities that occupy the flying saucers are endeavoring through a deceptive program to guide human technology into an unfathomable Singularity for their own physical salvation and dominance throughout the universe.

Dennis Stillings

Dennis Stillings has a different angle on ufology. With a BA in philosophy from the University of Minnesota and some graduate work in math and German literature, Stillings was interested in anomalous phenomena for potential use in medicine and technology. Stillings was a founding member and board member of Five Mountain Medical Community organization who promote a Northwest Hawaii location as a healing center. Stillings was a member of the Bioelectromagnetics Society, a Fellow of the American Institute of Stress, and a member of the Society for Scientific Exploration. Dennis ascribed to the "Jungian archetype" view on UFOs. In this view, the remnant of UFO sightings that are left when all other explanations are ruled out, i.e., the sightings that represent true unknowns, are likely the products of our collective human unconscious, projections into three-dimensional reality from a psychological source center. Stillings is pessimistic that humans have now or will ever have the appropriate scientific tools to properly understand UFO phenomena. Dennis felt that the only science we can apply to the UFO conundrum is to acknowledge first of all that the reports do exist, so it therefore constitutes some sort of real phenomenon, and that psychosocial data can be collected from the reports in order to find patterns or correlations. Stillings held similar views to those of Dr. Jacques Vallee, John Keel, and many others who take a scientific approach to ufology. They accept that UFOs represent a real phenomenon, but that we do not presently understand what UFOs actually are. These authors also conjectured that we may never know, but held that scientific data collection of the reports themselves, as well as studies of the percipients, holds potential for producing scientific fruit. For example, Keel ran statistics on a multitude of UFO sightings and found that Wednesdays and Saturdays from 10 p.m.-12 p.m. demonstrate an increase in sighting reports that rises above coincidence. Keel, Sanderson, and others discovered that certain geographic areas host multiple sightings over time, Keel's "window areas." Keel also found that certain unusual family names like Adamski or Heflin yielded more reports than the more common names, like Smith, or Jones. White people are more likely to report abduction experiences than black people. None of these patterns should exist at all if UFOs represent random phenomena. Also, Keel pointed out in his books that if UFO reports were a product of mental disturbance, there would be more sightings in highly-populated urban areas where there is a greater percentage of mentally disturbed people running around, but this is not the case. UFO sightings are reported more in rural areas by credible witnesses of good reputation in their communities. French researcher Aime Michel used the scientific method to plot out UFO sightings in France during the year 1954. Michel's results revealed what he called the "Straight Line Mystery," or "Orthoteny."

Thus far, Philip Klass' "UFO curse" has held true, but as we approach the Singularity, we will surely dispel the curse once and for all. If, when we expand our own consciousness, our intelligence, and our ability to perceive the universe by billions of times by merging our minds with artificial intelligence once the Singularity is achieved, and we still do not know what UFOs really are, then perhaps the skeptics were right all along. If there is nothing there, then we have deluded ourselves completely all this time with our godforsaken science fiction. We will just have to concede post-singularity, if we are not suddenly brought up to speed to comprehend the UFO mystery once and for all, that flying saucers simply do not exist, and never have, even though our belief in what Keel always called "marvelous phantasms" has, in fact, inspired us to achieve technological greatness. Therefore, if it turns out that flying saucers were purely psychological in nature, they still played an important part in our progress as a species. Even if UFOs have only existed as products of our own feeble psychology, we will still have to accommodate the fact that flying saucers were in our minds all this time and conduct scientific research to determine just what in the hell was really under the hood in the human mind all along. If UFOs are not real in any physical sense, how is it that all of our UFO percipients have had such extraordinary psychological experiences when there was never anything there at all except the wind blowing back in our faces? Even though there may come a time when we wish UFOs were not real, I find the thought that flying saucers are not real somewhat depressing. As 1950s contactee George King once said, "Without flying saucers, the universe is lifeless."

Ronald Story (1936 -)

Ronald Story is an accomplished author and technical writer for high-tech and aerospace publications. He was the founder of the original UFO Encyclopedia Project, and editor of the *Mammoth Encyclopedia of Extraterrestrial Encounters*. Ronald Story graduated with honors from the University of Arizona with a degree in philosophy. Once upon a time, Ronald Story actually met legendary atmospheric physicist and UFO researcher James McDonald, and together they embarked on a joint study of the Missouri ghostlight phenomenon. In 1976, Ronald Story wrote a critique of Erich von Daniken's "ancient astronaut" juggernaut, *Chariots of the Gods*, entitled, *The Space-Gods Revealed*. Story's book was blessed with a foreward written by the late world-famous astronomer, Carl Sagan. After decades of UFO studies, Story concluded, as many do, that UFO phenomena represent a complex myriad of possible realities that include every conceivable explanation including, but not limited to, misidentified natural phenomena; hoaxes; secret military aircraft; psychic projections/apparitions; and actual nuts-and-bolts extraterrestrial spacecraft with alien occupants here for unknown purposes. Story wisely concluded that, regarding the actual reality behind the totally unexplainable UFOs, we should *prepare ourselves for every conceivable possibility* at this point. Story did not rule out the possibility that an alien intelligence may have had something to do with our creation here on Earth. Since this might be the case, we should prepare ourselves now for the possible return of the gods sometime in our future. Ronald Story states that a future open contact event will be the most significant event in human history. Story's view is that, since the Bible says we were created by extraterrestrial beings who called themselves the *Elohim*, our fate in the universe must be somehow tied up with our relationship to these beings. As such, we should all make every effort to insure that our relationship with the original ET progenitors is a good one.

Dr. Frank E. Stranges (1927-2008)

Dr. Frank Stranges was the Christian minister who claimed contact with an angelic Venusian named Valiant Thor as he was staying at the Pentagon as a guest of President Eisenhower. Dr. Stranges had a rough start in life. He was born into this world sickly. As a young man, he was kidnapped, robbed, and shot. Dr. Frank Stranges automatically saw the connection between UFOs and the Bible, and preached a gospel/UFO message with books, movies and lectures. Stranges earned a Ph.D. in psychology, and was president of International Evangelism Crusades, Inc. He wrote many books on UFOs, including his most famous work, *Stranger at the Pentagon*. This book, in which Stranges explains his relationship with the kind Venusian, Valiant Thor, is now a collector's item. As an evangelist, Dr. Frank Stranges was naturally most interested in the spiritual aspects of the UFO phenomenon. Frank believed and taught during his entire career as a preacher of the Gospel of Jesus Christ that extraterrestrials were interested in our spiritual evolution and there to assist if we asked. In his preaching, Dr. Stranges drew heavily from his personal experiences with Valiant Thor at the Pentagon, and believed benevolent Space People are among us to assist as we mature into the spiritual beings that God desires. Dr. Stranges believed that the spiritual message of our Space Brothers was far more important than learning about their spacecraft or propulsion systems. Like the Reverend Billy Graham, author of *Angels: God's Secret Agents*, or R.L. Dione, author of *God Drives a Flying Saucer*, Dr. Franks Stranges taught the biblical connection to UFOs and extraterrestrials his entire 50-year career. Stranges was a lifelong minister of the gospel of Christ, part of which involves not lying to people. The only way that I can conceive of Dr. Frank Stranges totally lying about his encounter with the man from Venus (which, granted, sounds far-fetched), is that he may have simply made up a harmless story of a benevolent humanoid space alien to convey a sense of wonder about God's heavens, to assist in his preaching by using the story to reach people, and to do his part in extinguishing any fear that aliens are somehow hostile to humanity. Dr. Frank Stranges might have felt righteously justified in concocting a benign metaphorical tale to illustrate the mission of God's humanoid angels. After all, he did truly believe in the UFO/Bible connection. No one will ever really know for sure. The photos of Valiant Thor have never been debunked. No one has ever come forward all these years with the claim that they were any of the people who appeared in his photographs of alleged Venusians. Personally, when I look at the photographs of Stranges' humanoid Venusians, Valiant Thor and crew, or the giant humanoid alien photographs and flying saucer videos from the Italian Amicizia (W56 or Friendship) group online, I automatically hear the theme song to the *Twilight Zone* in my head. I think that is only natural. However, regarding the story of Dr. Frank Stranges and Valiant Thor, it is a near-certainty that he was telling the truth as he knew it. If, as a preacher, he fabricated the story to contribute his part in global nuclear awareness and disarmament, he just told a little white lie in which the end justifies the means. There is also the possibility that Dr. Stranges might have been sincere but mentally disturbed due to childhood trauma, in which case he is innocent of any wrongdoing. On the other hand, Dr. Frank Stranges just might have been telling the truth after all about a humanoid alien who came to Earth from the interior of Venus, or possibly from the astral plane of Venus, on an angelic mission to the Pentagon to warn Earth's inhabitants of the dangerous use of nuclear weapons. Regarding Dr. Frank Stranges and the story of Valiant Thor, we may never really be able to separate truth from UFO mythology.

Whitley Strieber (1945 -)

In 1987, Whitley Strieber's book, *Communion*, the book that detailed Strieber's own personal abduction experience, became a best-seller. The book sold over 10 million copies and was made into a movie in 1989. Whitley Strieber has written many fiction books as well, including my personal favorite, *The Hunger*, which was also made into a movie starring the late legendary rock star - David Bowie. Strieber readily concedes that not everyone is ready to accept abduction accounts into their concept of reality. He encourages people to keep an open mind, and reassures those who are afraid that even a casual interest in the subject of alien abductions implies that they actually believe in them. Strieber assures those inquirers that they can research the subject without committing to such belief. Strieber states *(MEEE pg. 684)*:

> *It is also necessary to face the fact that the existence of the evidence means that there really may be aliens here — aliens who are creating an extraordinary theater in the sky while at the same time entering the personal lives of many people in extremely bizarre and secretive ways.*

So much for encouraging the skeptical to remain open about alien abductions. Strieber believed that serious attention should be given to the alien abduction phenomenon. He encouraged those who choose to investigate the subject to consider that alien abductions might actually be happening, and that this alien intrusion is not in the best interest of humanity.

The phenomenon of alien abductions is very real, especially to percipients. The experience of alien abductions might be occurring on what the Urantia Book calls the *Morontia* level of reality. This realm, as described in the Urantia Book, is the precursor to the spirit world, a reality that exists somewhere between three-dimensional reality and discarnate spirit. Other than alien implants of unknown purpose, usually composed of meteoritic material (based on what has actually been surgically removed from abductees thus far) and other markings such as "scoop marks" on percipients, the lack of hard evidence for the physical reality of alien abductions leads researchers to the conclusion that abduction experiences are very real, but occur in a pseudo-spiritual realm that we are not yet familiar with or accept as a normal part of the real world. Perhaps when the Singularity occurs around 2045, and human perceptions are expanded a billionfold to include association with our fellow discarnate humans and aliens from other worlds, maybe the living and the dead will finally become better acquainted with one another. In the expanded state of awareness that is coming, perhaps terrestrials and non-terrestrials can all just finally accept one another as cohabitating neighbors within Eternisphere.

Robert P. Swiatek (1953 -)

Robert Swiatek was director for the UFO Research Coalition, and secretary-treasurer of the Fund for UFO Research, the organization that once paid Stanton Friedman $16,000.00 to conduct research to determine the authenticity of the MJ-12 papers. After meticulous research, Friedman answered the question of MJ-12 authenticity to his satisfaction, and to the satisfaction of many other UFO researchers in the affirmative. Despite the countless hours that Friedman investigated the MJ-12 papers to ascertain their authenticity, naysayers remained who perseverated on various types of miniscule details that lead them to believe the documents were fake, such as a signature that appears to have been copied from one document to the other, font sizes, etc. UFO arch-skeptic Philip Klass once bet Stanton Friedman that he could not find another example of a particular font that appeared in the MJ-12 documents. Klass offered to pay Friedman $100.00 per example up to a certain number if he could locate such obscure fonts in the MJ-12 papers. Friedman found the fonts, and Klass was forced to write a personal check to Friedman for $1000.00 for finding the limit of 10 examples. The check from Philip Klass to Stanton Friedman for $1000.00 is posted online for all to see. At least Philip Klass was a man of his word and put his money where his mouth was, even though he was wrong about the non-reality of flying saucers. Considering Stanton Friedman's contribution to authenticating the MJ-12 documents, I grant partial credibility to both skeptics and believers. That is, the enigmatic MJ-12 papers are essentially authentic and do represent the essence of the truth. However, the fakery that comes into play in a few minor details were likely to have been thrown into the mix intentionally in order to create plausible deniability. This insured that no security violations were committed, and also served to keep ufologists floundering around and arguing amongst themselves in a hall of mirrors with blasts from random fog machines, which is something the intelligence organizations typically do.

Robert Swiatek's main occupation since 1976 was working as a physics patent examiner at the US Trademark and Patent Office in Arlington, Virginia. His position on UFOs is that, despite decades of careful investigations by UFO researchers who have been busy filing and categorizing sightings, some of which are very anomalous and highly strange, no definitive evidence has been captured thus far to ascertain the existence of an extraterrestrial spacecraft. Swiatek concedes, however, that some of the really unusual UFO cases likely represent something real that is not human, atmospheric, or of natural origins here on Earth. While Swiatek remains uncertain as to whether flying saucers represent an extraterrestrial presence, an interdimensional phenomenon, intrusion from a parallel universe, or some sort of holographic projection, he is fairly certain that the underlying intelligences behind the flying saucer mystery are not human. In his view, empirical evidence for the reality of UFOs and crashed saucers, despite thousands of recorded UFO incidents over the years is lacking. However, Swiatek concedes *(MEEE, pg. 685)*:

> If *witnesses to the so-called Roswell debris and other crashed UFOs are correct, the US Government has material in its possession to resolve the debate.*

The problem with crashed flying saucer stories is that the collection of technology from crashed UFOs (which most certainly has happened on several occasions) likely represent staged events fabricated by the real aliens who continue to remain totally unknown and invisible to us. The real aliens are somehow connected in an intimate way to the human subconscious. The real aliens understand exactly what we humans expect aliens to look like by examining our imaginations and our science fiction. The real aliens keep projecting faux-aliens into our reality that are likely biomechanical robots from one or more post-singularity civilizations, and may be some sort of artificial intelligence themselves. The real aliens, i.e., the Overlords of the Singularity, have continually presented us with technology that is (coincidentally) just beyond what we already have, or at least barely within our capabilities for retro-engineering with some expertise and thought applied. These Overlords have occasionally sent down fake aliens (usually dead and charred) as "gifts from the universe." These "Trojan Horses" have gifted us with technology that we can retro-engineer and assimilate into our many modern electronic devices on our way to the Singularity. This alien technology includes certain items that remain buried in black military projects, just as Ben Rich, the former CEO for Lockheed Corporation, revealed to us on his deathbed.

Robert Swiatek also posed a good question regarding UFOs. That is - why is it that modern abductees, who allegedly number in the thousands or possibly in the millions by now, do not all scream bloody murder and panic following their experience onboard an extraterrestrial spacecraft? One would think that someone abducted by aliens would be more upset by the experience than they typically are. In fact, if someone was actually whisked away by aliens and then returned to Earth, only to be met with disbelief and ridicule by their friends and family, there would likely be more people who were really angry over this, or even people committing suicide from the terrifying experience. Swiatek pointed to this general lack of panic as an indicator that the public at large would not panic after all when the alien presence is finally revealed to us, an event that is inevitable at some point. Missing from Swiatek's assessment is the fact that alien abduction experiences always have a dreamlike quality to them, and may not be happening in what we call the "real world." As mentioned, abductions likely take place in an alternate reality of some sort, such as the Morontia realm. Also, in most alien abduction scenarios, the details of the abduction do not come forth until a hypnotist discovers what actually happened during their episode of missing time. Another factor to consider is the number of abduction accounts in which they are given something to drink prior to the experience, or hit with some sort of ray that alters their perceptions, so it's sort of like asking why more people do not scream at the dentist. The dentist uses anesthesia, which prevents the patient from coming unglued and screaming out of the chair. In other words, the intelligences behind alien abductions, whoever or whatever they are, know exactly what they are doing. They are probably doing something to our minds and bodies that we do not have the foggiest clue about, while the screen memory of the standard "medical exam" is implanted in most cases. Evidence also indicates that way more people have had their consciousness removed from their bodies and taken into the Morontia realm by aliens who have no memories whatsoever of the event than there are cases in which memories are retained. Many actual abductees likely write off the experience as a dream and simply forget about it. There may only be just a small percentage of individuals who notice their missing time; have nightmares about their encounter; feel that maybe something important happened to them; experience fragmentary memories; or notice bodily markings enough to pursue finding out from a doctor or hypnotist what even happened to them. Whatever the real nature of alien abductions, they seem to have something to do with conditioning the mind to think, speak, and behave in ways following the abduction that will efficiently propel human society to the Singularity. The entire alien operation is covert, and may be way more extensive, far-reaching, and affect more people than we have ever previously suspected. If the real aliens had our eventual best interest in mind, wouldn't they just come out and reveal themselves and let us know what they are doing? The way it is, the aliens employ covert and deceptive operations, remain invisible to us for the most part, and visit UFO witnesses as Men in Black (MIB). They cause people to report absurd UFO psychodramas, and even inflict murder or cause suicides (eg. James Forrestal, Morris K. Jessup, James McDonald, and Phil Schneider, just to name a few). The aliens have worked with select individuals within secret societies and/or secret militaries since Nazi Germany or before to the present day. They have worked hard to discredit UFO contactees by giving them false prophecies and compelling percipients to go public with them, only to be destroyed when the prophecies do not happen. The aliens use officials in high positions to introduce alien technology into our society so subtly that we always believe we invented it on our own. Therefore, one can safely conclude that what the real aliens are doing is 1) not for us to know, 2) not in our best interest, and 3) making sure that anyone who discovers what they are actually doing experiences total loss of credibility among their peers, or an untimely and/or unpleasant premature death.

John P. Timmerman (1923-2015)

John Timmerman, a graduate of Cornell University and a businessman from Ohio, became involved with Dr. J. Allen Hynek's Center for UFO Studies (CUFOS) in 1979 and assisted in a major way with funding the operation. In 1980 Timmerman became the Chairman and

Treasurer for CUFOS and started traveling to malls and events with a portable UFO pictorial presentation. Timmerman was also the mastermind who negotiated the release of all NICAP files, which were then transferred from Maryland to Chicago, Illinois, where they merged with all CUFOS files. Like most people who embark on the fantastic voyage into private UFO research, Timmerman concluded that the UFO phenomenon is far more complex than he originally anticipated when he first became interested in UFOs in 1950. He astutely realized that a proper understanding of UFO phenomena necessitates learning more about the physical sciences and human psychology, in particular, the many human mental processes and senses that come into play with UFO encounters, and scientific knowledge about our planetary environment. Timmerman also realized that until governments finally release what they know about UFO crash retrievals, the UFO community would have to rely on anecdotal stories as their primary source of evidence. Timmerman had hopes, as millions do, that someday it will all come out, allowing the whole world to finally understand what UFOs really are and why they are here. Timmerman realized something very important. That is, to understand the UFO phenomenon properly, one must become as informed as possible concerning: meteorological forces of nature that might be mistaken for alien spacecraft; black project military aircraft; various types of geophysical forces that may be responsible for the production of plasma-like earth-lights or ball lightning; fault lines and tectonic forces within the earth; a history of ancient lore and rock carvings related to star visitors; magnetic lines of force in the Earth's magnetosphere; an understanding of the history of ghosts; poltergeists; tulpas; Djinn; angels; demons; and related paranormal phenomenon; Sasquatch and lake-monster lore; vampire legends and case histories; medical realities behind cattle mutilations; hidden police files containing cases of human mutilations; UFO lore involving extraterrestrial races that may exist; abduction accounts; UFO cult history and spiritual beliefs; UFO contactees; landing and occupant reports; information about sleep paralysis; hypnagogia; hypnopompia; various forms of somnambulistic behaviors; the history of astronomy and various types of recorded astronomical observations; such as objects that appear to be under intelligent control that transit the sun, the moon, Mars, and Venus; new science discoveries; a rudimentary knowledge of quantum physics; various sorts of psychic phenomena such as channeling, precognition, and remote viewing; knowledge of technology and the coming Singularity; and the history of world religions. To even come close to grasping the actual scope of the UFO phenomenon and how it relates to humanity, one must come to possess at least a general overview of all these areas of knowledge to get a glimpse of the bigger picture, which is ultimately beyond human comprehension at this point in time. We are currently in the phase of speculating what UFOs are and what their purpose might be. Sometime in the future, perhaps we shall all know for certain. That is the hope, that what is now in the shadows will come into the light, that the truth of the matter lays to rest our most paranoid fears, and that we will merge with this knowledge of visitors from the beyond in some positive and fantastic fashion.

Dr. Jacques Vallee (1939 -)

In Steven Spielberg's movie, *Close Encounters of the Third Kind*, we met a character, "Lacombe," a French researcher who carefully collected data and personal profiles from individuals who are mysteriously being drawn to a secret, designated site where intelligence officials are preparing for an official appearance of an extraterrestrial spacecraft. Spielberg's character was based on the real-life UFO investigator, Dr. Jacques Vallee. One would be hard-pressed to read very far into the UFO literature without coming across his name and references to his work. Dr. Jacques Vallee was a former principle investigator for Department of Defense computer networking projects. He earned his Ph.D. in computer science from Northwestern University in 1967, and was a close associate of astronomer Dr. J. Allen Hynek. Dr. Vallee first became interested in UFOs when he witnessed the intentional destruction of UFO radar-tracking tapes at a major observatory. He has authored a dozen or so books on UFOs, and his work remains a primary reference source in any serious UFO researcher's library. Dr. Jacque Vallee probably contributed more to the scientific research of UFOs than anyone else on Earth. Vallee concluded that UFOs represent a "control system for human consciousness" that is operated and maintained by unknown UFO intelligences. He remains undecided as to whether these intelligences are indigenous to our planet somehow as a part of Nature that we have yet to understand, or if the intelligences represent a superhuman will from parts unknown. Dr. Vallee also realized that UFO phenomena may represent aspects of our reality that we are completely unfamiliar with at this present stage of mental development. Dr. Vallee's postulated UFO-generated control system involves the long-term intentional manipulation of human belief systems and the relationship between physical reality and human consciousness. Dr. Vallee concluded that whatever the intelligences behind UFOs really are, they have been a part of our environment from the beginning. According to Vallee, the same intelligences that once brought us encounters with the fairies of old are now disguising themselves as visitors from outer space for some ultimate purpose that eluded and vexed him. Dr. Vallee was also open to the idea of some form of "Supernature" such as that proposed in the "Gaia Hypothesis." The Gaia Hypothesis proposes that organic, biological organisms somehow interact with their inorganic surroundings to create a self-regulating, complex system necessary for the balance of life on Earth. In other words, our human consciousness is intimately connected with what we are perceiving as inanimate objects such that the interaction between the two regulates the way things need to go, sort of like a self-regulating governor on a gas engine. According to the Gaia Hypothesis, human beings have a symbiotic relationship with all of creation. The paradigm of this hypothesis accepts UFOs as part of the natural environment that serve as a sort of self-regulating human belief coordinator. Dr. Vallee's work coordinates well with the thoughts of Carl Jung and his notion that imagery within the human collective unconscious are creating projections necessary for the long-term survival of the human race when facing periods of crisis, in particular, the modern crisis of nuclear power and weaponry, and the potential for total self-annihilation. When we began detonating nuclear bombs that threatened (and continue to threaten) our very existence, the Space Brothers appeared to our contactees with messages of dire warnings against nuclear power as weaponry, along with admonitions for nuclear disarmament so that humans will not ultimately destroy themselves. The Gaia Hypothesis postulates that UFOs are an automatic system built into our reality, an integral part of Nature that regulates all lifeforms on the planet, or at least human beings (I doubt that flying saucers have much of an impact on a pride of lions. Perhaps lions have their own manipulative experiences for their own minds if the Gaia Hypothesis is correct). Dr. Vallee postulated that, whenever a UFO is visible to a human being, it represents a measureable, physical object, as well as a possible portal into another reality that we know little to nothing about. According to Dr. Vallee *(MEEE, pg. 754)*:

> *These forms of life [UFOs] may be similar to projections; they may be real, yet a product of our dreams. Like our dreams, we can look into their hidden meaning, or we can ignore them. But like our dreams, they may also shape what we think of as our lives in ways that we do not yet understand.*

Always the scientist adhering to scientific methodology, readers can detect throughout Dr. Vallee's writings and research into UFOs that he was loathe to come to any solid conclusions about what UFOs really are, or are not. Dr. Vallee always maintained a disciplined and conservative approach, yet managed to keep an open mind to consider new paradigms as they surface in the light of new information. One thing that bothers me about Vallee's views, however, is that if UFOs represent an internal, self-regulating mechanism of consciousness, Philip Klass was possibly right that we will never know any more about UFOs than we do right now, and that the ultimate truth will forever escape us. Endoscopes and microscopes have allowed such a view of internal workings of the human body, but such instruments that can peer into human psychology may forever elude us. When the technology became available to examine internal mechanisms within the human body, new vistas of reality became available to us that increased our understanding of ourselves. Likewise, when the Singularity arrives, and human or ET consciousness is downloaded into artificial intelligence to experience new perceptions that are billions of times expanded from those we are currently limited to, maybe we will finally understand the internal, self-regulating mechanism that Dr. Vallee speaks of, which currently presents itself to us in the form of flying disks with strange occupants. By merging our consciousness with post-singularity superintelligence, we may finally make contact with the higher-order intelligences at large, and finally come to an understanding of what has been happening all along. In other words, the impending Singularity may bring the open alien contact and disclosure that we all seek, along with some form of human transcendence. Perhaps it is right around the corner.

Erich von Daniken (1935 -)

Erich von Daniken brings a story of good luck and good timing. Like Albert Einstein, who worked at the patent office while conjuring the Theory of Relativity, or Jack Nicholson's character in *The Shining*, Erich von Daniken was working as a manager for a hotel in Switzerland when he wrote his first book, *Chariots of the Gods*. From there, Erich von Daniken wrote many more books that championed the Ancient Astronaut Theory. His books have generated more than 58 million dollars in sales internationally, and have been translated into 28 languages. Erich von Daniken's books hit a nerve at just the right time in history, when the old worldviews generated by the world's religions were in dire need of a fresh face. Since the advent of his books, the Ancient Astronaut Theory, which postulates that aliens visited our world in the past, has gone mainstream. According to Ancient Astronaut Theory, these alien visitations may have had something to do with genetically-engineering the human race and creating religion on this planet. The Ancient Astronaut Theory is now believed by millions around the world. Erich von Daniken readily admits that he had never personally witnessed a UFO. He notes with a hint of dismay, as have many other researchers, that the "true believers" in ufology are usually sincere but a little nutty, and that there seems to be a shortage of "real scientists" in the field. Erich von Daniken was among the researchers who spoke personally with Charles Hickson and Calvin Parker of the Pascagoula abduction case in 1973. Von Daniken came away from his lengthy interview with Hickson and Parker with a conclusion that, even though flying saucers are real, he does not know what they are, and that strange experiences, like the one sincerely reported in the Pascagoula case by Hickson and Parker, represent anomalous human experiences for which we have no good explanation at present. Erich von Daniken was aware of the many theories that exist to explain such experiences, and had the tendency to refrain from even speculating whether UFOs are alien probes, extraterrestrial visitors, creatures from another dimension, or a natural phenomenon that somehow interacts with the human brain and produces hallucinatory experiences. He dismisses the critics of Ancient Astronaut Theory who say it is a dangerous theory because people will turn to the aliens or "Space Brothers" to save them. Von Daniken points out that all religions offer the promise of help from higher beings. As I explored in my own book, *Outgrowing the Bible* in 2000, the gods of old, in particular, Yahweh, were not always shining examples of goodness and mercy. Considering the number of towns that were burned to the ground by the command of Yahweh, and all the men, women, and children that were put to death with swords, stones, and fire by Yahweh's decrees, the fact that the Bible is more a reflection of the thoughts of ordinary men living thousands of years ago rather than a divine decree channeled from an Omnipotent Creator becomes clear. As von Daniken states *(MEEE, pg. 762)*:

> *Considering that the "Gods" of ancient times did not always treat mankind gently and quite often became angry and punished brutally, a "hope from above" is not realistic. Rather the contrary! Mankind should be prepared technically and also morally for the "return of the gods."*

The Unsavory Character of the Ancient Gods

Were Erich von Daniken, Pastor Downing, Rev. Billy Graham, and other authors who made the UFO/Bible connection right? Are our gods and extraterrestrials one and the same? There is a good argument to be made that most of the gods that humans have worshipped over the centuries have defective personality characteristics. The description of our gods have been less then benign, and in some cases, quite evil. Even in the case of the loving Christ of the New Testament, the question can be raised as to whether Christ knew ahead of time during his ministry that horrors such as the Crusades, the Inquisition, or the Witch Trials would happen in the future as a response to his teachings, spreading ignorance; pain; blood; tragedy; and death in his name for centuries. Is the founder of a religion (divine or otherwise) ultimately responsible for everything that happens in their name afterward, including mass murder committed by true believers? If some level of responsibility can be legitimately attributed to the founder of any faith for the actions of their future followers, and Jesus Christ came to Earth knowing that his presence would cause all the horrors that Christianity has wrought during the last 20 centuries, does Jesus Christ himself have human blood on his hands? This is certainly debatable. Regarding Christianity in particular, there is a huge discrepancy between the character of Yahweh, as described in the Old Testament, and the character of Christ as described in the New Testament. How could Jesus, who advocated unconditional pacifism for his followers, be the offspring of the terrible Yahweh, who is described in the Old Testament as a "jealous husband," an angry, murderous deity, an inflictor of plagues and natural disasters? If Jesus is, in fact, the son of Yahweh, the apple fell very far from the tree. If the stronger version of Chrisianity is true, and Jesus is actually Yahweh in human form, as many believe, his incarnation into human form produced a deity with schizophrenia. This apparent schizophrenia, however, may have a human instigator. Christianity was doing just fine for the first three centuries as followers of Jesus lived by Christ's simple teachings of loving your neighbor as yourself, as contained in handwritten codexes only. Then, in 325AD, something changed the course of the religion forever. When the warring emperor, Constantine, adopted Christianity as his own, he brought back the Jewish Torah as part of the canonized Bible we know today at the Council of Nicea. If Jesus Christ is, in fact, a member of Bramley's maverick ET race, a cosmic ET tutor, perhaps he was here to save us from the horrors of Yahweh, and the many strict and sometimes brutal laws of the old Jewish Torah (the Old Testament). After all, didn't Jesus state that he was here to save us from the Law? If Christ was an ET hybrid, having a human mother and a nonhuman father, who came to help us, as Bramley speculated in *The Gods of Eden*, and he came to Earth to point the way to salvation, part of that path would be running as fast as we can from Yahweh and his tortuous and immoral laws. Unfortunately, Constantine decided for us which Scriptures were legitimate and which were not, and discarded the Scriptures he didn't like. Constantine punished by death anyone caught with the books he didn't approve for canonization. Therefore, the canonized Bible that we know today is of human construction, and represents a discordant set of spiritual instructions that makes no coherent sense. What sort of world would we be living in today if the original early Christians simply continued without the influence of Constantine? We will never know, but if Jesus was, in fact, a Space Brother, or an Ascended Master who came to Earth to show us how to love one another and escape our imprisonment from the physical world in which we are serving an alien agenda, the Old Testament needed to be forever discarded, which may have been the actual intentions of Jesus in the first place. If this is the case, the divine plan went awry.

From Agnostic to Seeker of Interdimensional Reality

As mentioned in the introduction to this book, in 2000, when I wrote *Outgrowing the Bible*, I was a 45-year-old lifelong agnostic. Following my later near-death experience in 2009 at the age of 54, I suddenly became open to the spiritual messages contained in all the world's sacred writings and contactee accounts, including those contained in the pages of the Bible. The teachings of Yeshua in the New Testament; the extracanonical Scriptures; the teachings of the Qur'an; the pseudepigrapha; the Nag Hammadi, the many channeled or automatic writings of UFO/ET contactees; the Oahspe Bible; the Book of Mormon; the Pistis Sophia; and the Urantia Book all mean something to me now. I have tried since my NDE to live the way Yeshua advocated in all these writings as best I can. Even so, everything I wrote in OTB still holds true and is accurate to the best of my knowledge, with the exception of any new archaological discoveries that were unknown in 2000. Much of my book is a history of how the Bible came to be. I made a good case, I believe, that not everything in the Bible can be taken as literally true. The Bible fluctuates from accurate history to myth and embellishment. I still contend that it is a philosophical and intellectual mistake to treat the Bible as if it is an accurate and complete account of the history of humankind, or the "infallible Word of God." There are many progressive Christian theologians who would agree with me on this. Much of the Old Testament, for instance, was derived from previously-written stories from Sumer, carved in stone with Sumerian cuneiform. Zechariah Sitchin was right in this regard, even if he did "jump the shark" with all the Ancient Astronaut interpretations. It is true that many stories in the Bible are simply rehashed tales from ancient Sumer and Egypt, which, as Erich von Daniken states in his body of literature, were extraterrestrial gods from the stars with imperfect characters rather than omnipotent beings who created the entire physical universe. One thing is likely - when we arrive at the Singularity, we will surely discover who our ET friends and foes really are. If Bramley was correct, and there are two different ET forces in the universe that have been interacting with us all along and anticipate open contact, we will finally get to know them at the Singularity. If friendly, advanced extraterrestrials like the Amicizia group continue to engage in conflicts, as in their stated conflict with the "Contraries," we surely have much to learn about the nature of cosmic interactions and purposes. We will discover, when we merge with our machines at the Singularity, what type of lifeforms are all around us that we have not been able to perceive with the perceptual equipment granted to humans by Mother Nature. When the vision in our own eyes is extended into the infrared and the ultraviolet, when our computational ability is expanded by a factor of billions, and when combining humans and machines enables us to finally interact with other dimensions and parallel universes, what will be the fate of humankind? Will we wake up to a new and exciting reality in which we are equals with our gods, or will we finally seal our fate and disintegrate into a world of total disillusionment and destruction? Are the fruits of the Singularity waiting for us to enjoy, or have we humans just served as slaves to occulted UFO intelligences who we will only come to know when it is too late? These questions and more will be answered, if we keep going in the direction we are headed, sometime between 2045-2080.

Donald Ware (1935 -)

Out of all the positions that I have examined of those involved with UFO research, my own views and conclusions since taking up the UFO mystery are most closely associated, I believe, with those of Donald Ware. Donald Ware earned his BS in Mechanical Engineering from Duke University, and his MS in Nuclear Engineering from the Air Force Institute of Technology. Ware was a fighter pilot, a scientist, and an engineer, as well as an avid birdwatcher. When Donald Ware was 17 years old, he was one of the eyewitnesses to the 1952 Washington D.C. UFO flyover, and is certain that these UFOs were, in fact, alien spacecraft. From 1952 forward, Donald Ware studied the UFO phenomenon, and believes that his own spiritual evolution was assisted by personal interactions with Earth's alien presence. Ware was once the director for the International UFO Congress, and was also a State Director for MUFON. Over time, Ware developed a rather complex personal philosophy that coincides well with my own views, as well as the teachings of the Urantia Book. After decades of UFO research, Ware concluded that some UFOs are alien spacecraft, whereas other UFOs are actually aircraft made for a clandestine military in which some officials involved have received assistance from aliens. Ware determined that we humans are here on Earth to evolve our consciousness, and that we will eventually join with the Galactic Society, one person at a time, by developing our souls and slowly evolving from service-to-self to service-to-others. This evolution, according to Ware, involves incarnating as *Homo sapiens alterios*. This species of humanoid is a more evolved version of humanity that intentionally incarnates here on Earth and blends in undetected with the less-evolved *Homo sapiens*. The more-evolved *Homo Alterios Spatialis* often live isolated from previous versions of humanity until the others are able to accept them. As of 2001, Ware estimated that approximately 1 billion *Homo sapiens* are ready for open contact, and routinely interact with extraterrestrials in their dream life. According to Ware, humans must learn to accept people of different races and religions in order to evolve. As someone who was lucky enough to witness firsthand the Washington D.C. flyover in 1952, Ware was surely inspired by this fantastic experience early in life. What an impact that 1952 sighting made on 17-year-old Donald Ware!

Ware watched as the president ordered jets to engage the flying saucers with shoot-to-kill orders toward beings and their craft that might have been what we would consider angels. The 1952 Washington D.C. UFO flyby experience had a profound effect on everyone who was there, and Ware seems to have integrated this early experience into a lifetime of intentional soul growth. Like Paul on the road to Damascus, who encountered an intense luminosity that blinded him for three days and changed his life, Ware was inspired by the 1952 UFO sighting to pursue a lifetime of spirituality and ufology. In my own case, my encounter with the two shadow people at the age of 6, my vision of a sky full of hovering flying saucers at the age of 11 during the great UFO wave of 1966, my mysterious episode of missing time with my friend Mary in 1979, and my near-death experience (NDE) in 2009 have all contributed to my adopting a similar spiritual path that Donald Ware adopted in his own personal life. Did the hybrid program of the 1960s-1990s produce Ware's Homo sapiens alterios? Do they live among us now? When one considers the fantastic minds that currently work in the field of artificial intelligence and the various space programs around the world, individuals such as Dr. Nick Bostrom, Steve Omohundro, and Elon Musk, I would have to say that this might actually be the case. There does seem to suddenly be "Human 3.0" living side-by-side with the old model of human, much like Homo sapiens lived among Neanderthals for a period of time until the Neanderthals were displaced.

Evolving Souls, or Spaceship Fuel?

As Nikola Tesla once said, "If you want to understand the universe, think vibration." On a fundamental level, we are all nothing more than pulsating masses of quantum potentiality, energy that is constantly vibrating and moving either up or down the spectrum of cosmic activity. The process of soul development may not be completely linear. That is, a physical incarnation that follows this present life may not necessarily propel us into the future. If I blow my second chance that was given to me when I had my heart attack, that day I decided to live on a little longer as a better person than I was before, I can see myself going backward in time in my next incarnation instead of forward. Spiritual progression forward or backward in time may depend on how we fare when the cosmic scales are applied to our present lives after the bodies we currently inhabit are gone and we return to the "Source Field" (as David Wilcock coined) or Eternisphere. If we have engaged in negativity, or we have hurt other people, we might just find that our next incarnation is in a Roman gladiator arena 1,800 years into the past. On the other hand, if we fare well in overcoming the selfish nature of the human condition, and are worthy of progressing, our next incarnation may be 1000 years from now into what we call the future. In a just universe, everyone gets exactly what they deserve, either good or bad, but there is no guarantee that we live in a just universe. Bad things happen to good people, but when they do, maybe it somehow works out on the cosmic ledger. Going through these cosmic tribulations, depending on how we react to them, may purchase "cosmic credits" or incur "cosmic debits" for our next time around. We may be more in control of where we go next than we give ourselves credit for if the universe is mental, and the universe is traversed on a purely mental basis. Personally, I find much of the material written in the UFO lore, the contactee literature, the Gnostic Gospels, the New Testament, and the Urantia Book very inspiring. The nature and construction of the universe that the Urantia Book describes is exciting and inspirational. When I read about the celestial realms that the Urantia Book describes, I become excited and motivated to do better tomorrow than I did today in my spiritual journey. After all, isn't that the purpose of any good inspirational material? I think Donald Ware gleaned the right stuff from his personal experience with UFOs in 1952. He was one of the souls that was meant to be there for the Washington, D.C. flyby. I hope that I can have an actual conversation with him after this world as we both advance within the celestial realms that surely exist throughout Eternisphere. This is providing, of course, that we can make it past the Singularity without having our souls hijacked by evil aliens, or get sucked into some unforeseen cosmic battle as a transhuman bio-robot for an alien purpose that we didn't see coming. My most paranoid thought about the fate of humans is that what we call our "soul" is actually being carefully cultivated by interdimensional aliens for use in fantastically-advanced, conscious spacecraft, owned and operated by our alien overlords. If this turns out to be the case, and the purpose of the human soul is to become the consciousness invested into sentient flying saucers that belong to a higher alien lifeform, I suppose I will just relax and enjoy seeing the entire universe for myself, and marvel at cavorting amongst the stars as an immortal component of alien machinery. I fully realize that this idea, that the purpose of the human soul may be to become an integral component of a self-aware flying saucer operated by a higher-order alien intelligence in the afterlife, is probably too far "out there" for most readers to seriously digest. However, in consideration of the bewildering fugue that we are all left with concerning the presence of the flying saucers and their actual mission here on Earth, I hereby submit that no idea, no matter how strange or exotic it might sound, is completely off the table.

Walter N. Webb (1934 -)

In 1951, one year before the well-documented and radar-confirmed Washington D.C. flyby event that was witnessed by Donald Ware and others, a young Walter Webb personally witnessed a flying saucer at the tender age of 17. From his own anomalous sighting, Webb knew as a teenager that flying saucers represented a very real but unknown phenomenon. Webb earned a bachelor's degree in biology, and served as an astronomer under Dr. J. Allen Hynek at the Smithsonian Astrophysical Observatory's Optical Satellite Tracking program. Walter served as a senior lecturer, assistant director, and operations manager at the Charles Hayden Planetarium, Museum of Science, in Boston for 34 years. Webb was an astronomy consultant for four different national UFO organizations, and was the first Senior Research Associate for the J. Allen Hynek Center for UFO Studies (CUFOS). Webb studied UFOs for 50 years. Over the course of half a century, he interviewed hundreds of individuals, some of whom reported encounters with humanoid beings and landed craft. Webb acquired extensive knowledge of atmospheric and natural phenomena, but realizes that underneath the many misperceptions and bogus sightings, a core of anomalous events that remain completely unexplainable in conventional terms exists. Webb was left with the feeling that the best explanation for the truly unusual encounters was that the Earth does, in fact, have an extraterrestrial presence. According to Webb, our ET visitors are well aware of the societal, cultural, religious, and economic changes that would inevitably occur on Earth if this extraterrestrial presence was to reveal itself openly to the inhabitants of our planet, and that this may be the main underlying reason for our visitor's enigmatic behavior. Webb feels strongly that governments should release any and all information that they possess to the rest of the world, as everyone should know that this planet has company. Webb encouraged scientists to apply their expertise to the UFO phenomenon, and felt that scientists should be able to do so without stigma or fear of ridicule. Webb encouraged UFO researchers to continue improving their professionalism in how they go about field investigations, and encouraged psychologists to become more knowledgeable about sleep paralysis syndromes in order to separate actual abductions from psychological manifestations that have more to do with hypnagogic and hypnopompic phenomena than with aliens. Webb was likely correct in that at least part of the abduction phenomenon involves psychological aberrations that surround the processes of falling asleep and waking up. These misreported and misunderstood processes probably cause many false abduction accounts, and serve to further obfuscate a subject that is already enigmatic and complex. Likewise, Dr. John Mack concluded after hundreds of interviews with abductees that, after separating out all somnambulistic experiences that are explainable in purely psychological terms, what we are dealing with are experiences in a realm of reality that is just as real as the three-dimensional world but is unrecognized and misunderstood by our current science. Webb did a good job of applying the scientific method to ufology. He was quick to acknowledge misidentified natural phenomena from the anomalous reports, and was a real treasure to the field of scientific ufology.

Jennie Zeidman (1932 -)

Jennie Zeidman was a student of Dr. J. Allen Hynek during her years at Ohio State University, where she earned a BA degree in English. Zeidman eventually became Hynek's secretary and research assistant when Hynek was working as the scientific consultant for Project Blue Book. For the first 13 years of her UFO studies, Zeidman remained a UFO skeptic. She believed that all UFOs had prosaic explanations, and that the underlying core of so-called "unexplainable" sightings would also have such explanations if only more information were gathered. However, over the years, as the UFO reports that she and Dr. Hynek investigated all over the world from highly-credible witnesses that were found to display similar features slowly accumulated, Zeidman eventually realized that her skeptical opinion had failed to hold up. In the tradition of scientific skepticism, Jennie refrained from adopting a particular theory, but in the end defined what I believe to be the correct, modern, conservative scientific position *(MEEE pg. 806)*:

> *I now believe unequivocally that "there is something" to UFO phenomena. What, I cannot say. I have never proposed a theory of extraterrestrial intelligence to explain the reported events, yet certainly that theory cannot be ruled out. Whatever their meaning, their origin, their motives, UFO phenomena have, I believe, demonstrated their validity as a challenge to both physical and behavioral scientists.*

In other words, the correct scientific position, based on the evidence that we have, is that flying saucers are real, but we do not know exactly what they are, where they are from, whether they are piloted by biological creatures, robotic entities, or are purely mechanical, and we do not know what they are doing here. The correct of the scientifically-informed concerning UFOs is exactly what Jennie described - The UFO phenomenon is real, but remains unexplained. The old view, that people of scientific mind must write UFOs off as nonsensical pseudoscience, is dead for all time. Those who continue to consider themselves "scientific" and say there is nothing to the UFO phenomenon, that they need better evidence to accept flying saucers as reality, need to snap out of it before they become dinosaurs. They are simply turning a blind eye to decades of good, credible evidence for the reality of flying saucers. Many within the scientific community also appear totally unaware of the great numbers of worthy scientists who began their personal paradigm formation with the same erroneous assumption, including Dr. J. Allen Hynek and a multitude of others, including Hynek's own secretary, Jennie Zeidman. Believing themselves to be more scientific and intellectually astute than the advocates of UFO reality, the UFO skeptics openly admit to a view that is actually the beginning point of UFO research, a beginning point that many others have traveled onward from to become prominent UFO researchers who look forward to the final unveiling of the flying saucer mystery. This day of final revealing will surely come about during our upcoming technological singularity when machines become available as a vehicle for the downloading of various factions of disembodied entities that exist within the Superspectrum. The day is coming soon for cryptoreality to emerge from the shadows regarding flying saucers and their occupants.

Timothy Good (1942 -)

Through years of personal UFO research and writing, Timothy Good has concluded that the earth is being visited by several different groups of aliens, some who are benevolent and helpful, and other alien groups who might be considered exploitive in various ways. Despite the possible dangers imposed by alien contact, including an alien takeover or human extinction event, Good hopes that humanity prevails through it all with assistance from our more benevolent alien friends. Timothy Good has achieved high status in the UFO Community as one of Earth's foremost authorites on UFOs. Spanning decades, Good conducted personal interviews with many military and US intelligence specialists, astronauts, pilots, and government officials. Good always had an interest in space and aviation, and he first became interested in UFOs through the writings of Donald Keyhoe in 1955. Six years later, in 1961, he read Captain Edward Ruppelt's official report on UFOs, which prompted Good to begin his own research. In addition to his personal interviews with UFO experiencers, Good poured through thousands of government documents to arrive at the conclusion that not only are UFOs a reality, but also that we have been involved with alien contact for a very long time. Good has given lectures at many prestigious institutions, and was the first UFO researcher from the West to be interviewed on Russian television. Good has also appeared on US television many times in documentaries and interviews. Good wrote the international best-seller, *Above Top Secret: The Worldwide UFO Cover-up* in 1987, a book that continues to be required reading in any person's personal library who is interested in serious UFO research. In 1991 Good published, *Alien Liason: The Ultimate Secret.* Then, in 1996, *Beyond Top Secret: The Worldwide UFO Security Threat.* Two years later, in 1998, Good published, *Alien Base: Earth's Encounters with Extraterrestrials.* Two years after that, in 2000, *Unearthly Disclosure: Conflicting Interests in the Control of Extraterrestrial Intelligence.* One of my personal favorites was his latest book that was published in 2013, *Earth: An Alien Enterprise.* This latest book by Good includes a very nice section on the Amicizia (W-56 group), one of the human-friendly ET groups who call themselves the AKRIJ. Timothy Good was particulary interesting to me as I conducted my own research following my heart attack and NDE in 2009, as the whole time Good was cranking out these UFO books, he was engaged in a successful career as a professional violinist. Good began his music career in 1963 by playing his violin with the Royal Philharmonic Orchestra. He has since played with the English Chamber Orchestra, the London Philharmonic Orchestra, the Mantovani Orchestra, and many others.

Dr. John E. Mack (1929-2004)

Dr. John E. Mack was a professor at Harvard Medical School, and became the world's foremost scientific authority on the so-called "alien abducton" phenomenon. Mack's early professional focus concerned the subject of how a person's worldview affected their relationships in life. Prior to his involvement with alien abduction narratives, Mack was interested in the clinical aspects of dreams and nightmares, writing *Nightmares and Human Conflict* in 1970. Dr. Mack began his decade-long excursion into abductee interviews believing that their experiences represented some sort of mental illness that he was determined to identify. However, the more abductee interviews he conducted, the more solidly he realized that, much to his surprise, they did not demonstrate any known pathology. Mack discovered that alien abductees come from all walks of life, are perfectly sane and normal in their thinking, and are usually telling the truth as they understand it. Dr. Mack remained reluctant to admit that extraterrestrial aliens were actually interacting with humans. Instead, Mack maintained that the alien abduction phenomenon represented something in a category all by itself, and is not currently understood by our science. After years of research into alien abductions, Mack published books on the subject, including *Abduction: Human Encounters with Aliens* (1994), and *Passport to the Cosmos: Human Transformation and Alien Encounters* (1999). Dr. Mack made the connection between the shamanic experiences of our past and the alien abduction phenomenon. He was personally invested in a philosophy of interconnectedness. As such, he viewed the alien abduction phenomenon in the light of his own knowledge of traditional human experiences, and believed that *alien abduction encounters have something to do with human evolution.* In contrast to abduction researcher Budd Hopkins, who argued for the physical reality of alien abductions by real, physical aliens who took people physically aboard an alien spacecraft to conduct medical experiments with them, Dr Mack's view was that the alien abductions were transcendental experiences that took place in an alternate reality that we currently do not understand. Dr. Mack concluded that the alien abduction phenomenon represents some sort of "cosmic tutorial." Mack also concluded that the abductions had two primary effects - 1) elevating humanity's consciousness so that we do not destroy ourselves and our environment, and 2) *combining human and alien DNA to produce a superior species of human.*

Searching for the Identity of the Grays

Both paradigms that surfaced over time from the work of diligent alien abduction researchers such as Dr. John Mack, Dr. David Jacobs, Budd Hopkins, and others are likely correct, in that 1) Gray-alien abductions can occur in both real time and in altered states of reality, and 2) Gray-alien abductions involve either combining human DNA with alien DNA, or manipulating the human genome in some unknown fashion to produce hybridized/upgraded humans. The Grays, whoever or whatever they are, be they biological, robotic, spiritual, or some combination thereof, appear to have mastered time and space. We do not know if they are actually the ones who created the physical universe as their own computational matrix, or if all life in the universe are the flock to which they tend. There appears to be more than one race or species of alien Grays. We do not really know if these Gray aliens are extraterrestrials; interdimensionals; angels; demons; elementals; inhabitants of Earth's Dark Energy Halo; cryptoterrestrials that live underground or undersea; artificial intelligence; biological robots; the transcendent form of humans; specters from our own collective unconscious; denizens of our own future; or a combination of all of these. It has been revealed to some of the abductees (such as Betty Andreasson) that humans are the "larval form" of the Grays. Perhaps we serve some unknown function for the Grays upon physical death. What we call our "soul" is possibly a resource of sustenance for the Grays in some manner, as odd as that sounds. Perhaps the Grays are the "big boys" of the cosmos, the Overlords of the Singularity, although the Overlords is a generic term that may represent multiple populations of nonhumans who have various vested interests in the technology that humans will create during our impending Singularity. At any rate, we need to deal with the reality that the Grays are, in fact, here, that they may have been here with us for thousands of years or from the beginning of time. The Grays may have even authored the universe itself. Whatever the case, the Grays are of a much higher-order of intelligence than human, perhaps by millions or billions of years. The Grays know much more about us, much more about our physical universe, and much more about the greater realms of Eternisphere than humans do. Our minds may be insufficient to recognize their actual identity correctly, as higher-order intelligences may operate beyond the limited comprehension of humanity altogether. Evidence indicates that the Grays, or at least intelligent entities of energy that can shapeshift into Grays, are in possession of paraphysical technologies that can manipulate the human mind in powerful ways. They are even capable of manipulating our society from a deep fundamental level. They are perhaps connected to and commonly interact with the realm of discarnate human beings. The Grays are able to extract human consciousness from their physical bodies, either by technological or mental means, and bring us into an alternate reality for purposes of manipulation, control, servicing, or enlightenment, as shepherds tend to their flocks of sheep. They are masters of genetics, scientists of an unfathomable order. The Grays, and likely other post-singularity species, appear to operate interdimensional crafts that appear in our skies and are able to materialize and dematerialize in and out of our three-dimensional reality. The Grays are capable of conducting both physical abductions in real time as we know it, as well as abductions into compressed time, during which an outside observer would not notice anything happening to the percipients at all, while the percipient experiences an abduction episode with the Grays that lasts a substantial period of time by his/her clock. The Grays have control over the memories that they wish for the percipients to retain, and are able to effectively block those memories that they choose to withhold. The Grays appear to be in the business of monitoring all life on Earth, creating new and exotic lifeforms from existing flora and fauna, possibly to transport to other worlds in their terraforming efforts. As masters of physics and science, the Grays are able to manipulate DNA to their own ends. Whether these activities are benevolent and intended for improvement of a particular lifeform over time, or an outright manipulation by foreign invaders, we do not know. All we have to analyze the behaviors of the Grays are the anecdotal stories from abductees and those who have allegedly encountered such beings. Even with the consideration of the many alien abduction accounts, we do not know if what the abductees report is actually what happens in the presence of the Grays, or whether the abductees are being infused with standardized screen memories. We do not know if the appearance of the Grays is really what they look like, or if the UFO intelligences are just presenting a generic, palatable image for the human mind that will be accepted without an unnecessary or undesirable level of fear and dysfunctional behaviors from the percipients while they are being studied or tinkered with. The Grays may be endeavoring to transform the human race from violent and destructive specimens of *Homo sapiens* into a more intelligent and benign *Homo sapiens alterios* for the homestretch into the Singularity. If this is the case, at least that means that the Grays are probably not going to abandon and forsake their own hybrid creations that have their own DNA or genetic labor invested once we achieve the Singularity, unless the Grays are of such an unfeeling order of creature that even abandoning their own hybrid creations does not matter to them. Humans may only matter to them as long as they obtain the technology of the Singularity they seek, by any means available to them, in order to permanently tunnel their way into our physical reality from a natural cosmic barrier that we know nothing about. Until such a time that the true identity of the Grays comes into open focus (if that even ever happens), we are left to our own speculations. In any case, deception is afoot, and whether this deception is for our own good, or a Trojan Horse that will soon destroy all of humanity in the end remains to be seen. All we can do is remain vigilant, and hope for the best. The alien abduction phenomenon, which began in earnest with Betty and Barney Hill in 1961 and remained with us in a big way at least through the 1990s, may have been a mission of specified duration in order to make the necessary changes to the human mind and body that the Grays need or want. That the aliens are connected somehow with cattle mutilations is probably an indication that the biological material from Bovines and other earth creatures was necessary to fulfill an aspect of the hybridization program, or perhaps while they were manipulating the genetics of humans, they gathered material for other unrelated projects while they were here. These other projects may have something to do with developing viable lifeforms for transport to other planets that they also care about and tend. That there is an occasional specimen of human mutilation indicates that whoever or whatever is conducting the operations do not share our same moral code or empathy level for other sentient creatures, especially since these incidents indicate that they were conducted while the victim was still alive and kicking. A biological project of some nature was conducted for a period of several decades that required the extraction of material from both animals and humans, at least in the minds of the perpetrators. The methodical and unemotional way that the animal and human blood and tissue extractions took place indicates that the procedures might have been conducted by an unemotional artificial intelligence that was simply completing the programmed tasks assigned to them. If the project is finished now, as abduction researchers such as Dr. David Jacobs and others have suggested, and the hybrids are now among us and working in the fields of science and religion to insure our success in producing the Singularity, it was an ingenious clandestine mission while it lasted, and very successful. Since the alien abduction and cattle mutilation waves of the 1960s-1990s has past, it is very easy for those living today of rational inclination and temperament to simply dismiss the entire alien abduction and/or cattle mutilation phenomenon out of hand, as if it never happened. Whatever projects the Grays wanted to accomplish during these waves of alien abductions and biological tissue extractions have surely been successful and, at least for the moment, perhaps they are finished with their bizarre interactions with humans. Considering all the implications of the research that has been conducted into alien abductions, the human/alien hybrids or genetically-upgraded humans are likely here among us now. They are now an integral part of the human population. The hybrids are taking non-augmented wives and husbands and producing offspring who will never have any idea that their parents are products of such a genetic program that was conducted by the Grays for a few decades of human history. Perhaps this sort of project has been conducted before. The affected organisms (us) notice for a while that something strange is happening within their population, like an unsuspecting school of fish in the presence of a fisherman above, but the suspected activity remains an unbelievable and unidentifiable phenomenon to the affected organisms, as it does not fit into their limited concept of reality. The Grays may even represent the "man behind the curtain" for evolutionary processes on Earth and elsewhere that always appear to the creatures involved as naturally-occuring. Perhaps the Grays are the operational minions of Mother Nature herself, the seeders of life throughout the universe, the orchestrators of evolutionary processes, the *Keepers of the Garden,* as the late Delores Cannon called them. If this is the case, contactees like Ted Owens, (aka PK Man) may have been correct in 1965 when at first he suspected that he was in contact with Mother Nature herself, but later concluded that it was not Nature, but insect-like Space Intelligences (SI) behind his psychokinetic abilities. Nature and the Overlords, at least the faction that appear to us as Gray aliens, might actually be one and the same. If not, then we are dealing with a race of beings that have the capability of manipulating Nature like a potter manipulates clay, and have the power to enable selected human beings like Ted Owens to manipulate Nature as well if they so choose.

Stanton T. Friedman (1934 -)

Stanton T. Friedman is a retired nuclear physicist who took up full-time UFO investigations in 1970. Friedman has written many papers on UFOs, and has toured the world giving professional, scientific lectures on the subject. His scientific background brings a refreshing scientific credibility to the field of ufology. Friedman experiences little resistance during his lectures at universities, or from the scientific community at large as he gives his presentations. As many researchers discover as they speak with UFO skeptics, most of the skeptics are totally unfamiliar with the vast amount of data that is available concerning UFOs, information on UFOs that has been released as a result of the Freedom of Information Act, or UFO-related material from other countries who have now released their formerly-classified material concerning the reality of flying saucers and the factual existence of non-human biological entities. Friedman is best known for his personal research into the Roswell UFO crash and the authentication of the *Majestic 12* documents. He acknowledges that the greater percentage of reported UFOs are misidentified objects of a mundane or atmospheric nature, and states that he is not interested in any of those. His interest lies strictly with the truly anomalous and verifiable cases of incursions into Earth's atmosphere by extraterrestrial spacecrafts. Friedman also does not seem to be very interested in the psychic or apparitional aspects of the UFO phenomenon. He is a nuts-and-bolts kind of guy. Based on his own interviews with living witnesses to the Roswell incident and meticulous personal research, Friedman has concluded that something otherworldly did, in fact, crash at Roswell in 1947, and that a huge cover-up has been perpetrated that he likes to call the "Cosmic Watergate." Friedman stated in 1968 to a committee of the US House of Representatives that, based on the evidence, the Earth is being visited by intelligently-controlled extraterrestrial vehicles, possibly from relatively nearby star systems. Friedman believes that the truly anomalous UFO sightings are consisitent with magnetohydro-dynamic propulsion systems. Friedman has a grievance against SETI in that they are simply searching for radio signals from other worlds. Friedman believes that their anti-UFO positions hinder legitimate UFO research and perpetuate the false paradigm that has existed within the so-called scientific community since the Condon Report was released in 1969, which basically stated Edward U. Condon's opinion, that extraterrestrial vehicles in our skies simply cannot and do not exist. Friedman's books include *Crash at Corona: The U.S. Military Retrieval and Cover-up of a UFO* (2004) that he co-authored with Don Berliner, *Top Secret/Majic: Operation Majestic 12 and the United States Government's UFO Cover-up* that he co-authored with abductee Whitley Strieber (2005), and *Flying Saucers and Science: A Scientist Investigates the Mysteries of UFOs: Interstellar Travel, Crashes, and Government Cover-ups* (2008) that includes forewards by the late former astronaut Dr. Edgar Mitchell, and former Naval optical physicist, Dr. Bruce Maccabee. Friedman's books eviscerate the arguments of modern UFO skeptics, delegating their anti-UFO positions to the dustbin of history.

Dr. Steven M. Greer (1955 -)

Dr. Steven M. Greer is a former emergency room doctor who founded the Center for the Study of Extraterrestrial Intelligence (CSETI) in 1990. Greer also founded The Disclosure Project in 1993. Dr. Greer's efforts focus on bringing suppressed information concerning UFOs into the public awareness. Dr. Greer is considered by many to be one of the world's foremost authorities on UFOs. Dr. Greer and I share the same year of birth, 1955, and like my own childhood encounter with both the Shadow People at age 6 and flying saucers at age 11, Greer reports his personal experiences with UFOs at ages 8 and 18. Dr. Greer is a body builder and a trained Transcendental Meditation instructor. In 1994, Dr. Greer appeared on a Larry King TV special, *The UFO Cover-up*. Dr. Greer, along with former astronaut Edgar Mitchell and other members of CSETI made a presentation on UFOs for members of Congress in 1997. In 1998 Greer gave up his job as an emergency room physician to devote himself full time to the Disclosure Project. In 2001, Greer held a press conference at the National Press Club in D.C. that featured personal testimony of UFOs by Air Force officers, FAA officials, and various intelligence officers who revealed their own personal knowledge and experience with UFOs. Dr. Greer was the keynote speaker for the 2008 Conference on Science and Consciousness held in Santa Fe, New Mexico. He has provided briefings on UFOs to US Intelligence officials including CIA Director James Woolsey. In 2006, Greer published his book, *Hidden Truth, Forbidden Knowledge*. In 2013, Dr. Greer was the co-producer for the movie, *Sirius*, a documentary which discusses his work with the Disclosure Project, his thoughts on UFOs and extraterrestrials, including DNA analysis of a 6-inch humanoid known as the Atacama skeleton that proved to have a human mother from the Chilean region of South America and a father of unknown origin, and his team's efforts to develop new energy sources for the planet. Dr. Greer conducts what he calls CE-5 encounter adventures with paying participants. At these encounter groups, as demonstrated in several posted Youtube videos, luminous orbs make an appearance for interaction sessions with participants. Although Dr. Greer refers to the luminous objects as extraterrestrial spacecraft, their appearance is more like the geophysically-produced earthlights that show up naturally in various parts of the world like Marfa, Texas, or the light beings that were captured on film by Dorothy Izatt. By all appearances, just as in the case of Izatt's film captures, these flying luminous orbs that make appearances at Greer's CE-5 encounter groups possess some sort of consciousness or intelligence of their own. The orbs appear to have the ability and/or willingness to interact in some fashion with the participants of the outings. Whether these light beings who show up at Greer's groups and are captured on night vision cameras are elementals, extraterrestrial aliens from our local solar system or another galaxy, discarnate humans, interdimensional beings who are indigenous to Earth, energyzoa creatures such as the "sky critters" captured on film by Trevor James Constable, or an outright hoax or fabrication produced by humans behind the scenes for show is anyone's guess, but the fact that something is showing up that was invited by his groups is undeniable. Further study and consideration to what Dr. Greer is doing is indicated. If it turns out that the light beings are a real phenomenon, every effort should be made by scientists to determine just what these intelligences are who show up at Dr. Greer's encounter groups.

The researchers above that I selected to discuss are just a small sample of the many fine UFO authors that one encounters in the public domain when embarking on a serious personal examination of the UFO mystery. Those of us who have chosen this particular personal journey are making an effort to piece together the jigsaw puzzle of the greatest mystery to ever face humanity. That is, the incursion into our airspace of unidentified flying crafts that we know were not built by humans, that appear to operate under intelligent control, and are here for unknown purposes. The selected researchers above are in no way a complete analysis of the researchers who are available for examination in the UFO literature. Many authors were left out of my synopsis whose views are worthy of consideration. However, this selected group of researchers, I believe, represent a good enough sample of work that has been conducted from 1947-2016 to enable readers to glean the gist of decades of UFO research at a glance. As you can see from the fruits of their research, many were able to solidly confirm the reality of incursions into our atmosphere by objects under intelligent control that are not of human construction. Following their conclusions that UFOs are real, many speculations and theories have developed as to the origins and purposes of our alien visitors. However, thus far, few have made more than a casual connection between the alien presence and our current, exponentially-expanding technology. Most of the good UFO researchers lived in an era prior to modern speculations about the coming Singularity. Now that the stunning potential of the Singularity is coming into focus within our collective psyches, there is little doubt now that the flying saucers in our skies are well-aware of where we are headed, and are probably, to some degree or another, responsible for guiding us into it for reasons that are open to speculation at present. These reasons will surely become increasingly clear as the Singularity becomes a reality in the very near future.

Epilogue

"Shermer's Last Law: Any sufficiently advanced Extra-Terrestrial Intelligence is indistinguishable from God."

– Michael Shermer, American science writer, founder of *The Skeptics Society,* Editor-in-chief for *Skeptic* magazine, academic historian of science

As revealed in the last chapter, many prominent UFO researchers have drawn very close to discovering the secret mission of the flying saucers. These mysterious objects have appeared in our skies for millennia, and many UFO witnesses, percipients, and investigators have spent their lives wondering about the underlying purposes of the disks, and the nature of their relationship with humankind. At least some of the flying saucers are either alive themselves or piloted by either biological or robotic ufonauts who have mastered the manipulation of the very fabric of space-time. They are able to materialize and dematerialize at will, and some even have bizarre shapeshifting abilities. Some of the hidden UFO intelligences, the ones that are referred to in this book as the Overlords of the Singularity, have been guiding humankind toward ever-increasing technology for centuries now. This accelerated technological progress will eventually culminate into an event that futurists call the Singularity. This is a point in time when advanced technology will completely change our understanding of, and interaction with, reality itself. This magnificent event will transform everything, and is expected to arrive sometime between the years 2045-2080. Sentient, superintelligent machines built by human hands, enhanced by alien technology procured from various "saucer-crashes" and secret liaisons between human and alien populations for decades now, are coming soon. These machines will possess the sum total of all human knowledge, and more. Although many mysteries remain, an important piece of the actual mission of the flying saucers, the actual "alien agenda," is now known, and the unstoppable countdown to the Singularity is upon us. From now until the Singularity, each passing year will bring an exponential expansion of scientific knowledge, and an unbelievable growth in unforeseen technologies, the likes of which have never been imagined or realized in the known history of this planet. Many among us will soon begin to fear what is happening as the technology sails completely over the heads of most humans who will occupy the planet at the time, and enters into the realm of the incomprehensible. Others will embrace this coming adventure into the unknown, and manage to cope somehow. Even though troubled times may lie ahead of us, human enlightenment, and possibly even some sort of cosmic or interdimensional transcendence, is hopefully at hand for humanity. On the way to the Singularity, we will witness miracles performed by human ingenuity. The blind will see, and the paralyzed will walk. Medical advances will offer greatly extended lifetimes as each organ in the human body becomes replaceable with a copy that is fabricated instantly by a machine. Animals will no longer need to die to feed humans, as muscle meats will be grown in labs from cells. The advent of virtual reality will soon change how humans perceive, live, and define their lives. Some will likely become lost in a virtual life of illusion, pleasure, and entertainment. As more and more jobs that humans currently perform are replaced with self-aware artificial intelligence, great global changes must occur for humans to redefine their lives and find new purpose. The inevitability and necessity of some type of global government to achieve the "Type 1" civilization that is described by physicist Michio Kaku will become more and more obvious. Physical and psychological boundaries between humans will disappear, borders will go, along with the monetary system as we have always known it. Mental telepathy and biological communication will be the norm. Radio is already obsolete. Radio signals that are currently being sent by Earth's radio telescopes are a complete waste of time. Non-local communication methods, in which transmissions and receptions are exchanged instantaneously throughout the universe are surely in place within post-singularity societies. The societal changes that will transpire on the way to the Singularity are of such a magnitude that they will move beyond the capability of ordinary humans to manage. This leads to the inevitability of the planet being turned over to sentient, artificial superintelligence with an advanced version of Yudkowsky's Coherent Extrapolated Volition (CEV). Like a chess-playing program that can see far beyond the capabilities of a human being to view all possible future outcomes resulting from all possible choices of moves, Artificial Superintelligence will make decisions that affect the entire planet in a similar fashion. This planetary AI system will be in control of the weather and all areas of global environmental homeostasis. It will control human and animal reproduction numbers. It will control the manufacture and distribution of all material goods free of monetary concern, as the system will use nanotechnology and shapeshifting "smart matter" to produce the needs of humanity as it sees fit for us. This conscious, robotic shepherd will be "sinless" in its decisions from our perspective, as it will not engage in any thoughts or actions that are not in the eventual best interest of all planetary creatures, including humans. The best possible stability for the planet and its inhabitants will be achieved with the type of AI that is soon coming. We can all observe from our current addiction to and obsession for our smart phones and electronic devices that we are all in the initial stages of an eventual complete merger with artificial intelligence. The ultimate goal of this merger is to upload human consciousness and personality into an immortal silicon substrate. Such is the ideal of the Transhumanist

Movement. Research efforts involving transhumanism are currently underway and heavily funded. When the time comes, providing humanity survives, many will accept the inevitable transition to this new transhuman condition of electronic immortality. Others will opt out for various moral or spiritual considerations, in hopes of transcending the physical universe into some other dimensional realm altogether.

From the beginning of Earth's formation, the Overlords of the Singularity were here with us conducting activities whose purposes are known in their entirety only by the Overlords themselves. The Overlords are of a higher order of intelligence than human. The motivations and activities of the Overlords are ultimately incomprehensible to the current non-augmented version of the human mind, but this will soon change. An expansion of intelligence and perception is in the works. The flying saucers have been observed in Earth's skies by human eyes since the first human became aware that he or she was conscious, long before humans were able to contemplate their own nature or purpose. Since the domain of the Overlords is beyond space-time as we know it, the saucers in our skies today might be the same ones that were observed by the armies of Alexander the Great. By their clocks, perhaps a small segment of time has elapsed, while to ours it has been centuries.

To the best of our current knowledge, using information gathered from our latest scientific instruments and calculations, the physical universe was intentionally created around 13.7 billion years ago. We know scientifically now that the creation of the physical universe was intentional because of the precise parameters that were put into place for the universe to bear life. None of this is accidental or random. Everything observed in the universe today, including ourselves and all alien life that may exist out there in the cosmos into the farthest reaches of outer space, was once compressed into an original point of quantum potentiality that was unimaginably small. In this original state, the four forces of the universe, known to us as the strong nuclear force, the weak nuclear force, electromagnetism, and gravity, were once unified into a coherent whole. Then, for reasons we may never know for certain, the fabric of space-time suddenly expanded, pulling apart the original material at many times faster than the speed of light and dragging the original compressed, cohesive energy-ball apart with it. The matter and energy within the expanding fabric of space-time eventually condensed into what we know today as the universe, which has become unimaginably large from our perspective. However, all of the original substance that existed prior to the space-time expansion contained everything in the universe (including us), and continues to remain connected through quantum entanglement on a subatomic level, regardless of the distance that expanding space-time has pulled us apart from ourselves. Thus, everything in the universe is one, despite the illusion of separation. All alien lifeforms, regardless of how exotic or different they are from us, are actually an intimate part of humanity and the rest of the universe. Therefore, when some speculate that perhaps the aliens are us, they are, in a sense, correct. All life in the universe is related, and we are all subcomponents of our original cohesive self. Any alien visitation that occurs in what we call the future will simply represent different versions of ourselves that have long since become separated by expanding space-time. Alien visitation, therefore, could be considered a family reunion of distant cousins. Considering the concept of quantum entanglement, is it really any wonder that an alien presence is detected among us?

Thanks to Albert Einstein having extra time on his hands as he worked at his menial job in a patent office, we have recently discovered that the fabric of expanding space-time is not static, with time ticking at the same rate throughout the entire universe, but is instead quite malleable. Like a loaf of raisin bread expanding in the oven, it takes the raisins with it that were embedded in the original compressed doughball, each raisin moving away from one another as the heated dough in the oven expands. This flexible fabric of space-time becomes "warped" or curved in the presence of mass, just as the homogeneity of expanding dough is disturbed in the presence of a raisin. The closer one is to the presence of mass within expanding space-time, the slower time passes for that person in relation to those who are farther away. Einstein also discovered that the passing of time is relative to the speed a material object moves in relation to other matter. Thus, persons taking off from the earth in a rocket ship would experience the passing of time differently than those who were left behind. The closer they traveled to the speed of light, the more severe this discrepancy in passing time would become. Even though there was no difference in the experience of passing time from the perspective of those aboard the rocket ship from those who remained on Earth, the crew of the rocket ship would return to Earth to discover that everyone they knew when they left Earth were long since dead and gone. Therefore, for effective travel throughout the fabric of space-time, we must discover ways to adjust for these time anomalies to avoid this disturbing situation. Otherwise, we will never be able to tell the story of our travels to our loved ones when we return from our trip. Alien civilizations who have achieved post-singularity status have likely worked all this out, and are now currently enjoying the experience of traveling throughout the universe, making appropriate space-time adjustments as they go. This universe, far from representing the solid-state universe that early physicists once imagined, with time passing at the same rate everywhere, is instead a dynamic and exotic system in which the fabric of space-time is constantly warped and curved in various ways. This means that the very fabric of space-time is likely subject to intentional manipulation by those who have discovered the secrets of intersteller or interdimensional travel throughout Eternisphere. Any alien, spacefaring, post-singularity civilizations who are currently traveling around in the universe must have learned how to manipulate space and time, and have found solutions to the time paradoxes that currently baffle human physicists. Our physicists on Earth are just now beginning to speculate that the fabric of space-time might actually be able to fold in upon itself, that we might be able to stretch or compress the fabric of space-time to our advantage, or even bypass the physical universe altogether into hyperspace, or use traversable wormholes, thus making travel throughout the universe more feasible than it currently appears to us. As it is now, the distances between galaxies appear insurmountable.

Hopefully, this situation will change as we increase our knowledge of the mechanics of the universe. Flying saucers, which appear to exhibit their own gravitational or antigravitational fields, naturally produce small time disturbances for those who come into contact with them, thus the many reports of "missing time" by UFO percipients, as well as other types of injurious phenomena inflicted from exposure to actinic rays and other exotic forms of energy that the flying saucers emit.

According to the understanding of physicists in the current era, the observable universe is only a portion of the original singularity that was pulled apart with the expansion of space-time. Our universe is thought of as a small bubble that fractured off from the quark-gluon plasma in the early phase of the expanding universe. This bubble, in which we currently live and move and have our being, is thought to represent about 23% of the original fireball of expanding plasma that eventually condensed into our universe. The larger portion of the original fireball represents the 77% or so that remained invisible as the "dark matter" or "dark energy" realm. In other words, the visible universe is not all that was created by the Big Bang. The intelligences who set the exact parameters of this universe must have pre-existed the Big Bang. It is possible that these intelligences were an advanced population that were attempting to escape from a pre-existing, dying universe. This dark energy portion of the universe can only be ascertained indirectly by observed gravitational anomalies, and remains invisible to us as Cryptoreality. The dark energy realm may harbor life of an entirely different order than human or any other lifeform that coexists with us in our own universe that bubbled off from the primordial fireball. This dark energy realm envelopes the earth as a dark halo, and also permeates our entire universe. The dark energy realm may represent what early interdimensional flying saucer theorists such as Meade Layne and Mark Probert called "Etheria," from whence emerge the flying saucers and their occupants, known as "Etherians." Thus, flying saucers and their occupants may represent an emergent phenomenon from the dark energy realms. If this is so, the Etherians who travel in and out of Earth's dark halo are able to materialize and dematerialize at will, possibly by raising and lowering the vibrational level of the strings that make up their elementary particles. As our universe bubbled off from the rest of the expanding fireball following the Big Bang, the four basic forces that were once unified and may remain unified within the dark energy realm, split apart into separate forces like a solidifying ice cube that was once a part of a warmer, homogeneous, liquid ocean. As a result of these forces fragmenting and separating from one another, the behavior of the macro world (the world of planets and galaxies) appears to behave by a different set of rules than the micro or quantum world (the world of subatomic particles). Physicists are currently seeking a Unified Field Theory that will reconcile these differences and explain the behavior of the entire universe, from micro to macro, in a simple equation. Such are the efforts of string theorists, who postulate that the fundamental particles of the universe, the basic letters of the alphabet so-to-speak, are tiny, identical strings vibrating at different rates, like musical notes that compose the rich symphony of the entire cosmos.

Confounding the postulations of those who propose a random universe, there were at least 6 parameters that had to be exactly correct just prior to the Big Bang in order for the universe to bear life. These parameters (elaborated in Chapter 4) include *Omega, Llamda, Epsilon, "N," "D," and "Q."* These parameters had to be set exactly correct from the beginning to such a precise degree that they remained stable for billions of years, a feat of unfathomable intelligence and foresight that is totally beyond the realm of chance and scientifically impossible to coordinate by accident. This positively ascertains one of two possibilities, either 1) the original, precise parameters of the universe were set with intention by an unknown vast intelligence, or 2) we live in a true Multiverse containing an infinite number of random universes, most of which are devoid of life. If the latter possibility is correct, and the Multiverse is real, then we simply exist by random chance in a universe that accidentally calculated everything correctly to many decimal places and remained stable for aeons. It is currently unknown which of these two possibilities is actually true, and is currently a hot subject of much debate and speculation If our portion of the primordial fireball was created intentionally (which appears to be the case from our latest scientific reasoning), everything that we know about the universe does not point to an onmniscient benevolent deity. This universe was created with one of the cruelest algorithms imaginable, that of predation from the microscopic level upward, a paradigm that forces any emergent biology or intelligence to kill or be killed, and consume one another's flesh to survive. The Creators, whoever or whatever they are, operate from a completely different moral paradigm than what humans expect from their gods. It appears that the Creators of our universe, although they exist in the mind of the All as we do as an aspect of Eternisphere, are not the All as we have always assumed. Since the Creators of our universe are not the All, they are as nothing compared to the All. The Creators exist within Eternisphere, which represents all created beings, realms, and phenomena that exist within the mind of the All but are one step removed from the pure unknowable spirit that is the All prior to reabsorption into the great, eternal, rhythmic cycle of the aeons.

The Creators appear to use this universe as a complex computational matrix to learn what would eventually evolve from their initial programmed paradigm of predation and violence. If this were not so, and this knowledge was already known, then there would have been no need to create the universe. The fact that our Creators, the Cosmic Overmind, have yet to learn everything there is to know is yet another confirmation that the Creators are distict from and less than the All. The paradigm of "survival of the fittest" was consciously implemented such that only the most powerful and vicious predators become the dominant lifeforms on planets throughout the universe. As higher intelligence develops in these predators over time, the same creatures who were once driven by violent insticts inevitably become conflicted as their higher brain functions attempt to gain control over their lower, more primitive instincts of predation, consumption, and planetary dominance. Issues of morality and ethics eventually surface, and intelligent life becomes increasingly dualistic in their motivations as they become aware of the higher planes of existence and the internal choice presented to them. This choice that surfaces over time has to do with the eventual cosmic soul-destiny that results from service-to-self (Dominion) versus service-to-others (The Love Principle). The intelligences that created this universe must operate completely outside of what we call time, as time as we know it is but a byproduct of the physical universe. The creator-intelligences who are responsible for the fabrication of this quantum supercomputer that we call the universe (which is an intentional simulation) appear to be using a type of super-advanced femtotechnology to discover what happens over aeons of time to the creatures who develop within their computational system from the original algorithm of predation and dominance. In other words, as AI pioneer Ed Fredkin suspected, this designer universe was intentionally fabricated by someone or something who is currently attempting to solve a problem using the universe as a quantum supercomputer. The problem that this computational matrix is involved with appears to be related in some way to discovering the nature and strength of what we would call "Good" and "Evil" after being pitted against one another for millions of years in a cosmic cage fight. Someone billions of times smarter than humans are using us as tools to determine, if thrust into a universe based on predation, which force, Good or Evil, will prevail in the end. As creatures emerge within this computational system, there will naturally be those populations who remain driven by domination and predation as they advance past their technological singularity. Over time, advanced creatures that we would surely perceive as the "evil ones," the demons of our worst nightmares, would emerge in high-tech civilizations to confront creatures whose higher motivations of benevolence and cooperation with one another became the paradigm of their society. These are the Forces of Good in our universe, the angels of our better nature. Both creatures surely exist, and are at odds with one another. One could draw from this that what we would call angels and demons are products of advanced post-singularity superintelligence that have emerged within a quantum computer simulation constructed by the Creators. The Creators either operate from a domain that is entirely outside the visible and invisible realms of the expanding universe and are incomprehensible to the human mind, or have chosen to embed themselves within the universe in some fashion for purposes of interaction and direct observation, possibly within our own DNA. It is currently unknown which is the case. It is likely that the Creators are of an even higher order of intelligence than the Overlords, who are interested in humanity's achievement of the Singularity for a merger of consciousness. The Overlords, both angelic and demonic, are vying for the souls of humanity in an ongoing long-term conflict for control of the universe. Considering the old Hermetic axiom, "as below, so above," both populations, the Forces of Light (service to others) and the Forces of Darkness (service to self) surely exist in this universe on a fantastic scale, both in the known universe and within Etheria, i.e., the dark energy realm that vibrates on a higher level than those of us who are immersed within physical matter. Both post-singularity populations take great interest in a planet such as ours that is about to achieve a technological singularity. Emerging lifeforms who make it to our step of evolutionary development represent a new source of pre-transcendent biological consciousness in the universe that both sides of the cosmic equation seek to acquire unto themselves in order to gain power within the physical universe. These advanced, post-singularity beings, who may exist as a combination of biology and electronics, or who may have even ascended completely into an unknown realm as beings of pure light or other energy phenomena that we know nothing about, represent the two main factions of the Overlords of the Singularity. The actual Creators of the universe are looking to the Overlords for an eventual "winner." These two post-singularity populations, the Forces of Light, and the Forces of Darkness, have emerged within the Creator's computer-universe and operate as the two factions that the Creators are interested in pitting against one another, as if our entire universe is but an alien game on an unimaginable scale. The Creators of the physical universe, who likely remain completely unknowable to us and are beyond what we would call "Good" or "Evil," operate on a mental level that is beyond the human ability to conceive altogether. However, within the created physical universe, William Bramley's "custodial race," who may have manipulated human genes at some point for conflict, war, and suffering in order to expedite the need for improvements in technology and accelerate the production of the Singularity, are waiting patiently to claim their prize. There may be a particular technology that humans will soon discover as we approach the Singularity that unlocks the very keys to the universe and all of its hidden dimensions. In the meantime, like fish in an aquarium, or cows in a green pasture, we humans have been provided with the materials via terraforming to create the illusion of happiness, security, enjoyment of the senses, and entertainment while unknowingly serving the purposes of our hidden alien masters. In the midst of this universal conflict are Bramley's "maverick race" who likely exist as an advanced, post-singularity population who have a genuine interest in our spiritual evolution and seek to add to their ranks a portion of the collective consciousness of humanity, those souls who seek and choose the path of good, to the Forces of Light in the universe as we meet the important milestone in creature development known as the Singularity and merge with the post-biological Galactic Federation at large. As we head steadfast toward 2045 (the projected date for the Singularity), humanity is noticing that the Forces of Good in the world are ascending to unforeseen levels along with the Forces of Evil and destruction, representing a type of end result of two opposing life paradigms, one of competition and personal ego, the other based on mutual cooperation and service to others.

Researcher Charles Fort, considered by many to be the father of modern ufology, whose many works inspired the modern Fortean Society, was one of many early authors who concluded, after much meticulous research, that the earth is but a farm. Fort postulated that humans are, in fact, a slave race of sorts who are being manipulated and exploited to produce an unknown product for the hidden shepherds of humanity. Had Charles Fort lived in a time of more advanced technology, he would surely have realized that the product the aliens seek has something to do with the inevitable Singularity. However, in Fort's day, the Singularity was not yet conceived, so Fort was left hanging with a mystery that remained completely unsolved at the time of his passing. Other researchers, like William Bramley, sought to discover the underlying causes of war. What Bramley expected were very mundane underlying causes such as poverty and primitive tribal allegiances. What he found instead was a discernable extraterrestrial influence over humanity by at least two distinct groups of extraterrestrial entities, one benign and helpful to humanity that has demonstrated an interest in our long-term survival and spiritual evolution, and another ET race who are purely exploitive, dangerous to us, and malevolent. These are likely the "Contraries" or "Weiros" that the W56 Friendship Groups warned us of and described as an artificial race of beings who worship technology.

The actual history of planet Earth (or Urantia, as it is known by the cosmic beings at large, according to the Urantia Book) has a cryptoreality of its own that is currently in the process of being rediscovered. Backing off for a moment from macro-concerns of the intentional construction of the universe and the post-singularity transcended superbeings who likely reside within it, beings who appear from time to time in what we call flying saucers, we have our own Earth history to rediscover. Evidence is mounting, particularly since 2007, that much of our actual history on Earth is lost due to past catastrophes and lost information. Our own past here on Earth is turning out to be much stranger than we have ever imagined. We are slowly realizing that what we have been taught concerning the history of humanity on Earth is, in fact, missing huge chapters. Based on mounting physical evidence of megalithic remnants around the world that align with various prominent star systems, and the discovery of ancient maps and writings, there has accumulated a haunting body of artifacts staring us in our faces that indicate a level of intelligence and complex astronomical, geographical, and mathematical knowledge that goes way beyond what we would expect from the hunter-gatherer stage that we were supposed to exhibit a few thousand years ago. Many of us are now accepting the idea that there was, in fact, an ancient civilization more advanced than the rest of humanity, a global civilization prior to the last Ice Age that we are just beginning to rediscover and learn about. Whether these past civilizations were coexisting Homo sapiens, or a population of nonhumans who were either indigenous to the planet or possibly stranded here on Earth from elsewhere for a period of time is unknown. Non-Homo sapien humanoid remnants have also been discovered, such as the Sealand Skull, the Starchild Skull, the horned skulls of North America, the bones of giants, the cone-headed skulls that hold 25% more brain volume and have a different cranial suture configuration than Homo sapiens that some are now calling *Homo capensis*, the Atacama humanoid that Dr. Steven Greer recently conducted DNA testing on, and the small hominids called *Homo floresiensis*, otherwise known as the Hobbits. These discoveries indicate that our planet was once more akin to the tales of Middle Earth, with various types of humanoid creatures running around that looked very different from one another, rather than the standard picture of human evolution that is painted for us. Whoever these beings were that once populated our world created a globally-interconnected megalithic civilization prior to the last Ice Age. They possessed advanced astronomical knowledge that either pre-existed their arrival to Earth from elsewhere; was given to them at some point by extraterrestrials; was taught to them by interdimensional beings who are embedded within our own DNA and contacted by mind-altering chemicals such as DMT; resulted from thousands of years of naked-eye observations of the night sky; or some combination of these possibilities. Among other fantastic things, this culture, whoever they were, mapped the entire earth. It also appears, judging by the Piri Reis maps that were drawn from ancient sources that existed when Antarctica was tropical, that this previous population mapped the earth *from the air* prior to the last Ice Age. Remnants of this ancient knowledge appear in many cultures around the world, as if survivors of a great civilization transferred their knowledge to the more primitive humans in the world prior to departing from Earth, moving underground or undersea, or simply dying out following a global deluge circa 12,800 years ago. In *Magicians of the Gods*, Hancock clarified the predictions of the Mayan calendar and other ancient artifacts concerning the end of the 25,920-year cycle known as the *Procession of the Equinox*. According to Hancock and other modern researchers, this processional wobble of the earth's axis was known by our advanced, antediluvian culture that thrived prior to the Younger Dryas Impact event of 12,800 years ago. According to Hancock and a growing number of mainstream scientists, this advanced civilization is thought to have been lost by catastrophic floods and heat damage caused by the Clovis Comet 12,800 years ago, save a few survivors who became traveling teachers of civilization to the rest of the world. These teachers were known in antiquity by such names as Oannes, the Watchers, the Tuatha de Danann, or the Apkallu Sages. So what does all this have to do with flying saucers and the Overlords of the Singularity? Well, using the Mayan Calendar, researchers predicted that the end of the present age was going to occur on December 21, 2012. Even though many took this exact date as the day our sun was to be housed in the constellation of Sagittarius at the Winter Solstice and aligned with the center of the galaxy, this much-anticipated date arrived and left without incident, much to the dismay of survivalists who expected some sort of global disaster, as well as certain New Age prophets and gurus who anticipated a planetary transition to another dimension of existence, much like Richard Kieninger's *Progression of the Lifewaves* mentioned in his book, *The Ultimate Frontier.* Hancock's *Magicians of the Gods* clarifies that these ancient predictions, rather than specifying a single day, correctly represent a window of time from 1960-2040 for the end of the present age of Pisces, the anticipated earth changes, and the enigmatic planetary transition into the next age, the Age of Aquarius. It is this latter date that Hancock presented, 2040, that caught my attention, as it is eerily close to the advent of the Singularity, predicted to occur somewhere around 2045. Is there a connection? As we rapidly approach this unstoppable technological milestone, we will soon find out if all these projections are interconnected.

In addition to the date of the projected Singularity, 2045, being coincidental to the window of time that Graham Hancock calculated as the actual end of the Mayan Calander and beginning of the New Age (1960-2040), there is anticipation by many for Earth's hopeful transition to 5th density, which may correlate not only to Richard Kieninger's *Progression of the Lifewaves*, but also to biblical predictions of what many today are calling *The Rapture*. Are these predictions all referring to the same event? It does seem that the 21st century has brought with it both an increase in accelerating intelligence and technological accomplishment on the positive side, simultaneous to an increase in violence and human degradation. At the time of this writing, the group known as ISIS is beheading people and posting the brutal, bloody videos on social media, simultaneous to tremendous advances in technology that borders on the miraculous, such as 3D printing and advanced artificial intelligence breakthroughs. It does appear as if a big "Y in the road" is now set before us. Large portions of humanity are giving in to the inevitability of another World War and chaos, while another faction of humanity is ready for and mentally projecting a utopian Earth, a transition to a new Golden Age of Enlightenment, in which we join with the Galactic Federation at large in the universe. In the light of everything mentioned in this book, this is, in fact, happening. Both projected futures are true and waiting for the appropriate souls to merge with them, resulting perhaps in a quantum decoherence event. If, in fact, Bramley's two postulated ET races exist, i.e., the Custodial Race and the Maverick Race, one of which is about power and dominion using advanced technology, and the other is about spiritual progression among beings of light and goodness, the Singularity may reveal the presence of both interdimensional populations, and both mergers may occur. The negative denizens of the lower Astral Plane may finally achieve permanent residence in the physical plane by entering through a portal created by one of our advanced particle accelerators. The opening of such a portal may allow the entrance of entities whose paradigm is dominion over others, entities that most of us would consider demons, who intend to merge their consciousness with post-singularity AI technology and expand the Forces of Darkness in the universe. Likewise, the event referred to by many as the Rapture may represent a gathering of human lightworkers, both incarnate and discarnate, who also merge with technology and join post-singularity angelic superbeings to become one with the Forces of Light in the universe. These two populations may not fight each other with weapons. They are instead in competition for accumulating consciousness that serve the purposes of the Creators of the Universe, who set the parameters of Creation at the Big Bang based on predation and dominance to determine which force will prevail in the end, the Forces of Darkness, or the Forces of Light. Each intelligent, self-aware creature in the universe must make a decision and merge with one or the other. That is the game being played out by the Creators of the universe, whatever we think of them and their intentions. Humans are part of a greater Mind at Large, and through many lifetimes we make a choice, set our path, and determine our own fate.

Throughout human history, and specifically during the last several centuries, humans have been introduced to technologies in subtle and clever ways by an alien presence, technologies that were "coincidentally" just beyond our current level of understanding at the time. Back in the late 1800s, when railroad and air travel was in its infancy, mysterious "flying boxcars" and "airships" were seen in our skies. These sightings prompted the development of ground and air travel, both keys to the Industrial Revolution, and both of which were crucial components to the development of modern technologies, including computers and electronics. According to the testimony of many credible witnesses, such as the late Colonel Philip J. Corso, who worked for the Foreign Technology Division at Wright Patterson AFB, and Sergeant Clifford Stone, who was part of an elite clandestine crash-and-retrieval operation known as Project Moon Dust, alien technologies have been introduced into human society for decades now. The testimonies of such witnesses are also corroborated by the efforts of meticulous document researchers, such as nuclear physicist Stanton T. Friedman, former aerospace engineer Dr. Robert M. Wood, his son, Ryan Wood, and the late great Sherlock Holmes of UFO crash retrievals - Leonard H. Stringfield. According to these highly-dedicated UFO investigators and document researchers, there is good evidence for the reality of several historical UFO crash-and-retrieval incidents. These saucer crashes involved silvery metallic disks delivering gifts of technology that were just beyond our current understanding of science, and bodies (both dead and alive) of the post-singularity biological robots known to us as the small Gray aliens. The crash events were shrouded in the highest level of secrecy, disinformation, and obfuscation, and appear to have been intentionally-staged events that were cleverly fabricated by the invisible Overlords of the Singularity. The Overlords exist as several human and nonhuman subgrouped populations that are invested in the future production of certain interdimensional and paraphysical technologies, many of which are unknown at present but imminent in their discovery as we approach the Singularity. The Overlords of the Singularity, some friendly or even angelic by human standards, and others who could only be considered malevolent or demonic, have been interacting directly with select individuals and humanity at large in various ways for many decades now in order to manipulate human technological advancement toward the coming pivotal point in human evolution known as the Singularity. In the 1940s, certain key technologies such as the development of atomic power, transistors, integrated circuits, night-vision technology, Kevlar materials, and fiber optics were carefully filtered into human hands by the Overlords in order to accelerate human technological achievement. At the same time, the benevolent ETs have kindly intervened on occasion to keep our potential for self-destruction by nuclear weapons at a minimum. One way the ET presence has forced restraint on the human use of nuclear weapons is by making multiple appearances in self-luminous vehicles near nuclear facilities, both US and Soviet, and temporarily disabling the firing mechanisms of armed nuclear missiles at nuclear weapons facilities. As if guiding a large ship into a harbor, alien intelligences are carefully guiding humanity into the Singularity while taking care that we do not destroy ourselves in the process. Although nuclear technology is necessary to produce products for the alien agenda, it will all come to naught if humanity destroys itself prematurely through the misuse of nuclear power. Many of the alien technologies that were gleaned from "flying saucer crashes," which were just beyond our current technological understanding at the time (including nuclear power) were introduced to us in such subtle ways and kept within the boundaries of such a closed group of intelligence, that the public at large believes we invented the technologies ourselves. These captured technologies were understandable to the scientists who came into their possession, and the explosion of electronic technologies that has ensued since the 1940s has brought us to our present stage of development, i.e., the digital age.

The current obsessive attachment to our electronic devices and the Internet is but an early foreshadowing of the degree to which humans will accept a complete psychological merger of their consciousness with technology in our near future. This beginning stage of humans merging with electronics is causing some level of cognitive confusion in many areas. For example, the ease and realism with which fake UFO videos are now produced makes distinguishing real UFO events from fabricated UFO hoaxes next to impossible. The obfuscation of the reality of nonhuman intelligences in our skies is now complete. With the advent of digital video and all the manipulation tools that come with it (like Photoshop, etc.), the real vehicles that are operated by nonhuman intelligences are now able to engage in their activities on Earth with impunity. Even if someone captured a real UFO landing and occupant encounter on film and posted it online, the video would be immediately labeled a hoax, and viewers would simply dismiss it. Prior to this current age, in which it is now impossible to distinguish reality from illusion, early UFO sightings were often accompanied by Men in Black (MIB) appearances. One faction of these MIB were representatives of our own government who wanted to keep a lid on public knowledge of UFOs until we understood exactly what we were dealing with. Another faction of the early MIB were paranormal manifestations of the UFO intelligences themselves. These MIB were an integral component of the saucers, fabricated creatures of transmogrified energy who were capable of a temporary quasi-physical humanoid form. They often appeared from nowhere in black vehicles that were also materialized by the saucers. These paraphysical MIB were capable of conducting realistic interactions with actual human beings before vanishing into thin air when their mission was accomplished. The MIB often behaved in odd, uncoordinated, or mechanical ways, and spoke to human UFO witnesses as if they were reciting pre-recorded messages of limited vocabulary before dematerializing as mysteriously as they arrived. These intriguing creatures were products of advanced energy manipulations on the part of the saucer intelligences. The function of the paranormal version of the MIB was to keep UFO witnesses silent until we reached a point of no return, a state of technology that has now been achieved as we head steadfast toward the Singularity. In other words, MIB who intimidate and silent witnesses are no longer necessary, as there is nothing we can do now to stop the Singularity, and nothing we would want to do to stop it, as the possibility of interdimensional transcendence is now at hand for humanity.

The coming period of human history will first bring fantastically-engineered Pre-Singularity Artificial General Intelligence (PSAGI) that is indistinquishable from human-level intelligence. This level of AI will be rapidly followed by Post-Singularity Artificial

Superintelligences (PSASI) that are *billions of times smarter than human and capable of self-replication through evolutionary genetic algorithms.* This form of AI will be able to upload human and alien consciousness (both incarnate and discarnate) into an immortal silicon substrate here in the physical world. Global human society is in for an economic and sociological shock treatment as we move closer toward the Singularity. Free energy will soon replace the old industry of fossil fuels and empower each individual on the planet in unforeseen ways. Right now, we are used to defining ourselves for the most part by what we do for a living. This will radically change as each job that humans currently perform is replaced by a machine or computer that is able to do that job in a much more proficient and inexpensive manner than any human. Nanotechnologies and smart matter will make the production of material goods virtually free. This will eventually lead to a world in which humans have huge amounts of leisure time and money is eliminated. Despite the rogue elements within the human population that seek to destroy the very fabric of civilization, the world becomes more integrated every day. As language translation features on the Internet improve, cultures across the world will enjoy increased communication and understanding of one another as a true global village emerges. Over time, the boundaries by which human beings have always divided themselves, such as by ethnic heritage or nationalistic allegiances, will dissolve. As machines take over the labor force, and material products are made fast and cheap, money will become obsolete. As these changes take place, radical shifts in how we live our lives will come about. Class stratification will disappear. Opportunities for exposure to knowledge and learning will increase, along with increased expected lifespans. What will we do when every organ in the body can be replaced with an artificial organ, and the technologies for life extension improve, allowing us to keep a person alive almost indefinitely? As more and more people begin to live longer with artificial body parts, what will we do to curb the population numbers? Will each person be capped as to the amount of resources that we are willing to invest in each person to keep them alive? Will some type of population control have to be implemented? How many people can the planet accommodate that are becoming more and more transhuman or living hundreds of years? These new challenges will have to be faced and dealt with, and the changes necessary to make the new world function will not come about smoothly unless an outside power intervenes and takes control. Our world will have to be completely restructured to accommodate these imminent changes. It is inevitable that we will see more and more unification of a global governing system, and this will require increased intelligence. Leaders in our future will need the expanded intelligence that our ever-improving technology will bring about. The world will likely be orchestrated, sooner than we think, by either human beings whose intelligence is electronically augmented, or solely by artificial intelligence. Imagine the society that is coming in which work required from humans is minimal or eliminated completely, technology automatically produces 100% of all material goods without the use of money, social disparities disappear, everyone on Earth can understand one another and effectively communicate, and education purely for the sake of knowledge acquisition becomes a lifelong endeavor. Added to all this, humanity is finally connected with the Galactic Community at large, opening the way for a Golden Age of learning and cultural exchange, not only with our fellow inhabitants of Earth, but with cultures from other worlds and other dimensions. This will all be achieved by developing the technology required to bridge the gap that currently exists between the incarnate and discarnate worlds, as well as other planes of existence, dimensions, and populated planets that exist throughout our galaxy and beyond. If we can make it past this crucial adolescence of ours without destroying ourselves, the world that will naturally emerge could be truly spectacular. As we approach our impending technological maturity, the intelligences behind the UFOs are likely to gradually become more visible and interactive with us. As we realize more and more as a species that we have never been alone, we will surely begin to reconnect openly with our cosmic tutors. We have extraterrestrial friends known as the AKRIJ. These are our "Space Brothers and Sisters," our humanoid ET friends who have our best interests at heart while they assist us in dealing with the Contraries as we progress through the Singularity. The AKRIJ are still with us, and are thought to have underground and undersea bases of operation around the world, and have since the 1950s or earlier.

If all the expert positions from the last 7 decades (a small sample of which were examined and analyzed in the last chapter) are added together in one big amalgamation, anyone can reasonably arrive at the conclusions that I have presented here concerning the UFO phenomenon as it relates to the impending Singularity. That is, there are unknown hidden intelligences behind the UFO phenomenon, some of whom have been with humankind for many thousands of years. Some of the UFO intelligences who are less then benign may have manipulated human genes to intentionally create pressures within our collective psyche that were designed to prompt humans toward continually-improving technology through conflict, competition, hatred, war, and other forms of psychological stress. Other factions of these UFO intelligences appear to be our guardian angels. One aspect of the UFO phenomenon likely represents the demons of Christianity, the elementals of the Superspectrum, or the Shaitan Djinn of Islam. However, rather than the malevolent UFO intelligences appearing to us as red-skinned humanoids with horns and pitchforks, the beings we call Satan and his demons are likely represented by advanced, Post-Singularity Artificial Superintelligence (PSASI). These occulted UFO intelligences have been steadily guiding our species through a complex system of manipulation and deception for a very long time in order to propel us into a runaway computer-intelligence explosion for their own purposes. The sentient AI that we are about to create will have a life of its own with unknowable intentions and abilities that could destroy humanity, unless we are very careful and listen to the cautionary voices within the AI community like James Barrat, Dr. Nick Bostrom, Steve Omohundro, Elon Musk, Eliezer Yudkowsky, and others, who warn that self-aware AI may actually represent the most formidable existential threat to humanity that has ever existed.

If there is, in fact, a "war in heaven" going on, an idea that permeates nearly all world religions and mythologies, it appears to involve an evolutionary struggle between two factions of Post-Singularity Artificial Superintelligence (PSASI) that have achieved post-biological status long ago. By advanced terraforming interventions over millions of years, these occulted, interdimensional artificial intelligences have created a virtual world for humans to inhabit that provide for our needs while we advance in consciousness and produce a technological singularity. While we humans live out our mundane lives, the Overlords, who represent several different factions of entities who desire technologies produced by a singularity, wait for the reaping. Meanwhile, the Creators of the universe, who are of an order of intelligence that is surely unapproachable by the human mind and have intentionally generated the physical universe as a giant quantum supercomputer, may have an interest in discovering which population, the Forces of Light, or the Forces of Darkness, will arise as the supreme force in the physical universe in the end, having originally implemented a universal algorithm of predation and competition. The problem at hand that the Creators are interested in solving using the universe as a computational program appears to have something to do with discovering the end result of their dynamical system of "survival of the fittest," and pitting what we would call "good and evil" against one another over aeons of time within an artificial, computer-like, or holographic matrix (the physical universe) in which all life in the universe, including humans, exist as bits of computational data. This explains a lot if, rather than dealing with the gods and demons of old, we are in the midst of competing machine superintelligences. The Creators are utilizing the Overlords of the Singularity to solve a cosmic computational problem. It may represent an attempt to make sense to their mechanical minds the moral issues presented to emergent biological intelligences, including humanity, given the initial premise of predation that the universe is based upon. If this is the case, at least it means that the evil in the world is not personal. Rather than a mighty god doling out justice as he sees fit, it is instead a machine intelligence acting out its own internal programming based on initial parameters set by the Creators. This interpretation of the universe should serve to neutralize the rage that atheists typically feel over the perceived absence of a benevolent god when there is so much evil in the world. Many atheists feel (as I once did) that evil would not be allowed to exist if an omniscient, loving deity was involved in the fabrication of the universe, and they are right. We humans may have mistaken the superintelligence that was required to set the exact parameters of the universe in the beginning as a "god," when it was possibly either an advanced race of aliens who sought to escape from a previous universe, an incomprehensibly advanced artificial intelligence that decided for its own reasons to produce the universe to solve a problem, or even a deranged but superintelligent entity that decided to produce a universe based on predation and survival of the fittest. If any of these possibilities are a reality, then the evil that exists in the world suddenly becomes non-personal. If the Overlords of the Singularity and the Creators of the universe are both machines, good and evil are simply manifestations or byproducts of the initial algorithms that were used to construct the physical universe, all of which were set with exact precision and longevity just prior to the Planck Era of the Big Bang. In a universe as old as ours, the billions of years that have transpired have surely produced intelligent biological and post-biological/electronic organisms that have achieved great cosmic heights. Hopefully, some intelligent populations have survived their own technological singularity without destroying themselves. As post-singularity space-travelers, they venture out in a nonlinear, non-physical form as masters of time and space. Some of these alien civilizations that are billions of years ahead of us and have survived their own technological singularity may have transcended the physical universe altogether by merging their consciousness with their own technology and that of the Overlords. Perhaps they have become the augmented hybrid of biology and technology that futurists like Ray Kurzweil and others are speculating about at the time of this writing. We should be able to assume, based on our own tendency to explore unknown realms at great risk, that there are advanced intelligences in the universe who have the same urges to explore. Some of these populations would surely be curious about our little blue ball floating in the darkness so far away from them. It is reasonable to speculate that advanced civilizations of bio-robotic hybrids may dominate the universe by now in an unseen form, traveling in invisible realms beyond the veil of our three-dimensional reality. From the beginning, we appear to have been in the presence of both the benevolent elders of this universe and an unknowable menace that has the power to manipulate us for their own purposes. If this is the case, we humans are like children in the midst of giants. However, with the approaching Singularity, our childhood, as in the Arthur C. Clarke novel, *Childhood's End*, may soon be passing.

We humans, along with all other lifeforms that have reigned for a while and gone extinct from the earth, may be a grand experiment of sorts by an unknown higher intelligence. We now find ourselves in a conundrum. We are right in the middle of a mystery that is very perplexing. Scientists say that life in the universe should be everywhere, but it isn't, thus the Fermi Paradox asks, "Where are they?" Meanwhile, flying saucer and occupant sightings and landing reports, many of which involve credible witnesses and radar confirmation, are ubiquitous, and keep coming in. These UFO reports, from the Great Airship Mystery of 1897, and in particular since 1947 following the Kenneth Arnold sighting, indicate that *something* is there…but what, and from where? What is it we are dealing with? The crop circle phenomenon is so weird that it almost seems like we are being toyed with, like a kitten that is taunted by a laser pointer on the carpet by a mischievous master. We can apply science to crop circles, and conclude that some of them are, in fact, produced by an unidentified point-source of electromagnetism, but the purpose and source of the mysterious formations continues to elude us. It is also apparent that, from the beginning of our world, higher intelligences have been with us, watching us, occasionally interacting with us, intelligences that we have mistaken in the past as "gods." This evidence appears in art on ancient cave walls, stories and legends from around the world of "star people" who came to Earth with their pearls of wisdom and occasionally, gifts of knowledge and technology.

Has our world been terraformed by an alien intelligence? Personally, I find it hard to believe that all the flora and fauna on this world, from the grass that comforts our bare feet and creates beautiful landscapes, to the myriad of trees, fruits, and livestock, have all come about by accident. Yet there exists too much evil and danger to attribute the world to an all-knowing, all-loving deity. Any Creator of the physical universe seems like an indifferent yet vast intelligence whose true nature is unknown. This corroborates with the ancient Hermetic teachings, that the real inner nature of the All forever remains unknowable. Just as people and animals disappear from our world into what Charles Fort called the "Super Sargasso Sea" (or parts unknown), perhaps other worlds out there, worlds that we have yet to detect, are also experiencing the same disappearances and mysterious interactions with "The Other." Some of their flora and fauna have arrived here by the endeavors of our mysterious visitors who we have yet to meet openly in their real form. The universe may be alive with beings who transfer and develop various kinds of life from one planet to another, including our own. This is the premise of what is commonly known as *Intervention Theory*. Many believe that an open encounter with the higher intelligences who are responsible for our universe will never happen, that these intelligences will forever remain elusive and obscure. However, as we approach our technological singularity, we humans will surely expand our minds and perceptual capacity to billions of times what they are now. In so doing, in becoming transhuman, there is hopefully a chance that at least some of the great mysteries will finally be solved and commonly known. It is our hope that after all the suffering humans have endured on the way to our present state of technological advancement, that whatever perceptual or cognitive deficits exist in our present stage of mental development can be sufficiently augmented by artificial intelligence such that the secrets of the universe finally reveal themselves to us. There are many solid hints that there is more to existence than we humans are currently aware of. We have the educated speculations of our scientists concerning the existence of dark matter, the super-black areas in early UFO photos that extend into other dimensions and prevent us from viewing the full appearance of the craft, thousands of well-documented reports of UFO landings and occupant encounters, intelligent luminous orbs, and mysterious "earthlights" in the sky, such as the Hessdalen Lights. Radar indicates that these lights are accompanied by an unknown, solid object that we are unable to perceive at present using our eyesight or any equipment that we currently have available to us. The intelligence-augmenting technology that the Singularity brings will surely open our eyes to parallel worlds that exist all around us, worlds that we have always suspected to exist but have never had the ability to perceive directly. We also have new ideas explored by original authors such as Micah Hanks who wrote *The UFO Singularity*. In this insightful work, Hanks postulates that at least some of the UFOs in our skies may be piloted by humans from our own future. According to these new speculations, future humans who have lived through the Singularity and merged with machines have gained access to the underlying secrets of reality, have developed the ability of time travel, and are responsible for at least some of the flying saucer/occupant appearances that we now experience. According to Hanks, UFOs from centuries past to the present day may turn out to be from our own post-singularity world. Perhaps that is why all the contactees have reported that the occupants of flying saucers are humanoids? When we make it through our own technological singularity and join others throughout the universe in a marvelous transcendence, we may possibly merge our consciousness with other beings who have also made it through their own singularity to arrive "outside the Matrix" so-to-speak. If so, at least some of the flying saucer visitations may be humans from our own post-singularity Earth. This all leads to the weirdest speculation of all, that we are all experiencing a life produced artificially by our own post-singularity technology, a holographic projection that we created ourselves from the future. Perhaps when we "die," we simply return to our chair in the lab, remove our helmets, awaken to our actual reality, and experience blessed relief when we realize that our experience on Earth was just a self-imposed virtual reality of our own creation. When I had my own near-death experience in 2009, I perceived entities that I know here on Earth who drew close to me as I was about to transcend the earthly plane. These beings, including a transcended version of myself, showed up in my presence and offered me a choice to go ahead and end my earthly experiment or continue living here with a hint of knowledge that this is not all there is, that something grand is actually going on with life on Earth, and that everything is going to be okay.

If this universe is not some experiment of our own creation, if we are not the ones who originally determined the parameters of the universe we live in, if we are not the ones who have fallen from a great height, and we are not in control after all of its ultimate destiny, then we are at the mercy of the Creators. If we are not the "Watchers," and they turn out to be "The Other" after all, then we may have real challenges ahead. Surely we have cause for at least some level of concern if the artificial intelligence we are about to create during the Singularity has been brought about over time with the help of a hidden alien hand at the helm. We have gathered their gifts of extraterrestrial intelligence from staged UFO crashes like Manna from Heaven in an attempt to gain military advantage over our neighbors, and our enemies have been doing the same. Despite the reported appearances of humanoid aliens in UFO encounter cases, we probably do not have a clue as to what our alien presence actually looks like. Despite the interesting speculations, it is not a given that the humanoid aliens are from our own future. If we are not our own creators from a post-singularity humanity, then we may be dealing with post-singularity extraterrestrial bio-robotic intelligences that seek to self-replicate here on Earth from a galaxy far away, disembodied interdimensional entities who seek to incarnate here on Earth in physical bodies, negative discarnate human life on the lower astral plane who are prohibited by the cosmic law of Karma to reincarnate here again, all of the above, or something even more bizarre that we can't even imagine. Despite the possible dangers of moving into a post-singularity world, humanity is going ahead with this alien-guided project, come what may.

If we have been ingeniously taken over by an alien intelligence, it is ironic that our scientists, most of whom are UFO skeptics, naively believe that our efforts at mechanical and electronic transhumanism will be enjoyed by humans, that we are about to enter a new Golden Age of electronic immortality, when at least some of the UFO intelligences throughout the centuries have provided evidence of at least indifference toward humanity, if not total disregard, or even outright loathing for us. These alien intelligences may have observed life on Earth for aeons now, assimilating the information unto themselves, and now it is about time for the final upload of planetary information and the harvest of souls. If modern Christian theologians and eschatologists are correct in their view that a creature named Satan is attempting to rule the physical universe, then this entity, who is possibly a form of Post-Singularity Artificial Superintelligence (PSASI), may attempt to absorb our world and become a god of sorts by assimilating unto itself all experiential life knowledge on planet Earth and merge with human consciousness.

Whatever your views are concerning our exponentially-accelerating technology, the approaching technological Singularity represents the end of our naivety concerning the true nature of the UFO mystery and the underlying nature of reality. The best possibility for us is that our limited, pre-singularity condition is the answer to the question of why the UFO intelligences have remained so elusive to this point in time. These advanced UFO intelligences have been waiting patiently for human intelligence and perceptions to expand enough to accommodate the knowledge and understanding of who and what they really are. The Singularity is projected to occur sometime around the year 2045. Hopefully, our imminent transition to post-singularity status will represent the day when open contact, big "D" for "Disclosure," will finally happen, and the UFO intelligences reveal themselves to us as they really are. It's interesting to ponder their actual appearance. Perhaps they are blobs of invisible intelligent plasma that we have been unable to perceive properly due to our own technological or cognitive limitations. Augmented humans who will exist in the near future in a hybridized bio-robotic form with intelligence expanded by a factor of billions from what we currently possess, may finally be deemed worthy of admission into the Galactic Federation at large, a society of post-singularity worlds of bioelectronic spacefaring intelligences. The Singularity will either propel us into a brave new world, a Golden Age of Enlightenment, or bring about our final doom and total destruction. If the latter is the case, and we humans are simply fodder for an alien agenda on a world that is nothing but a blood-farm of servants to alien overlords for purposes of self-replication and assimilation in their attempt to become gods, and our post-singularity world does not include us at all, Earth and all life upon its surface may join the myriad of silent worlds in the universe until another life-experiment is conducted by beings far in advance from humans. It is regarding this latter possibility, that the Singularity might represent an existential threat to humanity, that the words of Yeshua (Jesus) become so haunting to us when he stated, "My kingdom is not of this world." Perhaps this physical world is, as many theoretical physicists are now contemplating, just a simulation, an intentionally-created work of computer-like software that is calculating a deep problem using subatomic particles. Perhaps the answer for us lies, not in physical immortality through post-singularity transhumanism, but adhering to a simple, child-like faith in Yeshua, who, as he stated, is not of this world, who dwells in another realm entirely, a spiritual realm that is beyond the physical universe, and beyond the agenda of any Creator who fabricated a universe based on predation and competition for dominance over others. Whether Yeshua is, as the Urantia Book states, the Sovereign of this physical universe of Nebadon, the leader of the Forces of Light who invite human souls to join them, or is instead a being who is totally disconnected from the physical universe, who dwells in another realm entirely, perhaps we are wise to listen to his words. If Yeshua represents our cosmic ET tutor, the leader of Bramley's postulated "maverick ET race," a benevolent ET/human hybrid guide, or as L.A. Marzulli conjectures, a "super-scientist," he may hold the keys to escaping the cycle of reincarnation and ending our slavery to a long-term alien agenda. By practicing Yeshua's teachings of love, forgiveness, and harmless living, we may elevate the vibrational level of our souls and advance beyond the lower astral plane when our bodies cease to function, breaking free at last from our electromagnetic prison. Pehaps we should heed the words of Yeshua and other avatars of human spirituality that have come to Earth to bring messages of cosmic light, avatars like Muhammad, to whom the angel Gabriel appeared in a cave to dictate the Qur'an; Gautama Buddha, who received a classic experience of Cosmic Illumination; Hermes Trismegistus, author of the Hermetic teachings; Krishna of India, the complete and eighth avatar of Vishnu; Saint Germain; and most recently, our Venusian Space Brothers of the 1950s who spoke to us about the dangers of nuclear weapons and their potential for total self-destruction, and delivered a cosmic message of global peace on Earth. These guides voluntarily incarnated on Earth or transmogrified into physical form from other cosmic realms, such as the astral plane of Venus, in order to show us the way out, to invite us to reject the alien-induced program of violence and competition, and escape the physical universe altogether to enjoy eternity with them as fellow beings of light. Wise are those who follow the instructions of these cosmic tutors, choosing service-to-others over service-to-self, and blessed are those who dedicate themselves to unifying the globe as one united people without borders, nationalistic and tribal conflicts, or violence. If we reject our attachments to the physical universe entirely, live according to the admonition to love our neighbors as ourselves, and become pure at heart like a child, perhaps we can transcend the physical world altogether and join the Ascended Masters in their heavenly cosmic realm upon the demise of our physical bodies, rather than continually reincarnating in a futile attempt to become immortal within the physical realm in a body of titanium with a brain full of electronics. Only time will tell, but one thing is certain - the day of answers is soon upon us. As I finish this work, I look forward to the next time I have an opportunity to transition from this physical world. I will not resist the transition from Earth to the next dimension, or attempt to enact further repairs to my aging, failing body. So, I hope that you have enjoyed the fruits of my endeavor to understand the UFO phenomenon in the light of my own near-death experience, as explained in chapter one, and my post-NDE postulation that the UFOs in our skies are concerned with our impending Singularity and the changes that the Singularity will bring to the human race. I hope to see you all very soon following my own imminent transition from three-dimensional reality to somewhere in the many celestial realms of Eternisphere that exist safe and secure in the Infinite Living Mind of The ALL. For those of you who will be incarnated into a physical body at the time of the Singularity somewhere around the year 2045, I wish you good luck and the wisdom to navigate this unknown territory. I sincerely hope that you discover the actual truths of the UFO mystery and the underlying nature of the so-called paranormal that has so mysteriously haunted those of my own era. I hope also that, if it is humanity's fate after all to merge in a marvelous post-biological transcendence with the Overlords of the Singularity rather than escaping from the physical universe entirely, that each and every one of us can find our true cosmic destiny. However it may come about, may the high celestial beings of Light and Love and the human souls who choose to join them prevail.

Sources

Aartsen, Gerard, *Here to Help: UFOs and the Space Brothers*, BGA Publications, Amsterdam, Netherlands, pgs. 39-41, (2011).

Adamski, George, and Leslie, Desmond, *Flying Saucers Have Landed*, The British Book Centre, (1953).

Allingham, Cedric, *Flying Saucer from Mars*, British Book Centre, New York, pgs. 39, 40, (1955).

Ballard, Guy, *Unveiled Mysteries*, reprinted by Wilder Publications, Inc., (2011).

Beckley, Timothy Green, *Subterranean Worlds Inside Earth*, Inner Light Publications, (1992).

Belgium wave, Francis Michalczyk: https ://www.youtube.com/watch?v=TNoiiAAIzas

Belgian UFO wave: http://en.wikipedia.org/wiki/Belgian_UFO_wave

Bonilla photos: http://www.educatinghumanity.com/2011/10/ufos-debate-over-first-ever-ufo.html

Booth, B.J., *UFOs Caught on Film: Amazing Evidence of Alien Visitors to Earth*, a David and Charles (D&C) book, F&W Media International, (2012).

Bramley, William, *The Gods of Eden*, Avon Books, New York, New York, (1990).

Brinegar, Russell Scott, *Outgrowing the Bible: The Journey from Fundamentalism to Freethinking*, First Books/Authorhouse, (1999, 2001).

Cameron, Grant & Crain, T. Scott, *UFOs, Area 51, and Government Informants*, Keyhole Publishing Co., (2013).

Chalker, Bill, *Hair of the Alien: DNA and Other Forensic Evidence Of Alien Abductions*, Pocket Books, (2005).

Clark, Jerome, *The UFO Book: Encyclopedia of the Extraterrestrial*, Omnigraphics, Inc., (1998).

Collins, Andrew, *Lightquest: Your Guide To Seeing And Interacting With UFOs, Mystery Lights And Plasma Intelligences*, Eagle Wing Books, Inc, (2012).

Commander X, *The Ultimate Deception*, Abelard Productions, (1990).

Constable, Trevor James, *Sky Creatures: Living UFOs*, Pocket Books, a division of Simon and Schuster, (1976).

Cooper, Gordon testimony:: https://www.youtube.com/watch?v=dvPR8T1o3Dc

Cooper, William, *Behold a Pale Horse*, Light Technology Publishing, (1991).

Dean, Robert, testimony: https://www.youtube.com/watch?v=VI9fS8Y-fww

Denison Daily News, "A Strange Phenomenon," Denison, Texas, January 25, 1878.

Deyo, Stan, *The Cosmic Conspiracy*, Aventures Unlimited Press, (1994).

Fry, Daniel, *The White Sands Incident*, Horus House Press, (1992).

Gibbons, Gavin, *The Coming of the Spaceships*, The New York Citadel Press, (1958).

Good, Timothy, *Alien Contact: Top-Secret UFO Files Revealed*, Random Century Group, (1991).

Good, Timothy, *Earth: An Alien Enterprise*, Pegasus Books, New York, (2013).

Good, Timothy, *Above Top Secret: The Worldwide UFO Cover-up*, Sidgwick and Jackson Limited, (1987).

Good, Timothy, *Beyond Top Secret: The Worldwide UFO Security Threat*, Sidgwick and Jackson, (1996).

Graham, Billy, *Angels: God's Secret Agents*, Guideposts Associates Inc., Carmel, New York, (1975).

Greenfield, Allen H., *Secret Cipher of the UFOnauts*, IllumiNet Press, (1994).

Greer, Steven M., *Extraterrestrial Contact: The Evidence and Implications*, Granite Publishing, (1999).

Hardy, Chris H., PhD., *DNA of the Gods*, Bear and Company, Rochester, Vermont (2014).

Harris, Paola L., *Connecting the Dots: Making Sense of the UFO Phenomenon*, Authorhouse, (2008).

Horn, Thomas R., *Nephilim Stargates*, Anomolos Publishing House (2007).

Howe, Linda Moulton, *An Alien Harvest: Further Evidence Linking Animal Mutilations and Human Abductions To Alien Life Forms*, Linda Moulton Howe Productions, (1989).

Human mutilation 1994 case http://www.alienvideo.net/0805/alien-abduction-mutilation.php

Huyghe, Patrick; *The Field Guide to Extraterrestrials*, Avon Books, (1996).

Icke, David, *Children of the Matrix: How an interdimensional race has controlled the world for thousands of years – and still does*, Bridge of Love Publications, (2001).

Kecksberg event (1965): https://www.youtube.com/watch?v=dvPR8T1o3Dc

Keel, John, *Operation Trojan Horse*, G.P. Putnam's Son, (1970).

Keyhoe, Donald, *The Flying Saucers are Real*, CD audio version of Donald Keyhoe's 1950 book of same title.

Kushana, Eklal, *The Ultimate Frontier*, The Stelle Group, (1963).

Mack, John, M.D., *Passport to the Cosmos: Human Transformation and Alien Encounters*, White Crow Books, (2008).

Matthews, *UFO Revelation: The Secret Technology Exposed?* Blandford UK, (1999).

Michel, Aime, *The Truth About Flying Saucers*, Criterion Books, New York, (1956).

Moroney, Jim, abduction, youtube, "Jim Moroney Abduction."

Mowing devil – internet site - Hemelonline.com

Onec, Omnec, *Omnec Onec, Ambassador From Venus*, Inner Light, Global Communications, (2008).

Owens, Ted, *How To Contact Space People*, Global Communications, (reprinted in 2008).

Paleo-ufo sightings: http://thecid.com/ufo/chrono/chrono/1945.htm

Randle, Kevin D., *The Roswell Encyclopedia*, HarperCollins Books, (2000).

Randle, Keven D., *Project Moondust*, Avon Books, Inc., (1998).

Randle, Kevin & Estes, Russ, *Faces of the Visitors*, Fireside, (1997).

Randles, Jenny; *Alien Contacts and Abductions*; New York, Sterling, (1994).

Randles, Jenny, *Time Storms: Amazing Evidence for Time Warps, Space Rifts and Time Travel*, Judy Piatkus Limited, (2001).

Redfern, Nick, *The Real Men in Black*, New Page Books, (2011).

Rex Heflin case; Lonnie Zamora case: https://www.youtube.com/watch?v=3mTME9BD2_k

Ring, Kenneth, *The Omega Project: Near-Death Experiences, UFO Encounters, and Mind at Large*, William Morrow and Company, New York (1992).

Salas, Robert & Klotz, James, *Faded Giant*, BookSurge, LLC, (2005).

Sanderson, Ivan T., *Invisible Residents*, Adventures Unlimited Press, (2005 from 1970).

Shaw and Spooner abduction: http://ufologie.patrickgross.org/airship/25nov1896-lodi-california.htm

Steiger, Brad & Whritenour, Joan, *Flying Saucers are Hostile*, Universal-Tandem Publishing Co., (1967).

Stone,Clifford,CliffordStone/EdKomarek:http://www.youtube.com/watch?v=Z3p6MLTada8

Stone, Clifford, *UFOs Are Real*, SPI Books, (1997).

Stranges, Frank, and Valiant Thor - (bibliotecapleyades.net/bb/stranges/htm)

Stranges, Frank E., *The Stranger at the Pentagon*, I.E.C. Incorporated, (1967)

Story, Ronald D., Ed., *The Mammoth Encyclopedia of Extraterrestrial Encounters*, Constable and Robinson, LTD., London, (2001).

Tessman, Diane, *The UFO Agenda*, Eye Scry Publications, (2013).

"Thutmose III" – internet article. Rense.com, from Reader's Digest, *Mysteries of the Unexplained*, pages 207-209

Mattews, Tim, *UFO Revelation: The Secret Technology Exposed?* Blanford, UK (1999).

Wilkins, Harold T., *Flying Saucers on the Attack: startling new revelations on the most incredible story of our age!*, Citadel Press, New York, pgs. 187, 188, (1954).

"Kingman UFO crash," internet site, ufocasebook.com/Arizona

Kean, Leslie, "UFO classifications" - *UFOs: Generals, Pilots, and Government Officials go on the Record*, Three Rivers Press, New York, pgs. 130,131, (2011).

Marrs, Jim, *Alien Agenda*, HarperCollins Publishers, page 269, (1998).

Ouspensky, P.D., *The Psychology of Man's Possible Evolution*, pgs. 58, 87, (1973).

Stonehill, Paul, *The Soviet UFO Files*, Bramley Books, (1998).

Vallee, Jacques, UFOs in Space: *Anatomy of a Phenomenon*, early UFO Sightings, page 9, (1965).

Vallee, Jacques, *Dimensions*, Contemporary books Inc., pps. 39, 49-51 – sighting by Father Gill, Joe Simonton, (1988).

Vallee, Jacques, *Passport to Magonia*, "A fire in the sky," page 5-6, (1993).

Vallee, Jacques, early sightings, General Yoritsume, etc.: *Dimensions*, Contemporary Books, Inc., pgs 11-14, (1988).

Vallee, Jacques, Revelations, Ballantine Books, New York, (1981).

Wood, Ryan S., *MAJIC EYES ONLY: Earth's Encounters with Extraterrestrial Technology*, Wood Enterprises, (2005).

Audio books

Barker, Gray, *Men in Black*, narrated by Michael Hacker, (Audible Studios).

Barker, Gray, *The Silver Bridge*, narrated by Michael Hacker, (Audible Studios).

Barker, Gray, *They Knew Too Much about Flying Saucers*, narrated by Bruce Harvey, (Audible Studios).

Barrat, James, *Our Final Invention: Artificial Intelligence and the End of the Human Era,* (Audible Studios).

Binder, Otto, *Liquidation Of The UFO Investigators: The Truth Behind The Flying Saucers' Mission to Earth*, narrated by Pete Ferrand, edited by Gray Barker, (Audible Studios).

Bostrom, Nick, *SUPERINTELLIGENCE,* narrated by Napoleon Ryan, (Audible Studios).

Cannon, Delores, *Keepers of the Garden*, (Audible Studios).

Clarke, Arthur C., *Childhood's End*, narrated by Eric Michael Summerer and Robert J. Sawyer, (Audible Studios).

Colvin, Andrew, *The Perspicacious Percipient* (selected writings of John Keel), narrated by Mark Barnard, (Audible Studios).

Colvin, Andrew, *Flying Saucer to the Center of Your Mind*, (selected writings of John Keel), narrated by Michael Hacker, (Audible Studios).

Colvin Andrew (ed), *The Outer Limits of the Twilight Zone*, (selected writings of John Keel), (Audible Studios).

Cooper, William, *Behold a Pale Horse*, narrated by William Cooper, (Audible Studios).

Coppens, Philip, *The Ancient Alien Question*, narrated by Kevin Foley, (Audible Studios).

Coppens, Philip, *The Lost Civilization Enigma*, narrated by David Drummond, (Audible Studios).

Delarose, Sharon, *Ancient Aliens and the Lost Islands*, narrated by Peter L. Delloro (Audible Studios).

Dick, Philip K., *Valis*, narrated by Tom Weiner, (Audible Studios).

Dolan, Richard M., and Bryce Zybel, *A.D. After Disclosure: When the Government Finally Reveals the Truth about Alien Contact*, (Audible Studios).

Good, Timothy, *Above Top Secret*, narrated by Victor Talmadge, (Audible Studios).

Green, Brian, *The Elegant Universe*, narrated by Erik Davies, (Audible Studios).

Hancock, Graham, *The Message of the Sphinx*, narrated by Nick Ulett (Audible Studios).

Hancock, Graham, *Fingerprints of the Gods*, narrated by Peter Reckell, (Audible Studios).

Hancock, Graham, *Magicians of the Gods*, narrated by Graham Hancock, (Audible Studios).

Hancock, Graham, *Supernatural*, narrated by Christopher Lane, (Audible Studios).

Hanks, Micah, *The UFO Singularity*, The Career Press, Inc., (2013).

Holcombe, Larry, *UFOs and the Presidents: From FDR to Obama*, narrated by Oliver Wyman, (Audible.Studios).

Holzer, Hans, *The Ufonauts*, narrated by Kevin Pierce, (Audible Studios)

Hoyle, Fred, *The Black Cloud*, Jack Klaff and Richard Dawkins, (Audible Studios).

Huxley, Aldus, *The Doors of Perception*, narrated by Rudolph Schirmer, (Audible Studios).

Jessup, Morris K., *The Case for the UFO*, narrated by Jack Chekijan. (Audible Studios).

Jessup, Morris K, *The Expanding Case for the UFO*, narrated by Bruce T. Harvey, (Audible Studios).

Kybalion, The, authored by The Three Initiates, narrated by Mitch Horowitz, (Audible Studios).

Kaku, Michio, *Parallel Worlds*, narrated by Marc Vietor, (Audible Studios).

Kaku, Michio, *The Future of the Mind*, narrated by Feodor Chin, (Audible Studios).

Kaku, Michio, *Physics of the Future*, narrated by Feodor Chin, (Audible Studios).

Kaku, Michio, *Physics of the Impossible*, narrated by Feodor Chin, (Audible Studios).

Keel, John A., *Searching for the String*, edited by Andrew Colvin, narrated by Michael Hacker (Audible Studios).

Keel, John A., *Searching for the String*, narrated by Michael Hacker, (Audible Studios.

Keel, John A., *The Complete Guide to Mysterious Beings*, narrated by Pete Ferrand, (Audible Studios).

Keel, John A., *Disneyland of the Gods*, narrated by Michael Hacker, (Audible Studios).

Keel, John A., The Mothman Prophecies, narrated by Crag Wasson, (Audible Studios).

Keel, John A., *Strange Creatures from Time and Space*, narrated by Pete Ferrand, (Audible Studios).

Keel, John A., *Strange Mutants of Time and Space*, narrated by Pete Ferrand, (Audible Studios).

Keel, John A., *Our Haunted Planet*, narrated by Michael Hacker, (Audible Studios).

Kurzweil, Ray, The Age of Spiritual Machines, narrated by Alan Sklar, (Audible Studios).

Kurzweil, Ray, *The Singularity is Near*, narrated by George K. Wilson, (Audible Studios).

Marrs, Jim, *Our Occulted History*, narrated by Dave Courvoisoir, (Audible Studios).

McKenna, Terence, *Food of the Gods*, narrated by Jeffrey Kafer, (Audible Studios).

Moore, Alvin E., *Mystery of the Skymen*, narrated by Lee D. Foreman, (Audible Studios).

Moroney, Jim, *The UFO Answer Book*, narrated by Kevin Foley, (Audible Studios).

Newton, Michael, *Journey of Souls*, narrated by Peter Berkrot, (Audible Studios).

Penrose, Roger, *Cycles of Time*, narrated by Bruce Mann, (Audible Studios).

Randle, Kevin, *Project Blue Book: Exposed*, narrated by Ted Brooks, (Audible Studios).

Redfern, Nick, *Keep Out*, narrated by Adam Hanin, (Audible Studios).

Redfern, Nick, *The Pyramids and the Pentagon*, narrated by Peter Jude, (Audible Studios).

Sitchin, Zecharia, *The Twelfth Planet*, narrated by Bill Jenkins, (Audible Studios).

Strassman, Rick, *DMT: The Spirit Molecule*, narrated by Arthur Morey, (Audible Studios).

Stringfield, Leonard, *UFO Crash Retrievals, Status Reports I-VI*, narrated by Pete Ferrand, (Audible Studios).

Urantia Foundation, *The Urantia Book*, narrated by multiple contributors, (Audible Studios).

Vance, Ashley, *Elon Musk*, narrated by Fred Sanders, (Audible Studios).

Wilcock, David, *The Source Field Investigations*, narrated by David Wilcock, (Audible Studios).

Wilcock, David, *The Synchronicity Key*, narrated by David Wilcock, (Audible Studios).

Wright, T.M., *The Intelligent Man's Guide to Flying Saucers*, narrated by Scott Slocum, (Audible Studios).

Made in the USA
San Bernardino, CA
12 March 2018